Transforming Media Accessibility in Europe

Ann Marcus-Quinn · Krzysztof Krejtz ·
Carlos Duarte

Editors

Transforming Media Accessibility in Europe

Digital Media, Education and City Space
Accessibility Contexts

 Springer

Editors
Ann Marcus-Quinn 🆔
School of English
Irish, and Communication
University of Limerick
Limerick, Ireland

Krzysztof Krejtz 🆔
Eye Tracking Research Center
Institute of Psychology
SWPS University
Warsaw, Poland

Carlos Duarte 🆔
LASIGE, Faculty of Sciences
University of Lisbon
Lisbon, Portugal

ISBN 978-3-031-60048-7   ISBN 978-3-031-60049-4 (eBook)
https://doi.org/10.1007/978-3-031-60049-4

This Springer imprint is published by the registered company Springer Nature Switzerland AG
The registered company address is: Gewerbestrasse 11, 6330 Cham, Switzerland

If disposing of this product, please recycle the paper.

Foreword

Every time there is a major shift in technology accessibility must reinvent itself. It is similar to the feeling of having to pass "Go" when playing Monopoly starting a new with each advancement. You may collect money as you start anew round, or you may pass "Go" without collecting any. Regardless, the game continues, and your round starts again. I had the same feeling over the past 20 years. Accessibility was the game, it came with more or less funding, and I had to contend with the new technological landscape. First it was analog, then digital, and finally data driven. Each shift meant a new cycle of raising awareness, new terminology to be agreed and fixed, training to be updated, and eventually standardisation. Three technological shifts in 20 years have demanded an open attitude to change, endless energy, and an understanding of resilience. The commonalities across all these changes have been the research focus getting more complex, and the demography of end users becoming wider. Interdisciplinary research is seemingly the only way forward, with collaboration between disciplines, research groups, industry and academia, and research methodologies.

To continue with the Monopoly analogy, the first playing board represented the world of analog technology. The context was one-size-fits-all, and creative solutions were required to deliver accessibility services, such as audio description through the radio, or subtitling through teletext. Television and radio were considered a part of the family (Fabes et al. 1989) where all the members consumed the same content at the same time, and accessibility services such as audio description were almost unknown or difficult to access. WCAG already existed in version 1.0. This analog period coincided with the approval at the United Nations of the Convention on the Rights of Persons with Disabilities (2006) which politicised media accessibility. The most interesting issue during this period was the decision to transfer the responsibility for accessibility to the broadcasters and media content distributors—with the exception of videogames. In our Monopoly game analogy, this could be likened to drawing a Community Chest card that says: "Make x hours of your content accessible." Media content producers were excluded from any responsibility for accessibility, and this trend continues today. The benefits of applying Universal Design to media content creation and producing accessible by design remain an ideal rather than a reality. Research avenues and approaches in the analog era were vast. Accessibility had just started in academia, both as research in the field of Translation Studies, and in particular Audiovisual Translation (Orero 2005). Courses on media accessibility subtitling and audio description also began as part of Audiovisual Translation MAs (Amador et al. 2004). There was a time when understanding the reading speed for subtitles was interesting and funded by the European Commission (Matamala and Orero 2009) as it was challenging to define what information to prioritise in an audio description (Díaz Cintas et al. 2007).

The second time media accessibility had to be redefined was in response to the shift from analog to digital. The "one-size-fits-all" was dead, and the end user began to enjoy the freedom to choose (Orero et al. 2014): from the language to consume the media content to the position where subtitles could be placed and where to consume them (Rodríguez Alsina et al. 2012). This digital shift opened so many possibilities, but it also brought with it many new barriers such as accessibility to menus to name one. In this second round of Monopoly, a game of cat and mouse was also endlessly played. Industry came up with new developments, and accessibility solutions had to think creatively to ensure all citizens could benefit. The new possibilities such as the Hybrid Broadcast Broadband TV standard (Orero et al. 2015) changed workflows and gave a new life to broadcast by merging with the Internet. WCAG was more relevant than ever, but it was clear that in the digital world, research and manufacturing were performed in silos. Engineers rarely met psychologists to understand the effect of their developments in humans for a quality of experience, and often, IT development ignored human natural language communication. This digital world also added new formats, with the development of virtual worlds and XR. And yes, another round of Monopoly, fixing the terminology for virtual worlds, digital twins, metaverse, citiverse, avatar, and the digital human. How to produce and consume accessibility in virtual environments are capturing the interest of researchers and standardisation agencies (Montagud et al. 2020). Whilst enjoying the second round of Monopoly, now in a virtual format and fully interactive, industry is moving ahead.

The third round of Monopoly is happening now in the background. Artificial Intelligence seems to be capturing interest, but I feel that the shift is data driven—with manufacturers wondering on new business models for their products. At one point, videogames were the Monopoly streets of Mayfair and Park Lane, broadcasters have been the stations, and streaming platforms are Bond Street, Regent Street, and Oxford Street. Data brokers—the chancers—now own the card that will get you out of jail. Almost all accessibility services can be produced automatically—with several degrees of quality and acceptance. Research in media accessibility today is not only multidisciplinary, but it is also multitasking: whilst catching up with accessibility in virtual worlds, we need to start figuring out media accessibility in a data-driven market. The establishment of networks such as LeadMe is the way forward to create an inclusive digital society, human centric, and following Universal Design principles for all.

Prof. Pilar Orero🆔
Department of Translation
and Interpreting and East Asia Studies
TransMedia Catalonia
Barcelona, Spain

References

Amador, M., Carles D. & Orero, P. (2004). *e-AVT: A Perfect Match: Strategies, Functions and Interactions in an On-line Environment for Learning*. Topics in Audiovisual Translation, Ámsterdam, Benjamins, 141–153.

Díaz Cintas, J., Orero, P. & Remael, A. (Eds.) (2007). *Media for all. Subtitling for the Deaf, Audio description and Sign Language*. Amsterdam: Rodopi.

Fabes, R. A., et al. (1989). A time to reexamine the role of television in family life. *Family Relations, 38*(3), 337–41. JSTOR, https://doi.org/10.2307/585062. Accessed 28 Feb. 2024.

Matamala, A. & Orero, P. (Eds.) (2009). *Listening to Subtitles. Subtitles for the Deaf and Hard of Hearing*. Bern: Peter Lang.

Montagud, M., Orero, P., Fernández, S. (2020). Immersive media and accessibility: Hand in hand to the future. ITU Journal Discoveries. Special Issue: The future of video and immersive media. Geneva: ITU.

Orero, P. (2005). La inclusión de la accesibilidad en comunicación audiovisual dentro de los estudios de traducción audiovisual. *Quaderns de Traducció, 12*, 173–185.

Orero, P., Serrano, J., Soler, O., Matamala, A., Castella, J., Soto Sanfiel, M. T., Vilaró, A. & Mangiron, C. (2014). *Accessibillity to Digital Society: Interaction for All. Think Mind*. 188–191.

Orero, P., Martín, C. A. & Zorrilla, M. (2015). HBB4ALL: Deployment of HbbTV services for all. 2015 IEEE International Symposium on Broadband Multimedia Systems and Broadcasting.

Rodriguez-Alsina, A., Talavera, G., Orero, P. & Carrabina, J. (2012). Subtitle synchronization across multiple screens and devices. *Sensors, 12*(7), 8710–8731. https://doi.org/10.3390/s120708710.

UN CRPD https://www.un.org/development/desa/disabilities/convention-on-the-rightsof-Persons-with-disabilities.html.

Introduction

As we stand at the threshold of a new era in accessibility evidenced by the EU's broader efforts to enhance accessibility for everyone, it is with great pride and a sense of collective achievement that we present this collaborative work, born from the concerted efforts of the European Cooperation in Science and Technology (COST) Action LEAD-ME (CA19142). This book is not just a testament to the groundbreaking research and advancements in accessibility, but also a symbol of the power of collaborative European scientific endeavour. The essence of this book lies in its collaborative spirit. It reflects a confluence of ideas, a melting pot of cultures and methodologies, all united by a common goal: to push the boundaries of our understanding of accessibility. The chapters herein are more than just individual pieces of scholarship; they are a dialogue between different schools of thought, a debate between diverse approaches, and a harmonious blend of varied scientific traditions.

The COST Action LEAD-ME (Leading Platform for European Citizens, Industries, Academia, and Policymakers in Media Accessibility) is an initiative aimed at enhancing media accessibility in Europe. It operates under the strategic priorities of COST, an EU-funded organisation. These priorities include promoting and spreading excellence, fostering interdisciplinary research for breakthrough science, and empowering young researchers and innovators. LEAD-ME focuses on helping European stakeholders in the field of media accessibility comply with legal milestones set by European legislation. The action aims to induce a cultural change and create a new mindset in designing tools for professional and private activities, catering to the needs of all European citizens, including those with disabilities.

This book, *LEAD-ME: Transforming Media Accessibility in Europe* is a comprehensive exploration of the legal, technological, psychological, and societal aspects of media accessibility. The book is a result of the LEAD-ME project, which brings together researchers, educators, and practitioners to examine the critical role of media accessibility in Europe. It covers the legal foundations, showcases innovative technologies, and delves into real-world applications across sectors like education, culture, and smart cities. With case studies and future-focused insights, it is a valuable resource for anyone interested in fostering inclusivity through accessible media in a diverse Europe.

This book offers a holistic view of media accessibility, from legal frameworks to cutting-edge technologies and real-world applications. It's a one-stop resource for academics, policymakers, industry professionals, and advocates seeking in-depth knowledge. Readers gain access to exclusive research, innovative solutions, and best practices from a consortium of experts, making it a unique and authoritative source. With a forward-looking perspective, this book goes beyond existing knowledge to explore the evolving landscape of media accessibility in the digital age. It equips readers with insights into emerging trends, challenges, and opportunities, ensuring its relevance for years to come. Capacity building and knowledge exchange are central themes of the book, reflecting the project's commitment to developing a joint research agenda on accessibility and establishing a collaborative platform for stakeholders. The involvement of associations representing people with disabilities is particularly highlighted, ensuring that the discourse is inclusive and representative of the needs of all individuals.

As editors, we have sought to create a work that is not only academically rigorous but also accessible to a wider audience. We have organised the chapters into four parts that represent the various fields and expertise of accessibility by the members of the COST Action. These are; "Outside the Screen", "Learning and Education", "Inclusive Art and Society", and "Technological Innovations for Accessibility".

In the first chapter of the first part, Outside the Screen, Miroslav D. Vujičić (University of Novi Sad, Serbia), Uglješa Stankov (University of Novi Sad, Serbia), Biljana Basarin (University of Novi Sad, Serbia), Izabela Krejtz (SWPS University, Warsaw, Poland), Krzysztof Krejtz (SWPS University, Warsaw, Poland), and Dejan Masliković (Institute of Social Sciences, Belgrade, Serbia) endeavour to establish Tourism 5.0 as a holistic alternative to the prevailing concept of digital accessibility practices within the typically limited and task-focused tourism sector. This chapter critically examines the evolution from Industry 4.0 to Industry 5.0, drawing parallels with Tourism 4.0 and Tourism 5.0. The central focus of this chapter is placed on the imperative of technological accessibility, exploring how it takes precedence in the latest technological developments and contributes to the creation of more inclusive and fulfilling tourism experiences.

In the second chapter, Anna Warchol-Jakubowska (SWPS University, Warsaw, Poland), Iga Szwoch (SWPS University, Warsaw, Poland), Patryk Szczeciński (SWPS University, Warsaw, Poland), Izabela Krejtz (SWPS University, Warsaw, Poland), and Krzysztof Krejtz (SWPS University, Warsaw, Poland) explore accessibility in public transport, focusing on the case study of Warsaw capital city of Poland. The authors highlight the challenges faced by individuals with disabilities in urban spaces and shed light on the impediments encountered in navigating public transportation systems. The chapter underscores the importance of addressing challenges, legal frameworks, and the adoption of cutting-edge solutions to create a more inclusive and accessible urban transport environment.

The third chapter highlights the growing discussion of audio description techniques and accessibility in the context of museums. María Olalla Luque Colmenero (University of Granada, Spain) focuses on the diversity of methods and the need for a balance between objective and subjective audio descriptions.

In the fourth chapter, Krzysztof Krejtz (SWPS University, Poland), Daria Rutkowska-Siuda (University of Łódź, Poland), and Izabela Krejtz (SWPS University, Poland) present the novel concept of Gaze-Led Audio Description (GLAD) and its application for the accessibility of city space. Their chapter discusses how GLAD is promoting the creative development of inclusive travel experiences that are engaging and relevant for everybody enhancing the inclusiveness of architectural cultural heritage.

In the fifth chapter, Önder Islek (Aksaray University, Turkey) and Hatice Uyanik (Sinop University, Turkey) outline the significant challenges that people with disabilities encounter when they try to access higher education and employment. The authors detail how Aksaray University in Turkey is fostering more inclusive practices for a more equitable experience for all students.

The sixth chapter opens the second part, Inclusive Art and Society; Ferlanda Luna (University of Coimbra, Portugal) and Armela Maxhelaku (University of Tirana, Albania) address the potential of insurgent digital constitutionalism in establishing legal frameworks that ensure Internet security for both users and online platform managers; including private companies and government agencies. They discuss the importance of establishing legal environments in order to regulate the newly assigned responsibilities pertaining to the management of information.

In the seventh chapter, Estella Oncins (Universitat Autònoma de Barcelona, Spain) and Iris Serrat-Roozen (Universidad Internacional de Valencia, Spain) discuss the role of technology in Audiovisual Translation (AVT) and Media Accessibility (MA). The chapter presents the results of a three-year project, MediaVerse, aimed at designing and testing a framework to allow professionals and laymen to publish multimedia content that may be easily shared.

The eighth chapter details several projects aimed at making art accessible to visually impaired individuals. Aneta Pawłowska (University of Łódź, Poland), Adam Drozdowski (University of Łódź, Poland), Paulina Długosz (Muzeum Miasta Łodzi, Poland), and Magdalena Milerowska (University of Łódź, Poland) discuss how local museums have worked with academics to foster full cultural participation for people with sensory disabilities through digital technology, typhlographics, Braille books, and spatial objects, as well as offering sign language interpreted lectures, meetings, trips, and movie screenings.

In the ninth chapter, María Asunción Pérez de Zafra Arrufat (Universidad de Granada, Spain) and David Domínguez Escalona (Universidad de Granada, Spain) present a phased methodology that includes a literature review and sensory element analysis. Their project identifies innovative practices for creating accessible multisensory exhibitions which blur the boundaries of the conventional concert hall and exhibition space and can empower attendees with diverse abilities, foster social inclusion, and inspire future international endeavours in the realm of accessible contemporary arts.

Moving on to the third section, Learning and Education, in the tenth chapter, Alexandros Yeratziotis (A.G. Connect Deaf Limited, Cyprus), Thomas Fotiadis (University of Cyprus, Cyprus), Andrina Granić (University of Split, Croatia), and George A. Papadopoulos (University of Cyprus, Cyprus) present a descriptive systematic review of two major themes of media accessibility and inclusivity in the domain of education. Their chapter identifies the limited current state of the art in the area and stresses the need for further research.

In the eleventh chapter, Muhammet Bergiel (Karadeniz Technical University, Trabzon, Turkey), Gizem Dilan Boztaş (Karadeniz Technical University, Trabzon, Turkey), Beyza Güdek (Karadeniz Technical University, Trabzon, Turkey), Gabriela Neagu (Romanian Academy, Romanie), and Carlos Duarte (Universidade de Lisboa, Portugal) investigate the intricate dynamics within the field of media accessibility in education. Their chapter explores three major themes and highlights current challenges and gaps in the literature.

In the twelfth chapter, Muhammet Bergiel (Karadeniz Technical University, Trabzon, Turkey), Duygu Solak Bergiel (Trabzon University, Turkey), Carlos Duarte (Universidade de Lisboa, Portugal), Christos Mettouris (University of Cyprus, Cyprus), Evangelia Vanezi (University of Cyprus, Cyprus), Alexandros Yeratziotis (A.G. Connect Deaf Limited, Cyprus), and George A. Papadopoulo (University of Cyprus, Cyprus) critically assess the publicly available information provided by LMS providers on their accessibility. The chapter explores and compares the media accessibility features offered and adherence to established standards. This chapter provides educators, institutions, and learners with valuable insights, enabling them to make well-informed decisions in an era where digital learning has become ubiquitous.

In the thirteenth chapter, Ann Marcus-Quinn (University of Limerick, Ireland), Thomas Fotiadis (University of Cyprus, Cyprus), Alexandros Yeratziotis (A.G. Connect Deaf Limited), and George A. Papadopoulos (University of Cyprus, Cyprus) stress the imperative of accessibility in the context of eBooks specifically produced for the second-level education sector in both Ireland and Cyprus. The chapter explores accessibility features common to many school eBooks and highlights problematic issues associated with eBooks that have not been prepared with accessibility considerations as part of the publication process.

In the fourteenth chapter, Mariona González-Sordé (Universitat Autònoma de Barcelona, Spain) and Marina Pujadas-Farreras (Universitat Autònoma de Barcelona, Spain) present a case study which assesses the accessibility of online educational content, with a specific focus on second-language learning videos. Their chapter highlights the aspects that make educational videos accessible and inclusive.

In the fifteenth chapter, Giedrė Valūnaitė-Oleškevičienė (Mykolas Romeris University, Vilnius, Lithuania), Ebru Çavuşoğlu (Samsun University, Turkey), and Carlos Duarte (Universidade de Lisboa, Portugal) analyse the curricula of translation courses in Turkey, Portugal, and Lithuania and identify the need for practical recommendations in the analysed curricula on how teaching and assessment methods could be applied to ensure fair and equal possibilities and observing the four key digital accessibility principles in the study process. Their observations serve as a key factor for improving and creating curricula for technology-enhanced teaching and learning in Translation Studies.

In the sixteenth chapter, Miguel Ángel Oliva-Zamora (Universitat Autònoma de Barcelona, Spain) and María Eugenia Larreina-Morales (Universitat Autònoma de Barcelona, Spain) review the last decade of research in educational games and game accessibility. Based on this research, the authors suggest recommendations that will bring together players, teachers, developers, and researchers to create more interactive and engaging educational experiences for all.

In the seventeenth chapter, Sérgio Barbosa (University of Coimbra, Portugal) showcases how the Digital Literacy Pedagogical Sessions (#DLPS) have been exploited to empower and nurture young people's postdigital futures. Data from this chapter is derived from a participatory pedagogy approach adopted at Portuguese schools over two periods: 2021–2022 and 2022–2023.

In the eighteenth chapter, Marta Brescia-Zapata (Universitat Autònoma de Barcelona, Spain) and Sarah Anne McDonagh (Universitat Autònoma de Barcelona, Spain) outline the growing recognition of media accessibility as an educational asset in the classroom. In their chapter, they focus on the creation of non-professional audio description (AD) by secondary school students. This chapter contributes to the ongoing discourse, emphasising the need for flexible approaches and collaboration to further refine and standardise AD practices across diverse media formats.

In the nineteenth chapter, Ekrem Bahçekapılı (Karadeniz Technical University, Turkey) and Ahmet Ayaz (Karadeniz Technical University, Turkey) examine the use of assistive technologies designed to comprehend the challenges faced by individuals with hearing impairments. Their chapter elucidates how technological aids, developed for individuals with hearing impairments, support equal opportunities for those with hearing impairments.

In the twentieth chapter, in the final section, Technological Innovations for Accessibility, Juan Pedro Rica Peromingo (Universidad Complutense de Madrid, Spain) discusses how media accessibility has become a crucial aspect of content creation and distribution. This chapter examines how media accessibility training is being provided by university instructors and how this training aims to enable academic researchers and professionals to acquire the necessary knowledge to meet the needs of the deaf and blind communities.

In the twenty-first chapter, Iuliia Kostynets (National Academy of Management, Kyiv, Ukraine) and Valeriia Kostynets (National Economic University, Kyiv, Ukraine) consider the need for social adaptation for people with special needs and internally displaced people. The authors describe the use of digital media tools in the Ukraine to ensure accessibility and inclusivity in all areas of everyday life.

In the twenty-second chapter, Karolina Gabor-Siatkowska (Warsaw University of Technology, Warsaw, Poland), Izabela Stefaniak (Lazarski University, Warsaw, Poland), and Artur Janicki (Warsaw University of Technology, Warsaw, Poland) discuss the goal-directed therapeutic dialogue system that they have developed to provide additional therapy sessions to psychiatric patients where there is limited access to medical personnel.

In the final chapter, Vicente Bru García (University of Granada, Spain) and Silvia Martínez (University of Granada, Spain) focus on the need for standardisation in intersemiotic subtitling of sound effects and music in audiovisual products through the revision of standards and guidelines in subtitling for the D/deaf and hard of hearing (SDH) and the analysis of a corpus consisting of SDH from German, Spanish, and English Netflix series. This chapter underlines the importance of establishing quality guidelines to ensure access to leisure for people with hearing impairments and establishes a starting point in an interdisciplinary approach to subtitling sound effects and music.

This book looks towards the future, providing insights into emerging trends and challenges in media accessibility. It equips readers with the knowledge to navigate the evolving digital landscape, emphasising the ongoing need for innovation, awareness, and collaboration to achieve a truly inclusive and accessible media environment. This publication is an essential read for academics, policymakers, industry professionals, and advocates seeking a deep understanding of media accessibility. It is a unique and authoritative source that combines legal, technological, and practical perspectives, making it an invaluable addition to the field.

We extend our gratitude to all the contributors, whose work and invaluable insights have made this book possible. We also thank COST for providing us with the platform and support to undertake this ambitious project. Without this commitment to fostering transnational cooperation and networking among researchers and innovators, this book would not have been possible.

Contents

Outside the Screen

Accessibility in Tourism 5.0 Approach: Enabling Inclusive and Meaningful Tourist Experiences

Miroslav D. Vujičić⊙, **Uglješa Stankov**⊙, **Biljana Basarin**⊙,
Izabela Krejtz⊙, **Krzysztof Krejtz**⊙, and **Dejan Maslikovic**⊙

Abstract The advent of Industry 4.0 technologies, encompassing the Internet of Things (IoT), Big data analytics, artificial intelligence (AI), blockchain, location-based services, and virtual and augmented (VR/AR) reality systems, has revolutionized the tourism landscape, automating production and service delivery. As the momentum of Industry 4.0 propels us toward the tourism-specific concept of Tourism 4.0, questions arise about the ability of humans to keep pace with the rapid technological advancements and ensure these innovations genuinely benefit society. The ongoing debate prompts a call for humanizing Industry 4.0, echoed in the emerging concept of Industry 5.0, advocating for more responsible and humane technology approaches. Concurrently, voices championing Tourism 5.0 emphasize the need to align technology with diverse human tourism needs and enhance accessibility for a more inclusive and meaningful travel experience. Through this chapter, we endeavor to establish Tourist 5.0 as a holistic alternative to the prevailing concept of digital accessibility practices within the typically limited and task-focused tourism sector. This chapter critically examines the evolution from Industry 4.0 to Industry 5.0, drawing parallels with Tourism 4.0 and Tourism 5.0. The central focus of this chapter is placed on the imperative of technological accessibility, exploring how it takes

M. D. Vujičić (✉) · U. Stankov · B. Basarin
Faculty of Sciences, Department of Geography, Tourism and Hotel Management, University of Novi Sad, Nov Sad, Serbia
e-mail: miroslav.vujicic@dgt.uns.ac.rs

U. Stankov
e-mail: ugljesa.stankov@dgt.uns.ac.rs

B. Basarin
e-mail: biljana.basarin@gmail.com

I. Krejtz · K. Krejtz
Eye Tracking Research Center, Institute of Psychology, SWPS University, Warsaw, Poland
e-mail: ikrejtz@swps.edu.pl

K. Krejtz
e-mail: kkrejtz@swps.edu.pl

D. Maslikovic
Institute of Social Sciences, Belgrade, Serbia

3

precedence in the latest technological developments and contributes to the creation of more inclusive and fulfilling tourism experiences.

Keywords Industry 5.0 · Tourism 5.0 · Accessibility · Meaningful tourist experiences

1 Introduction

The Fourth Industrial Revolution, also known as Industry 4.0, is a conceptual framework that emphasizes the integration of advanced technologies such as robotics, artificial intelligence, and the Internet of Things (IoT) into manufacturing and supply chain operations to improve business flexibility, productivity, and efficiency. This integration also facilitates more informed decision-making and customization (Ustundag & Cevikcan, 2017). While the term "Industry 4.0" originated in the context of manufacturing and industrial processes, its principles and technologies have found applications and relevance in various other domains, from health care (Health 4.0), and education (Education 4.0), to finance and tourism (İyigün & Görçün, 2023; Starc Peceny et al., 2019). Industry 4.0 brings a positive and hopeful perspective regarding the impact of technology on society, economy, and overall human wellbeing (Vujičić & Stankov, 2022), and even the driver that can help achieve the sustainable development goals (SDGs) this decade (Herweijer et al., 2020). It is the belief that technological advancements and innovations have the potential to bring about positive changes, solve problems, and improve various aspects of life (Pencarelli, 2019). An inherent presumption exists that the operational efficacy of tourism information technology and other Industry 4.0 technological advancements is enhanced to the benefit of both tourists and society at large (Stankov & Gretzel, 2021). However, even technological marvels of the tourism industry frequently lack human-centered design (Stankov & Gretzel, 2020), and often even basic accessibility features (Cassia et al., 2020; Fernández-Díaz et al., 2022; Stankov & Filimonau, 2019).

The European Commission has implemented numerous initiatives to foster accessibility in Industry 4.0, including financial commitments toward training and development programs that furnish personnel with the knowledge and competencies required to navigate the continuously changing work environment (Duan & Da Xu, 2021). In recent years, however, a paradigm shift has been occurring pleading that a more comprehensive approach to Industry 4.0 is needed (Möller et al., 2022; Stankov et al., 2024).

Societies have recently encountered unprecedented challenges, including but not limited to global climate change, pandemics, hybrid and conventional warfare, and refugee crises, which account for this shift (Golovianko et al., 2023; Morar et al., 2022; Stankov et al., 2020, 2023a). In the era of digital advancements, there exists a persistent inclination to remedy all societal issues—be it corruption, pollution, or obesity—through the digital quantification, tracking, or gamification of human behavior. However, it is crucial to recognize that altering the incentives driving our moral, ethical, and civic conduct can potentially transform the very essence of these behaviors (Morozov, 2013). For processes to be resilient and sustainable, humans must be re-involved in organizational decision-making (Golovianko et al., 2023) providing value-driven development. In that sense Industry 5.0 approach has emerged (Xu et al., 2021).

As per the European Union, Industry 5.0 is a forward-thinking paradigm for the industrial sector. This approach goes beyond the conventional focus on basic efficiency and production, hence increasing the industry's importance within a wider societal context (Zizic et al., 2022). At the core of this approach is the emphasis on promoting well-being, employing state-of-the-art technologies to foster prosperity that transcends simple economic expansion (Hamdan et al., 2023). Industry 5.0 functions in a complementary manner to the well-established Industry 4.0 framework, placing distinctive emphasis on the contribution of research and innovation toward a sustainable, human-centric, and resilient industrial environment in Europe (Breque et al., 2021; Müller, 2020).

The tourism industry, inherently shaped by technological advancements, has witnessed a rapid evolution, catapulting it into a new era characterized by efficiency, innovation, and heightened connectivity (Cimbaljević et al., 2018; Radojević et al., 2023). As equivalent to Industry 4.0, tourism-specific use of technology can be referred to as Tourism 4.0 (Stankov & Gretzel, 2020; Starc Peceny et al., 2019). Tourism 4.0 is a novel tourism value ecosystem built upon a technology-intensive service production paradigm (Stankov & Gretzel, 2020). However, amidst this transformative journey, a notable consequence has emerged—certain segments of tourists have been inadvertently left behind (Gretzel & Stankov, 2021). In this sense, Tourism 5.0 as equivalent to Industry 5.0 is needed as a holistic approach to adopt a more human-oriented, sustainable, and resilient approach to using technology. This consists of responsible innovation that seeks to increase prosperity for all stakeholders—investors, workers, customers, society, and the environment—rather than focusing solely on profit maximization or cost-efficiency (Breque et al., 2021).

The need for the Tourism 5.0 approach stems from the dual factors of the relentless speed at which technology develops and the varying technological capabilities of individuals (Cimbaljević et al., 2023; Stankov & Filimonau, 2020). As technology becomes increasingly integral to every aspect of travel, ensuring universal accessibility has transitioned from being a mere consideration for tourism information provision (Domínguez Vila et al., 2020; Silva & Borges, 2020; Stankov et al. 2023) to an imperative need. With the progression of technology, it is anticipated that the degree of accessibility incorporation into the design of tourism services will increase exponentially (Kadijević et al., 2016) (see Fig. 1). This would be influenced not only by the technology itself (Industry 4.0) but also by a shift in perception regarding the significance of technology concerning the socio-economic environment and general welfare (Industry 5.0).

Industry 5.0 represents a paradigm shift that seeks to reconcile the benefits of technological achievements with a renewed emphasis on inclusivity (Bonello et al., 2024). The framework advocates for a holistic approach where the well-being and

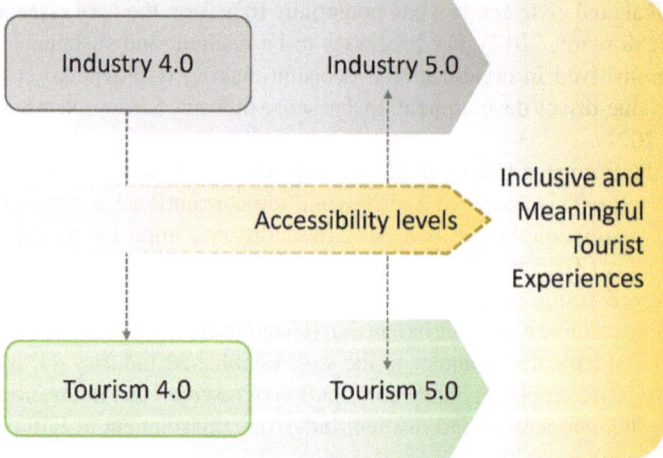

Fig. 1 Logical framework for the accessibility inclusion in the Tourism 5.0 approach (*Source* Contribution of the authors)

diverse needs of all individuals, including those who may face barriers due to technological disparities, are prioritized. This is particularly relevant in the context of the tourism industry, where experiences should be crafted to cater to a wide spectrum of travelers, irrespective of their technological proficiency or access to the latest innovations (Carlisle et al., 2021). The advent of Industry 5.0 introduces a unique opportunity to bridge the digital divide and create a more equitable travel landscape.

By aligning technological progress with the principles of human-centricity, sustainability, and resilience, Industry 5.0 can catalyze redefining the relationship between technology and tourism (Filimonau et al., 2022; Orea-Giner et al., 2022). The exploration of Industry 5.0 within the tourism industry presents an exciting prospect to leverage technology not only for its groundbreaking capabilities but also to ensure that its benefits are universally attainable, fostering a more inclusive and enriching travel experience for all.

To comprehend the implications of accessibility in designing the tourist experience within the Tourism 5.0 approach, a review of key existing concepts is essential. Consequently, this chapter undertakes an analysis of the literature on contemporary issues in Industry 4.0 and its transition to Industry 5.0. Initially, the chapter delves into the basic characteristics of Industry 5.0, resilience, human-centered design, and sustainability. It analyzes technology optimism as the underlying concept of Industry 4.0 and relates it to resilience in tourism crisis management. Second, the paper explores the human-centric approach as a core value of Tourism 5.0 and a path toward more sustainable development. Following that, the chapter further presents practical technologies for accessibility in Tourism 5.0 experiences throughout the travel phases. Thus, this chapter fills the gap in the literature regarding the place of accessibility in the transition from Tourism 4.0 toward Tourism 5.0. By outlining directions for future research, the chapter contributes further to the ongoing academic and practical discourse on the importance of technology accessibility in the area of information and communication technology (ICT) proliferation.

2   Resilience to the Crisis that Flows from Technology Optimism

In several industries, including tourism and hospitality, ICT has become a vital instrument for crisis management (Liu et al., 2015; Wilk-Jakubowski et al., 2022). In this context, ICT is not considered solely as a tactical tool, but also it serves as a strategic one. It is currently a critical component of all phases of tourism crisis management, as it is used to forecast (before), save or mitigate (during), and assist in recovery (after) (Dragović et al., 2019; Wut et al., 2021). Apart from the anticipated use of ICT solutions in crisis management scenarios (Kwok et al., 2021), smart environments and the ubiquitous presence of technology enable unique, unscripted, and creative applications (Gretzel et al., 2020). Except for vaccine development and medicine, the COVID-19 pandemic has revealed numerous exciting technology solutions in the fields of robotics, IoT and AI but also in consumer electronics and everyday Internet apps that are geared toward actively addressing newly emerging challenges (Thomas et al., 2021). As a result, the tourism industry and society as a whole, have gained confidence and optimism in their ability to deal with future crises through increased dependence on modern and sophisticated technology solutions (Berawi, 2021). This optimism could be related to, so so-called technology effect (Clark et al., 2016). This phenomenon implies that continuous exposure to technical breakthroughs would drive decision-makers to be overconfident in technology's ability to produce favorable outcomes, as that confidence builds an unconscious link between technology and success (Clark et al., 2016). Indeed, the implicit assumption that the technological innovations of Tourism 5.0 work better for tourists has already become commonplace in the tourism domain (Stankov & Gretzel, 2020). In essence, the technology effect has the concept of over-optimism at its core, and as such it could be viewed as a bias toward optimism in technology (Clark et al., 2016). The traditional concept of technology optimism is fueled by the fact that technological successes often come with game-changing results, such as revolutionizing industries, boosting sustainability, and improving the quality of life of many (Paro et al., 2021). Such events are highly notable, while on the other side, technology failures often go quietly, as they usually do not change the current state of affairs, and affect only a few (Case, 2015; Clark et al., 2016; Hatamura, 2009).

It must be noted that technology optimism has downsides of its own (Vujicic & Stankov 2022). For example, it could be problematic if it is viewed as a doctrine stating that the increasing number of technological advancements will sustain life as the human population grows. Many critical voices emerge in this case, such as the rising cost of pollution (Gonella et al., 2019), and the greenwashing of tech billionaires who contribute significantly to pollution, to name a few (Bove, 2021). Thus, there is always a lingering question about the true purpose of technology employ-ment or how technology is provided (Gonella et al., 2019). These issues and concerns continue to be critical even in the context of crisis management. This is particularly significant in the case of tourism technology optimism, which must always be viewed through a broader socio-economic lens (Røpke, 1996). Still, from a broader perspec-tive, this socially-responsible and empathic role during the crisis could further help in creating an image of tourism technology as more human-centered (Griffy-Brown et al., 2018).

The phenomenon of technology optimism holds a significant ramification for the question of the resilience of the tourism industry (Ivanov, 2021; Sharma et al., 2021). Thus, by building on the premises of technology optimism, Tourism 5.0 should fuel the idea that a strong influx of technology in tourism could encourage creative solutions, confidence, and activism in the tourism industry in times of crisis. Consequently, a shorter recovery period could be expected in the case of the technology-intensive and hyper-connected tourism industry.

Tourism 5.0 should enable balanced development by establishing adaptive capac-ities, but also corporate procedures that are resilient enough to provide stability, especially in value chains that provide support for critical human necessities like healthcare or security (Breque et al., 2021).

3 Human-Centric Approach as a Core Value of Tourism 5.0 and a Path Toward More Sustainable Development

Technology has emerged as a disruptive force in the tourism sector, transforming the way people plan, experience, and share their travel activities (Buhalis et al., 2019; Navío-Marco et al., 2018). During this technological growth, there is an increasing realization that a human-centric approach is required to ensure that tech-nical breakthroughs enhance and enrich the tourists' experience (Neuhofer et al., 2015; Stankov & Gretzel, 2020). This shift toward human-centricity signifies a change away from merely technological solutions and toward a more nuanced under-standing of visitors' different requirements, preferences, and aspirations (Neuhofer et al., 2012, 2013; Vujičić et al., 2022).

A human-centric approach to tourist technology, at its foundation, places people at the forefront of technological design and execution (Sheldon, 2020; Stankov & Gretzel, 2020). It aims to develop solutions that not only make use of the most recent technological advances but also resonate with the human experience, creating a seamless and meaningful relationship between tourists and technology (Gretzel, 2022; Stankov & Filimonau, 2021).

Personalization is a vital component of a human-centric approach (Buhalis & Amaranggana, 2015). Technology plays a critical role in building individualized journeys in an era when tourists want unique and specialized experiences. Personal-ization is transforming how tourists interact with and get value from technology, from

AI-driven recommendation engines that suggest places based on individual tastes to smart itinerary planning apps that adjust to real-time changes (Meehan et al., 2013; Ricci, 2020).

Furthermore, a human-centric approach takes into account the entire travel ecosystem, emphasizing the necessity of having a beneficial impact on local populations and the environment (Boes et al., 2016; Cassia et al., 2020). The human-centered approach values cultural sensitivity and local authenticity (Kovačić, et al., 2024; Vujičić et al., 2023). Technology is used as a facilitator to respect and enhance authentic cultural experiences rather than as a replacement for them (Anaya & Lehto, 2020; Lengyel, 2020). Augmented reality (AR) and virtual reality (VR) applications, for example, can provide immersive cultural experiences, allowing tourists to explore historical places or connect with local traditions respectfully and engagingly (Leung et al., 2022).

As discussed earlier in this chapter, accessibility is another critical dimension of a human-centric approach to tourism technology. Since, tourists represent one of the most diverse types of consumers, including a large group of people with disabilities. Many of them frequently face physical, sensory, cognitive, or cultural barriers in service provision and delivery. These barriers may occur in any of the typical tourist experience phases—inspiration-seeking, planning, booking, experiencing, and sharing, and they are not limited to any specific type of travel or a tourism setting. This could potentially further hamper the co-creation of tourist experiences for people with disabilities (and others), despite Industry 4.0 aiming to provide more sophisticated electronic/digital accessibility (e-accessibility) (Klironomos et al., 2006). At the same time, Industry 4.0 technologies have the innate qualities to mitigate many accessibility issues and turn them into possibilities by relying on tourists bringing their own devices and by promoting advanced approaches in system design and use. For instance, user-friendly interfaces, voice-activated systems, and other assistive technologies (Stankov et al., 2019) contribute to a more inclusive travel experience, ensuring that the benefits of technological innovation are accessible to all.

Technological advancements are progressively incorporating sustainable tourism practices, as evidenced by the proliferation of platforms that endorse environmentally conscious lodgings, conscientious travel decisions, and low-impact modes of transportation (Eiseman, 2018; Streimikiene et al., 2021).

The intersection of Industry 4.0 and sustainable tourism development holds significant promise for fostering responsible practices within the tourism sector (Ali & Frew, 2014). One key aspect of Industry 4.0 in sustainable tourism is the use of smart infrastructure and systems. Smart city technologies can be implemented to create more inclusive and user-friendly environments, such as smart transportation systems, barrier-free facilities, and augmented reality guides that cater to diverse needs (Cimbaljević et al., 2019). Moreover, Industry 4.0 can contribute to sustainability by optimizing resource management within the tourism industry. Smart energy solutions, waste reduction through data-driven insights, and the use of blockchain for transparent and eco-friendly supply chain management are examples of how technology can minimize the environmental footprint of tourism activities (Coca-Stefaniak, 2020; Frew, 2012; Gretzel, 2022).

4 Accessibility in Tourism 5.0 Experiences Through Travel Phases

In the nascent stages of the digital era, the focus of accessibility within the realm of tourism was primarily confined to the imperative of rendering tourism information more readily available on digital platforms, including websites and applications (Klironomos et al., 2006; Krstic, 2018). However, with the pervasive integration of ICT and their seamless convergence with the essence of tourism experiences, the significance of accessibility has undergone a profound transformation. No longer confined solely to the realm of information dissemination, accessibility has evolved into a paramount concern, intricately woven into the fabric of the entire tourism ecosystem (Filieri et al., 2021; Gajdošík & Marciš, 2019; Pisoni et al., 2021; Prahadeeswaran, 2023).

The technological landscape has shifted from merely providing information access to fostering inclusive and immersive tourism encounters (Bec et al., 2019). This paradigm shift underscores the broader realization that true accessibility extends beyond the digital realm, encompassing the entirety of the tourist journey. It now encompasses diverse dimensions, including but not limited to physical access to destinations, cultural inclusivity, and ensuring that technology serves as an enabler rather than a barrier for individuals with varying needs (O'Connor, 2022; Stankov et al., 2022b).

This evolution in the conceptualization of accessibility aligns with the dynamic nature of contemporary tourism experiences, where the emphasis is not solely on providing information (Vasiljević et al., 2009) but on facilitating meaningful and inclusive interactions (Câmara et al., 2023; Stankov et al., 2022a). As technology becomes increasingly integrated into every aspect of the travel industry, there is a growing acknowledgement that accessibility is not just a checkbox but a fundamental principle that should permeate the design and implementation of technological solutions in tourism.

Table 1 gives examples of technological approaches holding potential for broader use within Tourism 5.0 technologies across various phases of the tourist journey. Many examples are not limited to just one travel phase but can be useful in multiple phases or throughout the entire tourist experience. For instance, adaptive multi-modal interfaces shown in the "Experience phase" are expected to assist disabled people not only in all other phases but also in everyday activities.

The examples in Table 1 not only demonstrate commendable efforts in enhancing tourist experiences for individuals with diverse disabilities but also serve as integral components in everyday technology use for the mass consumers. This dual functionality establishes a fertile ground for developing user-centric technology across various domains, fostering cross-sectoral data exchange and innovation. These steps are crucial in realizing more sustainable and resilient approaches, aligning with the vision of Tourism 5.0.

It is evident from the examples in Table 1 that AI algorithms have the greatest potential for integration into every aspect of the travel experience, thereby facilitating

Table 1 Examples of accessible technological approaches holding potential for broader use in Tourism 5.0 (*Source* Contribution of authors)

Inspiration	Planning and booking	Experiencing	Sharing
• personalized trip recommendations • AR promotion • language translation • emotion analysis • reminder and notification system	• dynamic pricing and booking assistance • decrease of information and choice overload • voice-activated booking and real-time language translation • screen reader compatibility and accessible forms • predictive text and autocomplete, etc. • smart itinerary planning	• in-transit assistance • smart wearables for navigation • accommodation assistance (smart room controls, virtual concierge services) • accessible maps and navigation • multi-modal interfaces • AI-powered emergency assistance • health monitoring	• AI-powered customer service • feedback analysis • memory recall assistance • expense tracking and management • social media feeds

the use of technology (Chakraborty et al., 2023). For instance, through the analysis of a tourist's social media activity, past travel preferences, and travel history, they can provide personalized destination suggestions (Mukhopadhyay et al., 2022). An excellent illustration can be found in Istanbul. In a collaborative endeavor to enrich tourism and offer visitors seamless access to the city's abundant cultural wealth, the Istanbul Municipality has introduced a tourism campaign dubbed "Visit Istanbul". This initiative encompasses a web portal, AI tourist guide application, and a platform tailored for content creators (Kaburu, 2023). In addition, AI-powered chatbots (for instance, *Booking.com's* chatbot) and virtual assistants have the capability to interact with users to discern their preferences and offer customized travel recommendations (Hanji et al., 2024). As tourists explore new locales, AR applications can utilize AI to provide real-time navigation and information about historical sites, landmarks, and points of interest (Chen et al., 2020). Additionally, translation applications powered by AI can assist tourists in surmounting language obstacles through the provision of instantaneous translations of written or spoken text (Bulchand-Gidumal, 2022). Context awareness enabled by AI can optimize travel itineraries by analyzing historical data, weather conditions, and local events, while wearable devices with AI capabilities can analyze biometric data to determine a tourist's emotional state throughout the journey (Basarin et al., 2018; Santamaria-Granados et al., 2021). This data can be utilized to personalize the travel experience, for instance, by proposing tranquil activities or nearby points of interest following the tourist's disposition. From the standpoint of the providers, AI algorithms can evaluate current information on hotel rates, flight schedules, and other travel-related services to help customers locate the best offers. Dynamic tourism offers can be made, and using chatbots to speed up the booking process, make instant recommendations, and handle other tasks can save money (Ivanov & Webster, 2019; Nam et al., 2021).

5 Further Research and Practical Implementation Directions

By following the EU roadmap for Industry 5.0 (Breque et al., 2021; Pizoń & Gola, 2023), the tourism sector should follow a similar path in making Tourism 5.0 both practical and research agenda. In that sense, the several steps should be proposed.

- Profound Adopting the Human-Centric Approach to Digital Technologies Including Artificial Intelligence. Specifically, increasing the emphasis on user-centric design during digital technology advancements in the tourism sector. Significantly more emphasis should be placed on the value of user needs, preferences, and behavior comprehension to develop digital interfaces that are more personalized and intuitive.
- Investment in Digital Literacy Education. The implementation of digital literacy programs for both tourism industry professionals and tourists to ensure a better understanding of the technologies in use is a necessary step in the successful integration of Tourism 5.0 (Chaka, 2020; Kadijevich et al., 2020a, 2020b). This should include the promotion of awareness about the benefits and risks associated with digital technologies to empower both tourists and tourism workers to make informed choices (Zirar et al., 2023).
- Putting a Focus on Cultural Sensitivity. The development of AI systems that are culturally sensitive and respect local customs, traditions, and values is essential not only in European contests but most importantly on a global scale (Fatima et al., 2020; Goffi & Momcilovic, 2022; Ognjanović et al., 2019).
- Finding the Best Ways to Collaborate with Varied Tourism Stakeholders. Advocating for collaboration between technology developers, tourism businesses, government agencies, and local communities to ensure that technological applications align with the overall goals and values of the tourism industry (Stankov & Gretzel, 2021). This includes the promotion of dialogue and partnerships to address challenges and foster responsible innovation (Koops, 2015; Yildiz et al., 2023).

By incorporating these steps, the tourism industry can more systematically harness the benefits of Industry 5.0 technologies while prioritizing the well-being, satisfaction, and ethical considerations of tourists and other stakeholders.

Here, an important question can be asked: is accessibility merely a showcase of technological capabilities, a superficial gimmick akin to "ethics washing" (Wright, 2023)? The question that arises is whether accessibility initiatives within technology might also serve as a facade, potentially designed to project a positive image without a genuine commitment to true inclusivity.

This prompts a critical examination of whether accessibility efforts are authentic and meaningful (Stojsavljević et al., 2023) or merely symbolic gestures in the realm of technological progress. In that sense, more efforts should be put into exploring the journey from the rudimentary digitalization of tourism information to the current emphasis on holistic accessibility that should reflect a maturation in the understanding of the symbiotic relationship between technology and the tourism experience. From the practical perspective, tourism should showcase the industry's commitment to ensuring that technological advancements enhance, rather than impede, the diverse and enriching nature of travel experiences for all individuals, regardless of their unique requirements and backgrounds (Stankov & Gretzel, 2021). In particular, addressing issues such as privacy, transparency, and fairness in algorithmic decision-making seems to be a priority. The tourism industry should jointly propose the establishment of an industry-wide code of conduct to ensure responsible AI practices among stakeholders (Bulchand-Gidumal et al., 2023). In this regard, robust data privacy and security measures to protect tourist information from unauthorized access or misuse is a constant issue, despite different approaches to this matter among different tourism markets (Kadijevich et al., 2020a, 2020b; Line et al., 2020). In either case, advocating for transparent data practices, and ensuring that tourists are aware of how their data is collected, stored, and used is an important issue in the Tourism 5.0 approach.

6 Concluding Remarks

This chapter delves into the multifaceted dimensions of the Industry 5.0 approach, exploring its potential applications and implications for enhancing accessibility within the diverse tapestry of the tourism landscape. Through this chapter, we endeavor to form Tourist 5.0 as a holistic alternative to the prevailing concept of digital accessibility practices within the typically limited and task-focused tourism sector. Tourism 5.0, being an innovative concept, is thus receptive to numerous research avenues and the pursuit of creative concepts that will enable the development of more inclusive travel experiences that are engaging and relevant for consumers of all backgrounds.

Acknowledgements This chapter is based upon work from COST Action CA19142—Leading Platform for European Citizens, Industries, Academia and Policymakers in Media Accessibility (LEAD-ME) supported by COST (European Cooperation in Science and Technology); HORIZON TMA MSCA Staff Exchanges: ClearClimate (grant agreement No 101131220); and H2020-LC-GD-2020-3 GreenScent–Smart Citizen Education for a Green Future (grant agreement No 101036480) that have received funding from the European Union's Horizon 2020 research and innovation program. This chapter was also supported by the U.S. Embassy in Belgrade (grant number SRB10023GR0052).

References

Ali, A., & Frew, A. J. (2014). ICT and sustainable tourism development: An innovative perspective. *Journal of Hospitality and Tourism Technology, 5*(1), 2–16. https://doi.org/10.1108/JHTT-12-2012-0034

Anaya, G. J., & Lehto, X. (2020). Traveler-facing technology in the tourism experience: A historical perspective. *Journal of Travel & Tourism Marketing, 37*(3), 317–331. https://doi.org/10.1080/10548408.2020.1757561

Basarin, B., Lukic, T., Bjelajac, D., Micić Ponjiger, T., Stojićević, G., Stamenković, I., Đorđević, J., Djordjevic, T., & Matzarakis, A. (2018). Bioclimatic and climatic tourism conditions at Zlatibor Mountain (Western Serbia). *Időjárás, 122*, 321–343. https://doi.org/10.28974/idojaras.2018.3.6

Bec, A., Moyle, B., Timms, K., Schaffer, V., Skavronskaya, L., & Little, C. (2019). Management of immersive heritage tourism experiences: A conceptual model. *Tourism Management, 72*, 117–120. https://doi.org/10.1016/j.tourman.2018.10.033

Berawi, M. A. (2021). *Innovative technology for post-pandemic economic recovery*. IJTech—International Journal of Technology. https://ijtech.eng.ui.ac.id/article/view/4691

Boes, K., Buhalis, D., & Inversini, A. (2016). Smart tourism destinations: Ecosystems for tourism destination competitiveness. *International Journal of Tourism Cities, 2*(2), 108–124. https://doi.org/10.1108/IJTC-12-2015-0032

Bonello, A., Francalanza, E., & Refalo, P. (2024). Smart and sustainable human-centred workstations for operators with disability in the age of Industry 5.0: A systematic review. *Sustainability, 16*(1), Article 1. https://doi.org/10.3390/su16010281

Bove, T. (2021, June 8). *Techno-optimism: Why money and technology won't save us*. Earth.Org—Past | Present | Future. https://earth.org/techno-optimism/

Breque, M., De Nul, L., & Petridis, A. (2021). *Industry 5.0—Towards a sustainable, human-centric and resilient European industry*. Directorate-General for Research and Innovation.

Buhalis, D., & Amaranggana, A. (2015). Smart tourism destinations enhancing tourism experience through personalisation of services. In I. Tussyadiah, & A. Inversini (Eds.), *Information and communication technologies in tourism 2015* (pp. 377–389). Springer International Publishing. https://doi.org/10.1007/978-3-319-14343-9_28

Buhalis, D., Harwood, T., Bogicevic, V., Viglia, G., Beldona, S., & Hofacker, C. (2019). Technological disruptions in services: Lessons from tourism and hospitality. *Journal of Service Management, 30*(4), 484–506. https://doi.org/10.1108/JOSM-12-2018-0398

Bulchand-Gidumal, J. (2022). Impact of artificial intelligence in travel, tourism, and hospitality. In Z. Xiang, M. Fuchs, U. Gretzel, & W. Höpken (Eds.), *Handbook of e-tourism* (pp. 1943–1962). Springer International Publishing. https://doi.org/10.1007/978-3-030-48652-5_110

Bulchand-Gidumal, J., William Secin, E., O'Connor, P., & Buhalis, D. (2023). Artificial intelligence's impact on hospitality and tourism marketing: Exploring key themes and addressing challenges. *Current Issues in Tourism, 0*(0), 1–18. https://doi.org/10.1080/13683500.2023.2229480

Câmara, E., Pocinho, M., Agapito, D., & Jesus, S. N. de. (2023). Meaningful experiences in tourism: A systematic review of psychological constructs. *European Journal of Tourism Research, 34*:3403–3403. https://doi.org/10.54055/ejtr.v34i.2964

Carlisle, S., Ivanov, S., & Dijkmans, C. (2021). The digital skills divide: Evidence from the European tourism industry. *Journal of Tourism Futures, ahead-of-print*(ahead-of-print). https://doi.org/10.1108/JTF-07-2020-0114

Case, A. (2015). *Calm technology: Principles and patterns for non-intrusive design*. O'Reilly Media, Inc.

Cassia, F., Castellani, P., Rossato, C., & Baccarani, C. (2020). Finding a way towards high-quality, accessible tourism: The role of digital ecosystems. *The TQM Journal, 33*(1), 205–221. https://doi.org/10.1108/TQM-03-2020-0062

Chaka, C. (2020). Skills, competencies and literacies attributed to 4IR/Industry 4.0: Scoping review. *IFLA Journal, 46*(4), 369–399. https://doi.org/10.1177/0340035219896376

Chakraborty, N., Mishra, Y., Bhattacharya, R., & Bhattacharya, B. (2023). Artificial intelligence: The road ahead for the accessibility of persons with disability. *Materials Today: Proceedings, 80,* 3757–3761. https://doi.org/10.1016/j.matpr.2021.07.374

Chen, L., Xie, X., Lin, L., Wang, B., & Lin, W. (2020). Research on smart navigation system based on AR technology. *Fifth International Workshop on Pattern Recognition, 11526,* 104–110. https://doi.org/10.1117/12.2574673

Cimbaljević, M., Demirović Bajrami, D., Kovačić, S., Pavluković, V., Stankov, U., & Vujicic, M. D. (2023). Employees' technology adoption in the context of smart tourism development: The role of technological acceptance and technological readiness. *European Journal of Innovation Management.* https://doi.org/10.1108/EJIM-09-2022-0516

Cimbaljević, M., Stankov, U., & Pavluković, V. (2018). Going beyond the traditional destination competitiveness—Reflections on a smart destination in the current research. *Current Issues in Tourism,* 1–6. https://doi.org/10.1080/13683500.2018.1529149

Cimbaljević, M., Stankov, U., Demirović, D., & Pavluković, V. (2019). Nice and smart: Creating a smarter festival—The study of EXIT (Novi Sad, Serbia). *Asia Pacific Journal of Tourism Research,* 1–13. https://doi.org/10.1080/10941665.2019.1596139

Clark, B. B., Robert, C., & Hampton, S. A. (2016). The technology effect: How perceptions of technology drive excessive optimism. *Journal of Business and Psychology, 31*(1), 87–102. https://doi.org/10.1007/s10869-015-9399-4

Coca-Stefaniak, J. A. (2020). Beyond smart tourism cities—Towards a new generation of "wise" tourism destinations. *Journal of Tourism Futures, ahead-of-print*(ahead-of-print). https://doi.org/10.1108/JTF-11-2019-0130

Domínguez Vila, T., Alén González, E., & Darcy, S. (2020). Accessibility of tourism websites: The level of countries' commitment. *Universal Access in the Information Society, 19*(2), 331–346. https://doi.org/10.1007/s10209-019-00643-4

Dragović, N., Vasiljević, Đ., Stankov, U., & Vujičić, M. (2019). Go social for your own safety! Review of social networks use on natural disasters—Case studies from worldwide. *Open Geosciences, 11*(1), 352–366. https://doi.org/10.1515/geo-2019-0028

Duan, L., & Da Xu, L. (2021). Data analytics in Industry 4.0: A survey. *Information Systems Frontiers.* https://doi.org/10.1007/s10796-021-10190-0

Eiseman, D. (2018). Marketing sustainable tourism: Principles and practice. In M. Anthony Camilleri (Ed.), *Tourism planning and destination marketing* (pp. 121–140). Emerald Publishing Limited. https://doi.org/10.1108/978-1-78756-291-220181006

Fatima, S., Desouza, K. C., & Dawson, G. S. (2020). National strategic artificial intelligence plans: A multi-dimensional analysis. *Economic Analysis and Policy, 67,* 178–194. https://doi.org/10.1016/j.eap.2020.07.008

Fernández-Díaz, E., Jambrino-Maldonado, C., Iglesias-Sánchez, P. P., & de las Heras-Pedrosa, C. (2022). Digital accessibility of smart cities—Tourism for all and reducing inequalities: Tourism Agenda 2030. *Tourism Review, 78*(2), 361–380. https://doi.org/10.1108/TR-02-2022-0091

Filieri, R., D'Amico, E., Destefanis, A., Paolucci, E., & Raguseo, E. (2021). Artificial intelligence (AI) for tourism: An European-based study on successful AI tourism start-ups. *International Journal of Contemporary Hospitality Management, 33*(11), 4099–4125. https://doi.org/10.1108/IJCHM-02-2021-0220

Filimonau, V., Ashton, M., & Stankov, U. (2022). Virtual spaces as the future of consumption in tourism, hospitality and events. *Journal of Tourism Futures.* Scopus. https://doi.org/10.1108/JTF-07-2022-0174

Frew, A. A. (2012). *Information and communication technologies for sustainable tourism.* Routledge. https://doi.org/10.4324/9780203072592

Gajdošík, T., & Marciš, M. (2019). Artificial intelligence tools for smart tourism development. In R. Silhavy (Ed.), *Artificial intelligence methods in intelligent algorithms* (pp. 392–402). Springer International Publishing. https://doi.org/10.1007/978-3-030-19810-7_39

Goffi, E. R., & Momcilovic, A. (2022). Respecting cultural diversity in ethics applied to AI: A new approach for a multicultural governance. *Misión Jurídica: Revista De Derecho y Ciencias Sociales, 15*(23), 111–122.

Golovianko, M., Terziyan, V., Branytskyi, V., & Malyk, D. (2023). Industry 4.0 vs. Industry 5.0: Co-existence, transition, or a hybrid. *Procedia Computer Science, 217*, 102–113. https://doi.org/10.1016/j.procs.2022.12.206

Gonella, F., Almeida, C. M. V. B., Fiorentino, G., Handayani, K., Spanò, F., Testoni, R., & Zucaro, A. (2019). Is technology optimism justified? A discussion towards a comprehensive narrative. *Journal of Cleaner Production, 223*, 456–465. https://doi.org/10.1016/j.jclepro.2019.03.126

Gretzel, U. (2022). The Smart DMO: A new step in the digital transformation of destination management organizations. *European Journal of Tourism Research, 30*, 3002–3002. https://doi.org/10.54055/ejtr.v30i.2589

Gretzel, U., & Stankov, U. (2021). ICTs and well-being: Challenges and opportunities for tourism. *Information Technology & Tourism, 23*(1), 1–4. https://doi.org/10.1007/s40558-021-00198-2

Gretzel, U., Fuchs, M., Baggio, R., Hoepken, W., Law, R., Neidhardt, J., Pesonen, J., Zanker, M., & Xiang, Z. (2020). E-Tourism beyond COVID-19: A call for transformative research. *Information Technology and Tourism, 22*(2), 187–203. https://doi.org/10.1007/s40558-020-00181-3

Griffy-Brown, C., Earp, B. D., & Rosas, O. (2018). Technology and the good society. *Technology in Society, 52*, 1–3. https://doi.org/10.1016/j.techsoc.2018.01.001

Hamdan, A., Harraf, A., Buallay, A., Arora, P., & Alsabatin, H. (Eds.). (2023). *From Industry 4.0 to Industry 5.0: Mapping the transitions* (Vol. 470). Springer Nature Switzerland. https://doi.org/10.1007/978-3-031-28314-7

Hanji, S. V., Navalgund, N., Ingalagi, S., Desai, S., & Hanji, S. S. (2024). Adoption of AI chatbots in travel and tourism services. In X.-S. Yang, R. S. Sherratt, N. Dey, & A. Joshi (Eds.), *Proceedings of eighth international congress on information and communication technology* (pp. 713–727). Springer Nature. https://doi.org/10.1007/978-981-99-3236-8_57

Hatamura, Y. (Ed.). (2009). *Learning from design failures.* Springer Verlag.

Herweijer, C., Gawel, A., & Engtoft Larsen, A. M. (2020, January 20). *2030: From technology optimism to technology realism.* World Economic Forum. https://www.weforum.org/agenda/2020/01/decade-of-action-from-technology-optimism-to-technology-realism/

Ivanov, D. (2021). Digital supply chain management and technology to enhance resilience by building and using end-to-end visibility during the COVID-19 pandemic. *IEEE Transactions on Engineering Management*, 1–11. https://doi.org/10.1109/TEM.2021.3095193

Ivanov, S., & Webster, C. (2019). *Robots, artificial intelligence and service automation in travel, tourism and hospitality.* https://doi.org/10.1108/9781787566873

İyigün, İ., & Görçün, Ö. F. (2023). Introduction. In İ. İyigün, & Ö. F. Görçün (Eds.), *Health 4.0 and medical supply chain* (pp. 3–7). Springer Nature. https://doi.org/10.1007/978-981-99-1818-8_1

Kaburu, G. (2023). *Istanbul Municipality unveils AI-powered tourism apps to boost tourism.* https://www.cryptopolitan.com/istanbul-unveils-ai-powered-tourism-apps/

Kadijević, Đ., Odović, G., & Masliković, D. (2016). Using ICT and quality of life: Comparing persons with and without disabilities. *Computers Helping People with Special Needs, ICCHP 2016, Pt I, 9758*, 129–133. https://doi.org/10.1007/978-3-319-41264-1_18

Kadijevich, D. M., Masliković, D., & Tomić, B. M. (2020a). Dataset regarding access to information for persons with disabilities in Serbia. *Data in Brief, 32*, 106309. https://doi.org/10.1016/j.dib.2020.106309

Kadijevich, D., Maslikovic, D., & Tomic, B. (2020b). Familiarity with state regulations regarding access to information for persons with disabilities in Serbia. *International Journal of Disability, Development and Education, 69*, 1–11. https://doi.org/10.1080/1034912X.2020.1802646

Klironomos, I., Antona, M., Basdekis, I., Stephanidis, C., & EDeAN Secretariat for 2005. (2006). White Paper: Promoting design for all and e-accessibility in Europe. *Universal Access in the Information Society, 5*(1), 105–119. https://doi.org/10.1007/s10209-006-0021-4

Koops, B.-J. (2015). The concepts, approaches, and applications of responsible innovation. In B.-J. Koops, I. Oosterlaken, H. Romijn, T. Swierstra, & J. van den Hoven (Eds.), *Responsible innovation 2: Concepts, approaches, and applications* (pp. 1–15). Springer International Publishing. https://doi.org/10.1007/978-3-319-17308-5_1

Kovačić, S. Pivac, T., Solarević, M., Blešić, I., Cimbaljević, M., Vujičić, M.D., Stankov, U., Besermenji, S., & Ćurčić, N. (2024). Let us hear the voice of the audience: groups facing the risk of cultural exclusion and cultural accessibility in Vojvodina province (Serbia). *Universal Access in the Information Society, ahead-of-print*.

Krstic, N. (2018). Pain points of cultural institutions in search visibility: The case of Serbia. *Library Hi Tech, 37*. https://doi.org/10.1108/LHT-12-2017-0264

Kwok, P. K., Yan, M., Qu, T., & Lau, H. Y. K. (2021). User acceptance of virtual reality technology for practicing digital twin-based crisis management. *International Journal of Computer Integrated Manufacturing, 34*(7–8), 874–887. https://doi.org/10.1080/0951192X.2020.1803502

Lengyel, A. (2020). Authenticity, mindfulness and destination liminoidity: A multi-level model. *Tourism Recreation Research, 0*(0), 1–16. https://doi.org/10.1080/02508281.2020.1815412

Leung, W. K. S., Cheung, M. L., Chang, M. K., Shi, S., Tse, S. Y., & Yusrini, L. (2022). The role of virtual reality interactivity in building tourists' memorable experiences and post-adoption intentions in the COVID-19 era. *Journal of Hospitality and Tourism Technology, ahead-of-print*(ahead-of-print). https://doi.org/10.1108/JHTT-03-2021-0088

Line, N. D., Dogru, T., El-Manstrly, D., Buoye, A., Malthouse, E., & Kandampully, J. (2020). Control, use and ownership of big data: A reciprocal view of customer big data value in the hospitality and tourism industry. *Tourism Management, 80*, 104106. https://doi.org/10.1016/j.tourman.2020.104106

Liu, B., Pennington-Gray, L., & Klemmer, L. (2015). Using social media in hotel crisis management: The case of bed bugs. *Journal of Hospitality and Tourism Technology, 6*(2), 102–112. https://doi.org/10.1108/JHTT-08-2014-0036

Meehan, K., Lunney, T., Curran, K., & McCaughey, A. (2013). Context-aware intelligent recommendation system for tourism. In *2013 IEEE international conference on pervasive computing and communications workshops (PERCOM workshops)*, pp. 328–331. https://doi.org/10.1109/PerComW.2013.6529508

Möller, D. P. F., Vakilzadian, H., & Haas, R. E. (2022). From Industry 4.0 towards Industry 5.0. In *2022 IEEE international conference on electro information technology (eIT)*, pp. 61–68. https://doi.org/10.1109/eIT53891.2022.9813831

Morozov, E. (2013). *To save everything, click here: The folly of technological solutionism*. New York: PublicAffairs

Morar, C., Tiba, A., Jovanovic, T., Valjarević, A., Ripp, M., Vujičić, M. D., Stankov, U., Basarin, B., Ratković, R., Popović, M., Nagy, G., Boros, L., & Lukić, T. (2022). Supporting tourism by assessing the predictors of COVID-19 vaccination for travel reasons. *International Journal of Environmental Research and Public Health, 19*(2), Article 2. https://doi.org/10.3390/ijerph19020918

Mukhopadhyay, S., Jain, T., Modgil, S., & Singh, R. K. (2022). Social media analytics in tourism: A review and agenda for future research. *Benchmarking: An International Journal, 30*(9), 3725–3750. https://doi.org/10.1108/BIJ-05-2022-0309

Müller, J. (2020). *Enabling technologies for Industry 5.0—Results of a workshop with Europe's technology leaders*.

Nam, K., Dutt, C. S., Chathoth, P., Daghfous, A., & Khan, M. S. (2021). The adoption of artificial intelligence and robotics in the hotel industry: Prospects and challenges. *Electronic Markets, 31*(3), 553–574. https://doi.org/10.1007/s12525-020-00442-3

Navío-Marco, J., Ruiz-Gómez, L. M., & Sevilla-Sevilla, C. (2018). Progress in information technology and tourism management: 30 years on and 20 years after the internet—Revisiting Buhalis & Law's landmark study about eTourism. *Tourism Management, 69*, 460–470. https://doi.org/10.1016/J.TOURMAN.2018.06.002

Neuhofer, B., Buhalis, D., & Ladkin, A. (2012). Conceptualising technology enhanced destination experiences. *Journal of Destination Marketing & Management, 1*(1), 36–46. https://doi.org/10.1016/j.jdmm.2012.08.001

Neuhofer, B., Buhalis, D., & Ladkin, A. (2013). High tech for high touch experiences: A case study from the hospitality industry. In L. Cantoni, & Z. P. Xiang (Eds.), *Information and communication technologies in tourism 2013* (pp. 290–301). Springer Berlin Heidelberg. https://doi.org/10.1007/978-3-642-36309-2_25

Neuhofer, B., Buhalis, D., & Ladkin, A. (2015). Technology as a catalyst of change: enablers and barriers of the tourist experience and their consequences. In I. Tussyadiah, & A. Inversini (Eds.), *Information and communication technologies in tourism 2015* (pp. 789–802). Springer International Publishing. https://doi.org/10.1007/978-3-319-14343-9_57

O'Connor, E. (2022, September 26). *How technology can enhance diversity and inclusion.* WeAreTechWomen—Supporting Women in Technology. https://wearetechwomen.com/how-technology-can-enhance-diversity-and-inclusion/

Ognjanović, Z., Marinković, B., Šegan-Radonjić, M., & Maslikoviċ, D. (2019). Cultural heritage digitization in Serbia: Standards, policies, and case studies. *Sustainability, 11*(14), Article 14. https://doi.org/10.3390/su11143788

Orea-Giner, A., Muñoz-Mazón, A., Villacé-Molinero, T., & Fuentes-Moraleda, L. (2022). Cultural tourist and user experience with artificial intelligence: A holistic perspective from the Industry 5.0 approach. *Journal of Tourism Futures, ahead-of-print*(ahead-of-print). https://doi.org/10.1108/JTF-04-2022-0115

Paro, C. E., Ribeiro da Silva, H. M., Spers, E. E., Jugend, D., & Hamza, K. M. (2021). The technology effect, green consumption and age in propensity to collaborative consumption. *Cleaner and Responsible Consumption, 2*, 100008. https://doi.org/10.1016/j.clrc.2021.100008

Pencarelli, T. (2019). The digital revolution in the travel and tourism industry. *Information Technology and Tourism.* https://doi.org/10.1007/s40558-019-00160-3

Pisoni, G., Díaz-Rodríguez, N., Gijlers, H., & Tonolli, L. (2021). Human-centered artificial intelligence for designing accessible cultural heritage. *Applied Sciences, 11*(2), Article 2. https://doi.org/10.3390/app11020870

Pizoń, J., & Gola, A. (2023). Human–machine relationship—Perspective and future roadmap for Industry 5.0 solutions. *Machines, 11*(2), Article 2. https://doi.org/10.3390/machines11020203

Prahadeeswaran, R. (2023). A comprehensive review: The convergence of artificial intelligence and tourism. *International Journal for Multidimensional Research Perspectives, 1*(2), Article 2.

Radojević, B., Stankov, U., & Vujičić, M. D. (2023). Governing geospatial aspects of smart destination development—The case of Novi Sad, Serbia. *Geographica Pannonica, 27*(3), Article 3. https://doi.org/10.5937/gp27-44121

Ricci, F. (2020). Recommender systems in tourism. In *Handbook of e-tourism* (pp. 1–18). https://doi.org/10.1007/978-3-030-05324-6_26-1

Røpke, I. (1996). Technology optimism in a socio-economic perspective. *Journal of Income Distribution, 6*(2), 215–234.

Santamaria-Granados, L., Mendoza-Moreno, J. F., Chantre-Astaiza, A., Munoz-Organero, M., & Ramirez-Gonzalez, G. (2021). Tourist experiences recommender system based on emotion recognition with wearable data. *Sensors, 21*(23), Article 23. https://doi.org/10.3390/s21237854

Sharma, G. D., Thomas, A., & Paul, J. (2021). Reviving tourism industry post-COVID-19: A resilience-based framework. *Tourism Management Perspectives, 37*, 100786. https://doi.org/10.1016/j.tmp.2020.100786

Sheldon, P. J. (2020). Designing tourism experiences for inner transformation. *Annals of Tourism Research, 83*, 102935–102935. https://doi.org/10.1016/j.annals.2020.102935

Silva, F. M., & Borges, I. (2020). Digital accessibility on institutional websites of Portuguese tourism. In V. Ratten (Ed.), *Technological progress, inequality and entrepreneurship: From consumer division to human centricity* (pp. 67–85). Springer International Publishing. https://doi.org/10.1007/978-3-030-26245-7_5

Stankov, U., & Filimonau, V. (2019). Reviving calm technology in the e-tourism context. *Service Industries Journal, 39*(5–6), 343–360. https://doi.org/10.1080/02642069.2018.1544619

Stankov, U., & Filimonau, V. (2020). Technology-assisted mindfulness in the co-creation of tourist experiences. In Z. Xian, M. Fuchs, U. Gretzel, & W. Höpken (Eds.), *Handbook of e-tourism*. Springer. https://doi.org/10.1007/978-3-030-05324-6

Stankov, U., & Filimonau, V. (2021). Here and now—The role of mindfulness in post-pandemic tourism. *Tourism Geographies, 0*(0), 1–16. https://doi.org/10.1080/14616688.2021.2021978

Stankov, U., & Gretzel, U. (2020). Tourism 4.0 technologies and tourist experiences: A human-centered design perspective. *Information Technology & Tourism*. https://doi.org/10.1007/s40 558-020-00186

Stankov, U., & Gretzel, U. (2021). Digital well-being in the tourism domain: Mapping new roles and responsibilities. *Information Technology & Tourism, 23*(1), 5–17. https://doi.org/10.1007/ s40558-021-00197-3

Stankov, U., Filimonau, V., & Slivar, I. (2019). Calm ICT design in hotels: A critical review of applications and implications. *International Journal of Hospitality Management, 82*, 298–307. https://doi.org/10.1016/j.ijhm.2018.10.012

Stankov, U., Filimonau, V., & Vujičić, M. D. (2020). A mindful shift: An opportunity for mindfulness-driven tourism in a post-pandemic world. *Tourism Geographies, 22*(3), 703–712. https://doi.org/10.1080/14616688.2020.1768432

Stankov, U., Filimonau, V., Vujičić, M. D., Basarin, B., Carmer, A. B., Lazić, L., Hansen, B. K., Ćirić Lalić, D., & Mujkić, D. (2023a). Ready for action! Destination climate change communication: An archetypal branding approach. *International Journal of Environmental Research and Public Health, 20*(5), Article 5. https://doi.org/10.3390/ijerph20053874

Stankov, U., Gretzel, U., & Filimonau, V. (2022a). *The mindful tourist: The power of presence in tourism*. Emerald Publishing Limited.

Stankov, U., Gretzel, U., Vujičić, M. D., Pavluković, V., Jovanović, T., Solarević, M., & Cimbaljević, M. (2022b). The pandemic of loneliness: Designing smart tourism for combating loneliness. *Information Technology & Tourism, 24*(4), 439–455. https://doi.org/10.1007/s40558-022-002 34-9

Stankov, U., Vujičić, M. D., & Basarin, B. (2023). Enhancing energy management in tourism through accessible climate information services: A human-centered approach. In *International conference on power and renewable energy engineering*, Tokyo, Japan, 20–22 October, Tokyo.

Stankov, U., Vujičić, M.D, Orero, P., Gretzel, U. (2024). *Editorial: Accessibility of Tourism 4.0—Designing more meaningful and inclusive tourist experiences*. Universal Access in the Information Society, ahead-of-print.

Starc Peceny, U., Urbančič, J., Mokorel, S., Kuralt, V., & Ilijaš, T. (2019). Tourism 4.0: Challenges in marketing a paradigm shift. In *Consumer behavior and marketing [Working Title]*. IntechOpen. https://doi.org/10.5772/intechopen.84762

Stojsavljević, R., Vujičić, M. D., Stankov, U., Stamenković, I., Masliković, D., Carmer, A. B., Polić, D., Mujkić, D., & Bajić, M. (2023). In search for meaning? Modelling generation Z spiritual travel motivation scale—The case of Serbia. *Sustainability, 15*(6), Article 6.

Streimikiene, D., Svagzdiene, B., Jasinskas, E., & Simanavicius, A. (2021). Sustainable tourism development and competitiveness: The systematic literature review. *Sustainable Development, 29*(1), 259–271. https://doi.org/10.1002/sd.2133

Thomas, M. J., Lal, V., Baby, A. K., Rabeeh V. P. M., James, A., & Raj, A. K. (2021). Can technological advancements help to alleviate COVID-19 pandemic? A review. *Journal of Biomedical Informatics, 117*, 103787. https://doi.org/10.1016/j.jbi.2021.103787

Ustundag, A., & Cevikcan, E. (2017). *Industry 4.0: Managing the digital transformation*. Springer.

Vasiljević, Đ, Marković, S. B., Hose, T. A., Basarin, B., Lazić, L., Stojanović, V., Lukić, T., Vidić, N., Jović, G., Janićević, S., & Samardžija, D. (2009). The use of web-based dynamic maps in the promotion of the Titel loess plateau Vojvodina, Serbia, a potential geotourism destination. *Geographica Pannonica, 13*(3), 78–84. https://doi.org/10.5937/GeoPan0903078V

Vujicic, M. D., & Stankov, U. (2022). *Behind the smart: The hidden costs of tourism technology optimism.* Green Digital Accessibility, Barcelona. https://mapaccess.uab.cat/conference-presentations/behind-smart-hidden-costs-tourism-technology-optimism

Vujičić, M. D., Stankov, U., Pavluković, V., Štajner-Papuga, I., Kovačić, S., Čikić, J., Milenković, N., & Zelenović Vasiljević, T. (2023). Prepare for impact! A methodological approach for comprehensive impact evaluation of European capital of culture: The case of Novi Sad 2022. *Social Indicators Research, 165*(2), 715–736. https://doi.org/10.1007/s11205-022-03041-1

Vujičić, M. D., Stankov, U., & Vasiljević, Dj. A. (2022). Tourism at a crossroads—ignoring, adopting, or embracing alternative. In J. Kennell, P. Mohanty, A. Sharma, & A. Hassan (Eds.), *Crisis management, destination recovery and sustainability tourism at a crossroads.* Routledge.

Wilk-Jakubowski, G., Harabin, R., & Ivanov, S. (2022). Robotics in crisis management: A review. *Technology in Society, 68*, 101935. https://doi.org/10.1016/j.techsoc.2022.101935

Wright, J. (2023). The Development of AI Ethics in Japan: Ethics-washing Society 5.0? *East Asian Science, Technology and Society: An International Journal, 0*(0), 1–18. https://doi.org/10.1080/18752160.2023.2275987

Wut, T. M., Xu, J. (Bill), & Wong, S. (2021). Crisis management research (1985–2020) in the hospitality and tourism industry: A review and research agenda. *Tourism Management, 85*, 104307. https://doi.org/10.1016/j.tourman.2021.104307

Xu, X., Lu, Y., Vogel-Heuser, B., & Wang, L. (2021). Industry 4.0 and Industry 5.0—Inception, conception and perception. *Journal of Manufacturing Systems, 61*, 530–535. https://doi.org/10.1016/j.jmsy.2021.10.006

Yildiz, M., Pless, N., Ceyhan, S., & Hallak, R. (2023). Responsible leadership and innovation during COVID-19: Evidence from the Australian Tourism and Hospitality Sector. *Sustainability, 15*(6), Article 6. https://doi.org/10.3390/su15064922

Zirar, A., Ali, S. I., & Islam, N. (2023). Worker and workplace Artificial Intelligence (AI) coexistence: Emerging themes and research agenda. *Technovation, 124*, 102747. https://doi.org/10.1016/j.technovation.2023.102747

Zizic, M. C., Mladineo, M., Gjeldum, N., & Celent, L. (2022). From Industry 4.0 towards Industry 5.0: A review and analysis of paradigm shift for the people, organization and technology. *Energies, 15*(14), Article 14. https://doi.org/10.3390/en15145221

Accessible Public Transport: A Case Study of Warsaw

Anna Warchoł-Jakubowska⬤, Iga Szwoch⬤, Patryk Szczeciński⬤, Izabela Krejtz⬤, and Krzysztof Krejtz⬤

Abstract This chapter explores accessibility in public transport, focusing on the case study of Warsaw in Poland, and is structured into several key sections. In Sect. 2, the challenges faced by individuals with disabilities in urban spaces are discussed, shedding light on the impediments they encounter in navigating public transportation systems. Section 3 delves into the legal conditions surrounding accessibility, examining the international framework, national legislation, and the principles of universal design. A comprehensive review of existing accessibility solutions across various European cities is presented in Sect. 4, including accessible bus shelters equipped with access ramps and touchscreen directions and the integration of new technologies to enhance accessibility. Finally, Sect. 5 takes Warsaw as a central example of a European capital actively implementing innovative solutions in public transport accessibility. The chapter underscores the importance of addressing challenges, legal frameworks, and the adoption of cutting-edge solutions to create a more inclusive and accessible urban transport environment.

Keywords Accessibility · Public transport · Smart city · Mobility

A. Warchoł-Jakubowska (✉) · I. Szwoch · P. Szczeciński · I. Krejtz · K. Krejtz
Eye Tracking Research Center, Institute of Psychology, SWPS University, Warsaw, Poland
e-mail: awarchol-jakubowska@swps.edu.pl

I. Szwoch
e-mail: iszwoch@swps.edu.pl

P. Szczeciński
e-mail: pszczecinski@st.swps.edu.pl

I. Krejtz
e-mail: ikrejtz@swps.edu.pl

K. Krejtz
e-mail: kkrejtz@swps.edu.pl

© The Author(s) 2024
A. Marcus-Quinn et al. (eds.), *Transforming Media Accessibility in Europe*,
https://doi.org/10.1007/978-3-031-60049-4_2

1   Introduction

Accessibility is a key concept in creating urban agglomerations of the twenty-first century (UN, 2015). Eliminating barriers for people with physical and cognitive disabilities is also an obligation of public transport. Full access to city space is still a challenge for people with different disabilities who meet many barriers to cultural assets, public spaces, and public transport, during everyday functioning (The Ministry of Investment & Development, 2018). Accessible city space, infrastructure, and public transport improves inclusiveness and quality of live for people with disabilities and limited mobility. The general objective of the transport policy in Warsaw, the capital city of Poland, is to improve and develop the transportation system for everyone, regardless of their mobility, to travel safely (Office of Mobility & Transportation Policy, 2009). Later, in this chapter, we portray Warsaw public transport accessibility on the background of various European cities' solutions.

2   Challenges Faced by Individuals with Disabilities in Urban Spaces—Literature Review

People with disabilities come across several additional challenges in everyday life, and the sphere of urban spaces and public transportation is no different in that matter. Some of those have been addressed extensively in the literature, such as ramp access for people with mobility difficulties (Unsworth et al., 2021) or barriers arising from the architectural design of certain places like bus stops or stations (Boadi-Kusi et al., 2023), but certain not commonly thought of issues arise while delving deeper into the subject, making people with disabilities less prone to use public transportation systems (Park et al., 2023).

People using mobility devices are one of the groups affected by the lack of accessibility to public transportation. A systematic review collecting literature from 1995 to 2019 (Unsworth et al., 2021) highlighted issues surrounding the commute to and from public transport stops, such as uneven pavement, steps, narrow doorways, and bad street signage design. Reviewed studies also suggest difficulties such as a lack of space for wheelchair users inside vehicles, information being placed in places where it cannot be reached, boarding troubles (for example, a high-floor bus, in comparison with a low-floor one, which is a vehicle that has no steps between the ground and the vehicle floor at one or more entrances. This is necessary for easy entry and exit of people in wheelchairs and people with strollers). An additional challenge is posed by drivers being prejudiced and selecting whether to stop for a person using a mobility device, and improper ramp designs. Lifts are also not always available to access certain stations.

Public transportation also presents a challenge to people with visual impairments (Boadi-Kusi et al., 2023). Access to information is one of the most prominent issues, with notifications about approaching buses or trams being not available and not being notified accordingly when approaching the destination. Labels and information on overhead screens are often not designed with accessibility guidelines in mind, with e.g., small print, low contrasts, etc. (Park & Chowdhury, 2018). Voice announcements are reported to be not efficient—they can be delayed, unclear, have low volume, or just not be present (Starzynska et al., 2015). The bus layout can also be troublesome to people with visual impairments, due to no low-floor solutions available, having steps inside the bus, having no universal internal layout, and the nonexistence of standardized priority space for people with visual disabilities, as reported by Odame et al. (2020). The same authors put forward a lack of assistive technologies that encourage independent communication between drivers and people with disabilities.

People who are hard of hearing or deaf differently evaluate the levels of accessibility in public transportation, with most of the means of transport being valued as sufficiently or at most well equipped to assist those people accordingly (Orczyk & Mlodystach, 2022). The problems mentioned were incomprehensible voice systems, wrong information on displays (not updating times of departure or changes of platforms), and staff not being prepared to assist people with hearing impairments. Induction loops and sign language interpreters are not yet widely available at stations.

One of the most understudied groups are people with cognitive and intellectual disabilities, just recently gathering attention to the difficulties they may be facing (van Holstein et al., 2022). This group includes people with dementia, dyslexia, sensory issues, developmental disabilities, brain injuries, etc. (Carmien et al., 2005). However, it is important to also include people struggling with different psychiatric or psychological disorders that affect their cognitive state, such as depression or anxiety (Kircanski et al., 2012). Navigation across city, stations, or inside the means of transportation can be a demanding task requiring executive functioning for many (Fischer & Sullivan, 2002), and people with cognitive disabilities are put in the place of a new, unfamiliar public transportation user each time they try to reach a certain destination. They may encounter difficulties with remembering previously known paths and learning new, more complex, routes. Any changes such as delays or platform switches can go unnoticed and result in a failing attempt to travel. Risser et al. (2015) unveil the need to make public transportation available, due to the lack of other transport options for people with cognitive disorders and those who are often forced to stop driving a personal vehicle due to age or the progression of an impairment, and private companies offering special transportation options are difficult to find.

3   Legal Conditions

Poland's accession to the European Union in 2004 imposed many obligations regarding accessibility for citizens with disabilities (Trociuk, 2011). Implementation of EU standards includes, among other things, the elimination of architectural barriers that have a fundamental impact on how far people with disabilities can be independent as citizens. The United Nations Convention on the Rights of Persons with Disabilities of 13 December 2006, signed by Poland, imposed an obligation to equalize opportunities for people with disabilities and enable them to fully participate in all spheres of life on an equal basis with other citizens. The Ombudsman is a constitutional body protecting civil rights and freedoms and an independent body of equal treatment within the meaning of the Act of 3 December 2010 on the implementation of certain provisions of the European Union in the field of equal treatment (Journal of Laws of 2010, No. 254, item 1700). Below, we present an overview of European and national legislation that affects the solutions in Poland, taking into account equal treatment for all people. The list below is not an exhaustive collection of regulations, but it provides insight into the conditions considered when increasing accessibility in both Europe and Poland.

3.1 International Framework of Accessibility in Public Transport

In the global context, several key international documents and resolutions emphasize the importance of equal opportunities and accessibility for individuals with disabilities. Selected regulations are referenced below in chronological order. First, the resolution 48/96, known as the Standard Rules on the Equalization of Opportunities for Persons with Disabilities, adopted during the 48th session of the UN General Assembly on December 20, 1993, centers on accessibility as a fundamental principle. Principle 5 of this resolution highlights the critical role of accessibility in fostering equal opportunities across all aspects of social life. It urges states, organizations, and local authorities to recognize the significance of accessibility and initiate programs to enhance the physical environment, facilitate access to information, and improve interpersonal communication resources for individuals with disabilities.

Second, the Barcelona Declaration, adopted on November 28, 1995, during the City and the Disabled Conference, emphasizes policy objectives grounded in fundamental human rights and equal access to public life. Endorsed by over 400 cities, including Gdynia as the sole Polish city, the declaration prioritizes accessibility and calls for the elimination of barriers in public spaces and information. It aims to inspire local authorities to incorporate provisions for the integration of people with disabilities into their local legislation.

Recommendation No. 5/2006 of the Committee of Ministers of the Council of Europe, adopted on April 5, 2006, details the Council of Europe Action Plan to promote the rights and full participation of people with disabilities in society. It encourages Member States to adopt policies creating a barrier-free built environment.

The Convention on the Rights of Persons with Disabilities, a UN General Assembly Resolution A/RES/61/106 of December 13, 2006, reinforces the need for ensuring equal rights and opportunities. Emphasizing standardized spatial solutions, the convention aims to guarantee accessibility for all users. This resolution includes aspects such as accessibility of the architecture, public transportation, information and communication technologies, and other areas, to facilitate full participation of people with disabilities in society.

Regulation (EC) 1371/2007 of the European Parliament and the Council, issued on October 23, 2007, outlines the rights and obligations of rail passengers. Ensuring equal rights for people with disabilities and reduced mobility, the regulation emphasizes the principles of free movement, choice, and non-discrimination.

The European Disability Strategy 2010–2020, dated November 15, 2010, defines accessibility as providing individuals with disabilities equal access to the physical environment, transportation, information, and communication technology, as well as various facilities and services.

The Charter of Fundamental Rights of the European Union, dated 26 October 2012, particularly in Article 1, underscores the inviolable nature of human dignity. Article 26 recognizes the rights of persons with disabilities to ensure their independence, social integration, and community participation, while Article 21 prohibits discrimination based on disability.

3.2 National Legislation in Poland

The legal landscape in Poland, shaped by its commitment to inclusivity and equal opportunities for individuals with disabilities, encompasses several key provisions.

In the realm of transportation, the Transport Law Act, initiated on November 15, 1984, and subsequent amendments, places an onus on carriers to take proactive measures facilitating the use of transport by passengers, particularly those with reduced mobility and disabilities (Article 14(2)).

The Construction Law Act, implemented on July 7, 1994, reinforces the commitment to accessibility. Article 5.4 highlights the imperative to ensure facilities are accessible to individuals with disabilities, particularly addressing the needs of wheelchair users. Notably, this requirement applies to buildings constructed after 1995, emphasizing the forward-looking approach.

The Polish Constitution, enacted on April 2, 1997, serves as a cornerstone. Article 32(1) expressly prohibits discrimination on any grounds, reinforcing the nation's dedication to fostering a society free from unjust bias. Additionally, Article 69 places an obligation on public authorities to actively support people with disabilities in various aspects of their lives, including daily activities, employment, and social interactions.

The Lower House Resolution of August 1, 1997, known as the Charter of Rights of Persons with Disabilities, serves a declarative purpose. It affirms the inherent right of individuals with disabilities to lead independent, self-reliant, and active lives, explicitly prohibiting discrimination. While primarily aspirational, it reflects Poland's dedication to promoting a society where every individual, irrespective of ability, can fully participate and thrive.

The Act of August 27, 1997, focusing on vocational and social rehabilitation and employment of people with disabilities, aims to break down communication barriers.

Article 9, within this legislation, specifically targets architectural and transport obstacles, striving to enhance accessibility and participation in social life. Oversight of this Act falls under the responsibility of the Government Plenipotentiary for Disabled Persons, who works toward minimizing disability effects and societal barriers, as outlined in Article 34(1) and (6), (4).

Further regulations, such as the Minister of Infrastructure's Regulation dated April 12, 2002, set technical standards for buildings. Special considerations within this regulation are directed toward public utility buildings, especially those in various transport sectors, contributing to a more universally accessible infrastructure (74).

Lastly, the Railway Transport Act, enacted on March 28, 2003, with subsequent amendments, defines a comprehensive catalog of passenger rights. This legal framework underscores Poland's commitment to ensure a fair and accessible transportation system.

3.3   Universal Design

While writing about accessibility regulations, it is impossible to overlook the universal design rules. Universal design is designing products and environments to be accessible to all people, to the greatest extent possible, without the need for adaptation (Norwegian Ministry of the Environment, 2007). Products and environments should be designed to be used by people of all ages, abilities, and skills, taking into account factors related to mobility, vision, hearing, cognition, and environmental sensitivities (e.g., asthma or allergies). There are seven rules of universal design (Blaszczak & Przybylski, 2010):

Rule 1. The rule of equal opportunities—every person should have equal access to all elements of the environment: space, objects, buildings, streets, sidewalks, hospitals, schools, and means of transport. The space should be planned so that it does not require additional facilities for the people with disabilities or mothers with children in prams.

Rule 2. The rule of flexibility in use—assumes a variety of using the objects due to the capabilities and needs of users, e.g., scissors for the left-handed, and cinema seats for the people with disabilities.

Rule 3. Simplicity and intuitiveness in use—designing spaces and objects in such a way that their function is understandable to every user, regardless of their experience, knowledge, language skills, or concentration level, e.g., the way of marking space to avoid having to ask for directions.

Rule 4. The rule of perceptibility of information—information conveyed through objects and the structure of space should be multi-modal (visual, auditory, tactile).

Rule 5. Rule of error tolerance—its task is to minimize the risk of incorrect use of items and limit the adverse consequences of accidental and unintended use of a given item, including the design of elevators in public buildings for the evacuation of people with reduced mobility.

Rule 6. The rule of little physical effort during use—designing spaces and objects in such a way that their use is effective, comfortable, easy, and does not involve physical effort, e.g., low-floor buses and trams.

Rule 7. Rule of size and space sufficient for use—adapting urban space to the needs of its users, e.g., wide entrance gates to the subway, which will enable the use of this means of transport for people in wheelchairs.

4 Review of the Currently Existing Accessibility Solutions and the Future of Urban Transportation

In addition to the traditional solutions facilitating the use of public transport by people with disabilities, Smart Cities are increasingly being talked about. Komninos (2002) defines a Smart City as an area characterized by a high capacity for learning and innovation, having creative features, and Research and Development institutions, higher education, digital infrastructure, and communication technologies. Additionally, an important element of a Smart City is a high level of management efficiency. Lazaroiu and Roscia (2012) emphasize that a city can only be called intelligent when it optimizes available and new resources and potential investments. This goal can be achieved by supporting advanced information and communication technologies, especially in areas such as energy, technical infrastructure, public safety, waste management, and transport. It is worth noting that definitional problems result from differences in the perception of the essence of a Smart City in different regions. In the European Union, the concept of smart cities mainly focuses on clean energy, savings in energy consumption, and reducing CO_2 emissions (Sikora-Fernandez, 2013). In the United States, cities can be considered "smart" when they have developed human and social capital, traditional and modern communication infrastructure (transport and communication technologies), and their development is consistent with the theory of sustainable development (Krueger & Gibbs, 2008), supported by a participatory system of governance, which contributes to improving the quality of life. In Australia, however, the concept of a Smart City focuses on the creative industry and digital media (Murray et al., 2011). Finally, according to Hollands (2020), there is no clear definition of a Smart City. However, despite this, many cities aspire to be recognized as smart (Sikora-Fernandez, 2013).

Modern cities face the constant challenge of effectively managing the growing number of inhabitants and sustainable development while minimizing the negative impact on the environment. United Nations forecasts assume that by 2050, as much as 68% of the world's population will live in urban areas (United Nations, 2018). In the current era, cities constitute a significant share of global resources in terms of energy resources, as they consume as much as approximately 75% of the world's total energy (Mohanty et al., 2016). This constant energy consumption generates almost 80% of greenhouse gas emissions, resulting in serious and adverse environmental consequences (Nam & Pardo, 2011). In response to these challenges, the idea of Smart City was created, based on the use of innovative digital technologies, and is entering the mainstream of urban planning strategies. Business for Social Responsibility created a report to help cities identify how Smart City technologies can take a people-centric approach to benefit people with disabilities (Korngold et al., 2017). One of the key areas of transformation in the context of Smart City is facilitating access to public transport, which is a key element of urban infrastructure.

Public transport plays a fundamental role in the life of urban communities, influencing both the quality of life of residents and the functioning of the city itself. The introduction of modern digital technologies in the area of public transport, as an integral part of the Smart City concept, is not only a necessity but also an opportunity to create more effective, ecological, and accessible transport systems. When talking about the idea of a Smart City in the context of public transport, it is impossible not to mention the idea of Smart Mobility.

Smart Mobility is a cornerstone of a Smart City strongly associated with the transboundary haze (routing, digital transformation systems, and forecast of car traffic) decisions and policies of municipalities that are focused on the tools and innovations of data and communication (Tomaszewska & Florea, 2018). Simply put, Smart Mobility is a set of initiatives aimed at improving the mobility of people traveling both on foot, by public transport, and by private or other means of transport. Its result is a reduction in economic costs incurred by the natural environment and travel time (Aletà et al., 2017). An intelligent transport system is manifested mainly through the use of modern information technologies (but not only modern technologies) to ensure road safety, improve the efficiency of transport operations, and reduce the impact on the environment. Additionally, there are elements such as providing information for travelers, using automated vehicles, and monitoring safety while driving. The benefits resulting from the implementation of these systems include increasing the capacity of the road network by approximately 25%, significantly reducing the number of accidents by up to 80%, shortening travel times by approximately 50%, reducing exhaust emissions by approximately 40%, and reducing the costs of managing vehicle fleet and road infrastructure (ITS, 2012).

Many cities around the world have taken the idea of accessibility in public transport to heart and considered it important and necessary for the proper functioning of society. The concept of universal design for all is widely accepted in many countries and gains increasing adoption in middle- and low-income countries (Frye, 2019). To improve the availability of public transport for everyone in cities, various initiatives are undertaken, some of them are conceptually quite simple ideas that make life easier for residents, but several of the solutions deserve attention due to the level of technical advancement or ingenuity.

Thus, for example, some Slovak cities that have started public tenders for a public transport operator have created a group of requirements for the carrier that are necessary for everyone. Slovak cities are currently focusing on travel comfort, also for people with disabilities or people with strollers. Therefore, one of the most important requirements is that these machines should be low-entry. In addition, cities such as Nitra, Trencın and Levice in Slovakia included in their tender requirements such elements increasing the accessibility of public transport users as real-time data collection, camera system in buses, Wi-Fi access, mobile application (Bubelíny & Kubina, 2021).

In Maputo, Mozambique, a fairly simple system was tested that used raised bus platforms to help people with disabilities get on and off buses. The roadside platform provided a low-cost way to provide wheelchair access to standard buses at key locations along the route (Venter et al., 2004).

Many economical and creative solutions can make moving around much easier for many people. A very useful and accessible measure is the use of a clear color contrast at the edges of stairs or at the edges between the platform and doors in the train, which allows visually impaired people to enter and exit safely. An example of such a good design in, e.g., London is the subway, which was equipped with warning strips along the edges of the platform, which are characterized by contrasting colors and tangibility (Frye, 2019).

Another and more technically advanced solution supporting people with visual impairments is NaviLens (Sáez & Juan, 2017). Thanks to this system, people with visual impairments can move around the city, read signs placed at bus stops and metro stations, and receive directions via smartphones. This system effectively captures the new type of color QR codes, so that visually impaired people can read the information contained in the code without having to know exactly where NaviLens is located (NEOSISTEC, 2017). This system works successfully in cities such as New York and Barcelona.

For people with hearing or vision impairments, special systems are available to facilitate independent bus travel, such as sound signals warning about door opening and closing, common in many European cities. Moreover, such a system is recommended in the guidelines for designing accessible public transport (Rickert, 2007).

One of the most interesting ideas of using new technologies to support the mobility of people with disabilities is the system of intelligent sound signals introduced in the Helsinki metro on the Helsinki–Espoo line (Martinez, 2023). A kind of "sound and touch track" has been introduced there, which runs from the entrance to the elevators and down to the platform so that passengers can board the subway. At the next station, the path continues from the same metro doors to the exit. Sounders at the exit announce bus stops outside the station.

Additionally, real-time systems at bus stops, announcing the time until the next vehicle arrives, can be extremely helpful for people with hearing or vision impairments, while gaining the acceptance of all passengers (Frye, 2019). London can boast of such a solution. These elements are not only essential for safety but also provide helpful guidance for all passengers, including those with mobility and vision limitations.

Other, but already quite widely used, ideas to improve the availability of public transport are various types of applications that allow tracking the exact location of public transport vehicles in order to determine whether and when the desired public transport vehicle will arrive at our stop. There are many such initiatives, where a solution based on the GPS system is proposed, e.g., India (Vakula & Raviteja, 2017).

London offers a similar solution. The Countdown service is used to provide upto-date bus arrival data at all stops on London's transport network via the Internet, SMS, and road signs. In addition to providing live bus arrival times, the system also provides information on possible traffic disruptions and provides links to updates on London Underground services. Live information is transmitted using the most modern automatic vehicle location system, radio communication, and passenger information display system (Dudycz & Piatkowski, 2018). Singapore also invested in a similar initiative in 2008. Dedicated MyTransport.SG ecosystem, as the service is called, aimed to support travelers by providing an interactive map of bus and train stops, as well as a fare calculator. In 2011, a dedicated, integrated internet portal was introduced, extending its functionality to include road traffic information, the location of taxi stands, and details about vehicles and bicycles. In line with growing interest and developing opportunities, Singapore has also introduced a mobile version of the MyTransport.SG online portal (Dudycz & Piatkowski, 2018).

The above solutions, despite their advantages, also have some disadvantages. The main one is the fact that such a system is quite expensive, as it requires investing public money in GPS systems, or more generally, detection and tracking systems. An interesting development of the previous concept and coping with the economic disadvantages of previous solutions is the idea of Mobile Crowdsensing. This is an alternative solution because the crowd of passengers and their mobile devices are used to collect data, at virtually no cost. Farkas team has (Farkas et al., 2015) created an application called TrafficInfo and tested it in the city of Budapest. TrafficInfo is a simple and easy-to-use Android application that visualizes the city's public transport information in real-time on Google Maps. The real-time updates on schedule information are based on automatically detecting stopping events of public transport vehicles using passengers' mobile phones.

Other initiatives related to Smart Mobility are those undertaken to change the toll system. Currently, in Poland, we still rely on printed tickets available at unattended kiosks. As research by Pashkevich and colleagues (2021) using eye-tracking methods shows that such solutions are good, but not ideal. Foreigners needed almost twice as much time and more than twice as many glances to achieve the same goal as citizens. Here the idea used in London appears again—the Oyster Card. It is a form of electronic ticket used in public transport and works with radio frequency identification (RFID) technology. The reader transmits energy to the card via radio waves, using the phenomenon of electromagnetic induction to generate energy. This process activates the microchip on the Oyster card, allowing the reader to access the data stored on the card. In December 2012, Transport for London introduced the possibility of using a contactless debit, credit, or charge card to pay for tickets (Dudycz & Piatkowski, 2018). Similar solutions have been tested in Finland, Germany, and France (Guglielminetti et al., 2000).

5 Warsaw as an Example of a Central European Capital Implementing Innovative Solutions

The accessibility principles in Warsaw are defined by decree No. 1783/2022 of the Mayor of the Capital City of Warsaw dated December 1, 2022, referred to as the Accessibility Standards in Warsaw (Capital City of Warsaw, 2022). The document provides guidelines specifying the design of architectural elements, roads, sidewalks, green areas, and various components of public transportation.

The matters related to equal treatment are coordinated by the Commissioner for Equal Treatment in the Capital City of Warsaw (2022). The Commissioner works toward promoting equal treatment and non-discrimination in all areas of the city's functioning, including public transportation. The aim is to make Warsaw an increasingly inclusive city that is welcoming and conducive to living for individuals with various needs. The Commissioner coordinates the implementation of the Social Diversity Policy of the Capital City of Warsaw. This policy is a city-wide document describing the values and principles of equal treatment according to which Warsaw and municipal officials should operate. In the Warsaw City Hall, there is also a Commissioner for the President of the Capital City of Warsaw for Accessibility. The Commissioner focuses on activities aimed at enhancing architectural, digital, and informational communication accessibility for individuals with special needs in Warsaw.

According to data from the Central Statistical Office (CSO) (*People with disabilities in 2021*, 2022) in 2021, over 12% of the Polish population consists of individuals with various types and forms of disabilities. However, accessibility is important not only from the perspective of people with disabilities. Everyone can benefit from access to public transportation. This include parents with strollers and passengers with large luggage who fall under the group of individuals with limited mobility. Accessibility of public transportation, especially for people with disabilities, is a step toward combating social exclusion. Correct implementation of the accessibility principle will contribute to the implementation of the provisions of the United Nations Convention on the Rights of Persons with Disabilities at the European Union level (Center for European Union Transport Projects, 2021). More than half of trips made in Warsaw during the day are carried out by public transport (Office of Mobility & Transportation Policy, 2009). In 2022, over 863.4 million (863,445,768) passengers traveled on Warsaw Public Transport vehicles. This number increased by almost 37% compared to 2021. Within public transportation in Warsaw, one can travel using buses, trams, the metro, and the light rail.

5.1 Warsaw Trams

Tram communication in Warsaw is operated exclusively by the municipal company Warsaw Trams Ltd. Trams serve a significant part of passenger transport in public transport. As part of the accessibility initiative, Warsaw Trams primarily implements low-floor rolling stock, which is adapted for individuals with diverse needs. In 1996, there was one tram with a partially low-floor, and by the year 2000, there were already 30 such trams. In 2007, their number increased to 45, in 2013 to 231, in 2016 to 311, and by 2023, there are 434 low-floor trams, constituting over 66% of the fleet. The new rolling stock is intended to be quiet and monitored, equipped with ticket machines. Currently, high-floor trams are essentially used as additional vehicles during peak hours on weekdays, and on holidays and Saturdays, only individual high-floor trams operate. The low-floor ones are for now marked on the timetable.

Low-floor trams are equipped with systems to assist boarding and alighting, such as platforms facilitating access to the vehicle. Tram drivers are trained to assist passengers with disabilities boarding and disembarking from the vehicle. Additionally, low-floor trams are equipped with specially marked spaces for people with disabilities, usually located near the entrance, as well as spaces for elderly individuals and those with limited mobility. The trams provide space for wheelchairs, bicycles, and other mobile equipment.

Most trams use auditory announcements, informing passengers about upcoming stops and important announcements. Information screens are also present, displaying details about the route and stops. There are tactile markings on board trams to facilitate spatial orientation for visually impaired or blind passengers. When opening and closing tram doors, auditory signals are used to inform passengers about these operations. Moreover, the tram driver can activate an external auditory announcement with additional information for individuals with visual impairments.

5.2 Metro and Urban Bus Companies

As the Warsaw Metropolitan Transportation Authority report shows, Warsaw Trams is not the only transport company implementing accessibility principles. The city is actively working toward making transportation available to people with disabilities, the elderly, pregnant women, and others who may need assistance. All the operating buses are reported to have no basic barriers (Public Transport Authority in Warsaw, 2022b). Currently, all the buses are low-floor ones, with the ability to reduce the height difference between the vehicle and the curb. Each bus has electronic displays and voice announcements, informing about stops and route status. Several older vehicles are still, however, lacking this development. Most operating vehicles offer expandable platforms, enabling access to wheelchairs or carriages. All the doors have an assistance button on the outside and inside of the vehicle, which can signal the need to open up the platform. Proper sitting with special backrests and safety belts are available for wheelchair users.

The metro system in Warsaw has also introduced several solutions in the last few years. A hearing aid system was used for the first time at the new stations in 2022. Induction loops have been installed, i.e., devices that connect directly to hearing aids. Messages broadcast by loudspeakers at stations are simultaneously amplified in the telephones. Thanks to this, people using hearing aids will not be exposed to noise, interference, and echoes. All the metro stations are equipped with an elevator and special wide gates, as well as horizontal Braille markings across stations and platforms to help visually impaired people navigate smoothly. However, on some stations, elevators are only accessible from one part of the underground station, making it harder to navigate for people with a need for that kind of assistance. A convenience for passengers involves the installation of moving walkways, commonly seen at airports. They have been installed at one of the longest underground corridors of the metro system. This solution is particularly significant for passengers with limited mobility.

5.3   Accessibility of Stops and Stations

In the years 2021–2022, an audit of transportation stops was conducted on behalf of Warsaw Trams Ltd., and the auditors' recommendations set the direction for improvements in the municipal accessibility standards. Audit surveys were conducted at 596 tram stops in Warsaw and at one bus stop (Metro P locka 06). Selected parameters influencing accessibility were evaluated at each stop.

Several implemented solutions in Warsaw that received positive evaluations from auditors include the following:

Guidance System—Tactile Paths: Raised horizontal markings guide visually impaired individuals and warn of potential hazards. Two types are utilized: guiding elements (parallel lines) and warning signs (raised dots or buttons). These are applied on wide sidewalks, and main streets, leading to pedestrian crossings, and public transport stops.

Guiding Strips: Textured surface markings with parallel lines, having a minimum width of 25 cm. They indicate paths for individuals with visual impairments to pedestrian crossings, entrances, public spaces, and transport facilities.

Warning Strips: Textured surface markings with raised dots (bumps), with a width ranging from 30 to 50 cm. These strips mark hazardous areas like edges of stairs, ramps, platforms, and pedestrian crossings.

Attention Fields: Textured warning markings with raised dots, spanning a width of 50–90 cm. These fields mark changes in direction or branching of tactile paths, providing information about destination points.

Waiting Area: A special attention field within public transportation stops, designated at the height of the universally accessible second set of doors, with minimum dimensions of 90 × 90 cm.

Small Architecture: Elements and devices should be outside the obstacle-free path, with no sharp or angular edges for safety.

Rest Areas—Benches: One-third of benches have backrests and armrests for accessibility. Rest areas are placed near pedestrian traffic lanes, and bench materials include wood and plastics (avoiding uncomfortable metal seats).

Contrast Marking of Platform Edge: Warns visually impaired individuals of level differences, with recommended markings like a yellow strip, black contrasting strip, anti-slip gray surface, and warning strip.

Ticket Machines: Adapted to various disabilities, with several machines having different parameters. Ramp access, maneuvering space, Braille labeling, and touch guiding paths were considered.

Schedule Boards: Unrestricted access without obstruction, evenly illuminated, glare-free, and readable by all heights.

For the past 10 years, Warsaw Trams have been reconstructing platform stops to make them suitable for serving low-floor rolling stock. This involves adapting them to the platform level and marking the edges of the sidewalk, ramps, and other modifications, all in line with the accessibility standards. The modernization of tram stops includes extension, integration with bus stops, and the installation of visual and voice passenger information systems. In 2022, tests were conducted in Warsaw for markings for blind individuals at stops and on vehicles using QR codes and NaviLens software (Sáez & Juan, 2017). However, as of now, the Warsaw Public Transport Authority has not decided to implement solutions such as NaviLens.

6   Future Plans and Challenges

The availability of stations is a key issue in Warsaw (Office of Mobility & Transportation Policy, 2009). Most of the stations are marked as accessible to all, but several are still not available to everyone. The city provides an overview on the website, where they highlight all stations that are inaccessible for people with disabilities (Public Transport Authority in Warsaw, 2022a), with a substantial amount of them being in the city center. Existing accessible architecture for stations and key points for customer service in public transportation are pointed out in the accessibility declaration (Public Transport Authority in Warsaw, 2020). Existing accessibility solutions on main stations include elevators and escalators, parking spaces for people with disabilities, accessible toilets, communication systems across main points (such as railway stations), and audio induction loops. It is important to note that those solutions are most often available at major transportation hubs that are also designed to aid clients and travelers and therefore, have more advanced infrastructure.

A few promising developments have been mentioned in the Accessibility Plus Governmental program (The Ministry of Investment & Development, 2018), describing the current state of accessibility in Poland and presenting the foreseen actions to be taken in the years 2018–2025. Besides training for public transportation staff, describing accessibility and how to help people with disabilities, the document proposes creating a mobile app that collects all the data on accessibility in public transport and stations. It will record reports on the state of the stations and vehicles provided by users, as well as offer assistance after the sale of tickets. The application will also allow people to ask for assistance or flag noticed barriers. Twenty billions of

Polish Zlotys has been provided for the renovating 200 stations, creating the mobile app, and expanding the accessibility of the current transportation system by 20% until the end of the project.

In recent years, Warsaw's public transportation system has also recognized the challenges faced by passengers with cognitive and intellectual disabilities. One example is the Synapsis Foundation's campaign "Autism—My Whole Life." The videos from the series "Autism Misleads the Senses," filmed in urban spaces, including the metro and bus stops, are presented as part of training activities for drivers of public transportation vehicles in the capital city.

7 Summary

This chapter provided an overview of accessibility in the public transportation systems with a special focus on the city of Warsaw, emphasizing the city's commitment to inclusivity and equal opportunities. We started with the presentation of the legal international and national frameworks of accessible transportation. The accessibility of a city transportation system is framed within the Smart City concept, including Smart Mobility—intelligent and innovative solutions for transportation and mobility within urban areas. The accessibility guidelines in Warsaw present a holistic approach referring to transport vehicles, roads with sidewalks, bus and tram stops, and metro stations. Public transport vehicles are equipped with features like platforms, designated spaces for individuals with disabilities, and textual and auditory announcements. Tram stops feature guidance systems, waiting areas, and specific design solutions for benches, ticket machines, and schedule boards. The metro system in Warsaw introduces diverse accessibility solutions, including support systems for the hearing-impaired, induction loops, and tactile markings for the visually impaired. Recognizing challenges related to station and vehicle accessibility, Warsaw's public transportation system acknowledges the difficulties faced by passengers with cognitive and intellectual disabilities.

To sum up, Smart City and Smart Mobility are still open concepts, waiting for further development. For cities to become smart, they must continue to explore innovative solutions in the area of public transport. In comparison to other European and global solutions, Warsaw paints itself as a city focused on pursuing higher accessibility and is open to further, more innovative solutions, such as the usage of mobile apps (The Ministry of Investment & Development, 2018). Still, additional solutions and reworks of stations are needed for the public transport domain to be inclusive. These activities will not only improve the lives of residents but will also contribute to achieving sustainable development by minimizing the negative impact on the environment. As technology develops dynamically, Smart City will become not only a necessity but also a fascinating reality that shapes the urban space future.

Acknowledgements This chapter is based upon work from COST Action CA19142—Leading Platform for European Citizens, Industries, Academia and Policymakers in Media Accessibility (LEAD-ME) supported by COST (European Cooperation in Science and Technology).

References

Aletà, N. B., Alonso, C. M., & Ruiz, R. M. A. (2017). Smart mobility and smart environment in the Spanish cities. *Transportation Research Procedia, 24*, 163–170.

Błaszczak, M., & Przybylski, Ł. (2010). *Things are for people: Disability and the idea of universal design.* Wydawnictwo Naukowe Scholar.

Boadi-Kusi, S. B., Amoako-Sakyi, R. O., Abraham, C. H., Addo, N. A., Aboagye McCarthy, A., Gyan, B. O. (2023). Access to public transport to persons with visual disability: A scoping review. *British Journal of Visual Impairment*, 02646196231167072.

Bubelíny, O., & Kubina, M. (2021). Impact of the concept smart city on public transport. *Transportation Research Procedia, 55*, 1361–1367.

Capital City of Warsaw (2022). *Representative for equal treatment.* https://wsparcie.um.warszawa.pl/-/kto-koordynuje-sprawydotyczace-rownego-traktowania. Accessed November 22, 2023.

Carmien, S., Dawe, M., Fischer, G., Gorman, A., Kintsch, A., & Sullivan, J. F., Jr. (2005). Sociotechnical environments supporting people with cognitive disabilities using public transportation. *ACM Transactions on Computer-Human Interaction (TOCHI), 12*(2), 233–262.

Center for European Union Transport Projects. (2021). *People with disabilities in 2021.* https://www.cupt.gov.pl/archiwalna/images/publikacje/Dostepno. Accessed November 22, 2023.

Dudycz, H., & Piatkowski, I. (2018). Smart mobility solutions in public transport based on analysis chosen smart cities. *Informatyka Ekonomiczna. Prace Naukowe Uniwersytetu Ekonomicznego we Wrocławiu, 2*(48).

Farkas, K., Feher, G., Benczur, A., & Sidlo, C. (2015). Crowdsending based public transport information service in smart cities. *IEEE Communications Magazine, 53*(8), 158–165.

Fischer, G., & Sullivan, Jr., J. (2002). Human-centered public transportation systems for persons with cognitive disabilities. In *Proceedings of the participatory design conference* (Vol. 9, pp. 194–198).

Frye, A. (2019). *Disability inclusive public transport: practical steps to making public transport disability inclusive.* https://transport-links.com/wpcontent/uploads/2023/10/disability-inclusive-policy-brief-standard-version.pdf. Accessed January 3, 2024.

Guglielminetti, P., Buri, J., Tzieropoulos, P., & Garcia, S. (2000). Contactless ticketing: state-of-the-art and user impact. *WIT Transactions on the Built Environment, 50*.

GUS. (2022). *People with disabilities in 2021.* https://stat.gov.pl/obszary-tematyczne/warunk izycia/ubostwo-pomoc-spoleczna/osoby-niepelnosprawne-w-2021roku,26,3.html. Accessed November 22, 2023.

Hollands, R. G. (2020). Will the real smart city please stand up? Intelligent, progressive or entrepreneurial? In *The Routledge companion to smart cities* (pp. 179–199). Routledge.

ITS. (2012). https://pim.pl/its-wkracza-na-polskie-drogi/. Accessed November 22, 2023.

Kircanski, K., Joormann, J., & Gotlib, I. H. (2012). Cognitive aspects of depression. *Wiley Interdisciplinary Reviews: Cognitive Science, 3*(3), 301–313.

Komninos, I. (2002). *Product life cycle management* (pp. 1–26). Aristotle University of Thessaloniki.

Korngold, D., Lemos, M., & Rohwer, M. (2017). Smart cities for all: A vision for an inclusive, accessible, urban future. https://smartcities4all.org/wp-content/uploads/2017/06/Smart-Cities-for-AllA-Vision-for-an-Inclusive-Accessible-Urban-Futur...-min.pdf. Accessed January 3, 2024.

Krueger, R., & Gibbs, D. (2008). 'Third wave' sustainability? Smart growth and regional development in the USA. *Regional Studies, 42*(9), 1263–1274.

Lazaroiu, G. C., & Roscia, M. (2012). Definition methodology for the smart cities model. *Energy, 47*(1), 326–332. https://doi.org/10.1016/j.energy.2012.09.028. https://www.sciencedirect.com/science/article/pii/S0360544212007062. (Asia-Pacific Forum on Renewable Energy 2011)

Martinez, C. (2023). Our audio beacons guide the blind and visually impaired at the Helsinki subway. https://www.inclusivecitymaker.com/audio-beacons-blind-visually-impairedhelsinki-subway/. Accessed January 3, 2024.

Mohanty, S. P., Choppali, U., & Kougianos, E. (2016). Everything you wanted to know about smart cities: The internet of things is the backbone. *IEEE Consumer Electronics Magazine, 5*(3), 60–70.

Murray, A., Minevich, M., & Abdoullaev, A. (2011). Being smart about smart cities. *Searcher, 19*(8), 20.

Nam, T., & Pardo, T. A. (2011). Conceptualizing smart city with dimensions of technology, people, and institutions. In: *Proceedings of the 12th annual international digital government research conference: Digital government innovation in challenging times* (pp. 282–291).

NaviLens, Nuevos sistemas tecnologicos S.L. (NEOSISTEC). (2017). *NaviLens.* https://www.navilens.com/en/. Accessed November 22, 2023.

Norwegian Ministry of the Environment. (2007). *Universal design. Explanation of the concept.* http://www.universellutforming.miljo.no/. Accessed November 22, 2023.

Odame, P. K., Abane, A., & Amenumey, E. K. (2020). Campus shuttle experience and mobility concerns among students with disability in the university of Cape coast, Ghana. *Geo: Geography and Environment, 7*(2), e00093.

Office of Mobility and Transportation Policy. (2009). *The sustainable development strategy for Warsaw's transport system until 2015 and subsequent years.* https://www.wtp.waw.pl/wpcontent/uploads/sites/2/2019/06/strategia-zr. Accessed November 22, 2023.

UN (2015). *Transforming our world: The 2030 agenda for sustainable development.* https://sustainabledevelopment.un.org/content/documents/7891Transforming. Accessed April 3, 2024.

Orczyk, M., & Młodystach, L. (2022). Analysis of problems faced by the deaf while using public transport in a big city. *Transport Problems, 17.*

Park, J., & Chowdhury, S. (2018). Investigating the barriers in a typical journey by public transport users with disabilities. *Journal of Transport & Health, 10*, 361–368.

Park, K., Esfahani, H. N., Novack, V. L., Sheen, J., Hadayeghi, H., Song, Z., & Christensen, K. (2023). Impacts of disability on daily travel behaviour: A systematic review. *Transport Reviews, 43*(2), 178–203.

Pashkevich, A., Szarata, A., Burghardt, T. E., Jaremski, R., & Sucha, M. (2021). Operation of public transportation ticket vending machine in Kraków, Poland: An eye tracking study. *Sustainability, 13*(14), 7921.

Public Transport Authority in Warsaw. (2020). *Accessibility declaration.* https://ztm.bip.um.warszawa.pl/menuprzedmiotowe/Deklaracjadostepnosci/Deklaracja+dost. Accessed November 22, 2023.

Public Transport Authority in Warsaw. (2022a). *Availability of WTP.* https://www.wtp.waw.pl/mapy-schematy/dostepnoscprzestrzenna-wtp/. Accessed November 22, 2023.

Public Transport Authority in Warsaw (2022b). *Travel without barriers.* https://www.wtp.waw.pl/en/travel-without-barriers/. Accessed on November 22, 2023.

Rickert, T. (2007). *Bus rapid transit accessibility guidelines.* https://openknowledge.worldbank.org/server/api/core/bitstreams/0c697b93-6931-5439-b32b-e0db43d9a929/content. Accessed November 22, 2023.

Risser, R., Lexell, E.M., Bell, D., Iwarsson, S., & Stahl, A. (2015). Use of local public transport among people with cognitive impairments–A literature review. *Transportation Research Part F: Traffic Psychology and Behaviour, 29*, 83–97.

Sáez, M., & Juan, M. (2017). Navilens: Jornadas sobre tecnología de la información para una universidad accessible.

Sikora-Fernandez, D. (2013). Koncepcja smart city w założeniach polityki rozwoju miasta–polska perspektywa.

Starzynska, B., Kujawinska, A., Grabowska, M., Diakun, J., Więcek-Janka, E., Schnieder, L., Schlueter, N., & Nicklas, J.-P.G. (2015). Requirements elicitation of passenger with reduced mobility for the design of high quality, accessible and inclusive public transport services. *Management and Production Engineering Review, 6*(3), 70–76.

The Ministry of Investment and Development. (2018). *Program dostępność plus.* https://www.fun duszeeuropejskie.gov.pl/media/62311/Programdostepnoscplus.pdf. Accessed January 3, 2024.

Tomaszewska, E. J., & Florea, A. (2018). Urban smart mobility in the scientific literature—Biblio-metric analysis. *Engineering Management in Production and Services, 10*(2), 41–56.

Trociuk, S. (Ed.). (2011). The principle of equal treatment—law and practice. Accessibility of public infrastructure for people with disabilities. Analysis and recommendations. Office of the Ombudsman for Civil Rights.

United Nations. (2018). *68% of the world population projected to live in urban areas by 2050.* https://www.un.org/development/desa/en/news/population/2018-revision-ofworld-urb anization-prospects.html. Accessed on January 3, 2024.

Unsworth, C., So, M. H., Chua, J., Gudimetla, P., & Naweed, A. (2021). A systematic review of public transport accessibility for people using mobility devices. *Disability and Rehabilitation, 43*(16), 2253–2267. https://doi.org/10.1080/09638288.2019.1697382

Vakula, D., & Raviteja, B. (2017). Smart public transport for smart cities. In *2017 International conference on intelligent sustainable systems (ICISS)* (pp. 805–810).

van Holstein, E., Wiesel, I., & Legacy, C. (2022). Mobility justice and accessible public transport networks for people with intellectual disability. *Applied Mobilities, 7*(2), 146–162.

Venter, C., Rickert, T., Mashiri, M., & de Deus, K. (2004). Entry into high-floor vehicles using wayside platforms.

Subjectivity and Creativity Versus Audio Description Guidelines

María Olalla Luque Colmenero

Abstract For decades, different international guidelines on the field of audio description (AD) have been edited and supposedly followed by practitioners. There is general agreement on what should be included in terms of form, movement, colour, sound, perspective, and supporting information. According to all the guidelines, the style of audio description should be objective, not interpretative, although they do not specify what they mean by "objectivity". These guidelines are based on the fact that receivers interpret the work of art themselves. However, this idea is unconvincing, as the blind and partially sighted receivers are not on the same level as the sighted viewer in terms of visual and information selection. Moreover, the guidelines do not focus on the different strategies to create AD. This ambiguity is also reflected in the treatment of subjectivity and creativity, as they do not provide any clear definition and are untrustworthy, since they introduce subjective techniques while recommending being always objective. This incongruence, together with the view of art education at the centre of cultural mediation and accessibility nowadays, and its influence on access projects and AD programmes across Europe and beyond, is the base of this proposal. We aim to explore both the comprehensive role of subjectivity and creativity in the guidelines and some of the new trends on AD, such as metaphorical, synesthetic, with interpretative voices, and poetic in our museums, thanks to our practical research and practice during the past decade. This way, we may have a broader and more specific understanding of what their real subjective and aesthetic experience is.

Keywords Audio description · Subjectivity · Guidelines · Museums · Art education

M. O. L. Colmenero (✉)
University of Granada, Granada, Spain
e-mail: molc@ugr.es

© The Author(s) 2024
A. Marcus-Quinn et al. (eds.), *Transforming Media Accessibility in Europe*,
https://doi.org/10.1007/978-3-031-60049-4_3

1   Guidelines on Audio Description

Literature reviews play a very important role as a basis for all types of research, especially those dealing with novel and non-standardised practices, as they can be used for knowledge development, creation of new guidelines, improvement of practice, etc. AD is a translation of images into words that aims to help those with a visual impairment to construct a mental image of what they cannot see (Salzhauer and Sobol, 2003). While there is no international standard for the development of AD in any of its fields of application, there are guidelines and recommendations documents produced by different bodies and associations at national level. Most of them deal with video AD, whether for television, film or DVD, but there are also specific recommendations for other fields, including museums and the performing arts.

In the United States, there are general guidelines with sections dedicated to the different fields of application (television, dance, theatre and museums), and the same is true in the United Kingdom, where there are guidelines specific to the television context and others dedicated exclusively to the museum and historical heritage field. The latter are called *Museums, galleries and heritage sites: improving access for blind and partially sighted people* and have been developed by the RNIB (RNIB & Vocal Eyes, 2003) and the company Vocal Eyes. They include general measures for improving accessibility in museums, exhibitions and historical heritage sites, as well as specific recommendations for the development of audio-descriptive guides for these environments.

Various authors (Rai et al., 2010; Remael, 2005; Vercauteren, 2007) have analysed international standards on AD. For example, Vercauteren (2007) published research suggesting that it would be interesting to create a European AD standard, which has been partly carried out in the different ADLAB projects at European level: in 2011, the ADLAB project (Audio Description: Lifelong Access for the Blind) was created with the aim of defining and creating effective and reliable educational guidelines on the practice of audio description to provide access to most audiovisual products (ADLAB Project, 2019). Although there are numerous general guidelines on AD, there are none that specifically address a particular resource or category.

These guidelines are based on the fact that the recipients arrive at their own interpretations, under the protection of the most objective AD. However, this idea is not very convincing, as the visually impaired receiver is not on the same level as the sighted viewer in terms of visual and information selection, nor can they have the same tools for accessing information: Many blind people prefer other more multisensory ways of accessing visual information.

Eisner's perspective (2002) underscores that the primary objective of art education programmes should be the cultivation of learners' ability to experience aesthetics in their everyday lives. He emphasises that such aesthetic perception necessitates the capacity to slow down the process of perception, allowing for a meticulous examination and appreciation of visual qualities. It involves the active search for qualitative connections and a heightened awareness of the experiences they evoke.

This viewpoint on art education is closely aligned with cultural mediation, described as the educational approach involving the acquisition and negotiation of knowledge related to the arts, social phenomena, and scientific subjects. This is achieved through interactions, reactions, and creative responses. These perspectives collectively stress the significance of individual, subjective experiences, creativity, and dialogue within the realms of museums and art education.

However, subjectivity has been a point of contention within the domain of AD, particularly due to the inconsistency between various guidelines. Some advocate for a neutral or objective approach, while others argue in favour of more subjective descriptions, which have shown benefits for certain blind and partially sighted (BPS) visitors. For instance, Spanish, American, and French AD guidelines tend to favour objectivity, even within the context of visual arts. In contrast, British guidelines indicate that some BPS visitors prefer subjective descriptions when visiting museums (AENOR, 2005; Morisset & Gonant, 2008; RNIB & Vocal Eyes, 2003; Salzhauer Axel et al., 1996).

The discourse on subjectivity extends to the analysis of literary ekphrasis and narration in silent films and the performing arts, which serve as precursors to AD. Within the realm of film AD, various perspectives emerge. Benecke and Dosch (2004) suggested detailed physical descriptions instead of explicitly conveying the emotions of characters. In contrast, Vercauteren and Orero (2013) argued in favour of using emotional language, particularly for describing universal facial expressions. Kruger and Orero (2010) advocated the use of audio narration (AN) with some deviation from strict fidelity.

The exploration of subjectivity has also become a subject of investigation in the field of reception studies for AD. Research related to theatre suggests that audiences tend to respond positively to subjective ADs (Udo & Fels, 2009; Udo et al., 2010). In the realm of film (Walczak & Fryer, 2017), findings indicate that creative ADs may enhance the sense of "presence", creating a more immersive film experience, and ADs employing emotional language can elicit stronger emotional responses (Ramos, 2016).

Concerning AD for visual art, there exists a need to convey both clear and ambivalent visual cues, including the sensations they evoke in viewers. Neves (2012) emphasised the necessity of incorporating more subjective interpretations to enable visually impaired individuals to experience visual art at a level comparable to sighted individuals. Notably, several corpus-based studies have demonstrated the presence of subjective language in AD for visual art (Lima & Magalhães, 2013; Luque Colmenero, 2016, 2020; Soler Gallego, 2018).

In the following section, we will present a summary of the most important guidelines followed in AD practice in the UK and Spain, as these are two countries with guidelines.

1.1   Guidelines in the UK

In the UK, the project Talking Images: museums, galleries and heritage sites carried out by the RNIB in collaboration with the AD company Vocal Eyes resulted in the production of a guide entitled *The Talking Images Guide. Museums, galleries and heritage sites: improving access for blind and partially sighted people* (RNIB and Vocal Eyes, 2003), which includes measures to improve accessibility in these environments and specific recommendations for the production of AD guides. This document recommends following a series of guidelines which are summarised below:

- Involve people with DV in the development process.
- Use accessible technology.
- Link the AD guide to the other services offered by the museum.
- Plan the maintenance and updating of the guides at the beginning of the project.
- Include the general description of the museum, the duration and theme, the instructions for use and movement, and the information that forms part of the written text of the exhibition.
- Go from the general to the specific.
- Include the following specific elements: characteristics of the space, size of the element and type of support, particularities of each work, style, material and technique, impact of the work at first sight and the details that contribute to that impact.

Regarding the level of interpretation of the work, these guidelines state that a AD that is too objective and focussed on the location of the visual elements hinders understanding, while one that is more evaluative and interpretative is more attractive to the visitor and helps to maintain their attention, as it reflects the process of contemplation of the work and helps to build a sense of it, for example through elements such as colour. In the publication, there is a comparison between two ADs. These two versions were presented to a group of visually impaired people to gauge their impressions. The first version focuses on form, without interpreting it. If we analyse the tools they use to describe the shapes, we realise that they rely heavily on the elements that have already been described, i.e., some elements are understood in comparison with others, which is a kind of comparison or analogy at a figurative level. The second version includes a higher interpretative level. The first version was much more difficult to understand for the group, who also thought it was the longer of the two descriptions, although it is almost half as short.

We can relate this idea to the abstraction of the work, which requires common elements in order to be understood. In addition, the second description was considered more immersive, providing more visual information about the work. The use of colours and qualifying words, such as adjectives, was considered helpful in creating a mental image and thinking about the meaning of the work. They also felt that, after listening to it, they had something positive to talk about. As for the analogies used, although we also found comparisons with elements already described, the most striking for our research and, according to the results obtained, for the users were those that compare, as recommended by Snyder in the guidelines of the American Council of the Blind (Snyder, 2010), common and everyday elements with parts of the visual work, which transfer the experience of the work to the users' life experience.

1.2 Guidelines in Spain

In Spain, there are specific guidelines (AENOR, 2005) for the preparation of AD guides, which are set out below for comparison with those in the Anglo-Saxon context. They should contain the following:

- Instructions for handling the electronic device.
- Safety information (emergency exits), warning of places, or situations that may constitute a physical risk.
- Description of the space, including the following:

  - Location of the entrance
  - Location of the exit
  - Circulation route throughout the visitable space
  - Location of useful services, such as toilets, cafeteria, and shop
  - Location of accessible materials
  - Location of floor plans and other raised or tactilely significant information
  - Description of objects or environments, including:
  - Location of the placards with their data
  - Location of each piece within the ensemble of which it forms part.

- Use of concepts that are not exclusively visual, highlighting features whose sensory input channel is other senses.

When tactile access is possible, the AD guide should direct the exploration in a simple and orderly manner so that the BPS person can grasp the most significant aspects of the object, and when this is not possible, as is the case with pictorial works, the description should focus on the most significant data for capturing the work, expressly avoiding personal interpretations. The description of each object or environment should contain the appropriate terminology and include the most significant aspects.

The evolution of a field as new as AD is very rapid and changing and the AENOR standard does not cover all the fields in which it can be applied, so it is often the criterion of each museum, department or audio describer that prevails in AD guides. On the other hand, the standard does not make any direct reference to the use of figurative meaning, subjective language or analogies or metaphors, or even to language in general. It deals to a greater extent with the part related to accessibility and architectural barriers, be it the type of ramps or obstacles in the museum or the non-adaptation of its signs to Braille. It only alludes to the use of concepts that are not exclusively visual and features that have other senses as a sensory input channel, in a very similar way to the other guidelines we have analysed, which make translation through other senses their only general contribution to language.

2   Objective Versus Subjective Styles

All of these elements converge to give rise to what is termed the "objective" style. This term is used to describe AD that employs an objective language, focussing on informing about what can be seen without interpreting it. It is akin to a form of surface reading, emphasising what is overtly manifest (Kleege, 2016), or AD with a primary referential function whose purpose is to inform and describe (Bartolini & Manfredi, 2022).

The objective style aligns with the recommendations provided in existing guidelines for creating AD for visual art. Notably, Neves (2016) identifies three potential approaches, which are the objective, narrative, and interpretive styles, but only elaborates on the objective style. Furthermore, the objective style was identified as the preferred AD style by users in a study conducted by the RNIB and Vocal Eyes before the creation of their set of guidelines (RNIB & Vocal Eyes, 2003). More recently, a study conducted by Hutchinson and Eardley (2020), focussed on context and process, indicated that this style corresponds to the approach advocated and followed by professional audio describers.

It is true that, in general, and especially in the early AD guidelines, subjective judgements were not welcome and objectivity was favoured to avoid any manipulation or patronising attitude towards the public. However, it is not always clear what constitutes a subjective judgement or what kind of interpretation is more objective and could be included in the AD (Mazur & Chmiel, 2012). Udo and Fels (2009) argue that objective interpretation is impossible. Hyks admits that AD is always subjective and that, whether there is agreement on certain basic principles, audio describers will always see things differently and express it differently, from country to country, from company to company and also from person to person (2005). Corpus-based studies examining audio description (AD) for visual art have also unveiled less common approaches and characteristics (Lima & Magalhães, 2013; Soler Gallego, 2019, 2021; Luque Colmenero, 2020, 2021; Luque Colmenero & Soler Gallego, 2020, 2022) that have the potential to enhance accessibility in the realm of visual arts.

In the subsequent section, we will introduce some of these subjective styles, which are gradually gaining traction in museums across Europe and around the world. We will also outline their primary features and provide examples that illustrate their utility in various contexts.

3   New Audio Description Styles

In the realm of art and culture, museums have evolved into more than just repositories of historical artefacts; they have become metaphoric landscapes where the past and present merge into immersive experiences. In this section, we will present new styles of AD we can find in museums across Europe. They are metaphoric, gist, poetic, synesthetic, and interpretative voices, together with an explanation of their main features, which aim to prove their usefulness in different contexts. As these subjective styles continue to develop in museums across Europe and the world, we will delve into their essence by providing examples that underscore their profound usefulness in accessible cultural contexts for BPS people.

3.1   Metaphorical Styles

In a previous analysis (Luque Colmenero, 2016), we were able to determine that metaphor is used in the AD guides of art museums with the communicative function of transferring through the linguistic code that cannot be perceived through the visual channel. We compiled and analysed a corpus of approximately 35,000 words consisting of the intersemiotic translation text segments found in the AD guides of four museums, namely the Tate Modern in the United Kingdom and the MoMA, the Whitney Museum, and the Brooklyn Museum of New York in the United States. The results of this study indicated that metaphors, and especially novel, direct and deliberate metaphors, were widely used throughout the corpus.

An example of a deliberate metaphor found in the corpus was "the face like a wild mask". It was part of the AD of The Three Dancers, by Picasso, taken from the Tate Modern AD guide, and an example of a non-deliberate metaphor in the corpus is "soft white light", from the AD of "Home" by Mona Hatoum, also from the Tate Modern. General appearance of direct and deliberate metaphor in the academic genre is only 0.1%; in fiction, 0.4%; in conversation, less than 0.1%; and in press, 0.4% (Herrmann, 2013, p. 101). According to our analysis, more than 5.14% of the language used in the corpus is made up of metaphors of this type. The analysis also showed that higher levels of abstraction and conceptuality of the source text seem to be connected with higher percentages of deliberate metaphors in the target text. We have been able to show that metaphors are widely used across Spanish and European museums' AD nowadays (Luque Colmenero & Soler Gallego, 2020).

3.2 Gist Style

Another minority approach more and more used in museum AD is the one we have named "gist" style (Soler Gallego and Luque Colmenero, 2022). It has been developed by Claire Bartoli, a writer and actress who is blind, and who audio describes for art museums in Paris. This is a minority AD style from the point of view of selection and quantity of information (attention/salience), as well as the structure and connections (constitution/gestalt) built in the AD (Soler Gallego and Luque Colmenero, 2022).

Bartoli's AD of *Murs de peintures* (Walls of Paintings) by Daniel Buren for the AD guide of the Musée d'Art Moderne de la Ville de Paris is an enumeration of shapes, directions, and colours:

Black, white, black, white, black square.

Small red, white, red, white, red square.

Black square.

Large orange, white, orange, white orange, white, orange square.

Small blue, white, blue, white, blue rectangle.

Grey square.

Red rectangle.

It conveys the composition without using any lexis related to space and location. Instead, these formal components are implicitly indicated by means of the sequence in which they are enunciated through language.

3.3 Poetic Style

BPS visitors to museums can also experience the so-called poetic style. De Coster and Mühleis' propose that, instead of explaining the meaning of the ambivalent signs, audio describers could find in words the same "sensorial ambiguity" that can be found in sound or touch. This different approach could be addressed as "soundpainting", in line with the ekphrastic tradition. Ekphrasis, which Orero and Pujol (2007: 49) define as "a literary figure that provides the graphic and often dramatic description of a painting, a relief or other work of art", can include elements that can be considered objective, whereas other elements are completely subjective.

However, if the BPS person cannot have direct access to the work itself, they could also have access to an "alternative work of art". People who cannot see the work of art will not be able to relate to it as sighted people would do unless they gain access to the explicit and the implicit meanings of the piece. Furthermore, art is expression, and conveying the expressive nature of any work of art through words alone may be truly challenging. If only explicit signs can be expressed through words, then ways must be found to convey the feelings and sensations that are only invoked or raised through feelings. Poems, songs, literary works, etc. are widely used in different museums to fill this gap.

3.4 Synesthetic Style

Synaesthesia deals with a "confusion" between the bodily senses, although "exchange" between concepts and senses fits better within our area of study. Synesthetic metaphors, which have also been studied within cognitive approaches to metaphor (Steen et al., 2010), recreate a sensation through a sense that, while being alien to it, helps to understand it through body experience. The adjective "fluid", related to both a tactile and a visual experience, is introduced to describe the physical appearance of certain figures or the technique in an AD.

In a figurative work AD used during a multisensory visit with BPS people at the Alhambra of Granada, Spain, "Diego de Mendoza" (Luque Colmenero and Soler Gallego, 2020), the materials and the light depicted in the work are translated through contrasting synesthetic comparisons: "we can imagine the hardness and softness of the smooth marbles", "the warmth of the light on the stone" and "the brilliant coldness of the rings". The sense of touch serves here to translate Titian's use of light and his realistic technique. In another figurative work, "La salida de los moriscos", we find another example of a synesthetic metaphor built upon the touch-vision connection: "they offer a sensation of warmth, of powerful sunshine." This is directly related to the guidelines of Art Beyond Sight (Salzhauer Axel et al., 2003), which recommend the intersensorial translation of the artwork components and, specifically, suggest using tactile sensations to describe the surface of sculptural pieces and light in paintings. The synesthetic metaphor therefore contributes to creating a multisensory experience of the exhibit. This, according to a recent reception study by Eardley et al. (2016), seems to help BPS museum visitors create autobiographical memories, which are for these authors the end product that the visitor is seeking.

This is another example:

> Use of light and shadow in a painting can be explained by referring to the feeling one has when sitting in front of a window on a sunny day. The parts of the face and body that feel the warmth are said to be in the light. Those parts not being warmed by the sun are said to be in shade or shadow. (Salzauer et al., 2003, p. 8)

We can even go one step further and consider ADs created with a "sensological" point of view. Carlos Boyad is a researcher who has developed a field called "sensology". It is an approach designed to help people improve their quality of life by learning to perceive, express, organise and use their non-verbal world more effectively, which has an impact on intelligence, creativity and emotional balance. This approach also emphasises the importance of nurturing and preparing the brain to assimilate knowledge and focuses on fine-tuning sensory capacities. This has been proved to be effective with BPS visitors to museums (Soler and Luque, 2022).

Therefore, the aim must always be for the BPS person to perceive the whole of the work's contents and, furthermore, its artistic nature as previously stated, that is, to feel the inter-aesthetic tensions created in it. To appreciate a painting, therefore, is not only to see the different formal elements that compose it but to perceive and to be moved of the artisticity of the same one lived through the inter-aesthetic tensions.

3.5 Interpretative Voicing

We have already referred to the term "soundpainting" (Neves, 2012), but it does not only refer to poetry. It also brings together multiple sound "textures". Carefully chosen words and a careful direction of the voice to guarantee adequate tone of voice, rhythm and speech modulation can all work together with specific sound effects and music to provide emotions. In many ways, soundpainting goes against the grain of conventional museum AD, since it is openly subjective and interpretative in nature. By trying to capture and recreate artistic subtleties, it might be seen as a form of transcreation, particularly because it aims to "substitute" the original form by an equivalent and yet new art form.

Despite the fact that soundpainting may be interpretative or subjective in nature, it can still be loyal to the original piece of work in its effort to convey the messages and emotions of the first through new modes of expression (Neves, 2012). Soundpainting can inspire creative AD design to offer BPS users quality experiences.

4   Conclusion

In recent times, many studies have highlighted the complexity of encapsulating AD in a single typology that satisfies all the needs and expectations of users. Nowadays, an increasingly significant debate is taking place around AD techniques and accessibility. This dialogue has explored various dimensions of AD, such as the multiplicity of approaches (Soler Gallego, 2018) and its relationship with subjectivity and creativity (Luque Colmenaro & Soler Gallego, 2020), among other aspects.

We would need to carry out research focussed on reception, where BPS individuals evaluate and analyse the utility and effectiveness of AD with a subjectivity approach. These reception studies would offer a more accurate insight into how AD is perceived and experienced in practice, validating its real utility. We strongly believe museums, companies and professionals have to explore new ways of applying AD, from established guidelines into innovative and creative approaches.

Within the realm of AD for art, particularly when considering subjective and creatively driven approaches, the integration of technology may seem tangential at best. These methodologies prioritise nuanced interpretation and imaginative expression over standardised techniques or technological interventions. Consequently, the incorporation of technology in this type of AD often assumes a peripheral role, if it exists at all, as it does not align with the fundamental principles of subjectivity and creativity inherent in these processes. Rather than being perceived as a burgeoning trend or heralding a future direction, scholarly inquiry is directed towards understanding the intricate dynamics of human perception and interpretation within the context of AD. Thus, technology occupies a marginal, if not negligible, position within these discussions, as the emphasis remains firmly on the human experience of both BPS people and describers and the diverse perspectives that contribute to the multifaceted understanding of art.

After having explored the role of subjectivity and creativity in AD guidelines together with the current trends in research and practice, we can point at the need for a balance between objective and subjective AD, as some BPS visitors may prefer more interpretative and evaluative descriptions (Walczak & Fryer, 2017), and as museum education is adapting to new perspectives of enjoyment and to a wider and more profound approach to human rights and accessibility. This aligns with Hutchinson and Eardley's proposition from a few years back, which posited that the evolution of museum AD might involve offering a variety of AD styles, such as multiple shorter descriptions, or creative impressions (2019) and with Neves (2012), who has widely debated the inclusion of subjective and interpretive styles in AD. Also, the lack of consensus on what constitutes subjective judgement and the challenges in defining objective interpretation in AD may lead to more open approaches to AD.

We as academia have to present a strong will to carry out a further development of guidelines. There are recent on-going investigations leading to this. For example, Bisier (2023) has recently analysed the pertinence of the Spanish UNE 153020 norm. Since its publication in 2005, this standard has remained the only official document in Spanish regulating AD. However, despite significant advancements in the inclusion of these communities in the cultural sphere, the standard has not been updated in over seventeen years. With the implementation of the new General Audiovisual Communication Law in 2022, Spanish government mandates that audio described films comply with the quality standards outlined in the UNE standard. This has prompted a reevaluation of the document, aiming to provide a constructive review. However, we have to take to account that this document mostly deals with film AD, and the question should not be whether it has to be updated, as the author explains, but adapted to other types of AD, such as museum and performing arts. We understand new documents have to be created, not only prescriptive ones, but descriptive and practical texts that reflect the variety of experiences we can find in our increasingly accessible and multisensory museums.

Additionally, the significance of individual, subjective experiences, creativity, and dialogue in museums and art education is key, and we present insights into the evolving field of AD and the potential for enhancing accessibility and inclusivity in the realm of visual arts. Different styles of AD, including metaphorical, immersive, synesthetic, interpretative voices, and poetic styles have the potential to enhance the subjective and aesthetic experience of museum visitors.

Acknowledgements This chapter is based upon work from COST Action CA19142—Leading Platform for European Citizens, Industries, Academia and Policymakers in Media Accessibility (LEAD-ME) supported by COST (European Cooperation in Science and Technology).

References

ADLAB Project. (2019). ADLAB Project. http://www.adlabproject.eu/

AENOR. (2005). *Norma española UNE 153020: Audiodescripción para personas con discapacidad visual. Requisitos para la audiodescripción y elaboración de audioguías.* AENOR.

Bartolini, C., & Manfredi, M. (2022). Combining intersemiotic and interlingual translation in training programmes: A functional approach to museum audio description. *Status Quaestionis, 23,* 75–98. https://doi.org/10.13133/2239-1983/18225

Benecke, B., & Dosch, E. (2004). *Wenn aus Bildern Worte werden.* Bayerischer Rundfunk.

Eardley, A. F., Mineiro, C., Neves, J., & Ride, P. (2016). Redefining access: Embracing multi-modality, memorability and shared experience in museums. *Curator. the Museum Journal, 59*(3), 263–286.

Eisner, E. W. (2002). *The arts and the creation of mind.* Yale University Press.

Font Bisier, M. A. (2023). Análisis de la norma UNE 153020 sobre audiodescripción: ¿Debería modificarse tras diecisiete años de vigencia? *Ética y Cine Journal, 13*(1), 41–52.

Herrmann, J. B. (2013). *Metaphor in academic discourse: Linguistic forms, conceptual structures, communicative functions and cognitive representations.* LOT Dissertation Series, 333. Utrecht: LOT.

Hutchinson, R. S., & Eardley, A. F. (2019). Museum audio description: The problem of textual fidelity. *Perspectives, 27*(1), 42–57.

Hutchinson, R. S., & Eardley, A. F. (2020). The accessible museum: Towards an understanding of international audio description practices in museums. *Journal of Visual Impairment & Blindness, 114*(6), 475–487. https://doi.org/10.1177/0145482X2097195

Hyks, V. (2005). Audio description and translation. Two related but different skills. *Translating Today, 4,* 6–8.

Kleege, G. (2016). Audio description described: Current standards, future innovations, larger implications. *Representations, 135,* 89–101.

Kruger, J. L., & Orero, P. (2010). Audio description, audio narration: A new era in AVT. *Perspectives: Studies in Translatology, 18*(3), 141–142.

Lima, P. H., & Magalhães, C. M. (2013). A neutralidade em audiodescrições de pinturas: Resultados preliminares de um descrição via teoria da avaliatividade. In V. L. Santiago Araújo, & M. Ferreira Aderaldo (Eds.), *Os novos rumos da pesquisa em audiodescrição no Brasil* (pp. 73–87). Editora CRV.

Luque Colmenero, M. O. (2016). The embodiment of the metaphor: An analysis of the metaphors used to convey the human body in audio descriptive guides of museums for people with visual functional diversity. *E-AESLA, 2,* 326–334.

Luque Colmenero, M. O. (2020). Optionality for describing contemporary art: Deliberate metaphors as a tool for conveying subjectivity in audio description for visually impaired people. In O. Carrero Márquez, C. Monedero Morales, & M. Viñarás Abad (Eds.), *La nueva comunicación del siglo* XXI (pp. 166–181). Pirámide.

Luque Colmenero, M. O. (2021). "Como si sus ojos fueran soles": La marcación de la metáfora en la audiodescripción de arte para personas ciegas y con baja visión. *Trans, 25*(1), 333–347.

Luque Colmenero, M. O., & Soler Gallego, S. (2020). Metaphor as creativity in audio descriptive tours for art museums: From description to practice. *Journal of Audiovisual Translation, 3*(1), 64–78.

Mazur, I., & Chmiel, A. (2012). Audio description made to measure: Reflections on interpretation in AD based on the Pear Tree Project data. In A. Remael, P. Orero, & M. Carroll (Eds.), *Media for all: Audiovisual and media accessibility at the crossroads* (pp. 173–188). Rodopi.

Morisset, L., & Gonant, F. (2008). L'audiodescription: Principes et orientations. https://www.csa.fr/Media/Files/Espace-Juridique/Chartes/Charte-de-l-audiodescription

Neves, J. (2012). Multi-sensory approaches to (audio) describing the visual arts. *MonTi, 4*, 277–293.

Neves, J. (2016). Enriched descriptive guides: A case for collaborative meaning-making in museums. *Cultus, 9*(2), 137–154.

Orero, P., & Pujol, J. (2007). Audio description precursors: Ekphrasis and narrators. *Translation Watch Quarterly, 3*(2), 49–60.

Rai, S., Greening, J., & Petré, L. (2010). *A comparative study of audio description guidelines prevalent in different countries.* RNIB.

Ramos, M. (2016). Testing audio narration: The emotional impact of language in audio description. *Perspectives: Studies in Translation Theory and Practice, 24*(1), 1–29.

Remael, A. (2005). *Audio description for recorded TV, cinema and DVD. An experimental stylesheet for teaching purposes.* Artesis University College. Unpublished manuscript.

RNIB & Vocal Eyes. (2003). *The talking images guide. Museums, galleries and heritage site: improving access for blind and partially sighted people.* RNIB.

Salzhauer Axel, E., & Sobol, N. (2003). AEB's guidelines for verbal description. In E. Salzhauer Axel, & N. Sobol (Eds.). *Art beyond sight: A resource guide to art, creativity, and visual impairment* (pp. 229–237). AFB Press.

Salzhauer Axel, E., Hooper, V., Kardoulias, T., Stephenson Keyes, S., & Rosenberg, F. (1996). *Making visual art accessible to people who are blind and visually impaired.* Art Education for the Blind.

Salzhauer Axel, E., Hooper, V., Kardoulias, T., Stephenson Keyes, S., & Rosenberg, F. (2003). AEB's guidelines for verbal description. In E. Salzhauer Axel & N. Sobol Levent (Eds.), *Art beyond sight: A resource guide to art, creativity, and visual impairment* (pp. 229–237). New York: AFB Press.

Snyder, J. (2010). *Audio description guidelines and best practices.* American Council for the Blind. https://adp.acb.org/ad.html

Soler Gallego, S. (2018). Audio descriptive guides in art museums: A corpus-based semantic analysis. *Translation and Interpreting Studies, 13*(2), 230–249.

Soler Gallego, S. (2019). Defining subjectivity in audio description for art museums. *Meta: Translators' Journal, 64*(3), 708–733.

Soler Gallego, S. (2021). The minority AD: Creativity in audio descriptions of visual art. In M. Antona & C. Stephanidis (Eds.), *Universal access in human-computer interaction. Access to media, learning and assistive environments.* Springer.

Soler Gallego, S., & Luque Colmenero, M. O. (2022). User reception of minority and creative approaches to visual art audio description: Poetry, metaphor and synaesthesia. *Status Quaestionis, 23*, 53–74. https://doi.org/10.13133/2239-1983/18224

Steen, G. J., Dorst, A. G., Herrmann, J. B., Kaal, A., Krennmayr, T., & Pasmta, T. (2010). *A method for linguistic metaphor identification: From MIP to MIPVU.* John Benjamins.

Udo, J. P., Acevedo, B., & Fels, D. I. (2010). Horatio audio-describes Shakespeare's Hamlet: Blind and low-vision theatre-goers evaluate an unconventional audio description strategy. *British Journal of Visual Impairment, 28*, 139–155.

Udo, J. P., & Fels, D. I. (2009). Suit the action to the word, the word to the action: An unconventional approach to describing Shakespeare's Hamlet. Ted Rogers School of Information Technology Management Publications and Research, 16. http://digitalcommons-ryerson.ca/trsitm/16

Vercauteren, G. (2007). Towards a European guideline for audio description. In J. Díaz Cintas, P. Orero, & A. Remael (Eds.), *Media for all. Accessibility in audiovisual translation* (pp. 139–150). Amsterdam: Rodopi.

Vercauteren, G., & Orero, P. (2013). Describing facial expressions: Much more than meets the eye. *Quaderns Revista de Traducció, 20*, 187–199.

Walczak, A., & Fryer, L. (2017). Creative description: The impact of audio description style on presence in visually impaired audiences. *British Journal of Visual Impairment, 35*(1), 6–17.

Gaze-Led Audio Description (GLAD). Concept and Application to Accessibility of Architectural Heritage

Krzysztof Krejtz⬥, Daria Rutkowska-Siuda⬥, and Izabela Krejtz⬥

Abstract This chapter presents the concept of Gaze-Led Audio Description (GLAD) and its application for the accessibility of city space. Audio Description (AD) is created by domain experts who have deep knowledge of the audio-described matter but might have their own narrative biases. Many studies report that experts' perception and attentional patterns over the objects of their expertise are different from the perception of non-experts. As an unintended result, audio descriptions of architectural heritage created by experts, art historians or architects, might lose accessibility to non-experts. For example, often experts' views of historic buildings are based on reading diagrams of historic buildings, leading the description from a general presentation of the basic divisions of architectural structures. The descriptions then focus on the details leading from the lower to the upper parts. This type of audio description is useful in the analysis of monuments; however, it may not reflect the natural way of looking, which usually focuses initially on the dominant accent of the mass. In this chapter, we postulate that AD may benefit from adjusting it regarding the analysis of visual attention patterns of non-experts. We present some insights from empirical research.

Keywords Audio description · Eye tracking · Experts · Scanpath · Accessibility · Cultural heritage

K. Krejtz (✉) · I. Krejtz
Eye Tracking Research Center, Institute of Psychology, SWPS University, Warsaw, Poland
e-mail: kkrejtz@swps.edu.pl

I. Krejtz
e-mail: ikrejtz@swps.edu.pl

D. Rutkowska-Siuda
University of Łódź, Łódź, Poland
e-mail: daria.rutkowska-siuda@uni.lodz.pl

© The Author(s) 2024
A. Marcus-Quinn et al. (eds.), *Transforming Media Accessibility in Europe*,
https://doi.org/10.1007/978-3-031-60049-4_4

1 Introduction

Audio description (AD) is a widely used accessibility technique for Blind and Visually Impaired individuals (BVI). The general task of an audio describer is an inter-semiotic translation (Vandaele, 2012), which is a verbalization of the visual information needed to understand the visual content even without being able to actually see it by a viewer. A wide body of research has demonstrated the effectiveness of audio description in various applications for BVI (e.g., Szarkowska et al., 2013) and sighted people (e.g., Krejtz et al., 2012a, 2012b). As an accessibility technique AD has been relatively unchanged since its introduction which shows its robustness. However, new advances in visual attention research using eye-tracking method have demonstrated clear differences between experts and non-experts in the way they perceive the visual environment (Krejtz et al., 2023b). Prior expertise may change attention patterns over objects related to that domain and induce biases when experts are creating audio descriptions of these objects. In turn, such biases might lower the usability of audio descriptions created by experts for non-experts. Drawing on insights from eye-movement research, we may increase AD's usability, making it more universally designed. Extending the idea suggested by Orero (2007), we proposed an audio description that is organized around gaze patterns of non-experts, the Gaze-Led Audio Description (GLAD) (Krejtz et al., 2023a, 2023b).

In this chapter, we start with the literature review on AD and challenges related to its construction which professional audio describers face. Presenting the concept of attentional biases, we point out the potential biases in audio descriptions that might lower their accessibility features for non-experts. We claim that this potential risk is especially relevant to the fields that require a domain-specific knowledge (e.g., art or historical heritage) for object comprehension. We also present early ideas for overcoming these biases. On the example of existing accessibility systems for blind and visually impaired (BVI) individuals, we describe the idea of audio description of places and a novel approach to it called, gaze-led audio description (GLAD). The very core of its concept is to make use of the attentional patterns of non-experts to adjust audio descriptions of architectural art objects to facilitate their comprehension and understanding. The concept and its requirements are supported by the results of two empirical studies. The first one presents the qualitative analysis of BVI potential users' needs and expectations toward the accessibility system designed for sightseeing the city space (*Friendly City*) and the audio descriptions of places included in the *Friendly City* system (Krejtz et al., 2023a; Pawłowska et al., 2023). The second study qualitatively describes the eye-tracking results of attentional bias of experts in comparison with non-experts, both presented with AD while sightseeing the historical city of Łódź in Poland. The chapter ends with the proposition of gaze-led audio description and its application for a wide variety of fields facilitating the inclusion of BVI into the cultural heritage.

2 Background

2.1 Enhancing Access with Audio Description

Audio description is a narration translating what is visible into what is heard (Audio Description International, 2005; Fryer, 2010; Vandaele, 2012). AD was primarily created for the blind and visually impaired (BVI) individuals as an accessibility tool allowing for inclusive access to the visual content of cultural heritage (Independent Television Commission, 2000). AD is widely studied and used in practice as an additional narration between dialogues in films (Kruger, 2010; Orero, 2007; Remael & Vercauteren, 2007; Salway, 2007), theater (Fryer, 2010), opera performance (Cabeza-Caceres, 2010), sport shows (Mazur, 2020), or museum spaces (Cabeza-Caceres, 2010; Pawłowska & Sowińska-Heim, 2016; Szarkowska et al., 2016). For example, Szarkowska et al. (2016) created accessible content in a multimedia application guide containing a description of selected works of modern and contemporary art in museum spaces, (see also Pacinotti, 2017). In response to the needs of modern and contemporary art gallery visitors, the proposed guide with AD served as a guide explaining exhibition's meaning and content (Szarkowska et al., 2016).

Several studies have indicated the beneficial effects of AD on media content comprehension among visually impaired adult viewers (Frazier & Coutinho-Johnson, 1995; Pawłowska et al., 2019; Schmeidler & Kirchner, 2001) and children (Palomo, 2008). For example, Frazier and Coutinho-Johnson (1995) demonstrated that visually impaired participants who watched movies accompanied by AD achieved the same level of movie content comprehension as sighted viewers. Their level of movie content comprehension was also significantly better than those visually impaired who were presented with the same movies without AD (see also Peli et al., 1996). Similar results were found for educational TV shows (Schmeidler & Kirchner, 2001).

Listening to AD is beneficial to a much broader audience including sighted viewers when it is inserted between dialogues in the film. Eardley et al. (2017) noted that by stimulating imagery, AD can potentially enhance the experience of both sighted and BVI individuals. By creating a multi-sensory experience, enriched with narrative information, AD may increase the memorability of audio-described objects.

Krejtz et al. (2012a) in an experimental eye-tracking study, in primary school sighted children, demonstrated that AD guides children's attention toward described objects resulting, e.g., in more fixations on specific regions of interest in educational movies. AD also sustained attention of sighted viewers resulting in a better comprehension of the movie content (Krejtz et al., 2012a). After watching audio-described educational movies, children easily retrieved visual elements of the movies than their peers who watched the clips without AD and relied more on the recognition rather than based their decisions on the elimination heuristic (Krejtz et al., 2012b). Another series of multimedia learning experiments (Krejtz et al., 2016) corroborated that AD in a group of sighted young adults facilitates focal attention (see also Velichkovsky et al., 2005) when looking at still images of visual art which in turn enhances their comprehension and memorability.

In summary, studies on AD gathered sufficient evidence supporting the use of AD in both sighted and BVI users increasing the accessibility of visual content in various contexts. Therefore, creating audio descriptions is vital not only for extending access to visual content for BVI but also for supporting the understanding and experience of visual content for a broader audience.

2.1.1 Audio Description Challenges. What and How to Describe

The creation of accurate audio description faces several challenges: what to describe vs how to describe it (Vandaele, 2012), audio describer cognitive and emotional biases, and visual content specificity (movies, live shows, and places). Vandaele (2012) addressed the issue of narrativity of audio description in movies. He distinguished the problems of *how* and *what* to convert from a visual input into a verbal medium. The later problem of "what to detect and select" to preserve and enhance the visual narration of movies is causing more difficulties for audio describers (Vandaele, 2012). He also recognizes that audio describers may be biased by personal understanding of a movie narration. The proposed solution, "*a double hermeneutic-heuristic procedure*", shall help audio describers to understand and attend to their narrative emotions (narrative states of mind) to avoid bias. In the first step, the proposed procedure focuses on identifying narrative states. In the second step, it looks for the discursive triggers prompting these states (Vandaele, 2012).

Orero and Vilaro (2012) proposed using eye-tracking analysis on regular movie viewers to decide which details of the visual content should be audio-described. Following Navarrete (2005) they claim that AD should not extend to subtle visual elements that are hardly noticed by the sighted audience. The number of details according to Orero and Vilaro (2012, p. 304) "may reach the point of saturation where an audience can neither process nor remember any further details." That observation is in line with the literature on cognitive load theory which points out the limited cognitive resources for information processing (Sweller, 2010a, 2010b). Orero and Vilaró (2012) proposed that audio descriptions in films should be adjusted by prior eye-tracking research with the potential audience, e.g., BVI individuals. To our knowledge, this postulate has not yet been implemented.

2.1.2 Attention Bias of Audio Description Experts

Attention bias is a selection of some information while neglecting the other based on the viewer's characteristics (e.g., expertise, knowledge, preferences, and affect). Attention biases might be sourced in the emotional state or individual differences, e.g., the level of social anxiety when attending to socio-emotional signals (e.g., Krejtz et al., 2018). Cognitive biases are also related to the expertise in a certain domain while attending and/or processing information related to that domain. For example, the theory of long-term working memory proposes that experts have higher than non-experts limit of working memory when processing visual information related to the domain of their expertise (Cowan, 2001). On the other hand, *the information reduction hypothesis* claims that expertise causes better selectivity of relevant and neglect of irrelevant visual information (Haider & Frensch, 1999). Following *the eye-mind hypothesis* by Just and Carpenter (1980), which relates fixation duration with cognitive processing of attended information, better selectivity in experts should lead to longer fixation durations on relevant visual information (Kieras & Just, 2018). For example, in the context of architectural heritage that would be most of the elements of facade or other characteristics of built environments.

Gegenfurtner et al. (2011) based on the meta-analysis of 296 effect sizes in eye-tracking research on expertise differences in the comprehension of visualizations demonstrated consistent differences between attention patterns and characteristics between experts and non-experts. On average experts in comparison with non-experts had shorter fixation durations, more fixations on task-relevant areas, and fewer fixations on task-irrelevant areas. Presented findings support, in general, the hypothesis that experts encode and retrieve information more effectively than non-experts, select more relevant information, and demonstrate a wider visual span.

Gegenfurtner et al. (2011) in their meta-analysis also found significantly longer fixation duration for intermediates than for novices which suggests that expertise domain-relevant information processing is not yet fully automated in intermediates. Interestingly, the results of this meta-analysis showed that visual attention biases in experts are moderated by task and professional domain; however, the latter were not consistent (Gegenfurtner et al., 2011).

A more recent systematic review on the relation between gaze behavior and expertise (Brams et al., 2019) found more evidence on domain specificity of attentional bias and information processing. Summarizing 73 eye-tracking articles they concluded that the selectivity in attention allocation toward relevant visual information is a dominating element in most experts (most studies reported a bigger number of fixations of longer durations on relevant visual information), excluding medicine discipline experts. Interestingly, some studies assessing expertise in medicine report more structured scanning patterns in experts. Systematic visual attention strategies can enhance performance (e.g., Augustyniak & Tadeusiewicz, 2006; Vitak et al., 2012). Brams et al. (2019, p. 1) concluded that "large discrepancies in the outcomes of the papers reviewed suggest that there is not one theory that fits all domains of expertise."

Recently, Krejtz et al. (2023b) revealed differences between experts (art-history and architecture students) vs. non-experts (psychology students) in visual scanning of city architecture (buildings, churches, and monuments). In the eye-tracking experimental study, participants were instructed to scan and remember two-dimensional photos of architectural objects in the city of Łódź in Poland while their eye movements were recorded with a remote GazePoint HD (150 *Hz*) eye tracker. Experts' attentional patterns were more focal, meaning longer fixations were followed by shorter saccades. Additionally, they found that the more focal attentional pattern the better memory of the stimuli image was observed. Presented results suggest that experts in architecture and the art-history domain tend to process visual information about the architectural artifacts in a more deliberative way than non-experts, making sense of each detail of the building, e.g., presented in its façade (Krejtz et al., 2023b).

Also, Chmiel et al. (2010) used eye-tracking method and verbal reports to observe differences between what people normally looked at when watching scenes from a film and what audio describers included in AD of these scenes.

The above-mentioned examples of differences in attention patterns between experts and non-experts suggest that experts' perception of objects might be very different from the perception of non-experts (Castner et al., 2018; Chmiel et al., 2010). Consequently, audio descriptions created solely by experts in the field might be "unnatural" and less accessible for non-experts, which supports our claim of taking the perspective of non-experts while creating AD, by taking into account the knowledge from the analysis of visual attention patterns of non-experts.

2.2 Accessibility of City Built-Environments: Audio Description of Places

Audio description in city space can be implemented in smart-city assistive systems based on a combination of information and communication technology (ICT) and the Internet of things (IoT) proliferation, to help BVI visitors fully experience and appreciate the built environment, public art, or other landmarks. In a more general sense those systems are implementing Industry 4.0 conceptual framework and solutions (Ustundag & Cevikcan, 2018). To our knowledge, such systems mainly focus on navigation help through the city space, indoor navigation (Kuribayashi et al., 2021), or maintaining social distance (Kayukawa et al., 2020). Those accessibility solutions are commonly based on different technologies like Bluetooth to provide audio or tactile cues, audible traffic signals at intersections, tactile paving (raised bumps or patterns on the ground), audio-based way-finding systems in public buildings, and audio guides.

Among the most current ICT-based solutions for facilitating the accessibility of city space for BVI individuals, we might mention the following systems: *Mobility as a Service (MaaS)* (MaaS, 2016), *Safe Smart CLE, Wayfindr* (Wayfindr, 2018), *NaviLens* (NEOSISTEC, 2017), and *aBeacon* (Tech, 2018). Several cities, e.g., Barcelona in Spain, Marburg in Germany, Seattle in the USA, Louisville in the USA, Helsinki in Finland, Antwerp in Belgium, and Nijmegen in the Netherlands have implemented such systems to provide accessibility to the city space and enhance the well-being of BVI citizens and tourists. An interesting example is the *NaviLens* system in Barcelona, Spain, which currently boasts deployment of 9100 fiducial markers affixed in 161 metro stations and 2600 bus stops. *NaviLens* markers are visual fiducial markers, similar to well-known ArUco markers (Garrido-Jurado et al., 2014) or QR codes in color or monochrome (Saez et al., 2020), which can be scanned with smartphones to provide extended information about the navigation route and current location.

In terms of user interaction, He et al. (2020) proposed a light haptic cue-based wearable device PneuFetch that supports BVI people to locate and reach objects in a new environment. Kuribayashi et al. (2022) successfully tested a mobile-assistive *Corridor-Walker* system equipped with a LiDAR sensor to help blind individuals to avoid obstacles and recognize intersections while walking along indoor corridors. By generating a 2D map of the environment, the system alerts the user by vibrating and audio feedback when an obstacle or intersection appears on a selected walking path. As a result, blind individuals reported being less wall-dependent while walking straight and benefited from feedback about the intersections making their walking path less challenging. In another project, Kayukawa et al. (2020) combined an RGB-D camera (to detect the positions of target objects) and a LiDAR sensor (to create a 2D map of the surrounding environment) in *BlindPilot*, a system navigating blind individuals in city spaces, e.g., taking an empty seat in transport. Compared to sound-based navigation, the *BlindPilot* allowed reaching destinations faster and with greater safety. Kuribayashi et al. (2021) also proposed an interesting assistive *LineChaser* system based on an RGB smartphone camera to help blind individuals to find a queue and its end and allow a blind person to move forward as the line gets shorter. By estimating the position of a nearby person, the system detects whether the person stands in a queue, and it updates information about the distance to this person. Audio and vibration signals navigate the user through the line, suggesting when to move forward and stop.

Extending the use of AD to the outdoor experience potentially can make a difference in the city's built environment understanding and access. Although still relatively under-investigated, there are attempts to use AD in city space to increase the accessibility of architectural heritage and to enhance understanding of a built environment (Boys, 2014; Pacinotti, 2022). For example, Pacinotti (2022) provided guidelines for AD for bringing churches as places of worship to a broader audience within "A Sense of Place" project aimed at providing audio descriptions of buildings from the joint work of design students and blind and visually impaired volunteers. As the outcome, *VocalEyes* offers audio-described city tours providing the experience of examining architectural heritage and broader built environment from an audio describers' perspective (VocalEyes, 2007).

The present *Friendly City* Project aims at designing the city space accessibility system which will directly implement the AD of city spaces, especially historical architectural artifacts. The AD will be played on the user's smartphone after approaching an interesting spot in the city space (see Pawłowska et al., 2023).

3 Study 1. Needs and Expectations Toward Audio Description of Places

Audio descriptions of architectural objects in the city space are crucial to the architectural heritage accessibility system, especially for BVI users. Study 1 aim was to collect the needs and expectations of potential BVI users of the *Friendly City* system. Expectations of blind and visually impaired potential users might help adjust audio descriptions to their everyday usage. The nature of these expectations and needs requires a qualitative approach to the data obtained during in-depth interviews (IDIs).

Different expectations might also be related to the specific characteristics of the architectural objects. For the present qualitative study, eighty-six architectural objects have been selected. They all come from one industrial city formed in the early nineteenth century with its dynamic growth in the late nineteenth and early twentieth centuries. The selected architectural objects present various Neostyle forms, from Neo-Romanesque to Neo-Baroque. We also used twentieth-century modernist or social-realist buildings of various functions: sacral (14%), residential (34%), public utility (40%), and sculptures/monuments/murals (12%).

3.1 Study 1. Method and Qualitative Analysis Results

We have conducted in-depth interviews with 21 (15 females) visually impaired volunteers aged between 20 and 95 years old, recruited from members of the Polish Association of the Blind. None of the participants was visually impaired from birth. Eleven participants had a good knowledge of the city-built environment and architecture. The interviews started with questions related to usage and experience with digital media and technology and continued with questions related to knowledge of the city's architecture. Next, the general concept of the *Friendly City* architectural heritage accessibility system (Pawłowska et al., 2023) was presented by the interview moderator. The next set of questions was related to the expectations of the system and more importantly to the expectations toward the audio descriptions of the city-built environment. Participants were presented with examples of prepared audio descriptions for selected buildings representing various Neostyle forms and functions. The notes taken by the interview moderator were the subject of the following qualitative analysis. The analysis was of the basic interpretative analysis with the elements of thematic analysis (Lester et al., 2020) when it comes to the requested features of audio description required by potential BVI users.

BVI potential users expected architectural object descriptions and the *Friendly City* system to contain four groups of information: functional, basic metrics, core audio description, and contextual.

> **Functional information**. This type of information is expected to help BVI users navigate from the bus stop to the architectural object, the location of the object, etc. Participants unanimously stated that the distances to the object in the description should be in meters (local measure units of distance). They claimed it would help direct their attention toward the historical or urban context of place and object. Participants suggested introducing terms to locate the object near significant thoroughfares or squares. Their experience shows that these cues help them to establish contact with other people and passers-by while visiting the city independently without a human guide.

Basic metrics. This information is expected to include the name of the architectural object, authors' names, and year of creation. Participants expected to have basic information about the site's metrics before the core audio description. That information would help give a better understanding of the site by giving the historical or urban context of the place and object.

Core audio description. AD presents a detailed description of the object view. Study participants stressed that the audio description should be relatively short (2–3 min). Longer audio descriptions, according to the participants' opinions, became too challenging for their attention and negatively influenced comprehension. Participants claimed that shorter AD would be easier to remember and listen attentively.

Context and general information. BVI users explicitly expected that the *Friendly City* system and object descriptions would extend their general knowledge about architecture and cultural heritage. That is why they appreciated the use of professional terms, e.g., pilaster, paneling, rustication, and tympanum. Concordantly, they expected all terms to be defined and explained. It was also emphasized that context and general information needed to be kept as optional, available in the system on demand. Nearly half of the participants also wanted information about the interiors of the audio-described buildings.

3.2   Study 1. Results Summary

Qualitative results of the in-depth interviews with visually impaired people on the content of audio descriptions show that they expect not only a detailed description of the architectural objects. Potential BVI users of the *Friendly City* system requested features related to the historical context of the architectural artifacts and navigation to them from different parts of the city. According to BVI, audio description could include information on the cultural and spatial context of the buildings and other information extending their general knowledge of art and history. They also suggest that AD should be relatively short (up to 3 min). This poses another challenge for audio describers: how to include all relevant information in a short amount of time. Eye-tracking studies may help mitigate this challenge by showing *natural* visual attention allocated to certain elements of buildings in relatively short epochs, influencing the pace of certain moments of audio description.

4   Study 2. Eye-Tracking Research on Audio Description of Places

The concept of audio description of places in city space is relatively unaddressed in empirical research. There is no empirical evidence that AD can effectively guide the users' attention in the city space, e.g., to the audio-described elements of the architectural artifacts. Similarly, there is a lack of evidence that attention patterns differ between experts and non-experts in response to the AD of architecture in city space. To address these issues, we present preliminary results of an eye-tracking study on AD of places conducted in the wild, namely in the city space, as a part of the *Friendly City* project in Łódź (Pawłowska et al., 2023).

The architectural structure of the center of Łódź constitutes a unique historic complex. The compact, untransformed urban layout and buildings preserved to this day are a testimony to the development of an industrial city in the historicist period. Its classicist, symmetrical layout was laid out on a north–south axis and consisted of three main parts: Old Town, New Town, and Łódka, connected by the main axis defined by Piotrkowska Street. The streets intersect at right angles creating a characteristic checkerboard layout, strongly associated with the industrial cities of England and the United States. The legibility of this layout created in the nineteenth century and its basic development until the beginning of the twentieth century means that the main cultural and administrative institutions are concentrated in a relatively small area. This layout not only makes it easier to move around the city on foot for visually impaired people but also allows them to get to know the historic architecture in a relatively short time.

The vast majority of the buildings included in the *Friendly City* project are related to the period of the city's large-scale industrial development (the second half of the nineteenth century and early twentieth century). Objects created in recent decades were also included. They represent a variety of Neostyle forms: neo-Gothic, neo-Renaissance, neo-Baroque, eclecticism as well as Art Nouveau and Modernism. Each building thus has a different message expressed by the forms and details used, closely related to the building's function and its time of construction. In broader terms, one can say that the divisions of the massing, forms, and decoration used in architecture contain the cultural code of the city. The architectural heritage of Łódź is "decoded" with audio descriptions adapted to the needs of visually impaired people as well as tourists. The *Friendly City* system includes both individual descriptions of objects as well as 360° presentations of important points grouping monuments, such as the area of Plac Wolności (Church of the Holy Spirit, Town Hall, Tadeusz Kościuszko monument).

4.1 Study 2. Method

Thirty (28 females) volunteers (experts in fine arts and non-experts) participated in the study. The study was conducted in the Łódź city in Poland with a rich and unique architectural heritage. Participants were asked to take a route to visit three selected historical sites from the outside.

The routes were selected in terms of communication proximity, diversity of form, function, and time of construction. For example, Route 1—Former Polonia Hotel (neo-classical building from the early twentieth century, one of the most important hotels in Łódź, now adapted for residential purposes), St. Olga Church (sacred, orthodox building), Gustav Schreer Palace (representative building with neo-renaissance forms with the garden and factory premises); Route 2—Former Esplanade (Art Nouveau building with service and commercial functions, formerly one of the most important confectioner's houses), Tramway Station Centre (object from the beginning of the twenty-first century, modern tram shelter structure), and Unicorn sculpture, Place for the Stars (early twenty-first-century modern sculpture by Japanese artist Tomohiro Inaba).

The sites were audio-described, and those descriptions were presented to the participants while they were standing in front of the sites. Table 1 presents an exemplary fragment of the original AD that was read to participants while looking at the Esplanada Building (Fig. 1c, d). Participants' eye movements were collected with the PupilLabs (120 Hz) mobile video eye trackers while listening to audio descriptions. We present a qualitative analysis of visual scanning patterns with a focus on the comparison between two women experts in art history and two non-expert women while listening to the core part of the AD (presenting elements of the building). The participants were presented with the audio description of the aforementioned architectural objects to check their ability to guide the attention of the viewer in the most natural settings. The audio description is an essential part of the designed *Friendly City* system and that's why it was crucial to test its usefulness in this experiment before further development. In this very first study, the original AD was used to guide the users' attention. The major reason for it was to find potential problems in guiding the attention by the AD created in the original approach, potentially biased by the audio describers' expert knowledge.

4.2 Study 2. Qualitative Results

Attention patterns of an expert and a non-expert over two selected buildings (the Gustav Schreer Palace (Fig. 1a, b) and the Esplanada (Fig. 1c, d) were qualitatively analyzed by an expert in art history. Each recording lasted for approximately two minutes. Figure 1 presents a snapshot of the eye-movement patterns. Similar to Study 1, here we present the results of basic interpretive qualitative analysis (Lester et al., 2020, see also Krejtz & Krejtz, 2005).

4.2.1 Expert's Attention on the Gustav Schreer Palace

The expert initially focused her attention on the body of the building, the most decorative detail of the façade, and the upper window frame. She then looked at the entrances, briefly examining the spatial relationship of the building. While listening to the core AD, the observer focused her attention directly on the indicated elements focusing on them for a longer time, e.g., the whole of the window frames, and the horizontal stripes of the ground floor decoration. She then directed her attention for longer during the presentation of the ground floor window decoration, cornice, and

Table 1 Fragments of the core AD: original and gaze-led of the Esplanada building in the city of Łódź, depicted in Fig. 1c, d

Original audio description (AD)	Gaze-led audio description (GLAD)
The building was erected on a rectangular plan, with a one-story outbuilding adjacent to the east, invisible from the street. It is a one-story building painted in a light cream color, with a high, usable attic resembling another floor. The facade, i.e., the front wall facing Piotrkowska Street, can be divided into three horizontal zones. The ground floor is almost completely glazed. Through large rectangular windows, you can look into the interior, currently housing a restaurant. On the central axis, in a niche with a frame, there is a wooden, glazed door with a transom. To open it, grab the vertical metal handle, and pull it slightly toward you On the first floor, separated from the ground floor by a smooth strip of wall, the entire width of the facade is filled with a large window, framed from above by a slightly flattened arch, the shape of which is emphasized by a wide, fluted band on the sides. Its filling is a structure with ten glazed arcades. On the wall on the sides of the window, there is a bas-relief detail in the form of a pale green plant ornament climbing upwards, which slightly stands out against the cream background…	The building is painted a light cream color. The facade facing Piotrkowska Street can be divided into three horizontal zones. The top floor has a rich relief decoration. In the center there is a convexly carved caduceus, i.e., a winged stick—in this case resembling a glowing torch—entwined on both sides with snakes with heads turned toward each other. In Greek mythology, the caduceus was an attribute of the god Hermes, since modern times it symbolizes peace and trade On the first floor, the entire width of the façade is filled with a large window, framed from above by a slightly flattened arch. The window is divided into ten glazed arcades. From the top, the window is framed by a wide, fluted band, and at the bottom, it is closed by a belt with the name of the restaurant and the logo in an oval form. On the sides of the window frame, there is a bas-relief detail in the form of a pale green floral ornament climbing upwards, which slightly stands out against the cream background…

(a) (b)

(c) (d)

Fig. 1 Fragments of eye movements' scanpaths of expert and non-expert when looking at buildings while listening to AD in Study 2: Expert scanpath on Gustav Schreer Palace (**a**), Non-expert scanpath on Gustav Schreer Palace (**b**), Expert scanpath on Esplanade building (**c**), Non-expert scanpath on Esplanade building (**d**). *Note* Red and blue circles represent fixations, white lines represent saccadic eye movements, and numbers next to the blue circles represent fixation sequence

balcony. The viewer's attention did not explore the whole arrangement of divisions of the symmetrical massing, and it focused on the details indicated in the AD located only on the right side of the building.

4.2.2 Non-expert Attending the Gustav Schreer Palace

The non-expert initially focused her attention on the upper part of the body of the building and its central decoration in the form of a balcony with a decorative window and a finial—a cornice. Then her gaze followed the central axis from top to bottom, stopping for a longer time at the door decoration. She spent more time analyzing the individual parts of the object going from left to right. While reading the spatial context information, she followed with her eyes the parts indicated in the audio description. While listening to the Core AD, the observer focused her attention on the indicated parts of the description without focusing on the whole element but divided it into individual parts of the detail, she compared the same elements on the left and right. The gaze was guided in leaps and bounds. Then her gaze followed the read description, which focused on the central part of the solid, also guided in leaps and bounds.

4.2.3   Expert's Attention on the Esplanade Building

The viewer initially focused on the correlation of the building with the neighboring buildings. Then her gaze focused on the ground floor and directed toward the top of the building. Later, she returned to the lower floor, parts of which she examined from right to left. She successively examined each story according to this pattern. While listening to the core AD, her gaze wandered according to the description. For a longer time, her gaze stopped at the boundary of the first story and the finial, examining their relationship and the symmetrically arranged details. Without following the final part of the description any further, she examined the relationship of each part of the building to the neighboring buildings (height, width, and window frames). When the notion of a caduceus appeared in the AD, the viewer focused her gaze on it—not looking for it on the façade.

4.2.4   Non-expert Attending the Esplanade Building

The observer examined the building with her eyes walking from the ground floor upwards, from left to right, focusing her gaze on the visible details and accents of the story divisions. She then explored the object's relationship to neighboring buildings (the height of the floor layout) while listening to the basic metrics. Attention was then focused on the object's axis, with the gaze running from the lower toward the upper story, focusing for longer on the accent in the finial—the caduceus. As she heard the information about the neighboring objects, she shifted her gaze first to the left and then to the right. During the listening of the core AD, her attention was focused on the indicated lot. When the detail in the finial—the caduceus—was presented, the subject's attention only focused on it when the meaning of the term was developed.

4.3   Study 2. Results Summary

The perception of the audio-described buildings was probably influenced by the location of the buildings, and the Gustav Schreer Palace was more isolated from the factors of noise and convening traffic than the Esplanade Building. The viewers mostly focused their attention in the first stage on the spatial relationship of the object comparing (which is particularly evident in Esplanade Building) height relationships and details. In the Gustav Schreer Palace, the increased visual fixation of the non-expert is evident—it is three times that of the art historian. In the Esplanade Building, these differences are not so clear. The non-experts were more likely to focus first on the dominant features visible in the elevations such as the window frames, the entrance, the finial, and the accompanying details. The attention of non-experts was more likely to follow the read description than that of art historians. One might be tempted to say that the art historian's way of looking focuses on a broader field. When pointing out the lots and their detail, she does not focus on it for as long as the non-expert, concentrating more on examining the relationship between the elements.

5 Discussion and Conclusion. Toward Gaze-Led Audio Description

In this chapter, we reviewed the literature on audio description, exploring its diverse applications and associated challenges. Subsequently, we have provided concise summaries of the results of two empirical studies—one involving qualitative inter-views with BVI and the other employing eye-tracking method—both centered on the audio description of places.

Firstly, by integrating the aforementioned with the tenets of user-centered design (Abras et al., 2004; Norman, 1986, 1988), it is apparent that the development of audio description demands an active engagement of visually impaired users. Their qualitative perspectives, expression of requirements, and opinions assume a pivotal role in augmenting the effectiveness and pertinence of the AD creation process.

Secondly, following universal design principles (Błaszczak & Przybylski, 2010; Goldsmith, 2007), we posit that audio description should also be crafted with the subjective and attentional insights from typical users (non-experts). This inclusive approach seeks to address their specific needs, cognitive constraints (Carpena et al., 2019), and other relevant considerations, thereby promoting a more universally accessible and comprehensible audio description experience.

In their work, Krejtz et al. (2023a, 2023b) introduced the concept of Gaze-Led Audio Description (GLAD), a novel approach that leverages aggregated scanpaths of novices to adjust the content of audio descriptions. Their primary aim was to align the order of visual elements in the description with more natural, non-expert viewing patterns. This innovative methodology presents an opportunity to guide professionals in crafting gaze-cued narratives, seamlessly merging the expertise of art historians and professional audio describers with the attentional patterns exhibited by non-experts. The example of the implementation of the GLAD for architectural artifacts, in comparison with the original AD, is portrayed in Table 1.

Within the context of the *Friendly City* project, adaptations were made to the original audio descriptions to align with the layperson's perspective. The observation that individuals not versed in art history interpret the sequence and details of a building differently prompted the need for a tailored approach. The conventional AD structure, starting with the building's plan, location, and compositional scheme, followed by a systematic progression from lower to upper stories, was reconsidered.

Non-experts tended to focus their attention on key architectural features, such as the decorative finial and the entrance area of the ground floor. This alternative approach to viewing effectively captures the architect's intention, drawing the observer's attention to visually prominent elements enriched with symbolic detailing. Consequently, the audio description accents were repositioned to align with the natural gaze patterns of non-experts. The modified description not only adheres to their viewing habits but also incorporates additional information about the significance of specific details.

Notably, this enrichment of information responds to the preferences expressed by interviewees, who sought immediate explanations of symbols and terms during the audio description. By seamlessly integrating gaze-cued narrative adjustments and providing relevant context, the GLAD approach not only enhances accessibility for non-experts but also contributes to a more comprehensive and engaging experience of architectural descriptions.

In this chapter, we presented audio description as a core element of accessibility systems in various contexts with a special focus on bringing the architectural heritage of city space closer to a broader audience. We presented a qualitative analysis of scanning patterns with a focus on the comparison between experts in fine art and non-experts, which suggested that the visual attention of non-experts was guided by the audio description presented at the site. Traditional audio description, created by experts, is not free from biases stemming from their expertise. Referring to the empirical evidence about differences in visual scanning of architectural objects between experts and non-experts, Krejtz et al. (2023a) propose an innovative approach to the creation of AD. Eye-movement patterns of non-expert-sighted viewers may serve as guidelines for audio describers to focus in their narrations on parts of historical buildings that attracted the attention of non-experts. In turn, the gaze-led audio description may acquire a more natural experience of "seeing" spaces with audio description. The preference for Gaze-Led AD over traditional AD by sighted tourists and tourists with vision impairments requires additional testing. Nevertheless, the GLAD approach corroborates current literature suggesting that the use of eye tracking for enabling gaze-guided narratives enriches the tourist experience (Kiefer et al., 2018) and is in line with the Tourism 5.0 idea, promoting creative development of inclusive travel experiences that are engaging and relevant for consumers of all backgrounds (see Chap. 10 in this Volume).

Acknowledgements This work is a part of the project entitled *Friendly City* financed by the Polish National Center of Research and Development (NCBiR)—grant no. "Rzeczy sa dla ludzi/0106/ 2020". This publication is partially based upon work from COST Action LEAD-ME (CA19142) supported by COST (European Cooperation in Science and Technology). We would like to thank Dr. Katarzyna Wisiecka and Ms. Katarzyna Kuta for their help in eye-tracking data collection.

References

Abras, C., Maloney-Krichmar, D., & Preece, J. (2004). User-centered design. In W. Bainbridge (Ed.), *Encyclopedia of human-computer interaction* (Vol. 37, pp. 445–456). Sage Publications.

Audio Description International. (2005). *Guidelines for audio description*. http://www.adinternatio nal.org/ADIguidelines.html

Augustyniak, P., & Tadeusiewicz, R. (2006). Assessment of electrocardiogram visual interpretation strategy based on scanpath analysis. *Physiological Measurement, 27*(7), 597. https://doi.org/10. 1088/0967-3334/27/7/004

Błaszczak, M., & Przybylski, L. (2010). *Things are for people: Disability and the idea of universal design*. Wydawnictwo Naukowe Scholar.

Boys, J. (2014). Doing disability differently an alternative handbook on architecture, dis/ability and designing for everyday life. Routledge. ISBN 9780415824958

Brams, S., Ziv, G., Levin, O., Spitz, J., Wagemans, J., Williams, A. M., & Helsen, W. F. (2019). The relationship between gaze behavior, expertise, and performance: A systematic review. *Psychological Bulletin, 145*(10), 980–1027. https://doi.org/10.1037/bul0000207

Cabeza-Caceres, C. (2010). Opera audio description at Barcelona's Liceu theatre. In J. Diaz Cintas, A. Matamala, & J. Neves (Eds.), *Media for all 2: New insights into audiovisual translation and media accessibility* (pp. 227–237). Rodopi.

Carpena, F., Cole, S., Shapiro, J., & Zia, B. (2019). The ABCs of financial education: Experimental evidence on attitudes, behavior, and cognitive biases. *Management Science, 65*(1), 346–369. https://doi.org/10.1287/mnsc.2017.2819

Castner, N., Kasneci, E., Kübler, T., Scheiter, K., Richter, J., Eder, T., Huetting, F., Keutel, C., & Kasneci, E. (2018). Scanpath comparison in medical image reading skills of dental students: distinguishing stages of expertise development. In *Proceedings of the 2018 ACM symposium on eye tracking research & applications* (pp. 1–9).

Chmiel, A., Mazur, I., Vilaro, A., di Giovanni, E., Chmiel, P., & Orero, P. (2010). How audio description influences perception. A work-in-progress report on an international eye-tracking study. In *ARSAD 2010*.

Cowan, N. (2001). The magical number 4 in short-term memory: A reconsideration of mental storage capacity. *Behavioral and Brain Sciences, 24*(1), 87–114. https://doi.org/10.1017/S01 40525X01003922

Eardley, A. F., Fryer, L., Hutchinson, R., Cock, M., Ride, P., & Neves, J. (2017). Enriched audio description: Working towards an inclusive museum experience. In S. Halder, & L. C. Assaf (Eds.), *Inclusion, disability and culture: An ethnographic perspective traversing abilities and challenges* (pp. 195–207). Springer International Publishing. https://doi.org/10.1007/978-3-319-55224-8-13

Frazier, G., & Coutinho-Johnson, I. (1995). *The effectiveness of audio description in processing access to educational AV media for blind and visually impaired students in high school*. Audio Vision.

Fryer, L. (2010). Audio description as audio drama—A practitioner's point of view. *Perspectives, 18*(3), 205–213. https://doi.org/10.1080/0907676X.2010.485681

Garrido-Jurado, S., Munoz-Salinas, R., Madrid-Cuevas, F. J., & Martın-Jimenez, M. J. (2014). Automatic generation and detection of highly reliable fiducial markers under occlusion. *Pattern Recognition, 47*(6), 2280–2292. https://doi.org/10.1016/j.patcog.2014.01.005

Gegenfurtner, A., Lehtinen, E., & Saljo, R. (2011). Expertise differences in the comprehension of visualizations: A meta-analysis of eye-tracking research in professional domains. *Educational Psychology Review, 23*(4), 523–552. https://doi.org/10.1007/s10648-011-9174-7

Goldsmith, S. (2007). *Universal design*. Routledge. ISBN 9780080520209. https://doi.org/10.4324/9780080520209

Haider, H., & Frensch, P. A. (1999). Eye movement during skill acquisition: More evidence for the information-reduction hypothesis. *Journal of Experimental Psychology: Learning, Memory, and Cognition, 25*(1), 172–190.

He, L., Wang, R., & Xu, X. (2020). Pneufetch: Supporting blind and visually impaired people to fetch nearby objects via light haptic cues. In *Extended abstracts of the 2020 CHI conference on human factors in computing systems* (pp. 1–9). Association for Computing Machinery. https://doi.org/10.1145/3334480.3383095

Independent Television Commission. (2000). Guidance on standards for audio description.

Just, M. A., & Carpenter, P. A. (1980). A theory of reading: From eye fixations to comprehension. *Psychological Review, 87*(4), 329. https://doi.org/10.1037/0033-295X.87.4.329

Kayukawa, S., Ishihara, T., Takagi, H., Morishima, S., & Asakawa, C. (2020). Blindpilot: A robotic local navigation system that leads blind people to a landmark object. In *Extended abstracts of the 2020 CHI conference on human factors in computing systems* (pp. 1–9). Association for Computing Machinery. https://doi.org/10.1145/3334480.3382925

Kiefer, P., Adams, B., & Raubal, M. (2018). Gaze-guided narratives for outdoor tourism. In *Workshop on HCI outdoors: Understanding human-computer interaction in the outdoors at CHI 2018, Montréal, Canada* (pp. 1–6). https://doi.org/10.3929/ETHZ-B-000308968

Kieras, D. E., & Just, M. A. (2018). *New methods in reading comprehension research.* Routledge. https://doi.org/10.4324/9780429505379

Krejtz, K., & Krejtz, I. (2005). Metoda analizy treści–teoria i praktyka badawcza. In K. Stemplewska-Żakowicz, & K. Krejtz (Eds.), *Wywiad psychologiczny, 1*, 129–149.

Krejtz, I., Pawłowska, A., Milczarski, P., Rutkowska-Siuda, D., Hłobaż, A., Wendorff, A., Wisiecka, K., Śniegula, A., Duchowski, A. T., & Krejtz, K. (2023a). Towards accessible gaze-led audio description for architectural heritage. In *The 25th international ACM SIGACCESS conference on computers and accessibility (ASSETS '23).* https://doi.org/10.1145/3597638.3614509

Krejtz, K., Szczeciński, P., Pawłowska, A., Rutkowska-Siuda, D., Wisiecka, K., Milczarski, P., Hłobaż, A., Duchowski, A. T., & Krejtz, I. (2023b). A unified look at cultural heritage: Comparison of aggregated scanpaths over architectural artifacts. In *Proceedings of the ACM on Human-Computer Interaction, 7*(ETRA), 1–17. https://doi.org/10.1145/3591138

Krejtz, I., Szarkowska, A., Krejtz, K., Walczak, A., & Duchowski, A. (2012a). *Audio description as an aural guide of children's visual attention: evidence from an eye-tracking study.* Association for Computing Machinery. https://doi.org/10.1145/2168556.2168572

Krejtz, K., Krejtz, I., Duchowski, A., Szarkowska, A., & Walczak, A. (2012b). *Multimodal learning with audio description: An eye tracking study children's gaze during a visual recognition task.* https://doi.org/10.1145/2338676.2338694

Krejtz, K., Duchowski, A., Krejtz, I., Szarkowska, A., & Kopacz, A. (2016). Discerning ambient/focal attention with coefficient K. *ACM Transactions on Applied Perception (TAP), 13*(3), 1–20. https://doi.org/10.1145/2896452

Krejtz, K., Wisiecka, K., Krejtz, I., Holas, P., Olszanowski, M., & Duchowski, A. T. (2018). Dynamics of emotional facial expression recognition in individuals with social anxiety. In *Proceedings of the 2018 ACM symposium on eye tracking research & applications,* 1–9. Association for Computing Machinery. https://doi.org/10.1145/3204493.3204533

Kruger, J.-L. (2010). Audio narration: Re-narrativising film. *Perspectives. Studies in Translation Theory and Practice, 18*(3), 231–249. https://doi.org/10.1080/0907676X.2010.485686

Kuribayashi, M., Kayukawa, S., Takagi, H., Asakawa, C., & Morishima, S. (2021). Linechaser: Smartphone-based navigation system for blind people standing lines. In *Proceedings of the 2021 CHI conference on human factors in computing systems.* Association for Computing Machinery. https://doi.org/10.1145/3411764.3445451

Kuribayashi, M., Kayukawa, S., Vongkulbhisal, J., Asakawa, C., Sato, D., Takagi, H., & Morishima, S. (2022, sep). Corridor-walker: Mobile indoor walking assistance for blind people to avoid obstacles and recognize intersections. In *Proceedings ACM human-computer interaction, 6*(MHCI). https://doi.org/10.1145/3546714

Lester, J. N., Cho, Y., & Lochmiller, C. R. (2020). Learning to do qualitative data analysis: A starting point. *Human Resource Development Review, 19*(1), 94–106. https://doi.org/10.1177/1534484320903890

MaaS. (2016). *Mobility as a service alliance.* https://maas-alliance.eu/. Last accessed on December 30, 2022.

Mazur, I. (2020). Audio description: Concepts, theories and research approaches. In Ł. Bogucki, & M. Deckert, (Eds.), *The Palgrave handbook of audiovisual translation and media accessibility. Palgrave studies in translating and interpreting.* Palgrave Macmillan. https://doi.org/10.1007/978-3-030-42105-2_12

Navarrete, F. J. (2005). Sistema audesc: el fin de los susurros. *Seminario sobre medios de comunicacion sin barreras.*

NaviLens, NUEVOS SISTEMAS TECNOLOGICOS S.L. (NEOSISTEC). (2017). *Navilens.* https://www.navilens.com/en/

Norman, D. (1986). *User centered system design. New perspectives on human computer interaction.* United States: L. Erlbaum Associates Inc. ISBN: 0898597811

Norman, D. A. (1988). *The psychology of everyday things.* Basic Books.

Orero, P. (2007). Sampling audio description in Europe. In J. Diaz Cintas, P. Orero, & A. Remael (Eds.), *Media for all: Subtitling for the deaf, audio description and sign language* (pp. 111–125). Rodopi.

Orero, P., & Vilaro, A. (2012). Eye tracking analysis of minor details in films for audio description. *MonTI. Monografias de Traduccion e Interpretación, 4*, 295–319. https://doi.org/10.6035/MonTI.2012.4.13

Pacinotti, A. (2017). Audiodescrizione e accessibilita del patrimonio culturale: 'Ipotesi di linee guida per la descrizione della chiesa come opera d'arte totale [Unpublished master's thesis, University of Trieste].

Pacinotti, R. (2022). Audio describing churches: In search of a template. In C. Taylor & E. Perego (Eds.), *The Routledge handbook of audio description* (pp. 246–262). Routledge.

Palomo, A. (2008). Audio description as language development and language learning for blind and visual impaired children. In R. H. Parker & K. G. Garcıa (Eds.), *Thinking translation: Perspectives from within and without* (pp. 113–134). Brown Walker Press.

Pawłowska, A., Krejtz, I., Krejtz, K., Milczarski, P., Rutkowska-Siuda, D., Hłobaż, A., Wendorff, A., Drozdowski, A., Milerowska, M., Borowski, N., & Duchowski, A. (2023). Friendly city. Making architectural heritage accessible. *International Journal of Conservation Science, 14*(3), 1019–1032. https://doi.org/10.36868/IJCS.2023.03.15

Pawłowska, A., & Sowińska-Heim, J. (2016). *Audiodeskrypcja dzieł sztuki—metody, problemy, przykłady.* Wydawnictwo Uniwersytetu Łódzkiego; Muzeum Miasta Łodzi.

Pawłowska, A., Wendorff, A., & Sowińska-Heim, J. (2019). *Osoby z niepełnosprawnością i sztuka. Udostępnianie—percepcja—integracja.* Uniwersytet Łódzki.

Peli, E., Fine, E. M., & Labianca, A. T. (1996). Evaluating information provided by audio description. *Journal of Visual Impairment and Blindness, 90*, 378–385.

Remael, A., & Vercauteren, G. (2007). Audio describing the exposition phase of films: Teaching students what to choose. *Trans Revista de Traductologia, 11*, 73–93. https://doi.org/10.24310/TRANS.2007.v0i11.3099

Saez, J. M., Lozano, M. A., Escolano, F., & Pita Lozano, J. (2020). An efficient, dense and long-range marker system for the guidance of the visually impaired. *Machine Vision and Applications, 31*(57). https://doi.org/10.1007/s00138-020-01097-y

Salway, A. (2007). A corpus-based analysis of audio description. In J. Diaz Cintas, P. Orero, & A. Remael (Eds.), *Media for all: Subtitling for the deaf, audio description and sign language* (pp. 154–174). Rodopi.

Schmeidler, E., & Kirchner, C. (2001). Adding audio description: Does it make a difference? *Journal of Visual Impairment and Blindness, 95*(4), 198–212. https://doi.org/10.1177/0145482X0109500402

Sweller, J. (2010a). Cognitive load theory: Recent theoretical advances. In J. L. Plass, R. Moreno, & R. Brunken (Eds.), *Cognitive load theory* (pp. 29–47). Cambridge University Press.

Sweller, J. (2010b). Element interactivity and intrinsic, extraneous, and germane cognitive load. *Educational Psychology Review, 22*(2), 123–138. https://doi.org/10.1007/s10648-010-9128-5

Szarkowska, A., Jankowska, A., Krejtz, K., & Kowalski, J. (2016). Open Art: Designing accessible content in a multimedia guide app for visitors with and without sensory impairments. In Matamala, A., & Orero, P. (Eds.) *Researching audio description* (pp. 301–320). Palgrave Macmillan, London.

Szarkowska, A., Krejtz, I., Krejtz, K., & Duchowski, A. (2013). Harnessing the potential of eye-tracking for media accessibility. In S. Grucza, M. Płużycka, & J. Alnajjar (Eds.), *Translation studies and eye-tracking analysis* (Vol. 6, pp. 153–183). Peter Lang.

Tech, O. (2018). *aBeacon*. https://abeacon.okeenea.com/. Last accessed on December 30, 2022.

Ustundag, A., & Cevikcan, E. (2018). *Industry 4.0: Managing the digital transformation*. Cham: Springer. https://doi.org/10.1007/978-3-319-57870-5

Vandaele, J. (2012). What meets the eye Cognitive narratology for audiodescription. *Perspectives, 20*(1), 87–102. https://doi.org/10.1080/0907676X.2011.632683

Velichkovsky, B. M., Joos, M., Helmert, J. R., & Pannasch, S. (2005, July). Two visual systems and their eye movements: Evidence from static and dynamic scene perception. In *Cogsci 2005: Proceedings of the XXVII conference of the cognitive science society* (pp. 2283–2288). Stresa, Italy.

Vitak, S. A., Ingram, J. E., Duchowski, A. T., Ellis, S., & Gramopadhye, A. K. (2012). Gaze-augmented think-aloud as an aid to learning. In *Proceedings of the sigchi conference on human factors in computing systems* (p. 2991–3000). Association for Computing Machinery. https://doi.org/10.1145/2207676.2208710

VocalEyes (2007). *Sense of place case study: VocalEyes audio-described architecture tours*. https://vocaleyes.co.uk/services/museumsgalleries-and-heritage/architecture/case-study-vocaleyes-audio-describedarchitecture-tours/

Wayfindr. (2018). Itu-t f.921 (v2) (08/2018)—audio-based indoor and outdoor network navigation system for persons with vision impairment. *International Telecommunications Union*. https://www.itu.int/ITU-T/recommendations/rec.aspx?rec=13662lang=enteam. Last accessed December 30, 2022.

Achieving Accessibility on a Budget: Aksaray University's Strategy for Supporting Students with Disabilities

Önder Islek and Hatice Uyanik

Abstract Much emphasis has been put on the inclusivity of educational opportunities in international agreements, conventions, and declarations, with the valuable work that continues to be done globally. However, one area needs more attention for disability-inclusive international development, that is, higher education, which is still limited and not fully inclusive or accessible for individuals with disabilities globally (Covas & de Luna, 2019). This chapter presents a case study of the Aksaray University in the Republic of Türkiye. This chapter aims to deconstruct the Turkish social system with emphasis on education and employment first and show an example of how the current system is disrupted to ensure the proper application of international agendas that Türkiye is officially and legally a part of. For this chapter an eclectic approach is used combining a wicked problem frame with disability studies in education from a reconceptualist perspective. This chapter is arranged into four sections, including (a) background on education and employment in the Turkish legal and social system to understand the foundation of current systems that is a gateway or product of higher education for individuals with disabilities; (b) recent understanding of the inclusive, accessible, and nondiscriminatory higher education and where the Turkish higher education system stands in it for individuals with disabilities; (c) a case example of Aksaray University for how to disrupt the system by provision of the disability support services within the university; and (d) conclusion with future implications for policy, research, and practice.

Keywords Inclusion · Accessibility · University · Disability support services · Turkish higher education

Both Sustainable Development Goals for 2030 Agenda (SDG) 4 and Article 24 of the Convention on the Rights of Persons with Disabilities (CRPD) underline meaningful

Ö. Islek (✉)
The Department of Special Education, Aksaray University, Aksaray, Turkey
e-mail: onderislek@aksaray.edu.tr

H. Uyanik
The Department of Special Education, Sinop University, Sinop, Turkey

A. Marcus-Quinn et al. (eds.), *Transforming Media Accessibility in Europe*,
https://doi.org/10.1007/978-3-031-60049-4_5

and sustainable inclusive educational opportunities in various contexts. This focus extends to higher education which serves as a crucial gateway for people with disabilities, offering pathways to further education and employment (de Beco, 2019, p. 91). Scholars emphasize the term "reasonable accommodation" to eliminate the risk of inclusive education stopping after the formal or traditional schooling process and ensure the continuation of inclusivity throughout postsecondary educational settings (de Beco, 2019). The Universal Declaration of Human Rights (UDHR) also highlights the importance of equal accessibility to higher education for all (Kayess, 2019, p. 123). Despite ongoing global efforts, higher education still requires more focus on disability-inclusive international development, as it remains limited and not fully accessible for individuals with disabilities worldwide (Covas & de Luna, 2019).

To address and understand the multifaceted nature of this challenge, the Republic of Türkiye (hereafter Türkiye) was chosen as the case study. Türkiye is a state party to these international agendas and operates under a centralized top-down system, meaning that all stakeholders must adhere to policies and regulations regardless of their position, geographic location, or status within the community. Thus, this chapter aims to deconstruct the Turkish social system with emphasis on education and employment first and show an example of how the current system is disrupted to ensure the proper application of international agendas that Türkiye is officially and legally a part of. This chapter is arranged into four sections, including (a) background on education and employment in the Turkish legal and social system to understand the foundation of current systems that is a gateway or product of higher education for individuals with disabilities; (b) recent perspectives on inclusive, accessible, and nondiscriminatory higher education, and an analysis of the current state of the Turkish higher education system in relation to individuals with disabilities; (c) a case study of Aksaray University, illustrating how the provision of disability support services can disrupt and improve the system.

To address the multifaceted nature of the aforementioned challenge, the authors adopt an eclectic approach. First they deconstruct the inclusive postsecondary education within the framework of a wicked problem, which provides a better understanding of *the critical issues* (for a detailed explanation of the wicked problem, please see Rittel & Weber, 1973; Zhao et al., 2019). Next, the authors employ disability studies in education as a conceptual approach to explore *why* and *how* these issues arise (Bacon & Baglieri, 2020). It is important to note that both authors have firsthand multicultural disability experiences, positioning them closer to a reconceptualist understanding of disability (Connor & Olander, n.d.).

1   Introduction

According to the latest statistics from the Turkish Statistical Institute (Turk Stat), in 2023, the country's population has surpassed 85 million, solidifying its status as one of the most populous nations in the region. Numbers show that the proportion of the working age group (15–64) was 67.7% in 2020, while the proportion of the children age group (0–14) was 22.8%, and the proportion of the older population (over 65) was 9.5%. On the other hand, the average age of the overall Turkish population is 33.5 years old. This data suggests that Türkiye has a relatively young population, and an important portion of the Turkish population is still of school age.

According to Turk Stat's most recent data, the population of people with disabilities in Türkiye constitutes a sizable portion of the overall demographic landscape. Even though the number of people with a disability is uncertain due to a lack of a recent and consistent data collection, there are few studies regarding the population with a disability in Türkiye. In a statistical study carried out by the Prime Ministry Administration for People with Disabilities in 2002, it was found that the percentage of people with disabilities in Türkiye, including those with chronic diseases, is 12.29% (of the total population), totaling 8,431,937 individuals. However, a different perspective emerged from the 2011 Population and Housing Survey in Turkey, indicating that the percentage of the population with at least one disability, such as in seeing, hearing, speaking, walking, climbing stairs, holding or lifting something, learning, doing simple calculations, remembering, and concentrating compared to peers (aged three or older) is 6.9%, equivalent to 4,876,000 people. The breakdown shows that the disability rate is 5.9% among men and 7.9% among women. It is also worth noting that the 2011 survey did not consider persons with multiple impairments as a separate category (Arun, 2014; Turkish Statistical Institute, 2015).

The term "disability" encompasses a range of conditions, including physical, sensory, intellectual, and developmental disabilities. Turk Stat categorizes individuals based on the type and severity of their disabilities; however, it is difficult to access accurate data regarding the exact number of people with a disability and types of disability in Türkiye. Since the World Health Organization (WHO) anticipates the disability rate to be around 16% of the population, it can be speculated that there are around 14 million people with a disability in Türkiye. Understanding the educational and employment status of individuals with disabilities is essential for gauging societal inclusivity. Therefore, a general overview of the education and employment of individuals with a disability in Türkiye is provided below.

2 Background

2.1 Education System for Students with Disabilities as a Gateway to Higher Education

Legal context: Following the international agenda, the right to education for everyone was first recognized as a basic human right in the UDHR in 1948 (Raja & Giannoumis, 2019; Yazicioglu, 2020). This was further emphasized through inclusion practices in the CRPD and SDGs, which were subsequently incorporated into the National Constitution of Türkiye. Article 10 guarantees equal rights and freedom for all citizens, strongly opposing discrimination based on socially constructed or inherent characteristics such as language, race, color, gender, political thought, philosophical belief, religion, sect, and disability. Article 42 protects the educational and training rights of all citizens. The constitution also includes measures to prevent exclusionary practices and privileges granted to unintended persons or groups not within vulnerable populations. State and administrative organs work together to uphold the principle of equality as the rule of law.

Although several laws and regulations have emphasized the needs of people with disabilities since the early years of the establishment of the republic, a turning point in the legal system was the takeover of the management of special education services by the Ministry of National Education in 1950 from the Ministry of Health and Social Aid (Ozturk, 2019). Furthermore, the foundations of the current special education system were established with the legislation titled "Children with Special Education Needs Law No. 2916" in 1983. While this law was protecting the education rights of students with disabilities between 4 and 18 years old, the "Statutory Decree on Special Education Services No. 573" in 1997 furthered the educational rights for mainstream and vocational education for students with disabilities and detailed the process with the addition of concepts including inclusion, early intervention, individualized education programs, and parent involvement in educational processes.

The second major turning point in Turkish laws and regulations was the enactment of the "Regulation on Special Education Services" in 2000, with revisions in 2004 and a major reorganization in 2006 (Cavkaytar et al., 2017; Ozturk, 2019). The current version with detailed definitions and implementation processes was established in 2012. Concurrently, the operations and activities of private rehabilitation centers were regulated by the "Turkish Disability Act No. 5378" in 2005 and the "Private Educational Institutions Act No. 5580" in 2007 (Cavkaytar et al., 2017; Ozturk, 2019). These legislative revisions underscore the importance of ensuring equal opportunities in lifelong education for individuals with disabilities while prohibiting direct and indirect discrimination. They protect fundamental rights and freedoms, strengthen respect for inherent dignity and implement preventive measures against disability-based discrimination. This action might be recognized as the first step toward changing the understanding of disability as an intersectional and critical social construct and not merely a health issue that should be fixed. These legislations and regulations advocate for the involvement of multiple state parties within the centralized national system and stakeholders to ensure the best possible approach is followed.

Civic applications and social practices context: In the last seventeen years that statistics are available for formal schooling, there has been a major improvement regarding special education and students with disabilities in Türkiye. Table 1 gives the official numbers for students, schools, and teachers for both special and mainstream education populations within the formal schooling system for the 2022/3 and 2006/7 academic years (Ministry of National Education, n.d.). The analysis of Table 1 data shows that although students receiving special education in the formal schooling system rapidly increased in seventeen years with a 1455.54% rate and their representation within the mainstream student population increased to 2.55%, the growth in the number of teachers is still insufficient to meet the rapid increase in students with disabilities receiving special education. This suggests that the education system may be unable to adequately respond to the needs of this population in terms of recognition, diagnosis, accommodation, and support services while also ensuring the least restrictive environment and inclusive practices.

Based on the data from the Turkey Disability Survey (Turkish Statistical Institute, 2002); 66.09% of individuals with intellectual disabilities, 53.01% of individuals with speech disorders, 36.9% of individuals with deafness or hard of hearing, 34.9% of individuals with blindness or vision impairment, and 29.5% of people with physical disabilities are reported as illiterate. Additionally, according to the Turkish Statistical Institute (2022a, 2022b), the professions of special education teaching, teaching for individuals with intellectual disabilities, teaching for individuals with deafness or hard of hearing, and teaching for individuals with blindness or vision impairment are four professions among the top ten professions that received high employment in 2021. However, combined with the information in Table 1, this increase is still far from meeting the rapid increase of students with disabilities receiving special education in formal schooling. The latest official statistics tailored to individuals with disabilities that are available via the Turkish Statistical Institute are the Turkish Disability Survey (2002), the Problems and Expectations of People with Disabilities Survey (2010), and the Population and Household Survey (2011). These surveys are all older than a decade, which suggests the requirement of recent data that is either collected with similar methods or combined with data-merging or data-fusing methods that would provide more detailed information on the population with disabilities in Türkiye.

The mismatch between the steep increase in students with disabilities within the education system and the educational support, services, and accommodations provided is highlighted by several scholars (Girli & Atasoy, 2012; Göl, 2014; Gül & Vuran, 2015; Güleryüz, 2014; Sazak-Pinar & Güner-Yildiz, 2013). Research suggests the dissatisfaction of students with disabilities with the provided materials, supports, and services, especially with STEM classes such as math (Bayram et al., 2015) and physics (Ünlü et al., 2010), and overall unhappiness with the overall educational experiences (Işlek, 2017). Furthermore, various researchers have documented far more negative experiences of students with disabilities in mainstream schools, including incidents of physical abuse (Girli & Atasoy, 2012; Güleryüz, 2014; Yekta, 2010).

Multiple studies also reflected the knowledge of and perspectives toward the inclusion construct of educators in mainstream classrooms that highlight multiple shortcomings, including limited knowledge on inclusion in general (Batmaz & Çermik, 2019; Deniz & Çoban, 2019; Söğüt & Deniz, 2018) and specific knowledge such as Individualized Education Plan (IEP) preparation (Karakiş, 2023; Söğüt & Deniz, 2018), lack of communication with students with disabilities (Öztürk et al., 2024), lack of materials and types of equipment (Batmaz & Çermik, 2019; Deniz & Çoban, 2019), family-related obstacles (Batmaz & Çermik, 2019), limited time (Batmaz & Çermik, 2019; Karakiş, 2023), physical and behavioral characteristics of students with disabilities (Öztürk et al., 2024); classroom size and inability for physical arrangements (Batmaz & Çermik, 2019; Karakiş, 2023; Öztürk et al., 2024; Üçler

Table 1 Distribution of special and mainstream education population

	Students			Schools			Teachers		
	2006/7	2022/3	%*	2006/7	2022/3	%*	2006/7	2022/3	%*
Special education	32,027	507,804	1455.54	489	1859	280.16	6296	19,536	210.29
Mainstream education	19,383,060	19,904,679	2.69	56,388	75,019	33.04	679,880	1,154,383	69.79
Special/Mainstream %**	0.16	2.55	N/A	0.86	2.47	N/A	0.92	1.69	N/A

Note N/A refers to not available for calculation
*Percentage increase from 2006–7 to 2022–3 of the number of the same group of education population (special/mainstream education)
** Percentage of the number of special education group within the mainstream population for the given year

et al., 2021), curriculum intensity and absence of knowledge on organization of teaching processes (Batmaz & Çermik, 2019; Üçler et al., 2021), workload (Batmaz & Çermik, 2019; Öztürk et al., 2024), absence of guidance counselors (Batmaz & Çermik, 2019), and lack of support education classrooms (Batmaz & Çermik, 2019), lack of training on general inclusive practices, measurement and evaluation, and instructional adaptations (Ceyhan & Alici, 2023; Girgin, 2021; Öztürk et al., 2024; Karakiş, 2023; Üçler et al., 2021).

Research also suggests that although some teachers preserve positive attitudes towards inclusion (Çankaya, 2010; Çankaya, & Korkmaz, 2012; Kaya, 2016), more teachers have negative attitudes towards inclusion (Demir & Acar, 2011; Engin et al., 2014; Gündüz, 2015; Ilk, 2014; Sadioğlu et al., 2012, 2013; Turk, 2011; Yatgin et al., 2015). Even some teachers expressed unwillingness to teach students with disabilities (Sanir, 2009) and consider them a burden due to their disability (Soyyiğit, 2013) and the perpetrators of the academic failure of their peers without disabilities (Gündüz, 2015; Ilk, 2014; Sadioğlu et al., 2013). Teachers feel that their desires are not taken into consideration (Saraç & Colak, 2012), and students with disabilities should be educated in segregated schools (Deniz & Çoban, 2019). Finally, Söğüt and Deniz (2018) highlighted that all concerns are valid in both the rural and urban schools, albeit the situation is much more concerning in the schools in the rural part of Türkiye.

Other research focused on parents of school-age children with disabilities to understand inclusion in the Turkish education system. Participant parents in various studies underlined the absence of special education services (Yazcayir & Gürgür, 2021). Their psychological experiences often included anxiety, avoidance, guilt, burnout, self-neglect, and child-centered life (Tümlü & Akdoğan, 2022), likely exacerbated by concerns regarding the education of their children with disabilities (Melekoğlu, 2014). Although some research suggests parents are content with inclusive practices but expect better educational provisions such as social development (Yigen, 2008), parents cited that better communication and reciprocal information-sharing with teachers with better governmental support on family inclusion (Içyüz, 2016). Consequently, the current atmosphere and context on educational inclusion suggest snowballing unmet needs of various stakeholders and a lack of support, services, and accommodations that are accessible and sustainable within the system. Therefore, a comprehensive revision of the system, both horizontally and vertically, is required to better fulfill the needs of stakeholders to approach and adopt a more inclusive approach for everyone.

2.2   Employment System for Students with Disabilities as a Product of Higher Education

Legal context: According to the December 2021 data of the Turkish Statistical Institute (2022a, 2022b), the general labor force participation rate in Türkiye is 71.7% for men, 34.5% for women, and 52.9% in total. Conversely, accessing recent and

accurate data regarding people with a disability in Türkiye is challenging. Nevertheless, a comprehensive study based on administrative records was conducted nevertheless with the
European Union member states, that is the Population and Housing Survey in 2011.
According to the data, the labor force participation rate of the population with at
least one disability is 35.4% for men and 12.5% for women; in total, it is 22.1% in
Türkiye (Turkish Statistical Institute, 2011). The remarkable difference can be seen
when this population is compared to the general population participating in the labor
force, which is 71.7% for men and 34.5% for women; in total, it is 52.9% in Türkiye
(Turkish Statistical Institute, 2011). Another striking point from the statistics is the
gender inequality toward women for both citizens with and without disabilities, with
a wider gap for women with disabilities.

Since Türkiye adopted the European tradition of advancing the inclusion of individuals with disabilities in the workforce, mandatory employment quotas in labor
markets were introduced (Altan, 1999). According to this mandate, a minimum of
3% of the workforce should comprise individuals with disabilities in private-sector
businesses with over 50 employees, whereas the minimum employment requirement
is set at 4% for contract workers in the public sector (2003, Article 30). Similarly,
public institutions are mandated to ensure that at least 3% of their civil servants are
individuals with disabilities (Yılmaz, 2020). Implementation of this policy enhanced
the opportunities for individuals with disabilities to join the workforce. Within a
decade, the number of employed people with a disability surpassed 19,000 in 1982.
However, the results still were not at the desired level. Therefore, starting from 2005,
new measurements were introduced. One of the landmarks is introducing the 5738
Law on Disabled People in 2005. Article 14 of the law explicitly prohibits all forms
of discrimination in the labor market based on disability. Furthermore, the law (2005,
Article 122) stipulates imprisonment (ranging from one to three years) for those who
obstruct the hiring of individuals due to *hateful treatment of differences,* including
disability.

The Turkish Disability Act (2005, Article 14) places the onus on the state to
offer vocational training, rehabilitation services, and support for individuals with
disabilities in establishing their own businesses. Specifically, the Turkish Employment Agency (Türkiye Iş Kurumu [IŞKUR]) is tasked with identifying suitable candidates for job openings and providing job training. IŞKUR is also authorized to impose
fines if a company fails to adhere to the minimum employment requirement. These
fines contribute to a special public fund, which is allocated to nonprofit organizations
(NGOs). The NGOs use these funds to provide project grants aimed at enhancing the
employability of individuals with disabilities (Article 30). Furthermore, the same law
(Article 14) assigns the responsibility for providing reasonable accommodations in
workplaces to relevant public institutions and employers. In addition, the purchase of
assistive technologies, including software, is exempt from both value-added (Article
3) and customs taxes (Article 12).

On the other hand, in the 2000s, there was a push for a comprehensive analysis
of jobs and occupations, aiming to designate suitable job types for specific disabilities. However, this project was misguided as it relied on the medical model of
disability, assuming that individuals with disabilities could only perform certain jobs

based on their physical, mental, and/or intellectual differences. This discriminatory stance was codified in the 2005 Turkish Disability Act. In 2014, a new article was introduced, granting individuals with disabilities the freedom to choose their own occupation without restrictions, replacing the article on job and occupation analysis. Finally, the Turkish Disability Act (2005, Article 14) officially recognized sheltered workshops. Defined as specially designated state-supported workplaces that provide occupational rehabilitation and employment for individuals with disabilities, these workshops began operation primarily after the 2013 bylaw and predominantly cater to individuals with cognitive disabilities, including intellectual disabilities and mental health disorders.

Despite the improvement in legislation over time, the unemployment rate of individuals with disabilities remains higher than the general population (Metin et al., 2011). Notably, more than one-third of individuals with a disability were illiterate, whereas the overall illiteracy rate was around 10%. These statistics show that citizens with disabilities face significant disparity and challenges to joining the workforce. This situation suggests a revision within the system to eliminate systemic oppression and overall discrimination, while the first step might be to reconceptualize the laws and regulations from a more reconstructive approach than the understanding of the medical model of disability. This root change might have a positive effect on the implementation of the legal procedures in societal systems by reducing the bias toward individuals with disabilities to access, join, and maintain their work and employment.

Civic applications and social practices context: A survey conducted in 2011 by the Ministry of Family and Social Policies (Metin et al., 2011) on private-sector employees and managers to gauge employers' perspectives on working with individuals with disabilities revealed that small-scale firms were less compliant with the regulations and the overall rate of employment was below the legally mandated quota, although many of the enterprises did hire individuals with disabilities. Additionally, the 2011 survey highlighted a correlation between educational attainment and the sectoral distribution of employment (Metin et al., 2011). Almost half of workers with disabilities completed primary school, followed by 45% with a secondary school diploma, and some 7% with a university diploma. Due to the overall low educational attainment among individuals with disabilities, they were concentrated in junior/ entrance occupations (35.5%) and clerical support work (31.3%). Only 7.9% of individuals with disabilities were employed in skilled professional work (Metin et al., 2011). The survey also revealed that most employers (71%) were aware of their legal obligation regarding the minimum employment requirement (Metin et al., 2011). Larger enterprises demonstrated a higher awareness of legislation on the employment of individuals with disabilities and employers' legal obligations. Most employers (71%) cited the legal obligation as their main reason for employing individuals with disabilities, while 22% mentioned a sense of social responsibility. This suggests that removing the quota may significantly limit the employment of individuals with disabilities. Only 7% of employers reported employing individuals with disabilities because they were suited for a particular job. Half of the employers who did not employ individuals with disabilities stated they were unable to find a qualified person with a disability suitable for the job and/or sector.

The survey results indicated that employer attitudes toward hiring varied according to the type of disability. The majority of employers expressed a preference for employing people with orthopedic disabilities (40.9%). The least preferred groups were people with cognitive disabilities, including intellectual disabilities (4%) and those with mental health disorders (3.8%) (Metin et al., 2011). Given the historical context of extra-legal exclusion, the educational attainment level of individuals with disabilities in Türkiye remains notably lower than that of the general population. All interviewees highlighted that the low educational attainment of individuals with disabilities poses a significant obstacle to their employment. Those specializing in job-matching services for individuals with disabilities noted that university graduates tend to secure jobs more easily than primary and secondary school graduates, a pattern that mirrors the general population (Metin et al., 2011). However, interviewees also pointed out that educational qualifications do not shield individuals with disabilities from discrimination. When asked about the impact of discriminatory attitudes from employers and human resources personnel toward disabled university graduates, most respondents affirmed that such discrimination exists by offering only low-skilled jobs. In addition, it is stated that job training designed to increase skills that are truly marketable would increase the employability of adults with disabilities. Numerous other interviewees shared a high level of awareness regarding the exclusionary impact of the ableist social environment, extending to cities, transportation, housing, and workplaces. One form of discrimination highlighted in the interviews was the pseudo-employment of individuals with disabilities, where employers, in informal agreements, register individuals with disabilities as employees solely for social security coverage without actual employment. These discriminatory strategies, aiming to avoid fines for non-compliance, were criticized by interviewees, who pointed out that such agreements often serve the purposes of both parties, with some individuals with disabilities seeking them out to benefit from full social security coverage without actually working (Metin et al., 2011).

As highlighted previously, one of the major deficiencies in the implementation of the employment quota in the Turkish context lies within its definition of the target group of employers—specifically, private enterprises hiring more than 50 employees. It is worth noting that industrial enterprises employing fewer than 50 workers constitute approximately 98% of all industrial enterprises in the Turkish economy (Bayülken, 2017) and contribute to 45% of industrial employment. Consequently, the target group's definition of the employment quota restricts its broader applicability in an economy dominated by small and medium-sized enterprises. On the other hand, despite Turkey having a robust legal framework safeguarding individuals with disabilities from employment discrimination, there are still discriminatory laws that, in practice, hinder their entry into specific professions or positions. For instance, the Judges and Prosecutors Law still portrays disability as a disqualifying condition for becoming a judge or prosecutor (Ataman et al., 2023).

In summary, according to the Turkey Disability Survey 2002, 78.29% of individuals with disabilities over 15 years old are not in the labor force. The employment rate is 25.61% in urban areas and 17.76% in rural areas. Only 6.71% of women having disabilities are working. The employment rate of persons with disabilities over age 12 is 22.19% (Metin et al., 2011), and 52.45% of individuals with disabilities are not included in any social security system (Firat, 2010). In addition, the research revealed that hidden disabilities, including mental health or emotional disorders, and cognitive disabilities, including intellectual and developmental disabilities, are the most disadvantaged and non-preferred group within the disability community within the workforce (Metin et al., 2011). This study also shows that individuals with chronic diseases or physical or orthopedic disabilities are generally favored with higher expectations over individuals with mental or multiple disabilities and individuals with blindness and visual impairment on employment accounts (Metin et al., 2011), which clearly shows the discrepancy between disability types and lower expectations from individuals with cognitive disabilities or mental health disorders.

Since the abovementioned figures and research highlight the multiple aspects of both legislation and implementation negativities for individuals with disabilities to access, join, and maintain their work or employment, one possible way to disrupt these negative aspects might be allocating and using inclusive and higher education as a medium to produce better opportunities for individuals with disabilities within the workforce. Thus, the next section focuses on how an inclusive and accessible higher education system might be approached.

3   The Inclusive, Accessible, and Nondiscriminatory Higher Education

With the wicked problem frame and Disability Studies in Education approach in mind, the authors approached disability as a culturally and socially constructed construct that is not equivalent to the impairment, and neither belongs to a simple dichotomy of disability-non-disability perspective (Goodley, 2017). This understanding stems from first, adopting a reconstructivist approach, that is the social model of disability, and second, placing social justice and equity close to the center when tackling multiple issues. The previous sections of this chapter discussed the widespread challenges of inclusion and accessibility from multiple perspectives. This examination aimed to understand why these challenges persist. The main issue now is how to create an inclusive and accessible higher education structure for all stakeholders, including those with and without disabilities. This structure should enable institutional transformation to address and disrupt inequities. Such changes would impact both pre-existing and future processes, helping to break down systemic oppression within society.

Students with disabilities often face lower enrollment and higher dropout rates when compared to their peers without disabilities in higher education. Multiple stakeholders attribute this to unclear decision-making processes within higher education institutions. These unclear processes lead to negative experiences for all stakeholders, including a lack of general knowledge and collaboration needed to create more inclusive environments. As a result there is more ignorance and fewer proactive efforts toward inclusion (Ristad et al., 2024). However, a report on diversity, equity, and inclusion in European higher education institutions (Claeys-Kulik et al., 2019) shows that seeing disability equality as an explicit value, an institutional social responsibility, or a legal obligation that regulates the systems is much higher than seeing it as a recruitment strategy or quota for students or staff. Additionally, the understanding of diversity includes a broad range of groups represented on-campus. However, the concept of intersectionality (e.g., disability and gender and/or migration background) is mostly considered as the next step for the future (Claeys-Kulik et al., 2019). Another research study addresses accessibility challenges and criticizes the engagement of all stakeholders in the development of accessible information and communication technology (ICT). Accessibility should be understood not as a simple concept but as a complex one involving current and potentially new power imbalances when all stakeholders participate. Therefore, participatory action research or case studies specific to the university space and atmosphere might be a better approach to understand and deconstruct this complex system while accounting for its unique culture, politics, and social structure (Seale et al., 2020).

Another significant accessibility issue involves the accessibility of both print, hard-copy, and digital material for students with disabilities in higher education. While institutions are required to provide options and accommodations for students for enhanced learning processes, they are still requiring students to disclose their disability to access these options (Hurley, 2020; Moriña Díez, 2022). Yet only 30% of students self-disclose their disabilities (Hurley, 2020). Thus, it is imperative to provide room for learning opportunities, safe spaces, and a welcoming culture that respects diversity and dignity for students and staff with disabilities. This approach can transform the organizational structure and culture benefitting all stakeholders. It is especially important during periods of rapid change, such as the onset of COVID-19, as it helps reduce resistance and improve comprehension and adaptability to changes, such as the introduction of new software (Kishira & Sasaki, 2023).

One way to advocate for change and reorganization of the higher education system to expand the learning opportunities and accessible experiences for inclusive and accessible higher education is to provide disability support services for students with disabilities (Bacon & Baglieri, 2021; Mendoza-González et al., 2022). Mendoza-González and colleagues (2022) provided eight guidelines for establishing and maintaining an office providing accessibility supports and services, including; (a) curricular adjustments, (b) reasonable adjustments for physical, social, and attitudinal environment, (c) inclusive student mobility, (d) inclusive employability fostering, (e) awareness of disability and accessibility, (f) integration of office of accessibility services within the organizational structure, (g) internal structure, and (h) quality assessment. Griesmeyer-Krentz et al. (2022) further analyzed how disability support services administrators can use their positions as change agents in the higher education institution to create an institutional culture of accessibility with the following points, including (a) overcoming institutional challenges via developing a partnership with stakeholder-allies, (b) advancing proactive accessibility in addition to reactivating accommodation including shifting the narrative from compliance-focused to a more human-centered approach, (c) shifting understanding on learning space from physical to multifaceted learning, including digital spaces. Elaborating on these research findings, it might be a better approach to bridge online and on-campus learning opportunities for students with disabilities, which might provide a more flexible learning experience for them to enhance their engagement; indeed, this reflects on a continuum of support and services that require disability support services staff to be more proactive in meeting these needs (Seale et al., 2015; Young, 2023). Researchers suggest several strategies for improving the overall learning experience for students with disabilities in higher education. First, they emphasize the need to recognize the lack of an inclusive university concept. This recognition is crucial for expanding inclusive education opportunities in higher education. The researchers propose an ecological-integrated inclusive model, characterized as multilevel, multidimensional, multifocal, and diachronic (Damiani et al., 2024). This model operates within a tripartite framework, such as (a) micro level, including special education, digital and assistive technology, (b) meso level, including research- and evidence-based education; and (c) macro level, including universal inclusive education (i.e., Universal Design) (Damiani et al., 2024). Fovet (2021) highlights the importance of the ecological model to balance stakeholder engagement when using the universal design principles in higher education to design an approach that is uniquely owned by the specific higher education institution and reduce the resistance that might be more inclined to be political or organizational than situated within the value system of stakeholders.

3.1 *Where Does the Turkish Higher Education System Stand in Inclusive, Accessible, and Nondiscriminatory Higher Education for Individuals with Disabilities?*

The Turkish Higher Education Law 2547, enacted in 1981 and revised multiple times since then, is the main legislation governing higher education in Türkiye. Nevertheless, this law does not contain any information regarding students with disabilities. The main legislation about the rights of students with disabilities in higher education is the "Higher Education Institutions Disabled Persons Consultation and Coordination Regulation", which is prepared in accordance with Law No. 5378 of the Disability Act and published in 2010. In accordance with the said regulation, the responsibility of establishing disability support services unit is given to higher education institutions. According to regulations for forming disability support services, higher education institutions must assign a coordinator, who is either a lecturer or an assistant specialized in disability or a related field. This coordinator operates under the chairmanship and responsibility of a vice-rector. Disability support services directly affiliated with the rectorate are established to identify the administrative, physical, housing needs, and social and academic needs of disabled students, to determine what needs to be done to meet these needs, to plan, implement, and develop the works to be carried out and to evaluate the results of the works carried out. The working procedures and principles of the units are determined by higher education institutions. In addition, all costs of providing services to students with a disability must be paid from the higher educational institutions' own budgets.

The term *disability* defined in Article 1-c) (2014) students with disabilities are defined as those who have difficulties in adapting to social life and meeting their daily needs due to losing their physical, mental, spiritual, emotional, and social abilities to various degrees due to any reason, congenital or later, and who have difficulties in protecting themselves. It refers to higher education students who need care, rehabilitation, counseling, and support services. The Council for Higher Education draws very flexible guidelines regarding disability support services even though they have so many responsibilities. Since the Council for Higher Education does not mandate specific professionals who should be hired for disability support services (except an academic faculty and vice-rector) nor create a budget to hire the necessary staff, often the universities establish disability support services but cannot offer any effective services to meet needs of students with disabilities. Therefore, there is a growing body of research that captures the dissatisfaction of the university students with disabilities in Türkiye (Aydın, 2012; Bicer & Iscan, 2020; Erdogan, 2019; Kurt, 2017; Sevinç & Çay, 2017).

In Türkiye, all candidates who want to study at a university must take a centralized exam, which takes place once every year. Based on their exam scores, individuals are accepted into university programs. Table 2 details, the number of candidates with disability who applied to take the university exam.

Data in Tables 2 and 3 show the significant discrepancy between the applicants and disability types, meaning that some individuals with disabilities experience more hardship than others. In 2016, the number of students with disabilities accepted into university programs was as follows: 1,278 in 4-year undergraduate programs and 1,545 in 2-year associate degree programs, totaling 2,823 students with disabilities. The data indicates that the majority of students with disabilities could not apply to the university entrance exam, and more than half of those who did apply were not admitted to a university program. In the 2022/23 academic year, there were 6,950,142 students enrolled in 208 higher education institutions. Among them, 54,206 were students with disabilities (Council for Higher Education, n.d.). Most of these students were in 2-year associate degree programs, with only 236 pursuing master's degrees and 48 enrolled in doctoral programs. Additionally, 89% of students with disabilities participated in distance education programs rather than face-to-face education (Council for Higher Education, n.d.). This high percentage of students with disabilities in distance education suggests that due to poor accessibility, many students with disabilities prefer distance learning over attending on-campus programs.

In addition, a general gender divide can be seen among university students with disabilities. 35,088 of this population are men and 19,118 are women (Council for Higher Education, n.d.). Considering that disabled women experience multifaceted discrimination compared to men, both due to their disability and being women,

Table 2 Number of applicants taken the university entrance exam

Years	2012	2013	2014	2015	2016	2017
Students	3937	4852	3842	4964	6015	6859

Source Higher Education Council; https://engelsiz.yok.gov.tr/Documents/Toplantilar/Macid_Mel ekoglu.pdf

Table 3 Percentage of applicants taken the university entrance exam based on the type of disability

Type	2012	2013	2014	2015	2016	2017
VI (%)	30.2	28.8	39.2	29.5	27.0	24.8
HI (%)	16.6	18.3	21.1	21.6	18.9	18.1
PD (%)	34.3	32.0	39.7	29.3	26.5	26.1
OD (%)	16.8	19.3	N/A	19.6	23.1	26.4
TD (%)	2.0	1.7	N/A	N/A	4.6	4.6

Note VI: Applicants with blindness or visual impairment; HI: Applicants with deafness or hearing impairment; PD: Applicants with physical disabilities; OD: Applicants with other disabilities; TD: Applicants with temporary disabilities; N/A: Not available
Source Higher Education Council; https://engelsiz.yok.gov.tr/Documents/Toplantilar/Macid_Mel ekoglu.pdf

this rate is not surprising. On the other hand, students with physical disabilities and students with blindness and visual impairment have relatively higher access to higher education than other disability groups (Council for Higher Education, n.d.). With the decisions taken in recent years, the Council for Higher Education aims to increase student diversity among disability populations, such as those with autism or deafness and hearing impairment. The Council for Higher Education acknowledges that, although efforts to increase accessibility in higher education have gained momentum, they have not yet reached the desired level. Therefore, few individuals with disabilities can get into a university program (Table 4). Moreover, it is important to have information regarding the services offered to the few students with a disability who could get into a university program.

The current higher education context has multiple challenges to tackle prior to enhancing the learning experience in an inclusive and accessible nondiscriminatory environment. These challenges include significant deficiencies and inconsistencies in instructional adaptations and assistive technology, and access to lecture notes (Bavli et al., 2020; Gündoğar, 2020), dissatisfaction with disability support services due to

Table 4 Percentage of university placement of students with disabilities by years

Years	2012	2013	2014	2015	2016
Percentage (%)	49.2	49.3	49.5	45.4	46.9

Source Higher Education Council; https://engelsiz.yok.gov.tr/Documents/Toplantilar/Macid_Mel ekoglu.pdf limited staff (Gündoğar, 2020), insufficient knowledge of the academic staff on inclusive and accessible teaching and university-wide system of supports for readiness for academic staff for inclusive teaching (Gündoğar, 2020; Özkul et al., 2016), major accessibility issues of digital content of university, including university websites (Şerefoğlu & Henkoğlu, 2019) and websites of university disability support services (Emiroğlu, 2015), and library services (Kazak, 2008), and finally, the need for more inclusive and systematic wide variety supports for students, including academic support (Bavli et al., 2020; Genç & Koçdar, 2020).

Higher education is an important agent of change for individuals with disabilities because it creates employment opportunities and improves future working conditions (Kotera et al., 2019). For instance, research has shown that individuals with disabilities who have a university degree have approximately four times more job opportunities than their peers with disabilities who do not pursue higher education (Lamichhane, 2012). Thus, higher education can help individuals with disabilities overcome adversity, gain greater independence, and achieve a better quality of life (Järkestig Berggren et al., 2016; Moriña & Orozco, 2021). Despite the advantages of higher education, individuals with disabilities face a number of barriers in their education journey, which hinder them from getting into a university program, including the high rates of discrimination (Girli et al., 2016), and limited awareness of challenges students with disabilities face in higher education (Bavli et al., 2020). This research suggests that even those who could get into a university program are not guaranteed a nurturing experience.

To summarize, the chapter has deconstructed the education and employment opportunities for individuals with disabilities in Türkiye with underlying problems. The second section explained how inclusive and accessible higher education might propose a medium to disrupt the inequity and the demanding need for inclusive and accessible higher education for students with disabilities, especially in Türkiye. Special attention should be paid to taking the necessary measures to ensure the full participation of students with a disability in higher education. The next section provides an example of how Aksaray University, reconstructs its system by the provision of disability support services as change agents. This effort is part of its journey toward becoming a more inclusive and accessible higher education institution despite having limited and low resources.

4   A Case Example of Aksaray University

The university is located in Aksaray, a city in the Central Anatolia region of Türkiye. Aksaray is known as a transit town, particularly for those traveling between Ankara, Konya, and Nevsehir. However, it is also home to some historical buildings, including the Grand Mosque, the Egri Minaret (Türkiye's version of the Leaning Tower of Pisa), and the Kizil Minaret Cami (mosque with a red minaret). Aksaray University was officially founded in 2006, but its origins can be traced back to 1986 when the Technical Sciences Vocational School was established. This school was a department

Table 5 Number of students with a disability at the Aksaray University

Disability type	Number of students
Chronic health problems	10
Visual impairment and blindness	14
Hard of hearing and deafness	6
Physically disability	22
Specific learning disability	4
Emotional and behavioral disorder	2
Intellectual disability	4
Total	62

Source Aksaray University Disability Support Services (2023): https://engelsiz.aksaray.edu.tr/hizmetler?l=en

of the Selçuk University and then the Nigde University when it opened in 1992 (Aksaray University, 2023). The university became Aksaray University in 2006. With 12 faculties on offer, there is an expansive range of courses available for students to study. These include education, engineering, and Islamic studies. The university also boasts 17 research centers, six vocational schools, three institutes, one college, and one training and research hospital (Aksaray University, 2023).

In the 2023/4 academic year, the number of students who were studying for a 2-year associate degree was 4661, 4-years bachelor's degree was 12,260, master's degree was 2879, and doctorate degree was 183, a total of 19,983 students (Council for Higher Education, n.d.). In the 2023/4 academic year, in total, 62 students with disabilities were studying at Aksaray University. More details regarding students with disabilities at Aksaray University are provided in Tables 5 and 6. It is important to note that due to stigma and prejudices, many students with disabilities prefer not to self-disclose their disability. Consequently, the number of students with disabilities who attend Aksaray University is uncertain and is anticipated to be higher than official statistics when considering the students with hidden or non-disclosed disabilities.

5   Accessibility Provisions at the Aksaray University

As discussed earlier in this chapter, the main legislation regarding the rights of students with disabilities and higher education is the "Higher Education Institutions Disabled Persons Consultation and Coordination Regulation", this regulation is prepared in accordance with Law No. 5378 of the Disability Act. In line with national legislation, Aksaray University is one of the first universities in Türkiye to take the necessary measures to support students with disabilities. Therefore, in 2013, under the vice-rector, a member of the academic faculty was assigned as disability services coordinator at Aksaray University. Later, an office was allocated to the disability support services. With these developments, the Aksaray University

Table 6 Types of degrees studied by the students with disabilities at the Aksaray University

Faculties	Departments	Number of students with disability
Faculty of Economics and Administrative Sciences	Political Science and Public Administration	4
	Business	3
	Finance	3
Engineering Faculty	Electrical Electronics Engineering	1
Sports Science Faculty	Coach Training	7
	Sports Management	5
	Physical Education Teacher	3
Faculty of Medicine	Veterinary	4
Islamic Science Faculty	Islamic Studies	4
Faculty of Education	Social Studies Teacher	3
	Guidance and Psychological Counseling Teaching	2
	Early Childhood Education	3
	Turkish Language Teacher	2
	Special Education	3
Aksaray Vocational School of Social Sciences	Public Relations and Promotion	1
Institute of Sciences	Ma Geology Engineering	1
Communication Faculty	Public Relations and Advertising	3
Faculty of Arts and Sciences	Garden Farming	1
Aksaray Vocational School of Technical Sciences	Laborant and Veterinary Health	1
Institute of Social Sciences	Master of Management and Organization	1
	Master of Early Childhood Education	1
Faculty of Arts and Sciences	History	2
	Turkish Language	3
Institute of Sciences	Master of Geological Engineering	1
Total		62

Source Aksaray University Disability Support Services (2023): https://engelsiz.aksaray.edu.tr/hiz metler?l=en

Disability Support Services was established officially (Aksaray University, 2023). In 2016, the "Aksaray University exam practice directive for students with disabilities" was approved in the Aksaray University Senate. According to the Senate, the purpose of this directive is to address and eliminate possible problems that students with disabilities may encounter in course and exam practices while enrolled in associate, bachelor's, master's, and doctoral programs at Aksaray University. In this context, the directive aims to ensure equal opportunity in education and to organize practices for students with disabilities to conduct exams on equal terms with their peers and in a fair manner (Aksaray University, 2023).

The first author of the chapter was assigned officially as the coordinator of the Disability Support Services at Aksaray University after his complaints and requests for appropriate services for students with disabilities similar to those he encountered during his own higher education experience in Türkiye, the USA, the UK, and Canada. Although the Disability Support Services existed prior to his appointment, the orientation and activities were limited. Thus, the first action after the appointment was to ascertain the number of students with disabilities at Aksaray University. The alternative option was to hire relevant professionals, including disability advisors and accessibility professionals. However, this was not an option due to limited financial resources and the shortage of experts in the country. With the existing conditions' limitations, the first author reached out to the academic staff in the faculty of education and the department of special education who have diverse backgrounds and expertise related to disability field. This group of eight proactive academic staff allocated some of their time to volunteer to aid the Disability Support Services in meeting the needs of students with disabilities. The first task was to develop a service delivery model. The initial step of the service delivery model included information sessions via informative presentations for all faculty and departments on disability, legal rights and responsibilities, and inclusive approaches for accessible lectures. These sessions lasted for two months. The second step was to appoint representatives from each faculty, college, and center, and these representatives found sub-representatives from each department. Through this service delivery model, Disability Support Services staff, volunteering academic staff, collaborated with faculty, centers, and representatives. These representatives then communicated with their department representatives, and these department representatives would identify students with special needs within their department and would refer them to the Disability Support Services. The Disability Support Services staff would meet with each student with disabilities one-on-one and discuss their rights and support needs. Based on these discussions an informative letter outlining the students' support needs and accommodations would be prepared. These letters were then delivered to all professors who are teaching the particular student ensuring they had access to lectures, learning materials, buildings, and social life.

With a proactive group of volunteer academic staff from the Department of Special Education, the disability support services, which had no staff except the coordinator, were able to provide students with disabilities access to university life similar to their non-disabled peers. These efforts highlighted the need for accessibility and encouraged the university management to take necessary measures to create an accessible environment for all. In 2018, the university management board published guidelines that all staff must follow to ensure equal opportunities for all students, including those with various disabilities. As a result, all buildings, including faculties, classrooms, libraries, and recreation areas such as food courts, gyms, and pools, were modified to meet the needs of people with disabilities. For example, buildings that were not accessible were equipped with ramps or elevators. All classrooms now have adjustable desks to accommodate wheelchair users and individuals who need desks at different heights. Additionally, all classrooms and offices are equipped with Braille labels. Simply put, wherever needed, ramps, elevators, accessible restrooms, and other features have been provided to ensure that students with disabilities can easily navigate the campus.

Addition to adjustments to the physical environment, essential services such as note-taking assistance, alternative exam arrangements, and other reasonable accommodations are provided free of charge. These services are made possible by hiring part-time student employees and recruiting volunteers. The special education department trains these student employees and volunteers on how to meet the needs of students with disabilities and monitors the services provided. Despite facing several limitations, Aksaray University management has worked hard to create resources for purchasing technological devices to help students with disabilities access learning materials, lectures, and social activities. Funding for these devices comes from various departments, including the Department of Construction and Technical Affairs, the Department of Health, Sports, and Culture, the Department of Financial Affairs, the Department of Information Technology, the Library and Documentation Department, and the faculties, such as the Faculty of Education. Additionally, some projects have secured external funding to purchase assistive technology for students with disabilities. Devices purchased include magnifiers, voice recorders, Braille embossers, tactile graphic machines, screen magnifiers, screen readers, wheelchairs, and canes.

Aksaray University has been offering scholarships and part-time employment opportunities to support financially needy students. Part-time employed students were referred to the disability support services to help meet the needs of students with disabilities by providing services such as note-taking, producing accessible textbooks, and assisting with laboratory experiments or social activities. In 2022, the "Aksaray University Exam Practice Directive for Disabled Students" was updated to align with standards similar to those in developed countries. These updates offer students with disabilities alternative exam arrangements, such as extended time, separate quiet rooms, or the use of assistive technologies during exams based on their needs. Additionally, Aksaray University offers accessible housing options for students with disabilities, including wheelchair-accessible rooms, ramps, and other features to ensure full participation in campus life. These accommodations are not limited to physical adaptations but also include support for participating in all educational and social aspects of university life. The specific accommodations depend on the individual needs of each student and are determined in collaboration with the Disability Support Services and the Department of Special Education. Awareness programs are conducted on important occasions such as International Disability Day to foster understanding and sensitivity among faculty, staff, and students about the needs of individuals with disabilities. These programs aim to create an inclusive and supportive campus community and encourage volunteers to assist in making the university more inclusive. In recent years, the Turkish Council of Higher Education has taken actions to improve access to universities for individuals with disabilities. One such action is the "University without Barriers" project, launched in 2018. This initiative aims to improve access to higher education for students with disabilities by enhancing accessibility in physical spaces, socio-cultural activities, and education. Under this program, universities meeting the required criteria are eligible for University Accessibility Flag Awards and University Accessibility Program Medal Awards. These efforts have been recognized by the Council for Higher Education, and Aksaray University has received several awards for its commitment to becoming an inclusive university for all. Some of these awards are presented in the appendix below.

6 Conclusion

Türkiye is still a developing nation, and there are several measures to be taken to create an equal society and include all citizens with disabilities. Despite existing challenges, there are some positive improvements to enhance life quality of people with disabilities. The number of students who are benefiting from educational services, especially the number of students attending inclusive schools, is increasing significantly. Even though this is an important improvement, there is evidence indicating that these students' needs could not be met under the existing conditions. Therefore, students with disabilities face a number of barriers to accessing education and developing the necessary skills for the labor market. Consequently, they face significant challenges in accessing higher education and employment. Even though there are positive improvements in legislation, there are serious issues in the implementation of this legislation. Therefore, a comprehensive reform is needed on the rights of people with a disability across all age groups. Nevertheless, despite such major challenges, with the willingness and effort of professionals who are willing to go the extra mile, university students at Aksaray University could be served to meet their needs. The main motivation for writing this chapter is to show that despite all institutional and system-wide barriers, it is possible to lead change in our society. We would like to conclude this chapter by expressing appreciation and gratitude to our colleagues at the Department of Special Education and the university management board for supporting the creation of a more inclusive university. Hopefully, in the near future all states and individuals take the necessary measures to create an accessible society for all.

Acknowledgements This chapter is based upon work from COST Action CA19142—Leading Platform for European Citizens, Industries, Academia and Policymakers in Media Accessibility (LEAD-ME) supported by COST (European Cooperation in Science and Technology).

Appendix

Rewards of the Aksaray University for Inclusive Efforts

"Barrier-Free University Flags are given in three categories. Orange flags are given to those that provide 'accessibility in spaces', green flags are given to those that provide 'accessibility in education', and blue flags are given to those that provide 'accessibility in sociocultural activities'."

In addition, "it is also announced the candidacy of the universities that cannot meet the required standards to receive the flag but have done good work in this regard. Universities that get at least 75 points according to the post-evaluation criteria will receive the flag. The ones that receive between 50 and 75 points are announced as flag candidate universities".

In addition to flags, departments and programs that are accessible to different disability groups are awarded with the "Barrier-Free Program Medal". "For example, the adaptation of the visually impaired to the English Language and Literature department is different from the adaptation of the hearing impaired. Therefore, this medal is given to the departments that make their programs accessible to different disability groups, in line with their work".

The flags won by the universities are valid for three years. At the end of this period, the university must re-apply according to the criteria. If the application is not made, the flag will be removed.

Source https://engelsiz.yok.gov.tr/DuyuruBelgeleri/engelsiz_universite_bayrak_odulleri_Bilgi.pdf

https://www.yok.gov.tr/Sayfalar/Haberler/2022/engelsiz-universite-odulleri-basvurulari-basliyor.aspx

In 2023 barrier-free university flag awards from the Council of Higher Education to "Barrier-Free Universities": in the ranking of universities with the most flags, the Aksaray University came second with 23 flags.

	2023 Barrier-free university flag awards
	ORANGE FLAG
1	Tourism Faculty
2	Social Sciences Institute
3	Vocational School of Health Services
4	New Social Facility Building
5	Architecture and Design Faculty
6	School of Foreign Languages
7	Health Sciences Institute
8	Communication Faculty
9	Institute of Science
	GREEN FLAG

(continued)

(continued)

	2023 Barrier-free university flag awards
1	Tourism Faculty
2	Faculty of Education
3	Communication Faculty
4	Faculty of Islamic Sciences
5	School of Foreign Languages
	BLUE FLAG
1	Vocational School of Health Services
2	Architecture and Design Faculty
3	Health Sciences Institute
4	Social Sciences Institute
5	Medical School
6	Communication Faculty
7	Tourism Faculty
8	School of Foreign Languages
9	Faculty of Islamic Sciences

	2023 space accessibility award candidate medal
	ORANGE FLAG
1	Guzelyurt Vocational School
2	Eskil Vocational School
	GREEN FLAG
1	Vocational School of Health Services
2	Health Sciences Institute
3	Architecture and Design Faculty
4	Aksaray Social Sciences Profession Vocational School
5	Social Sciences Institute
6	Institute of Science and Science
7	Medical School
	BLUE FLAG
1	Ortakoy Vocational School
2	Institute of Science
3	Guzelyurt Vocational School
4	Eskil Vocational School
5	Aksaray Social Sciences Profession Vocational School

Source https://engelsiz.yok.gov.tr/HaberBelgeleri/2023/2023-engelsiz-universite-odulleri-odul-ala nlar.pdf

In 2022, barrier-free university flag awards from the Council of Higher Education to "Barrier-Free Universities": in the ranking of universities with the most flags, Aksaray University came first with 27 flag awards and 4 program medals (DECORATION).

	2022 Barrier-free university flag awards
	ORANGE FLAG
1	Athletics Complex and Tribune
2	Scientific and Technological Application and Research Center Building
3	Faculty of Economics and Administrative Sciences
4	Xystus
5	Indoor Swimming Pool
6	Medico Social Support Services
7	Engineering Faculty
8	Ortakoy Vocational School
9	Vocational School of Social Sciences
10	Social Facility Building
11	Social Life Center
12	Vocational School of Technical Sciences
13	Faculty of Medicine and Central Classrooms Building
14	I Application and Research Center Building
15	Faculty of Veterinary Medicine
	GREEN FLAG
1	Faculty of Arts and Sciences
2	Faculty of Economics and Administrative Sciences
3	Engineering Faculty
4	Faculty of Health Sciences
5	Sports Science Faculty
	BLUE FLAG
1	Faculty of Education
2	Faculty of Arts and Sciences
3	Faculty of Economics and Administrative Sciences Central Campus
4	Engineering Faculty
5	Faculty of Health Sciences
6	Sports Science Faculty
7	Vocational School of Technical Sciences
8	Faculty of Veterinary Medicine

The disabled program decoration of 2022
Aksaray University and relevant disability groups

Faculty name	Program badge	Disability group
Faculty of education	Science teaching	Visually impairment
	Music teaching	Visually impairment
	Social studies teaching	Physically disability
	Turkish teacher	Visually impairment

Source https://www.yok.gov.tr/HaberBelgeleri/Haber%20%C4%B0%C3%A7erisindeki%20Belg
eler/Dosyalar/2022/2022-engelsiz-universite-odulleri-od%C3%BCl-alanlar.pdf

	2021 Barrier-free university flag awards
	ORANGE FLAG
1	Faculty of Islamic Sciences
2	Auditorium
3	Library Building
4	Rectorate Building
5	Faculty of Health Sciences
6	Faculty of Sports Sciences Main Campus
	GREEN FLAG
1	Vocational School of Technical Sciences
2	Faculty of veterinary medicine

The Aksaray University ranked second with nine flag awards

	Candidacy for 2021 award
	ORANGE FLAG
1	Xystus
2	Indoor swimming pool
3	Faculty of Economics and Administrative Sciences
4	Faculty of Engineering
5	Social Facility Building
6	Faculty of veterinary medicine

	Candidacy for accessibility in education 2021
	GREEN FLAG
1	Sports Science Faculty

	Socio-cultural 2021 candidate for accessibility in activities
	BLUE FLAG
1	Tourism Faculty
2	Central Campus

Source   https://engelsiz.yok.gov.tr/HaberBelgeleri/2021/02-2021-engelsiz-universite-odulleri/
2021-engelsiz-universite-odulleri-odul-alanlar.pdf

References

Aksaray University. (2023). Official university website. https://www.aksaray.edu.tr/?l=en

Aksaray University Disability Support Services. (2023). Official website. https://engelsiz.aksaray.edu.tr/hizmetler?l=en

Altan, Ö. Z. (1999). Türkiye'de sakatlarin istihdam edilerek korunmalarini öngören sosyal politikalar yeniden yapilanirken [During the reconstruction of the social policies provisioning the employment of people with impairments in Türkiye]. *Anadolu Üniversitesi İktisadi ve İdari Bilimler Fakültesi Dergisi, 15*(1), 403–436.

Arun, Ö. (2014). Disability in Turkey: The risks in being disabled for accessing educational opportunities. *Akdeniz İnsani Bilimler Dergisi, 4*(1), 53–62.

Ataman, S., Karaaslan, Ö., Kösretaş, B., & Yavuz, M. (2023). The opinions of Turkish civil servant employees with disability and their working experience. *Kalem Eğitim ve İnsan Bilimleri Dergisi, 13*(2).

Aydın, A. (2012). Görme engelli üniversite öğrencilerinin bilgi erişim sorunları üzerine yapılmış bir araştırma [A study on information access problems of visually impaired university students]. *Bilgi Dünyası, 13*(1), 93–116.

Bacon, J., & Baglieri, S. (2021). Perspectives of students labeled intellectually disabled at college: Using disability studies in education as a lens to contemplate inclusive postsecondary education. *Journal of Disability Studies in Education, 2*(1), 27–49.

Baglieri, S., & Bacon, J. (2020). Disability studies in education and inclusive education. In *Oxford research encyclopedia of education*.

Batmaz, G., & Çermik, H. (2019). Sınıf öğretmenlerinin kaynaştırma öğrencilerine yönelik yaptıkları öğretimsel düzenlemelerde karşılaştıkları engeller ve aldıkları destekler [The obstacles faced by classroom teachers in their instructional arrangements for mainstreaming students and the support they receive]. *Eğitim Kuram Ve Uygulama Araştırmaları Dergisi, 5*(1), 27–38.

Bavlı, B., Korumaz, M., & Akar, E. (2020). Visually impaired mentally sighted: An inclusive education case. *International Journal of Progressive Education, 16*(6).

Bayram, G. I., Corlu, M. S., Aydın, E., Ortaçtepe, D., & Alapala, B. (2015). An exploratory study of visually impaired students' perceptions of inclusive mathematics education. *British Journal of Visual Impairment, 33*(3), 212–219.

Bayülken, Y. (2017). *Oda Raporu: Küçük ve Orta Ölçekli Sanayi İşletmeleri [Chamber report: Small and medium sized industrial enterprises]*. Makina Mühendisleri Odası.

Biçer, D. F., & Işcan, I. (2020). Engelli bireylere üniversite kütüphanelerinde verilen hizmetlerde toplam kalite uygulamalarına yönelik nitel arastirma [Qualitative research on total quality practices in services provided to individuals with disabilitys in university libraries]. *Kafkas Üniversitesi İktisadi Ve İdari Bilimler Fakültesi Dergisi, 11*(1), 60–80. https://doi.org/10.36543/kau iibfd.2020.ek1.003

Çankaya, Ö. (2010). *İlköğretim 1. kademede kaynaştırma uygulamalarının sınıf öğretmenlerinin görüşlerine göre değerlendirilmesi* [Evaluation of inclusion practices in primary school 1st level according to the opinions of classroom teachers]. Master's thesis, Selçuk University.

Cankaya, Ö., & Korkmaz, İ. (2012). İlköğretim i. Kademede kaynaştirma eğitimi uygulamalarinin sinif öğretmenlerinin görüşlerine göre değerlendirilmesi [Primary education level I. evaluation of inclusive education practices in primary education according to the opinions of classroom teachers]. *Ahi Evran Üniversitesi Kırşehir Eğitim Fakültesi Dergisi, 13*(1), 1–16.

Cavkaytar, A., Uyanık, H., & Yücesoy Özkan, S. (2017). Republic of Turkey. In M. L. Wehmeyer, & J. R. Patton (Eds.), *The Praeger International handbook of special education* (pp. 251–264). International Praeger. http://www.abc-clio.com/ABCCLIOCorporate/product.aspx?pc=A4262C

Ceyhan, Ş. S., & Alici, S. (2023). Güzel sanatlar lisesinde çalgi eğitimi alan kaynaştirma öğrencilerine ilişkin öğretmen görüşleri (Bursa ili örneği) [Teachers' opinions on inclusion students receiving instrument education in fine arts high school (Bursa province example)]. *Uludağ Üniversitesi Fen-Edebiyat Fakültesi Sosyal Bilimler Dergisi, 24*(44), 133–149.

Claeys-Kulik, A. L., Jørgensen, T. E., & Stöber, H. (2019). *Diversity, equity and inclusion in European higher education institutions* (p. 51). European University Association Asil.

Connor, D. J., & Olander, L. (n.d.). *How medical and social perspectives of disability influence models of inclusive education in the USA.* academia.edu.

Council for Higher Education. (n.d.). *Higher education knowledge management system.* https://istatistik.yok.gov.tr/

Council for Higher Education. (n.d.). *Number of enrollment to university by students with disabilities.* https://engelsiz.yok.gov.tr/Documents/Toplantilar/Macid_Melekoglu.pdf

Council for Higher Education Commission for Students with Disabilities. (2018). *Internal documents.* https://www.mevzuat.gov.tr/MevzuatMetin/1.5.2547.pdf

Council for Higher Education Commission for Students with Disabilities. (n.d.). *Official website.* https://engelsiz.yok.gov.tr/

Covas, C. B., & de Luna, M. A. C. (2019). Advocacy for inclusive education. In G. de Beco, S. Quinlivan, & J. E. Ford (Eds.), *The right to inclusive education in international human rights law* (pp. 269–303). Cambridge University Press.

Damiani, P., Guaraldi, G., Genovese, E., & Lotti, A. (2024). *An ecological-integrated framework for an inclusive academia* (No. 11804). EasyChair.

de Beco, G. (2019). Comprehensive legal analysis of Article 24 of the convention on the rights of persons with disabilities. In G. de Beco, S. Quinlivan, & J. E. Ford (Eds.), *The right to inclusive education in international human rights law* (pp. 58–92). Cambridge University Press.

Demir, M. K., & Seçil, A. (2011). Kaynaştirma eğitimi konusunda tecrübeli sinif öğretmenlerinin görüşleri [Opinions of experienced classroom teachers on inclusive education]. *Kastamonu Eğitim Dergisi, 19*(3), 719–732.

Deniz, E., & Çoban, A. (2019). Kaynaştirma eğitimine ilişkin öğretmen görüşleri [Teacher opinions on inclusive education]. *Elektronik Sosyal Bilimler Dergisi, 18*(70), 734–761.

Emiroğlu, B. G. (2015). Üniversitelerin engelli destek ofislerinin web sayfalarinin erişilebilirlikleri [Accessibility of the web pages of universities' disability support offices]. *Journal of Educational Sciences & Practices, 14*(27).

Engin, A. O., Tösten, R., Kaya, M. D., & Köselioğlu, Y. S. (2014). İlköğretim öğretmenlerinin kaynaştirma uygulamasiyla ilgili tutum ve görüşlerinin *değerlendirilmesi (Kars ili örneği)* [Evaluation of primary school teachers' attitudes and opinions about inclusion practice (The case of Kars province)]. *Kafkas Universitesi. Sosyal Bilimler Enstitusu, 13*, 27–44.

Erdoğan, Ö. (2019). *Erişilebilir üniversiteler kapsamında engelli öğrenci birimlerinin engelli öğrenciler açısından değerlendirilmesi* [Evaluation of disabled student support services in terms of students with disabilities within the scope of accessible universities]. Master's thesis, Adnan Menderes University.

Firat, S. (2010). People with disabilities in Turkey: An overview. *Information Technologies, Management and Society, 3*(2), 51–54.

Fovet, F. (2021). Developing an ecological approach to the strategic implementation of UDL in higher education. *Journal of Education and Learning, 10*(4), 27–39.

Genç, H., & Koçdar, S. (2020). Determining needs and priorities of learners with special needs for support services in an open and distance learning context in Turkey. *Open Praxis, 12*(3), 359–382.

Girgin, İ. (2021). Eğitimcilerin kaynaştırmaya yönelik mesleki gelişim ihtiyaçları [Educators' professional development needs for inclusion]. *OPUS International Journal of Society Researches, 18* (Eğitim Bilimleri Özel Sayısı), 4151–4175.

Girli, A., & Atasoy, S. (2012). *Kaynaştirmaya yerleştirilen zihin yetersizliği veya otistik özellikleri olan öğrencilerin okul yaşantilari ve akranlariyla ilişkilerine ilişkin görüşleri* [Opinions of students with intellectual disability or autism placed in mainstreaming about their school experiences and their relationships with their peers]. *Dokuz Eylül Üniversitesi Buca Eğitim Fakültesi Dergisi, 32*, 16–30.

Girli, A., Sarı, H. Y., Kırkım, G., & Narin, S. (2016). University students' attitudes towards disability and their views on discrimination. *International Journal of Developmental Disabilities, 62*(2), 98–107.

Göl, B. (2014). *Kaynaştırma eğitimi alan görme yetersizliği olan ve gören öğrencilerin akran ilişkilerinin incelenmesi* [Investigation of peer relations of students with visual impairment and sighted students receiving inclusive education]. Master's thesis, Gazi University.

Goodley, D. (2017). *Disability studies: An interdisciplinary introduction.* SAGE.

Griesmeyer-Krentz, J., Griffen, J., & Tevis, T. (2022). Institutional access through a culture of accessibility: The role of disability services providers as institutional change agents. *Canadian Journal of Disability Studies, 11*(3), 92–128.

Gül, S. O., & Vuran, S. (2015). Normal sınıflara devam eden özel gereksinimli öğrencilerin kaynaştırma uygulamasına ilişkin görüşleri ve karşılaştıkları sorunlar [Opinions of students with special needs attending regular classes about mainstreaming and the problems they face]. *Eğitim ve Bilim, 40*(180), 169–195.

Güleryüz, B. (2014). *Sınıf öğretmenlerinin ve sınıf öğretmeni adaylarının kaynaştırma eğitimine ilişkin görüşlerinin belirlenmesi* [Determining the views of classroom teachers and prospective classroom teachers on inclusive education]. Master's thesis, Karaelmas University.

Gündoğar, A. N. (2020). *Yükseköğretime devam eden görme engelli öğrencilere yönelik öğretimsel uyarlamalar hakkındaki görüşler* [Opinions on instructional adaptations for visually impaired students attending higher education]. Master's thesis, Hasan Kalyoncu Üniversitesi.

Gündüz, A. (2015). *Özel ve devlet ilkokullarındaki birinci sınıf kaynaştırma öğrencilerinin akademik başarılarına ilişkin öğretmen görüşleri* [Teachers' views on the academic achievement of first grade mainstreamed students in private and public primary schools]. Master's thesis, Çanakkale Onsekiz Mart University.

Hurley, T. A. (Ed.). (2020). *Inclusive access and open educational resources e-text programs in higher education.* Springer Nature.

Içyüz, R. (2016). *İşitme kayıplı çocuğu kaynaştırmaya devam eden ebeveynlerin sorunlarının ve gereksinimlerinin belirlenmesi* [Determining the problems and needs of parents whose children with hearing loss continue to be mainstreamed]. Master's thesis, Anadolu University.

Ilk, G. (2014). *Sosyal bilgiler ogretmenlerinin kaynastirma uygulamalarina yonelik goruslerinin ve deneyimlerinin incelenmesi* [Investigation of social studies teachers' views and experiences on mainstreaming practices]. Master's thesis, Istanbul University.

Işlek, Ö. (2017). An investigation into the balance of the school curriculum content for pupils with a visual impairment in Turkey (Doctoral dissertation, University of Birmingham).

Järkestig Berggren, U., Rowan, D., Bergbäck, E., & Blomberg, B. (2016). Disabled students' experiences of higher education in Sweden, the Czech Republic, and the United States—A comparative institutional analysis. *Disability & Society, 31*(3), 339–356.

Karakış, H. (2023). *Ortaokul öğretmenlerinin kaynaştırma eğitimindeki yeterlilik düzeyleri ile bireyselleştirilmiş eğitim programı hazırlama ve uygulama süreçlerinin incelenmesi* [Investigation of the competency levels of secondary school teachers in inclusive education and their individualized education program preparation and implementation processes]. Master's thesis, Balıkesir University.

Kaya, A. (2016). *Türkçe öğretmenlerinin kaynaştırma eğitimi ve özel gereksinimli öğrencilere ilişkin görüşleri* [Turkish teachers' views on mainstreaming education and students with special needs]. Master's thesis, Gazi University.

Kayess, R. (2019). Drafting Article 24 of the convention on the rights of persons with disabilities. In G. de Beco, S. Quinlivan, & J. E. Ford (Eds.), *The right to inclusive education under international human rights law* (pp. 122–140). Cambridge University Press.

Kazak, M. (2008). Görme engellilere yönelik kütüphanecilik hizmetlerinde Türkiye'deki son gelişmeler: Gazi Üniversitesi Merkez Kütüphanesi görme engelliler bölümü örneği [Recent developments in librarianship services for the visually impaired in Turkey: The case of Gazi University Central Library visually impaired section]. *Türk Kütüphaneciliği, 22*(2), 216–221.

Kishira, H., & Sasaki, G. (2023). Information and communication technology use by students with disabilities in higher education during the COVID-19 pandemic. *Universal Access in the Information Society*, 1–15.

Kotera, Y., Cockerill, V., Green, P., Hutchinson, L., Shaw, P., & Bowskill, N. (2019). Towards another kind of borderlessness: Online students with disabilities. *Distance Education, 40*(2), 170–186.

Kurt, G. (2017). Engelli Öğrencilerin Yaşam ve Eğitim Kalitesi Algısı Bolu İl Örneği [Disabled Students' Perception of Quality of Life and Education, Bolu Province Example]. *Researcher, 5*(2), 100–121.

Lamichhane, K. (2012). Employment situation and life changes for people with disabilities: Evidence from Nepal. *Disability & Society, 27*(4), 471–485.

Lord, J. E. (2019). Advancing the right to inclusive education in development cooperation. In G. de Beco, S. Quinlivan, & J. E. Ford (Eds.), *The right to inclusive education under international human rights law* (pp. 304–345). Cambridge University Press.

Melekoğlu, M. A. (2014). Special education today in Turkey. In *Special education international perspectives: Practices across the globe* (pp. 529–557). Emerald Group Publishing Limited. https://doi.org/10.1108/S0270-401320140000028024

Mendoza-González, R., Luján-Mora, S., Otón-Tortosa, S., Sánchez-Gordón, M., Rodríguez-Díaz, M. A., & Reyes-Acosta, R. E. (2022). Guidelines to establish an office of student accessibility services in higher education institutions. *Sustainability, 14*(5), 2635.

Metin, A., Ridvanoglu, S., Akgun, U., Gergin, S., Aktas, C., Gokmen, F., Çerezci, E. T., Yildirim, F., Dokmen, Z., Mamatoglu, N., Ozugurlu, M., Karabulut, E., Aydin, A., Aydin Koc, F., & Koc, A. C. (2011). *An analysis of the labour market based on disability*. Ministry of Family and Social Policy: General Directorate of Services for Persons with Disabilities and Elderly People. https://www.aile.gov.tr/media/42387/an-analysis-of-the-labour-market-based-on-disability.pdf

Ministry of National Education (n.d.). Official Statistics. sgb.meb.gov.tr

Moriña Díez, A. (2022). When what is unseen does not exist: Disclosure, barriers and supports for students with invisible disabilities in higher education. *Disability & Society*, 1–27.

Moriña, A., & Orozco, I. (2021). Spanish faculty members speak out: Barriers and aids for students with disabilities at university. *Disability & Society, 36*(2), 159–178.

Özkul, A. E., Hepkul, A., Tutal, O., & Arı, S. (2016). Yükseköğretimde engelli öğrencilerin desteklenmesinde öğretim elemanlarinin rolü, tutumlari ve deneyimleri. *Journal of Exercise Therapy & Rehabilitation, 3*.

Öztürk, H. A., Berber, Z., Aytekin, A., Tüter, M., & Çetin Yüce, B. (2024). Türkiye'de kaynaştırma eğitimi ve uygulamaları [Inclusive education and practices in Turkey]. *Avrasya Sosyal ve Ekonomi Araştırmaları Dergisi, 11*(1), 300–315.

Öztürk, M. E. (2019). The Turkish history of special education from the Ottoman period to the present day. *International Journal of Academic Research in Education, 5*(1–2), 25–30.

Raja, D. S., & Giannoumis, G. A. (2019). Harnessing technology to realize the right to inclusive education. In G. de Beco, S. Quinlivan, & J. E. Ford (Eds.), *The right to inclusive education in international human rights law* (pp. 346–372). Cambridge University Press.

Republic of Turkey. (1982). *Constitution*. Retrieved from https://acikerisim.tbmm.gov.tr/items/c35b2a7b-3df5-4ef6-9144-14da48e35277

Ristad, T., Østvik, J., Horghagen, S., Kvam, L., & Witsø, A. E. (2024). A multi-stakeholder perspective on inclusion in higher education: Ruling on fragile ground. *International Journal of Educational Research Open, 6,* 100311.

Rittel, H. W., & Webber, M. M. (1973). Dilemmas in a general theory of planning. *Policy Sciences, 4*(2), 155–169.

Sadioğlu, Ö., Batu, E. S., & Bilgin, A. (2012). Sınıf öğretmenlerinin özel gereksinimli öğrencilerin kaynaştırılmasına ilişkin görüşleri [Classroom teachers' views on mainstreaming students with special needs]. *Uludağ Üniversitesi Eğitim Fakültesi Dergisi, 25*(2), 399–432.

Sadioğlu, O., Bilgin, A., Batu, S., & Oksal, A. (2013). Problems, expectations, and suggestions of elementary teachers regarding inclusion. *Kuramda ve Uygulamada Egitim Bilimleri, 3*(3), 1760–1765. https://doi.org/10.12738/estp.2013.3.1546

Sanir, H. (2009). *Kaynastirma egitimine devam eden ogrencilerin akademik ogrenme ile ilgili karsilastiklari sorunlarin ogretmen ve aile gorusleri acisindan degerlendirilmesi* [Evaluation of the problems faced by students in inclusive education regarding academic learning from the perspectives of teachers and parents]. Unpublished master thesis, Selcuk University.

Saraç, T., & Çolak, A. (2012). Kaynaştırma uygulamaları sürecinde ilköğretim sınıf öğretmenlerinin karşılaştıkları sorunlara ilişkin görüş ve önerileri [Opinions and suggestions of primary school classroom teachers about the problems they face in the process of mainstreaming practices]. *Mersin Üniversitesi Eğitim Fakültesi Dergisi, 8*(1), 13–28.

Sazak-Pinar, E., & Guner-Yildiz, N. (2013). Investigating teachers' approval and disapproval behaviors towards academic and social behaviors of students with and without special needs. *Educational Sciences: Theory and Practice, 13*(1), 551–556.

Seale, J., Georgeson, J., Mamas, C., & Swain, J. (2015). Not the right kind of 'digital capital'? An examination of the complex relationship between disabled students, their technologies, and higher education institutions. *Computers & Education, 82,* 118–128.

Seale, J., King, L., Jorgensen, M., Havel, A., Asuncion, J., & Fichten, C. (2020). Engaging ignored stakeholders of higher education accessibility practice: Analysing the experiences of an international network of practitioners and researchers. *Journal of Enabling Technologies, 14*(1), 15–29.

Şerefoğlu, H., & Henkoğlu, T. (2019). Türkiye'deki üniversite web sitelerinin görme ve işitme engelli kullanıcılar açısından erişilebilirliklerinin değerlendirilmesi [Evaluation of accessibility of university websites in Turkey for visually and hearing impaired users]. *Yükseköğretim ve Bilim Dergisi, 1,* 111–122.

Sevinç, I., & Çay, M. (2017). Fiziksel engelli bireylerin üniversite eğitimi sirasinda karşilastiklari sorunlar (Akdeniz üniversitesi örneği) [Problems faced by physically individuals with disabilitys during university education (Akdeniz university case)]. *Selçuk Üniversitesi Sosyal Ve Teknik Araştırmalar Dergisi, 13,* 219–238.

Söğüt, D. A., & Deniz, S. (2018). Sınıf öğretmenlerinin bireyselleştirilmiş eğitim programı (BEP) hazırlamada karşılaştıkları güçlükler ve kaynaştırma uygulamalarına ilişkin görüşlerinin değerlendirilmesi [The difficulties faced by classroom teachers in preparing individualized education program (IEP) and the evaluation of their opinions on inclusion practices]. *Erzincan Üniversitesi Eğitim Fakültesi Dergisi, 20*(2), 423–443.

Soyyiğit, T. (2013). *Sınıf öğretmenlerinin değer tercihleriyle kaynaştırmaya yönelik tutumları arasındaki ilişkininin incelenmesi: Pendik ilçesi örneği* [Examining the relationship between classroom teachers' value preferences and their attitudes towards inclusion: The case of Pendik district]. Master thesis, Yeditepe University.

Tümlü, G. Ü., & Akdoğan, R. (2022). Persistence in the face of ecological challenges: A phenomenological study of parents of children with disabilities in Turkey. *International Journal for the Advancement of Counselling, 44*(1), 17–38.

Türk, N. (2011). *İlköğretim okullarında uygulanan kaynaştırma eğitimiyle ilgili sosyolojik bir araştırma* [A sociological research on inclusive education in primary schools]. Master's thesis, Süleyman Demirel University.

Turkish Disability Act. (2005). Law on disabled people and on making amendments in some laws and decree laws, law no: 5378 (Engelliler Hakkinda Kanun, no: 5378). http://www.refworld. org/docid/4c445e652.html

Turkish Employment Agency (Türkiye İş Kurumu [İŞKUR]). (n.d.). Official website. https://www. iskur.gov.tr/en

Turkish Statistical Institute. (2002). *Turkish disability survey.* data.tuik.gov.tr

Turkish Statistical Institute. (2010). *Problems and expectations of people with disabilities survey.* data.tuik.gov.tr

Turkish Statistical Institute. (2011). *Population and household survey.* data.tuik.gov.tr

Turkish Statistical Institute. (2015). *News Bulletin: 2015 UNFPA theme for world population day is vulnerable populations in emergencies.* Retrieved from https://data.tuik.gov.tr/Bulten/Index? p=Dunya-Nufus-Gunu-2015-18617

Turkish Statistical Institute. (2022a). *Higher education employment indicators.* data.tuik.gov.tr

Turkish Statistical Institute. (2022b). *Labor force statistics.* data.tuik.gov.tr

Üçler, A. M., & Yikmiş, A. (2021). Kaynaştirma öğrencisi bulunan Türkçe öğretmenlerinin öğretim uyarlamalarina ilişkin yaptiklari çalişmalarin belirlenmesi [Determining the studies of Turkish teachers with mainstreaming students on teaching adaptations]. *Abant İzzet Baysal Üniversitesi Eğitim Fakültesi Dergisi, 21*(3), 1023–1043.

Ünlü, P., Pehlivan, D., & Tarhan, H. (2010). Ortaöğretim kurumlarinda öğrenim gören görme engelli öğrencilerin fizik dersi hakkindaki düşünceleri [The thoughts of visually impaired students studying in secondary education institutions about physics course]. *Gazi Eğitim Fakültesi Dergisi, 30*(1), 1–15.

Yatgın, S., Sevgi, H. M., & Uysal, S. (2015). *Sınıf öğretmenlerinin, kaynaştırma eğitimine ilişkin görüşleri ve çeşitli değişkenlere göre mesleki tükenmişliklerinin incelenmesi* [Classroom teachers' views on inclusive education and their professional burnout according to various variables]. *Abant İzzet Baysal Üniversitesi Eğitim Fakültesi Dergisi.*

Yazcayir, G., & Gurgur, H. (2021). Students with special needs in digital classrooms during the covid-19 pandemic in Turkey. *Pedagogical Research, 6*(1), 1–10.

Yazicioglu, Y. (2020). An Analysis of the national legislation in terms of inclusive education in Turkey. *European Journal of Educational Sciences, 7*(2), 49–69.

Yekta, Y. (2010). *Kaynaştırma uygulamaları yapılan ilköğretim okullarına devam eden zihinsel engelli bireylerin eğitim yaşantılarına yönelik görüşlerinin betimlenmesi* [Describing the views of individuals with intellectual disabilities attending primary schools with inclusive practices on their educational experiences]. Master's thesis, Abant Izzet Baysal Üniversitesi.

Yiğen, S. (2008). *Çocuğu ilköğretim kademesinde kaynaştırma uygulamalarına devam eden anne-babaların kaynaştırmaya ilişkin görüş ve beklentileri* [Opinions and expectations of parents whose children attend mainstreaming practices at primary school level about mainstreaming]. Unpublished master's thesis, Anadolu University.

Yilmaz, V. (2020). An examination of disability and employment policy in Turkey through the perspectives of disability non-governmental organisations and policy-makers. *Disability & Society, 35*(5), 760–782.

Young, S. (2023). *Students with hidden disabilities' perceptions of online versus on-campus education, and disability support services.* Master's thesis, Technological University Dublin.

Zhao, Y., Wehmeyer, M., Basham, J., & Hansen, D. (2019). Tackling the wicked problem of measuring what matters: Framing the questions. *ECNU Review of Education, 2*(3), 262–278.

Inclusive Art and Society

Digital Constitutionalism and the Data Economy

Ferlanda Luna⬡ and Armela Maxhelaku⬡

Abstract The recent development of virtual data processing has brought about an entirely new perspective on the issues of regulation and the access to information. Information, in turn, has become a crucial component of the changing dynamics of the global market. It is crucial to address the potential of insurgent digital constitutionalism in establishing legal frameworks that ensure Internet security for both users and online platform managers, including private companies and government agencies. This applies to the usage and dissemination of data. With the development of technology, data management has become an important asset in the market. Considering these conditions, it is essential to establish legal frameworks in order to regulate the newly assigned responsibilities pertaining to information.

Keywords Fundamental rights · Digital constitutionalism · Law regulation · Data economy · Digital technology

1 Introduction

The evolution of fundamental rights has gone through three important phases: first, second, and third-generation rights, which correspond, respectively, to the enshrinement of individual freedoms and economic and social rights, and the rights known as diffuse and collective rights since they do not have a specific addressee but affect the whole of society, such as the right to an ecologically balanced environment. There is also a fourth dimension, which includes democracy, pluralism, and the right to information (Novelino, 2009).

There is also a current argument that defends the existence of a fifth dimension of fundamental rights related to information and communication technologies. Holanda

F. Luna (✉)
University of Coimbra, Coimbra, Portugal
e-mail: ferlandaluna@ces.uc.pt

A. Maxhelaku
University of Tirana, Tirana, Albania
e-mail: armela.maxhelaku@fdut.edu.al

© The Author(s) 2024
A. Marcus-Quinn et al. (eds.), *Transforming Media Accessibility in Europe*,
https://doi.org/10.1007/978-3-031-60049-4_6

(2007a, 2007b) states that the contemporary world has required legislative frameworks to make progress in seeing how technology has transformed legal relationships. Laws now need to adapt to a virtual reality. In addition to the rights understood as providing services that, to be realized, require positive action by the state through public policies (Gonçalves, 2018a, 2018b), the right to information also involves the actions of private entities.

What matters now is facing the reality that technology and globalisation have brought to society. The absence of normative commands that impose limits on the digital landscape encourages self-regulation on the part of large companies that process data to meet market demands. From this perspective, human rights have created a breeding ground for new laws that set limits on data management. Human rights can reach both businesses and government policies through their universality (Suzor, 2020).

In the age of easy and rapid dissemination of information, the regulation of data traffic brings a scenario of concern Suzor (2020) and an insurgent market with new conceptions of buyers and sellers Frontier Technology Quarterly (2019). In this way, this paper seeks to discuss how "digital constitutionalism" and the concept of the data economy have been creating a new market and regulation scenario for large companies that own information and how regulatory advances have contributed to making the present and future of computerisation legally viable to ensure rights.

The digital revolution has brought about significant changes in contemporary society, particularly in our legal systems and constitutional norms. Current constitutions were developed for a different era and are currently dealing with the difficulties posed by the digital revolution. The constitutional charters provide guidance on safeguarding our physical well-being but do not explicitly address the protection of our digital identity. The utilisation of digital technology has the potential to address imbalances in power among constitutional actors. However, traditional constitutional texts fail to acknowledge these new possibilities. One interesting development in response to this situation is the rise of what can be referred to as "Internet bills of rights." The documents presented are non-binding declarations that promote constitutional principles for a digital society. Celeste (2023), the successful implementation of digital transformation necessitates the adoption of constitutional standards that safeguard and uphold human rights. Without these standards, the progress of constitutionalism within the realm of digital transformation would be impossible to achieve. One aspect that requires attention is the necessity for a normative definition and regulation of the right to access the Internet European Law Institute (2021).

Most states, establish the right to access the Internet through specific legislation. This approach allows for the implementation of ratified conventions and recommendations from international organisations while also avoiding the need to amend the constitution. However, it is important to consider the incorporation of constitutional ideas, concepts, and doctrines into the "body of the Constitution." This is because the constitution, being the most powerful legal document, must address the global processes of social and legal modernisation Korniienko et al. (2022).

Concerns such as safeguarding individual privacy, mitigating algorithmic bias, and reconciling the disparity between the right to public access to information and data under the control of a select few have emerged as challenges brought about by the digital age. Protecting digital rights should, therefore, be incorporated into public policies in order to achieve a more equitable equilibrium of interests and rights among various stakeholders Song and Ma (2022). The possibility of protection gaps and evolving values over time indicate that, in the digital age, new fundamental rights must be considered. This exercise in thought provokes an innovative examination of essential rights as opposed to exclusively implementing established rights. This classification of legal concerns novel issues that emerge as a result of the implementation of emerging technologies for which there are presently no established rights. The EU's right to data protection, the right to be forgotten, and the right to data portability, as defined in the GDPR, are instances of recently introduced rights (Custers, 2022).

From the perspective of businesses and consumers, it is crucial that regulatory frameworks effectively safeguard consumer data, irrespective of technological advancements. To prevent regulatory obsolescence and innovative subversion by businesses, it is essential that legal and protective parameters be formulated with a technology-neutral approach. However, in addition to imposing limitations, we advise regulators to collaborate closely with businesses to ascertain how the proposed regulations are likely to be implemented in practice (Quach et al., 2022). The influence of big data technologies on privacy (and consequently human dignity) covers everything from group privacy and high-tech profiling to data discrimination and automated decision-making. It becomes particularly important when individuals share personal information in the online context at various stages of their lives, with varying levels of awareness.

Here, individuals frequently have the ability to present their ideas and findings. It is concerning how easily data miners can access and exploit freely available data from social networks and other sources linked to an IP address for profiling purposes.

There is a significant concern when it comes to big data regarding the potential for re-identification of individuals even after their data has been anonymised. It is possible for this to happen by utilising de-anonymisation technologies that have become more accessible due to the enhanced computational capabilities of modern personal computers. This allows for identifying the original personal data (Da Bormida, 2021).

2 Digital Constitutionalism

It is clear from looking at the global effects of the new General Data Protection Regulation (2018) that the GDPR will have a significant impact in at least three key areas. There are several important aspects to consider in relation to data protection regulations. These include the right to erasure, which is also known as the "right to be forgotten," as outlined in Article 17 of the GDPR. Additionally, the territorial scope of the regulation, determined by Article 3 of the GDPR, is a crucial factor to take into account. Another significant consideration is the commission's decisions on the adequacy of data protection in third countries, which are regulated under Article

45 of the GDPR. Lastly, it is worth noting that multinational companies that fail to comply with the regulation may face substantial penalties, as defined in Article 83 of the GDPR (Rubinstein & Petkova, 2018).

The ECJ has consistently upheld strict data protection standards when it comes to tech companies. This means that IT providers offering services within the EU internal market are required to comply with EU data protection laws. As a result, data subjects are given enhanced protection under these laws. In this context, the ECJ has acknowledged a right to be forgotten, which has been subsequently incorporated into the GDPR and adopted by various other courts (Fabbrini & Celeste, 2020). Fundamental rights are the greatest representation of the constitution of a democratic state, guaranteeing the exercise of individual freedoms and respecting the limits of life in society (Carvelli & Scholl, 2011). The first declaratory text to illustrate the birth of fundamental rights was the Declaration of the Rights of Man and of the Citizen, representing the historical moment of the French Revolution, considered to be first-dimension rights, whose holder is the individual without state interference for the exercise of individual freedom (Bonavides, 2009). The second dimension presents state action as one of its facets; from this perspective, the state starts intervening to provide social welfare. Bonavides (2009) adds that the fundamental rights that correspond to this categorisation include social, cultural, economic, and other rights attributed to the community.

For Bobbio (2004), third-dimension rights, which were included in the 1948 Universal Declaration of Human Rights, represent the protection of the rights of humanity, such as the environment and culture. These are inalienable rights that belong to the whole of society. First-generation rights (civil and political rights), which include classic, negative, or formal freedoms, emphasise the principle of freedom and second-generation rights (economic, social, and cultural rights), which are identified with positive, real, or concrete freedoms, emphasise the principle of equality, third-generation rights, which materialise powers of collective ownership attributed generically to all social formations, enshrine the principle of solidarity and constitute an important moment in the process of development, expansion, and recognition of human rights, characterised as unavailable fundamental values by the note of an essential inexhaustibility (Lafer, 1995).

In the context of the fourth dimension of fundamental rights, Bonavides (2009) argues that "political globalisation in the sphere of legal normativity introduces fourth-generation rights, which, incidentally, correspond to the final phase of institutionalisation of the social state. Thus, understood as rights that govern the democratic social order, fourth-generation rights outline the first parameters for regulating information.

Some consider them to be fourth-dimension rights (Novelino, 2009), and others fifth Holanda (2007a, 2007b). At this point, it is worth discussing how digital constitutionalism presents itself as a tool for measuring rights and enabling responsible and ethical use in the virtual environment. The norms that aim to regulate digital (Gill et al., 2015) space must be based on the following premises: substantive content, political community, formal recognition and legitimacy, and degree of scope.

These dimensions seek, respectively, to guarantee an environment that promotes individual freedoms and the articulation of rights, political action through directive documents that announce universal principles that should be applied in the use of the Internet, formal expression of documents that have the content of announcing rights and duties, and, finally, the degree of comprehensiveness, with the aim of avoiding empty determinations that only have the scope of establishing criteria that apply to specific situations, since the rules that should govern the digital sphere presuppose universal applicability (Gill et al., 2015). In turn, digital constitutionalism can be categorised as follows: fundamental rights and freedom; general limits on state power; Internet governance and civic participation; privacy and surveillance rights; access and education; openness and stability of networks; economic rights and responsibility (Gill et al., 2015).

There are significant considerations that the authors have broken down within this division with the intention of guiding the process for managing data, acts, and rights within the Internet. Based on this categorisation and subdivisions, the categorisation would be as follows:

- Basic or Fundamental Rights and Freedoms: This category includes freedom of speech and expression; freedom of information; freedom of (religious) belief; freedom of association and protest; the right to personal security and dignity; protection of children; non-discrimination; and cultural and linguistic diversity.
- General Limits on State Power: Encompassed here are democracy and the rule of law; the right to due process; and the right to legal remedies.
- Internet Governance and Civic Participation: This area covers multi-stakeholder and participatory governance; transparency and openness; open data; the right to participation; and digital inclusion.
- Privacy Rights and Surveillance: Included are privacy rights; data protection; control and self-determination; the right to anonymity; protection from surveillance; the right to use encryption; and the right to be forgotten.
- Access and Education: This encompasses the right to access; speed and affordability; access and skills in the workplace; user awareness and education; and media and digital literacy.
- Openness and Stability of Networks: This includes security of the network, net neutrality, open standards, interoperability and non-fragmentation, stability and reliability of the network, free and open source software, and device rights.
- Economic Rights and Responsibilities: This section contains information on innovation, competition, economic development, intellectual property, intermediary liability, corporate responsibility, and consumer protection (Gill et al., 2015).

Based on these categories, it is possible to understand how digital constitutionalism has established itself as a normative guideline to guide actions within digital spaces as well as to settle any conflicts. It should be noted, in turn, that the guidelines described above are in line with human rights, respecting the individual as a person and as a community. In this way, it is pertinent to make a correlation with the law that is already in force on the European scene, the General Data Protection Regulation (GDPR) (2018), which was systematised using seven principles as a basis, enshrined in Article 5 of the GDPR. These principles guide the normative rules that follow them through guiding values such as limitation and specific purpose of use, as well as responsibility for unauthorised use and measures that seek to prevent harmful conduct. The attempt to regulate intangible space is exemplified by some rules that have sought to regulate permissible and prohibited conduct, such as the Marco Civil da Internet, Brazil (2014, 2018), the General Data Protection Law, Law No. 13,709, was inspired by the General Data Protection Regulation (GDPR) (2018).

From this perspective, human rights formed the basis for the creation of the rules already in force as well as the new laws still under discussion to define the margins of action in the handling of data. Another point that should be considered is the instructive role of this process since human rights can reach businesses, government policies, and the agents who make their information available on the Internet daily through their universality (Suzor, 2020). In addition, Suzor (2020) points out that to change this "status of freedom" on the Internet, it is also necessary for users to understand the responsibility and importance of making efforts to use the digital space democratically. Internet intermediaries enjoy broad discretion to create and enforce their rules in almost any way they see fit. They make decisions based on their own vision of how they want users to behave, their business plans, and commercial interests, as well as in response to their exposure to legal risk and potential bad publicity (Suzor, 2020).

Despite the harmful nuances of technology in terms of computerisation and the ease with which controversial content can be shared, culminating in misinformation and the spread of untrue news Mendes and Fernandes (2021), it is also necessary to recognise the benefits of democratising access to knowledge through digital platforms. According to research by the United Nations, which gave rise to the report Measuring Digital Development: Facts and Figures in 2019, 4.1 billion people have Internet access, corresponding to 53.6% of the world's population. Although these are significant figures for a connected society, there is another side. There are more than 3.1 billion people who don't take advantage of what the Internet has to offer.

From this angle, according to the list of rights outlined above, in addition to providing a regulated space, digital constitutionalism is also linked to the promotion of rights, which is to enable more people to be inserted into the Internet and exercise their rights to access information, education, privacy, and transparent, lawful, and responsible use of the data made available. In this vein, Boaventura states that regulation, through the tools available to the law, is an indicator for resolving social tensions and includes political measures. The author also states that it is one of the ways of protecting universal rights so that parameters and criteria that cannot be delegitimised can be established, even if they are applied in different contexts. Based on this logic, the rise of regulation in the digital landscape aims to ensure the uniform application of the limits imposed and the rights in order to provide the security and legal viability necessary for the expansion of this segment.

An interesting aspect of the GDPR is its capacity to extend its jurisdiction to international organisations that may not be based in the EU. With the implementation of the GDPR guidelines, this ruling has the potential to significantly impact global tech companies by mandating compliance for non-EU data controllers and processors who target individuals in the EU. It is worth noting that although there has been an increase in the number of large international companies being fined for violations, the majority of these fines in the past two years have been imposed on companies based in the EU, providing solely to European clients. Consequently, smaller companies have generally faced more substantial fines during the time period under examination. When analysing the percentage of annual revenue, it is observed that smaller fines imposed on national companies tend to be relatively higher, even when considering the outlier fines exceeding €1 million. While the largest fines may seem immense, they still fall short of reaching the maximum limit. On the other hand, the smaller fines come much closer to hitting the maximum limit, which is either 2 or 4% of the annual turnover amount. It is evident that the GDPR poses a greater risk to smaller national European companies compared to large international tech companies with significant global influence and higher web traffic (Wolff & Atallah, 2021).

3 Data Economy

The globalisation of the economy has brought new contours to the performance of activities in the digital sphere. What differentiates transactions involving data from other economic activities is basically established on two pillars: there is no express definition between the agents involved in the relationship as buyers, sellers, or consumers, and, on the other hand, the price does not follow the law of supply and demand (Frontier Technology Quarterly, 2019). The data economy has significant implications for distribution matters, which are heavily influenced by legal arrangements and entitlements. This phenomenon has various consequences, including increased commercialisation and government monitoring, the concentration of market power in monopolistic companies, negative environmental impacts, the transformation of labour into temporary and outsourced forms, the exacerbation of existing racial and social inequalities, and the widening gap between developed and developing nations. Technological advancements and network effects further amplify these distributive effects. The global data economy is regulated by international laws that promote trade liberalisation, often favouring technology corporations primarily located in the Global North. Algorithmic decision-making is now being used by international organisations and domestic welfare agencies to determine eligibility for welfare and humanitarian assistance (Vatanparast, 2021).

The data economy was organised around a "digital curtain" that obscured its practices from lawmakers and the general public for the majority of its existence. Even though the data originated from the private activities of customers, it was regarded as company property and a proprietary secret (Rahnama & Pentland, 2022). The heterogeneity of consumer privacy concerns can impact the effectiveness of the social planner's data regulation policy. The optimal amount of data changes depending on the relationship between consumer privacy concerns and consumer type in different scenarios. This relationship can be positively correlated, negatively correlated, or uncorrelated. There can be significant variations in different scenarios, indicating the need for policy intervention by the social planner in certain cases while being ineffective in others (Wang et al., 2022). The diversity of consumer privacy concerns has an impact on the firm's data collection practices, which consequently influences the effectiveness of data regulation policies (Wang et al., 2022). The data economy is governed by guidelines that conventional economic theories cannot yet explain. Unlike any product in circulation today, data, as a new member of the production chain, presents a challenge to legislation and economic regulation. Furthermore, the pricing of data depends on the context in which it is inserted and how it is intended to be used.

One aspect that sets informational capitalism apart is its impact on legal institutions and the granting of quasi-legal entitlements. Additionally, it is reshaping markets in unprecedented ways. The use of data for governance has the potential to supplant traditional methods such as law and markets for organising society. Given that the nature of data is not competitive, technology firms often claim quasi-property rights and charge for data access (Vatanparast, 2021). Existing literature reveals three main consensuses in the field of big data-driven management innovation. Firstly, the utilisation of big data has become a valuable asset for companies in the digital economy, enhancing their ability to adapt and thrive.

Furthermore, the utilisation of big data resources enhances companies' learning capabilities. For instance, by utilising big data analysis and processing, companies can enhance their capacity for exploratory and applied organisational learning. Furthermore, the process of creating value from big data necessitates that companies adapt, adjust, and update their key structures and capabilities. Companies must navigate the resistance of their established procedures and business models in order to maximise the benefits of big data analysis in decision-making (Xu, 2021).

Data is increasingly a critical factor in production, complementing labour and physical capital. But unlike capital or labour, data is non-depletable. The use of data by many does not diminish its quantity or value. On the contrary, the use of the data by many may increase its value. At the same time, data can become less relevant and less valuable over time. The value of data, unlike physical capital, also depends on its unique characteristics. An individual data point can carry little value, but its value can multiply manifold when aggregated and analysed with other relevant data Frontier Technology Quarterly (2019).

The companies at the top of the data economy pyramid are Google, Facebook, Uber, Airbnb, Netflix, Amazon, Apple, Microsoft, and others, also known as "data companies." The giants of the market, Apple, Amazon, Facebook, Google, and Microsoft, had a turnover of more than 3 trillion dollars in 2018. Another impasse that arises is the monopoly exercised by these companies in the market. The report states: "The net effect on the economy can be negative, depressing overall employment, investment, and aggregate demand" Frontier Technology Quarterly (2019). Through the analysis of consumer portraits, consumer content, and consumer behaviour prediction, customised suggestions are provided for goods and services, enabling consumers to develop a stronger affinity for products. Consumer preference is often overlooked in the traditional approach to defining the relevant market by substitution (Frontier Technology Quarterly, 2019).

In addition to the economic clashes, Mendes and Fernandes (2021) draw attention to the ideological influence and intentional production of information that these companies have: instead of being merely passive agents in the intermediation of content produced by third parties, companies like Facebook, Google, and Amazon are able to interfere in the flow of information by filtering, blocking, or mass reproducing content produced by their users. This interference in the flow of information is also characterised by the intensive use of algorithms and big data tools that allow platforms to manipulate and control the way in which private content is propagated in a non-transparent way (Mendes & Fernandes, 2021).

The great contradiction experienced by this "new economy" is the accessibility and volume of data provided daily on websites, and the questions that arise are many: who is actually benefiting? How can users of online platforms protect themselves from possible illegal conduct? What is the responsibility of the owners of the information if it is used incorrectly or in a different way than what was agreed upon? In response to these questions, Mendes and Fernandes (2021) infer that the realisation of information and privacy rights is shifting from the public to the private sphere. In order to keep up with the fast-paced growth of the Internet and digital economy, it is crucial to enhance the standards used to evaluate the relevant market. The operational model of Internet platform operators poses challenges in accurately determining market share using traditional sales-based calculations. When examining this case, it may be worth exploring the possibility of incorporating additional factors to determine the relevant market. These factors could include the size of the user base, the scale of data, the impact of network effects, and the level of control over key facilities.

On the one hand, the data economy is radically transforming many economic activities and creating new levels of prosperity. On the other hand, it presents the possibility of a perilous dystopia, where participants in the data economy can face chronic trust deficits and insecurity (Frontier Technology Quarterly, 2019). Privacy-enhancing technologies (PETs) provide a promising solution to the ongoing conflict between privacy and the data economy. Some examples of PETs are differential privacy, federated learning, on-device computation, zero-knowledge proof, and secure multi-party computation Johnson (2022).

The performance of data on the Internet is used as a tool to induce society's way of thinking and acting, directly influencing the decisions made (Suzor, 2020). The network itself is organised to serve people anywhere in the world, transmitting information immediately (Lévy, 1999). In this area, companies have played a discretionary role in disseminating information and using data to meet their own needs and the interests of the market. In short, digital constitutionalism requires us to develop new ways of limiting abuses of power in a complex system that includes many different governments, businesses, and civil society organisations. The difficult task of digital constitutionalism is to build consensus about how power over the Internet should be shared and limited, how those limits may be imposed, and by whom (Suzor, 2020).

In order to curb this discretionary process, Suzor (2020) advocates the creation of laws that provide a substantial structure so that these relationships can be conducted in the public interest and within the moral limits of society. Faced with the challenges posed by this new system, the author points out that this is the time to discuss the creation of new ways of regulating activities in the digital sphere. Internet governance is, therefore, an indispensable issue. For Kurbalija (2016), governance outlines a reference framework with the aim of enabling communication between agents and decision-making. The current era of Internet governance is closely linked to the concept of digital constitutionalism.

The aim of digital constitutionalism is to reconsider how the exercise of power should be constrained and justified in the era of digital technology (De Gregorio & Radu, 2022). This governance model explores the decentralisation of state sovereignty, focusing on the traditional criterion of jurisdiction. The creation and implementation of legal norms are shifting away from the traditional focus on the United States and towards non-governmental entities. The transnational nature of network governance necessitates that constitutional courts consider the various ways in which international actors interact in the regulation of the Internet when assessing the constitutionality of domestic laws (Mendes & Fernandes, 2021). Since the data economy is in the present, it is undeniable that this situation is already showing signs that it will develop and reach more and more people in the present and the future. Thus, with a view to structuring paradigms that consider development, security, and human rights, in 2017, the United Nations Development Group proposed guidelines for handling data in the coming years, such as through UN Global Pulse, ensuring the production of reports that contribute to monitoring the use of data (Frontier Technology Quarterly, 2019).

In addition, the United Nation (2014) introduced actions such as monitoring and supervising how private entities are handling data in order to prevent possible abusive conduct. The UN World Data Forum in 2018 addressed statistical migrations allied to the objectives of the 2030 Agenda for Sustainable Development, and the 2017 Forum dealt with policies to improve the programmes used in government action (Frontier Technology Quarterly, 2019). Following this path, the European Law Institute (ELI), in partnership with the American Law Institute (ALI) in 2021, outlined potential principles that can be applied to transactions involving data. The document constitutes initial steps towards the implementation of general rules involving transactions with data, including in the draft document some clauses that could be present in contracts, such as the designation of the intellectual property of data, privacy and limitation, and determination of the use of the information collected. Another important mechanism that is being studied with the possibility of use is economic participation in the profits arising from the use derived from the data. Since the scope and multiplicity of the management of the information made available generate revenue, this should be shared.

Although not formalised before the international community, the discussion of this document and the observations made throughout the text demonstrate the willingness to draw the lines that will define how contracts involving data and information will be regulated and economically treated. Between laws, contracts, clauses, companies, and users, the data economy presents itself in a scenario, despite many uncertainties and obstacles, that is promising for the growth of the economy and the expansion of information technologies, which if well-managed, will contribute to the development of society by expanding access and making human rights effective in their various dimensions.

4 Conclusion

This research paper sought to discuss the roots, trends, innovations, and dilemmas of regulation in the context of digital constitutionalism linked to human rights. In light of the research carried out, which is a field that is in the process of being refined, it can be seen that the main normative guidelines have served as the basis for legislation in various countries, which demonstrates the commitment of nations to demarcating the boundaries of this new business space. On the other hand, despite the advances made so far, these are still insufficient in the face of the magnitude that computerisation and data sharing have become in the globalised era. There are still regulatory gaps governing financial transactions involving data. As a result, this creates instability both for those who use data as their main raw material and for users and consumers, who, in many cases, do not have the opportunity to know how their personal data is collected, used, and stored.

In terms of legal and economic regulation, the data economy is an imminent and unavoidable reality, which means that regulatory guidelines and the market need to define the extent to which activities that handle data can be established for fear of becoming a convenient scenario for illegal activities. On the other hand, the expansion of these businesses is led by information fronts that have a differentiated technological structure, which creates a less competitive environment for the resources these companies use. In view of the above, small and medium-sized companies are not able to be on an equal footing in terms of enabling the application of data processing in accordance with current legislation, which dismantles the market, leaving the same economic circle of organisations holding the financial opportunities provided by this ubiquitous asset of data handling.

The challenges begin as we come to understand the reality that needs to be addressed. We cannot treat the data economy as a future issue requiring greater legal rigidity and economic regulation. It is an urgent matter that must be managed now to ensure that all agents involved in the production cycle can utilize its benefits in compliance with the law. This will help make the data economy an economically viable activity across all proposed levels: legislative, financial, organizational, transparency, and parity with the consuming public.

Acknowledgements This chapter is based upon work from COST Action CA19142—Leading Platform for European Citizens, Industries, Academia and Policymakers in Media Accessibility (LEAD-ME) supported by COST (European Cooperation in Science and Technology).

References

Bobbio, N. (2004). *A era dos direitos* (9th ed.). Elsevier.

Bonavides, P. (2009). Curso de direito constitucional. Malheiros Editores.

Brazil. (2014). Marco Civil da Internet, Brazilian Federal Law No. 12,965 of April 23, 2014.

Brazil. (2018). General Data Protection Law, Law No. 13,709.

Carvelli, U., & Scholl, S. (2011). Evolução histórica dos direitos fundamentais: Da Antiguidade até as primeiras importantes declarações nacionais de direitos. Retrieved January 21, 2022, from https://www2.senado.leg.br/bdsf/bitstream/handle/id/242914/000926858.pdf?sequence=1

Celeste, E. (2023). *Digital constitutionalism: The role of internet bills of rights.* Routledge. Available at https://search.ebscohost.com/login.aspx?direct=true&db=nlebk&AN=3349887&site=ehost-live on January 11, 2024.

Custers, B. H. M. (2022). New digital rights: Imagining additional fundamental rights for the digital era. *Computer Law & Security Review, 44*, 1–13. https://doi.org/10.1016/j.clsr.2021.105636. https://ssrn.com/abstract=4329235. Accessed on November 10, 2023.

Da Bormida, M. (2021). The big data world: Benefits, threats and ethical challenges. In *Ethical issues in covert, security, and surveillance research* (pp. 76). December 9, 2021.

De Gregorio, G., & Radu, R. (2022). Digital constitutionalism in the new era of internet governance. *International Journal of Law and Information Technology, 30*(1), 68–87. https://doi.org/10.1093/ijlit/eaac004

European Law Institute. (2021). ALI-ELI principles for a data economy: Data transactions and data rights. https://www.europeanlawinstitute.eu/fileadmin/user_upload/p_eli/Projects/Data_Economy/Principles_for_a_Data_Economy_Final_Council_Draft.pdf

Fabbrini, F., & Celeste, E. (2020). The right to be forgotten in the digital age: The challenges of data protection beyond borders. *German Law Journal, 21*, 55–65. https://doi.org/10.1017/glj.2020.14

General Data Protection Regulation (GDPR). (2018). Article 5. Official *Journal of the European Union, L 119*/1–88.

Gill, L., Redeker, D., & Gasser, U. (2015). Towards digital constitutionalism? Mapping attempts to craft an internet bill of rights. Berkman Center Research Publication No. 2015–15

Gonçalves, M. E. (2018). *Em tempos de crise e de austeridade, de que valem os direitos sociais?* (pp. 87–101).

Gonçalves, P. (2018). The role of the state in realising rights: Services and public policies.

Holanda, A. (2007a). The impact of technology on legal relationships: The need for legislative frameworks.

Holanda, I. W. C. (2007b). O negócio virtual e segurança jurídica. Retrieved January 20, 2022, from https://egov.ufsc.br/portal/conteudo/o-neg%C3%B3cio-virtual-eseguran%C3%A7a-jur%C3%ADdica-0

Johnson, G. (2022). *Economic research on privacy regulation: Lessons from the GDPR and beyond.* National Bureau of Economic Research Working Paper No. 30705. http://www.nber.org/papers/w30705

Korniienko, P. S., Plakhotnik, O. V., Blinova, H. O., Dzeiko, Z. O., & Dubov, G. O. (2022). *Contemporary challenges and the rule of law in the digital age* (pp. 1002–1001).

Kurbalija, J. (2016). Uma introdução à governança da internet. CGI.

Lafer, C. (1995). Desafios: Ética e política. Siciliano.

Lévy, P. (1999). Cibercultura (C. I. da Costa, Trans.). Editora 34.

Mendes, G., & Fernandes, V. (2021). Digital constitutionalism and constitutional jurisdiction: A research agenda for the Brazilian case. Forthcoming in *The rule of law in cyberspace: Democracy, disinformation and social networks.* Springer, 2022. Retrieved October 6, 2023, from https://ssrn.com/abstract=3769947 or https://doi.org/10.2139/ssrn.3769947

Novelino, M. (2009). The fourth dimension of fundamental rights: Democracy, pluralism, and the right to information.

Quach, S., Thaichon, P., Martin, K. D., Weaven, S., & Palmatier, R. W. (2022). Digital technologies: Tensions in privacy and data. *Journal of the Academy of Marketing Science, 50*, 1299–1323. https://doi.org/10.1007/s11747-022-00845-y

Rahnama, H., & Pentland, A. S. (2022). The new rules of data privacy. *Harvard Business Review.* Retrieved November 10, 2023, from https://hbr.org/2022/02/the-new-rules-of-data-privacy

Rubinstein, I., & Petkova, B. (2018). The international impact of the general data protection regulation. In M. Cole, & F. Boehm (Eds.), *Commentary on the general data protection regulation.* Edward Elgar Publishing. Forthcoming. https://ssrn.com/abstract=3167389

Song, L., & Ma, C. (2022). Identifying the fourth generation of human rights in the digital era. *International Journal of Legal Discourse, 7*(1), 83–111. https://doi.org/10.1515/ijld-2022-2065

Suzor, N. (2020). Human rights and data management: Limitations and responsibilities.

United Nations. (2014). A world that counts: mobilising the data revolution for sustainable development. Retrieved from https://www.undatarevolution.org/wp-content/uploads/2014/11/A-World-That-Counts.pdf

United Nations Department of Economic and Social Affairs, Economic Analysis and Policy Division. (2019). Frontier technology quarterly. Retrieved January 5, 2022, from https://www.un.org/development/desa/dpad/wp-content/uploads/sites/45/publication/FTQ_1_Jan_2019.pdf

Vatanparast, R. (2021). The code of data capital: A distributional analysis of law in the global data economy. juridikum, 1/2021, 98–110. https://ssrn.com/abstract=3832471

Wang, J., Dou, Y., & Huang, L. (2022). Regulating the collection of data as a factor of production: An economic analysis. Retrieved from https://ssrn.com/abstract=4215107 or https://doi.org/10.2139/ssrn.4215107

Wolff, J., & Atallah, N. (2021). Early GDPR penalties: Analysis of implementation and fines through May 2020. *Journal of Information Policy, 11*, 63–103. https://doi.org/10.5325/jinfopoli.11.2021.0063

Xu, X. (2021). Research prospect: Data factor of production. *Journal of Internet and Digital Economics, 1*(1), 64–71. https://doi.org/10.1108/JIDE-09-2021-005

Making Copyright Management Agile: Challenges and Opportunities in Audiovisual Translation and Media Accessibility for a New Digital Era

Estella Oncins⊚ and Iris Serrat-Roozen⊚

Abstract Digital interactive accessibility services must enable human interaction with the media content beyond consumption, ensuring that people can perceive, understand, navigate, and interact with the content and contribute to it. All these new types of interactions are also a field of study in audiovisual translation (AVT) and media accessibility (MA), as translation is a form of human–computer interaction (HCI) (O'Brien, Translation Spaces 1:101–122, 2012). Therefore, the role of technology in AVT/MA is a key aspect not only in the process of creation, but also for distribution, delivery, and consumption. This tendency is expected to grow in the coming years as "technology is also the basis of tools to translate or adapt content and tools to consume content" (Matamala in Accessibilitat i traducció audiovisual, 2019). The progressive transition from Web 2.0 to Web 3.0, with the irruption of recent technologies such as blockchain and artificial intelligence (AI), is opening up innovative forms of communication and interaction for users in the digital world. Yet, challenges in relation to intellectual property rights (IPR) management in AVT/MA remain a major concern (Orero et al., 2023; Serrat-Roozen & Oncins, 2023). The following chapter presents the results of a series of focus groups held with professionals and researchers from the different fields of the AVT and MA in the frame of the European project MediaVerse. This three-year project was aimed at designing and testing a framework to allow professionals and laymen to publish multimedia content that may be easily shared. Results presented highlight user's needs and expectations from AVT/MA professionals in relation to copyright management, through the use of blockchain technology to protect and recognise IPR for professionals in these fields.

Keywords Audiovisual translation · Media accessibility · Copyright management · Blockchain technology · Artificial intelligence

E. Oncins (✉)
Universitat Autònoma de Barcelona, Bellaterra, Spain
e-mail: estella.oncins@uab.cat

I. Serrat-Roozen
Universidad Internacional de Valencia, Valencia, Spain
e-mail: iris.serrat@professor.universidadviu.com

© The Author(s) 2024
A. Marcus-Quinn et al. (eds.), *Transforming Media Accessibility in Europe*,
https://doi.org/10.1007/978-3-031-60049-4_7

121

1 Introduction

The incessant penetration of technological tools and solutions opens the doors to new user interactions in the areas of audiovisual translation (AVT) and media accessibility (MA). Technological solutions and products are increasingly being used in our daily activities and even determine our social communication. The role of technology in the fields of AVT and MA is a key aspect not only in the process of creation, but also for the distribution, delivery, and consumption of content.

There is an increasing number of technologies which are being incorporated in all fields of the translation and digital/media accessibility industry. In this regard, various researchers in the AVT and MA fields have described the so-called audiovisual translation workstation as a workstation that changes continuously and is moving towards cloud-based solutions (Díaz Cintas and Massidda 2019; Oziemblewska & Szarkowska, 2022). In the case of subtitlers, this convergence to the cloud allows both language service providers (LSPs) and subtitlers to centrally manage multiple subtitle files, track changes, introduce quality assurance (QA) processes, and integrate other tools (Oncins, 2022). In most cloud-based subtitling tools, technology central, enhancing work efficiency and reducing costs. However, this often compromises output quality and creates ambiguity around data ownership in AVT and MA works. Yet, technology can also offer solutions. By integrating blockchain, AI, and smart contracts, professionals in AVT and MA can move towards a fairer system, especially in managing the copyrights of their works.

1.1 AVT and MA Modalities: Not Shaken but Stirred

It should be noted that the technological acceleration in the audiovisual and multimedia sector has also increased the risk of people being excluded from enjoying media products and services, or the risk of providing *fake accessibility* (Serrat-Roozen, 2023), as it is crucial to ensure that digital content not only includes the essential features for accessibility, but also implements them accurately and effectively. This issue has been recognized through the concept of media accessibility (Matamala, 2019). Although research and practice in MA was initially framed as a domain within AVT studies, AVT and MA studies are guided by different questions. While AVT focuses mainly on the process of translation, and research in this field is framed in issues related to linguistic aspects, MA analyses the world in terms of access (Greco, 2016). Thus, making a distinction between AVT and MA does not mean excluding one or the other, since some accessibility issues may be related to translation and vice versa. Similarly, AVT and localisation are two convergent fields which share more similarities than differences (Mejías-Climent, 2021). In this regard, one of the required competences for professionals in this field is to be familiar with specific features of screen translation, such as subtitling and dubbing, for the localisation of audio and cinematic assets (Mangiron, 2007). Finally, accessibility in the video game field has mainly received the attention of the industry, especially in the design phases of the product, with the production of a number of game accessibility guidelines (Game accessibility guidelines, n.d.). Yet, accessibility in relation to video games "remains an overlooked area in translation studies" (Mangiron, 2018).

Given this context, MA and AVT professionals would greatly benefit from a dynamic copyright management system, leveraging the opportunities presented by recent developments. Copyright issues in these fields are at a critical juncture. The integration of emerging technologies like blockchain within the new Web 3.0 environment can empower content creators to enhance the visibility of their work. The earlier version of the web, known as Web 1.0, was primarily a read-only medium, while Web 2.0 allowed for greater interactivity with read/write capabilities. Now, the emerging version of the web, Web 3.0, is considered to be a technologically advanced medium that not only facilitates read/write capabilities but also enables a machine to carry out some of the thinking that was previously expected only of humans. This progress in technology also brings with it new challenges and opportunities for generating digital content that should be born accessible (Orero, 2020), and enhance accessibility in the digital world to its fullest extent. In particular, blockchain technology allows for the minting of digital assets by creating a digital representation typically in the form of a digital file or a link to a digital file. This file is then associated with a unique token on the blockchain, which serves as proof of ownership (see Fig. 1). This creates the opportunity to bring translators and content creators out of anonymity, making their work visible and ensuring they bear the associated responsibilities (Orero et al., 2023). The integration of blockchain technology in translation workflows could substantially contribute to improving translation and media accessibility quality, in particular for the corresponding professional and economic recognition of professionals in these fields.

2 Copyrights Management in AVT and MA

There is no international-unified legal framework in terms of copyright management in the translation field. Even if there is an international legal framework on copyright management, each EU country has its own copyright laws, and an agency to manage the rights. The different EU countries have substantially modified their intellectual property rights (IPR) laws in order to transpose the different European Directives in this subject as a step to harmonise copyright (Margoni, 2016; Orero et al., 2023; Serrat-Roozen & Oncins, 2023). In the case of Spain, the last reform took place in 2021 in order to transpose the European Directives 2019/789[1] and 2019/790.[2] Yet, the current copyright regime remains outdated and unworkable in the digital era, especially with the increasing widespread use of machine translation (MT) across all translation sectors (Morkens & Lewis, 2019). For instance, in Spain there is the

---

[1] See: https://eur-lex.europa.eu/legal-content/ES/TXT/?uri=CELEX%3A32019L0789.

[2] See: https://eur-lex.europa.eu/legal-content/ES/TXT/?uri=CELEX%3A32019L0790.

DAMA organisation (Derechos de Autor de Medios Audiovisuales), which is in charge of managing the copyright of the different agents in the audiovisual field, including professionals in the AVT field. Still, professionals in video game localisation are bound with strict non-disclosure agreements, particularly in the case of major video game companies. At the same time, most work delivered by MA professionals does not fall under copyright protection (Orero et al., 2023).

Generally, there are two different types of copyright: moral rights and economic rights (Serrat-Roozen & Oncins, 2023). Moral rights are personal, indisputable, and inalienable. Some of these rights exist in perpetuity; for example, the right of the author to be acknowledged and the right to the integrity of works. Recognition of the authorship and integrity of works are the most important moral rights, together with the right to share this work. Economic rights and rights of exploitation are transferable rights and do have time limits. Their duration depends on the legislation in each country (i.e. in Spain, they last for the lifespan of the author and following the death of the author they belong to the inheritors for a further 70 years). This means that they can be sold, ceded, or shared with third parties, whether this is for economic purposes or not. Hence, the ownership of rights of exploitation does not always belong to the author, since the latter may have ceded or sold these to a third party or organisation, such as an editor or compiler.

2.1 Copyright and the Question of Originality/Creativity

The translator's profession is undergoing significant changes, and AI is demanding a rethink of what translating entails today. In this regard, it is advisable to take into account central issues such as the creativity and originality of a work, an issue which most organisations in the different translation fields are already demanding. In the near future, translations will likely be labelled based on whether and to what degree AI has been used, a practice already implemented in localisation processes. Currently, in the case of machine aided translations, "the question of copyright is particularly challenging and complex, and it is mostly overlooked by many national legislations" (Debussche & Troussel, 2014: 103).

Additional challenges linked to the increasing use of technologies in AVT and MA include the quality of the final output, the high level of post-editing, as well as the degree of creativity that certain content requires. Thus, according to Debussche and Troussel (2014: 100), "the protection of translations will indeed depend on the nature of the original text". In this regard, the more creative, complex or original the source, the more likely it is that its translation will be original as well.

Translators may have grounds to claim copyright of a translated text to which they have made an original contribution as a derivative or adapted work, depending on the contract (Tong King, 2020) and the perceived degree of originality (Debussche & Troussel, 2014). This is subject to the rights of the original author as recognised by the Berne Convention (World Intellectual Property Organisation 1979). While this principle might apply to different fields of translation, in the case of AVT and

MA copyrights related to creativity and originality are missing mainly due to strict signed contracts. Furthermore, in many occasions, when AVT professionals send their work to language service providers, these professionals find that they do not own the copyright, a fact that many consider a violation of these rights (Nikolic & Bywood, 2021). According to Moorkens and Lewis (2019: 481), "at present, benefits are rarely passed to the translator, meaning that, while an initial translation may be costly, secondary uses are very inexpensive". Thus, it is necessary to open a debate in relation to AVT and MA assets, data ownership, and the copyrights that derive from it.

2.2   Copyrights and Data Ownership in AVT and MA

Ensuring data ownership and security is essential for maintaining the trust of users with their working systems and tools. The key lies in how to make data sharing trusted and secure. Blockchain technologies can help to achieve this goal via consensus mechanisms through the network to guarantee data sharing in a tamperproof way embedded with smart contracts. Blockchain technology can provide tools to make users owners of their data, through authentication and controlled data access. In addition, as in the case of educational settings the blockchain uses encryption and hashes techniques to secure the stored data and facilitates a secure way to access data from various locations.

Therefore, the use of blockchain technology could be a possible solution for translators in the fields of AVT and MA, as this technology allows including metadata to track the authors' copyrights. Metadata is important for the definition of preferences defined by authors on how their works should be repurposed (Moorkens & Lewis, 2019) and at the same time which copyrights should be respected. Blockchain constitutes one of the technologies underpinning the MediaVerse platform and its IPR management system.

3   MediaVerse

The MediaVerse project was aimed at designing and testing a framework to allow professionals and laymen to publish multimedia content that could be easily shared and licenced following a user-centred copyright management model. The appeal of blockchain to AVT and MA works can be seen in the possibility to ensure data ownership and security, thus maintaining the trust of users with their working systems and tools without the need for a central governing body (Qureshi & Megías Jiménez, 2021). Any professional working in these fields should be able to create and mint their own works (Orero et al., 2023).

The MediaVerse copyright management tool provides a machine-readable format for content creators to handle the legal aspects of copyright. The platform also provides a legal framework to allow storage and registration of assets and smart negotiation of (multimedia) content to manage revenues.

To this aim, the MediaVerse project identified the following seven blockchain-based solutions that could help content creators to address the main challenges related to copyright management in the audiovisual sector:

1. Decentralised digital content ecosystem: power and ownership return to creators.
2. New pricing options: new options for creators to earn by selling content.
3. Monetisation of content: content creators can establish direct relationships with customers.
4. Distribution of royalty payments: near real-time payments based on smart contracts.
5. From digital rights management (DRM) to smart contract: transparent and "self-execute" right management underlying smart contracts.
6. Attribution: blockchain increases the visibility and availability of the information regarding copyright ownership.
7. Copyright management: blockchain enables content owners to directly manage their works.

3.1 Methodology

Since the development of the blockchain technology within the MediaVerse platform remained at a proof of concept level, the testing sessions held were of a theoretical evaluative nature. To this aim, a set of small-scale focus groups with experts in the different AVT and MA modalities were favoured to allow for a higher interaction among participants. Three focus groups involving active professionals in the different modalities of AVT and MA were organised between January and April 2023.[3]

The evaluation procedure was designed following social science qualitative research methods (Bryman, 2021). The structure of the sessions was the same for all groups and lasted a maximum of 90 min. First, an introduction on the MediaVerse project and its aims was provided. Second, a short introduction about the methodological approach for the use of blockchain technology as part of the MediaVerse platform to manage moral and economic copyrights was explained (see Fig. 1). Finally, a set of questions were posed to participants for discussion.

At the end of the session, an online questionnaire was sent to participants. It included an open question related to the possible use of the MediaVerse platform in their working context, and a list of the possible MediaVerse blockchain-based solutions that could apply to the fields of AVT and MA. The main objectives of these focus groups were to first gather and analyse data from users to understand the existing workflow for production, distribution, and monetisation of digital assets in their fields. And second, to gain information about professionals' needs and expectations

---

[3] Ethical clearance was previously obtained by the UAB Ethical Committee and ethical procedures were strictly followed to ensure compliance with EU existing regulations and codes of conduct.

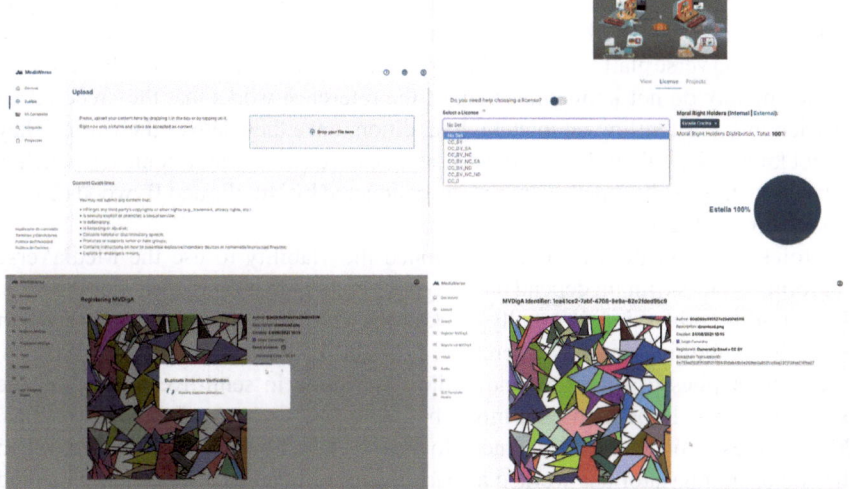

Fig. 1 MediaVerse blockchain-based registration of digital assets

of the blockchain technology to manage copyrights of digital assets in their working contexts.

3.1.1 Demographics

In terms of demographics, there were three groups. The first group consisted of five audiovisual translation professionals in the subtitling field. The second group consisted of five media accessibility professionals working in different modalities (AD, SDH, live subtitling, and subtitling for the scenic arts). Finally, the third group consisted of four professionals in video game localisation and accessibility. All participants reported to be active professionals in their corresponding field. They were all based in Spain, with Spanish/Catalan as their main target languages.

The mean reported technological skills were "advanced". The mean reported level of knowledge about copyright management and IP was "medium", and the mean reported level of knowledge about blockchain was "low".

3.1.2 Extracted Conclusions

Question 1: *[Do you think that the MediaVerse platform could be used in the professional world of translation and/or audiovisual translation? Does it have any advantage over the current way of managing the different modalities of AVT and accessibility in the media?]*

In the case of professionals in the AVT field, most participants reported managing their copyrights through the Spanish organisation DAMA. Still, participants, agreed that the MediaVerse platform would be especially relevant in the case of film festivals, as they mainly do not know the origin of the reference works that they receive for translation (i.e. subtitling templates). In addition, once they deliver their work, they do not know where their delivered work will be used (i.e. country/context), which is in line with the results reported by a study conducted by Nikolic and Bywood (2021), reported in Sect. 2.1.

Professionals in the MA field questioned the viability to use the MediaVerse platform, as the use might depend on the type of content to be uploaded. For instance, live subtitling professionals usually work in the abstract, as various people are part of the live subtitling process. Therefore, it might be difficult to assign copyrights. The same applies to subtitling and audio description in semi-live events, i.e. the performing arts. In both cases it might be due to the "ephemeral nature" (Oncins, 2015) of these works, as there is a need to modify them for each performance. When the author or translator has worked as part of a crowdsourced effort, their input and therefore degree of ownership is less clear (Moorkens & Lewis, 2019). In the case of audio description (AD), copyrights are in a grey area and copyright management might differ depending on the country. For instance, while AD in Spain is not eligible for copyright, in other European countries such as France and Germany authors can claim copyrights in AD.

Finally, professionals working in the video game localisation and accessibility field reported that it might be difficult to use this platform in the environment of large video game developers (Triple A). This fact is mainly due to the existence of non-disclosure agreements (NDAs) or "observance of copyright laws" (Bernal-Merino, 2007: 2). At the same time, then according to participants, the platform could be used in the context of "indie" games that usually work with smaller budgets and with decentralised workflows, as no central platform is used to manage the assets.

Question 2: *[Within the framework of accessibility and audiovisual translation files (i.e. media accessibility assets) rights management, authors have the moral right over the assets they create. This can never be sold. Thus, assets should be somehow "watermarked" for moral ownership. Do you agree?]*

According to professionals in the AVT field, authors should have the moral right over the asset they create. This is something that has been achieved in the last years mainly thanks to the work conducted by professional associations in the AVT sector, such as ATRAE and DAMA in the case of Spain.

In contrast, professionals in the field of MA working on accessibility services such as AD and SDH do not receive the corresponding recognition of the moral rights over the assets they create, as these are not considered literary creations. Therefore, they do not have the right to claim the authorship of such assets. Even if participants in the MA field reported an improvement in recent years on the recognition of the works that they create, they also reported that most times users do not even consider that there is a professional person behind the generation of the corresponding accessibility services. This might be due to the increasing use of speech recognition technologies along with automation processes, especially in the different types of subtitling (live, semi-live, and pre-recorded), a fact that poses a major challenge in terms of copyright recognition. As such, the ownership of subtitles created through an automatic speech recognition technology remains unclear. There is no specific legal framework considering such issues; "it is necessary to apply the general principles related to authorship and transfer of rights" (Debussche & Troussel, 2014: 103).

Finally, all participants working in video game localisation and accessibility reported that moral rights of their works should always be recognised. This is a claim that has been around in the sector for years, especially through social media campaigns like #TranslatorsInTheCredits.[4] Some agencies do not allow professionals to even mention the titles of the video games they work on. In addition, there is also a lack of recognition of other agents involved in the localisation process, such as reviewers and "testers".

Question 3: *[Should authors be able to establish the economic rights and rights of exploitation?]*

Most participants in AVT reported to be sceptical in relation with establishing both economic and exploitation rights. The reason behind this might be related to the problem of monetising the works they deliver. This seems to be unattainable for participants due to the contracts they have to sign with the agencies/clients in relation with the economical exploitation of the assets they create, which is in line with research reported by Moorkens and Lewis (2019). However, participants agreed that authors should be involved in the negotiations to establish the exploitation rights of their works, also depending on the foreseen reuse. In the case of MA participants, it was reported that economic and exploitation rights might have a short term.

This may be due to the fact that productions, especially in the performing arts, are limited and subject to modifications. Therefore, most professionals in this modality do not register their works. In the case of participants in video game localisation, it was reported that economic and exploitation rights should be agreed at a joint level among all agents involved in the localisation process, which, contrary to other more traditional AVT modalities, is more iterative (Bernal-Merino, 2007; Mangiron, 2018). An additional problem reported in this field was that the localisation of videogames is considered a work derived from the "computer industry" and does not generate exploitation rights.

Finally, an important question raised by participants in the field of video games localisation was also the creative nature of their works. According to participants, the creativity in videogames localisation can be often greater than in the subtitling or dubbing of audiovisual products.

---

[4] https://slator.com/online-movement-pushes-that-translators-be-named-in-game-credits/.

3.2 Satisfaction Questionnaire

At the end of the session, an online questionnaire was sent to participants. The first question was related to the possible use of the MediaVerse platform in their professional contexts. In this regard, 75% of participants replied positively and 25% replied "maybe". It needs to be stressed that participants reporting "maybe" could be due to their superficial knowledge of the project, as the aim of the focus group remained at a theoretical level. The reported common advantages of the MediaVerse platform in relation with copyright management across the different groups were mainly the benefit of easy-to-share content, not depending on large companies, as well as decentralisation and easy access for everyone, ensuring that the generated content is always available and authorship can always be recognised. This could also allow giving control back to creators over their own content. Therefore, copyright management could be structured in a more systematic way, as the platform allows you to monitor your own work (and trace it: who acquires it, who modifies it, etc.).

Conversely, reported common disadvantages of the MediaVerse platform in relation to copyright management across the different groups were the challenge to "recruit" a broad group of users. In most cases, clients require a more traditional way to handle copyrights. Copyright management conflicts with the commercial interests of many companies. Questions related to bureaucracy and excessive commodification of intellectual authorship were also reported as downsides.

At the end of the questionnaire, a final question was included with the different blockchain-based solutions for copyright management envisaged within the MediaVerse project. Participants were asked to rate their relevance in relation with their working contexts. Aggregated data from all focus groups are presented in Table 1.

According to reported results, the most relevant blockchain-based solutions were copyright management, attribution, and decentralisation. In terms of copyright management and attribution through blockchain, this technology is considered relevant as it enables content owners to directly attribute copyrights and manage their works. Thus, it might increase the visibility and availability of their works. Finally, the importance of working in a decentralised digital content ecosystem allows for returning power and ownership to creators.

4 Conclusion

The trend in the use of technologies in AVT is expected to increase in the coming years, and will clearly have an impact on AVT, as it is a sector that has so far been eminently artisanal (Oncins, 2022). As highlighted by Kenny (2022: 33), "audiovisual content is thus becoming just the latest in a long line of commercial products whose markets can be expanded through machine translation". In this regard, the question of copyright management is considered a common problem across the

Table 1 Summary of reported replies on the relevance of blockchain-based solutions in AVT and MA

	1	2	3	4	5	I don't know	Mean	Standard deviation	Median
Decentralised digital content ecosystem: power and ownership return to creators									
Number of replies	0	0	0	5	7	2	4.58	0.51	5.00
New pricing options: new options for creators to earn by selling content									
Number of replies	0	1	1	6	5	1	4.15	0.90	4.00
Monetisation of content: content creators can establish direct relationships with customers									
Number of replies	0	2	2	3	7	0	4.07	1.14	4.50
Distribution of royalty payments: near real-time payments based on smart contracts									
Number of replies	0	1	4	5	4	0	3.86	0.95	4.00
From digital rights management (DRM) to smart contracts: transparent and "self-execute" right management underlying smart contracts									
Number of replies	0	0	4	6	4	0	4.00	0.78	4.00
Attribution: blockchain increases the visibility and availability of the information regarding copyright ownership									
Number of replies	0	0	1	4	8	1	4.54	0.66	5.00
Copyright management: blockchain enables content owners to directly manage their works									
Number of replies	0	0	1	3	9	1	4.62	0.65	5.00

different AVT and MA modalities. Both fields are moving towards a cloud-based environment with an increasing number of technologies involved in the process to reach a faster and more cost-effective work. Still, the question of copyright recognition and effective management remains unsolved.

According to gathered results from the study, while the mean reported level of "technological skills" was advanced, the mean reported level of knowledge about blockchain technology was "low". This means that the potential of blockchain technology remains unknown to most professionals. It is important to highlight that blockchain technology is expected to be crucial in the new decentralised Web 3.0 environment, and it could also prove to be an effective tool for fair and collaborative copyright management. This is especially relevant because, while workflows in all modalities are moving towards the cloud, the creativity and reuse of existing works are neither traced nor always protected with copyrights, at least in the Spanish context.

This fact is directly related to copyright management, as the reported level of knowledge about copyrights was medium. It seems that professionals do not to always have a clear idea of the rights they generate, especially in MA. The recognition of moral rights might have a direct impact on the reputation of all professionals in these fields. In this regard, the role of associations to promote the recognition of copyrights is crucial, particularly in the case of MA and video game localisation.

The MediaVerse platform is considered particularly relevant for the copyright management of small and medium-sized enterprises (SMEs) and freelancers. While technologies are available, there are no existing platforms that allow for an easy-to-use management of the copyrights. In Web 3.0, decentralisation is one of the key aspects, along with authorship. The way new emerged technologies are increasingly being used, and the way in which they are merging in the different AVT and MA fields, should ensure a fairer ecosystem for professionals in these fields.

It should be stressed that copyright management in the digital media value chain differs across countries. The results gathered from this series of focus groups are limited to the Spanish context, as most participants were active professionals and/or academics in this country. Further research needs to be conducted not only in other countries but should include other sectors/industries involved in content production, media preparation, content distribution, monetisation, and consumption of digital media assets, in relation with the use of blockchain for the copyright management of digital media assets.

Acknowledgements This chapter is based upon work from COST Action CA19142—Leading Platform for European Citizens, Industries, Academia and Policymakers in Media Accessibility (LEAD-ME) supported by COST (European Cooperation in Science and Technology).

Disclaimer This article has been partially funded by the TransMedia Catalonia research group through the SGR funding scheme (Catalan Government funds 2021SGR00077, Xarxa AccessCat (2021XARDI00007), MediaVerse (957252), GreenScent (101036480), and ClearClimate (101131220).

References

Bernal-Merino, M. A. (2007). Challenges in the translation of video game. *Tradumàtica: traducció i tecnologies de la informació i la comunicació, 5.* https://raco.cat/index.php/Tradumatica/art icle/view/75761

Bryman, A. (2021). *Social research methods* (6th ed.). Oxford University Press.

Diaz-Cintas, J., & Massidda, S. (2019). Technological advances in audiovisual translation. In M. O'Hagan (Ed.), *The Routledge handbook of translation and technology* (pp. 255–270). Routledge.

European Commission, Directorate-General for Translation, Debussche, J., Troussel, J. (2014). In J. Debussche, & J. Troussel (Eds.), *Translation and intellectual property rights—Final report.* Publications Office, 2014. https://doi.org/10.2782/72107

Greco, G. M. (2016). On accessibility as a human right, with an application to media accessibility. In A. Matamala, & P. Orero (Eds.), *Researching audio description. New approaches* (pp. 11–33). Palgrave Macmillan.

Kenny, D. (Ed.). (2022). *Machine translation for everyone: Empowering users in the age of artificial intelligence.* Language Science Press. (Translation and Multilingual Natural Language Processing, 18). https://doi.org/10.5281/zenodo.6653406

Mangiron, C. (2007). Video games localisation: Posing new challenges to the translator. *Perspectives, 14*(4), 306–323. https://doi.org/10.1080/09076760708669046

Mangiron, C. (2018). Game on! Burning issues in game localisation. *Journal of Audiovisual Translation, 1*(1), 122–138. https://doi.org/10.47476/jat.v1i1.48

Margoni, T. (2016). The harmonisation of EU copyright law: The originality standard. In M. Perry (Ed.), *Global governance of intellectual property in the 21st century: Reflecting policy through change* (pp. 85–105). Springer.

Matamala, A. (2019). *Accessibilitat i traducció audiovisual.* Vic: Eumo Editorial

Mejías-Climent, L. (2021). Between audiovisual translation and localization: The case of Detroit: Become Human. In Mario Bisiada (Ed.), *Empirical studies in translation and discourse* (pp. 199–219). Language Science Press. https://doi.org/10.5281/zenodo.4450093

Moorkens, J., & Lewis, D. (2019). Copyright and the reuse of translation as data. In M. O'Hagan (Ed.), *The Routledge handbook of translation and technology. Routledge translation handbooks* (pp. 469–481). ISBN 9781138232846.

Nikolic, K., & Bywood, L. (2021). Audiovisual translation: The road ahead. *JAT: Journal of Audiovisual Translation, 4*(1), 50–70. https://doi.org/10.47476/jat.v4i1.2021.156

O'Brien, S. (2012). Translation as human–computer interaction. *Translation Spaces, 1*(1), 101–122.

Oncins, E. (2015). The tyranny of the tool: Surtitling live performances. *Perspectives, 23*(1), 42–61. https://doi.org/10.1080/0907676X.2013.793374

Oncins, E. (2022). Traducció automàtica: La tecnologia (in)visible de la traducció audiovisual. *Revista Tradumàtica. Tecnologies de la Traducció, 20,* 302–311. https://doi.org/10.5565/rev/tradumatica.317

Orero, P. (2020). Born accessibility as a way towards normalisation and inclusion of all citizens in a democratic and participatory society. In *International conference for the promotion of educational innovation,* vol. 6, 2020. https://ddd.uab.cat/record/234303

Orero, P., Fernández-Torner, A., & Oncins, E. (2023). The visible subtitler: Blockchain technology towards right management and minting. *Open research Europe.* https://doi.org/10.12688/openreseurope.15166.1

Oziemblewska, M., & Szarkowska, A. (2022). The quality of templates in subtitling: A survey on current market practices and changing subtitler competences. *Perspectives: Studies in Translation Theory and Practice, 30*(3), 432–453. https://doi.org/10.1080/0907676X2020.1791919

Qureshi, A., & Megías Jiménez, D. (2021). Blockchain-based multimedia content protection: Review and open challenges. *Applied Sciences, 11*(1), 1.

Serrat-Roozen, I. (2023). Accessibility and standards in online subtitling: From quantity to quality in making videos accessible. In C. Pena Díaz (Ed.), *The making of accessible audiovisual translation* (pp. 107–126). Peter Lang.

Serrat-Roozen, I., & Oncins, E. (2023). Towards a decentralized solution for copyrights management in audiovisual translation and media accessibility. In *Proceedings of the international conference HiT-IT 2023,* pp. 177–187, 7–9 July 2023, Naples, Italy. https://hit-it-conference.org/wp-content/uploads/2023/07/HiT-IT-2023-proceedings.pdf

Tong King, L. (2020). Translation and copyright: Towards a distributed view of originality and authorship. *The Translator, 26*(3), 241–256. https://doi.org/10.1080/13556509.2020.1836770

The Inclusivity of Art in City Space. Activities of Researchers from the University of Lodz to Support People with Sensory Disabilities. A Case Study from Lodz (Poland)

Aneta Pawłowska[iD], **Adam Drozdowski**[iD], **Magdalena Milerowska**[iD], and **Paulina Długosz**[iD]

Abstract Projects dedicated to addressing the accessibility of art for visually impaired individuals have been conducted at the Institute of Art History, University of Lodz, since 2013. This chapter focuses on four projects realized in collaboration with local museums, all aiming to support the full participation of people with sensory disabilities in culture. These projects employ digital technology, as well as dedicated typhlographics, Braille books, and spatial objects. Additionally, lectures, meetings, trips, and movie showings are interpreted into sign language. Such initiatives align with the positive changes brought by the Polish Accessibility Act. The most significant projects include "Lodz Art Against the Background of European Art. Excluded/Included" (2019–2022) and "Friendly City. Supporting the Independence of Visually Impaired People in Using the Public Transport Network in Lodz," which includes an application for locational information and local architectural monuments (2021–2024). Both projects are funded by the National Center for Research and Development. Drawing from years of research experience, this chapter presents various methods and forms of using both tactile and digital tools to support audio description.

Keywords Lodz · Inclusive accessibility · Museums · Audio description

A. Pawłowska (✉) · A. Drozdowski · M. Milerowska
Institute of Art History, University of Lodz, Lodz, Poland
e-mail: aneta.pawlowska@uni.lodz.pl

A. Drozdowski
e-mail: adam.drozdowski@uni.lodz.pl

M. Milerowska
e-mail: magdalena.milerowska@uni.lodz.pl

P. Długosz
Museum of the City of Lodz, Lodz, Poland

1   Introduction

Between 2019 and 2022, the International Council of Museums (ICOM) undertook efforts to develop a new definition of a museum. This new definition expands the scope of these institutions' activities and sets new guiding principles for fulfilling their statutory missions. Key aspects of this new vision include openness to multi-culturalism, participation, and activities promoting sustainable development. These principles significantly influence exhibition formats and the accompanying linguistic narratives in contemporary museums. Additionally, one of the most important tasks for museology in the twenty-first century has been established: ensuring broad accessibility to cultural heritage for all audiences, including individuals with various disabilities ("Report on the ICOM Member Feedback for a new museum definition. Independent analysis & report elaborated for the ICOM Define Committee", 2021).

Contemporary museum activity strategies have evolved in response to positive social changes related to equality and social inclusion, as well as legal and statutory regulations that recommend or mandate specific solutions.The most important Polish legal acts supporting people with various needs in equal access to socio-economic life and cultural goods are: the Charter of the Rights of Persons with Disabilities (1997) ("Karta Praw Osób Niepełnosprawnych", 1997), the UN Convention on the Rights of Persons with Disabilities (2006) ("Karta Praw Osób Niepełnosprawnych", 1997), ratified in Poland in 2012, and the Recommendation CM/Rec 14 of the Committee of Ministers for Member States on the participation of disabled people in political and public life ("Zalecenie CM/Rec(2011)14 Komitetu Ministrów dla państw członkowskich w sprawie uczestnictwa osób niepełnosprawnych w życiu politycznym i publicznym z dn. 16 listopada 2011 r., 2011").

A new perspective in developing solutions for a diverse group of museum visitors is the increasingly widespread use of the principles of universal design principles in the field of architecture (Kuryłowicz, 1995) and various spheres of social life (Błaszczak & Przybylski, 2010). In Poland, the importance of universal design was affirmed by the "Act of July 19, 2019, on Ensuring Accessibility for People with Special Needs." This act officially mandated the use of universal design solutions and required all public entities to ensure accessibility in architecture, digital information, and communication. A direct outcome of this legislation is the government program "Accessibility Plus," which led to the implementation of several initiatives. One such initiative is the research grant "Friendly City: Supporting the Independence of People with Visual Impairments in Using the Public Transport Network in Lodz," which includes applications for location information and local architectural monuments.

Literature and source materials regarding contact with and reception of works of art by people with disabilities can be divided into three categories:

• **Publications and scientific studies**: Among the most important publications related to the theoretical aspect of research on the reception of works of art are: Maria Poprzęcka, *Inne obrazy: oko, widzenie, sztuka. Od Albertiego do*

Duchampa, (Poprzęcka, 2009); Georges Didi-Huberman, *Devant l'image: question posée aux fins d'une histoire de l'art*, (Didi-Huberman, 1990); Rudolf Arnheim, *Art and Visual Perception. A Psychology of a Creative Eye*, (Arnheim, 1990); Freeman Tilden, *Interpreting our heritage*, (Freeman, 2007). The idea that knowledge allows one to see is also present in the texts of an iconic avant-garde artist who worked in Lodz, Władysław Strzemiński, who emphasized the role of thought, experience and visual awareness being the result of the development of society (Strzemiński, 1969).

- **Legal and normative acts and government recommendations**, which officially introduce the requirement to use universal design solutions, as well as the introduction by all public entities of architectural, digital and information and communication accessibility. A vital part of this group of publications are also the documents issued by International Council of Museums (ICOM) and International Council on Monuments and Historic Sites (ICOMOS). Among them, particularly important documents include the ICOM *Code of Ethics for Museums* and the ICOMOS *Charter for the Interpretation and Presentation of Cultural Heritage*.
- **Reports, statistical summaries and training materials**, which in Poland are issued by National Institute for Museums (NIMOZ) and foundations supporting people with disabilities (i.e., *Audiodeskrypcja* foundation based in Białystok, Poland).

The chapter is structured as follows: Section 2 regards the history of research conducted at the University of Lodz, it shows the background for more recent and currently developed projects. Sections 3 and 4 describe activities undertaken in the "Art from Lodz Against the Background of European Art" and "Friendly City projects", focusing on their goals, methods of achieving them, eventual challenges and difficulties faced by both organizers and beneficiaries. Section 5 considers the Industrial Doctorate realized in cooperation with the Museum of the City of Lodz, as a way of building theoretical foundations for further development of methods of making art and information more available to users with various impairments. The chapter is ended with a conclusion and clear recommendations regarding making historic buildings available to people with special needs.

2   History of Research and Worked Out Solutions

The "Friendly City" project is one of the activities undertaken at the Institute of Art History of the University of Lodz, in the field of making art accessible to people with visual impairments. Before presenting the basic concepts, it is essential to highlight the preliminary solutions piloted in Lodz and its region. It is also important to note that all developed approaches were consistently consulted with the final beneficiaries— people with sensory disabilities—as well as museum curators and educators. Key questions addressed during the implementation of all accessibility projects include:

- What and how should we, as a society, but also scientists, do to make social inclusion even greater?
- What kind of message would be full and clear for people with non-standard needs?
- How to make it easy to convey, but also to understand?
- What makes it modern and suitable for the twenty-first century?

Research into ways of supporting people with visual disabilities began at the University of Lodz in the academic year 2013/2014 as part of the course "Audio Description of Works of Art" under the supervision of Prof. Aneta Pawłowska from the Department of Art History of the University of Lodz. During the classes, a group of students, in consultation with blind audio describer Barbara Szymańska from the "Audiodekrypcja" Foundation in Białystok, prepared a description of the key space of the Museum of Art in Lodz, the Neoplastic Room designed by Władysław Strzemiński in 1948. Separate descriptions were made for the artistic objects exhibited within. The course was intended to introduce the topic of verbal description of works of art, so that it meets the needs of people with advanced visual impairment (i.e., audio description of artistic objects) to the interest of art historians (Pawłowska, 2015). The classes conducted in subsequent years were carried out using the project method in cooperation with local cultural institutions (Museum of Art in Lodz, Museum of the City of Lodz, Museum of the Factory in Manufaktura, Museum of Independence Traditions). The classes' main goal was to familiarize students with the principles of making art accessible to people with visual impairments, with particular emphasis on the ability to create audio descriptions. For students, it was also an opportunity to learn about the realities of work in institutions that could be their potential places of employment. During classes, working in groups, they tested their skills in practice and consolidated the acquired knowledge in the field of history of art and the region.

The following academic year, another group of students prepared audio descriptions for the second branch of the Museum of Art in Lodz-ms2. The institution boasts one of the world's oldest publicly exhibited collections of modern art. A key part of the collection are works of art that are non-figurative. Working with paintings seemingly devoid of narrative made students aware of the importance of using precise vocabulary while creating descriptions, but above all, the need for constant consultations and gaining feedback on the effects of their work from people with visual impairments. Since the beginning of research and implementation of activities related to audio description, the Institute of Art History of the University of Lodz has been continuously cooperating with local associations of visually impaired people. The regularly organized meetings highlight the significant role that emotions play in the perception of a work of art. This emphasizes the challenging task of an audio describer, who must verbally convey colors and the relationships between elements in a composition. The goal is to enable people with visual impairments to achieve a comprehensive perception of the artwork, rather than merely becoming superficially familiar with its appearance. (Drozdowski & Pawłowska, 2019).

While implementing projects, prepared descriptions are not limited to sculptures or paintings. This diversity was particularly visible in the case of the project carried out at the Museum of the City of Lodz, located in the former palace of the Poznański family. In 2015, students worked on descriptions of the interiors and their furnishing elements (e.g., furniture, fireplaces, decorations, everyday items, etc.), supporting the "Museum at Your Fingertips" project (2015), created as part of the "Accessible Culture" program of the Ministry of Culture and National Heritage. The aim of the activities was to adapt the Museum of the City of Lodz for the use of people with non-standard needs.

To promote the active and independent participation of people with visual impairments in engaging with art, researchers from the University of Lodz developed a special mobile application for the private Factory Museum located in the Lodz shopping and entertainment center, Manufaktura. The application's task is to help future users navigate the facility. The project was developed in collaboration with three faculties of the University of Lodz: the Faculty of Philosophy and History, the Faculty of Philology, and the Faculty of Physics and Applied Computer Science. This interdisciplinary cooperation resulted in a guidance system with dedicated audio descriptions. The solution was repeatedly evaluated by the final beneficiaries—people with various visual impairments and histories of eyesight loss. It is based on a mobile application and a system of guiding markers (beacons), which enable visually impaired visitors to independently explore urban spaces or exhibitions by directing them to specific locations and describing the appearance of these spaces or objects (Fig. 1). Although the audio description has been prepared, and the application developed, it turned out to be too expensive for the privately owned museum to commercialize. This highlights that financial constraints can sometimes prevent the implementation of prepared solutions, either entirely or partially, depending on the decisions of private owners. Solutions like this can be used by all people using a smartphone or smartwatch application. The application was supposed to be free, and was prepared as compatible with both IOS and Android environments (Drozdowski et al., 2019). This project called "I See Because I Hear: audio description—contemporary support for people with visual impairments in contact with art" was awarded at the INTARG 2020 International Fair of Economic and Scientific Innovations (Drozdowski et al., 2019).

The key conclusions drawn from projects that supported Lodz museologists with human resources, recruited from art history students at the University of Lodz, were twofold. First, it is essential to sensitize audio describers to the critical importance of well-constructed verbal descriptions. Second, the subjective input of people with visual disabilities is invaluable when consulting on these descriptions of works of art. The experiences and recommendations for proceeding with the above activities were presented in the academic textbook by Aneta Pawłowska and Julia Sowińska-Heim entitled "Audio Description of Works of Art. Methods, Problems, Examples" (Pawłowska & Sowińska-Heim, 2016).

Fig. 1 Screenshots of the application. The first one guides viewers to the next object on the exhibition tour, and the second shows part of the audio description prepared

3 "Art from Lodz Against the Background of European Art"

As part of the Operational Program Knowledge Education Development 2014–2020, which is financed by the EU, a team of employees of the Institute of Art History of the University of Lodz and the Museum of the City of Lodz, made an attempt at answering the question: How to encourage the viewer to have more frequent and open contact with museums and art?

The goal of the project "Art from Lodz Against the Background of European art. Excluded/Included" POWR.03.01.00-00-T141/18 (project director—Aneta Pawłowska) was to familiarize recipients from the Lodz Voivodeship, seniors and school youth with visual or hearing impairments, with issues related to broadly understood visual arts (paintings, sculptures, installations, murals and objects of decorative art) and architecture (Pawłowska & Długosz, 2020). The activities were aimed at disseminating regional cultural heritage among non-standard higher education recipients.[1] In the project, it was important to take action in the context of the current and, above all, projected demographic situation of the voivodeship's population. Data collected in June 2023 shows that over 600,000 people living in the area are senior citizens. The last data on people with disabilities collected in 2021, shows

---

[1] For the purpose of the article, authors use this term to describe senior students (after 60—retirement age in Poland) and students with various disabilities. The term is correlated with Polish standards and practice of long life learning (Kukła & Duda, 2020).

that almost 400,000 declared legal or biological disability.[2] The project, carried out from February 2019 to September 2022 involved 693 people with visual, hearing and other disabilities from the Lodz Voivodeship. In the additional, fourth year (until September 30, 2023), another 219 people were invited to the project, and the group of beneficiaries was expanded to include cultural animators.

To better illustrate the phenomena, concepts, and characteristics of different eras, beneficiaries had access to typhlographics (graphic reliefs made using the thermoforming technique) that depicted buildings, architectural details, and other related aspects of Lodz and European architecture. These typhlographics became one of the most important tools for understanding monuments. A crucial factor in presenting buildings through typhlographics is selecting an appropriate façade that is both characteristic and visually identifiable with the landmark. When describing architecture, it is also important to present the monument's floor plan, typically limited to the ground floor. However, for twentieth and twenty-first-century architecture, where floor layouts can vary significantly, it is beneficial to illustrate a combination of several floors. Additionally, three volumes of the textbook series "Lodz Art in Europe, European Art in Lodz" were developed (Pawłowska & Długosz, 2021, 2022a, 2022b). The publications were done in enlarged black print, correlated with dot notation in Braille. Each volume is divided into several shorter topics, discussing important phenomena and styles in art, as well as selected artists. Individual topics are complemented by audio descriptions adjacent to full-page, colorful, convex graphics (typhlographics) (Fig. 2).

The participants significantly improved their qualifications in contact with art and knowledge of the language used to describe works of art. They also strengthened their life skills, such as special orientation or overcoming communication barriers and improved their Polish. The participants generally stated that their involvement in the project boosted their knowledge on art and culture. This was also measured by using pre-tests and post-tests in which outcomes (in the first year of the project duration) are presented on graphs (Figs. 3 and 4).

The activities developed in the project showed how, without interfering with the fabric of the monument, and with a small financial outlay, it is possible to bring the recipient closer to the work of art. One of the alternative forms, which does not interfere with the structure of the building and allows for getting to know it, is using audio description (written or recorded in Polish Sign Language) combined (or standing alone) with typhlographics. The correlated impact on hearing and touching enables visually impaired people to have significant access to architectural monuments. This may be particularly important in the broader context of independent exploration of art, which goes beyond the competence of museums or galleries.

---

[2] The statistics are available at Statistics Poland (GUS) website: [stat.gov.pl]. Statistics from previous years were published in (Kaleta & Matysiak, 2018) and (Cmela, 2014).

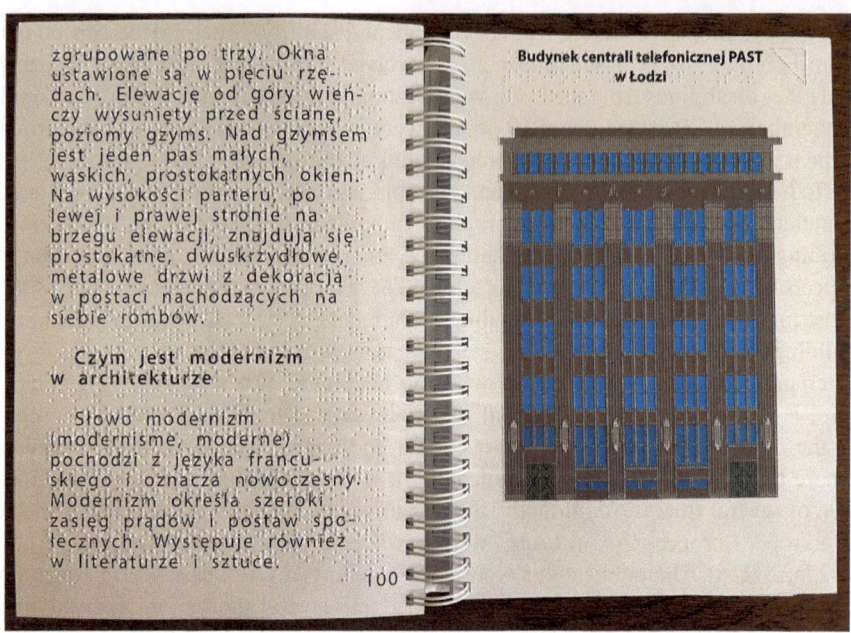

zgrupowane po trzy. Okna
ustawione są w pięciu rzę-
dach. Elewację od góry wień-
czy wysunięty przed ścianę,
poziomy gzyms. Nad gzymsem
jest jeden pas małych,
wąskich, prostokątnych okien.
Na wysokości parteru, po
lewej i prawej stronie na
brzegu elewacji, znajdują się
prostokątne, dwuskrzydłowe,
metalowe drzwi z dekoracją
w postaci nachodzących na
siebie rombów.

**Czym jest modernizm
w architekturze**

Słowo modernizm
(modernisme, moderne)
pochodzi z języka francu-
skiego i oznacza nowoczesny.
Modernizm określa szeroki
zasięg prądów i postaw społecznych. Występuje również
w literaturze i sztuce.

100

Budynek centrali telefonicznej PAST
w Łodzi

Fig. 2 Examplary pages from the "Lodz Art in Europe, European Art in Lodz" textbook, show-casing the topic: "What is modernism in architecture?" and a correlated typhlographic of the PAST telephone exchange building, 1928

4 The "Friendly City" Project—Boosting Activity

The project "Friendly City. Supporting the independence of people with visual impairments in the use of the public transport network in Lodz, including applications regarding location information and local architectural monuments" (implementation 2021–2024, grant holder Aneta Pawłowska) is a joint effort of employees of the Institute of Art History of the University of Lodz and the University of Social Sciences and Humanities in Warsaw (SWPS). The main goal of the project is to improve the accessibility of cultural heritage for people with visual impairments, focusing on the space of the historic city with unique 19th-century buildings. The main aim of the project is to develop an application that makes it easier for the visually impaired people to navigate around Lodz, but it will also be dedicated to foreign tourists (available languages: Polish, English, Spanish and Ukrainian). In Poland, people with vision problems have significant difficulties in moving around and visiting or exploring cities on their own. In result, they are not fully independent, nor do they enjoy much aesthetic experiences. The appearance of eclectic monuments or whole building complexes and its urban context seem particularly difficult to perceive by people with visual impairments.

Lodz is the first city affected, but also treated as a pilot center. The scalability of IT solutions will allow them to be introduced in other European cities (e.g., within

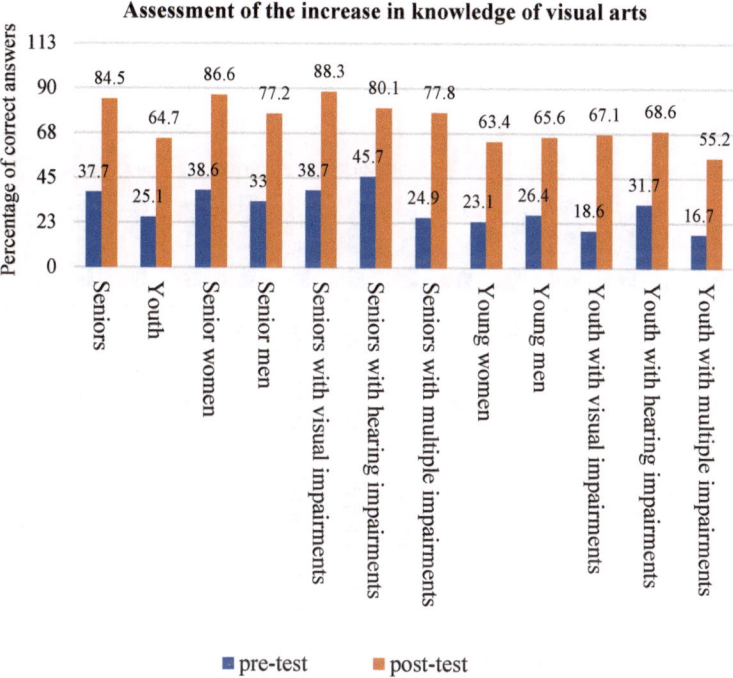

Fig. 3 Graphs showing assessment of growth of knowledge, measured by using pre- and post-tests

the prestigious group of universities associated with the European University of Post-industrial Cities (UNIC) network, of which the University of Lodz is a member).

It is important to note the variety of level of accessibility among the historic buildings in Lodz. The ones that are best prepared for visiting by visitors with disabilities are currently, primarily museums and galleries. In the project however, the area of interest of scholars was wider and included buildings and whole complexes, that are characteristic of the urban fabric and represent a wide range of public utility, not only relating to culture. These include 19th-century tenement houses, former industrialists' palaces, churches, but also buildings erected in recent years, such as the Fabryczna Railway Station or the EC1 complex.

The combination of experience in creating audio description and eye-tracker research (oculograph) (Krejtz et al., 2024), in which effects will be presented in a form of a free application for smartphones, smartwatches and other devices in the IoS and Android environment is intended to increase the level of independence in mobility and experiencing cultural goods, and set to break the current barriers of visually impaired people in the field of tourism. Application users will receive precise voice messages regarding location and information on selected objects through their own devices. The final product will contain five paths with the most interesting objects that can be visited "from the level of a passer-by". One of the functions prepared

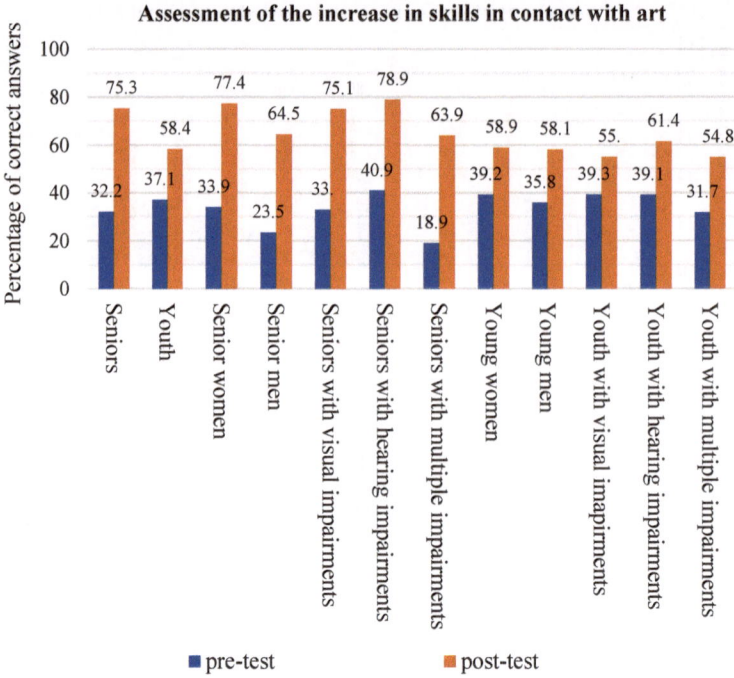

Assessment of the increase in skills in contact with art

Fig. 4 Graphs showing assessment of growth of skills, measured by using pre- and post-tests

for users will be the ability to independently create routes with their favorite objects (Pawłowska et al., 2023a, 2023b).

There will be over eighty historically and culturally interesting places on the map of Lodz, selected and described by art historians. All of them have been provided with an audio description consisting of the property's "bio", a detailed description of the style and architectural details, and additional information (fun facts and historical information related to a given place). The texts were prepared according to the established rules resulting from the principles of audio description, professional description of a work of art, the outcomes of eye-tracking tests and consultations with people with various visual impairments.

Participants of the consultations were members of the Polish Association of the Blind (PZN)—branch in Sieradz, the Lodz District—Lodz—Gorna Circle and the Municipal Circle No. 3 Lodz-Centrum. The consulting group was varied in terms of age, eye-sight loss history and educational background (Fig. 5.). Interviews with this target group have been conducted since the beginning of 2022 and have contributed a lot of important remarks to the development of audio descriptions. One of the problems was adapting the language of the descriptions to make it as understandable and as accessible as possible for those using the application. Many hours of conversations with people from PZN led to the selection of two solutions for constructing the audio description content. The first is providing given technical terms in the field of architecture (tympanum, pilaster, portal, etc.), with simple two- or three-word explanations in brackets. This solution freed people who were not sufficiently proficient in using the mobile application from searching for explanations in the resident dictionary program, and thus made the application easier to use and more thorough. The second proposed solution, which additionally enriches the application's functions, is a glossary explaining the more difficult terms broadly (Krejtz et al., 2023).

During the development of audio descriptions, numerous walks around Lodz were conducted. Testers, consisting of both sighted and visually impaired individuals, were recruited for the project to provide feedback on the clarity of the texts presented. During this process, sighted people wore eye trackers that recorded the movement of their eyemovements. Based on the tests, audio descriptions were created according to the hierarchy of points that most frequently attracted the participants' gaze. In the next stage of refining the descriptions, both versions (the one consulted with the Polish Association for the Blind (PZN) and the one based on the eye-tracking results) were read to visually impaired consultants. Their feedback on the usefulness of the audio descriptions was collected through a survey prepared by SWPS employees. (Pawłowska et al., 2023a, 2023b).

Fig. 5 Consultation meeting for the early drafts of the application, 2023. Due to technological progress, mobile phones have become the basic tool for exploring space for the visually impaired. Hence, the authors notice that retirees are willing to engage in work on such applications. Although it is difficult to determine what percentage of the final users of the application will be seniors, they constitute a significant group that should not be forgotten when designing mobile solutions

The application will be coordinated with Totupoint navigation and information system (http://www.Totupoint.Pl/Strona.Php?Nazwa=start). The installation of the system's wireless tag network took place in the last quarter of 2023, but the list is still being supplemented. What is important the process is noninvasive, it does not interfere with the edifice's structure permanently (i.e., there is no need for drilling holes, the device can be mounted using a special adhesive tape) and does not significantly interfere with the visual sphere of objects. The tags were placed at both public transport stops, and the monuments indicated in the project. Within the principles of universal design, the developed system will be incorporated into the urban tourist infrastructure and public transport (buses, trams and stops). It is worth mentioning that the stage of preparing cooperation agreements with MPK (local public transport) and managers of buildings such as the Grand Theater, District Court or Fabryczna Railway Station caused the most difficulties. These problems were mainly issues of time-consuming bureaucracy, permissions for placing the devices on historical buildings had to be obtained from both current users or owners and the Provincial Office for the Protection of Monuments. However, in each of the places selected for the project, researchers met with a remarkably friendly reception and full support for the initiative. It should be added that a significant problem hindering the smooth implementation of the projects schedule are large-scale works in the center of Lodz, such as the prolonged renovation of Freedom Square, where several navigation and information devices are planned to be placed.

The finalization of project activities aims to address the main research question: how can the availability of architecture for all its recipients shape their attitudes toward it, and what new standards can be established for the dissemination of cultural goods? Lodz, a city reflecting the history of the 19th-century textile industry, has the potential to become an inclusive place, widely accessible to people with disabilities and tourists from abroad.

5 "The Industrial Doctorate"—Good Practices in Museology and Language

The implementation of the described projects was not only an opportunity to create specific tools and solutions supporting access to culture for the widest possible audience, but also paved the way for their permanent implementation in Polish cultural institutions. An attempt to further standardize and introduce said changes to the area of museum practice was conducted during the period October 2018–June 2023 as part of the doctoral studies in the second edition of the grant program of the Ministry of Science and Higher Education "Industrial Doctorate". The research work carried out was entitled "Assessment and verification of modern methods of translating the visual code of an art object and a historical object into a descriptive language in the educational space of a museum exhibition". Its main part was realized at the Museum of the City of Lodz—an interdisciplinary institution located in a former factory owner's residence, which is a symbol of the industrial city. The aim of the research project was to comprehensively implement a new methodology and accessibility standards for the design of language message systems in exhibition spaces. Reflections obtained through the implementation of the previously described university projects, as well as surveys with disabled beneficiaries conducted within them, allowed for the development of key research assumptions. The primary goal of the work was to analyze and verify the linguistic methods currently used in museum practice to support the perception and knowledge of a visual object ("Act of November 21, 1996, on museums", 1996),[3] which is an exhibit or a work of art. The assessment was carried out in terms of their effectiveness, compatibility with the competences of a modern recipient and accessibility in the case of recipients with special needs (including, above all, recipients with visual impairments and intellectual disabilities). The main research problem was an attempt to answer the question of what a universal formula of a linguistic message in a museum should look like, how can it fulfill not only informational or educational functions, but through its structure and method of communication could become a tool supporting the cultural and social inclusion of the recipient, and also implement the universal design requirements. The solution to the problem outlined above assumed the implementation of a number of projects in the scope of standard activities of the Museum of the City of Lodz, within which research (qualitative and quantitative) was carried out on the effectiveness of traditional and modern types of linguistic messages present in the space and educational activities of museum institutions. Research was conducted with the museum's audience (surveys, observations, interviews and eye tracking) in order to identify their needs and habits in terms of activities undertaken while visiting museum exhibitions and the attitudes they adopt when contacting a visual object. It should be emphasized that the direction of this research and some of the tools used to conduct it (including typhlographics and audio description texts assessed by respondents) were a direct result of the experience, conclusions and material results of previous projects of the University of Lodz. Their introduction into museum practice was carried out by preparing pilot (and later partial and main) solutions for the space of new permanent and temporary exhibitions (e.g., through leaflets accompanying exhibitions in the ETR—easy to read formula, audio descriptions, pre-guides) along with their evaluation (Długosz, 2022).

Then, based on the collected results, an improved system of methods and tools was prepared, which, after evaluation and pilot implementation, was standardized to become a formula that could also be used in other museums and cultural institutions. The final stage of implementation was the adoption at the Museum of the City of Lodz of "Standards for Communication and Information Accessibility in the Exhibition and Educational Spaces of the Museum of the City of Lodz", taking into account

---

[3] In the light of described research, a visual object may be treated as a museum object. According to Art. 21.1.: "museum objects are movable and immovable property owned by the museum and entered into the inventory of museum objects. Museum objects constitute a national asset", i.e., any item that enters museum collections. For the purposes of research work, this area has been narrowed down to works of art and historical objects (artifacts), the perception of which is largely or significantly based on their aesthetic features.

and specifying the solutions that turned out to be the most effective tools during the research [i.e., texts written in simple Polish in accordance with the principles of plain language (Piekot & Maziarz, 2014), which were recognized as the lowest common denominator of other language systems present in museum spaces], as well as the introduction of a system of linguistic messages that meet these principles to all permanent exhibition spaces.

6   Conclusions and Recommendations Regarding Making Historic Spaces, Buildings and Objects Available to People with Special Needs

The conclusions and experiences resulting from the projects described above, obtained during many years of research by scholars and museologists from Lodz, allowed for the development of a number of recommendations and good practices related to making cultural goods available to people with various needs. They can be described by determining three basic aspects of the activities undertaken in the fields of:

- **Cooperation**, in which it is vital to involve the future recipients of the designed solutions (including people with various degrees and types of disabilities), as well as the administrators or organizers responsible for the space provided (i.e., museums and exhibition institutions, private owners of historic buildings, representatives of city authorities, etc.).
- **Communication** (both during the implementation of the accessibility project and as an effect of its results), which assumes starting from the simplest and most accessible messages toward more advanced linguistic forms. Thanks to that, instead of adapting a previously prepared wide range of content, it should first be prepared in a simplified form (in accordance with the rules of simple Polish and using elements of ETR texts), and then developed into more extensive variants or adapted to specific information transmission channels (sound, e.g., audio description or visual, e.g., supplemented with translations into Polish sign language).
- **Polysensory**, thanks to which, depending on the needs of the respondents' various senses, they can freely and flexibly choose the most convenient solutions. An example may be the desire to integrate words and images, in example, by combining text and graphic content within tools supporting the tour (such as captions, boards and typhlographics). In this respect, exhibition plans or diagrams are particularly useful. They can be used to present in the form of a mind map the spatial arrangement of individual issues and thematic sequences within an exhibition or a more complex work of art. As research shows, the support most expected by the recipient from the linguistic narrative in the museum space is the ability to understand the material arrangement and the general curatorial concept of the exhibition, which is therefore read as an integrated, ordered message.

Considering the challenges of modern times and rapidly developing technologies, we would like to point out the potential of building digital accessibility, e.g., by creating dedicated applications, an example of which can be the activities for the Factory Museum in Manufaktura and the project "Friendly City. Supporting the independence of people with visual impairments in the use of the public transport network in Lodz, including applications regarding location information and local architectural monuments" described in this chapter. The implemented methods are particularly important because they do not interfere with the historic fabric of the building. Moreover, the use of this type of tools allows to explore monuments independently and frequently return to the content, which translates into deeper knowledge and satisfaction from gaining it. The digitally based methods are also easier to disseminate, standardize and optimize costs, which will translate into their universality and availability.

Acknowledgements Project titled "Art from Lodz Against the Background of European art. Excluded/Included" POWR.03.01.00-00-T141/18, co-financed by European Funds; implemented under the Knowledge Education Development Operational Program entitled "The Third Mission of the University"; competition no. POWR.03.01.00-IP.08-00-3MU/18, regarding the development of education programs and implementation of teaching activities, courses, training for non-standard higher education recipients under Priority Axis III: Higher Education for the Economy and Development; Action 3.1 Competences in higher education. The project is implemented by the University of Lodz in partnership with the Museum of the City of Lodz.

Project titled "Friendly City. Supporting the independence of people with visual impairments in the use of the public transport network in Lodz, considering the application regarding location information and local architectural monuments" Agreement No. Things are for people /0106/2020-00, implemented by the University of Lodz in partnership with SWPS University of Humanities and Social Sciences in Warsaw, project co-financed by European Funds.

Research project titled "Evaluation and verification of modern methods of translating the visual code of an art object and a historical object into a descriptive language in the educational space of a museum exhibition" carried out as part of the doctoral studies of the second edition of the grant program of the Minister of Science and Higher Education "Industrial Doctorate" (Agreement No. 0083/DW/2018/02 of November 28, 2018).

This chapter is based upon work from COST Action CA19142—Leading Platform for European Citizens, Industries, Academia and Policymakers in Media Accessibility (LEAD-ME) supported by COST (European Cooperation in Science and Technology)

References

Arnheim, R. (1990). *Art and visual perception*. University of California Press.
Błaszczak, M., & Przybylski, Ł. (2010). *Rzeczy są dla ludzi. Niepełnosprawność i idea uniwersalnego projektowania*. Wydawnictwo Naukowe.
Cmela, P., & Ryszard. (2014). *Niepełnosprawni w województwie łódzkim*. Zakłady Wydawnictw Statystycznych.
Didi-Huberman, G. (1990), *Devant l'image: question posée aux fins d'une histoire de l'art*. Editions de Minuit.
Długosz, P. (2022). The 21st-century Museum—in search of a space for the integration of image and word. *Art Inquiry. Recherches sur les Arts, 24*, 57–172.

Drozdowski, A., & Pawłowska, A. (2019). Audiodeskrypcja dzieł sztuki jako wsparcie osób niewidomych i słabowidzących w przestrzeni muzealne. *Problemy Edukacji, Rehabilitacji i Socjalizacji Osób Niepełnosprawnych, 28*(1), 73–88.

Drozdowski, A., Hłobaż, A., & Pawłowska, A. (2019). Audiodeskrypcja-przedmiot akademicki, praktyka muzealna czy wyzwanie dla informatyków? In *Osoby z niepełnosprawnością i sztuka. Udostępnianie—Percepcja—Integracja* (pp. 57–74). Uniwersytet Łódzki.

Freeman, T. (2007). *Interpreting our heritage.* University of North California Press.

http://www.totupoint.pl/strona.php?nazwa=start (n.d.).

Kaleta, I., & Matysiak, A. (2018). *Ludność, ruch naturalny i migracje w województwie łodzkim.* Zakłady Wydawnictw Statystycznych.

Karta Praw Osób Niepełnosprawnych. (1997). *Monitor Polski. Dziennik Urzędowy Rzeczypospolitej Polskiej, 50,* 970. https://isap.sejm.gov.pl/isap.nsf/download.xsp/WMP19970500475/O/M19970475.pdf

Krejtz, K., Krejtz, I., Rutkowska-Siuda, D., & Pawłowska, A. (2024). *Gaze-led audiodescription (GLAD).* In this publication.

Krejtz, K., Pawłowska, A., Rutkowska-Siuda, D., Hłobaż, A. (2023). A unified look at cultural heritage: Comparison of aggregated scanpaths over architectural artifacts. *Proceedings of the ACM on Human-Computer Interaction, 7*(ETRA), 1–17.

Kukła, D., & Duda, W. (2020). Non-standard higher education recipients as an important area of the university's third mission. Examples of good practices of Polish and German universities. *Edukacja Ustawiczna Dorosłych, 1,* 8–17.

Kuryłowicz, E. (1995). *Projektowanie uniwersalne: Udostępnianie otoczenia osobom niepełnosprawnym.* Centrum Badawczo Rozwojowe Rehabilitacji Osób Niepełnosprawnych.

Pawłowska, A. (2015). Sztuka audiodeskrypcji – audiodeskrypcja sztuki – koncepcja nowej metody z zakresu upowszechniania sztuk wizualnych. In Twórczość, pasja, Uniwersytet. Kategoria zaangażowania w dydaktyce akademickiej (pp. 49–63). Uniwersytet Łódzki.

Pawłowska, A., & Długosz, P. (2020). Wykluczeni/Włączeni. Teoria i praktyka udostępniania sztuki osobom chorym i z niepełnosprawnościami w perspektywie muzealnej i akademickiej. *Rocznik Muzeum Wsi Mazowieckiej w Sierpcu, XI,* 41–54.

Pawłowska, A., & Długosz, P. (2021). *Lodzka sztuka w Europie europejska sztuka w Lodzi* (T. 1). Wydawnictwo Uniwersytetu Łódzkiego.

Pawłowska, A., & Długosz, P. (2022a). *Architektura w Lodzi* (T. 2). Uniwersytet Łódzki.

Pawłowska, A., & Długosz, P. (2022b). *Lodz i awangarda* (T. 3). Wydawnictwo Uniwersytetu Łódzkiego.

Pawłowska, A., & Sowińska-Heim, J. (2016). *Audiodeskrypcja dzieł sztuki Metody, problemy, przykłady.* Wydawnictwo Uniwersytetu Łódzkiego. https://dspace.uni.lodz.pl/bitstream/handle/11089/42784/Pawlowska-Audiodeskrypcja.pdf?sequence=2&isAllowed=y

Pawłowska, A., Rutkowska-Siuda, D., Hłobaż, A., Wendorff, A., Drozdowski, A., & Milerowska, M. (2023a). Friendly city. Making architectural heritage accessible. *International Journal of Conservation Science, 14*(3), 1019–1032.

Pawłowska, A., Rutkowska-Siuda, D., Wendorff, A., Milczarski, P., Krejtz, I., Hłobaż, A., Wisiecka, K., Duchowski, A.T., Krejtz, K., & Sniegula, A. (2023b). Towards accessible gaze-led audio description for architectural heritage: Evidence from an eye-tracking study. In *ASSETS'23: Proceedings of the 25th international ACM SIGACCESS conference on computers and accessibility* (vol. 59, pp. 1–5). Association for Computing Machinery.

Piekot, T., & Maziarz, M. (2014). Styl „plain language" i przystępność języka publicznego jako nowy kierunek w polskiej polityce językowej. *Acta Universitatis Wratislaviensis. Język a Kultura, 24*(3588), 307–324.

Poprzęcka, M. (2009). *Inne obrazy: oko, widzenie, sztuka. Od Albertiego do Duchampa.* Słowo/Obraz Terytoria.

Report on the ICOM Member Feedback for a new museum definition. Independent analysis & report elaborated for the ICOM Define Committee. (2021). https://icom-europe.mini.icom.museum/wp-content/uploads/sites/24/2021/07/ICOM-Define-Consultation-2-Results-Report-enVF.pdf

Strzemiński, W. (1969). *Teoria widzenia*. Wydawnictwo Literackie.

The Act of November 21, 1996, on museums as "museum object" (Art. 21.1). (1996).

Zalecenie CM/Rec (2011). *14 Komitetu Ministrów dla państw członkowskich w sprawie uczestnictwa osób niepełnosprawnych w życiu politycznym i publicznym z dn. 16 listopada 2011 r.* (2011). https://niepelnosprawni.gov.pl/container/dokumenty-miedzynarodowe/dokumenty-rady-europejskiej/Zalecenie%20CM%20Rec(2011)14.pdf

Contemporary Art and Audio Accessibility from Translation Studies: An Essential Binomial in Current Artistic Creations

María Asunción Pérez de Zafra Arrufat and David Domínguez Escalona

Abstract BioArt is an interdisciplinary research project that focuses on contemporary art. It aims to advance the field of universal accessibility in experimental artistic spaces, emphasizing multisensory experiences. Utilizing a phased methodology that includes a literature review and sensory element analysis, the project identifies innovative practices for creating accessible multisensory exhibitions. In collaboration with researchers and artists with and without disabilities, the exhibition aims to blur the boundaries of the conventional concert hall and exhibition room by creating experimental visual and sound works based on the analysis of movement patterns in individuals with permanent or temporary disabilities, such as Parkinson's disease tremors or spinal cord injuries. Bioart will offer accessible experiences targeting diverse groups, such as visitors with hearing impairments. This chapter explores the barriers present in contemporary exhibitions and addresses them by implementing alternative accessibility measures for the deaf and hard of hearing. These measures include vibrating backpacks to translate the music track played in the room's soundscape, sign language translation, easy-to-read displayed information, and multichannel information. Contemporary art can provide fully accessible experiences for deaf and hard-of-hearing visitors when considering them from the concept design, even if the sound is a key concept. For this purpose, new approaches and accessibility solutions have to be considered to translate the sound experience through other channels (haptic, visual, or the sense of smell). Expected benefits include empowering attendees with diverse abilities, fostering social inclusion, and inspiring future international endeavors in the realm of accessible contemporary arts.

Keywords Accessibility · Contemporary art · Deaf · Sign language · Design for all

M. A. Pérez de Zafra Arrufat (✉) · D. Domínguez Escalona
Universidad de Granada, Granada, Spain
e-mail: arrufat@ugr.es

D. Domínguez Escalona
e-mail: domiesca@ugr.es

© The Author(s) 2024
A. Marcus-Quinn et al. (eds.), *Transforming Media Accessibility in Europe*,
https://doi.org/10.1007/978-3-031-60049-4_9

1 Introduction

Contemporary art has the potential to be a powerful tool for promoting accessibility and inclusion for people with disabilities. The intersection of contemporary art and disability justice has been a subject of scholar research, with a focus on rethinking inclusion in arts education and addressing barriers to social inclusion for disabled individuals within the arts. The UN Convention on the Rights of Persons with Disabilities emphasizes the importance of ensuring accessibility to cultural goods and services, highlighting the obligation of states to adopt measures enabling persons with disabilities to utilize their artistic potential (Leahy & Ferri, 2022). However, despite these efforts, access to arts and culture for people with disabilities remains inconsistent (Leahy & Ferri, 2022).

The potential of contemporary art to foster social connectedness and belonging for individuals with severe and enduring mental health problems has been explored, indicating the role of artistic practices and spaces in promoting a sense of belonging for this demographic (Gratton, 2019). Moreover, the participation of people with learning disabilities in mainstream arts and culture has been a subject of participatory action research, shedding light on the need for consistent access to such opportunities (Gratton, 2019).

Inclusive education through the arts has been identified as a potential avenue for reviving inclusive education, with reflections on the implications for professionals involved in this process (Parr, 2006). Additionally, the role of art therapy and disability aesthetics has been examined, emphasizing the importance of understanding the intersection between art practice and disability discourse (Allan, 2014). Furthermore, the arts have been recognized as a space that welcomes disability self-representation and alternate ways of knowing, drawing on principles of disability studies, and the political agenda of disability art to imagine otherwise (Solvang, 2017).

The experiences of disabled artists, including their creativity and the environmental barriers they face, have been highlighted, emphasizing the essence of creative activities in deriving artistic value from painful experiences and creating numerous possibilities (Badía, 2023; Gabriel, 2022):

> My work as an artist focuses on the validation of error, the challenge to stereotypes of beauty and behavior. I seek an alternative path by researching the coexistence between normative and non-normative individuals. My identity as "disabled" is fundamental since I constantly need to claim that my body and the way I move are different. My source of inspiration comes from experiences and the relationship my body has with society. Some of my performances involve confronting the audience with a sense of discomfort caused by the different rhythms that people with disabilities have compared to normativity. I really enjoy reversing the roles present in society and bringing them into my own artistic realm.

(Badía, 2023)

Furthermore, critical disability arts contribute to discourses about vision, visuality, and spectatorship in the arts, highlighting the significance of inclusive representation and participation (Bunch, 2021). Art making has been shown to have a transformative impact on specific populations such as the health of individuals living with psychiatric disabilities. It emphasizes the value of art as a practical strategy for personal and group transformation in community arts studios (Howells & Zelnik, 2009). Additionally, the evolving norms and values surrounding the politics of inclusion and access play a pivotal role in shaping the opportunities available to disabled artists (Bang & Kim, 2015; Hsueh, 2021). Moreover, the lack of support, guidance, and community for neurodivergent artists underscores the need for inclusive spaces within disability arts and activist communities (Gold, 2021).

The concept of beauty in art is a complex and often subjective domain, steeped in cultural, historical, and personal aesthetics. Traditionally, beauty has been associated with harmony, balance, and the pleasure derived from sensory experiences. Artistic beauty transcends mere visual appeal to encompass a resonance with the viewer's inner sense of what is profound, stirring, and sublime. It can manifest in myriad forms, challenging traditional norms and evoking emotions ranging from tranquility to discomfort, thereby expanding our understanding of what is considered beautiful. Beauty in art is not static but dynamic, evolving with societal shifts and individual perceptions, inviting continuous dialogue and reflection on the aesthetic values that shape our interaction with the world. The transition from traditional forms of art like paintings and sculptures to performance art and immersive experiences marks a significant evolution in the art world. This shift represents a move away from the passive consumption of art toward a more interactive and experiential engagement. Performance art breaks the confines of the canvas and pedestal, often unfolding in museums and unconventional spaces like warehouses, streets, or natural landscapes. It invites the audience to become part of the art itself, engaging directly with the artists and the environment. This form of art blurs the boundaries between creator and spectator, art and life, fostering a deeper, more personal connection with the work. It reflects a contemporary understanding of art as a dynamic event rather than a static object, emphasizing process over product and experience over observation. This trend toward experiential art has expanded the role of museums and galleries, transforming them into spaces of live interaction, dialogue, and sensory exploration. According to Escalona (2012), the concept of beauty:

> (...)It's hard to set it, because beauty is what has been stripped of all kinds of prejudice. Learned standards are not good and the very concept of beauty already stick out like a sore thumb. To me, it's more interesting to talk about beautiful situations, those small accidents that pull you out of the routine and show you the world in a different light. To keep playing, and to perform pirouettes on what is known. That is beautiful.

(Escalona, 2012)

Greco (2019) posits that accessibility studies encompass a broad range of disciplines, and there has been a sequential evolution from particularist views toward a universalist perspective. This universalist perspective acknowledges that media accessibility (MA), as defined by Szarkowska et al. (2013) and cited by Greco (2016: 11), is:

The field of research concerned with the theories, practices, technologies, and tools that enable access to media products, services, and environments for people who are unable to access or adequately access content in its original form.

(Greco, 2016: 11)

This domain shares aspects of its knowledge base with audiovisual translation (AVT), which Chaume (2004: 30) characterizes as:

A type of translation distinguished by the particular nature of the texts being transferred across languages. These objects, as implied by the name, deliver (translatable) information through two simultaneously encoding communication channels: the acoustic channel (acoustic vibrations through which we receive words, paralinguistic information, soundtracks, and special effects) and the visual channel (light waves through which we receive moving images, as well as posters or signs with written texts, etc.). In semiotic terms, (…) its complexity lies in a sign-based structure that combines verbal (written and spoken) and non-verbal information, encoded according to different systems of signification simultaneously.

(Chaume, 2004: 30)

Both MA and AVT are framed within translation studies and, in turn, partially within accessibility studies (AS). Accessibility studies within the artistic context incorporate various digital and analog elements that also involve the discipline of translation and interpretation to reach all audiences (Arrufat Pérez de Zafra & Álvarez De Morales Mercado, 2019). Considering accessibility in cultural spaces is crucial for both the visitors and the artists with disabilities. They have reflected on their commitment to welcome and engage all members of society. To get to this point, different international initiatives have played a vital role, such as the UN Convention on the Rights of Persons with Disabilities, which emphasizes the importance of ensuring accessibility of cultural goods and services. They enable persons with disabilities to utilize their artistic potential (Leahy & Ferri, 2022). Museums are transforming, moving beyond physical access to embrace multisensory experiences, thereby enriching the visitor's engagement with art and history (Kellouai, 2023). This includes tactile exhibits, audio descriptions, and sign language tours, allowing every visitor to experience the collections fully. Similarly, concert events are redefining the auditory experience for the deaf and hard of hearing through advanced technology like vibrating platforms and wearable haptic devices (Contreras Pérez, 2023; García López et al., 2022). These innovations translate sound into tactile sensations, enabling a more inclusive and holistic enjoyment of music. Furthermore, easy-to-navigate layouts, clear signage, pictograms and accessible online content cater to a wide range of cognitive and physical abilities (Niimah & Maina, 2019; Kamran, 2021; Weiss, 2013). By implementing such diverse accessibility strategies, museums and concert events are not only complying with legal requirements but are also embracing the deeper ethos of equality and inclusion, ensuring that culture and entertainment are truly for everyone.

In the context of education, aesthetics and art play a significant role in enhancing creativity and learning, particularly in children, emphasizing the value of art in education (Adu-Agyem & Enti, 2009). Furthermore, the pedagogical encounters with disability justice art exhibitions have the potential to disrupt and shift perspectives through encountering works of art, highlighting the transformative power of art in challenging societal norms and perceptions (Gross & Keifer-Boyd, 2022). Museums and cultural environments have the potential to contribute to combating stereotypes and enriching perceptions. They emphasize the value of further learning opportunities in these spaces (Kanari & Souliotou, 2021). Additionally, the documentation of works by physically disabled artists serves as a valuable resource for art and special education (Osei-Poku & Acheampong, 2010).

The intersection of art, technology, and accessibility has become a prism through which the artistic experience can be reexamined and redesigned, opening new pathways for inclusion and universal participation. The BioArt project, initiated at the University of Granada, embodies this convergence. Focusing on creating multisensory experiences through experimental visual and sound works, the project aims to blur the conventional boundaries between the concert hall and the art gallery, advocating for broader inclusion. This innovative approach presents a unique opportunity to explore and expand the boundaries of accessibility in art, while challenging traditional perceptions of ability and disability.

The concept of universal design, underlying the philosophy of the BioArt project, is based on the premise that accessibility should not be an afterthought but an intrinsic principle in artistic creation. This perspective is essential to understand the project's approach to accessibility, which seeks not only to adapt existing art to be more accessible but also to create art with the explicit intention of being accessible from its inception. This approach reflects a paradigm shift in how we conceive accessibility, emphasizing the need for proactive engagement rather than corrective reactions.

Accessibility in art, especially in experimental ways integrating visual and sound elements, presents unique challenges. The audience for these works is inherently diverse, encompassing a wide spectrum of sensory and cognitive abilities. To address this diversity, BioArt adopts an interdisciplinary methodology that amalgamates accessible translation and interpretation, neurophysiology, music, and visual arts. Collaboration among artists, scientists, and accessibility experts is fundamental to this approach, enabling a deeper understanding of how different people experience art.

At the core of the BioArt project is the analysis of movement patterns of people with disabilities, including those suffering from diseases like Parkinson's or spinal cord injuries. This approach not only serves to inform artistic creation but also to emphasize the representation of these experiences in the art itself. Such representation not only increases awareness of these conditions but also challenges dominant narratives about disability, promoting a more nuanced and empathetic understanding.

2   Multisensory Translation Considerations for Sign Language Speakers

Museum spaces have conceptually evolved in recent decades to become places with educational and communicative purposes (Soler-Gallego, 2012). In 1974, the International Council of Museums (ICOM) advocated for the establishment of Departments of Education and Cultural Action, offering a new definition for this institution:

> A museum is a non-profit institution, permanent, in service to society and its development, open to the public, which acquires, conserves, researches, communicates, and exhibits, for purposes of study, education, and enjoyment, material evidence of humanity and its environment.

(ICOM, 2007, p. 3)

One of the current challenges museums face is to disseminate knowledge to the public while acknowledging the inherent diversity of their visitors. Universal accessibility is the cross-cutting tool that can facilitate full social participation at different levels (Chaymae, 2023). This concept is internationally recognized and unified through the International Convention on the Rights of Persons with Disabilities, ratified by most countries. This is of special interest because it ensures the protection of everyone's rights, regardless of where they live, their culture or language, where they travel, or reside. There are universal values that by law must be respected. Museums, housing significant parts of historical and cultural heritage within their walls, as previously mentioned, bear the responsibility to meet society's needs. Nevertheless, it is crucial that the assurance of rights is not limited to isolated good practices (Juncá, 2011).

Accessibility in the artistic context through sign language has traditionally been considered in a linear way, as a resource created ad hoc by external. It is a complementary resource that hasn't any link to the creation process nor being part of the essence of the artist and the work.

Translation allows guiding the visitor through the room using audiovisual material such as sign language guides. It shows the contents of part or all the exhibited pieces. Accessibility is limited to its informative function because it acts as a bridge of communication. As pointed out in the introduction, art and accessible translation are two disciplines that have recently had more and more interactions and spaces of creation and confluence. These spaces have allowed offering resources to users that have opened windows of knowledge to many people. Some of those *windows* have been videos of the artwork and guided tours in the natural language of many Spanish deaf people, Sign Language (Abasolo Elices & Arrufat Pérez de Zafra, 2023). However, it is necessary to question whether a measure like translation into another language can really offer the viewer an immersive and equitable experience. Is there a hundred percent equivalent translation of a written text into sign language? Is it the same to translate from an oral, audiovisual, or written source text? Will the target text offer a completely equal experience to the one experienced by users who access the information through the auditory or visual channel with a written or spoken Spanish text?

Undoubtedly, a text contains a semantic and cultural load that can be complex to translate or that may lose nuances and gain others when translated. In the mere description of the location of an artwork, the visual-spatial nature of sign languages allows offering more precise information with fewer linguistic signs.

Moreover, it is important to consider that an oral or audiovisual text in Spanish contains paralinguistic information that plays an essential role in the communication process. For example, the volume of the voice, the speed at which a person speaks, the tone, the silences, etc. All these elements are part of the text and, when we translate into sign language, they automatically become part of the target text.

Perhaps at this point, the following question has suddenly appeared: Why do signed texts have to add automatically paralinguistic information? The answer is simple, a written text rarely contains these types of elements. They can be observed in literary texts, where the author may spend a few sentences describing the tone or intensity of the person speaking, but it is not the most common in other types of texts. In sign language, as it does not have an official written representation, the translator or interpreter adds this type of information to the target text.

One of the most well-known dubbing actors in Spain has been Pepe Mediavilla, voice of characters like Gandalf from the Lord of the Rings, Star Trek's Spock, or Morgan Freeman in many of his films. His deep voice has brought Tolkien's texts closer to thousands of followers, and his warm, intimate, and intense interpretation has gone down in history on his YouTube channel (Mediavilla, 2016). This special sparkle that his interpretation has is a light that any translation or interpretation into sign language can shed, as every text is ultimately enriched by the intonation, intensity, pauses, and interpretation that the sign language speaker impregnates in it. For this reason, it is possible to affirm that in this process of creation, it may be utopian to think that the information can really be neutrally translated into sign language.

Moreover, in the artistic context, the elements richly utilize sensory channels, and translating or seeking equivalent experiences through another sensory channel makes it arduously complex to obtain a target text with an identical meaning in which all the nuances of the original can be perceived and interpreted in the same way.

This can be observed with greater incidence in those texts that require intersemiotic translation or those that are per se multisensory texts. From a Deleuzian perspective (1977), an event cannot be conceptualized as a fixed entity, but its entity and identity are extensive dynamic. This allows it to be understood through the relationships that are established. If we focus on the event of a contemporary art exhibition, the multisensory experiences and the different ways of interacting with the work allow blurring the traditional linear and static perception to open paths that had not been previously considered through *aesthetic reason* (Maillard, 1998). In the process of blurring these lines, this path can be taken, returning to the origin or to the place where all possible forms exist, the Jaos in Hindu mythology (Escalona, 2024). This way of creating through multisensoriality and being aware of the different possibilities of interaction with the work constitutes a paradigm shift in the artistic context.

3 Users Diversity for Audio Accessibility

The landscape of audio accessibility in contemporary creations is a rich tapestry of diverse users, each with unique needs and experiences. Among these, individuals with hearing loss represent a significant group (Smith et al., 1998). The spectrum of hearing loss varies widely, from mild to profound, necessitating different levels of accommodation. For instance, those with partial hearing loss may benefit from amplified sound systems or hearing loop technologies in galleries and concert halls (Lopez et al., 2020). Meanwhile, individuals with profound hearing loss might rely more on visual or tactile interpretations of sound, such as visual sound representations or vibrating tools that allow them to experience the rhythm and intensity of sound (Quittner et al., 1994). This differentiation in needs underscores the importance of versatile and adaptable sound accessibility solutions in contemporary art and performance spaces.

Another vital group consists of diverse sign language speakers, who bring a unique cultural and linguistic perspective to the experience of sound in art (López et al., 2018). Sign languages, with their rich visual-spatial grammar and expression, offer a different mode of experiencing sound-related art. Translating textual content into sign language, or offering sign language translations of musical performances, not only makes these experiences accessible but also adds a new dimension to them. It's crucial for creators and curators to collaborate with the translators to ensure that their translations are sensitive and contextually relevant (Hindley et al., 1994).

Hearing users who are temporarily unable to hear due to contextual reasons, such as being in a talk or having a temporary hearing impairment, also benefit from sound accessibility features (Abascal & Nicolle, 2005). This group's needs highlight the importance of universal design in sound accessibility. Features designed for those with permanent hearing disabilities can also enhance the experience for those facing temporary auditory challenges. For example, providing subtitles or written descriptions for audio guides in museums not only aids those with permanent hearing loss but also assists visitors in a crowded and noisy gallery where the audio might be difficult to hear (Koo et al., 2008). This approach not only ensures inclusivity but also enhances the overall visitor experience, demonstrating that accessibility features can have widespread benefits.

Furthermore, the needs of deaf children, elderly people, and individuals with multiple disabilities must be considered (Moffatt et al., 2004). Deaf children, in their developmental years, require sound accessibility that supports their learning and engagement with art. Interactive, visually stimulating, and tactile elements can be pivotal in fostering their appreciation and understanding of sound-based art. Elderly individuals might face age-related hearing loss and could benefit from similar accessibility tools designed for those with permanent hearing impairments. For people with multiple disabilities, a holistic approach that considers all their needs is essential (Holone & Herstad, 2013). By considering the varied and sometimes overlapping needs of these diverse groups, creators can ensure that contemporary art and sound experiences are truly inclusive and enriching for all.

4   Sensory Accessibility in BioArt Design

In this endeavor to blur the conventional boundaries between music and art, concert spaces and exhibition centers, the current project has embarked on challenging and expanding traditional methods of accessibility for people with hearing impairments or in a context where a hearing person might have a similar experience (Arrufat et al., 2022: 227). Through the implementation of innovative technologies and inclusive practices, BioArt seeks to create an artistic space where the auditory experience is accessible and enriching for all visitors, including those with hearing impairments.

One of the key accessibility strategies in the BioArt project is the use of sign language to provide essential information at the entrance of the exhibition hall. This measure is realized through an introductory text displayed on an interactive digital screen, designed to capture attention and facilitate access to information. The same text is also accessible on visitors' mobile devices via a strategically placed and easily scannable QR code. Upon scanning the code, users can instantly access the information, with the added benefit of being able to view the video according to their usual preferences, such as the size of visual elements, screen brightness, contrast, and other aspects that enhance user experience.

Furthermore, in an effort to encompass the diverse accessibility needs of visitors, the integrated sign language playback system has been enriched with several adjustable options. Users have the freedom to select the playback speed, tailoring it to their comprehension pace and comfort. In addition, subtitles for deaf synchronized with sign language can be activated. They are helpful not only for individuals that speak in sign language and can visualize a term that they don't know, but also for those visitors who may be learning sign language. To ensure comprehensive accessibility, the option to access the full text of the presented information is provided, allowing users with different preferences and needs to enjoy a fully inclusive and enriching experience. This flexibility and adaptability in information has been conscientiously designed by the team for this artistic experience.

This approach not only facilitates access to information for deaf individuals but also elevates sign language to an artistic and expressive medium in its own right. By integrating sign language prominently, the project challenges conventional notions of storytelling and communication in the artistic space, underscoring the importance of linguistic and cultural diversity.

Another innovation is the use of vibrating backpacks to translate the sounds of soundscapes into geolocated vibrations (Fig. 1).

This technology allows users with hearing impairments to experience music and sound in a completely new way, through tactile sensations (Silvestri & Falk, 2023). This method of sound translation opens up new possibilities for the perception and appreciation of sound art, challenging our traditional understandings of how music and sound are experienced. These backpacks create a multisensory experience that aligns auditory and tactile stimuli. This synchronization not only enhances the artistic expression but also deepens the emotional and cognitive engagement of the audience.

Fig. 1 Primavera sound. *Source* Fundación Music For All (2022). https://www.facebook.com/fun
dacionmusicforall/posts/pfbid025ogAJJhJmWmwbmKoCiumfvccuZq2FJKNhh4GjGkJBugEnNx
xZVkwc2KfeXJ9RMLpl

This approach positions sound art at the intersection of technology, sensory experience, and artistic innovation, inviting a broader audience to immerse themselves in
a holistic art experience.

Additionally, the project incorporates an unconventional approach to subtitles
for the deaf in its audiovisual material. Instead of limiting itself to a mere textual
transcription of dialogue and auditory information, the subtitles aim to capture the
essence and emotional tone of the content, providing a richer and more nuanced
experience for people with hearing impairments. This innovative approach not only
enhances accessibility but also enriches the aesthetic experience of audiovisual art.
By doing so, the subtitles become an integral part of the artistic expression, akin
to a narrative voice that conveys not just words but the atmosphere, rhythm, and
emotional depth of the audio. This method transcends traditional subtitling, turning
it into an art form in itself, one that respects the integrity of the original content
while offering a new layer of meaning and engagement. The subtitles are carefully
crafted, considering the timing and placement on the screen to complement the visual
elements, thus creating a harmonious and immersive experience.

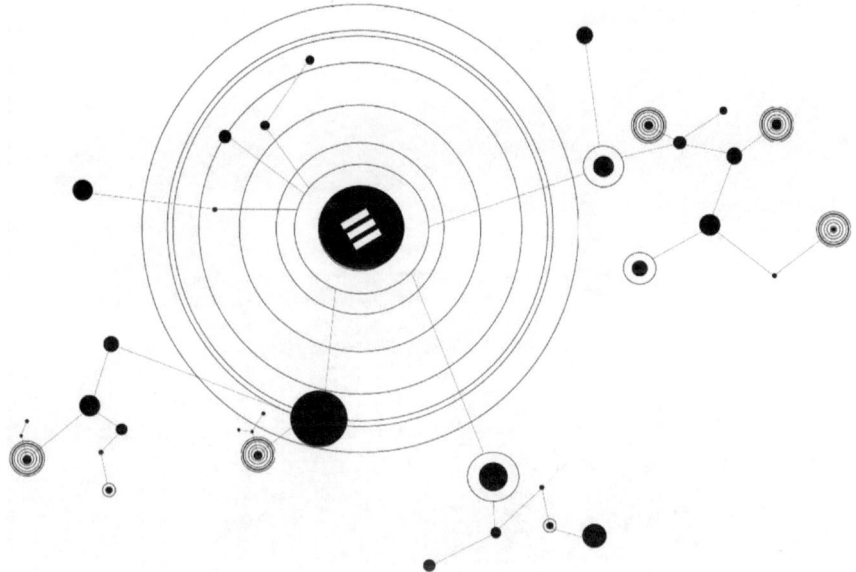

Fig. 2 Nocturno No.2 op.9. *Source* Alvaro Escalona (2023)

The artwork displayed combines visual rhythms with auditory elements to create a multidimensional sensory experience. This piece or alternative musical score has been designed to be showcased in an alternative format (Fig. 2).

It invites not just the eyes but also the hands to explore its contours and textures. The concentric circles and interconnected nodes suggest a cosmic dance of planets or the intricate pathways of neural networks. Such a piece becomes a tactile soundscape, where each relief and texture is a note to be felt, allowing visitors, especially those who are musicians to create, imagine, and "hear" through touch. This fusion of tactile and visual stimuli exemplifies a progressive move in contemporary art toward the concept of design for all, providing a profound experience that speaks to the interconnectedness of our senses. The artwork offers an immersive exploration that is as much about feeling as it is about individual creation.

Within the questioning of the limits of the concert hall and the exhibition room with the created sound art pieces, the harp of a piano has been included, whose parts have been dismantled like a puzzle. This is a particularly resonant choice with the ideas of John Cage, a pioneer in the use of prepared pianos. In a prepared piano, the sounds of the instrument are altered by inserting objects between or on the strings, resulting in a transformation of the traditional piano. However, the one that has been created is not a prepared piano per se, although it has been converted into a new instrument capable of creating a new range of sounds. The piece *Nada I* is the result of the integration of new technology to produce and maximize sounds (Fig. 3).

For this piece, vibratory speakers (vibration transducers) have been used, operating under a different principle than conventional speakers. Instead of emitting

Fig. 3 *Nada I. Source* Alvaro Escalona and David Escalona (2023)

sound waves through the air, the vibrations they generate are transmitted through any solid surface they are in contact with (a table, a window, or even human bone). The effectiveness of the transmission will depend on the physical properties of the surface, such as its density and rigidity. When the vibratory speaker is in contact with the human body, as with bone conduction headphones, the vibrations are transmitted through the bones of the skull to the inner ear, bypassing the middle ear. This allows the person to perceive the sound without the need for sound waves to travel through the air and enter through the outer ear. In art and sound installation, they can be used to make a specific surface emit sounds, opening new possibilities in terms of sound exploration and its interaction with space and materials using new technologies. If the surface on which a vibratory speaker is placed is the wooden base of a piano harp, as in "Nada Brahma I", designed to resonate, it will become part of the piano's acoustic system. The curious thing about this sound installation is that the strings vibrate indirectly, creating a unique combination of sounds generated by the vibratory speaker and the harmonics of the piano strings. From several vibratory speakers, placed on its surface, various pieces will be played that, as electronic miniatures, have been composed from a series of graphic scores, whose symbols have been inspired by seismic swarm maps. Each of these sound micropieces is a reinterpretation of classic piano works that music students play and marked the composer's youth, such as the Moonlight Sonata. The sounds that are heard are emitted from the piano harp through four vibratory speakers. The piano has become a large music box, but it is a metaphor for our body, for the world we inhabit. It seems as if the piano's sonorous

Fig. 4 Cliczz. *Source* David Escalona (2023)

body becomes the theater of the world and vice versa. Its strings vibrate and project the sound of different sonic textures that fill the main room with resonances.

Within the project, one element that serves as a cohesive nexus for the experience is the scent of a beehive's honeycomb (Fig. 4).

This concept originates from the tattoo of the model featured in the exhibition, where nature plays a pivotal role. The sense of smell is engaged through this element, creating a multisensory bridge between the visual art and the viewer's olfactory perception. The aroma of honeycomb permeates the space, drawing visitors deeper into the artwork's narrative and symbolizing the intricate connection between humanity and nature. This olfactory dimension not only adds depth to the visual aesthetics but also evokes the natural world's raw beauty and complexity, enhancing the immersive quality of the exhibition and creating a visceral connection to the artwork.

In the exhibition, a conscientious effort has been made to ensure cognitive accessibility through the implementation of easy-to-read texts. These texts adhere to principles of clarity and simplicity, avoiding complex sentence structures and employing straightforward language to accommodate the visitors. This approach reflects an inclusive mindset, acknowledging that cognitive accessibility is as crucial as physical accessibility in the arts. By considering the cognitive load and processing demands of their content, the exhibition curators have made a decisive step toward inclusivity. The elements of the exhibition are designed with intuitive navigation and concise informational signage, which minimizes potential cognitive barriers. The consideration of these elements aim to invite a broader audience to engage with the art in a way that is meaningful, democratizing the artistic experience.

Collectively, these strategies exhibit a profound commitment to inclusion and innovation within the realm of sensory auditory accessibility. BioArt endeavors not merely to render art accessible to a broader audience but also to explore and push the boundaries of how art can be experienced and enjoyed. This holistic and creative approach to auditory accessibility benefits not only individuals with hearing impairments but also enhances the artistic experience for all visitors, fostering a deeper and more empathetic understanding of diversity and inclusion in art. Contemporary art has the potential to offer fully accessible experiences for deaf and hard-of-hearing visitors, even when sound is a central concept. To achieve this, BioArt has considered new approaches and accessibility solutions to translate the auditory experience through other channels—haptic, visual, or olfactory. The BioArt project challenges and enriches our collective understanding of art and the aesthetic experience, signaling a transformative step in how we interact with and appreciate the sensory dimensions of artistic works.

5   Conclusions

The comprehensive examination of multimodal accessibility in contemporary artistic creations reveals two particularly significant conclusions. Firstly, the integration of diverse accessibility tools, such as tactile systems, sign language translations, and visual representations of sound, underscores the importance of a specific approach in artistic spaces. This approach not only caters to a wide spectrum of sensory needs but also enhances the overall experience for all audiences, regardless of their sensory abilities. Such inclusivity not only aligns with the principles of universal design but also promotes a deeper, more empathetic understanding of the diverse ways in which people perceive and interact with art. The adoption of these inclusive practices signifies a paradigm shift in the conception of art and accessibility, moving away from a one-size-fits-all approach to a more nuanced, tailored experience that acknowledges and values the diversity of sensory experiences.

Secondly, the collaborations between artists, musicians, and accessibility experts have been instrumental in pushing the boundaries of what is possible in sound accessibility. These interdisciplinary collaborations have led to innovative solutions that transcend traditional accessibility measures, offering new ways for people with sensory impairments to engage with art. For instance, the use of technology to convert audio art into visual or tactile formats not only provides access to individuals with hearing impairments but also introduces a new dimension of artistic expression. These advancements are not just technical triumphs; they are reshaping the cultural narrative around art and accessibility. They challenge preconceived notions of who can enjoy art and how it can be experienced, fostering a more inclusive cultural landscape where the diversity of human experience is not just accommodated but part of the narrative.

Acknowledgements This chapter is based upon work from COST Action CA19142—Leading Platform for European Citizens, Industries, Academia and Policymakers in Media Accessibility (LEAD-ME) supported by COST (European Cooperation in Science and Technology).

References

Abascal, J., & Nicolle, C. (2005). Moving towards inclusive design guidelines for socially and ethically aware HCI. *Interacting with Computers, 17*(5), 484–505. https://doi.org/10.1016/j.int com.2005.03.002

Abasolo Elices, A., & Arrufat Pérez de Zafra, M. A. (2023). Protocolo para la traducción a lengua de signos o señas de textos especializados: aproximación desde el proyecto Al-Musactra. *Revista de Estudios de Lenguas de Signos REVLES*. In: R. H. González-Montesino y M. C. Bao-Fente (Eds.), *La interpretación de lenguas de signos/señas en España e Hispanoamérica: periferia de la propia periferia* (Vol. 5, pp. 167–183). https://www.revles.es/index.php/revles/article/vie w/130

Adu-Agyem, J., & Enti, M. (2009). Learning: The role of aesthetics in education. *Journal of Science and Technology (Ghana), 29*(1). https://doi.org/10.4314/just.v29i1.46464

Allan, J. (2014). Inclusive education and the arts. *Cambridge Journal of Education, 44*(4), 511–523. https://doi.org/10.1080/0305764x.2014.921282

Arrufat Pérez de Zafra, M. A., & Álvarez De Morales Mercado, C. (2019). Aproximación episte-mológica a la traducción y la accesibilidad en el contexto digital: Propuesta de una taxonomía. *mAGAzin Revista intercultural e interdisciplinar* (Vol. 27, pp. 17–41). https://doi.org/10.12795/ mAGAzin.2019.i27.02

Arrufat Pérez de Zafra, M. A., Álvarez de Morales Mercado, C., & Olivencia Carrión, M. A. (2022). Análisis del diseño universal de la comunicación digital y las pautas de accesibilidad al contenido digital WCAG 2.1. In: R. Arroyo González, E. Fernández-Lancho & D. Brao Serrano (Eds.), *Investigación en comunicación inclusiva y multilingües* (pp. 227–236). Comares.

Badía, C. (2023). Conociendo a la artista Costa Badía. *ANIDA: Revista de arte y escuela, 3*, 39–42.

Bang, G., & Kim, K. (2015). Korean disabled artists' experiences of creativity and the environmental barriers they face. *Disability & Society, 30*(4), 543–555. https://doi.org/10.1080/09687599.2015. 1030065

Bunch, M. (2021). Blind visuality in bruce horak's "through a tired eye". *Studies in Social Justice, 15*(2), 239–258. https://doi.org/10.26522/ssj.v15i2.2456

Chaume, F. (2004). *Cine y traducción*. Cátedra

Chaymae, K. (2023). Accesibilidad museística y experiencias multisensoriales en el arte contem-poráneo: El contexto marroquí y el museo Muhammad VI. Universidad de Granada. https://dig ibug.ugr.es/handle/10481/81906

Contreras Pérez, M. (2023). Accesibilidad y traducción accesible en la música en directo: el caso de la Fundación Music for All. Trabajo de fin de grado. Available in https://digibug.ugr.es/han dle/10481/82849

Deleuze, G., & Guattari, F. (1977). Introducción: rizoma. *Pre-Textos*.

Escalona, D. (2012). *«El arte no es una profesión. Es una actitud»*. Diario ABC. https://www.abc. es/cultura/cultural/abci-arte-entrevista-david-escalona-201207190000_noticia.html

Escalona, D. (accepted). Acontecimiento, pájaros y heridas. Aproximación a la poética de Chantal Maillard y David Escalona. *Anales de Historia del Arte*.

Gabriel, J. (2022). Disrupting discipline: A discrit critique of behavior "management" in the art room. *Research in Arts and Education, 2022*(3). https://doi.org/10.54916/rae.125084

García López, A., Batán, D. Souto Rico, M., & Flys, E. (2022). Nuevos dispositivos tecnológicos universales para la mejora de los estudios y la percepción musical. *Dykinson*, 427–442.

Gold, B. (2021). Neurodivergency and interdependent creation: breaking into Canadian disability arts. *Studies in Social Justice, 15*(2), 209–229. https://doi.org/10.26522/ssj.v15i2.2434

Gratton, N. (2019). People with learning disabilities and access to mainstream arts and culture: A participatory action research approach. *British Journal of Learning Disabilities, 48*(2), 106–114. https://doi.org/10.1111/bld.12303

Greco, G. M. (2016). On accessibility as a human right, with an application to media accessibility. En A. Matamala y P. Orero (Eds.), *Researching audio description. New approaches* (pp. 11–33). Palgrave MacMillan. https://doi.org/10.1057/978-1-137-56917-2_2

Gross, K., & Keifer-Boyd, K. (2022). Pedagogical encounters with the indigeneity & disability justice art exhibition. *Research in Arts and Education, 2022*(3). https://doi.org/10.54916/rae. 125085

Hindley, P., Hill, P., McGuigan, S., & Kitson, N. (1994). Psychiatric disorder in deaf and hearing impaired children and young people: A prevalence study. *Journal of Child Psychology and Psychiatry, 35*(5), 917–934. https://doi.org/10.1111/j.1469-7610.1994.tb02302.x

Holone, H., & Herstad, J. (2013). Rhyme: Musicking for all. *Journal of Assistive Technologies, 7*(2), 93–101. https://doi.org/10.1108/17549451311328772

Howells, V., & Zelnik, T. (2009). Making art: A qualitative study of personal and group transformation in a community arts studio. *Psychiatric Rehabilitation Journal, 32*(3), 215–222. https://doi.org/10.2975/32.3.2009.215.222

Hsueh, S. (2021). Politics of inclusion and lessons of access from disabled artists. https://doi.org/10.14236/ewic/pom2021.6

ICOM. (2007). *Development of the Museum Definition according to ICOM Statutes (1946–2001)*. http://archives.icom.museum/hist_def_eng.html

Juncà, J. A. (2011). *Accesibilidad universal al patrimonio cultural: Fundamentos, criterios y pautas. Real Patronato sobre Discapacidad*. http://hdl.handle.net/11181/3292

Kanari, C., & Souliotou, A. (2021). The role of museum education in raising undergraduate preservice teachers' disability awareness: The case of an exhibition by disabled artists in Greece. *Higher Education Studies, 11*(2), 99. https://doi.org/10.5539/hes.v11n2p99

Kamran, A. (2021, September 13). The Power of Pictograms: A study and guide on how to create inclusive navigational signage using pictograms to address low situational literacy [MRP]. OCAD University. https://openresearch.ocadu.ca/id/eprint/3513/

Koo, D., Crain, K., LaSasso, C., & Eden, G. (2008). Phonological awareness and short-term memory in hearing and deaf individuals of different communication backgrounds. *Annals of the New York Academy of Sciences, 1145*(1), 83–99. https://doi.org/10.1196/annals.1416.025

Leahy, A., & Ferri, D. (2022). Barriers and facilitators to cultural participation by people with disabilities: A narrative literature review. *Scandinavian Journal of Disability Research, 24*(1), 68–81. https://doi.org/10.16993/sjdr.863

Lopez, M., Kearney, G., & Hofstadter, K. (2020). Seeing films through sound: Sound design, spatial audio, and accessibility for visually impaired audiences. *British Journal of Visual Impairment, 40*(2), 117–144. https://doi.org/10.1177/0264619620935935

López, M., Kearney, G., & Hofstadter, K. (2018). Audio description in the UK: What works, what doesn't, and understanding the need for personalising access. *British Journal of Visual Impairment*. https://doi.org/10.1177/0264619618794750

Maillard, C. (1998). Filosofía en los días críticos: "Diarios 1996–1998". *Pre-textos*.

Mediavilla, J. (Director). (2016, August 19). Un cuento élfico: la princesa Mie, de Tolkien. https://www.youtube.com/watch?v=BpcOk4o368Q

Moffatt, K., McGrenere, J., Purves, B., & Klawe, M. (2004). *The participatory design of a sound and image enhanced daily planner for people with Aphasia*. https://doi.org/10.1145/985692. 985744

Niimah, I., & Maina, J. (2019). Differences in navigation behaviour based on literacy levels within a tertiary healthcare complex in northwest Nigeria. In Laryea, S. & Essah, E. (Eds.), *Procs West Africa Built Environment Research (WABER) Conference* (pp. 451–466), August 5–7, 2019, Accra, Ghana.

Osei-Poku, P., & Acheampong, B. (2010). The disabled and art: Selected artifacts of Ghanaian physically disabled artists as a resource for teaching and learning. *Journal of Science and Technology (Ghana), 30*(2). https://doi.org/10.4314/just.v30i2.60547

Parr, H. (2006). Mental health, the arts and belongings. *Transactions of the Institute of British Geographers, 31*(2), 150–166. https://doi.org/10.1111/j.1475-5661.2006.00207.x

Quittner, A., Smith, L., Osberger, M., Mitchell, T., & Katz, D. (1994). The impact of audition on the development of visual attention. *Psychological Science, 5*(6), 347–353. https://doi.org/10.1111/j.1467-9280.1994.tb00284.x

Silvestri, J. A. & Falk, J. L. (2023). And the beat goes on: Using music to transform classes for deaf students with multiple disabilities through universal design. *Odissey,* 76–81.

Smith, L., Quittner, A., Osberger, M., & Miyamoto, R. (1998). Audition and visual attention: The developmental trajectory in deaf and hearing populations. *Developmental Psychology, 34*(5), 840–850. https://doi.org/10.1037/0012-1649.34.5.840

Soler-Gallego, S. (2012). *Traducción y accesibilidad en el museo del siglo XXI.* Tragacanto.

Solvang, P. (2017). Between art therapy and disability aesthetics: A sociological approach for understanding the intersection between art practice and disability discourse. *Disability & Society, 33*(2), 238–253. https://doi.org/10.1080/09687599.2017.1392929

Weiss, A. (2013). Museum signage design and implementation. *Graphic Communication.* https://digitalcommons.calpoly.edu/grcsp/93

Learning and Education

An Overview of Media Accessibility and Inclusivity in the Educational Domain

Alexandros Yeratziotis⊙, Thomas Fotiadis⊙, Andrina Granić⊙, and George A. Papadopoulos⊙

Abstract Educational technology has advanced considerably over the past two decades, yet media accessibility and inclusion still require significant improvement. These areas remain major barriers for many students with disabilities. This descriptive systematic review aims to provide an overview of current research, offering a concise analysis of key concepts related to media accessibility and inclusivity in education. The review examines the frequency and prominence of these themes in research. Recognized journals from the Web of Science (WoS) database were searched without a specified timeframe, resulting in the critical analysis of 14 review articles published between 1998 and 2023. The findings reveal a limited state of the art in this area, highlighting the need for further research and development. An in-depth analysis indicates that themes of inclusivity and accessibility appear with varying frequency, influenced by several factors. These factors include regulatory standards, the direct impact on disabled learners, the emergence of new technologies, and the historical prominence of inclusivity in research literature and the interdisciplinary nature of accessibility.

Keywords Education · Media · Accessibility · Inclusivity · Systematic review · Frequency · Current state of research

A. Yeratziotis (✉)
A.G. Connect Deaf Limited, Nicosia, Cyprus
e-mail: alexis@connectdeaf.com

T. Fotiadis · G. A. Papadopoulos
Department of Computer Science, University of Cyprus, Nicosia, Cyprus

A. Granić
Faculty of Science, University of Split, Split, Croatia

© The Author(s) 2024
A. Marcus-Quinn et al. (eds.), *Transforming Media Accessibility in Europe*,
https://doi.org/10.1007/978-3-031-60049-4_10

1   Introduction

Over the last two decades, the use of technology in education has significantly increased, proving to be an effective tool for facilitating and enhancing learning. (Ortiz-Jiménez et al., 2020). Benefits of digital technologies, such as learning management systems (LMSs), digital learning materials, and massive open online courses (MOOCs), both for students and faculty, are well documented. A systematic review in Granić (2022) comprehensively explores theoretical perspectives and practical approaches regarding the acceptance and adoption of educational technology. Thorough analysis of 47 studies has been conducted to identify the key factors influencing successful educational technology adoption. Examining user aspects, task and technology aspects, as well as social aspects, the findings highlight significant predictors such as system accessibility (found to be greatly affecting intention of using mobile learning), self-efficacy, subjective norm, enjoyment, facilitating conditions, computer anxiety, and technological complexity. E-learning emerges as the most validated technology delivery mode, followed by m-learning, LMSs, and social media services, with most studies conducted in higher education environments. Despite existing research, the review suggests future exploration avenues, including predictive validity for emerging teaching strategies, validation of less-explored factors like perceived playfulness and social media usage, examination of cost-effective solutions, and integration with established theories from various fields to enhance explanatory power.

Equitable access for students with disabilities, however, remains a work in progress. Inaccessibility of digital technologies was reported as one of the main barriers experienced by students with disabilities pursuing higher education in particular (Kimball et al., 2016; Moriña, 2019). Design and implementation of technology has a significant influence on whether access is enhanced. Complying to usability and accessibility standards helps ensure that digital technologies do not become exclusionary tools, avoiding the digital disability divide (Ortiz-Jiménez et al., 2020). Interestingly, and equally importantly, faculty members were found to generally have positive attitudes towards inclusive education, which bodes well to influencing their willingness to contribute towards that goal (Rao, 2004). Understanding the needs of users with disabilities and involving them in the design process of inclusive and accessible technology extend beyond that of educational context alone.

In addition to the above, the comprehensive literature review in Ahlin and Hiddinga (2023) explores the impact of various communication technologies, including specialized ones like cochlear implants (CI) and generally accessible ones like text messaging and social media, on the socialities of deaf and hard-of-hearing (DHH) individuals, particularly adolescents and young adults. It was shown that such tools do not automatically increase inclusion for everyone and that, for a more inclusive approach to take place, DHH people needed to be involved in the design process of such applications. Grounded in the concept of "deaf anthropology," the review emphasizes ethnographic studies as the most suitable method for understanding the nuanced complexities of DHH socialities, allowing for a range of visual methods tailored to the needs of DHH individuals. The analysis delves into the influence of CI on belonging and identity within the "deaf world" and "hearing world," contrasting it with the smoother integration of generic technologies like social media. While CI adoption has sparked debates, generic technologies, despite potential inequalities, have provided new avenues for socialization beyond local networks. The study calls for deeper theoretical exploration of communication technologies' role in relation to deafness and underscores the importance of participatory methods in inclusive technology design, moving towards a more respectful and inclusive approach for DHH individuals.

Social media nowadays has a significant influence on students' academic life. Some ways in which it is being used within this context is to try and influence critical thinking, collaboration, and knowledge construction amongst students and faculty alike (Boateng & Amankwaa, 2016). Exploring how social media is used in education by individuals with disability, and how these serve as tools for building supportive communities, (Sweet et al., 2020) conducted an in-depth thematic analysis. A total of 59 articles were reviewed, identifying six major related themes (community, cyber-bullying, self-esteem, self-determination, access to technology, and accessibility). Overall, online interactions seem to support and empower individuals, foster collaboration and networking, and facilitate the acquisition or exchange of valuable knowledge. On the downside, affording and accessing technology prove to be a hindering factor, due to the low income associated with the disabled. Accessibility itself incurs extra costs. Also, not all cyber environments, including social media platforms, are universally accessible, leading to isolation rather than socializing. By refining aspects of community, domain, and practice, more effective and positive social media practices can be applied. Further research is needed to ensure that social media becomes inclusive for everyone.

Types of technology, learning strategies, research issues, and learning environments have also been singled out as important dimensions in analysing trends of technology-based learning in specific applications (Lin & Hwang, 2019). This in turn further highlights the importance of exploring the needs of learners when using technologies from multiple dimensions (Fernández-López et al., 2013). Moreover, valuable information can be collected by determining the appropriateness and effectiveness of digital technologies for different types of disabilities at different school ages, leading to the enhancement of teaching quality and learning performance (Ok et al., 2016).

1.1 Research Gap

To the best of the authors' knowledge there is limited research in the field, highlighting the need for an overview of the current status of media accessibility and inclusivity in the educational domain. Within this context, particular emphasis is placed on the media domains, specifically audiovisual and multimedia, as well as the accessibility domains, particularly cognitive, visual, and auditory. Hence, this overview aims at addressing this concern with the following three main research questions (RQs):

- RQ1. How can the current state of the art be summarized as an overview?
- RQ2. How prominent are the notions of media accessibility and inclusivity in the educational domain?
- RQ3. Which are the most prominent themes affecting media accessibility and inclusivity in the educational domain?

In answering the aforementioned RQs, both research and educational practices can benefit. Contributions towards a better understanding of media accessibility and inclusivity in the educational domain, foremost, will benefit the learners and can act as a catalyst to decision-makers too.

2   Research Approach

The overview focuses on understanding the current state of research on media accessibility and inclusivity in education. To ensure a comprehensive yet focused review, a search was conducted in the Web of Science (WoS) Current Contents Connect (CCC) database to cover representative literature from recognized journals. This chapter discusses the results of that search.

The literature review was not bounded by any time-based constraints. The search was conducted using relevant terms connected with Boolean operators "OR" and "AND", specifically ("education*" OR "learn*") AND ("technolog*") OR ("inclusive technolog*" OR "assistive technolog*"). Additionally, since we were interested in determining whether the studies contain references to specific media domains (i.e. audiovisual, multimedia) and accessibility domains (i.e. cognitive, visual, and auditive), the search terms "media" AND ("accessib*" OR "inclusiv*") were combined with the aforementioned ones using the operator "AND". Truncation was used to cover all variations of some keywords; for example, the search term "technolog*" was used to search for literature that included the word "technology" as well as "technologies". The search string used in its complete form is the following:

("education*" OR "learn*") AND ("technolog*" OR "inclusive technolog*" OR "assistive technolog*") AND ("media" AND ("accessib*" OR "inclusiv*"))

Specific search terms related to the publication topic, thus including the title, abstract, and author keywords, were sought (i.e. the filter "TOPIC" was selected). Moreover, inclusion criteria were defined for this review, enabling the selection of studies that reported on accessible and inclusive media used in technologies for the purpose of education or learning. Besides, the studies needed to be review articles, published in peer-reviewed journals, written in the English language and reporting on empirically evaluated research.

The literature search was conducted in September 2023, and the publications that included specified search terms in the publication topic were identified ($N = 250$).

From these, only review articles, which were peer-reviewed journal publications and written in English, were further considered ($N = 36$). Since two duplicate publications were returned, the number of review articles considered were thus reduced ($N = 34$).

Subsequently, title, abstract, author keywords, keywords plus, and full text of the filtered literature were analysed to ensure publication suitability and relevance, and the qualified publications were retained. This resulted in narrowing the number further ($N = 14$) and leaving for more detailed analysis review articles that were found to be compliant with the purpose of this study.

3   Results

The analysis of the selected 14 review articles found to be compliant with the purpose of this paper is presented and discussed below.

3.1   Publication History and Distribution by Countries

The trend of publication frequency between the years 2014 and 2023 is illustrated on Fig. 1. All the identified studies ($N = 14$) have been published in the timespan of the past 10 years, reflecting the recent attention given to the researched domain. There was a plateau in relevant studies in the immediate aftermath of the pandemic, counterbalanced by the upwards curve followed since then. Given the prominence of the notions discussed in this paper and the continuous emergence and development of new technologies and media, this trend is expected to continue in the coming years.

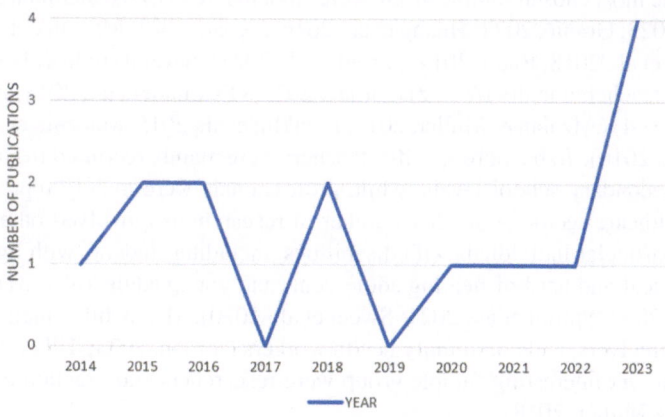

Fig. 1 Publication history

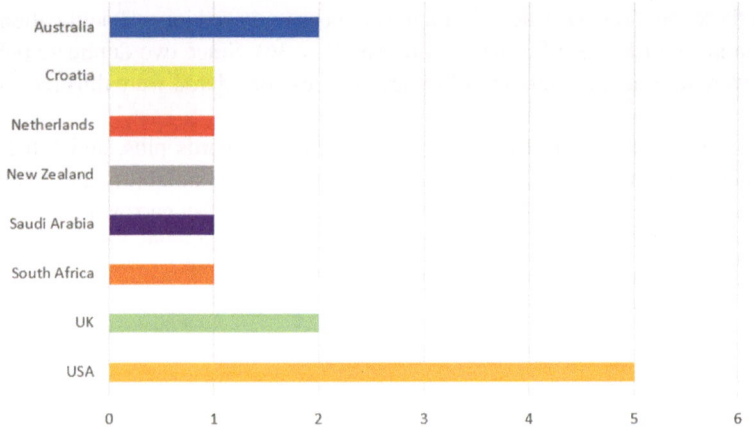

Fig. 2 Distribution of selected review articles by country

What also becomes evident is the spread of researcher interest worldwide (see Fig. 2). Most of the identified studies were conducted in the USA ($N = 5$), followed by the UK and Australia ($N = 2$). In the rest of the countries, only single studies were piloted (alphabetical order): Croatia, Netherlands, New Zealand, Saudi Arabia, and South Africa.

3.2 Type of Participants and Sample Size

Regarding the types of participants/users involved in the reviewed studies, those were diverse and in some cases included more than one type within the same study. Overall, the most chosen sample group were students ($N = 8$) (Alshammari & Fayez Alanazi, 2023; Granić, 2022; Huang et al., 2016; Jordan, 2023; Mącznik et al., 2015; O'Connor et al., 2018; Radu, 2014; Sproul et al., 2021). Several studies also engaged respective teachers/faculty ($N = 2$) (Jordan, 2023; O'Connor et al., 2018) or professionals ($N = 4$) (Afzalan & Muller, 2018; Franklin et al., 2015; Mącznik et al., 2015; Rolls et al., 2016). To be more specific, teachers were mainly recruited from elementary and secondary school levels, while professionals were mainly representative of the healthcare sector. A smaller number of research also involved other participants, in particular individuals with disabilities, including students with light sensitivity and deaf and hard-of-hearing adolescents and young adults ($N = 3$) (Ahlin & Hiddinga, 2023; Sproul et al., 2021; Sweet et al., 2020). Meanwhile others involved parents, caregivers, and community health workers (Jordan, 2023; Till et al., 2023). A different, yet interesting sample group were researchers and practicing planners (Afzalan & Muller, 2018).

In studies where the sample sizes were reported (Alshammari & Fayez Alanazi, 2023; Granić, 2022; Huang et al., 2016; Jordan, 2023; Mącznik et al., 2015; O'Connor et al., 2018; Rolls et al., 2016; Sweet et al., 2020; Till et al., 2023), these varied with the smallest (3) and largest (8586) samples of individuals with disabilities originating from the same study (Sweet et al., 2020). What is also notable is the domination of smaller sample sizes up to 400 participants ($N = 8$) compared to the number of larger sample sizes.

4 Discussion

The 14 review articles that form our literature corpus demonstrate how media accessibility and inclusivity are discussed in various educational contexts, such as healthcare education. The analysis reveals that these key concepts appear with varying frequency, with accessibility being more prominently featured than inclusivity in most articles.

Moreover, further related ideas are discussed. The integration of messaging apps in education is addressed, with emphasis placed on their potential in low- and middle-income countries (Jordan, 2023). A focus on the impact of communication technologies on deaf and hard-of-hearing individuals and an emphasis on the need for inclusive technology design through the involvement of the deaf community are visited in Ahlin and Hiddinga (2023). Digital health interventions for maternal and child health in low- and middle-income countries are explored, with challenges such as insufficient consideration of community perspectives and the exclusion of key players being pointed out (Till et al., 2023). The transformative influence of technology on nursing education in Saudi Arabia and the need for adequate training and the integration of emerging technologies are all discussed (Alshammari & Fayez Alanazi, 2023). Factors influencing the adoption of educational technology are explored, with emphasis placed on the importance of system accessibility and self-efficacy (Granić, 2022). Focus is also placed on guidelines for the safer use of digital media for light-sensitive students (Sproul et al., 2021). Social media's role in building supportive communities for individuals with disabilities is analysed, and challenges related to accessibility and affordability are identified (Sweet et al., 2020). Social media's role in healthcare education is explored, while factors such as motivation, accessibility, and digital literacy are also mentioned (O'Connor et al., 2018). Online participatory tools are explored, and concerns about social injustices and the importance of ensuring inclusiveness are highlighted (Afzalan & Muller, 2018). Changes in reading patterns influenced by Internet technologies are investigated, touching upon the accessibility and affordability of smart technologies (Huang et al., 2016). An assessment of online technologies in physiotherapy education takes place along with an identification of benefits related to accessibility and practical skills enhancement (Mącznik et al., 2015). Virtual communities in health care are discussed, recognizing ease of access as enhancing perceived benefits (Rolls et al., 2016). The affordability and approachability of ICT tools employed in health care are both examined (Franklin et al., 2015). Finally, augmented reality in education is explored, recognizing its wide accessibility, while factors influencing its effectiveness are also addressed (Radu, 2014).

Through an overview of the 14 review articles, the key themes of inclusivity and accessibility emerge with varying degrees of frequency, with the latter appearing in all review articles under consideration ($N = 14$) compared to the former ($N = 9$). This prominence can be attributed to several factors currently rendering one more widely researched than the other, including, but not limited, to:

- the regulatory standards pertaining to accessibility (it itself can be considered part of inclusion and therefore can provide a more focused target for policymakers).
- the fact that accessibility links directly with the disabled, itself a well-researched area.
- the emergence of new technologies, including (generative) artificial intelligence and virtual reality, and how these may enhance accessibility in educational settings.
- inclusivity's prominence in the research literature prior to the years under study in this paper. This has by no means exhausted all possible research avenues, and it has, however, also brought attention to the importance of making things accessible to users.
- accessibility itself is an interdisciplinary field, calling upon contributions from technology, education, social sciences, and disability studies, inter alia. Therefore, as these individual fields develop, more combined studies are expected to take place.

Table 1 presents the incidence of those themes as well as several highly related indicative key notions that fall under each of the two major themes according to their relevance, along with studies looking at those themes and notions. The list is obviously non-exhaustive, but it serves to show how commonly these related notions occur in our corpus. Below follows an analysis of the findings.

4.1 Interpreting the Results for Media Accessibility Theme

For the media accessibility theme, the notions of accessibility and its derivatives (access, accessible, and inaccessible) were present in all studies reviewed ($N = 14$) which points to the prominence and significance of the term as a research area. Technologies ($N = 14$) and user experiences/user satisfaction ($N = 13$) were equally highly-researched terms. Both these were expected to feature high on this list, given that (a) technologies is the underlying concept of the overall scope of this paper and (b) users are the reason such technologies are developed and researched in the first place, rendering their experiences and general views important. Policies and regulations relating to media accessibility were also frequently researched ($N = 9$), which is testament to the fact that rendering media accessible to users regardless of their means, backgrounds, location, etc., is slowly becoming the norm rather than the exception to the rule. Having access regulated ensures that accessibility is not a privilege like it used to, but a right of all. Related notions like sensory ($N = 5$), navigation ($N = 4$), subtitles/transcripts ($N = 3$), and captions ($N = 1$) appeared in the search in

Table 1 Incidence of themes relating to media accessibility and inclusivity

Category	Incidence of key notions	Indicative sample research
Media accessibility	Access ($N = 14$)	Jordan (2023)
	Technologies ($N = 14$)	Ahlin and Hiddinga (2023)
	User experience/satisfaction ($N = 13$)	Granić (2022)
	Policies/regulations ($N = 9$)	Sweet et al. (2020)
	Affordability ($N = 6$)	Afzalan and Muller (2018)
	Sensory ($N = 5$)	Huang et al. (2016)
	Navigation ($N = 4$)	Radu (2014)
	Subtitles/transcripts ($N = 3$)	Mącznik et al. (2015)
	Captions ($N = 1$)	Ahlin and Hiddinga (2023)
Media inclusivity	Interactivity ($N = 14$)	Alshammari and Fayez Alanazi (2023)
	Participation ($N = 14$)	Franklin et al. (2015)
	Platform ($N = 13$)	O'Connor et al. (2018)
	Integration ($N = 12$)	Till et al. (2023)
	Collaboration ($N = 11$)	Till et al. (2023)
	Diversity ($N = 10$)	Granić (2022)
	Exclusion ($N = 10$)	O'Connor et al. (2018)
	Inclusion ($N = 9$)	Sproul et al. (2021)
	Format ($N = 5$)	Jordan (2023)
	Usability ($N = 5$)	Sweet et al. (2020)
	Respect ($N = 5$)	Afzalan and Muller (2018)

more limited numbers, which might be an indication that even though accessibility was the overarching theme with a striking prevalence among the researched notions indeed, not all of its parameters were equally researched. This is not to necessarily say that such notions warrant less attention, but rather that the scope of the reviewed papers may have been such that more emphasis was placed on some umbrella terms and less on more nuanced ones.

4.2 Interpreting the Results for Inclusivity Theme

For the media inclusivity theme, the notions of inclusivity and its derivatives (inclusion, inclusive, and inclusiveness) were present in the majority of studies reviewed ($N = 9$). Like mentioned above, inclusivity appears less frequently in the review articles compared to accessibility. In fact, it might cause surprise that most of the key notions identified in this category and which link to inclusivity appear more frequently in the review articles than inclusivity itself. Ever-present are the notions of interactivity and participation ($N = 14$), which makes sense given that such terms are at the core of inclusivity. The notions of platform ($N = 13$) and integration ($N = 12$) also feature highly, drawing direct links to how technology is employed in an effort to help make environments more inclusive. Collaboration ($N = 11$) was one of those terms that not only appeared in the majority of studies but was also highly prevalent among the key notions. This is in complete alignment with pedagogical developments of the past two decades or so, which have placed collaboration at the forefront of learning. Diversity ($N = 10$) and exclusion ($N = 10$) also feature higher in prominence than inclusivity. Lastly, terms like format, usability, and respect appear similarly among them ($N = 5$). Results here indicate that inclusivity as a notion is widely researched, while the same can be said for a number of its major parameters.

4.3   Addressing the Research Questions

Returning to the RQs posed in the introduction section, the literature overview reveals a limited current state of the art in the area. This can be attributed to educational technology's relatively recent rise to prominence and the even more recent development of areas like media accessibility and inclusivity. Further development is imminent though, as new technologies are emerging at a fast pace (e.g. virtual reality and artificial intelligence), giving rise to a whole new set of possibilities and research areas. Addressing RQ2, the notions of media accessibility and inclusivity currently show themselves somewhat prominent in the educational domain but only just. In line with the discussion above, they appear to be under-researched to date. Although both notions have received some attention, there is still a lot of ground to cover, particularly research that looks at the two in tandem. Finally, RQ3 enquired which themes affecting media accessibility and inclusivity in the educational domain are most prominent. Themes closely linked to accessibility included technologies, user experiences and user satisfaction, and related policies and regulations governing and/ or ensuring equitable access. On the other hand, interactivity of online educational environments, user participation and collaboration, platform setup and integration of tools and other sources were the themes being more closely linked to inclusivity.

5   Conclusions and Future Work

Scarcity of literature on educational technology accessibility (Brito & Dias, 2020) is a more general concern. Media accessibility and inclusivity can be considered as an important part of this broader problem. Published works have conducted comparative analysis on educational technology and others documented problems experienced by students with disabilities to cope with educational technology. Two main concerns highlighted in Brito and Dias (2020) are accessibility of the educational technology, i.e. LMS in this study and accessibility of the contents published in the educational technology. We share similar observations from the contents perspective especially, as the conducted review has made a two-fold contribution to the research area under study. Firstly, it exposed the limited current state of the art, and secondly, it revealed the need for educational technologies to be more compliant to usability and accessibility standards to ensure inclusive education. Continuous development of new educational technologies to support diverse users, including those with disabilities, further emphasizes the priority and attention that this requires.

In the overview of the 14 review articles, the key themes of inclusivity and accessibility emerged with varying degrees of frequency, with the latter and its derivatives (access, accessible, and accessibility) appearing in all review articles under consideration ($N = 14$) compared to the former and its derivatives (inclusion, inclusive, and inclusiveness) ($N = 9$). This prominence can be attributed to several factors discussed in detail in Sect. 3.3.

The limited current state of the art in this area highlights the need for further research. In light of recent findings, this chapter could be expanded to provide a more comprehensive review, supported by a literature map. This map would represent the landscape of media accessibility and inclusivity in education, summarizing the purpose of each code category. Such an approach would contribute directly to this specific research area by guiding researchers on where contributions can be made. Additionally, future research could focus on identifying the types of learning content that can be effectively taught using emerging technologies, such as VR and AI, and how these should be designed to ensure accessibility and inclusivity.

Acknowledgements This chapter is based upon work from COST Action CA19142—Leading Platform for European Citizens, Industries, Academia and Policymakers in Media Accessibility (LEAD-ME) supported by COST (European Cooperation in Science and Technology).

References

Afzalan, N., & Muller, B. (2018). Online participatory technologies: Opportunities and challenges for enriching participatory planning. *Journal of the American Planning Association, 84*(2), 162–177.

Ahlin, T., & Hiddinga, A. (2023). Technological socialities: The impact of information and communication technologies on belonging among deaf and hard-of-hearing people. *Sociology Compass, 17*(5), e13068.

Alshammari, A., & Fayez, A. M. (2023). Use of technology in enhancing learning among nurses in Saudi Arabia; a systematic review. *Journal of Multidisciplinary Healthcare, 31*, 1587–1599.

Boateng, R., & Amankwaa, A. (2016). The impact of social media on student academic life in higher education. *Global Journal of Human-Social Science, 16*(4), 1–8.

Brito, E., & Dias, G. P. (2020). LMS accessibility for students with disabilities: The experts' opinions. In *2020 15th Iberian Conference on Information Systems and Technologies (CISTI)* (pp. 1–5). IEEE.

Fernández-López, Á., Rodríguez-Fórtiz, M. J., Rodríguez-Almendros, M. L., & Martínez-Segura, M. J. (2013). Mobile learning technology based on iOS devices to support students with special education needs. *Computers & Education, 61*, 77–90.

Franklin, N. C., Lavie, C. J., & Arena, R. A. (2015). Personal health technology: A new era in cardiovascular disease prevention. *Postgraduate Medicine, 127*(2), 150–158.

Granić, A. (2022). Educational technology adoption: A systematic review. *Education and Information Technologies, 27*, 9725–9744. https://doi.org/10.1007/s10639-022-10951-7

Huang, S., Orellana, P., & Capps, M. (2016). US and Chilean college students' reading practices: A cross-cultural perspective. *Reading Research Quarterly, 51*(4), 455–471.

Jordan, K. (2023). How can messaging apps, WhatsApp and SMS be used to support learning? A scoping review. *Technology, Pedagogy and Education, 32*(3), 275–288.

Kimball, E. W., Wells, R. S., Ostiguy, B. J., Manly, C. A., & Lauterbach, A. A. (2016). Students with disabilities in higher education: A review of the literature and an agenda for future research. In M. B. Paulsen (Ed.), *Higher Education: Handbook of Theory and Research* (pp. 91–156). Springer.

Lin, H. C., & Hwang, G. J. (2019). Research trends of flipped classroom studies for medical courses: A review of journal publications from 2008 to 2017 based on the technology-enhanced learning model. *Interactive Learning Environments, 27*(8), 1011–1027.

Mącznik, A. K., Ribeiro, D. C., & Baxter, G. D. (2015). Online technology use in physiotherapy teaching and learning: A systematic review of effectiveness and users' perceptions. *BMC Medical Education, 15*(1), 1–2.

Moriña, A. (2019). Inclusive education in higher education: Challenges and opportunities. *Postsecondary Educational Opportunities for Students with Special Education Needs, 18*, 3–17.

O'Connor, S., Jolliffe, S., Stanmore, E., Renwick, L., & Booth, R. (2018). Social media in nursing and midwifery education: A mixed study systematic review. *Journal of Advanced Nursing, 74*(10), 2273–2289.

Ok, M. W., Kim, M. K., Kang, E. Y., & Bryant, B. R. (2016). How to find good apps: An evaluation rubric for instructional apps for teaching students with learning disabilities. *Intervention in School and Clinic, 51*(4), 244–252.

Ortiz-Jiménez, L., Figueredo-Canosa, V., Castellary López, M., & López Berlanga, M. C. (2020). Teachers' perceptions of the use of icts in the educational response to students with disabilities. *Sustainability, 12*(22), 9446.

Radu, I. (2014). Augmented reality in education: A meta-review and cross-media analysis. *Personal and Ubiquitous Computing, 18*, 1533–1543.

Rao, S. (2004). Faculty attitudes and students with disabilities in higher education: A literature review. *College Student Journal, 38*(2), 191–198.

Rolls, K., Hansen, M., Jackson, D., & Elliott, D. (2016). How health care professionals use social media to create virtual communities: An integrative review. *Journal of Medical Internet Research, 18*(6), e166.

Sproul, J., Ledger, S., & MacCallum, J. (2021). A review of digital media guidelines for students with visual light sensitivity. *International Journal of Disability, Development and Education, 68*(2), 222–239.

Sweet, K. S., LeBlanc, J. K., Stough, L. M., & Sweany, N. W. (2020). Community building and knowledge sharing by individuals with disabilities using social media. *Journal of Computer Assisted Learning, 36*(1), 1–1.

Till, S., Mkhize, M., Farao, J., Shandu, L. D., Muthelo, L., Coleman, T. L., Mbombi, M., Bopape, M., Klingberg, S., van Heerden, A., & Mothiba, T. (2023). Digital health technologies for maternal and child health in Africa and other low-and middle-income countries: Cross-disciplinary scoping review with stakeholder consultation. *Journal of Medical Internet Research, 25*, e42161.

Media Accessibility in Education: Combining Bibliometric Study and Literature Review

Muhammet Berigel[ID]**, Gizem Dilan Boztaş**[ID]**, Beyza Güdek**[ID]**, Gabriela Neagu**[ID]**, and Carlos Duarte**[ID]

Abstract Media accessibility in education is vital for inclusive learning. It ensures that all students can engage with educational content, regardless of their abilities. By offering accessible formats like closed captions, transcripts, and audio descriptions, barriers to learning are eliminated. Media accessibility benefits not only those with sensory impairments but also students with learning disabilities, language barriers, or different learning preferences. Legislation and scientific studies emphasize the importance of media accessibility in education. From a methodological point of view, we will use the bibliometric study and literature review. By applying criteria specific to the two methods of analysis (keywords, language of writing documents, type of journal, number of citations, etc.), we will select articles that correspond to the objectives of the research. From an empirical point of view, theories such as social-cognitive theory, social constructivism or media richness theory will guide us in analyzing the data and establishing relevant conclusions for this field. The results we obtained confirm the importance of the study of specialized literature through specific methods and techniques in the development of new perspectives in the field of media accessibility.

Keywords Media accessibility · Education · Bibliometric analyses · Literature review

M. Berigel (✉) · G. D. Boztaş · B. Güdek
Karadeniz Technical University, Trabzon, Turkey
e-mail: muhammetberigel@gmail.com

G. Neagu
Research Institute for Quality of Life, Romanian Academy, Bucharest, Romania

C. Duarte
LASIGE, Faculdade de Ciências da Universidade de Lisboa, Lisbon, Portugal

© The Author(s) 2024
A. Marcus-Quinn et al. (eds.), *Transforming Media Accessibility in Europe*,
https://doi.org/10.1007/978-3-031-60049-4_11

187

1 Introduction

In an era dominated by the digital transformation of educational practices, the accessibility of media in learning environments emerges as a critical concern, especially for individuals with disabilities. As the landscape of educational resources expands to include a myriad of media formats, ranging from online courses to audiovisual materials, the imperative to ensure equitable access becomes increasingly pronounced. This chapter embarks on a comprehensive exploration of the intersection between media accessibility and education, guided by a bibliometric analysis of contemporary research trends. Rooted in the recognition of the transformative potential of media in education, our inquiry seeks to unravel the nuanced challenges and opportunities that shape the accessibility landscape.

The proliferation of digital media in education, encompassing diverse formats such as Massive Open Online Courses (MOOCs) and multimedia presentations, underscores the need for a comprehensive understanding of accessibility. Recognizing that media serves as a pivotal vehicle for knowledge dissemination, our inquiry delves into the multifaceted dimensions of accessibility. From accommodating individuals with disabilities to addressing diverse learning styles, the contextualization of media accessibility within the educational landscape sets the stage for our exploration.

In this chapter, we present the outcomes of a bibliometric analysis of articles on media accessibility and education. We searched Scopus, a widely used bibliometric database, for this study. The sample of this study consists of peer-reviewed journal articles published between 2013 and 2022. As a result of the query, 100 studies were obtained. After removing publications that were not peer-reviewed or were written in a language different from English, the size of the corpus was reduced to 50 studies. Then, the studies were meticulously reviewed, and it was determined that 17 studies were outside the scope of the study. For this reason, the final dataset to be used in the study consists of 33 studies. These studies were reviewed in detail according to the criteria, keywords, method/methodologies, used technologies, study areas/scope, and working scales/sample of study. The analysis of the review results found eleven clusters. Results of study reveal the current situation of media accessibility in education.

In the remainder of the chapter, we start by contextualizing media accessibility in the domain of education. This is followed by the presentation of the methodology employed and the findings from the bibliometric study. The chapter concludes with a discussion of the findings.

2   Literature Review

Our analysis uses bibliometric analysis as a method, which is considered a recent method easy to use due to (1) the existence of a large number of documents—articles, book chapters, and legislative documents—to which researchers have free access; (2) the development of analysis programs—Gephi, Leximancer, and VOSviewer—which facilitate the work of researchers and lead to results and conclusions relevant for the academic, scientific environment; and (3) the accelerated development of cross-disciplinary studies that can be analyzed in a much more efficient manner by applying bibliometric analysis.

Due to the development of scientific literature in all fields, the methodology of their analysis has been diversified. Thus, for similar objectives, some authors opt for meta-analysis, document mapping, or systematic literature review. It is very important to understand what the particularities of each method are and what is the most suitable option considering the proposed objectives, the volume of documents to be analyzed, etc. A systematic literature review is a theoretical approach used to review relevant documents in a particular field, where documents are selected based on certain criteria of relevant databases (Okoli, 2015). If the systematic review proposes an aggregation of primary studies in terms of research results and investigates whether the results are consistent or contradictory, the mapping study aims to classify the relevant literature based on defined analysis categories (Kitchenham et al., 2010). Unlike the two previous methods, bibliometric analysis is a computer-assisted scientific review that can provide not only a greater amount of information about topics and authors but also relational information on a given topic (Han et al., 2020). Considering the topic addressed by us in this chapter, we consider bibliometric analysis much more appropriate to use.

2.1   Historical Evolution of Media Accessibility in Education

The development of media accessibility solutions for educational settings has been a long and ongoing process, reflecting both the changing needs of learners and the advancement of technology. Early efforts focused on providing access to printed materials for individuals with visual impairments, such as braille transcription and audio recordings (American Printing House for the Blind, 2023). As technologies such as television and video emerged, so did the need for solutions to make these media accessible to a wider range of learners. In the 1970s and 1980s, closed captioning and descriptive video narration (DVN) began to be developed and adopted, providing access to auditory content for individuals who are deaf or hard of hearing (U.S. Department of Justice, 2023).

The advent of the Internet in the 1990s spurred developments in web accessibility, with initiatives such as the Web Content Accessibility Guidelines (WCAG) emerging to address digital inclusivity (W3C, 2023). This era also witnessed the integration of technologies like screen readers, sign language interpreters, and multimedia transcripts to enhance educational content accessibility. Notable milestones include the implementation of Section 508 in the United States, setting standards for electronic and information technology accessibility in federal agencies (Access Board, 2023).

In recent years, there has been a growing focus on making educational technology accessible, including software, learning management systems, and educational games. This has led to the development of a variety of tools and techniques, such as alternative input methods, alternative output methods, and assistive technologies (Haleem et al., 2022). More recently, the rise of artificial intelligence has presented new opportunities for personalized and adaptive learning experiences. Machine learning algorithms are being explored to automatically generate captions, transcripts, and alternative formats, showcasing a paradigm shift in addressing accessibility challenges (Pereira & Duarte, 2023).

2.2 Theoretical Frameworks and Models for Media Accessibility

Media accessibility in educational contexts is grounded in various theoretical frameworks and models that emphasize the importance of inclusive and equitable learning environments for all students, regardless of their individual abilities or disabilities. These frameworks provide a foundation for understanding the significance of media accessibility and the role it plays in promoting inclusive education.

One of the most influential frameworks for media accessibility in education is the universal design for learning (UDL). UDL is a set of principles and guidelines for creating learning experiences that are accessible to all learners, including those with disabilities (Burgstahler, 2013). The three main principles of UDL are as follows:

1. Multiple means of representation: Provide learners with various ways to access and process information, such as text, images, audio, and video.
2. Multiple means of action and expression: Provide learners with various ways to demonstrate their understanding, such as writing, speaking, drawing, and using assistive technologies.
3. Multiple means of engagement: Provide learners with various ways to connect with and motivate themselves to learn, such as choice, personalization, and collaboration.

Social-cognitive theory, developed by Albert Bandura, posits that learning occurs through a combination of observation, imitation, and social interaction (Bandura, 1977). This theory has been applied to media accessibility in education to understand how media can be used to promote positive social interactions and self-efficacy among students with disabilities. For instance, educational videos with closed captioning and descriptive video narration can provide deaf and hard-of-hearing students with access to the same social and emotional cues as their hearing peers, fostering their inclusion and participation in the learning environment.

Social constructivism, a theory of learning that emphasizes the role of social interaction in the construction of knowledge, has informed the development of media accessibility tools and practices (Vygotsky, 1978). For example, online discussion forums and collaborative learning environments can be made accessible to students with disabilities through features like text-to-speech and real-time captioning, enabling them to participate fully in these social learning spaces.

The social model of disability, originating in the disability studies field, posits that disability results from societal barriers rather than inherent impairments (Oliver, 1996). Applied to media accessibility, this model emphasizes the importance of removing barriers in educational content to ensure equitable access for all learners, aligning with inclusive pedagogical principles.

In the realm of technology, the media richness theory offers insights into the selection of communication media based on their ability to convey information (Daft & Lengel, 1986). Applied to educational media, this theory suggests that the richness of content should be preserved across various formats to accommodate different learning styles and preferences. Consequently, educators must consider the inherent richness of different media when designing accessible educational materials.

These theoretical frameworks collectively form a foundation for understanding the significance of media accessibility in educational contexts, emphasizing the principles of inclusivity, proactive design, and the removal of barriers to learning.

2.3 Impact of Media Accessibility on Learning Outcomes

Research provides valuable insights into the impact of multimedia and digital technologies on student learning outcomes, retention rates, and academic achievement. Birch et al. (2010) explore the impact of multiple representations of content using multimedia on learning outcomes. While the experiment did not show a significant improvement in learning performance, students reported favorable perceptions of multimodal learning elements, suggesting that such approaches enhance comprehension and retention.

Burgstahler and Cory (2008) investigated the influence of captioned videos on student learning. The findings indicated that students exposed to captioned videos exhibited improved comprehension and retention of content compared to those without captions. This underscores the significant role of media accessibility, particularly captions, in supporting diverse learning styles and reinforcing educational content.

In the realm of online learning, Cavanaugh et al. (2004) investigated the impact of multimedia design principles, including accessibility features, on student achievement in online courses. The results indicated that courses incorporating these principles led to higher student satisfaction, engagement, and improved learning outcomes.

Srivastava (2012) emphasizes the growth of multimedia within the education sector and its acceleration in recent years. The study acknowledges the potential of multimedia learning resources in supporting concept development, allowing teachers to focus on facilitating learning while students engage with interactive multimedia elements. The Educomp Smart Class program, discussed in the paper, demonstrates positive impacts on students, fostering curiosity and aiding in the understanding of complex concepts.

Poquet et al. (2018) conducted a systematic review of video-based learning from 2007 to 2017, synthesizing the effects of manipulating video presentation, content, and tasks on learning outcomes. The findings highlight the importance of addressing the gap between large-scale data analysis on video interaction and experimental findings, suggesting a direction for future research in video-based learning.

Agisni et al. (2023) delve into the effectiveness of multimedia learning and its impact on student achievement. The study acknowledges the advantages of multimedia, including enhanced visual appeal, support for diverse learning styles, improved information retention, and enhanced understanding of complex concepts. The effectiveness of multimedia learning is contingent on factors such as design, student characteristics, learning objectives, and technological infrastructure.

Pradana (2023) focuses on the impact of digital media on student learning at the university level. The research aims to improve students' perceptions of the utility of digital media in the classroom. While the study recognizes the practicality and less labor-intensive nature of using digital media, it underscores the importance of addressing factors like the quality of instructional materials, technological equipment availability, and trainer assistance.

In conclusion, the collective findings suggest that multimedia and digital technologies have the potential to positively impact student learning outcomes, retention rates, and academic achievement. However, the effectiveness of these approaches depends on various factors, including design considerations, technological infrastructure, and the quality of instructional materials. Addressing these factors is crucial for maximizing the benefits of media accessibility in education.

2.4   Technological Advances in Media Accessibility

The evolution of multimedia technologies has significantly influenced the educational landscape, as evident in the works of Almara'beh et al. (2015) and Barnard (1992). Almara'beh et al. emphasize the transformative impact of multimedia on education, citing the convergence of satellite, computers, audio, and video to create dynamic learning environments. The integration of multimedia not only enhances interaction between teachers, students, and courseware but also provides innovative ways to make learning more dynamic and applicable to real-world scenarios.

Bahja et al. (2021) address the challenges and opportunities arising from technological changes in higher education. The ubiquity of the Internet and smartphones has made information more accessible, prompting a shift in student reliance from traditional classroom resources to online platforms. The study underscores the need to adapt pedagogical approaches to effectively integrate technology into higher education, especially in the post-pandemic era.

Molnár and Szűts (2014) delve into the profound impact of mobile communication and media devices on learning mechanisms. Students' reliance on online sources, social networking sites, and the shift from teachers as information sources to methodological guides are highlighted. The study emphasizes the effectiveness and efficiency of modern learning environments supported by information and communication technologies (ICTs) in higher education.

Kistan (1996) underscores the role of multimedia in narrowing information gaps, emphasizing its contribution to creating rich learning environments. Multimedia not only enriches learning but also empowers individuals to apply technology as both users and developers, contributing to societal development.

Nicolaou et al. (2019) explore the integration of audiovisual media technologies in technology-enhanced learning and teaching methodologies. The paper emphasizes the transformative effects of contemporary advancements in science and technology on education, especially in media studies, where audiovisual media technologies play a crucial role.

Mfreke et al. (2020) highlight the indispensable role of media technology in teaching and learning. The rapid growth of information and communication technology (ICT) is shown to have brought remarkable changes to education in the twenty-first century. However, the study also identifies challenges, such as the need for instructors and learners to acquire essential skills and a prevalent negative attitude toward media technology.

Hong and Shin (2015) focus on the application of multimedia and wireless technology in education. The study explores the use of mobile and wireless multimedia tools, examining available resources for learning and suggesting ways to integrate these tools for effective education. It also considers the role of smartphones, applications, and modern mobile technologies in enhancing the learning environment.

In summary, the discussed papers collectively highlight the transformative role of multimedia, mobile communication, and audiovisual media technologies in shaping the landscape of media accessibility tools and services in education. These advancements have not only changed the way information is accessed and disseminated but also prompted the need for educators to adapt pedagogical approaches and methodologies to meet the evolving demands of the digital era.

2.5 Challenges and Future Directions in Media Accessibility

Implementing media accessibility in education faces multifaceted challenges and barriers that impede its seamless integration. Resource constraints, including limited budgets and technical expertise, present a significant hurdle for educational institutions seeking to adopt and implement media accessibility solutions (Zhang et al.,

2020). The lack of awareness among educators and content creators about the importance of media accessibility, coupled with a dearth of knowledge regarding available tools and guidelines, further compounds the challenge (Matamala & Orero, 2019). Additionally, the existence of varied and evolving accessibility standards contributes to confusion and inconsistencies in the implementation of accessible media across different educational platforms (Fathauer & Rao, 2019; Oncins & Orero, 2021). Technological gaps, where educational technologies and platforms may not uniformly support accessibility features, contribute to disparities in the accessibility of digital learning materials (Tare et al., 2022). Moreover, resistance to change, whether rooted in institutional inertia or individual reluctance, poses a formidable barrier to the widespread integration of media accessibility solutions in educational settings.

Looking ahead, potential future directions and trends in media accessibility research and implementation offer promising avenues for improvement. Artificial intelligence (AI) stands out as a key area, with the potential for AI-driven personalization of media accessibility features based on individual learning preferences (Carbonaro, 2021; Wald, 2021). Exploring how emerging technologies like virtual and augmented reality can enhance accessibility in immersive educational environments is another intriguing direction (Scavarelli et al., 2021). The development of cross-platform integration for accessibility features, ensuring uniform access to media content across various educational platforms, is an area warranting further exploration. User-centered design principles can be leveraged to refine and improve the design of media accessibility tools, considering diverse user needs and preferences (Ortiz-Escobar et al., 2023). Research advocating for policies that promote the integration of media accessibility in educational settings, addressing systemic barriers, is crucial for creating an inclusive learning environment.

3 Methodology

The study was carried out in two stages. In the first stage, bibliometric analysis was carried out, and 50 articles were analyzed. As a result of bibliometric analyses, general statistical analysis information about the studies was obtained. In the second stage, 50 studies were examined in detail, and 33 of them were examined in detail as literature review.

3.1 Bibliometric Analysis

Bibliometric analysis is a numerical analysis method that allows the application of mathematical and statistical methods to text data such as journals and books (Pritchard, 1969). The history of bibliometric analysis dates to the 1950s (Wallin, 2005). However, this method has gained popularity in parallel with the creation of large-scale bibliographic databases (Zupic & Čater, 2015). Bibliometric analysis is based on two basic procedures, performance analysis and scientific mapping (Cobo et al., 2011). Performance analysis includes measuring the performance of countries, institutions, authors, or regions according to publication outputs and citations. In other words, performance analysis is used to reveal the contributions of different research components. Scientific mapping, on the other hand, focuses on explaining the relationships between research components (Donthu et al., 2021). Both were used in this study.

3.2   Search Strategy, Data Collection, Data Preprocessing, and Data Analysis

The creation of the appropriate corpus is one of the most important steps in literature studies. To select relevant studies for this review, a study had to conform to the following criteria: (1) published between 2013 and 2022; (2) published in a Scopus database; (3) focused on media accessibility; (4) articles in English. In this context, Scopus, a widely used bibliometric database, was used in this study. The sample of this study consists of peer-reviewed journal articles published between 2013 and 2022. The Scopus database was searched using the following query for title, summary, and keywords.

- (("media accessibility" OR "accessibility in media" OR "accessible media" OR "media inclusion") AND (educat* OR learn* OR teach*))

As a result of the query, 100 studies were obtained. Studies whose type was specified as an article and whose language was written in English were included in the scope, probably because they underwent a rigorous evaluation process. Thus, the number of corpora to be used in the study was reduced to 50 studies. Then, the studies were meticulously reviewed, and it was determined that 17 studies were not suitable for the scope of the subject. For this reason, the final dataset to be used in the study consists of 33 studies. These studies were reviewed in detail according to the criteria's, keywords, method/methodologies, used technologies, and study areas/ scope. The process is summarized in Fig. 1.

Preprocessing of data is an important step in determining the effectiveness of an analysis. During the data preprocessing of bibliometric studies, singular–plural expression of keywords, synonyms, and the use of abbreviations should be considered. In addition, the spelling of author names, which is important in determining the intellectual structure, should also be checked. Accordingly, in the study, synonymous keywords were identified and reduced to a single word. In addition, the arrangement was made by matching singular and plural. No contradictions were observed regarding the author names.

VOSviewer software was used during the data analysis phase. In the performance analysis, citation rates were considered to determine the best journals in the field. Co-citation analysis, which relates the relationship between authors to the amount

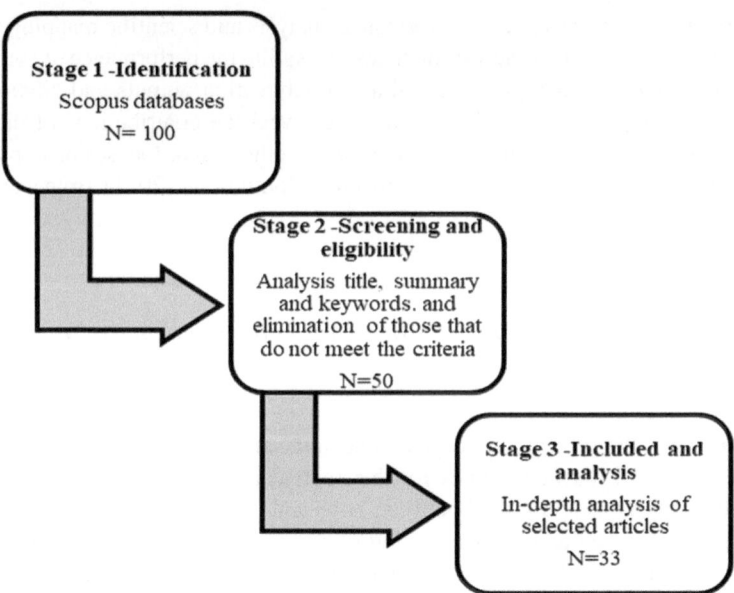

Fig. 1 Document selection process

of co-citation, was conducted for the intellectual structure of the field (White & Griffith, 1981). Authors with at least five citations were included in the co-citation analysis. Co-author analysis, which is an indicator of collaboration, was carried out to determine the social structure (Zupic & Čater, 2015). Authors who received at least one citation were included in the co-authorship analysis.

4　Findings and Results

4.1　Findings Obtained from Bibliometric Analyses

Performance Analysis. When Fig. 2 is examined, it is seen that the number of publications related to media accessibility in education has a fluctuating trend until 2018. It showed increasing momentum between 2018 and 2019. However, the number of publications between 2020 and 2022 remains constant.

The stability in the number of publications related to media accessibility in education between 2020 and 2022 could be attributed to various factors, including the global impact of the COVID-19 pandemic. The unprecedented challenges posed by the pandemic may have redirected research efforts and resources toward urgent issues related to remote learning, digital education, and technology integration in response to widespread disruptions in traditional educational practices. Additionally, during

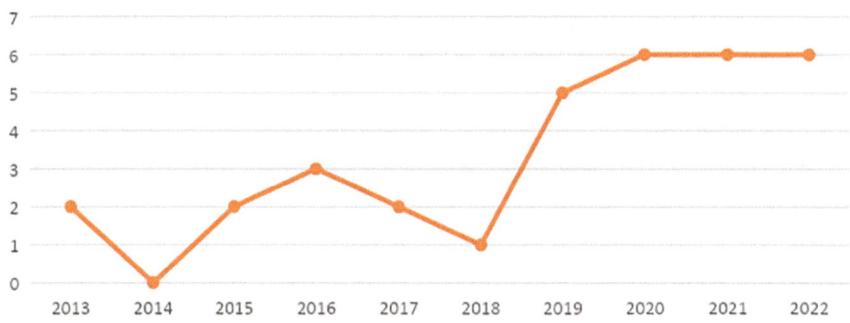

Fig. 2 Change in the number of publications over the years

this period, researchers and educators may have been focused on adapting to new instructional formats and addressing immediate concerns rather than producing a significant volume of publications in the field of media accessibility.

The most influential journals. As a result of the citation analysis carried out to determine the most important journals in media accessibility research in education, it was determined that there were 27 journals that received at least one citation out of 30 journals. As a result of the analysis, the top ten journals with the highest citation value are shown in Table 1.

When Table 1 is examined, it is seen that the most influential journal is the Journal of Specialized Translation. This journal is followed by the journal "Linguistica Antverpiensia, New Series—Themes in Translation Studies". It is also interesting that there are journals from various fields such as medicine, language education, and history among the ten most influential journals in this field.

Structure of the author co-citation network. As a result of the co-citation analysis, it was determined that there were 1890 authors in the bibliography of the study.

Table 1 Ten most influential journals on media accessibility in education

Source	Documents	Citations
Journal of specialised translation	1	64
Linguistica Antverpiensia, new series—themes in translation studies	2	13
Procedia Manufacturing	1	11
Journalism and mass communication educator	1	10
History compass	1	9
Eclinicalmedicine	1	8
Medical science educator	1	8
Monografias de Traduccion e Interpretacion (Montı)	1	8
Interpreter and translator trainer	2	8
Universal access in the information society	1	7

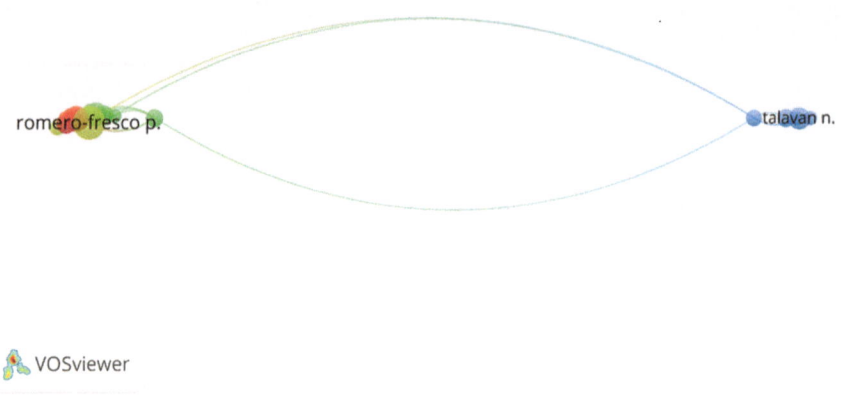

VOSviewer

Fig. 3 Co-citation network map

Twenty six of these authors received at least five citations. The common citation network created by the relevant authors is shown in Fig. 3.

When Fig. 3 is examined, it is seen that four different clusters are formed. The positions of the circles representing the clusters indicate the likelihood of authors to cite similar studies. However, the focus of authors on similar topics in a cluster is directly proportional to the distance of the circles symbolizing the authors. Considering this context, both the authors of the red (Diaz-Cintas J., D. Kiraly et al.), green (D. I. Fels, I. Fryer, G. M. Greco et al.), and yellow (P. Romero-Fresco and C. Eugeni) clusters potentially work on very similar topics both among themselves and with other authors. The distance from the center of the blue (A. Ibanez Moreno, N. Talavan, Lertola et al.) cluster indicates that they focus on different issues than the authors in other clusters. However, the closeness of the circles indicates that the authors of the blue set focus on similar issues within themselves.

Structure of cooperation between countries. With the co-authorship analysis, it was aimed to reveal the social structure of the field. Countries with at least one publication and at least one citation were included in the analysis. Sixteen out of 21 countries met the inclusion criteria. However, Australia, Spain, China, Czech Republic, Germany, Norway, Turkey, and United States are not included in the analysis as they are not affiliated with any country. The co-authorship map reflecting the cooperation between countries is shown in Fig. 4.

The country co-authorship map consists of three different clusters. Each cluster has an equal number of countries. Belgium has the highest total link strength (TLS = 2) in the red cluster. In the blue cluster, Spain (TLS = 4) is the country with the highest total link strength, while in the green cluster, United Kingdom (TLS = 3) ranks first in terms of total link strength. When Fig. 4 is examined, it is seen that Spain and United Kingdom are the most effective countries in terms of media accessibility in education. In addition, the co-authorship map on a country basis shows that collaborations in the field of media accessibility in education are still limited to a certain geography.

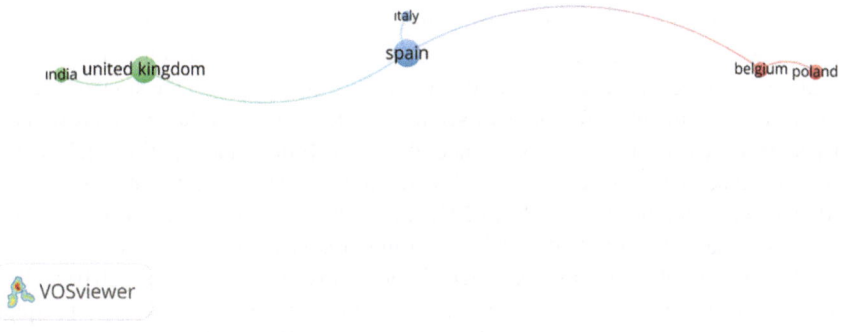

Fig. 4 Co-authorship map by country

Research Themes of Media Accessibility in Education. The common word analysis map made to examine the change of research themes of the field according to time is shown in Fig. 5. The analysis was carried out over 140 words.

When Fig. 5 is examined, it is seen that 11 clusters are formed. Looking at the common word analysis map, it is noticed that the most frequently used keyword is "audio description". This keyword is followed by the keywords "accessibility" and "audiovisual translation". In addition, it is seen that cluster 1, cluster 4, cluster 7, and cluster 10 belong to the studies carried out between 2018 and 2020. It is noticed that cluster 2 and cluster 8 cover the studies between 2016 and 2018, and cluster 3 covers the works of 2020 and beyond. On the other hand, it is noteworthy that some of the cluster 2 and cluster 11 are keywords originating from the studies of 2016. Cluster 5 and cluster 6 consist of keywords for the 2022 period.

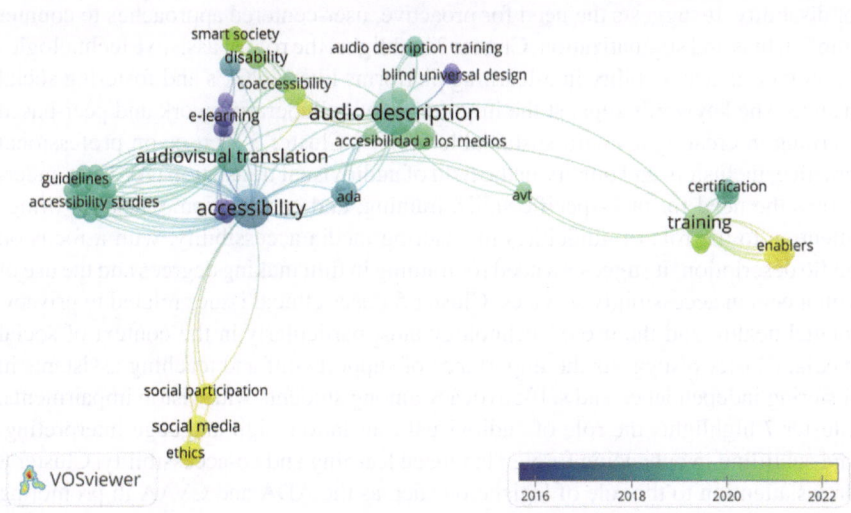

Fig. 5 Co-word analysis map

The observed clustering pattern in bibliometric analysis, with specific clusters associated with distinct time periods, suggests a temporal evolution in the research landscape of media accessibility in education. The prominence of the keyword "audio description" as the most frequently used term underscores a sustained interest in this aspect of accessibility. The prominence of "accessibility" and "audiovisual translation" as subsequent keywords reflects broader themes in the field. Clusters 1, 4, 7, and 10 focusing on studies from 2018 to 2020 may indicate a concentrated research effort during this period, possibly driven by emerging trends, technological advancements, or educational policy changes. Clusters 2 and 8 covering studies from 2016 to 2018 suggest an earlier wave of research, perhaps laying the groundwork for subsequent investigations. Cluster 3, representing works from 2020 and beyond, could signify a response to the challenges posed by the COVID-19 pandemic and the subsequent surge in interest in digital education and accessibility. Clusters 5 and 6, consisting of keywords for the 2022 period, indicate a more recent shift or a continued focus on specific aspects of media accessibility, possibly reflecting ongoing developments or emerging research directions.

The presence of keywords from 2016 in clusters 2 and 11 may suggest enduring themes or foundational concepts that have persisted over time. Overall, the clustering based on time periods likely reflects the dynamic nature of research in media accessibility in education, influenced by technological advancements, societal changes, and evolving educational priorities.

Figure 6 provides a visual representation of the clusters of keywords derived from the literature review.

The clusters of keywords suggest a multifaceted approach to media accessibility and education. Cluster 1 emphasizes the importance of integrating accessibility studies into curriculum design, drawing on critical theory and the social model of disability. It suggests the need for proactive, user-centered approaches to counter implicit bias and stigmatization. Cluster 2 highlights the role of assistive technologies in promoting accessibility in e-learning platforms like MOOCs and fostering social justice. The keywords suggest the importance of collaborative work and peer-based learning in creating a smart, sustainable society. Cluster 3 focuses on professional practice, inclusion, and quality in the field of audiovisual translation (AVT). It underscores the need for task-specific skills, training, and certification. Cluster 4 brings attention to the role of guidelines in ensuring media accessibility, with a focus on audio description. It suggests a need for training in film making degrees and the use of volunteers in accessibility services. Cluster 5 raises ethical issues related to privacy, mental health, and the use of technology aids, particularly in the context of social media. Cluster 6 suggests the importance of support staff and teaching assistants in fostering independence and self-advocacy among students with vision impairments. Cluster 7 highlights the role of audiovisual translation, sign language interpreting, and subtitling in enhancing foreign language learning and co-accessibility. Cluster 8 draws attention to the role of legislation such as the ADA and CVAA in promoting accessibility and the importance of pedagogy in meeting these standards. Cluster 9 emphasizes the role of creative subtitling and universal design in accessible filmmaking. Cluster 10 suggests the importance of training and course design in audio

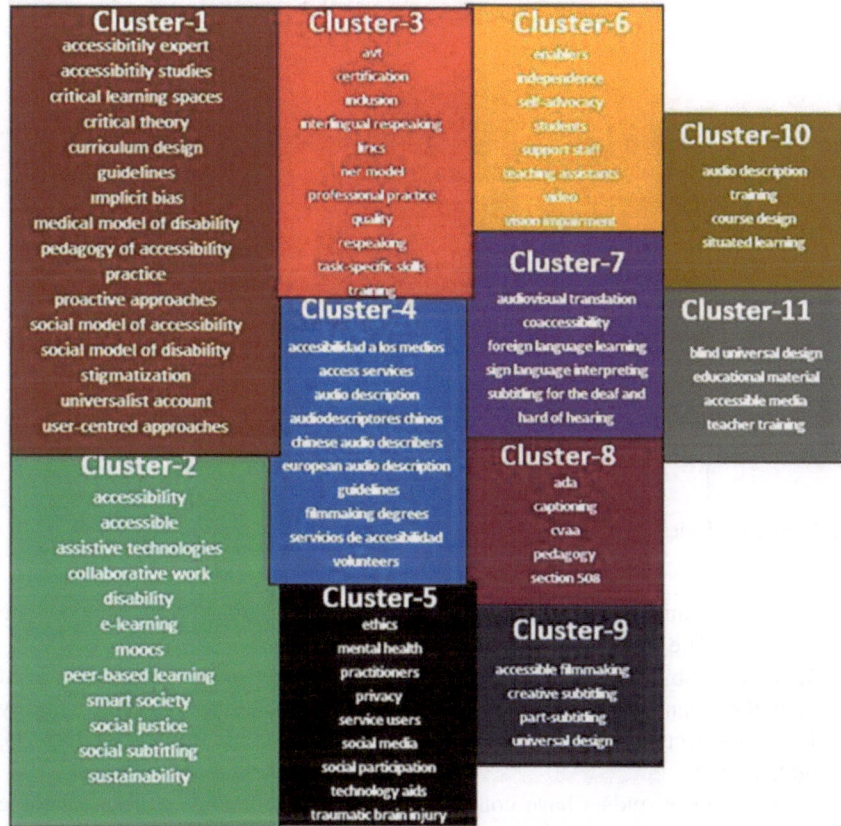

Fig. 6 Clusters and keywords

description, with a focus on situated learning. Finally, cluster 11 emphasizes the need for teacher training and the design of accessible educational material, particularly for the blind.

These clusters collectively underscore the need for a comprehensive, multidisciplinary approach to media accessibility and education, encompassing curriculum design, assistive technologies, professional practice, ethical considerations, legislative compliance, and teacher training.

Systematic Literature Review. In the second part of study, 33 articles were reviewed in detail according to the criteria: keywords, method/methodologies, used technologies, and study areas/scope. There are 33 studies derived from rigorously filtered data. Figure 7 shows that these studies were carried out using different methods.

The most preferred method is the qualitative method, and there are 16 qualitative studies including reviews. Another preferred method is quantitative: 11. In the quantitative studies, the survey method was mostly preferred. There are also two

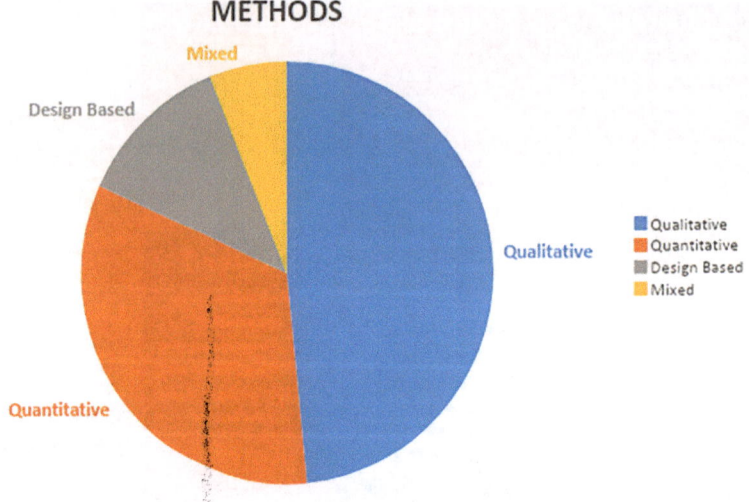

Fig. 7 Methodologies of articles

studies that use mixed methods, in which qualitative and quantitative methods are used together. The remaining four studies are design-based.

Media accessibility in education is divided into different areas of study. Presented in Fig. 8, these can be categorized as individuals with disabilities (11), accessibility (8), learning effect (8), individuals with disabilities and accessibility (3), ethics (1), and addiction (1).

However, other studies have considered different technologies. These include audio or video works for individuals with disabilities. According to study data,

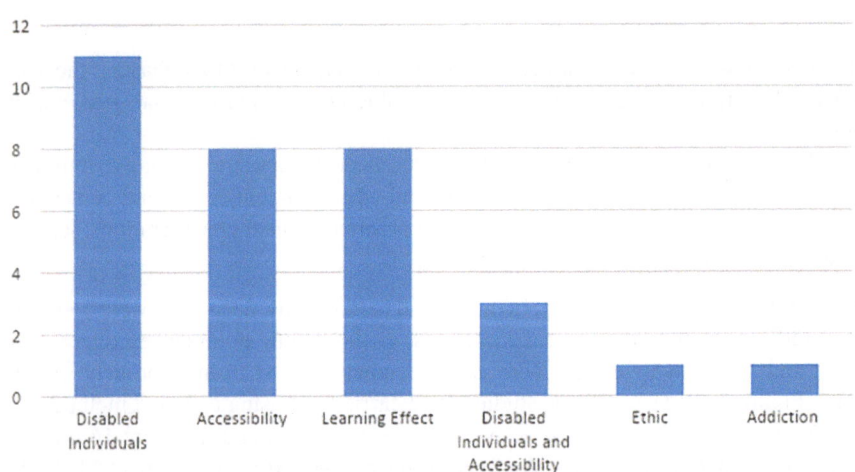

Fig. 8 Research field/scope of studies

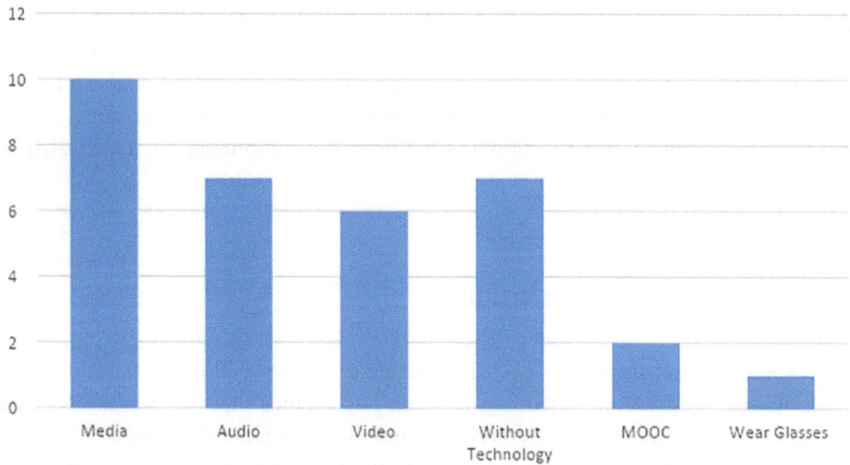

Fig. 9 Used technology in articles

presented in Fig. 9, TV is a widely preferred media tool. Massive Open Online Courses (MOOC) is the topic of two different studies. In the 33 studies, seven studies did not mention technology or did not use technology.

The literature review findings provide valuable insights into the methodologies, research scope, and technological dimensions of studies on media accessibility in education. The prevalence of qualitative methods, including reviews, in 16 out of 33 studies suggests a strong inclination toward exploring the subjective experiences, perceptions, and qualitative aspects of media accessibility. This qualitative focus may be indicative of a nuanced understanding of the lived experiences of individuals with disabilities in educational settings.

The prominence of quantitative methods in 11 studies, particularly through survey methodologies, underscores a commitment to empirical data collection and statistical analysis. This suggests a complementary effort to quantify and generalize findings regarding media accessibility and its impact on education.

The presence of two studies utilizing mixed methods signifies a recognition of the multifaceted nature of the research topic. This approach allows researchers to capture both the depth of qualitative insights and the breadth of quantitative data, providing a more comprehensive understanding of media accessibility in education. The categorization of studies based on their research scope reveals varied focal points. The emphasis on individuals with disabilities (11 studies) aligns with a growing awareness of inclusivity in education. The attention to accessibility (8 studies) and learning effects (8 studies) highlights the multifaceted nature of the relationship between media and education. The exploration of ethics and addiction in one study each reflects a recognition of the broader societal implications of media accessibility.

The diversity in technologies considered in the studies, ranging from traditional media like TV to modern platforms like MOOCs, indicates a dynamic landscape. The omission of technology in seven studies may suggest a focus on theoretical or conceptual aspects, highlighting the need for a balanced exploration of both practical applications and theoretical underpinnings in media accessibility research. In conclusion, the reviewed literature showcases a rich tapestry of research methodologies, scopes, and technological considerations, emphasizing the multidimensional nature of media accessibility in education and the need for comprehensive approaches to address this complex field.

5 Discussion and Conclusion

The examination of the results reveals intricate dynamics within the field of media accessibility in education, shedding light on key themes that bridge the literature review and empirical findings. In this discussion, we delve into three focused themes, namely intersectionality in media accessibility, emerging technologies and media accessibility, and challenges and gaps in current research.

5.1 Intersectionality in Media Accessibility

The identified research themes showcase the importance of adopting an intersectional lens when addressing media accessibility in educational settings. Considering the diverse needs of individuals with disabilities highlighted in the literature (Díaz Cintas & Remael, 2021), it is imperative to evaluate how these themes capture the nuanced experiences of different user groups. Our analysis aligns with the perspectives from Romero-Fresco et al. (2020), integrating factors such as disability type, cultural background, and educational context to understand the intricacies of ensuring equitable access to educational media. This discussion underscores the necessity of tailoring accessibility solutions to the multifaceted identities of learners.

5.2 Emerging Technologies and Media Accessibility

Building on the literature's emphasis on technological advancements shaping media accessibility (Zupic & Čater, 2015), our analysis explores the intersection of identified themes with emerging technologies. The literature's discussions on MOOCs and technological preferences (Donthu et al., 2021) guide our evaluation of how these themes anticipate and respond to challenges and opportunities posed by new technologies. This exploration accentuates the dynamic nature of the field, emphasizing the need for adaptive strategies to harness the potential of emerging technologies positively. As technology continues to evolve, the identified themes provide a foundation for future-proofing media accessibility in education.

5.3 Challenges and Gaps in Current Research

Rooted in the literature's insights into bibliometric study methodologies (Zupic & Čater, 2015), our analysis identifies challenges and gaps within the current state of media accessibility research in education. Drawing from the literature's emphasis on study inclusion criteria and rigorous evaluation processes (Donthu et al., 2021), we assess how the identified themes contribute to addressing or exacerbating these challenges. By reflecting on the literature's anticipation of methodological challenges, our discussion prompts the formulation of research questions that guide future directions for more robust and inclusive media accessibility research. This critical evaluation lays the groundwork for advancing the methodological rigor and depth of research in the field.

5.4 Limitations of the Research

Like all research, this work also has several limitations, and the results should be interpreted with this in mind. First, the inclusion criteria that guided the selection of studies for this bibliometric analysis may have influenced the results obtained. Some relevant studies may have been excluded. Second, the 70 papers included in the final selection were not distributed in such a way as to reflect a possibly generalized situation.

5.5 Concluding Remark

In conclusion, this discussion offers a nuanced understanding of the results, positioning them within the broader context of existing literature. The synthesis of theoretical perspectives and empirical findings not only contributes to the academic discourse on media accessibility but also informs actionable recommendations for researchers, educators, and policymakers committed to fostering inclusive educational environments.

Acknowledgements This chapter is based upon work from COST Action CA19142—Leading Platform for European Citizens, Industries, Academia and Policymakers in Media Accessibility (LEAD-ME) supported by COST (European Cooperation in Science and Technology).

References

Agisni, A., Novari, D., Leander, G., Prawirawan, B. U., & Pohan, A. H. (2023). The effectiveness of multimedia learning: A study on student learning. *Priviet Social Sciences Journal*, 9–11.

Almara'beh, H., Amer, E. F., & Sulieman, A. (2015). The effectiveness of multimedia learning tools in education. *International Journal of Advanced Research in Computer Science and Software Engineering*, 761–764.

American Printing House for the Blind. (2023). Retrieved from American Printing House for the Blind: Mission, History, and Services: https://aphmuseum.org/. https://aphmuseum.org/

Bahja, M., Kuhail, M. A., & Hammad, R. (2021). Embracing technological change in higher education. In L. Waller, & S. Waller (Eds.), *Higher education—New approaches to accreditation, digitalization, and globalization in the age of covid*. IntechOpen.

Bandura, A. (1977). *Social learning theory*. Prentice-Hall.

Barnard, J. (1992). Multimedia and the future of distance learning technology. *Educational Media International*, 139–144.

Birch, D., Sankey, M., & Gardiner, M. (2010). The impact of multiple representations of content using multimedia on learning outcomes. *International Journal of Instructional Technology and Distance Learning*, 3–19.

Burgstahler, S. E., & Cory, R. C. (2008). Indicators of institutional change. In S. E. Burgstahler & R. C. Cory (Eds.), *Universal design in higher education: From principles to practice*. Harvard Education Press.

Burgstahler, S. E. (2013). *Universal design in higher education: Promising practices*. DO-IT, University of Washington.

Carbonaro, A. (2021). Modelling educational resources to support accessibility requirements. In *2021 IEEE 18th Annual Consumer Communications & Networking Conference (CCNC)* (pp. 1–5). IEEE.

Cavanaugh, C., Gillan, K. J., Kromrey, J., Hess, M., & Blomeyer, R. (2004). *The effects of distance education on k–12 student outcomes: A meta-analysis*. Learning Point Associates.

Cobo, M., López-Herrera, A., Herrera-Viedma, E., & Herrera, F. (2011). Science mapping software tools: Review, analysis, and cooperative study among tools. *Journal of the American Society for Information Science and Technology*, 1382–1402.

Daft, R. L., & Lengel, R. H. (1986). Organizational information requirements, media richness and structural design. *Management Science*, 554–571.

Díaz Cintas, J., & Remael, A. (2021). *Subtitling: Concepts and practices*. Routledge.

Donthu, N., Kumar, S., Mukherjee, D., Pandey, N., & Lim, W. M. (2021). How to conduct a bibliometric analysis: An overview and guidelines. *Journal of Business Research*, 285–296.

Fathauer, L., & Rao, D. M. (2019). Accessibility in an educational software system: Experiences and Design Tips. In *2019 IEEE Frontiers in Education Conference (FIE)* (pp. 1–8). IEEE.

Haleem, A., Javaid, M., Qadri, M. A., & Suman, R. (2022). Understanding the role of digital technologies in education: A review. *Sustainable Operations and Computers*, 275–285.

Han, J., Kang, H.-J., Kim, M., & Kwon, G. H. (2020). Mapping the intellectual structure of research on surgery with mixed reality: Bibliometric network analysis (2000–2019). *Journal of Biomedical Informatics*.

Hong, S. R., & Shin, I. Y. (2015). The application of multimedia and wireless technology in education. *Indian Journal of Science and Technology*, 1–11.

Kistan, C. (1996). Multi media in education: emerging technology and our information gaps. In *1996 IEEE International Conference on Multi Media Engineering Education. Conference Proceedings* (pp. 313–318). IEEE.

Kitchenham, B. A., Budgen, D., & Brereton, O. P. (2010). The value of mapping studies—A participant-observer case study. In *14th International Conference on Evaluation and Assessment in Software Engineering (EASE)* (pp. 1–9). Keele University.

Matamala, A., & Orero, P. (2019). Training Experts in inclusive practices for an equity on access to culture in Europe. In S. Halder, & V. Argyropoulos, (Eds.), *Inclusion, equity and access for individuals with disabilities: Insights from educators across world* (pp. 263–280). Springer Nature.

Mfreke, U. J., Ismail, S., & Isong, M. B. (2020). Teaching and learning with media technology. *International Journal of Innovations in Engineering Research and Technology*, 296–300.

Molnár, G., & Szűts, Z. (2014). Advanced mobile communication and media devices and applications in the base of higher education. In *2014 IEEE 12th International Symposium on Intelligent Systems and Informatics (SISY)* (pp. 169–174). IEEE.

Nicolaou, C., Matsiola, M., & Kalliris, G. (2019). *Technology-enhanced learning and teaching methodologies through audiovisual media.* Education Sciences.

Okoli, C. (2015). *A guide to conducting a standalone systematic literature review.* Communications of the Association for Information Systems.

Oliver, M. (1996). *Understanding disability: From theory to practice.* Red Globe Press.

Oncins, E., & Orero, P. (2021). *Let's put standardisation in practice: accessibility services and interaction* (pp. 71–90). Hikma.

Ortiz-Escobar, L. M., Chavarria, M. A., Schönenberger, K., Hurst, S., Stein, M. A., Mugeere, A., & Rivas Velarde, M. (2023). Assessing the implementation of user-centred design standards on assistive technology for persons with visual impairments: A systematic review. *Frontiers in Rehabilitation Sciences.*

Pereira, L. S., & Duarte, C. (2023). *AI and media accessibility, an overview.* Retrieved from https://lead-me-cost.eu/resources/LEAD-ME_AIandAccessibility.pdf

Poquet, O., Lim, L., Mirriahi, N., & Dawson, S. (2018). Video and learning: A systematic review (2007–2017). In *Proceedings of the 8th International Conference on Learning Analytics and Knowledge* (pp. 151–160). Association for Computing Machinery.

Pradana, H. D. (2023). The Impact of Digital Media on Student Learning at University. Jurnal Ilmu Pendidikan (JIP) STKIP Kusuma Negara Jakarta, 1–8.

Pritchard, A. (1969). Statistical bibliography or bibliometrics. *Journal of Documentation*, 348–349.

Romero-Fresco, P., & Eugeni, C. (2020). Live subtitling through respeaking. In Ł Bogucki & M. Deckert (Eds.), *The Palgrave handbook of audiovisual translation and media accessibility* (pp. 269–295). Palgrave Macmillan.

Scavarelli, A., Arya, A., & Teather, R. J. (2021). Virtual reality and augmented reality in social learning spaces: A literature review. *Virtual Reality*, 257–277.

Srivastava, S. (2012). A study of multimedia & its impact on students' attitude. In *2012 IEEE International Conference on Technology Enhanced Education (ICTEE)* (pp. 1–5). IEEE.

Tare, M., Shell, A. R., & Jackson, S. R. (2022). Student engagement with evidence-based supports for literacy on a digital platform. *Journal of Research on Technology in Education*, 177–187.

U.S. Access Board. (2023). Retrieved from IT Accessibility Laws and Policies. https://www.section508.gov/manage/laws-and-policies/

U.S. Department of Justice. (2023). ADA Standards for Accessible Design. Retrieved from https://archive.ada.gov/doj_responsibilities.htm

Vygotsky, L. S. (1978). *Mind in society.* Harvard University Press.

W3C. (2023). Retrieved from Web Content Accessibility Guidelines (WCAG) 2.2: https://www.w3.org/TR/WCAG22/

Wald, M. (2021). AI data-driven personalisation and disability inclusion. *Frontiers in Artificial Intelligence.*

Wallin, J. A. (2005). Bibliometric methods: Pitfalls and possibilities. *Basic & Clinical Pharmacology & Toxicology*, 261–275.

White, H. D., & Griffith, B. C. (1981). Author cocitation: A literature measure of intellectual structure. *Journal of the American Society for Information Science*, 163–171.

Zhang, X., Tlili, A., Nascimbeni, F., Burgos, D., Huang, R., Chang, T.-W., et al. (2020). Accessibility within open educational resources and practices for disabled learners: A systematic literature review. *Smart Learning Environments.*

Zupic, I., & Čater, T. (2015). Bibliometric methods in management and organization. *Organizational Research Methods*, 429–472.

Media Accessibility in E-Learning: Analyzing Learning Management Systems

Muhammet Berigel⊙, Duygu Solak Berigel⊙, Carlos Duarte⊙,
Christos Mettouris⊙, Evangelia Vanezi⊙, Alexandros Yeratziotis⊙,
and George A. Papadopoulos⊙

Abstract Distance education and online learning gained significant importance, especially during the COVID-19 pandemic, as well as in response to new needs and trends in the digital age. Learning Management Systems (LMS) are one of the main instruments for formal and informal learning activities. Learners, educators, and potential new customers need LMS that are accessible to instructors and other users with disabilities, as well as produce accessible content for students. Accessibility standards, as Section 508, EN 301 549, ADA (Americans with Disabilities Act), and WCAG (Web Content Accessibility Guidelines), serve as the basis for evaluating LMS providers commitment to inclusivity. This study presents a critical assessment of the publicly available information provided by the LMS providers on their accessibility. It explores and compares the media accessibility features offered and adherence to established standards. This chapter aims to provide educators, institutions, and learners with valuable insights, enabling them to make well-informed decisions in an era where digital learning has become ubiquitous. Moreover, results of the study highlight the need for enhanced accessibility features and improved usability in creating accessible and inclusive LMS. Key themes arising from the review of LMSs regarding their accessibility features and compliance with established standards are presented.

Keywords Learning management systems · Accessibility · Assistive technology

M. Berigel (✉)
Karadeniz Technical University, Trabzon, Turkey
e-mail: muhammetberigel@gmail.com

D. S. Berigel
Trabzon University, Akçaabat, Turkey

C. Duarte
LASIGE, Faculdade de Ciências da Universidade de Lisboa, Lisbon, Portugal

C. Mettouris · E. Vanezi · G. A. Papadopoulos
Department of Computer Science, University of Cyprus, Nicosia, Cyprus

A. Yeratziotis
A.G. Connect Deaf Limited, Nicosia, Cyprus

A. Marcus-Quinn et al. (eds.), *Transforming Media Accessibility in Europe*,
https://doi.org/10.1007/978-3-031-60049-4_12

209

1 Introduction and Background

In recent years, the integration of technology into education has brought about trans-formative changes in the way learning is delivered and accessed. Learning Manage-ment Systems (LMS) have emerged as powerful tools that facilitate the creation, management, and delivery of educational content in both traditional and online settings. While the adoption of LMS platforms has led to increased convenience and flexibility, it has also raised concerns regarding equitable access for all learners, including those with disabilities. As digital learning continues to evolve, the accessi-bility of LMS becomes a critical consideration in ensuring that education is truly inclusive. Moreover, characteristics and features that could transform LMS into advanced LMS from a technical perspective include learner profiling; customiza-tion/personalization/differentiated learning; ubiquitous learning; active knowledge making; multimodal meaning; recursive feedback; collaborative intelligence; and metacognition. Although implementation and adoption of the aforementioned are relatively slower in pace, learners and educators would benefit immensely, especially as these evolve over the next few years. We foresee such technologies having a signif-icant role in enhancing equity, accessibility, inclusion, diversity and understanding and support for learners and therefore propose that they generally be considered more in the development of LMS.

1.1 Accessibility Standards and Regulations

To address the issue of digital accessibility, various international standards and regu-lations have been established. Notable among these are Section 508 of the Reha-bilitation Act, the European Standard EN 301 549, the Americans with Disabilities Act (ADA), and the Web Content Accessibility Guidelines (WCAG) developed by the World Wide Web Consortium (W3C). These standards provide a framework for evaluating the accessibility of digital platforms, including Learning Management Systems. Institutions and organizations have increasingly recognized the importance of adhering to these standards to ensure that their educational content and platforms are accessible to individuals with disabilities.

Section 508 (U.S. General Services Administration, 2023) refers to a critical component of the Rehabilitation Act of 1973 in the United States, which mandates that federal agencies make their electronic and information technology accessible to people with disabilities. This includes Learning Management Systems (LMS) used in digital education. Compliance with Section 508 ensures that students and educators with disabilities have equal access to educational resources and opportunities. In the context of digital education, Section 508 plays a pivotal role in fostering inclusivity and eliminating barriers for individuals with diverse needs.

Across the Atlantic, the European Standard EN 301 549 (ETSI, CEN, & CENELEC, 2021) establishes accessibility requirements for ICT products and services, including those used in education. Developed by the European Telecommunications Standards Institute (ETSI), this standard aims to create a more inclusive digital environment. EN 301 549 considers a wide range of disabilities and ensures that learning materials and platforms, including Learning Management Systems, are designed to accommodate diverse learners. In the realm of digital education, adherence to this standard enhances accessibility, creating an environment conducive to learning for all.

The Americans with Disabilities Act (ADA) (U.S. Department of Justice Civil Rights Division, 2008) is a landmark piece of legislation in the United States that prohibits discrimination against individuals with disabilities. In the context of digital education, ADA compliance is crucial for ensuring that online learning platforms, including Learning Management Systems, are accessible to all students and educators. ADA extends beyond federal agencies to cover a broader spectrum, emphasizing the importance of inclusivity in the digital education landscape.

The Web Content Accessibility Guidelines (WCAG) (W3C, 2024) provide a comprehensive set of recommendations for making web content, including educational materials on Learning Management Systems, more accessible. Developed by the Web Accessibility Initiative (WAI), these guidelines are internationally recognized and serve as a benchmark for digital inclusivity. Adhering to WCAG ensures that educational content is perceivable, operable, and understandable by a diverse audience, reinforcing the principles of universal design in the realm of digital education.

1.2   Digital Inclusion in Education

The concept of digital inclusion in education goes beyond compliance with accessibility standards; it embodies the principle that all learners, regardless of their abilities, should have equal access to educational opportunities. Accessible LMS platforms play a pivotal role in removing barriers to learning for individuals with disabilities. A study by Burgstahler and Cory (2008) highlights that accessible online learning environments not only benefit students with disabilities but also enhance the overall learning experience for all students by providing diverse means of engagement and interaction.

Accessible LMS platforms encompass a range of features and technologies designed to accommodate different types of disabilities. These include video subtitles to aid individuals with hearing impairments, easy navigation and interactivity options for intuitive use, screen reader support for visually impaired users, accessible text editors for content creation, support for accessible course content, high-contrast themes for improved visibility, and keyboard accessibility for those who rely on keyboard navigation.

While substantial progress has been made in improving the accessibility of LMS platforms, challenges persist. These challenges range from ensuring that accessibility features are effectively implemented to keeping pace with evolving technologies.

Future research in this domain should address the practical implementation of accessibility standards and explore innovative solutions to enhance the overall usability of LMS platforms for individuals with disabilities.

In conclusion, the accessibility of Learning Management Systems is a pivotal aspect of modern education, reflecting the commitment to inclusivity and equitable access to knowledge. This literature review sets the stage for a comprehensive examination of LMS platforms, evaluating their adherence to accessibility standards and the presence of key accessibility features. The study aims to contribute to the ongoing dialogue on accessible digital education, providing valuable insights for educators, institutions, and learners alike.

1.3   Literature Review on Accessibility in LMS

In the literature, many papers explore whether LMS conform to accessibility standards and the level to which they do. Most LMS include accessibility barriers that make the creation of accessible e-learning environments difficult for teachers and administrators (Calvo et al., 2014). Calvo et al. (2014) evaluated the accessibility of the Moodle authoring tool with a study focused on visual impairment. According to the World Health Organization (WHO), an estimated 2.2 billion people have a near or distance vision impairment (WHO, 2023). Visually impaired users confront numerous difficulties daily when accessing web pages and online content. The authors mention two studies (Creven, 2003; Disability Rights Commission, 2004) that concluded that visually impaired users using screen readers were found to take three times as long as non-disabled users to complete a given task. Common problems faced by screen reader users include the lack of labels associated with controls like inputText, complex Web page structures and layouts, the lack of alternative texts for images, the impracticality of certain navigation techniques, inadequate color contrasts used, and incorrect size of elements (Disability Rights Commission, 2004).

Especially in LMS, visually impaired users often face difficulties in accessing online courses or learning content, while visually impaired teachers and administrators face difficulties in uploading their learning materials and managing their courses (Calvo et al., 2014). It is important to note here that, regarding LMS, besides the system itself, all documents and resources created by the teachers and presented via the LMS should also be accessible. For example, screen reader users require alternative text in all images, while hearing-impaired users require appropriate subtitles for videos (Calvo et al., 2014).

Regarding studies that evaluate LMS according to accessibility guidelines, it is mentioned that in most studies, LMS like Moodle, dotLRN, Blackboard ATutor, and Sakai have been found to contain serious barriers to accessibility with respect to WCAG 1.0 and ATAG 2.0 (Calvo et al., 2014; Iglesias et al., 2014; Power et al., 2010). Accessibility problems for visually impaired users in Moodle were also found in the diverse images used to convey information and the lack of headings in the application (Moreno et al., 2012). Hence, Moodle did not conform to ATAG 2.0 or WCAG 2.0.

Calvo et al. (2014) conclude with recommendations for improving the accessibility of Moodle interface and the content created therein, the most important of which are: checking the accessibility of any external elements before using them in Moodle, avoiding common accessibility errors, and providing mechanisms to enable authors to avoid mistakes such as buttons for the cancellation of each task, mechanisms to undo actions executed, functionalities to periodically save the actions executed to prevent information loss, ways to save user preferences regarding auto-saving, colors, font size, etc.

In Iglesias et al. (2014), a comparative study of the accessibility of three LMS, Moodle, ATutor, and Sakai, was conducted as regards the compliance of each system with ATAG 2.0 and each system's user interface with WCAG 1.0. The results of the study indicate that indeed barriers to accessibility exist in each of the three systems evaluated. More to the point, the authors conclude that ATutor facilitates the creation of accessible learning content better than the other two LMS. However, problems were observed in all three LMS that would likely limit their accessibility for certain groups of users like elderly people and people with disabilities. Such accessibility barriers could partially or completely exclude these users from interacting with the LMS (Iglesias et al., 2014).

Regarding accessibility of mobile applications for LMS, a recent study showed that many educational mobile apps remain inaccessible to users with disabilities who require accessibility features such as talkback or screen reader features (Aljedaani et al., 2023; Brito & Dias, 2020). The authors in Aljedaani et al. (2023), Brito and Dias (2020) explore the accessibility status of the Blackboard mobile app, a well-known and widely used LMS. They have conducted a survey on students' perceived usability of the Blackboard mobile app, where 1308 hearing students and 65 deaf and hard-of-hearing students participated. In addition, the authors collected and analyzed 15,478 user reviews from the Google Play Store to identify any accessibility issues. The outcome of this study was that most deaf and hard-of-hearing students found difficulty in using the Blackboard mobile app compared to hearing students. For example, the lack of captions in some videos caused problems for deaf students, as they could not hear what the teacher was saying and solely relied on captions. This problem was reported for both live-streaming content and pre-recorded videos. The app store analysis showed that only 31% of the reviews reported violations of accessibility principles that apps like Blackboard must comply with. The study highlights these violations and their corresponding implications to support LMS frameworks in becoming more inclusive for all users.

We aim to provide a complementary study by examining compliance with accessibility standards and key accessibility features regarding the 10 most widely used Learning Management Systems, a combination that no other work studied so far.

2 Methodology

The methodology for this study involved a critical assessment of the publicly available information provided by the LMS providers. This included reviewing provider Web sites, product documentation, and marketing materials to identify the accessibility features and limitations of their LMSs. The information was then analyzed using a content analysis approach (Krippendorff, 2019) to identify patterns, themes, and trends in the data. An overview of the methodology is presented in Fig. 1.

2.1 Research Objective

This study aims to assess the reported accessibility standards compliance and the availability of key accessibility technology features within the 10 most widely used Learning Management Systems (LMS). The primary focus is to provide an overview of the current accessibility status of these LMS platforms as reported by their providers.

2.2 Selection of Learning Management Systems

A purposive sampling method is employed to select the 10 LMS platforms for examination. These platforms are chosen based on their popularity and extensive usage in

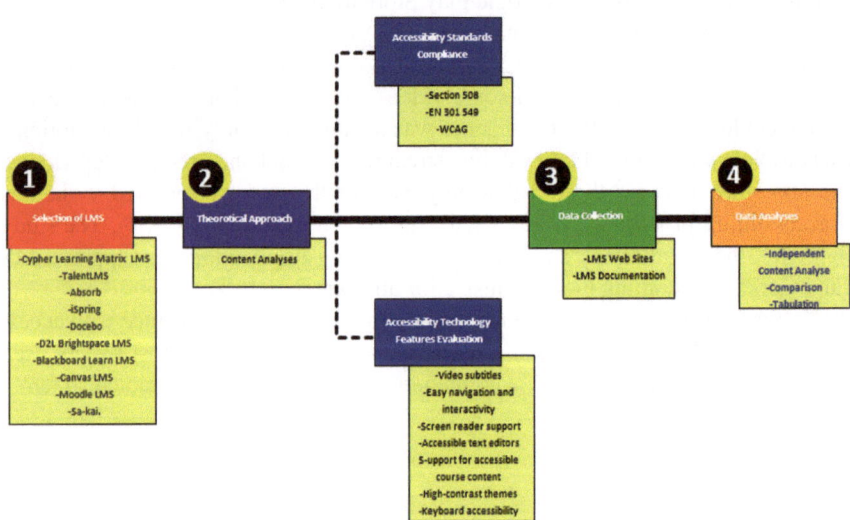

Fig. 1 Study methodology

educational settings, ensuring the representation of a broad spectrum of users. The selected LMS platforms, presented in Table 1 include Cypher Learning's MATRIX LMS, TalentLMS, Absorb, iSpring, Docebo, D2L Brightspace LMS, Blackboard Learn LMS, Canvas LMS, Moodle LMS, and Sakai.

2.3 Accessibility Standards Compliance

In our study, we undertook a compliance check of accessibility standards for LMS. The selection of the accessibility standards was based on their global acceptance, comprehensive coverage, and relevance to digital learning environments. We chose Section 508, the EN 301 549, and WCAG 2.0 and 2.1. Section 508 was selected due to its broad application within the U.S. federal agencies and its emphasis on electronic and information technology. The EN 301 549 was chosen for its extensive applicability in the European market and its focus on ICT products and services. WCAG 2.0 and 2.1 were selected for their worldwide acceptance and their specific guidelines for web content accessibility. Moreover, these standards collectively provide a comprehensive framework for digital accessibility, thus ensuring that our compliance check was thorough. We then proceeded to scrutinize the LMS information provided by vendors to determine their compliance with these selected standards. This involved a detailed analysis of vendor documentation and product specifications, enabling us to assess the degree to which each LMS adhered to the chosen accessibility standards.

2.4 Accessibility Technology Features Evaluation

A comprehensive examination of accessibility technology features and functionalities available within each LMS platform is conducted based on the information each LMS provider provides for their platforms. The key features assessed include:

1. Video Subtitle: The presence of options for adding subtitles or captions to video content.
2. Easy Navigation and Interactivity: The extent to which the LMS interface facilitates easy navigation and interaction for users with disabilities.
3. Screen Reader Support: The compatibility of the LMS with popular screen reader software.
4. Accessible Text Editors: The availability of text editors that offer accessibility features for content creation.
5. Support for Accessible Course Content: The LMS's capacity to host and deliver course materials in accessible formats.
6. High-Contrast Themes: The provision of high-contrast themes to accommodate users with visual impairments.

Table 1 Assessment of the various LMS according to their support of accessibility standards and features

LMS	Standards			Technologies/features						
	Section 508	EN 301 549	WCAG	Video subtitles	Easy navigation and interactivity	Screen reader support	Accessible text editors	Support for accessible course content	High-contrast themes	Keyboard accessibility
Cypher learning MATRIX LMS	+	–	+	–	+	+	+	+	+	+
TalentLMS	Partial	–	+	–	+	+	+	+–	+	+
Absorb	–	–	+	+	+	Partial	+	Partial	Partial	+
iSpring	+	–	+	+	+	+	+	+	+	+
Docebo	+	+	+	+	+	+	+	+	+	+
D2L Brightspace LMS	+	+	+	+	+	+	+	+	+	+
Blackboard learn LMS	+	–	+	+	+	+	+	+	+	+
Canvas LMS	+	–	–	+	+	–	Partial	+	+	+
Moodle LMS	+	–	+	+	+	+	+	+	+	+
Sakai	+	–	+	+	Partial	+	+	+	+	+

7. Keyboard Accessibility: The ease with which users can navigate and interact with the LMS using only keyboard input.
8. Standards Compliance: The accessibility standards the LMS is reported to comply with.

2.5 Data Collection

Data collection is performed on each platform's Web site and documentation, looking specifically for information related to each of the accessibility technology features identified before.

2.6 Data Analysis

The findings from the assessment of each LMS are analyzed independently. Compliance with accessibility standards and the availability of technology features are reported in Table 1.

A comparative analysis is carried out to juxtapose the accessibility performances of the 10 LMS platforms. This analysis highlights variations in standards compliance and the presence of technology features across the platforms.

3 Findings

In the study, detailed analysis and reviews were carried out for ten LMS, and accessibility reviews were carried out for each LMS.

3.1 Cypher Learning's MATRIX LMS

Cypher Learning's MATRIX LMS incorporates several features that contribute to a more inclusive learning environment. The platform offers keyboard navigation, screen reader support, accessible text editors, and high-contrast themes, ensuring that users with diverse needs can navigate and engage effectively. The provision of closed captions, transcripts, and subtitles for multimedia content reflects an understanding of the importance of multiple modalities for learning. Additionally, the platform's adherence to accessibility standards, including Section 508 and WCAG, reinforces its dedication to creating an inclusive digital education space. However, the absence of video subtitles as an accessibility feature may pose challenges for users who rely on them. Furthermore, the lack of reported compliance with EN 301 549 raises questions about the platform's accessibility in the European context.

3.2   TalentLMS

TalentLMS integrates multiple features fostering an inclusive experience in online learning. The platform offers strong support for easy navigation, screen reader compatibility, accessible text editors, high-contrast themes, and keyboard accessibility, addressing the needs of users with diverse abilities. Full compliance with WCAG is evident, emphasizing a dedication to recognized international accessibility standards. However, notable gaps exist in the absence of video subtitles and partial support for accessible course content. The lack of video subtitles may pose challenges for users who rely on them for comprehension, limiting the platform's inclusivity in multimedia learning scenarios. While TalentLMS acknowledges alignment with Section 508 and ADA requirements, the partial compliance suggests potential challenges in meeting all aspects of these regulations. Additionally, the non-reporting of EN 301 549 compliance raises questions about the platform's accessibility in the European context.

3.3   Absorb LMS

Absorb LMS incorporates various features to foster inclusivity in online learning. The inclusion of video subtitles, easy navigation, and interactive elements, along with accessible text editors and keyboard compatibility, reflects a comprehensive approach to addressing diverse user needs. The platform's alignment with WCAG standards is evident in the introduction of screen reader compatibility, enabling text-to-speech engines, and the option to customize reading orders for improved readability. While Absorb LMS has made commendable strides in accessibility, there are notable gaps. Partial screen reader support and partial availability of high-contrast themes suggest areas where further improvements can enhance the experience for users with disabilities. Additionally, the absence of reported Section 508 and EN 301 549 compliance raises questions about the platform's adherence to specific accessibility standards, particularly in the U.S. and European contexts. The platform's initiatives to make multiple-choice and true or false questions accessible for screen readers and keyboard users, along with support for timed and video pages, align with WCAG requirements. However, the inaccessibility of elements like tooltips and audio, as well as the limited compatibility of themed templates with accessibility standards, indicates areas for enhancement.

3.4   iSpring LMS

iSpring LMS offers a comprehensive suite of accessibility features, contributing to an inclusive online learning experience. The platform provides video subtitles, easy navigation, screen reader support, accessible text editors, and high-contrast themes, addressing the needs of users with diverse abilities. Notably, iSpring LMS achieves Section 508 compliance, reinforcing its commitment to accessibility standards in the U.S. The LMS provider underscores iSpring's commitment to inclusivity, emphasizing alignment with WCAG 2.1 standards. The unique publishing format enabling learners to switch to accessibility mode is a commendable feature, enhancing text readability, simplifying navigation, and ensuring compatibility with prominent screen readers like JAWS, VoiceOver, and NVDA. The encouragement for authors to rely on text, include meaningful data in questions, and ensure accessibility of audio and video content reflects a proactive approach to content creation. However, the absence of reported compliance with EN 301 549 raises questions about the platform's accessibility in the European context. While the provider highlights the availability of accessibility features, a more explicit acknowledgement of adherence to additional international standards would provide a more comprehensive understanding of iSpring LMS's global accessibility compliance.

3.5   Docebo LMS

Docebo LMS exhibits a comprehensive set of features that contribute to an inclusive online learning experience. The platform provides video subtitles, easy navigation, screen reader support, accessible text editors, high-contrast themes, and keyboard accessibility, addressing the diverse needs of users. Docebo's commitment to accessibility is evident through its compliance with key standards, including WCAG 2.1, U.S. Section 508, and European EN 301 549 V3.1.1, showcasing a global commitment to inclusivity. The provider emphasizes Docebo's dedication to accessibility, extending beyond legal requirements to a broader goal of inclusivity. The platform's impact on various aspects of the learning experience, from registration to layout, underscores a holistic approach to accessibility. Noteworthy features include the "skip to main content" option for users of assistive technology, enabling efficient navigation. While Docebo's commitment to accessibility is commendable, the acknowledgment that content uploaded by users must be made accessible without content checks raises considerations for ensuring comprehensive inclusivity. It would be beneficial for Docebo to implement content checks or provide clearer guidance to users on creating accessible content to enhance the overall accessibility of the platform.

3.6   D2L Brightspace LMS

D2L Brightspace Learning Management System offers an extensive array of features to create an inclusive learning environment. The platform provides video subtitles, easy navigation, screen reader support, accessible text editors, high-contrast themes, and keyboard accessibility, aligning with stringent standards including WCAG 2.1, Section 508, and EN 301 549. Brightspace's dedication to accessibility extends beyond compliance, emphasizing a comprehensive approach to enhancing the educational experience for all users. The LMS provider underscores Brightspace's commitment to accessibility, detailing specific features that contribute to a more inclusive learning community. The integration of an HTML Editor with an Accessibility Checker is a commendable initiative, ensuring content pages are free from common accessibility issues. Encouraging proper usage of headings for visually impaired students signifies a thoughtful consideration of diverse learning needs. Brightspace's organization options, such as modules and sub-modules, contribute to smooth navigation, fostering an intuitive learning experience.

3.7 Blackboard LMS

Blackboard LMS incorporates a range of features that align with recognized standards such as WCAG 2.1 Level AA and Section 508. The platform provides video subtitles, easy navigation, screen reader support, accessible text editors, high-contrast themes, and keyboard accessibility. The structure of Blackboard Learn pages reflects a thoughtful design with a logical heading structure, consistent H1 and H2 usage, and hidden elements to improve navigation. Replacing frames with DIVs and iFrames contributes to better page accessibility, and the use of landmarks based on ARIA further enhances the platform's accessibility. The implementation of industry-standard keyboard navigation patterns demonstrates a commitment to providing an accessible interface. However, the absence of reported compliance with EN 301 549 raises questions about the platform's accessibility in the European context. While the platform's comprehensive accessibility features are commendable, ensuring transparency on European standards compliance would provide a more holistic understanding of Blackboard LMS's accessibility initiatives.

3.8 Canvas LMS

Canvas Learning Management System incorporates various features designed to create an inclusive learning environment. The platform provides video subtitles, easy navigation, support for accessible course content, high-contrast themes, keyboard accessibility, and Section 508 compliance. The use of modern HTML and CSS technologies, along with manual testing for popular screen readers and browsers, signifies a proactive approach to ensuring compatibility with assistive technologies. Region-based navigation using ARIA landmarks enhances page traversal for users relying on keyboard navigation. However, the partial availability of accessible text editors is a gap that could impact the experience for users with certain disabilities. While Canvas encourages direct communication with third-party developers to ensure compliance, the variability in standards for integrated tools raises considerations for a consistent user experience.

3.9   Moodle LMS

Moodle Learning Management System offers a comprehensive set of features designed to create an inclusive learning environment. The platform provides video subtitles, easy navigation, screen reader support, accessible text editors, high-contrast themes, keyboard accessibility, and Section 508 compliance. Moodle's dedication to adhering to multiple accessibility standards, including WCAG 2.1, ATAG 2.0, and ARIA 1.1, underscores a commitment to recognized benchmarks. The acknowledgement that accessibility is an ongoing process of continuous improvement, with a focus on user feedback and expert testing, reflects a proactive approach to evolving user needs and technical environments. The platform's compliance with WCAG 2.1 AA ensures that authoring and evaluation tools align with robust accessibility criteria. Additionally, the provision of features and integrations, such as the Accessibility Starter Toolkit, further supports educators in creating accessible content. However, the absence of reported compliance with EN 301 549 raises questions about the platform's accessibility in the European context.

3.10   Sakai LMS

The Sakai Learning Management System provides various features designed to establish an inclusive learning environment. The platform provides screen reader support, accessible text editors, high-contrast themes, keyboard accessibility, and Section 508 compliance. Notably, the inclusion of Quick Access links, a Tool Menu, and a content area designed to be navigable with Access keys enhances ease of navigation and interactivity. The responsive design accommodating various screen sizes and guidance for users to modify text size and color/contrast settings contribute to a user-friendly interface. The absence of information regarding video subtitle support leaves uncertainty about the platform's multimedia accessibility. While the system likely adheres to recognized guidelines such as WCAG and Section 508, explicit mention of these standards would provide greater clarity for users seeking specific accessibility information.

4 Discussion

The section delves into a comprehensive exploration of key themes arising from the critical assessment of LMSs regarding their accessibility features and compliance with established standards. Through a systematic evaluation of prominent LMS platforms, this study has identified recurring themes, including the presence of critical accessibility features, compliance gaps, content creation and guidelines, user interaction and navigation, and global accessibility considerations. These themes encapsulate the intricacies of digital accessibility in educational technology, shedding light on both commendable practices and areas for improvement within the LMS landscape. As we navigate through each theme, we aim to unravel insights into how LMSs contribute to or hinder inclusive learning practices and digital accessibility. By initiating this discussion, we seek to foster a deeper understanding of the current state of LMS accessibility, laying the groundwork for future advancements that will facilitate a more inclusive and equitable digital education landscape.

4.1 The Presence of Critical Accessibility Features

The first theme centers on the identification and examination of critical accessibility features present in various LMSs. Notably, LMS platforms such as iSpring, Docebo, and D2L Brightspace have demonstrated a commendable commitment to inclusivity by incorporating essential features like video subtitles, screen reader support, accessible text editors, and high-contrast themes. These features cater to users with diverse needs, ensuring that individuals with visual impairments, hearing impairments, or motor disabilities can effectively engage with the learning content. For instance, iSpring's accessibility mode and Docebo's "skip to main content" option exemplify a user-centric approach to accommodate different learning styles and preferences. While Canvas and Blackboard also exhibit strong commitments to accessibility, Canvas's partial availability of accessible text editors highlights a nuanced aspect, emphasizing the need for comprehensive toolsets. The exploration of this theme underscores that the inclusion of critical accessibility features is foundational for fostering an inclusive digital learning environment. Brito and Dias (2020) found that it is important for the LMS to allow compatibility with external tools, which can in turn be adapted according to learner needs. This is a preferred approach in comparison with directly embedding facilities into the LMS. This approach would support learners with disabilities in using the adapted software and hardware needed, such as scroll wheels, touch screens, hands-free touchpads. It is thus imperative for developers to first be aware of these accessibility concerns and second develop compatible applications. This form of compatibility would further enhance the LMS under this theme. Rashikj-Canevska et al. (2021) likewise emphasize the importance of creating different types of accessibility plug-ins to ensure LMS offer greater accessibility. These extend to plug-ins with support for text-to-speech engine for blind students, a mode for sign language support for deaf students, mode supporting dyslexic students, and speech-to-text mode for motor impaired students.

4.2 Compliance with Accessibility Standards

The second theme revolves around the examination of Learning Management Systems' adherence to established accessibility standards. Several platforms, including Docebo, iSpring, and D2L Brightspace, showcase a robust commitment to compliance with recognized standards such as WCAG, Section 508, and EN 301 549. These standards are designed to ensure that digital content is accessible to users with disabilities, emphasizing factors like perceivability, operability, and understandability. The inclusion of video subtitles, easy navigation, and screen reader support aligns with these standards, reflecting a proactive effort to meet the diverse needs of users (Batanero-Ochaíta et al., 2021). However, the absence of reported compliance with EN 301 549 in some cases raises questions about the platforms' accessibility in the European context. The discussion on this theme delves into the importance of aligning with recognized standards to guarantee a universally accessible learning environment and highlights the need for consistent reporting across different jurisdictions to ensure global inclusivity (Ingavélez-Guerra et al., 2023).

Examining LMS platforms through the lens of accessibility standards reveals the commitment of these platforms to providing a learning environment that caters to all. The discussion of this theme contributes to a broader understanding of how platforms can proactively engage with established benchmarks, fostering an inclusive space for learning. It also prompts considerations about the challenges associated with varying standards across different regions and the importance of a unified approach to digital accessibility in education.

4.3 Content Creation and Guidelines

Content creation plays a pivotal role in ensuring an inclusive learning experience, and the third theme underscores the strategies adopted by LMS platforms to guide authors in creating accessible content. Notably, platforms like iSpring LMS take a proactive approach by providing unique publishing formats and accessibility modes. These features empower authors to simplify navigation, enhance text readability, and ensure compatibility with prominent screen readers. The discussion on this theme delves into the multifaceted aspects of accessible content creation, including the encouragement to rely on text, inclusion of meaningful data in questions, and addressing the accessibility of audio and video content. These guidelines are crucial for fostering an environment where educational materials are perceivable and comprehensible to a diverse audience, accommodating different learning styles and preferences.

The exploration of this theme prompts considerations about the role of LMS platforms in shaping content creation practices. It raises questions about the integration of content creation guidelines directly into the authoring tools of LMSs, ensuring that accessibility considerations are seamlessly woven into the fabric of educational material development. Additionally, the theme invites discussions on the collaborative efforts between LMS providers and educational institutions in educating authors about the significance of accessible content creation. This theme highlights the transformative potential of content creation guidelines in shaping a digital educational landscape that is inherently inclusive and caters to the diverse needs of learners. The lack of work in this area is highlighted and remains a main obstacle preventing the use of LMS by learners with disabilities. According to Brito and Dias (2020), teachers also have a role to play under this theme, like in providing captions for images or tables or not uploading content in the form of a scanned PDF unless such content can be converted by OCR software.

4.4 User Interaction and Navigation

The fourth theme revolves around the critical aspects of user interaction and navigation within LMSs. Seamless navigation is imperative for an inclusive learning environment, and LMS platforms address this through various features. Region-based navigation using Accessible Rich Internet Applications (ARIA) landmarks and organizational options like modules and sub-modules contribute to a smoother learning experience. Furthermore, the use of HTML Editors with integrated Accessibility Checkers emerges as a noteworthy practice, ensuring that content pages are devoid of common accessibility issues. The discussion on this theme encompasses the importance of providing features that facilitate intuitive navigation, especially for users who rely on keyboard navigation or screen readers. Additionally, the theme encourages reflections on the ongoing advancements in user interface technologies and their implications for enhancing accessibility.

4.5 Global Accessibility Considerations

The fifth and final theme delves into the global accessibility considerations of LMSs, particularly the questions raised about their accessibility in the European context. This theme underscores the necessity for international standards compliance to ensure inclusivity on a global scale. The absence of reported compliance with EN 301 549 in some LMSs raises pertinent questions about their accessibility in the European landscape. The theme invites considerations about the complexities of adhering to diverse accessibility standards and regulations in different parts of the world. It raises questions about the strategies LMS providers employ to navigate these variations and ensure their platforms meet the expectations of users globally. This discussion also opens avenues for exploring the evolving nature of global accessibility standards and the role of LMSs in shaping and adapting to these standards. In conclusion, the theme on global accessibility considerations prompts a deeper understanding of the challenges and opportunities associated with ensuring that digital educational platforms cater to a diverse and global user base. It emphasizes the need for collaborative efforts in standardizing accessibility practices to create a truly inclusive digital learning environment worldwide.

Inclusive learning practices can be significantly enhanced through the robust implementation of digital accessibility features in LMSs. The themes identified underscore the importance of providing a diverse range of accessibility features to cater to users with varying needs. LMSs play a pivotal role in fostering inclusivity by ensuring compliance with established standards such as WCAG, Section 508, and EN 301 549. To further support inclusive learning practices, LMS providers should prioritize closing compliance gaps, especially concerning video subtitles, to ensure equitable access to multimedia content. Moreover, a collaborative effort between LMS providers, educators, and content creators is crucial to promote adherence to content creation guidelines that prioritize accessibility. By addressing global accessibility considerations and maintaining transparency about compliance with international standards, LMSs can contribute to creating a digital learning environment that is accessible and inclusive for all learners and educators.

5 Conclusions

This study provides a comprehensive analysis of Learning Management Systems (LMSs) with a focus on their accessibility features and adherence to established standards. The literature review establishes the backdrop by emphasizing the transformative impact of technology on education and the ensuing challenges related to equitable access for diverse learners. The critical assessment of LMSs through a content analysis methodology revealed recurring themes, such as the presence of critical accessibility features, compliance gaps, content creation and guidelines, user interaction and navigation, and global accessibility considerations. These themes shed light on the complexities and opportunities within the LMS landscape concerning digital accessibility. The exploration of each theme contributes valuable insights into how LMSs either facilitate or hinder inclusive learning practices. The themes collectively underscore the importance of robust digital accessibility implementation and adherence to international standards to foster inclusivity in digital education.

As we conclude this study, it is essential to acknowledge the avenues for future research in the realm of LMS accessibility. While this research provides a foundational understanding of current practices and challenges, there is a need for in-depth investigations into the user experience and impact of accessibility features on diverse learners. Future studies could employ user testing methodologies to evaluate the effectiveness and usability of specific accessibility features identified in this research. Additionally, longitudinal studies could track the evolution of LMS accessibility, considering the dynamic nature of both technology and accessibility standards. Collaborative efforts between LMS providers, educators, and accessibility experts could be explored to develop best practices and guidelines that address the identified gaps and elevate the overall accessibility landscape. Moreover, extending this research to encompass a more extensive array of LMS platforms and updates would provide a more nuanced understanding of the diverse approaches to digital accessibility in education. Lastly, knowing that LMS have a crucial role in mediating knowledge processes, gamification and game elements are commonly being used nowadays to engage learners and enhance the learning experience. It is however important that learners with disabilities can also access and experience equally these gamified learning resources too and this portrays another important avenue of future research (Schimmelpfeng & Ulbricht, 2021).

Acknowledgements This chapter is based upon work from COST Action CA19142—Leading Platform for European Citizens, Industries, Academia and Policymakers in Media Accessibility (LEAD-ME) supported by COST (European Cooperation in Science and Technology).

References

Aljedaani, W., Alkahtani, M., Ludi, S., Mkaouer, M. W., Eler, M. M., Kessentini, M., & Ouni, A. (2023). The state of accessibility in blackboard: Survey and user reviews case study. In *Proceedings of the 20th International Web for All Conference* (pp. 84–95). Association for Computing Machinery.

Brito, E., & Dias, G. P. (2020, June). LMS accessibility for students with disabilities: The experts' opinions. In *2020 15th Iberian Conference on Information Systems and Technologies (CISTI)* (pp. 1–5). IEEE.

Batanero-Ochaíta, C., De-Marcos, L., Rivera, L. F., Holvikivi, J., Hilera, J. R., & Tortosa, S. O. (2021). Improving accessibility in online education: comparative analysis of attitudes of blind and deaf students toward an adapted learning platform. *IEEE Access, 9.*

Burgstahler, S. E., & Cory, R. C. (2008). *Universal design in higher education: From principles to practice.* Harvard Education Press.

Calvo, R., Iglesias, A., & Moreno, L. (2014). Accessibility barriers for users of screen readers in the Moodle learning content management system. *Universal Access in the Information Society*, 315–327.

Creven, J. (2003). Access to electronic resources by visually impaired people. *Information Research: An International Electronic Journal, 156.*

Disability Rights Commission. (2004). *The web: Access and inclusion for disabled people: A formal investigation.* The Stationery Office (TSO).

ETSI, CEN, CENELEC. (2021). EN 301 549 v3.2.1 Accessibility requirements for ICT products and services. Retrieved from https://www.etsi.org/deliver/etsi_en/301500_301599/301549/03.02.01_60/en_301549v030201p.pdf

Iglesias, A., Moreno, L., Martínez, P., & Calvo, R. (2014). Evaluating the accessibility of three open-source learning content management systems: A comparative study. *Computer Applications in Engineering Education*, 320–328.

Ingavélez-Guerra, P., Otón-Tortosa, S., Hilera-González, J., & Sánchez-Gordón, M. (2023). The use of accessibility metadata in e-learning environments: A systematic literature review. *Universal Access in the Information Society, 22*, 445–461.

Krippendorff, K. (2019). *Content analysis: An introduction to its methodology*. SAGE Publications.

Moreno, L., Iglesias, A., Calvo, R., Delgado, S., & Zaragoza, L. (2012). Disability standards and guidelines for learning management systems: Evaluating accessibility. In *Information resources management association, virtual learning environments: Concepts, methodologies, tools and applications* (pp. 1530–1549). IGI Global.

Power, C., Petrie, H., Sakharov, V., & Swallow, D. (2010). Virtual learning environments: Another barrier to blended and e-learning. In *Computers helping people with special needs* (pp. 519–526). Springer.

Rashikj-Canevska, O., Tasevska, A., Orechova, M., Dias, G. P., & Haubro, H. (2021). *Accessible learning management systems: Students' experiences and insights*.

Schimmelpfeng, L. E., & Ulbricht, V. R. (2021). Accessible learning management system (LMS) for disabled people: Project development based on accessibility guidelines, gamification, and design thinking strategies. In *The role of gamification in software development lifecycle*. IntechOpen.

U.S. Department of Justice Civil Rights Division. (2008). *Americans with Disabilities Act of 1990, As Amended*. Retrieved from https://www.ada.gov/law-and-regs/ada/

U.S. General Services Administration. (2023). *Section508.gov*. Retrieved from https://www.sectio n508.gov/

WHO. (2023, August 10). *Blindness and vision impairment*. Retrieved from http://www.who.int/ mediacentre/factsheets/fs282/en/

W3C. (2024). WCAG 2 Overview. Retrieved from https://www.w3.org/WAI/standards-guidelines/ wcag/

Accessibility of e-books for Secondary School Students in Ireland and Cyprus

Ann Marcus-Quinn⬤, Thomas Fotiadis⬤, Alexandros Yeratziotis⬤, and George A. Papadopoulos⬤

Abstract Across the EU, an increasing number of second-level schools are using digital materials (Baron in How we read now: Strategic choices for print, screen, and audio. Oxford University Press, 2021; Hsieh and Huang in Educ Inf Technol 25:1285–1301, 2020). Such resources must be inclusive and accessible (Marcus-Quinn and Hourigan in Irish Educ Stud 41:161–169, 2022). Accessibility is paramount if students, particularly students confronting disabilities or learning impediments, are to experience equitable educational outcomes. While a multitude of school text-books presently offer electronic book (e-book) alternatives, tailored for download and engagement via digital platforms, a significant number of these lack purposeful adaptation for online dissemination, thereby undermining their optimal accessibility. Some studies of e-book use at third level have found that undergraduate students notice accessibility features that e-books do not offer, such as customization of text display, the facility to highlight and annotate text, or the inclusion of interactive features such as embedded media content (Pierard et al. in Undesirable difficulties: investigating barriers to students' learning with e-books in a semester-length course, 2019). There have been few similar studies for other education sectors. Accessibility features play a crucial role in making the digital learning experience more successful and also help students succeed in their studies. This chapter discusses the imperative of accessibility in the context of e-books specifically produced for the second-level education sector in both Ireland and Cyprus. The chapter will explore accessibility

A. Marcus-Quinn (✉)
University of Limerick, Limerick, Ireland
e-mail: Ann.Marcus.Quinn@ul.ie

T. Fotiadis · G. A. Papadopoulos
University of Cyprus, Nicosia, Cyprus
e-mail: fotiadis.f.thomas@ucy.ac.cy

G. A. Papadopoulos
e-mail: papadopoulos.george@ucy.ac.cy

A. Yeratziotis
A.G. Connect Deaf Limited, Nicosia, Cyprus
e-mail: alexis@connectdeaf.com

229

A. Marcus-Quinn et al. (eds.), *Transforming Media Accessibility in Europe*,
https://doi.org/10.1007/978-3-031-60049-4_13

features common to many school e-books and highlight problematic issues associated with e-books that have not been prepared with accessibility considerations as part of the publication process.

Keywords Accessibility · Equity · e-books · Education · Schools

1 Introduction

The transformation in the materiality of textbooks requires a redefinition of their significance and a substantial evolution in teaching and learning methodologies. It is imperative that all stakeholders involved in the design, production, and consumption of e-books and digital teaching and learning materials investigate, as technologies evolve, how learners can best engage with the text (Kepic Mohar, 2020). Digital materials are being used in post-primary level education in both Ireland and Cyprus. Digital material, including e-books, is produced in both a formal context (publishers with a formal publication process and quality checks) and an informal context (teachers producing digital content). Each context has problems associated with it. Our goal in this chapter is to analyze the current situation and discuss how we can support educators in the two countries to create accessible digital content. This chapter suggests some solutions that may help in generating and creating better, more accessible digital material and e-books. In this chapter, we discuss the data made available by the Department of Education (Cyprus) and similar data available in Ireland. We discuss issues around accessibility that teachers have reported in their community. We also examine the issues that can arise from teachers creating their own content and what teachers as content creators can do to try and overcome these barriers and create accessible digital content and e-books.

2 e-books in Education

There is a growing body of research in recent years which looks at the use of e-books in educational settings. Some studies have suggested that to increase the availability of e-books, the production process will need to evolve from current manual methods to a more automated system. Automating the process would facilitate publishers in maintaining a consistent brand across a digital library's collection or creating customized editions for particular audiences (Carriço et al., 2005; Lopes et al., 2006). A study carried out by Almekhlafi (2021) on the effect of e-books on preservice student teachers' achievement and perceptions in the United Arab Emirates (UAE) has made several recommendations for all stakeholders including the Ministry of Education. Some of these recommendations are specific to the UAE, but some could be considered by other Departments of Education and Ministries of education. These include the provision of comprehensive professional development and training for teachers which is focused on the effective development and use of e-books. The study also recommends that the education sectors forge partnerships with reputable publishing companies and that schools be equipped with the necessary technological infrastructure which is crucial for the effective use and accessibility of e-books for all students. In 2023, a study exploring the impact of traditional materials versus electronic textbooks (via mobile applications) on English vocabulary development among university students also examined the benefits and challenges of using mobile devices. This study found that using e-books on mobile devices was effective in enhancing vocabulary learning in both short and long terms, with benefits including episodic learning, easy access to materials, and increased motivation, but faced challenges like health concerns and distractions from other apps. Despite limitations such as the inability to control for all variables and the focus on only one aspect of vocabulary knowledge, the study provides evidence that electronic textbooks on mobile devices can significantly improve vocabulary learning in EFL students. However, the authors suggest the need for further research to explore the broader impacts of mobile-assisted vocabulary learning across different demographics and learning contexts (Xodabande & Hashemi, 2023). It is clear that more research is necessary to identify the potential limitations and benefits of incorporating e-books into the teaching and learning environment.

3 The Use of e-books and Digital Materials in Ireland and Cyprus

As more secondary schools across the EU begin to integrate e-books into their curriculum, accessibility should play a critical role in the decisions made. Ensuring that digital textbooks are accessible aids every student. Accessibility features which promote inclusivity, flexibility, and personalized learning result in better academic results and a fairer learning environment for all students (Marcus-Quinn, 2022; Marcus-Quinn et al., 2022). In this chapter, our analysis is based on information shared by the education community in Ireland and primary survey data collected in Cyprus. This approach was adopted due to the wealth of relevant discussions, opinions, and information shared online, which provided valuable perspectives for our analysis. Using both this publicly available data and the targeted survey data allowed us to include both countries in our study, ensuring a broader comparative scope, while acknowledging the methodological differences in data collection between the two countries. This strategy highlights the adaptability of our research design to navigate the varied landscapes of data availability and accessibility in different geographical contexts.

In Ireland, there are various publishers and platforms that offer e-books tailored for educational purposes. Some popular publishers for second-level schools include Edco, Folens, and CJ Fallon. In recent years, these publishers have started to offer digital versions of many of their textbooks. The e-book may not be specifically designed for online consumption and may be a PDF version of the hardcopy book. The majority of school textbooks available as e-books come with a single-user license. Some publishers offer a direct download after purchase, while others may provide access through a specific platform or app. Some publishers will have their own platforms or apps where students can access the purchased e-books, and this includes additional interactive features, resources, and updates. When selecting an e-book, teachers should be able to check the level of compatibility with assistive technology. This entails verifying that the e-book integrates seamlessly with widely used assistive tools such as screen readers, braille displays, and voice recognition systems. A challenge arises when an e-book, associated with a school textbook, is merely a PDF replica of the print version without any advanced accessibility or interactive features (Marcus-Quinn, 2024). Typographic choice is an example of an issue that will significantly impact the usability of an e-book as typographic variations should be determined based on whether the material will be consumed hardcopy or electronically. One such issue concerns the display of italicized text, especially when combined with bold. Many fonts struggle to correctly render a Bold Italic style, which is often used for emphasis, highlighting quotations, referencing older texts, or indicating foreign words. This becomes notably problematic in History e-books where such emphasis is used more frequently.

Historically, accessibility solutions provided by publishers in Ireland have been tailored to individual needs. For instance, if a student needed an accessible version of a course text, they would request it through their teacher. "Accessible" usually implies a text modified to cater to the student's specific requirements. Educational and academic textbook publishers represented by the Irish Educational Publishers' Association (IEPA) handle these needs individually. While publishers strive to meet all requests, they cannot always promise the availability of a specific title or format, but they have established procedures to cater to these accessibility demands, often providing customized textbooks for students with special needs. However, this process requires significant administrative effort for both those requesting the service and those providing a solution. For example, if a student or their parent/guardian wishes to acquire an accessible text from the IEPA, the IEPA's centralized Special Needs Access Policy necessitates both parental permission and confirmation from the school's principal for the student in question. The steps for acquiring accessible texts include:

1. Filling out the IEPA Special Needs Access Request Form available on the IEPA Web site at https://iepa.ie/.
2. Submitting this form to the appropriate publishers via the listed email addresses (given that multiple educational publishers exist in Ireland).
3. The relevant publisher will communicate the conditions for access, including payment, proof of purchase, copyright agreements, and data retention policies.
4. Once the prior steps are completed, the student will receive the files or access.

Similar processes are also employed in other EU member states to obtain accessible e-books.

Many publishers do not have a central online facility to gather feedback from teachers and students about the effectiveness and usability of e-books. A central facility would enable publishers to capture usability more effectively and would help in making better informed design decisions in future and would also allow them to optimize the learning experience for all students.

4 Cyprus

In accordance with extant directives issued by the Cyprus Ministry of Education, Sport, and Youth, educational materials, specifically textbooks, are presently distributed to students in a printed format. Within the framework of the Cyprus Educational System, books used include materials from the Curriculum Development Unit (C.D.U./M.O.E.C.), the Greek Agency for Publishing School Textbooks (O.E.B.Δ.), and various alternative sources. The graphical representation below is the total number of books used at all levels of education (Fig. 1).

Concurrently, an electronic version in Portable Document Format (PDF) is accessible for download via the Ministry's Educational Portal (https://schools.ac.cy/). Supplementary materials, including supporting documentation, presentations, applications, simulations, and analogous content, are also disseminated through subject-specific webpages. Notably, the instructional manuals and publications originating from the Cyprus Ministry of Education, Sport, and Youth are presently unavailable in electronic book (e-book) format, at least within the current operational framework. A small number of books are posted on the Web site of CTI in the form of e-books and, consequently, are also accessible to teachers in Cyprus as Interactive School Books,

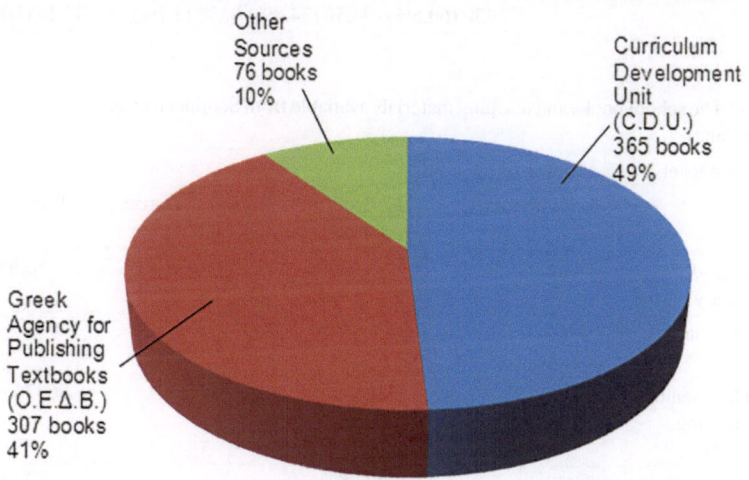

Fig. 1 The total quantity of books utilized in Cyprus education system at all levels

of which the materials are categorized by class or subject (http://eBooks.edu.gr/eBo oks/). In the context of their teaching, teachers may use e-books obtained from other sources as a means of enriching a lesson. However, there is no reliable data (e.g., research) at this point that records the degree of usability and accessibility or the ways of pedagogical utilization of e-books by the teachers in Cyprus (Table 1).

As teachers in Ireland have complete autonomy in terms of where they source their textbooks (hardcopy and e-books), it is almost impossible to conduct a direct comparison with the context in Cyprus. The process by which teachers choose their textbooks can vary by school and is typically influenced by several factors, including curricular requirements, school policy, teacher preference, resource evaluation, budget considerations, and student needs. However, the majority of Irish schools using traditional books will use the online bookshop schoolbooks.ie an Irish online retailer that specializes in the sale of schoolbooks and educational materials. Teachers will also use digital resources available from Scoilnet.ie; Scoilnet is the Department of Education's official portal for Irish education and was originally launched in 1998. The Web site is currently managed by Oide Technology in Education on behalf of the Department of Education. Scoilnet collaborates with practicing teachers to maintain and manage the content on the Web site (Table 2).

Table 1 The set of student's textbooks for the 2021–2022 school year and their sources (Cyprus)

Education level	Number of book titles			
	C.D.U.	CTI	Other sources	Total
Elementary/pre-primary	101	40	–	141
Secondary general education	154	63	26	243
Secondary technical vocational education and training	183	149	8	340
Total	438 (60.5%)	252 (34.8%)	34 (4.7%)	724 (100%)

Table 2 The school books and teaching materials available from Scoilnet for the 2022–2023 school year (Ireland)

Education level	Number of book titles			
	Schoolbooks.ie	Scoilnet resources	Teacher resources Schoolbooks.ie	Total
Elementary/pre-primary	1790	15,042	13	16,845
Secondary junior cycle	570	6381	2	6953
Secondary senior cycle (leaving certificate)	567	8530		9097
Total	2,927	29,953		32,880

5 The Education Community

The international education community collaborates extensively to support the use of digital materials and e-books, fostering a network of shared knowledge and resources. Educators worldwide exchange best practices and innovative teaching strategies through online platforms, webinars, and international conferences. Online forums and professional learning communities offer spaces for teachers to discuss challenges and solutions in integrating technology into the classroom. The next section discusses the use of e-books in both Ireland and Cyprus.

6 Ireland

The education community in Ireland is very solution-focused as is evidenced by the nature and frequency of the online discourse relating to digital resources for teaching and learning in schools. The Computers in Education Society of Ireland (CESI) is an organization dedicated to the advancement of computers in education. It was formed in 1973, and its mission is to support teachers and educators in integrating technology effectively into teaching and learning processes. The online community of CESI is quite active and serves as a platform for educators across Ireland to share resources, experiences, and ideas related to using technology in education. The CESI mailing list provides support and answers to common questions. While CESI has a specific focus on fostering a community around the use of technology in education, the professional service branch of the Department of Education offers a more structured and comprehensive range of professional development services across all areas of teaching and learning, including curriculum support and implementation. CESI's approach is more community-driven and informal, based on the sharing of ideas and experiences, while Oide provides formal training and resources, aligned with national educational policies and goals.

7 Challenges Associated with e-books and Digital Materials in Ireland

Every August, as schools reopen after the summer break, members of various online discussion groups within the education community, including CESI, share their experiences of how they have managed problems with technology. The purpose of the discussion list managed by the CESI is to facilitate discussion of the ICT issues faced by teachers in schools in Ireland. Anyone on the web can view these discussions. Discussions in recent years have focused on digital resources including e-books and supplementary materials provided by publishers to primary school classes. At the start of the last academic year, members discussed the prevailing challenges relating to e-books as outlined in the section below.

Members discussed the potential value of having one central repository/access point to all e-books. They referred to the ongoing proposition for Irish publishers to transition to a unified app for all e-books. However, despite being proposed repeatedly over the past two decades, this idea has not been realized, indicating a clear lack of inclination from publishers to consolidate e-book offerings in one application. It is indeed difficult to understand why school textbooks cannot be made accessible in a manner analogous to standard e-books. Where such a transition has been made access and distribution have been streamlined, thereby enhancing the user experience for a wide array of users (Cooke, 2017; Scott et al., 2022).

Accessibility features of e-books are also discussed in terms of the challenges posed. At a minimum, users expect to be able to adjust fonts, themes, and reading modes according to their needs and preferences. Many users are using a diverse range of devices to access the material and expect digital material and e-books to be optimized for various devices with responsive design factored in from the beginning of the design and development process to allow users to access material on various devices, including tablets, smartphones, and e-readers (Clark & Mayer, 2016).

Members of many education Communities of Practice regularly complain that e-books are platform agnostic and are not accessible and fully functional across different e-book platforms and operating systems or that content is only available online and cannot be accessed off-line. During the pandemic, university libraries had to overcome barriers in delivering digital materials including e-books, and the lessons learned from this activity should now impact how access to material can be managed at second level (Whitfield et al., 2021). Users expect to be able to download e-books to read at their convenience. It is also often the case that teachers can only access a publisher's app via the computer that they have downloaded it to with an assigned login provided by the publisher. This login is unique to each teacher. Therefore, if a teacher is unexpectedly absent and has their laptop at home, a substitute teacher cannot access the app on another device.

Members of this education community also frequently highlight the challenges associated with the licensing of e-books. Digital Rights Management (DRM) technologies prevent the unauthorized copying and distribution of e-books. However, this can limit legitimate uses, such as sharing an e-book with students or transferring it to different devices for classroom use. There is little in the research literature pertaining to perpetual licenses at second level, but there is research published which highlights and discusses issues with such licenses at third level (Bulock, 2014). Some schools have purchased a perpetual license, and when they experience problems, they cannot cancel their subscription.

Obsolete technology is also often discussed in the online spaces. In the late 1990s, many teachers started to incorporate material from CD ROMs into their teaching practice (Glasgow, 1997; Shamir & Korat, 2006). Many language hardcopy books are still sold with a CD ROM despite many households not having any compatible hardware to play the audio material. Similarly, when digital schoolbook publishing was in its nascent stages, several publishers opted to design their books using Flash.

However, Adobe officially discontinued Flash at the end of 2020, ceasing updates and distribution of the Flash Player (Keizer, 2017). The obsolescence of Flash means that any teaching materials (like interactive web applications, animations, or multimedia content) that were created using Adobe Flash may no longer be accessible or functional on modern devices and browsers. Educators and institutions have had to update or replace these materials with alternatives that use more modern and supported technologies.

Research on interactivity and e-books is growing. Some studies exploring young children's educational experiences with e-books indicate that straightforward, repetitive interactive elements within e-books, which keep the reader engaged in the narrative, neither significantly aid nor hinder learning (Etta & Kirkorian, 2019). There are many examples where the e-book is essentially a PDF version of their printed book with little or no interactivity, annotation options, audio or video. Book publishers can enhance their e-book offerings in various ways to make them more appealing, user-friendly, and competitive in the rapidly evolving digital marketplace. The expectations that educators and end users have of e-books have grown in recent years, and people now expect an enhanced user experience with interactive features. Users of e-books expect to be offered integrated interactive elements such as multimedia, hyperlinks, and quizzes to engage readers better. Depending on the subject matter, users also expect that digital content will incorporate audio, video, and visual content to enrich the reading experience. Many users would also like to see improved search functionality and ease of navigation within e-books.

Separate to these issues, parent representatives regularly take to the media to complain about the business model and pricing of e-books. For many students, the e-book that accompanies the hardcopy book can only be accessed once using a code printed on the inside cover of the hardcopy book. The code usually has a timed expiry (often three years). This means that e-books cannot be shared with younger siblings. Many parents are highly critical of this practice and believe that e-books should be priced more competitively, considering the lack of printing and distribution costs.

8 Cyprus

As mentioned earlier in this chapter, in Cyprus, there is a gap in research on the accessibility of e-books for secondary education; consequently, to address this need, primary research was undertaken, drawing upon insights furnished by educational staff in Cyprus. The acquisition of survey data has facilitated the discernment of the applicability of the research framework in negotiating diverse geographical settings wherein data may be scarce or challenging to access.

The assimilation of e-books is becoming increasingly important in modern educational methods in Cyprus, as it is in many other places around the world. e-books offer numerous advantages, such as portability, interactivity, and accessibility, which have revolutionized how students engage with educational materials. However, ensuring that all students, including those with special needs, have equal access to e-books is still a significant concern in Cyprus' education sector. There is widespread recognition in Cyprus of the transformative potential of e-books in enabling learning experiences that go beyond traditional boundaries.

There is a visible increase in the use and recognition of the advantages of e-books in the educational sector of Cyprus. Majority of the educators are now incorporating e-books into their teaching methods, indicating the widespread acceptance of digital learning resources in Cyprus's educational institutions. Additionally, e-books are highly favored for their ability to enhance accessibility for students with special needs. The flexibility and versatility of e-books are considered highly valuable, as they enable educators to cater to the varied learning styles and requirements of their students. The positive attitude toward e-books in Cyprus demonstrates their potential as an effective tool to improve the quality of education and promote inclusivity in the learning environment.

Despite the widespread recognition of the benefits associated with e-books, there are still challenges when it comes to accessing them. One of the main issues is the difficulty of accessing e-books across different online platforms. This highlights the need for streamlined access mechanisms to make e-books more widely available. Another important consideration is to incorporate flexible and adaptable design features into e-books to ensure that everyone, regardless of their abilities, can access them. These challenges emphasize the need for proactive measures to enhance e-book accessibility in Cyprus. It is important to address these issues to promote inclusivity and ensure that all students have equal access to educational resources.

In Cyprus, there is a significant need for training seminars that can provide educators with the necessary skills to integrate e-books effectively into their teaching practices. This requires the creation of specialized spaces with suitable technological infrastructure that can facilitate easy access and utilization of e-books. Additionally, it is crucial to ensure that students have access to electronic devices and continuous internet connectivity to enhance their access to e-books. These efforts are essential in promoting inclusivity and equal access to educational resources for all students.

Educators in Cyprus have reached a consensus about the importance of having e-book licenses available at their institutions. However, there is a need for clearer guidelines and support structures to facilitate the procurement and licensing of e-books, ensuring accessibility for all students. It is essential to continuously improve accessibility challenges to maintain the efficacy of e-books as educational tools. These actions are necessary for promoting educational equity and enhancing learning outcomes in Cyprus.

In conclusion, the use of e-books in education is highly valued in Cyprus, particularly for its potential to create inclusive learning environments. However, to fully realize this potential, there are challenges that need to be addressed such as accessibility issues and providing adequate training and support for both educators and students. This is especially important to ensure that individuals with special needs have equal access to educational resources. By implementing the recommendations of stakeholders and committing to continuous improvement, educational stakeholders in Cyprus can harness the power of e-books to enhance learning experiences and promote educational equity and inclusion across diverse student populations.

9 Challenges Associated with e-books and Digital Materials in Cyprus

Teachers who incorporate e-books into their lessons often encounter the challenge of ensuring accessibility for students with special needs. They also emphasize the significance of a flexible and adaptable design for e-books, positively influencing their educational value. Many teachers adjust font size or color, signaling dissatisfaction with the default settings. It is noteworthy that schools or institutions play a pivotal role in providing digital resources and e-books, with over half of the teachers indicating that their respective institutions possess licenses for online book usage. However, a considerable number of teachers remain unaware of whether their institutions hold such licenses, underscoring the need for more information about the availability of digital resources within the educational community.

For teachers who abstain from using e-books, the primary obstacle appears to be a lack of familiarity with new technologies, implying a need for teacher training. Nonetheless, the incorporation of e-books can render teaching more engaging for students by fostering increased interactivity in the classroom. The accessibility of e-books for students with special needs is also crucial, highlighting the necessity for equal access to educational materials. The majority of respondents agreed that an educational platform offering e-books across all subject areas, especially for students with special needs, would be exceedingly useful and beneficial.

The importance of a flexible and adaptable design for e-books is emphasized to meet the diverse needs of readers. Nevertheless, challenges in accessing various platforms persist, with a notable percentage of teachers reporting that they have not experimented with them. Many teachers remain uncertain about the existence of licenses for e-books in schools and institutions. Finally, teacher training emerges as a crucial component for the effective support of students with special needs through the utilization of e-books.

10 Designing for Accessibility in e-books

Publishers can maximize accessibility in e-books by incorporating features like adjustable text sizes, alternative text for images, and screen reader compatibility to cater to diverse needs, including those of visually impaired readers. Additionally, ensuring compatibility with various platforms and devices, and providing options for customizable layouts and text-to-speech functions, can greatly enhance the usability and inclusiveness of digital reading materials. Some publishers have developed bimodal-bilingual e-books to enhance accessibility. Both theoretical and practical evidence supports the idea that early exposure to sign language (SL) through effective teaching methods enhances the written literacy of deaf children (Clark & Mayer, 2023; Cooper et al., 2020; Joy et al., 2021). The RISE e-book, a collaborative effort between Gallaudet University and Swarthmore College (Cooper et al., 2020), is a bilingual-bimodal project aimed at promoting reading. This e-book offers classic children's books and incorporates sign language to create a shared reading experience for deaf children and their parents. Presently, the e-books are accessible in American, Korean, Nepali, Fiji, Japanese, and Brazilian sign languages. Mirus and Napoli's research (2018) has highlighted the efficacy of bimodal-bilingual e-books for both deaf children and hearing adults (Mirus & Napoli, 2018). They emphasized the growing demand for bimodal-bilingual e-books for recreational purposes, fostering pre-literacy skills, and the necessity for educational e-books tailored for academic knowledge acquisition. Mirus and Napoli have highlighted the limited availability of such e-books.

The GLOSSING system involves representing signs in written form using capital letters (and other indicators for pointing signs, classifiers, etc.) to convey the meaning of each sign in accordance with GSL syntax (Joy et al., 2021). The same methodology is applied to fairytales, oral stories, and picture stories. All printed materials can be accessed in PDF or in HTML formats on the official Web site of the Publishing House of the Department of Education "ITYE Diofantos" http://eBooks.edu.gr/new/allmat erial.php. Textbook content is organized into meaningful units, ranging from individual vocabulary items to sentence-level expressions for vocalization, presentation in Greek Sign Language (GSL), and incorporation of interactive subtitles. Materials for teaching GSL as a primary language utilize a simple GLOSSING system and are transcribed in both GSL and written Greek. By incorporating glossing in these ways, e-books can become more accessible to the deaf and hard of hearing community, ensuring that they have equal opportunities to access information and education.

Reading applications have also reached a sufficient level of maturity to support interactive EPUB 3; the standard for digital books and publications. EPUB3 enhances the capabilities of its predecessor (EPUB 2) by offering a richer reading experience and greater accessibility features, and the format could be instrumental in shaping the future of digital publishing, providing authors, publishers, and developers with the tools to create rich, interactive, and accessible digital reading experiences (Prasetya et al., 2020). However, screen reader assistive technology currently faces challenges in effectively interacting with multimedia and interactive EPUB 3 content as the interactive EPUB3 format is not yet fully compatible with apps and screen readers (Nakajima et al., 2013).

Veliz et al. conducted a study (Véliz et al., 2017) on the impact of sign language (SL) augmented digital books for deaf learners. Employing a participatory development model, preliminary findings suggest that enhancing SL-based instructions with books enhances comprehension. The Visual Language and Visual Learning (VL2) project at Gallaudet University developed a storybook application for mobile devices, augmenting SL content with English text to facilitate reading and language acquisition for early and emerging readers. In contrast, the SMARTSign project (Joy et al., 2021) is a mobile application used alongside physical books. Users can capture a picture of the story, and the SMARTSign AR mobile application automatically converts it into the corresponding sign. While not specifically focused on textbook learning, Hariharan, Al-hkhazraji, and Huenerfauth proposed a web-based tool (Hariharan et al., 2018) for translating words to American Sign Language (ASL) to enhance accessibility. Initial results indicate that participants prefer having support tools in their interfaces compared to having none. This research introduces SignText, a web-based tool designed for learning textbook lessons in sign language. Findings suggest that learning through sign language improves students' scores compared to traditional textbook-based learning. Currently, SignText supports sign language-based learning for a limited number of lessons, with pre-recorded sign videos provided by instructors on the web page. Qualitative analysis indicates a preference among respondents for watching their instructor sign. Further investigation is needed to assess the effectiveness of signs produced by different signers within the SignText application. Presently, SignText only includes one chapter for learning, and expanding content may pose challenges for sign instructors. Thus, automating the content generation process could significantly benefit both instructors and students.

Regarding the young DHH (deaf and hard of hearing) children, research undertaken by Wauters and Dirks (2017) explored interactive storybook reading through e-books on tablets. Parents participated in a program to learn interactive reading strategies, such as asking open-ended questions and connecting stories to their child's personal experiences. The results, involving 18 DHH children aged one to three, revealed that parents engaged in similar interactive reading behaviors with both e-books and print books. The study concluded that e-books offer additional opportunities for interactive reading with DHH children, particularly noting the portability of tablets and their capacity to store a large collection of e-books. Similarly, Messier and Wood (2015) investigated the use of e-books with embedded vocabulary instruction for 18 children with cochlear implants (aged four to nine). The study found that using e-books with embedded vocabulary instruction, as opposed to traditional storytelling, resulted in greater benefits for expressive labeling, definition generation, and enhanced retention of expressive vocabulary.

Designing an accessible e-book for students with motor impairments is crucial for ensuring inclusivity in an educational content. Incorporating principles from the Web Content Accessibility Guidelines (WCAG) is foundational. Jankovic (2021) specified guidelines on keyboard accessibility which is essential, as it allows users with motor impairments to navigate the e-book seamlessly using only a keyboard, providing a comprehensive insights into creating a keyboard-accessible interface, emphasizing the importance of allowing users to operate the e-book without relying on fine motor skills.

To enhance accessibility further, publishers could consider integrating voice command options into the e-book. Voice-based interaction can be a valuable alternative for individuals with motor challenges, offering a hands-free method of navigating through content. Studies, such as "Voice-based Interaction in the Automobile: Understanding the Effects of Cognitive Load on Task Performance," emphasize the effectiveness of voice commands in reducing cognitive load and improving task performance, demonstrating the potential benefits for users with motor impairments (Cooper et al., 2020).

User testing also plays a crucial role in refining the design and ensuring its effectiveness for students with motor impairments. Engaging individuals with diverse motor abilities in the testing process provides valuable insights into the usability of keyboard controls and voice command features. Resources like the Interaction Design Foundation's guidance on "Involving Users in the Design Process" emphasize the importance of user feedback in creating a more inclusive and user-friendly educational experience (Jankovic et al., 2021). Through a holistic approach that combines WCAG guidelines, voice command integration, and user testing, an accessible e-book can be crafted to meet the diverse needs of students with motor impairments.

Creating an accessible e-book for students with cognitive impairments involves thoughtful design to enhance comprehension and ease of navigation and the guidelines and recommendations established by Hashim et al. (2021) are very useful. For cognitive accessibility, it is important to emphasize clear and consistent presentation of information, adhering to guidelines on reading level and consistent navigation. These guidelines stress the importance of using plain language and organizing content in a way that minimizes cognitive load, making it more accessible for students with cognitive impairments (Hashim et al., 2021). Incorporating interactive elements that provide additional context and support understanding is another key aspect of designing for accessibility in e-books. Features such as tooltips or guided tutorials, which can assist students with cognitive challenges in grasping complex concepts can be exploited. This aligns with the WCAG principle of creating content that is not only perceivable but also understandable, ensuring that students with cognitive impairments can engage with the material more effectively (Shahzad, 2018).

Regular user testing involving individuals with cognitive impairments is also essential for refining the e-book's design. Obtaining feedback on the clarity of language, the effectiveness of interactive elements, and the overall usability of the e-book can guide iterative improvements. This user-centered design approach, supported by resources such as the Interaction Design Foundation's "Involving Users in the Design Process," emphasizes the importance of incorporating user feedback to create an e-book that truly meets the cognitive accessibility needs of diverse students (Sun et al., 2023). By implementing these principles and continually refining the design based on user insights, an accessible e-book for students with cognitive impairments can contribute to a more inclusive educational experience.

11   Conclusion

The global trend toward digitization in education, including the increasing use of e-books, has been steadily growing. The EU is developing and implementing initiatives to improve accessibility across all aspects of daily life for all EU citizens. The Web Accessibility Directive and numerous other projects work toward implementing a digital education strategy. This work involves promoting digital literacy and ensuring that educational materials are accessible digitally. E-books will be under much more scrutiny in the near future due to the European Accessibility Act.

This chapter underscores the vital importance of accessibility in the realm of digital educational materials, particularly e-books, for second-level education in

Ireland and Cyprus. The increasing reliance on digital resources in schools across the EU brings to the forefront the need for inclusivity and accessibility in educational content. As evidenced by the experiences of undergraduate students, the absence of essential accessibility features in e-books—such as text customization, annotation capabilities, and interactive media—can significantly impede the learning experience, especially for students with disabilities or learning challenges. This chapter highlights that while many school e-books incorporate some accessibility features, there remains a substantial gap in those not specifically designed with accessibility in mind. Addressing these shortcomings is not just about enhancing digital textbooks but is fundamentally about ensuring equitable access to education. Future efforts in the publication of educational materials must prioritize accessibility from the outset, ensuring that all students, regardless of their learning needs, have equal opportunities to benefit from the digital learning revolution.

Acknowledgements This chapter is based upon work from COST Action CA19142—Leading Platform for European Citizens, Industries, Academia and Policymakers in Media Accessibility (LEAD-ME) supported by COST (European Cooperation in Science and Technology).

References

Almekhlafi, A. G. (2021). The effect of E-books on preservice student teachers' achievement and perceptions in the United Arab Emirates. *Education and Information Technologies, 26*, 1001–1021.

Baron, N. (2021). *How we read now: Strategic choices for print, screen, and audio.* Oxford University Press.

Bulock, C. (2014). Tracking perpetual access: A survey of librarian practices. *Serials Review, 40*(2), 97–104.

Carriço, L., Duarte, C., Lopes, R., Rodrigues, M., & Guimarães, N. (2005). Building rich user interfaces for digital talking books. In *Computer-Aided Design of User Interfaces IV: Proceedings of the Fifth International Conference on Computer-Aided Design of User Interfaces CADUI'2004 Sponsored by ACM and jointly organised with the Eight ACM International Conference on Intelligent User Interfaces IUI'2004*, 13–16 January 2004, Funchal, Isle of Madeira (pp. 335–348). Springer, Netherlands.

Clark, R. C., & Mayer, R. E. (2023). *E-learning and the science of instruction: Proven guidelines for consumers and designers of multimedia learning.* Wiley.

Clark, R. & Mayer, R. (2016). *Learning science through instruction: An evidence-based approach.* Wiley.

Cooke, R. (2017). ProQuest eBook central. *The Charleston Advisor, 19*(2), 39–43.

Cooper, J. M., Wheatley, C. L., McCarty, M. M., Motzkus, C. J., Lopes, C. L., Erickson, G. G., et al. (2020). Age-related differences in the cognitive, visual, and temporal demands of in-vehicle information systems. *Frontiers in Psychology, 11*, 1154.

Etta, R. A., & Kirkorian, H. L. (2019). Children's learning from interactive eBooks: Simple irrelevant features are not necessarily worse than relevant ones. *Frontiers in Psychology, 9*, 2733.

Glasgow, J. N. (1997). It's my turn! Part II: Motivating young readers using CD-ROM storybooks. *Learning & Leading with Technology, 24*(4), 18–22.

Hashim, N. L., Matraf, M. S. B., & Hussain, A. (2021). Identifying the requirements of visu-ally impaired users for accessible mobile E-book applications. *JOIV: International Journal on Informatics Visualization, 5*(2), 99–104.

Hariharan, D., Al-khazraji, S., & Huenerfauth, M. (2018). Evaluation of an English word look-up tool for web-browsing with sign language video for deaf readers. In *Universal Access in Human-Computer Interaction. Methods, Technologies, and Users: 12th International Confer-ence, UAHCI 2018*, Held as Part of HCI International 2018, Las Vegas, NV, USA, July 15–20, 2018, Proceedings, Part I 12 (pp. 205–215). Springer International Publishing.

Hsieh, Y., & Huang, S. (2020). Using an E-book in the secondary English classroom: Effects on EFL reading and listening. *Education and Information Technologies, 25*, 1285–1301.

Jankovic, N. (2021). The alerting effect occurs in simple–but not compound–visual search.

Jankovic, J., Hallett, M., Okun, M. S., Comella, C. L., & Fahn, S. (2021). *Principles and practice of movement disorders E-book*. Elsevier Health Sciences.

Joy, J., Balakrishnan, K., & Madhavankutty, S. (2021). SignText: A web-based tool for providing accessible text book contents for Deaf learners. *Universal Access in the Information Society*, 1–7.

Keizer, G. (2017). FAQ: How apple, google, microsoft and Mozilla will eliminate adobe flash. Computer World, July, 31.

Kepic Mohar, A. (2020). The materiality of textbooks. In T. Schilhab & S. Walker (Eds.), *The materiality of reading*. Aarhus Universitetsforlag.

Leporini, B., & Meattini, C. (2019, May). Personalization in the Interactive EPUB 3 Reading Expe-rience: Accessibility Issues for Screen Reader Users. In *Proceedings of the 16th International Web for All Conference* (pp. 1–10).

Leporini, B., Minardi, L., & Pellegrino, G. (2019, September). Interactive EPUB3 vs. Web Publi-cation for Screen Reading Users: the Case of 'Pinocchio' Book. In *Proceedings of the 5th EAI International Conference on Smart Objects and Technologies for Social Good* (pp. 235–238).

Lopes, R., Duarte, C., Simões, H., & Carriço, L. (2006). On the road to rich digital books. In *2nd National Conference in Human Computer Interaction*.

Marcus-Quinn, A. (2022). The EU accessibility act and web accessibility directive and the implica-tions for digital teaching and learning materials. *Routledge Open Research*. https://doi.org/10.12688/routledgeopenres.17581.1

Marcus-Quinn, A. (2024) Digital Resources for Second Level: The importance of accessible e-books. *Ireland's Education Yearbook 2023* (pp. 201–203). https://irelandseducationyearbook.ie/downloads/IEYB2023/Ireland%27s%20Education%20Yearbook%202023.pdf

Marcus-Quinn, A., & Hourigan, T. (2022). Digital inclusion and accessibility considerations in digital teaching and learning materials for the second-level classroom. *Irish Educational Studies, 41*(1), 161–169.

Messier, J., & Wood, C. (2015). Facilitating vocabulary acquisition of children with cochlear implants using electronic storybooks. *Journal of Deaf Studies and Deaf Education, 20*(4), 356–373.

Mirus, G., & Napoli, D. J. (2018). Developing language and (Pre) literacy skills in deaf preschoolers through shared reading activities with bimodal-bilingual eBooks. *Journal of Multilingual Education Research, 8*(1), 10.

Nakajima, T., Shinohara, S., & Tamura, Y. (2013). Typical functions of e-Textbook, implementation, and compatibility verification with use of ePub3 materials. *Procedia Computer Science, 22*, 1344–1353.

Prasetya, D. D., Wibawa, A. P., Hirashima, T., & Hayashi, Y. (2020). Designing rich interactive content for blended learning: A case study from Indonesia. *Electronic Journal of e-Learning, 18*(4), 276–286.

Pierard, C., Svihla, V. L., Clement, S. K., & Fazio, B. S. (2019). *Undesirable difficulties: Inves-tigating barriers to students' learning with EBooks in a semester-length course*. College & Research Libraries (forthcoming).

Scott, R. E., Jallas, M., Murphy, J. A., Park, R., & Shelley, A. (2022). *Assessing the value of course-assigned eBooks.*

Shahzad, H. (2018). *E-book accessibility* (Master's thesis, OsloMet–Oslo Metropolitan University).

Shamir, A., & Korat, O. (2006). How to select CD-ROM storybooks for young children: The teacher's role. *The Reading Teacher, 59*(6), 532–543.

Sun, T. S., Gao, Y., Khaladkar, S., Liu, S., Zhao, L., Kim, Y. H., & Hong, S. R. (2023). Designing a direct feedback loop between humans and convolutional neural networks through local explanations. *Proceedings of the ACM on Human-Computer Interaction, 7*(CSCW2), 1-32.

Véliz, S., Espinoza, V., Sauvalle, I., Arroyo, R., Pizarro, M., & Garolera, M. (2017). Towards a participative approach for adapting multimodal digital books for deaf and hard of hearing people. *International Journal of Child-Computer Interaction, 11*, 90–98.

Wauters, L., & Dirks, E. (2017). Interactive reading with young deaf and hard-of-hearing children in eBooks versus print books. *The Journal of Deaf Studies and Deaf Education, 22*(2), 243–252.

Whitfield, S., Bergmark, M., Dawson, P., Doganiero, D., & Hilgar, R. (2021). Rider University: Keeping resources available through the pandemic & construction. *Journal of Interlibrary Loan, Document Delivery & Electronic Reserve, 29*(3–5), 97–104.

Xodabande, I., & Hashemi, M. R. (2023). Learning English with electronic textbooks on mobile devices: Impacts on university students' vocabulary development. *Education and Information Technologies, 28*(2), 1587–1611.

Examining the Accessibility of Online Educational Content: A Case Study of Second-Language Learning Videos

Mariona González-Sordé⬤ and **Marina Pujadas-Farreras**⬤

Abstract The digital age has transformed the ways we approach education, customizing learning experiences to cater to student preferences. However, this transition often neglects the needs of many learners, making both physical and online classrooms not fully accessible. Although experienced organizations have shared instructions on how to create accessible educational content and how to design inclusive learning platforms, when it comes to how this is put into practice, much remains to be done. This case study assesses the accessibility of online educational content, with a specific focus on second-language learning videos, specifically on those aimed at adult non-native Catalan learners and created by the Catalan Government. The study investigates two series: "Ep! Escolta i Parla" (*'Hey! Listen and Learn'*) and "Màgia per conversar" (*'Magic to Conversation'*). Five videos from each series were chosen for evaluation, culminating in around 20 min of analyzed material. The evaluation criteria encompass audio description, subtitles, subtitles for the deaf and hard of hearing, language clarity, and speech rate. Our study successfully highlighted the aspects that make educational videos accessible or not accessible, and the fact is that there is a long way to go in terms of inclusive and public educational resources.

Keywords Media accessibility · Inclusive education · E-learning · Catalan learning · Second-language learning

1 Introduction

Digitalization has changed the way we understand education. The professional practice of teaching any subject in any level of education has been reshaped to provide a more comfortable learning experience for some students. Online learning can be

---

M. González-Sordé (✉) · M. Pujadas-Farreras
Universitat Autònoma de Barcelona, Bellaterra, Spain
e-mail: mariona.gonzalez@uab.cat

M. Pujadas-Farreras
e-mail: marina.pujadas@uab.cat

© The Author(s) 2024
A. Marcus-Quinn et al. (eds.), *Transforming Media Accessibility in Europe*,
https://doi.org/10.1007/978-3-031-60049-4_14

advantageous and offer more opportunities for students with disabilities, as some physical barriers are excluded and as some accessibility servings are more easily applied to a digital classroom (Arachchi et al., 2017; Barron et al., 2004; Kent, 2015, 2016; Salomoni et al., 2007). Nevertheless, the digital progress of educational environments has overlooked the need of some students, and online classrooms are often also not fully accessible or not designed with accessibility in mind (Arachchi et al., 2017; Roberts et al., 2011; Nganji, 2012).

This is the starting point of our study, which aims to review the accessibility of online learning environments, more specifically of educational videos, which are very commonly used in second-language learning. The focus of the study will be in analyzing the accessibility of videos aimed to adult non-native learners of Catalan, due to the familiarity of the authors with the context and since there is content created by public entities that claim to strive for universal access to their resources (see Sect. 1.2).

The accessibility of online educational platforms and content has been researched and some efforts to develop enhanced online learning environments have been performed, especially by researchers in Computer Science. Salomoni et al. (2007) took into consideration both the sensory and motor needs of the user and the technical characteristics of the device they used and developed an e-learning platform that is able to adapt its own materials to the user that is browsing it and their needs. Batanero et al. (2017) tested an adaptation of a Moodle platform following some accessibility principles and they created a system design of the learning platform that could be personalized with additional disability configurations. Luephattanasuk et al. (2011) proposed a method to present questions in an accessible format using WCAG and developed a prototype tool to check whether the accessibility of the question was compatible with NVDA screen reader software. They tested questions of different types (true or false, multiple choice, fill-in gaps) and their prototype showed to work and assess the completion with WCAG successfully, although the tool should be tested with its blind end users. The latest study presented rather than the learning platform. This is an overlooked aspect of e-learning that we will put the focus on in our study. The study aims to show some aspects of online educational videos that can easily be assessed in terms of accessibility and to evaluate some educational materials that the Catalan Government designs for initial Catalan learners.

In this chapter, we will provide an overview of accessibility in online education and delve into the profile of second-language Catalan learners. Following that, we will explain the methodology used in our analysis, present the results, and engage in a discussion of these findings.

1.1 Accessible Online Education

Ensuring universal access to education should not only be a government's aspiration, but their duty. Article 26 of the Universal Declaration of Human Rights (UN General Assembly, 1948) states that "everyone has the right to education, [which shall be free and compulsory] in the elementary and fundamental stages. [...] Higher education shall be equally accessible to all on the basis of merit." For education to be accessible, we should aim for equity (fairness) rather than equality. And for education to be equitable, opportunities and resources need to be designed and distributed with the needs of everyone in mind, so everyone can reach the same outcomes and benefits. Going back to Article 26 of the UDHRL: not everyone will have the merits to access higher education if they have not undergone inclusive elementary education, if their learning needs have not been met, or if any physical or cognitive difficulty that they may have experienced has been overlooked. In the context of Catalonia, the Department of Education of the Catalan Government agreed on and published an accessibility plan (Departament d'Educació, 2019). This plan was unfortunately only applied to the communications from the department and not to public education practices. Additionally, money recently destined to accessibility in the public educational centers (ACN, 2023) is mainly aimed to topple architectural barriers. Media accessibility and the need to include students with sensory and cognitive disabilities in public strategies and policies should not be left unnoticed.

Media accessibility barriers escalate in the online learning environment. The barriers that traditional education presents for some students add onto the mostly sensory and cognitive obstacles that digital environments and hardware can also present: information communicated exclusively through a visual channel, auditory content that is not written down, hard to navigate digital environments, hardware not adapted to all visual needs, etc. In addition, teachers also often seem to struggle with online teaching environments, which require a certain level of digital literacy and intuition to navigate, and which differ from their traditional teaching skills and know-how (Sánchez-Cruzado et al., 2021). It is important to bear in mind that online education can engender accessibility barriers in terms of (1) content, (2) platform, and (3) hardware (W3 Consortium, 2023b). In order to provide teachers and learning designers with the resources to make online content and platforms as accessible as possible, a few organizations and institutions have collected recommendations and published guidelines, standards, and policies (e.g., W3C, ADA[1]) and some projects that are working for these instructions to be put into practice in online education appeared recently (e.g., IDE@ and IMPACT projects[2]).

In terms of standards, there is an extensive ISO norm on "Individualized adaptability and accessibility in e-learning, education and training" (ISO, 2023b), which aims to facilitate the matching of digital learning resources to learners' accessibility needs and preferences.

---

[1] "Web Content Accessibility Guidelines (WCAG) 2.1" by W3C, "Guidance on Web Accessibility and the ADA" by the ADA.

[2] Implementing a Digital E-learning @lternative (IDE@) (https://portalrecerca.uab.cat/en/projects/implementing-a-digital-e-learning-lternative-3).

Inclusive Method based on the Perception of Accessibility and Compliance Testing (IMPACT) (https://portalrecerca.uab.cat/en/projects/inclusive-method-based-on-the-perception-of-accessibility-and-com-4).

The W3 consortium has also published some recommendations and collected resources on accessible online learning, referring to their Web Content Accessibility Guidelines and always following the consortium's approach to web accessibility. These four aspects should be assessed for any online content to evaluate its accessibility and detect the areas that need to be improved:

(1) "Perceivable—Information and user interface components must be presentable to users in ways they can perceive.

(2) Operable—User interface components and navigation must be operable.

(3) Understandable—Information and the operation of the user interface must be understandable.

(4) Robust—Content must be robust enough that it can be interpreted reliably by a wide variety of user agents, including assistive technologies."

Understanding WCAG 2.0 .(W3 Consortium, 2023a, in Understanding the Four Principles of Accessibility)

Finally, the Disabilities, Opportunities, Internetworking, and Technology (DO-IT) Center at the University of Washington shared a list of recommendations for teaching an accessible online course (Burgstahler, 2021) and presented a section on inclusive pedagogy specially dedicated to neurodiverse students:

(1) Some of the recommendations on course materials encourage to:

– "Use clear, consistent layouts, navigation, and organization schemes.

– Provide concise text descriptions of content presented within images.

– Use large, bold, sans serif fonts on uncluttered pages with plain backgrounds.

– Caption videos and transcribe audio content."

(2) And some of the recommendations on inclusive pedagogy encourage to:

– "Recommend videos and written materials to students where they can gain technical skills needed for course participation.

– Provide multiple ways for students to learn (e.g., use a combination of text, video, audio, and/or image; speak aloud all content presented on slides in synchronous presentations and then record them for later viewing).

– Address a wide range of language skills as you write content (e.g., use plain English, spell out acronyms, define terms, avoid or define jargon)."

20 Tips for Teaching an Accessible Online Course. (Burgstahler, 2021)

Having presented the above, professionals could find it helpful to have more specific and extensive guidelines on designing and teaching online courses in an accessible way; but it is also true, as we will present in the present study, that sometimes, the already-existing recommendations are often overlooked and not followed in online education.

1.2 Accessibility in Catalan as a Second-Language Learning

According to the last Catalan language policy report (Departament de Cultura, 2020), 36.4% of the residents in Catalonia were born in other regions of Spain or foreign countries. Furthermore, the foreign population is more prominently represented within the working-age demographic, particularly among individuals aged 20–54, with a noticeable concentration between 25 and 39 years old. On the other hand, residents from other regions of Spain tend to be over 65 years old.

According to the language policy report, which references the data from a survey conducted by the Department of Culture and the Statistical Institute of Catalonia (Departament de Cultura and Institut d'Estadística de Catalunya, 2018), 49% of the 1,380,720 people born in a foreign country that lived in Catalonia did not speak Catalan, and 62.5% did not know how to write in this language. Among residents from other parts of Spain (a total of 1,301,357) 38.9% did not speak Catalan and 72.1% did not know how to write in Catalan.

For individuals who could speak Catalan, they learned it through their daily life, regardless of whether they were foreigners or came from other regions of the country. Among foreigners, 37.3% reported learning Catalan primarily in their daily interactions, closely followed by language schools at 31.2%. Meanwhile, among residents from other parts of the country, a significant majority of 54.2% learned Catalan in their everyday lives, with the second most common setting being at work, where they learned from colleagues, accounting for 21.6%. Additionally, among foreigners, 61.7% indicated that they wished to improve or learn Catalan, while 27.7% of residents coming from other parts of Spain said the same. The age group that expressed the greatest interest in learning Catalan was those aged 30–44, with 43.6% showing interest. Following closely, the second most interested age group was those aged 45–64, with 40.3% displaying interest in learning the language.

Other Catalan-speaking regions of Spain register similar percentages of immigrants than Catalonia. Nevertheless, Catalonia has been more actively promoting the need to learn Catalan, although newcomers show a general higher interest in learning Spanish (Bori & Petanović, 2017).

Data strongly suggests a demand for self-paced learning resources tailored to adults, and a noteworthy percentage of residents who were born in other countries have expressed an interest in learning Catalan. Additionally, the data reveals a trend among those who already know Catalan, with a preference for acquiring oral language skills over written language proficiency. Furthermore, non-regulated, informal learning methods appear to be more prevalent in the Catalan learning context. The inclination toward non-regulated learning may be because the primary age group among migrants falls within the working-age bracket, which can potentially restrict their opportunities for structured and formal learning.

A recent study (Massaguer Comes et al., 2023) shows that at the Consortium for Language Standardization (CPNL) (the public agency that offers Catalan courses in Catalonia) it is common for classrooms to have students with very different profiles in terms of their native languages, educational levels, levels of motivation, and contact with Catalan outside the classroom, but tend to overlook that students can also differ in their sensorial and cognitive abilities. While diversity can enrich learning and provide an opportunity to learn from each other, the coexistence of diverse academic profiles and the lack of optimal tools and adaptations can also make it challenging to conduct sessions effectively (Massaguer Comes et al., 2023).

Catalan learners in the CPNL in many cases do not use their knowledge nor socialize in Catalan outside the classroom (Massaguer Comes et al., 2023). The main causes range from having a low educational level or not aiming for positions that require knowledge of Catalan to lacking access to Catalan-speaking social networks and not identifying or perceiving themselves as potential members of these groups in the future (Massaguer Comes et al., 2023). Again, the list of contributing factors does not mention sensorial or cognitive diversity, which should have been considered, as these impediments would probably be very relevant on whether a student succeeds not only in the acquisition of a certain level of language knowledge in the classroom, but also in the ability to use this knowledge in their everyday life.

2   Method

This section will provide an overview of the methodology employed in our analysis, the characteristics of the materials we examined, and the findings derived from this analysis.

2.1   Sample Description and Selection Criteria

In this study, we analyze the accessibility of two video series aimed at Catalan learners. The first series was created by the Secretariat of Language Policy and CPNL, while the second series was created by the Secretariat of Language Policy. These two series were selected as they were produced by public entities entrusted with the normalization and education of Catalan.

The video series "Ep! Escolta i Parla" ('*Hey! Listen and Learn*'), hereafter referred to as "Series 1," is addressed to students who lack literacy skills or are unable to use written language to learn. It comprises 21 videos, each spanning 1–4 min, that are divided in three difficulty modules. According to the series description, upon completion of the course, students typically attain a proficiency level approximately equivalent to A2 on the Common European Framework of Reference for Languages.

The video series "Màgia per a conversar" ('*Magic for Conversation*'), hereafter referred to as "Series 2," has the objective of providing supplementary resources for students engaged in language tandems while learning Catalan. Comprising a collection of 25 videos, each spanning 1–3 min, the series features magic performances designed to inspire discussion topics.

Table 1 Overview of analyzed videos

Series 1	Duration	Series 2	Duration
Consells pràctics U2 (*'Practical advice U2'*)	1:35	E1. Els monuments (*'E1. The monuments'*)	1:56
Això és un amic U9 (*'This is a friend U9'*)	2:43	E2. La caixa d'espases (*'E2. The box of swords'*)	2:09
L'entrevista de feina U8 (*'Work interview U8'*)	2:14	E3. El trencaclosques (*'E3. The puzzle'*)	2:16
Em preparo per a una entrevista de feina U8 (*'Getting ready for a work interview U8'*)	1:53	E4. L'elefant (*'E4. The elephant'*)	2:13
El programa de ràdio U7 (*'The radio programeU7'*)	1:55	E5. Veritats i mentides (*'E5. Truths and lies'*)	2:13
Total duration	10:22	**Total duration**	10:47

We chose a sample of five videos from each video series, resulting in an approximate duration of 10 min of material for each individual series. In total, we analyzed around 20 min of content. The specific videos were chosen with an effort to ensure similar lengths and total duration, enabling a comparable analysis. In Table 1, a compilation of the analyzed chapters and their respective durations is presented.

3 Analysis and Results

In order to gauge the accessibility of the video series, we examined the video samples to determine if the creators had made them accessible to diverse student profiles. Since these materials are intended to enhance and promote the learning of Catalan and were developed by public entities, ensuring accessibility to a diverse range of students would contribute to better achieving this goal.

We performed a corpus analysis, following Arias-Badia and Matamala's (2023) methodology, to determine the level of sentence complexity (sentence length and average verbs per sentence) and the distribution of parts-of-speech (PoS), that is, the usage of adjectives, nouns, verbs, and adverbs. This analysis was performed with the online tool SketchEngine and had the aim of helping determine if the videos followed easy-to-understand recommendations such as short and simple sentences and using a verbal style (European Accessible Information Working Group, 2011; Commission, 2012). An easy-to-understand language would mean that the contents are accessible to a wider variety of student profiles. We also manually looked at the speech rate by calculating the words per minute (wpm) and syllable per second (sps) rate.

For accessibility for students with visual impairments, we focused on the information given in the video images to see if this information was also present in the audio and if it was necessary for the comprehension of the videos (AENOR, 2005).

In terms of accessibility for students with hearing difficulties, we checked whether the videos included subtitles and subtitles for the deaf and hard of hearing (SDH) that communicated audio information or audio cues necessary for the comprehension of the video that would otherwise not be transmitted through the visual channel (AENOR, 2012).

Corpus analysis

In Series 1, most videos feature very concise sentences, typically consisting of 6–8 words, and usually containing only a single verb. This is a result of the videos being designed as dialogues involving two or more characters. The one exception is the first video, "Consells pràctics," which is a monologue. Nevertheless, even in this monologue, the average sentence length remains relatively short at 15 words, and the sentences tend to contain an average of 2.8 verbs per sentence. This could suggest a certain degree of sentence complexity, but it is important to note that most of these sentences are coordinated with connectors such as "and" or "but."

In contrast, Series 2 features monologues where a single person addresses the audience. In these videos, the average sentence length falls in the range of 10–15 words, with each sentence typically including 2–3 verbs. The sentence structure in Series 2 is slightly more complex compared to Series 1, incorporating both coordinated and subordinated structures (Table 2).

When it comes to the distribution of parts-of-speech (PoS), specifically, the percentage of content words that are verbs, nouns, adverbs, and adjectives, there is a difference observed between the two series. Typically, an average sentence should contain more nouns than verbs. However, upon closer examination of the results, it

Table 2 Mean length and mean verb per sentence

Series 1	Mean length	Mean verb per sentence
Consells pràctics U2	15.8	2.8
Això és un amic U9	7.6	2.5
L'entrevista de feina U8	6.7	1.3
Em preparo per a una entrevista de feina U8	8.2	1.8
El programa de ràdio U7	8.3	1.7
Series 2		
E1. Els monuments	10.7	2.4
E2. La caixa d'espases	13.5	2.7
E3. El trencaclosques	15.8	3.3
E4. L'elefant	10.3	2.12
E5. Veritats i mentides	14.8	3.2

becomes evident that not only do the videos adopt a verbal style, but also the quantity of verbs used is unusually high in some of the videos.

Throughout the five analyzed videos, Series 2 maintains a relatively consistent use of verbs, ranging between 35 and 37% of the lexical words. Conversely, in Series 1, there is a wider range, with most videos falling between 32 and 39% in terms of verb usage. One video in Series 1 stands out as an outlier, with a 50% use of verbs.

When it comes to the use of nouns, Series 1 exhibits again a broader range, with noun usage percentages spanning from 31 to 45% across its videos. In contrast, Series 2 maintains a narrower range, showing noun usage percentages between 33 and 39%.

A notable difference becomes apparent when comparing verb and noun usage. Series 2 consistently employs both verbs and nouns in nearly equal proportions, with only a slight 2–4% difference in usage between them. However, Series 1 tends to favor either verbs or nouns more prominently. In Series 1, the difference between the percentage of verbs and nouns often falls within a range of 9–11%, indicating a preference for one over the other. However, there are two outliers in Series 1. One video exhibits a 19% higher usage of verbs compared to nouns, while another video in Series 1 shows nearly equal verb and noun usage, with just a 1% difference. It is worth noting that using more verbs makes the language easier to understand. In this case, both series show a higher-than-average verb usage (Figs. 1 and 2).

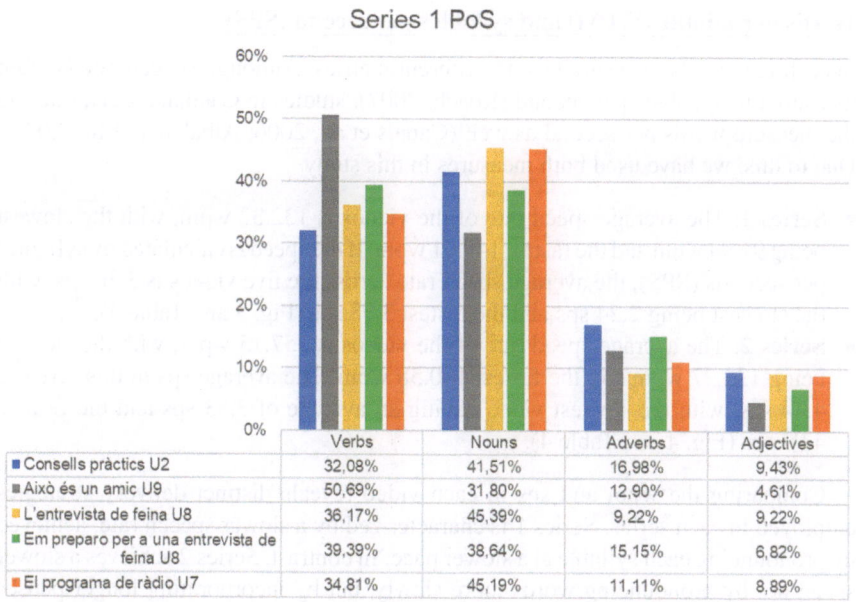

	Verbs	Nouns	Adverbs	Adjectives
■ Consells pràctics U2	32,08%	41,51%	16,98%	9,43%
■ Això és un amic U9	50,69%	31,80%	12,90%	4,61%
■ L'entrevista de feina U8	36,17%	45,39%	9,22%	9,22%
■ Em preparo per a una entrevista de feina U8	39,39%	38,64%	15,15%	6,82%
■ El programa de ràdio U7	34,81%	45,19%	11,11%	8,89%

Fig. 1 Series 1 PoS

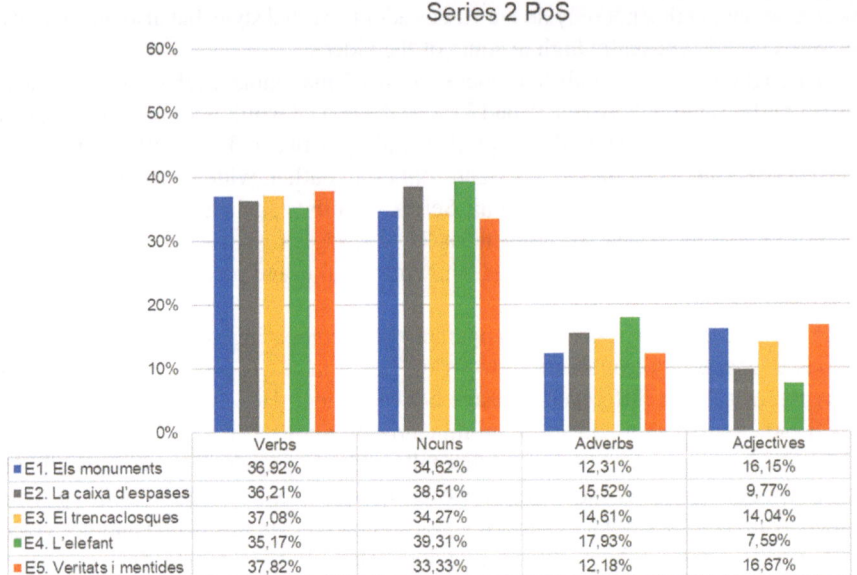

	Verbs	Nouns	Adverbs	Adjectives
■ E1. Els monuments	36,92%	34,62%	12,31%	16,15%
■ E2. La caixa d'espases	36,21%	38,51%	15,52%	9,77%
■ E3. El trencaclosques	37,08%	34,27%	14,61%	14,04%
■ E4. L'elefant	35,17%	39,31%	17,93%	7,59%
■ E5. Veritats i mentides	37,82%	33,33%	12,18%	16,67%

Fig. 2 Series 2 PoS

Words per minute (WPM) and syllables per second (SPS)

Speech rate can be measured using different metrics. Although speech rate is often measured in syllables per second (Roach, 2007), studies in Catalan speech rate use the measure words per second as well (Canals et al., 2006; Albaladejo Mur, 2020). Due to this, we have used both measures in this study.

- **Series 1**: The average speed rate of the videos is 132.32 wpm, with the slowest being 91.94 wpm and the fastest 149.01 wpm. If the speed is calculated by syllables per seconds (SPS), the average speed rate across the five videos is 3.30 sps, with the slowest being 2.24 sps and the fastest 3.78 sps (Fig. 3 and Table 3).
- **Series 2**: The average speed rate of the videos is 157.15 wpm, with the slowest being 135.27 wpm and the fastest 180.58 wpm. The average sps in this series is 4.44 sps, with the slowest video having an average of 3.83 sps and the fastest, 4.97 sps (Fig. 4 and Table 4).

Comparing the wpm and sps in each video reveals distinct delivery strategies employed in each series. Series 1 is characterized by a slower speech rate, achieved by pronouncing each syllable at a slower pace. In contrast, Series 2 achieves a slower speed not by pronouncing words more slowly, but by incorporating longer pauses between sentences. This contrast becomes evident when we examine two specific videos: "Em preparo per a una entrevista de feina U8" from Series 1 and "E4. L'elefant" from Series 2. The first video has an average speed of 143.75 wpm and

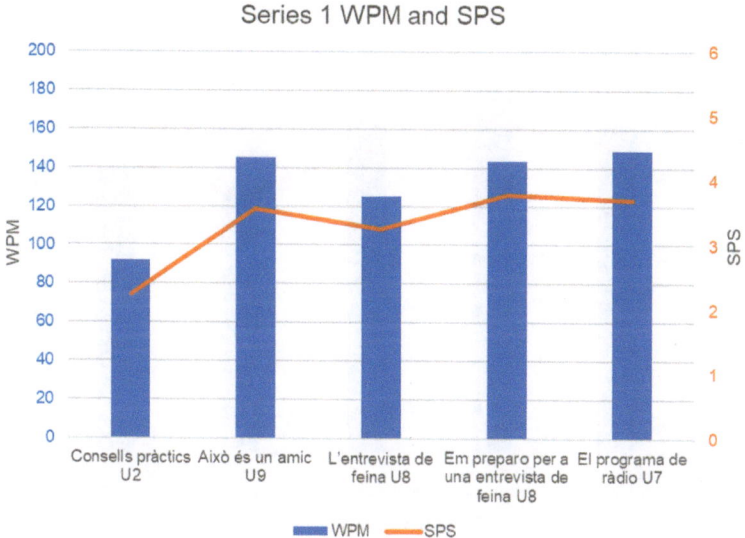

Fig. 3 Series 1 speech rate

Table 3 Series 1 speech rate

Video	WPM	SPS
Consells pràctics U2	91.94	2.24
Això és un amic U9	145.56	3.56
L'entrevista de feina U8	125.54	3.24
Em preparo per a una entrevista de feina U8	143.75	3.78
El programa de ràdio U7	149.01	3.70

3.78 sps, while the second video exhibits a lower wpm average at 135.27 wpm but a higher sps average, measured at 3.83 sps.

Another example are the videos "Això és un amic U9" and "El programa de ràdio U7" from Series 1, which have an average speed rate of 145.56 wpm and 3.56 sps and 149.01 wpm and 3.70 sps, respectively. In contrast, the video "E5. Veritats i mentides" from Series 2 has a lower wpm average, at 141.05 wpm, but a higher sps rate, 4.40 sps.

Finally, it is worth mentioning that both series are available on YouTube, which allows the users to slow down the video if needed.

Audio description (AD), subtitles, and subtitles for the deaf and hard of hearing (SDH)

In case there are students with hearing difficulties or visual impairments in the course, including AD, subtitles and SDH in any audiovisual content are essential (Table 5).

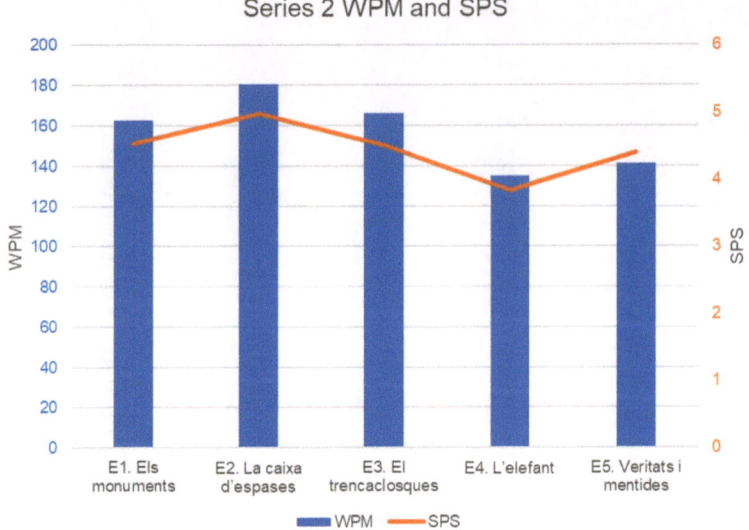

Fig. 4 Series 2 speech rate

Table 4 Series 2 speech rate

Video	WPM	SPS
E1. Els monuments	162.53	4.53
E2. La caixa d'espases	180.58	4.97
E3. El trencaclosques	166.31	4.50
E4. L'elefant	135.27	3.83
E5. Veritats i mentides	141.05	4.40

Table 5 Overview of AD, subtitles, and SDH features

	AD	Subtitles	SDH
Series 1	×*	×	×
Series 2	×	✓	×

*Alternative resources are provided

Audio description

- **Series 1**: There is no AD option offered, but the organization that has created the content provides transcripts of clips that include descriptions of some relevant actions. Other types of information are lost without the visual channel.
- **Series 2**: There is no AD option offered, and there is information lost without the visual channel. However, the topic of the videos being focused on magic is not as relevant as the series' main goal, which is providing conversation topics for

language pairs. The users can still answer to the verbal prompts even if they do not see the magic trick.

Subtitles

- **Series 1**: The videos do not include any subtitles, but the organization that has created the content offers transcripts of the clips that include some actions and the dialogue between characters.
- **Series 2**: The videos include manually generated subtitles of good quality in Catalan. Sometimes the subtitles do not meet optimal accessibility conditions and appear and disappear too quickly, but YouTube has the option to slow down the video, allowing you to also view the subtitles at a more relaxed pace.

Subtitles for the deaf and hard of hearing (SDH)

- **Series 1**: The videos do not include any subtitles, nor any audio information through the visual channel. This information is also not available in the transcription of the actions and the dialogue that is available to the students. If the audio channel is suppressed, no relevant information about the plot is omitted, but some audio effects are missed.
- **Series 2**: The subtitles available in the videos in Series 2 do not provide any additional audio information besides the speech of the speaker. Nevertheless, not much information is lost, as the videos focus on a magician that speaks over a musical background.

In summary, both series showed some good accessibility practices, such as using an easy-to-understand language, but lacked some relevant others, like AD or SDH, which could potentially exclude users with sensory disabilities (Table 6).

Table 6 Overview of the analyzed parameters' results

	Series 1	Series 2
Easy-to-understand	Yes	Yes
Average speed rate	132.32 wpm 3.30 sps	157.15 wpm 4.44 sps
AD	No Some actions described in the transcripts provided	No
Subtitles	No Transcriptions of the dialogues provided	Yes Manually generated subtitles
SDH	No	No

4 Discussion

The objective of this study was to gauge the accessibility of these video series. To do so, we focused on linguistic aspects, speech rate, and the presence of AD, subtitling, and SDH.

In terms of linguistic aspects, the results show that both series adhere to practices of easy-to-understand language, which is any simplified language variety that aims to make information easier to understand (ISO, 2023a) and is thus accessible to different types of users. For example, in terms of sentence length, Series 1's average ranges from 6 to 8 words, while Series 2 ranges from 10 to 15. To put these results into perspective, the average length found in easy-to-understand texts is 12–17 words (Arias-Badia & Matamala, 2023). Furthermore, in AD, which is characterized for having short and concise sentences (Taylor, 2015), we see averages like 12 in film AD (Arias-Badia & Matamala, 2023), 13 in opera AD (Hermosa-Ramírez, 2021), and 8 in short films AD (Matamala, 2018).

If we look at the average number of verbs per sentence, Series 1 has between 1 and 2 verbs and Series 2 between 2 and 3. Series 1 shows results closer to film AD again (Arias-Badia & Matamala, 2023). As mentioned, in Series 1, the sentences with more than one verb are coordinated with connectors such as "and" or "but," while in Series 2, there are also some subordinated structures. However, this is not an indication of a higher sentence complexity, given that in Easy-to-Read texts (the easiest version of easy-to-understand) copulative or adversative coordinated sentences are acceptable, as well as subordinated causal, final, temporal, conditional, and comparatives sentences (García Muñoz, 2012).

Finally, the PoS analysis shows unexpected results. While other studies identify nouns as the dominant category (Arias-Badia & Matamala, 2023; Hermosa-Ramírez, 2021), in Series 1, two of the three videos have verbs as the dominant category, while in Series 2, it is three out of five videos. These results are quite positive, since they align with the European Commission's recommendations (2012), which recommend using more verbs for easier comprehension.

While Series 2 shows slightly longer sentences with more verbs, it is important to remember that this series is addressed to more advanced students than Series 1. Considering this, both Series 1 and 2 are accessible in terms of linguistic aspects.

Regarding speech rate, the average in Catalan oral language is 120–150 wpm (Canals et al., 2006), while the recommendation for oral discourse is 150 wpm (Albaladejo Mur, 2020). Since the material we have analyzed is addressed to Catalan second-language learners, ideally the results should be within these parameters or lower. Series 1 follows these recommendations, with all the videos falling within the 120–150 wpm average or lower. In contrast, in Series 2 three of the videos have a speed rate higher than 150, while the remaining two keep to the average established by Canals et al. (2006).

However, when looking at another speech rate measure, syllables per second, the results are different. Series 2's results are closer to the average established by

Cremades Cortiella (2016) and Cicres Bosch (2008), at 4.92 sps and 6.45 sps, respectively. The range for Series 2 is 3.83 sps–4.97 sps, while Series 1 exhibits a slower pace, ranging from 2.24 sps to 3.78 sps. In essence, Series 1 proves to be quite accessible in terms of speed for both measures, whereas determining the accessibility of Series 2 is more challenging because; while it exceeds the average in wpm, its sps falls within the average range. Series 2 is addressed to more advanced learners, which might account for the faster speed, but it might also pose some difficulties to some students with varied needs. Nonetheless, it is important to note that the viewing platform of both series enables users to adjust the video speed, mitigating any potential drawbacks associated with a faster pace.

One of the main accessibility issues of both series is the lack of AD. Although Series 1 provides a transcription that narrates some of the actions of the characters, the resource is not perceivable and requires a certain level of autonomous research from the user. AD would not only help students with visual impairments to engage with the video the same way as their peers, but would also help auditory learners to stay focused and point out relevant visual information (Krejtz et al., 2012). Another big accessibility issue is the lack of SDH in both video series. Although they present good-quality subtitles, these do not present a text description of auditory information other than the dialogue.

5 Conclusions

Through our small study and theoretical exploration of accessible e-learning audiovisual resources, we have been able to firstly discuss the importance of overcoming the possible barriers than any online educational content or platform may present by taking accessibility into account from the early stages of their design and providing students with accessibility services and secondly to demonstrate through our study that this is nowadays not a common practice, even when the resources are created by public institutions that have been taking steps toward their communications being universally accessible (Generalitat de Catalunya, 2022, 2023).

In the specific context of our study, both Series 1 and Series 2 demonstrate accessibility to students with diverse needs. Series 1's language is easy-to-understand, with a slower speed and video transcriptions containing image descriptions, making it inclusive for all students. Despite lacking AD or SDH, Series 1 is designed in a way that minimizes information loss. In contrast, Series 2, while sharing an easy-to-understand language and a slower pace, provides subtitles but lacks AD or SDH, resulting in information loss for students without access to the visual content. This underscores the critical need for educational materials to either be fully accessible from their design or to provide the necessary accessibility features.

We aim for this chapter to foster multidisciplinary research with one common goal: to make online educational environments as accessible as possible. Online resources should make learning easier and accommodate everyone rather than being an additional obstacle for some people to access education.

Acknowledgements Both authors have received funding from COST Action LEAD-ME (CA19142) supported by COST (European Cooperation in Science and Technology).

Marina Pujadas-Farreras is also a FI grant holder from the Catalan Government (2022FI_B 00097). She is part of the research group TransMedia Catalonia, funded by Secretaria d'Universitats i Recerca del Departament d'Empresa i Coneixement de la Generalitat de Catalunya, under the SGR funding scheme (ref. code 2021SGR000077). She is part of the project WEL (PID2022-137058NB-I00), funded by MCIN/AEI/10.13039/501100011033 and by "ERDF A way of making Europe". This chapter is based upon work from COST Action CA19142—Leading Platform for European Citizens, Industries, Academia and Policymakers in Media Accessibility (LEAD-ME) supported by COST (European Cooperation in Science and Technology).

References

Accessible Information Working Group. (2011). *Make it easy: A guide to preparing easy to read information.* https://inclusionireland.ie/wp-content/uploads/2020/10/makeiteasyguide2011.pdf

ACN. (2023). Una seixantena de centres educatius podran millorar l'accessibilitat dels seus espais. *Social.Cat,* 2023. https://www.social.cat/noticia/19282/una-seixantena-de-centres-edu catius-podran-millorar-laccessibilitat-dels-seus-espais

AENOR. (2005). *UNE 153020:2005 Audiodescripción para personas con discapacidad visual. Requisitos para la audiodescripción y elaboración de audioguías.*

AENOR. (2012). *UNE 153010:2012 Subtitulado para personas sordas y personas con discapacidad auditiva.*

Albaladejo Mur, M. (2020). *Presentacions orals en públic.* Diputació de Barcelona. https://reposi tori-dsf.diba.cat/public_resources/wiki_prod/2139POP/2139POP.pdf

Arachchi, T. K., Sitbon, L., & Zhang, J. (2017). Enhancing access to ELearning for people with intellectual disability: Integrating Usability with Learning. *In Human-Computer Interaction— INTERACT, 2017,* 13–32. https://doi.org/10.1007/978-3-319-67684-5_2

Arias-Badia, B., & Matamala, A. (2023). Audio description from an easy-to-understand language perspective: A corpus-based study in catalan. *Jostrans: The Journal of Specialised Translation.* https://jostrans.org/issue40/art_arias.pdf

Barron, J. A., Laura, F., & Barron, A. E. (2004). E-Learning for everyone: Addressing accessibility. *Journal of Interactive Instruction Development, 16*(4), 3–10.

Batanero, C., Fernández-Sanz, L., Piironen, A. K., Holvikivi, J., Hilera, J. R., Otón, S., & Alonso, J. (2017). Accessible platforms for E-learning: A case study. *Computer Applications in Engineering Education, 25*(6), 1018–1037. https://doi.org/10.1002/cae.21852

Bori, P., & Petanović , J. (2017). The representation of immigrant characters in Catalan as a second language textbooks: A critical discourse analysis perspective. *Lengua y Migración/Language and Migration, 9*(2), 61–75. http://hdl.handle.net/10017/31879

Burgstahler, S. (2021). *20 tips for teaching an accessible online course.* DO-IT Disabilities, Opportunities, Internetworking, and Technology. https://www.washington.edu/t/20-tips-teaching-acc essible-online-course

Canals, R., Esteban, M., & Ribas, J. (2006). La lectura a les comarques de Girona. *Lletres. Revista de Girona, 234,* 37–43. https://core.ac.uk/download/pdf/132550448.pdf

Cicres Bosch, J. (2008). *Aplicació de l'anàlisi de l'entonació i de l'alienació tonal a la identificació de parlants en fonètica forense.* Universitat Pompeu Fabra. http://hdl.handle.net/10803/7504.

Cremades Cortiella, E. (2016). El tempo como factor discriminante en el análisis forense del habla: Análisis descriptivo en hablantes bilingües (catalán-español). *Estudios Inter-lingüísticos, 4*(4), 13–35. https://dialnet.unirioja.es/servlet/articulo?codigo=5757433&info=res umen&idioma=ENG

Departament de Cultura. (2020). *Informe de Política Lingüística 2020*. https://llengua.gencat.cat/web/.content/documents/informepl/arxius/ipl2020.PDF

Departament de Cultura, and Institut d'Estadística de Catalunya. (2018). *Enquesta d'usos lingüístics de la població 2018*.

Departament d'Educació. (2019). *Pla d'accessibilitat Del Departament d'Educació 2019–2021*. Barcelona. https://hdl.handle.net/20.500.12694/1180

European Commission. (2012). *How to write clearly*. Publications Office. https://op.europa.eu/s/y41f

García Muñoz, Ó. (2012). *Lectura Fácil: Métodos de Redacción y Evaluación*. Real Patronato sobre Discapacidad. https://www.plenainclusion.org/sites/default/files/lectura-facil-metodos.pdf

Generalitat de Catalunya. (2022). Nova guia per aprendre a comunicar en llenguatge planer. *Serveis Digitals i Experiència Ciutadana*. 2022. https://atenciociutadana.gencat.cat/ca/detalls/noticia/Nova-guia-per-aprendre-a-comunicar-en-llenguatge-planer

Generalitat de Catalunya. (2023). Comunicació Clara. *Serveis digitals i experiència ciutadana. apoderar la ciutadania*. 2023. https://atenciociutadana.gencat.cat/ca/apoderar-la-ciutadania/comunicar/llenguatge-planer/index.html

Hermosa-Ramírez, I. (2021). The hierarchisation of operatic signs through the lens of audio description: A corpus study. *MonTI. Monografías de Traducción e Interpretación, 13*(June), 184–219. https://doi.org/10.6035/MONTI.2021.13.06

ISO. (2023a). *ISO/IEC 23859-1. Information technology—User interfaces—Part 1: Guidance on making written easy to read and easy to understand*. https://www.iso.org/obp/ui/#iso:std:iso-iec:23859:-1:dis:ed-1:v1:en

ISO. (2023b). *ISO/IEC 24751-[1–4]. Information technology individualized adaptability and accessibility in e-learning, education and training*.

Kent, Mike. (2015). Disability and ELearning: Opportunities and barriers. *Disability Studies Quarterly, 35*(1). https://doi.org/10.18061/dsq.v35i1.3815

Kent, M. (2016). Opportunities for ELearning, social media and disability. In E. Katie, & M. Kent (Eds.), *Disability and social media. Global perspectives* (pp. 191–99).

Krejtz, K., I. Krejtz, A. Duchowski, A. Szarkowska, & A. Walczak. (2012). Multimodal learning with audio description. In *Proceedings of the ACM Symposium on Applied Perception* (pp. 83–90). ACM. https://doi.org/10.1145/2338676.2338694

Luephattanasuk, N., A. Suchato, & P. Punyabukkana. (2011). Accessible QTI presentation for web-based e-learning. In *Proceedings of the International Cross-Disciplinary Conference on Web Accessibility* (pp. 1–4). ACM. https://doi.org/10.1145/1969289.1969323

Massaguer Comes, M., A. Flors-Mas, & X. Vila. (2023). *De l'aprenentatge a l'adopció de la llengua catalana: cap al cicle d'acompanyament als usuaris del Consorci per a la Normalització Lingüística*.

Matamala, A. (2018). One short film, different audio descriptions. Analysing the language of audio description created by students and professionals. *Onomázein, 41*, 185–207. https://ddd.uab.cat/record/199423

Nganji, J. T. (2012). Designing disability-aware E-learning systems: Disabled students' recommendations. *International Journal of Advanced Science and Technology, 48*(6), 61–70.

Roach, P. (2011). *English phonetics and phonology. Glossary*.

Roberts, J. B., Crittenden, L. A., & Crittenden, J. C. (2011). Students with disabilities and online learning: A Cross-institutional study of perceived satisfaction with accessibility compliance and services. *The Internet and Higher Education, 14*(4), 242–250. https://doi.org/10.1016/j.iheduc.2011.05.004

Salomoni, P., Mirri, S., Ferretti, S., & Roccetti, M. (2007). Profiling learners with special needs for custom E-learning experiences, a closed case? In *Proceedings of the 2007 International Cross-Disciplinary Conference on Web Accessibility* (pp. 84–92). ACM Press. https://doi.org/10.1145/1243441.1243462

Sánchez-Cruzado, C., Campión, R. S., & Sánchez-Compaña, M. T. (2021). Teacher digital literacy: The indisputable challenge after COVID-19. *Sustainability, 13*(4), 1858. https://doi.org/10.3390/su13041858

Taylor, C. (2015). The language of AD. In A. Remael, N. Reviers, & G. Vercauteren (Eds.), *Pictures painted in words: ADLAB audio description guidelines* (pp. 46–55). EUT Edizioni Università di Trieste. http://hdl.handle.net/10077/11838

UN General Assembly. (1948). Universal declaration of human rights.

W3 Consortium. (2023a). *Understanding WCAG 2.0. A guide to understanding and implementing web content accessibility guidelines 2.0. 2023.* https://www.w3.org/TR/UNDERSTANDING-WCAG20/

W3 Consortium. (2023b). *W3C accessibility guidelines (WCAG) 3.0. W3C. 2023.* https://www.w3.org/TR/wcag-3.0/

Accessibility in Technology-Enhanced Curricula: A Comparative Study in Portugal, Turkey, and Lithuania

Giedrė Valūnaitė-Oleškevičienė, **Ebru Çavuşoğlu**, and **Carlos Duarte**

Abstract While using technology to enhance teaching and learning, it is essential to make sure that none of the learners is excluded. Therefore, curriculum design should be done in such a way that it should not be left to students to adapt. This chapter focuses on the legal prerequisites officially applied in each researched country. According to the survey on the EU law on accessibility, the constitutions of Lithuania and Portugal foresee the availability of education for all citizens. Also, the currently available constitution in Turkey recognizes accessibility to education. Recently, the European Accessibility Act covered accessibility matters of products and services and requires legal adaptation in all the member countries, which lays a sound background for accessibility implementation in education. The current study analyzes the curricula of the translation courses of the Translation and Interpreting Department of Samsun University in Turkey, the Language Sciences Department of Lisbon University in Portugal, and the Institute of Humanities of Mykolas Romeris University in Lithuania by checking how the four main principles of digital accessibility (perceivable, operable, understandable, and robust) are observed in the existing curricula. The analysis identifies the need for practical recommendations in the analyzed curricula on how teaching and assessment methods could be applied to ensure fair and equal possibilities and observing the four key digital accessibility principles in the study process. The practical points should serve as a key factor for improving and creating curricula for technology-enhanced teaching and learning in translation studies.

Keywords Accessibility · Technology-enhanced education · Accessibility legislation · Translation studies curricula · University studies

G. Valūnaitė-Oleškevičienė (✉)
Mykolas Romeris University, Ateities 20, 08303 Vilnius, Lithuania
e-mail: gvalunaite@mruni.eu

E. Çavuşoğlu
Faculty of Economics Administrative and Social Sciences, The Department of Translation and Interpreting, Samsun University, Samsun, Turkey

C. Duarte
LASIGE, Faculdade de Ciências da Universidade de Lisboa, Lisbon, Portugal

© The Author(s) 2024
A. Marcus-Quinn et al. (eds.), *Transforming Media Accessibility in Europe*,
https://doi.org/10.1007/978-3-031-60049-4_15

265

1 Introduction

In today's modern world, technology profoundly influences various facets of life, necessitating continual adaptation to its evolving developments. Education is certainly one of those areas that requires embracing technology to be able to create an effective teaching and learning environment. Availability of the latest technological tools, the profile of the students who are keen on using technology in their everyday lives, and the online components of many coursebook materials compel the educational environment to assimilate technology. In line with this, the notion of accessibility has gained a pivotal position in education as well.

The notion of media accessibility is tightly related to the development of legal prerequisites directed to the implementation of human equality and participation in society. According to Greco (2018), accessibility has become a proactive principle for human rights and can be used as an important instrument in international and national policies. The author stresses that media accessibility focuses on access to media products, services, and environments for all people who might not be able to get access due to linguistic, sensory, or other barriers. Thus, legal regulations, especially the European Accessibility Act, and related international and national legislation play an important role in media accessibility implementation. The process of media accessibility implementation is also strengthened by the Web Accessibility Initiative providing the four principles of accessibility,[1] as defined by the Web Content Accessibility Guidelines (WCAG)[2] focused on accessibility requirements and international standards.

Education is one of the areas where research has been carried out in various directions focusing on a multitude of issues including accessibility. In the research on the didactics of audiovisual translation, Díaz-Cintas (2008) observes the need for consistent attention on examining pedagogical issues in audiovisual translation by focusing on both theoretical and practical perspectives. The research on media accessibility has broadened the accessibility studies, and accessibility research has become a field embracing many specific domains which resulted in accessibility studies becoming acknowledged interdisciplinary research (Greco, 2018). Media accessibility is one of the areas that focuses both on research and the implementation of education and training. It deals with both practical and theoretical issues in accessibility education and is directed toward the specific pedagogical issues related to accessibility. It analyses not only the courses in which accessibility is a curricular topic but also examines current media practices and accessibility issues in the related research areas. However, there is a need to broaden the perspective by including research and the implementation of education and training in other fields and domains that have been influenced by accessibility.

To provide equal opportunities for all students in an educational environment, the curriculum design must involve and embrace students with disabilities. Doyle et al. (2002) emphasize the key role of accessible curriculum design and put forward that

[1] https://www.w3.org/WAI/fundamentals/accessibility-principles/.
[2] https://www.w3.org/WAI/standards-guidelines/wcag/.

with the aim of creating sources that are "usable and accessible," design guidelines like WCAG offer suggestions to make sure that information can be reached by as many people as possible. The main goal of this research is to analyze the curricula of the translation courses by checking how the four main principles of digital accessibility (perceivable, operable, understandable, and robust) are observed in the existing curricula and highlight the need for improving curricula for technology-enhanced teaching and learning in translation studies.

2   Accessibility in Technology-Enhanced Education-Related Research

Blending technology into education requires certain infrastructure, and this brings up the issue of accessibility. Fast dissemination of technology has been observed in education as well as online education specifically with the fast-developing technological advancement. Education has become intertwined with technology in terms of the curricula and the materials used during classes as well. Therefore, in education, to be able to access information via technology has become a required medium to succeed and create a change in academic and professional life (Yu, 2002). The issue of accessibility in the field of education has gained momentum as a research topic.

Fairness, equal opportunities, and human rights have been on the agenda of the United Nations since its beginnings. Pursuing equal opportunities is very important as it embraces human diversity and promotes possibilities for everybody to exercise their freedom of expression and participate in the information society to the full extent. In the twenty-first century, two treaties have been developed to ensure equal opportunities and move toward the fulfillment of universal human rights and the promotion of fundamental freedoms. Greco and Jankowska (2020) discuss the shifts of media accessibility to universal approaches directed to user-centered and proactive views. The authors highlight various pedagogical and theoretical implications stressing the need to move beyond audiovisual translation and translation research embracing the interdisciplinary field of accessible studies. Seale (2013) analyses social, educational, and political factors behind making e-learning accessible in higher education. The author stresses the importance of giving a "voice" to disabled students to acquire valuable insights into their relationships with technologies and institutions of higher education. Lee (2017) provides a historical overview of the conceptualization of distance education and the related discussion in relation to the complex and multi-dimensional issues of increasing the accessibility of university education. Cumming and Rose (2022) discuss Universal Design for Learning (UDL) suggesting it as a framework to guide higher education teachers in the planning and delivery of their courses. The authors advocate that effective implementation of UDL allows all students to access course materials, removing the need for some of them to actively seek support and disclose their disabilities.

Faculty needs to be a driving factor in ensuring that learning materials and tools are accessible, but also in instilling accessibility as a topic in curricular units. However, research indicates that faculty have concerns about unfamiliarity with the content (Soares et al., 2020), including accessibility barriers, available assistive technology, and legislation (Sanderson et al., 2022), insufficient time or institutional support (Kawas et al., 2019), and a lack of program- and field-level learning objectives (Shinohara et al., 2018). Still, when such goals are supported and pursued, findings highlight how important they are considered by students (Kramer, 2020).

3   National Backgrounds

3.1   Portugal

Several studies have focused on the accessibility of higher education institutions in Portugal, shedding light on various aspects of this important topic. Ismail et al. (2020) examined the accessibility of higher education institution Web sites in Portugal. Their analysis revealed a wide variation in accessibility status among Web sites, with some institutions having highly accessible platforms while others faced significant accessibility barriers. The authors emphasized the need for inclusive web platforms that cater to persons with disabilities.

In a similar vein, Eusébio et al. (2022) explored the preparation of future tourism professionals for accessible tourism (AT) in Portuguese higher education institutions. Their findings indicated a lack of specific learning outcomes related to AT in curricula, as well as a lack of knowledge and resources among staff. The authors recommended incorporating specific AT learning outcomes, offering dedicated AT courses, providing resources and support for teachers, and fostering collaboration with stakeholders to enhance the preparation of future professionals.

Furthermore, Martins and Moriña (2023) investigated resilience factors in students with disabilities at a Portuguese university. Their study identified resilience, self-esteem, family support, subjective well-being, and psychological well-being as protective factors that contribute to adaptation and inclusion in higher education. The authors also acknowledged the ongoing challenges posed by accessibility barriers on campus, highlighting the need for interventions and support services to promote student success and inclusion.

The digital competence of higher education teachers in Portugal was examined by Moreira et al. (2023). The authors focused on the digital competence of teachers at a distance learning university. Their findings revealed a range of digital competence levels among teachers, with some demonstrating high levels of proficiency while others were less comfortable with digital technologies. The authors emphasized the importance of providing opportunities for professional development and training to enhance teachers' digital competence.

Soares et al. (2020) focused on the design of learning outcomes in higher education curricula. The authors emphasize the importance of specific, measurable, achievable, relevant, and time-bound learning outcomes that are aligned with program goals and objectives. The article discusses challenges such as defining outcomes for complex skills and balancing specificity with flexibility. Recommendations include identifying program goals, brainstorming specific skills and knowledge, and reviewing outcomes for alignment.

In terms of physical accessibility, Martins et al. (2018) explored attitudes toward inclusion in higher education at a Portuguese university. The study identified positive attitudes toward inclusion, but also highlighted challenges such as a lack of disability awareness, insufficient resources, and physical barriers. The authors recommended training for staff, improved accessibility, an inclusive curriculum, and the development of an inclusive campus culture to create more inclusive environments in higher education institutions.

Overall, these studies collectively contribute to our understanding of the accessibility of higher education institutions in Portugal. They highlight the importance of inclusive web platforms, the preparation of future professionals, the resilience of students with disabilities, and the digital competence of teachers. The findings underscore the need for comprehensive strategies and interventions to address accessibility barriers and promote inclusivity in higher education settings in Portugal.

3.2 Turkey

Starting from the fact that technology has taken an essential role in the education field, developing a curriculum to enhance student learning by integrating technology can be considered the primary purpose of educators. Unlike traditional methods where there happens to be a direct knowledge transfer, a new and modern understanding of education emphasizes the significance of the learner. Thus, learner-centered classrooms are essential to sustain high motivation for the students. Sezer points out the value of technology in education and advertises the involvement of technology in education as the integration of components such as the learning environment, conditions, circumstances, resources, and so on that are effective in learner development (Sezer, 2017).

The topic of technology-enhanced education has been researched in the context of Turkey from various aspects such as students' attitudes toward and their readiness for technology-enhanced history education in Turkish high schools (Turan, 2007), the effectiveness of technology-enhanced science classrooms (Sezer, 2017), technology-enhanced learning in EFL students (Haidari et al., 2019), challenges of creating technology-enriched classrooms in Turkey (Kurt, 2014), analysis of the micro-context dimension of the technology-enhanced learning environment (Ustunel & Tokel, 2018), and student perception of technology-enhanced learning environment in second language learning and the curriculum development (Gürleyik & Akdemir, 2018). While a wide variety of studies have been conducted in different areas of education, the common point of all is the fact that there is an obvious need to accept the huge role of technology in education in today's world.

3.3   Lithuania

In the Lithuanian context, research on accessibility analyzes the whole education system. Dudaitė et al. (2018) discuss accessibility at school by concluding that there is a need to extend working hours in school to create preconditions for wider possibilities of providing additional education, health, social, and cultural services at school.

The research on accessibility in higher education reveals some aspects of the possibilities to enhance accessibility. Navickienė and Vainorytė (Navickienė & Vainorytė, 2015) analyze the improvement of access to higher college education in Lithuania by applying a variety of e-learning forms. In their analysis, they observe that accessibility of higher education is improved by employing a wider variety of e-learning forms. Leišytė et al. (2019) analyze the main reforms in the Lithuanian higher education system, paying special attention to the actors involved as well as the increase of the component of accessibility.

Galkiene and Monkeviciene (2021) analyze the application of the Universal Design for Learning (UDL) approach highlighting research possibilities aimed at enriching already existing educational practices of inclusive education embracing accessibility and providing teachers with more tools for achieving better efficiency of education. Researchers discuss the importance of inclusive e-learning and teaching environments, the preparation and enrichment of educational practices for the inclusion of students with disabilities, and the digital competence of teachers. The findings observe the necessity for comprehensive strategies to address accessibility and promote inclusion in higher education.

4   Four Main Principles of Accessibility

The four principles of accessibility,[3] as defined by the Web Content Accessibility Guidelines (WCAG), are perceivable, operable, understandable, and robust.

1. Perceivable: This principle ensures that information and user interface components are presented in a way that can be perceived by all users, including those with visual or hearing impairments. This includes providing alternatives for non-text content, offering captions and audio descriptions for multimedia, and ensuring sufficient color contrast.

---

[3] https://www.w3.org/WAI/fundamentals/accessibility-principles/.

2. Operable: This principle focuses on making web content and navigation operable for all users. It involves providing keyboard accessibility, giving users enough time to read and interact with content, avoiding content that can cause seizures or physical reactions, and making it easy to navigate and find information.
3. Understandable: This principle emphasizes the need for content to be clear and understandable to all users. It involves using plain language, organizing, and presenting information in a logical manner, providing instructions and error messages that are easy to comprehend, and making sure that users can avoid and correct mistakes.
4. Robust: This principle ensures that web content can be interpreted reliably by a wide range of user agents, including assistive technologies. It involves using standard and accessible technologies, ensuring compatibility with different browsers and devices, and providing fallback options for content that may not be supported.

In the context of higher education, these principles can be applied to ensure that all students and instructors, regardless of their abilities, can access and engage with educational materials and resources. For example, providing captions and transcripts for lecture videos would make them perceivable for students with hearing impairments. Making course Web sites and learning management systems keyboard accessible would ensure operability for students with mobility impairments. Using clear and concise language in course materials would enhance understandability for students with cognitive disabilities. Lastly, using standard and accessible technologies in online learning platforms would ensure robustness and compatibility with assistive technologies used by students with disabilities. By adhering to these principles, higher education institutions can create an inclusive learning environment that benefits all students.

5 Legal Requisites in Lithuania, Portugal, and Turkey

One of the important legislation documents on equal opportunities is the EC Directive 2006/54/EC[4] of the principle of equal opportunities and equal treatment of men and women in matters of employment and occupation. Provisions include the following: individuals, opportunities for education, training, employment, career development, and empowerment without being disadvantaged based on disability, sex, race, language, religion, economic or family situation, etc. In addition, there is recently published European Standard EN 17161[5] (2019) "Design for All—Accessibility following a Design for All approach in products, goods and services—Extending the range of users." The document sets the European standard and specifies requirements for the design, development, and provision of products, goods, and services that are accessible and can be used by all users including those with

---

[4] https://www.legislation.gov.uk/eudr/2006/54.

[5] https://www.en-standard.eu/bs-en-17161-2019-design-for-all-accessibility-following-A-design-for-all-approach-in-products-goods-and-services-extending-the-range-of-users/.

disabilities. In the twenty-first century, it sets the background for the development of any accessible products and services aiming at inclusion, personalization, and all members of society.

5.1 Legal Background in Lithuania

In Lithuania, the legislation has also been adopted as the document of the Republic of Lithuania Law on Equal Treatment (Last amended on 7 May 2019—No XIII-2105). This document aims to ensure the application of the legal acts of the European Union and the monitoring and control of the implementation of the Convention of the United Nations on the Rights of Persons with Disabilities. The part of the document concerning education foresees that educational institutions, as well as higher education and research institutions, aim to ensure that education programs, textbooks, and teaching aids do not promote discrimination on grounds of sex, race, nationality, citizenship, language, origin, social status, belief, convictions or views, age, sexual orientation, disability, ethnic origin or religion and makes sure that equal opportunities are observed and implemented.

5.2 Legal Background in Portugal

In Portugal, accessibility in education is governed by several laws and regulations. The basis is the Constitution of the Portuguese Republic that, in its article 74,[6] establishes equal access to education for all citizens, regardless of their physical or intellectual disabilities, setting the foundation for inclusive education. In 1973, the Basic Law of the Educational System[7] outlined the fundamental principles of the Portuguese educational system, including provisions for students with special educational needs. This law emphasizes the right to an inclusive education and the need to provide appropriate support and accommodations for students with disabilities. Later, the Decree-Law 3/2008[8] establishes the legal framework for the inclusion of students with special educational needs in mainstream schools. This was later updated, in 2018, through Decree-Law 54/2018[9] which establishes the legal regulation for inclusive education. In what concerns access to Higher Education, since 1992,[10] the different regulations for the national calls for application to higher education have reserved a percentage of the vacancies for students with special education needs.

[6] https://www.parlamento.pt/sites/EN/Parliament/Documents/Constitution7th.pdf.

[7] https://diariodarepublica.pt/dr/en/detail/act/5-1973-421823.

[8] https://diariodarepublica.pt/dr/en/detail/decree-law/3-2008-386871.

[9] https://diariodarepublica.pt/dr/en/detail/decree-law/54-2018-115652961.

[10] https://diariodarepublica.pt/dr/en/detail/decree-law/296-A-1998-173481.

With the increasing ubiquity of digital resources in education, and more recently, of online communication services that can also support education purposes, it is also important to highlight legislation that applies to digital accessibility. Portugal was one of the first European states to legislate about the access rights to digital information for people with special needs. The Resolution of the Council of Ministers 97/99[11] establishes that Web sites published by public bodies from the publication date of the resolution onwards should support interaction through audio, visual, and haptic interfaces. In 2007, the Resolution of the Council of Ministers 155/2007[12] established the conformance level (at level A of the WCAG 1.0) required from Web sites of public bodies. Five years later, the Resolution of the Council of Ministers 91/2012[13] updates the level of conformance to level A or level AA of the WCAG 2.0, depending on the type of service. More recently, the Decree-Law 83/2018[14] transposes into Portuguese law the European Web Accessibility Directive,[15] clearly identifying higher education institutions as one of the entity groups the law applies to.

5.3   Legal Background in Turkey

The current study bases its ground on the matter of accessibility. Although not involved in the constitution in the frame of the EU, Turkey also has the legal prerequisites officially applied covering accessibility in education. Dated 2005, the currently available constitution[16] has an article that also focuses on education and training. The legislation declares the aim of the law as follows:

> Turkey: Law No. 5378 of 2005 on Disabled People and on making amendments in some laws and decree-laws: "The objective of this Law is to prevent disability, to enable the disabled people to join the society by taking measures which will provide the solution of their problems regarding health, education, rehabilitation, employment, care and social security and the removal of the obstacles they face and to make the necessary arrangements for the coordination of these services" Law No. 5378 on Disabled People.[17]

As can be inferred from the stated aim of the law, in the case of disabled people, under the provision of laws, some legal measures are put forward to protect the right to education for all students to include them by not letting them be exposed to any type of hindrance.

---

[11] https://diariodarepublica.pt/dr/en/detail/tipo/97-1999-428656.

[12] https://diariodarepublica.pt/dr/en/detail/tipo/155-2007-642547.

[13] https://diariodarepublica.pt/dr/en/detail/resolution-of-the-council-of-ministers/91-2012-191863.

[14] https://diariodarepublica.pt/dr/en/detail/decree-law/83-2018-116734769.

[15] https://eur-lex.europa.eu/legal-content/EN/TXT/?uri=CELEX%3A32016L2102.

[16] https://www.un.org/development/desa/disabilities/wp-content/uploads/sites/15/2019/11/Turkey_Turkish-Disability-Act-TDA-No.-5378-of-2005.pdf.

[17] https://disabilityin.org/country/turkey/.

As stated under Article 15 with the title of Education and Training, the current constitution protects the rights of disabled people and serves for the availability of equal rights in education for all by creating an inclusive atmosphere with non-disabled people. Regarding higher education, which is the scope of the current study, the declaration under the same article mentions:

> The Counselling and Coordination Centre for Disabled People is established in order to carry out works within the Higher Education Council on the procurement of tools and equipment, preparation of special class material, enabling the preparation of education, research and accommodation environments suitable for the disabled people in order to facilitate the education life of the disabled university students The operation methods and principles of the Counselling and Coordination Centre for Disable Disabled People are arranged by the regulation which is prepared jointly by the Ministry of Health, the Ministry of National Education, Higher Education Council and the Administration on Disabled People.

As can be seen from the above-mentioned part of the article, the current law on disabled people prohibits discrimination and creates equal education opportunities for all students. However, when it comes to practicing what is written on paper, in Turkey, most people or institutions have not been attentive toward the special needs of disabled people. In the same context, Ari and Inan confirm this fact and posit:

> There is a general lack of awareness in Turkey, concerning the needs and capabilities of individuals with disabilities. Some people are unconcerned and justify this lack of awareness by claiming that individuals living with a disability are rare and do not warrant much attention. (Ari & Inan, 2010)

Even though it is part of an educational policy, in developing countries like Turkey, how effectively the inclusion of disabled students in the mainstream education system works is a crucial point to consider.

6   Research Methodology

According to the definition, the research subject involves "everything that represents the so-called social reality, that is, communities and social collections, social institutions, social processes and phenomena (Sztumski, 1995)." Following this approach, the first step of the research includes the analysis of the documents underlying the provided educational courses. The subject of the research presented here is the analysis of the curricula of the translation courses of the Translation and Interpreting Department of Samsun University in Turkey, the Language Sciences Department of Lisbon University in Portugal, and the Institute of Humanities of Mykolas Romeris University in Lithuania by checking how the four main principles of digital accessibility (perceivable, operable, understandable, and robust) are observed in the existing curricula. The study aims to answer the research question if the general legislation of the EU and of the countries of the curricula analyzed are reflected in the descriptions of the study courses.

7 Analysis of the Translation Studies Courses Considering Accessibility Principles

7.1 Research Findings

Lithuania In our study, we analyze the curricula considering the four principles of accessibility (perceivable, operable, understandable, and robust), defined by the WCAG. The Lithuanian curriculum of translation studies has the purpose of preparing professional translators–editors having general philological education and comprehensive knowledge about the culture of the countries of the study languages (English and one more foreign language—French, Spanish, German, Norwegian, Chinese, or Korean), theoretical principles of translation and editing and able to translate and edit texts in humanities and social sciences. It foresees classical admission requirements based on competition scores, by taking into consideration the regulations of the Lithuanian Ministry of Education, Science and Sport. It could be observed that admission is open to all persons fulfilling the competition requirements; however, focused future research could be helpful in looking into how accessibility is ensured for all groups of the population and if the competitive entry is really based on the materials prepared in compliance with the four principles in order to ensure that all students, regardless of their abilities, can access and engage with the materials and resources.

Teaching and learning methods include:

- lectures, seminars, and classes.
- individual and group work on analytical tasks focused on selection of theoretical material and analysis; problem-based teaching, case studies; mind maps, situation simulations, and role plays.
- written assignments completed applying translation software, translation tools, and databases.
- creative tasks and written assignments in translation and editing.
- interactive study methods including work in language laboratories, using Web sites, education technologies, and Moodle platform Projects, individual and group presentations.

Assessment methods include oral examination, didactic testing, self-check, progress tests; individual and group presentations, projects, reflection, feedback; written assignments, essays, translations, and their written analysis; reflection, self-evaluation, peer assessment, and achievement portfolio. On the surface, the curriculum complies with the legislation on accessibility as it foresees the variety of teaching and assessment methods that could be applied to individual cases to ensure accessibility. The variety of teaching and learning, and assessment methods including audio, written, creative, interactive, web technology-guided tasks and activities could ensure the observation of the four principles of accessibility such as perceivable meaning that information is presented in a way that can be perceived by all users, operable meaning that the content is operable for all users including possibilities of easy navigation in finding information, understandable meaning that the content is understandable for all users, and robust meaning that the content can be interpreted by all users with possibilities of using assistive technologies. However, the choice of the methods is left to the teaching staff which again requires focused research on how the teaching staff implements accessibility in practice and if the staff is ready and can observe the four principles to ensure that all students can access and engage with educational materials and resources.

Also, it is pointed out that there are various forms of support available to students coping with academic, financial, social, psychological, personal, and other problems and provide them with the necessary recommendations. It could be observed that students are provided with individual support to cope with crises of psychological character as well as with communication, academic, and other problems. In addition, the students' survey results reveal that most of the survey participants recognize receiving academic support from the teaching staff (77%). However, it would be also interesting to investigate the cases of the remaining 23% looking for reasons behind not being satisfied with the support received. On the surface, while analyzing documents, it appears that the EU accessibility principles are integrated into the Lithuanian legal system and the analyzed curriculum of the translation studies complies with the accessibility principles. However, for future research, it would be relevant to carry out a qualitative study to get deeper into the voices of the research participants on how the documented accessibility principles are implemented in real-life studies.

Turkey There is no doubt that the burgeoning field of technology supports the domain of education in many aspects. However, integrating technology into education and maintaining a curriculum mediated through online resources and accessible to all students equally may create intricacies. Within this context, to provide an in-depth look into the issue mentioned, the curriculum of the Translation and Interpreting Department of Samsun University in Turkey is examined within the frame of the four main principles of digital accessibility (perceivable, operable, understandable, and robust) as taken part in WCAG.

The Turkish higher education system requires students to take a university entrance exam after graduation from high school, and based on the score, they receive they are placed in the universities. The students with disabilities take the same test as well with the supervision of a minimum of two different invigilators who help them according to their needs during the exam process. At Samsun University, the curriculum of the Translation and Interpreting program mentions the overall purpose of the bachelor's degree as educating the candidates of translators who will be able to translate and interpret effectively within the various professional areas of translation as professional translators equipped with both academic and professional knowledge. Moreover, a third language is offered to the students (German, Spanish, and French) through the acquisition of the selected language in all eight semesters. All students have the opportunity for a double major as well.

The classes are taught face-to-face in a classroom that is equipped with a projector and internet connection. Although the methods changed depending on the preference of the lecturer and the nature of the class, generally the approaches consist of lectures, seminars, and hands-on activities within a group, pair, or an individual. Mostly, the classes are divided into theory and practice. The materials used in the class or the assignments are distributed to the class via LMS (learning management system).

The assessment process is conducted by placing considerable importance on the multiple intelligences, and various types of implications are conducted such as creative projects (video blogs, podcasts, short films, etc.), translation projects, presentations, individual, group, and/or pair work, and written assignments.

All in all, regarding accessibility for all students throughout the courses taught in the department, it would be possible to say that all four principles are sufficiently apparent. Either in class or online, the content is delivered in a way that there is no difficulty in perceiving the content with the guidance of the lecturers or tutors when needed. The web content and the required tools are in a standard format with accessible technologies. For instance, for the visually impaired student, the digital documents for the class are provided in a Word format since it is the only form that is compatible with the student's personal computer. Via the learning management system (LMS), the students have access to web content and navigation that are operable for all users. The lecturers upload extra materials intending to clarify the content of the course and make sure there is no confusion for the students.

Portugal The Translation course at the School of Arts and Humanities of the University of Lisboa provides professional training in translation for the native language and back-translation for a foreign language, developing skills related to various text types, including literary, scientific, technical, and audiovisual texts, as well as mastery of tools and technologies to support translation. The program covers seven foreign languages: Catalan, English, French, German, Italian, Romanian, and Spanish.

The admission requirements align with the standard higher education admission criteria in Portugal. The process involved two admission examinations: one for Portuguese language and another for a chosen foreign language (French, English, German, and Spanish). Although admission is open to all qualifying candidates, further investigation is recommended to assess the accessibility of the medium used for the admission examinations.

The teaching and learning methods outlined in the syllabi of various course units include classes, seminars, individual and group work, analysis of relevant theoretical materials, written assignments, use of translation software and tools, translation and editing tasks, as well as individual and group presentations. Evaluation methods encompass written examinations, class participation, individual and group projects and presentations, and achievement portfolios. While these methods cater to diverse functional needs, practical limitations exist, with not all methods available in every unit. This could result in instances where certain individual needs may not be addressed.

An additional consideration pertains to the tools introduced and explored in the course. Students are acquainted with various translation support tools, including automated and crowdsourced options, as well as tools for captioning. Ensuring the accessibility of these tools is crucial, aligning with the four principles of accessibility. Furthermore, integrating the topic of accessibility into the curricular units using these tools would enhance the overall effectiveness of the course.

7.2 Discussion

The analysis of the curricula considering the four principles of accessibility defined by the Web Content Accessibility Guidelines (WCAG) in the three countries reveals that there is a variety of teaching and learning methods prescribed in the curricula including:

- lectures, seminars, and classes.
- individual and group work on analytical tasks: selection of theoretical material and analysis; problem-based teaching, case studies; mind maps, situation simulations, role plays.
- written assignments completed applying translation software, translation tools, and databases.
- creative tasks and written assignments in translation and editing.
- interactive study methods: work in language laboratories, using Web sites, education technologies, and Moodle platform Projects, individual and group presentations.

Similarly, assessment methods allow the lecturers to apply various methods including oral examination, didactic testing, self-check, progress tests; individual and group presentations, projects, reflection, feedback; written assignments, essays, translations, and their written analysis; reflection, self-evaluation, peer assessment, and achievement portfolio. The curricula also foresee the use of various web-based technologies such as translation support tools, LMS (like Moodle), and installed classroom technology such as multimedia and language laboratories.

It appears that the curricula comply with the legislation on accessibility as it foresees the variety of teaching and assessment methods that could be applied to individual cases to ensure accessibility as the methods include audio, written, creative, interactive, web technology-guided tasks and activities and could ensure the observation of the four principles of accessibility: perceivable envisioning information presented in a way that can be perceived by all users; operable prescribing the content being operable for all users including possibilities of easy navigation in finding information, understandable foreseeing the content to be understandable for all users, and robust instructing that the content can be interpreted by all users with possibilities of using assistive technologies.

However, the choice of the methods is left to the teaching staff which requires focused research on how the teaching staff implements accessibility in practice and if the staff is ready and can observe the four principles to ensure that all students can access and engage with educational materials and resources. The analyzed curricula provide a general framework but do not foresee detailed guidelines for the teaching staff. Also in Lithuania, there are various forms of support available to students to enable them to cope with academic, financial, social, psychological, personal, and other problems.

8 Conclusions

On the surface, while analyzing documents, it appears that the EU accessibility principles are integrated into the Portuguese, Lithuanian, and Turkish legal systems and the analyzed curricula of the translation studies generally comply with the accessibility principles prescribing a wide choice of teaching and learning, and assessment methods, the use of various web-based technologies and installed classroom technology. However, the curricula of the translation studies are formulated in a general way, and a closer consideration reveals that not much information is provided on the practical recommendations or guidelines on how teaching staff could implement the principles of accessibility in real classroom environments, and on how they can choose or adapt the appropriate methods of teaching and assessment. There could be possible risks of certain limitations and possible instances where individual student needs might not be addressed due to the lack of detailed guidelines.

The issue of accessibility in educational settings has a pivotal role in creating an efficient teaching–learning environment for both the teachers and the students. Therefore, the awareness of accessibility through the guidelines should be enhanced so that in the real setting of the classroom, all principles can appear by taking into consideration all students equally.

For future research, it would be relevant to carry out a qualitative study to get deeper into the voices of the research participants on how the documented accessibility principles are implemented in real-life study environments.

Acknowledgements This chapter is based upon work from COST Action CA19142—Leading Platform for European Citizens, Industries, Academia and Policymakers in Media Accessibility (LEAD-ME) supported by COST (European Cooperation in Science and Technology).

References

Ari, I. A., & Inan, F. A. (2010). Assistive technologies for students with disabilities: A survey of access and use in Turkish Universities. *Turkish Online Journal of Educational Technology*, 40–45.

Cumming, T. M., & Rose, M. C. (2022). Exploring universal design for learning as an accessibility tool in higher education: A review of the current literature. *The Australian Educational Researcher*, 1025–1043.

Díaz-Cintas, J. (2008). Introduction: The didactics of audiovisual translation. In J. Díaz-Cintas (Ed.), *The didactics of audiovisual translation*. John Benjamins.

Doyle, C., Robsen, K., Ball, S., & Campy, D. (2002). *Accessible curricula: Good practice for all*. UWIC Press.

Dudaitė, J., Indrašienė, V., Jegelevičienė, V., & Prakapas, R. (2018). Accessibility of education and support for a learner after formal education: a case of Lithuania. Society, integration, education: Proceedings of the international scientific conference (pp. 103–115). Rezeknes Academy of Technologies.

Eusébio, C., Alves, J. P., Rosa, M. J., & Teixeira, L. (2022). Are higher education institutions preparing future tourism professionals for tourism for all? An overview from Portuguese higher education tourism programmes. *Journal of Hospitality, Leisure, Sport and Tourism Education.*

Galkiene, A., & Monkeviciene, O. (2021). *Improving inclusive education through universal design for learning.* Springer.

Greco, G. M. (2018). The nature of accessibility studies. *Journal of Audiovisual Translation*, 205–232.

Greco, G. M., & Jankowska, A. (2020). Media accessibility within and beyond audiovisual translation. In Ł Bogucki & M. Deckert (Eds.), *The Palgrave handbook of audiovisual translation and media accessibility* (pp. 57–81). Palgrave Macmillan.

Gürleyik, S., & Akdemir, E. (2018). Guiding curriculum development: Student perceptions for the second language learning in technology-enhanced learning environments. *Journal of Education and Training Studies.*

Haidari, S. M., Yelken, T. Y., & Akay, C. (2019). Technology-enhanced self-directed language learning behaviors of EFL student teachers. *Contemporary Educational Technology*, 229–245.

Ismail, A., Kuppusamy, K. S., & Paiva, S. (2020). Accessibility analysis of higher education institution websites of Portugal. *Universal Access in the Information Society*, 685–700.

Kurt, S. (2014). Creating technology-enriched classrooms: Implementational challenges in Turkish education. *Learning, Media and Technology*, 90–106.

Kawas, S., Vonessen, L., & Ko, A. J. (2019). Teaching accessibility: A design exploration of faculty professional development at scale. In *Proceedings of the 50th ACM Technical Symposium on Computer Science Education* (pp. 983–989). Association for Computing Machinery.

Kramer, H. (2020). *Preliminary results from a survey to measure the benefits of accessibility and universal design topics in course curricula.* SIGACCESS Access. Comput.

Lee, K. (2017). Rethinking the accessibility of online higher education: A historical review. *The Internet and Higher Education*, 15–23.

Leišytė, L., Rose, A.-L., & Želvys, R. (2019). Higher education reforms in Lithuania: Two decades after Bologna. In B. Broucker, K. De Wit, J. C. Verhoeven, & L. Leišytė (Eds.), *Higher education system reform: An international comparison after twenty years of Bologna* (pp. 179–195). Brill.

Martins, M., Borges, M., & Gonçalves, T. (2018). Attitudes towards inclusion in higher education in a Portuguese university. *International Journal of Inclusive Education*, 527–542.

Martins, M. H., & Moriña, A. (2023). Resilience factors in students with Disabilities at a Portuguese University. *Pedagogika*, 110–128.

Moreira, J. A., Nunes, C. S., & Casanova, D. (2023). Digital competence of higher education teachers at a distance learning University in Portugal. *Computers*, 169.

Navickienė, V., & Vainorytė, B. (2015). Improvement of accessibility of higher college education in Lithuania applying forms of e-learning. REEP: Rural environment. Education. Personality [elektroninis išteklius]. In *8th International Scientific Conference* (pp. 139–147). Latvia University of Agriculture.

Sanderson, N. C., Kessel, S., & Chen, W. (2022). What do faculty members know about universal design and digital accessibility? A qualitative study in computer science and engineering disciplines. *Universal Access in the Information Society*, 351–365.

Seale, J. (2013). *E-learning and disability in higher education: Accessibility research and practice.* Routledge.

Sezer, B. (2017). The effectiveness of a technology-enhanced flipped science classroom. *Journal of Educational Computing Research*, 471–494.

Shinohara, K., Kawas, S., Ko, A. J., & Ladner, R. E. (2018). Who teaches accessibility? A survey of U.S. computing faculty. In *Proceedings of the 49th ACM Technical Symposium on Computer Science Education* (pp. 197–202). Association for Computing Machinery.

Soares, D., Carvalho, P., & Dias, D. (2020). Designing learning outcomes in design higher education curricula. *International Journal of Art & Design Education*, 392–404.

Sztumski, J. (1995). *Wstęp do metodologii i technik badań społecznych [Introduction to social research methodologies and techniques].* Wydawnictwo Śląsk (The Silesia Publishers).

Turan, I. (2007). Student readiness for technology-enhanced history education in Turkish high schools (Order No. 3284637). University of Pittsburgh. Available from ProQuest Dissertations & Theses Global. (304828184). https://www.proquest.com/dissertations-theses/student-readiness-technology-enhanced-history/docview/304828184/se-2

Ustunel, H. H., & Tokel, S. T. (2018). Distributed scaffolding: Synergy in technology-enhanced learning environments. *Technology, Knowledge and Learning*, 129–160.

Yu, H. (2002). Web accessibility and the law: recommendations for implementation. *Library Hi Tech*, 406–419.

Cognitive Accessibility in Educational Games: A Set of Recommendations

Miguel Ángel Oliva-Zamora and María Eugenia Larreina-Morales

Abstract Educational games aim to teach players new knowledge or skills in an entertaining manner. However, they are often not accessible for players with disabilities, hindering their right to education. For players with cognitive disabilities and learning difficulties, it may be particularly challenging to determine the response to the game's visual, auditory, and haptic stimuli. This chapter presents a set of recommendations to develop educational games that are accessible to these players. To that aim, a literature review was conducted comprising the past ten years of research about educational games and game accessibility. Ten papers were selected, which take diverse approaches to the topic: some review existing research, while others focus on the development of an accessible educational game. All of them address cognitive disabilities and learning difficulties, but some also include recommendations for visual, hearing, and motor accessibility. The review of these papers shows that, to develop an accessible game for players with cognitive disabilities and learning difficulties, it is recommended to provide stimuli through several channels of communication, to allow the game's pace to be customizable, and to design simple but engaging content, among other features. Although these recommendations are not universally applicable to every educational game, they are a first step to bring together players, teachers, developers, and researchers to create more interactive and engaging educational experiences for all.

Keywords Accessibility · Cognitive disabilities · Learning difficulties · Educational games · Literature review

M. Á. Oliva-Zamora (✉) · M. E. Larreina-Morales
Universitat Autònoma de Barcelona, Barcelona, Spain
e-mail: miguelangel.oliva@uab.cat

M. E. Larreina-Morales
e-mail: mariaeugenia.larreina@uab.cat

A. Marcus-Quinn et al. (eds.), *Transforming Media Accessibility in Europe*,
https://doi.org/10.1007/978-3-031-60049-4_16

283

1   Introduction

In a world of three billion gamers, video games are everywhere—in our homes, workplaces, gyms, hospitals, and classrooms (Tran, 2023). Video games' purpose is not just to entertain. In fact, there is a whole subgenre, known as serious games, which are employed in diverse contexts and disciplines. Among them, educational games aim to teach players certain knowledge or skills. Applied both to formal and informal educational contexts, they engage and motivate learners by using achievement systems such as points, levels, rankings, and challenges (Laine & Lindberg, 2020). Research shows that, if they are designed adequately and they tailor to players' needs, educational games have pedagogical potential (Calvo-Ferrer, 2015; Fokides, 2018; Oliveira et al., 2023).

However, most video games, including educational ones, often present accessibility barriers that hinder and even prevent persons with disabilities from playing (IGDA-GASIG, 2021). In the context of educational games, these barriers affect every person's right to education, information, and technology recognized in the Convention on the Rights of Persons with Disabilities (CRPD) (United Nations, 2008). Players with sensory disabilities such as blindness or deafness may not be able to access the visual or auditory stimuli of the game, while providing input can be the biggest challenge for players with motor disabilities. In the case of players with cognitive disabilities or learning difficulties, the issue lies in determining the response to visual, auditory, and haptic stimuli before providing the adequate input through the controller. For example, complex instructions or unclear goals may cause players to not know what to do next, preventing them from progressing in the game (Yuan et al., 2011).

Solutions related to cognitive accessibility include wording instructions in simple language, giving players the option to review the goals at any point during gameplay, and providing hints to aid progress (AbleGamers, 2018). The implementation of these features depends on the mechanics of the game. It should be tackled at the design stage of the development cycle, so that accessibility is integrated into the game's budget and workflow (Barlet & Spohn, 2012).

In the past few years, cognitive accessibility in serious games has been examined in academic research. For example, Salvador-Ullauri et al. (2020a, 2020b) performed a systematic literature review to determine how sensory, cognitive, and motor disabilities were addressed in serious games. They focused on web-based games, which should follow the Web Content Accessibility Guidelines, also known as WCAG (W3C World Wide Web Consortium, n.d.). After analysing several therapeutic and educational games, they concluded that few developers include accessibility in their games. In another study, Dutra et al. (2021) conducted a systematic literature mapping of guidelines to develop accessible video games. They offered a series of recommendations for cognitive accessibility mainly based on serious games, even though their search accounted for all disabilities and all kinds of video games. The wideness of their scope can be seen in the terms of their search string (related to guidelines, games, and people with disabilities in general), and in the fact that they included two non-serious games in their sample. These examples, among other research in treatment and rehabilitation contexts (Derks et al., 2022; Francillette et al., 2021; Shapoval et al., 2022), show the growing interest in cognitive accessibility in video games. However, there is a research gap regarding educational games (von Gillern & Nash, 2023).

Therefore, it is pertinent to analyse the state of the art of cognitive accessibility in educational games. This chapter aims to be a resource for game developers and researchers by identifying and gathering recommendations about developing educational games with cognitive accessibility features. This is reflected in the primary research question (PRQ): what recommendations are available in the literature to design educational games with cognitive accessibility features? To deepen the understanding and contextualize the recommendations, the following secondary research questions (SRQ) have been defined: what methods are employed in developing recommendations for cognitive accessibility in educational games? (SRQ1); and who are the targeted players in the recommendations? (SRQ2).

The paper is organized as follows. Firstly, the concept of educational games is defined. Secondly, cognitive accessibility in video games is presented, emphasizing its importance for education. Thirdly, the methodology of the systematic search is explained and selected papers are analysed. Then, a set of recommendations to develop educational games with cognitive accessibility features derived from the literature is presented. Lastly, conclusions and future avenues for research are outlined.

2 Educational Games

Serious games have a purpose other than entertainment, and their applications range from formal and informal education to industry training, social awareness, and health care (Wilkinson, 2016). While *gamification* means applying game elements to other domains, such as incorporating a ranking on a pedometer mobile app, serious games are explicitly designed to teach players specific information or skills (Kenwright, 2017).

When compared to traditional teaching methods, the interactivity element in video games may contribute to players' engagement and interest in learning, which may result in increased knowledge and retention of information (Riopel et al., 2019). Educational games take different forms and address several topics, such as computer programming in MIT Media Lab's *Scratch*, USA history in MECC's *Oregon Trail*, or marine wildlife in E-Line Media's *Beyond Blue*. Moreover, games that were originally designed for entertainment may also be applied in educational settings (Martinez et al., 2022). For example, there is a website created by Microsoft that offers resources about how to use the game *Minecraft* for educational purposes addressed to institutions, teachers, and learners (Minecraft, 2023).

According to teaching practice and academic research, educational games bring several cognitive, emotional, and social benefits to students. First, games may enhance cognitive skills such as critical thinking, problem-solving, decision-making, and long-term retention of information (Barz et al., 2023; Reynaldo et al., 2021). Second, the active participation of the player in education may elicit emotions, engagement, and motivation to learn (Plass et al., 2015; Vankúš, 2021). Lastly, and particularly in multiplayer modes, educational games may promote communication and teamwork among students (Mikropoulos & Iatraki, 2023; Sun et al., 2018).

However, some scholars question educational games' pedagogical advantages, particularly because there is a lack of research on how games are used in actual teaching practices (Backlund & Hendrix, 2013), and on how they compare to traditional teaching approaches (Hainey et al., 2016). In addition, there are concerns about games turning complex issues into an oversimplified, playable product, and the ideological implications this entails (Sanford et al., 2015). In spite of all, authors highlight the learning benefits of these games and their overall potential as educational tools of the future (Girard et al., 2013; Lau et al., 2017). This potential, of course, entails designing them with accessibility in mind, or their benefits may be compromised, particularly for learners with disabilities or difficulties.

3   Cognitive Accessibility

Cognition is an umbrella term that refers to "mental tasks, including conceptualizing, planning, sequencing thoughts and actions, remembering, interpreting subtle social cues, and manipulating numbers and symbols" (LoPresti et al., 2008, p. 29). Thus, according to ISO standards, cognitive accessibility means preventing or avoiding barriers related to tasks that involve cognition (Steel & Janeslätt, 2017). The issue may be approached, as originally described by Marks (1997), from two angles: first, according to the medical model of disability, the product or service stays the same and users improve their performance via training and rehabilitation if they want to use it, and second, according to the social model of disability, the product or service changes to cater for users' accessibility needs, aiming to include as many people as possible (Retief & Letšosa, 2018).

Whereas the medical model sees disabilities as an illness, the social model considers them one of the many traits of a person. The latter is therefore less stigmatizing and more inclusive than the former. In fact, there is a trend in sociopolitical environments of adopting the social model, as can be seen in policies such as the aforementioned CRPD (United Nations, 2008). Following the same principle, this chapter is concerned with including everyone in education, regardless of their (dis)abilities, as summarized by Wolff (2009, p. 406): "Changing the world rather than the person is a way of accepting individuals in their differences, rather than making them adapt to the world".

Persons with cognitive disabilities and learning difficulties may find it challenging to learn in the traditional classroom. According to Eurostat (European Statistics Department, n.d.), they tend to stop studying before ending secondary education. Among the reasons, one common theme seems to be that they feel socially alienated

(Cobb et al., 2006). This might be worsened by the lack of transparency: some disabilities are noticeable from a young age, but learning difficulties might not start posing barriers until higher education (Tops et al., 2012); at that point, the inability to progress adequately might affect self-esteem, which is frustrating and stigmatizing at the same time (Abraham et al., 2002). In this respect, serious games represent a way of creating accessible paths to education. This is where initiatives such as the Universal Design Learning (Rao & Meo, 2016) gain importance: if lessons offer several ways of accessing and processing information, learner diversity will not pose any barriers to education.

In the case of video games, cognitive accessibility is particularly important, since they are interactive and, therefore, entail a cognitive load that is superior to the one required in other non-interactive audio-visual products (Mangiron, 2012). Some mainstream video games include cognitive accessibility features, such as *Gears 5* (The Coalition, 2019), which allows pausing videos at any time and turning off notifications, or *Grounded* (Obsidian Entertainment, 2020), which allows to customize the rate and the amount of auto-savings, and includes a "creative" mode that can work as a training ground. However, other games, even if they are widely recognized (and even prized) for their accessibility, lack dedicated settings for cognitive features. It is the case of *The Last of Us Part I* (Naughty Dog, 2022) or *God of War: Ragnarök* (SIE Santa Monica Studio, 2022), which include presets for visual, hearing and motor accessibility, but not for cognitive.

There are also several guidelines that address cognitive accessibility in video games, such as the Game Accessibility Guidelines (GAG) (Ellis et al., 2017), the Accessible Player Experiences (APX) (AbleGamers, 2018), the Cognitive Accessibility Guide (Cassidy, 2019), and the Xbox Accessibility Guidelines (XAG) (Microsoft, 2023). An important contribution of these guidelines to our research is that they show the diversity of potential players and, consequently, potential students. After all, the guidelines take people with intellectual disabilities (such as Down syndrome), learning difficulties (such as dyslexia), and mental health issues (such as depression) into consideration. These may seem too different, but all affect cognition in some way: in the cited examples, mental tasks related to comprehension and attention might be at stake (Franceschini et al., 2012; Keller et al., 2019; Laws et al., 2016).

However, these guidelines are not specific to educational games. While some recommendations may be applicable, it may be challenging for developers to choose which ones are relevant for their games, especially due to their great level of detail and technicality. Aiming to ease the creation of an educational game with cognitive accessibility, this chapter gathers a series of recommendations that could be useful during that process.

4 Methodology

A literature review was conducted to identify recommendations for developing educational games that take cognitive accessibility into account. This methodology consists of carefully reading and critically assessing what is known about a certain topic (Bryman, 2012). To that end, a systematic search was performed in several databases to gather pertinent documents. Then, recommendations about how to develop an educational game with cognitive accessibility features were extracted.

Firstly, these five databases were chosen due to their importance in the research world and in social research in particular: Web of Science (WoS), SAGE Journals, ProQuest, Google Scholar, and Scopus. The following search string was entered in all of them:

"game accessibility" AND cogniti* AND educati*

The term *game accessibility* ensures that results are related to the area of interest, and the terms *cogniti** and *educati** are truncated to include variances such as *cognitive* or *cognition*, and *educational* and *education.*

Secondly, the search was conducted, retrieving a total of 159 documents: 1 in WoS, 3 in SAGE Journals, 40 in ProQuest, 55 in Google Scholar, and 60 in Scopus (Table 1).

Thirdly, duplicates were identified and erased. Then, by reading the title, abstract, discussion, and conclusion, papers were included on the corpus according to the following selection criteria: to be peer-reviewed to ensure results are based on research evidence; to be published after 2013 to ensure representativeness of the current research landscape; to be written in English or Spanish (both working languages of the researchers); and to include recommendations for game development (Table 2). Likewise, these exclusion criteria were applied: to not have access to the full text, and to not be related to game accessibility, cognition, or education (Table 3).

After the process, ten documents were included in the corpus. The systematic search may be summarized as follows (Fig. 1).

All accepted papers were read through for data extraction, which consisted of noting the following information on a Microsoft Excel spreadsheet: title, author, date of publication, methods (SRQ1), targeted disability (SRQ2), and recommendations for game development (PRQ).

Table 1 Results of the systematic search by database ($N = 159$)

Database	Results
Web of Science	1
Sage Journals	3
ProQuest	40
Google Scholar	55
Scopus	60

Table 2 Criteria followed to include studies in the review

Inclusion criteria
Peer-reviewed
Published after 2013
Written in English or Spanish
With recommendations

Table 3 Criteria followed to exclude studies in the review

Exclusion criteria
No access to the document
Not related to game accessibility
Not related to cognition
Not related to education

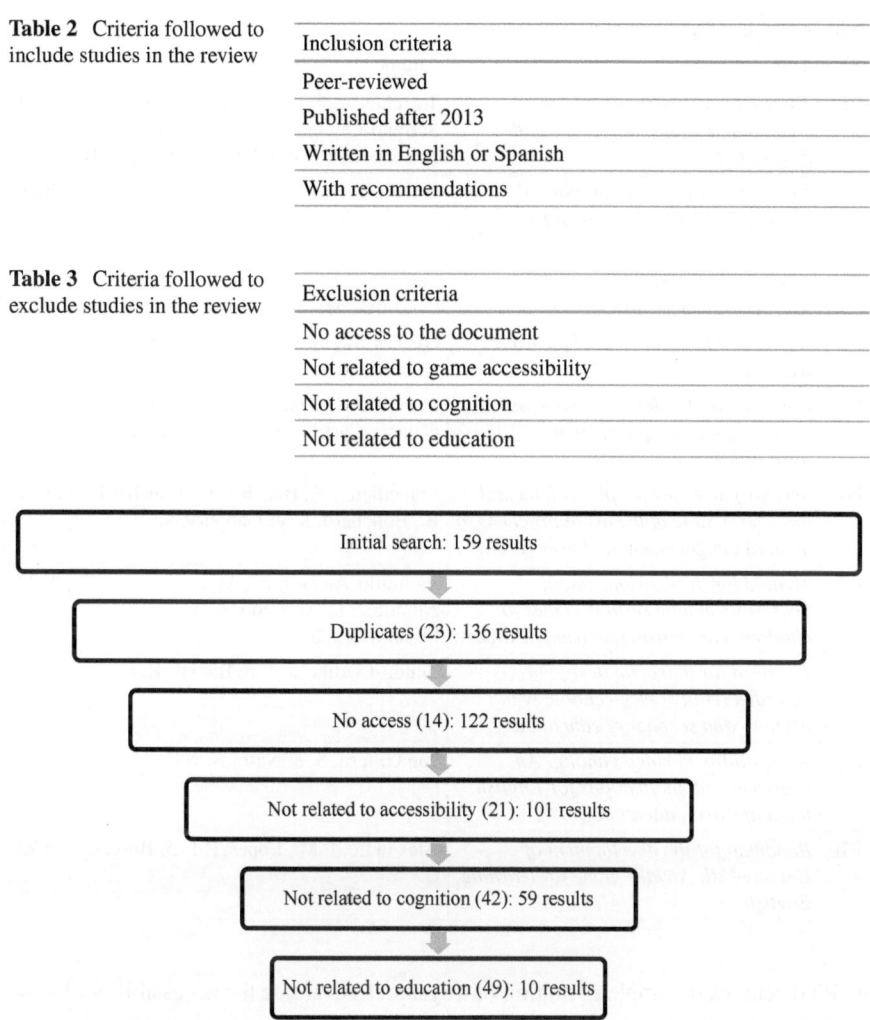

Initial search: 159 results

Duplicates (23): 136 results

No access (14): 122 results

Not related to accessibility (21): 101 results

Not related to cognition (42): 59 results

Not related to education (49): 10 results

Fig. 1 Systematic search overview

5   Results and Discussion

After performing the systematic search and the review of the retrieved documents, ten papers were selected (Table 4). They are sorted by date of publication.

With the aim of contextualizing the content of the papers before reviewing their accessibility recommendations, their core concepts are summarized hereunder:

- P1 uses the video game *My First Day at Work* to present the steps of developing an accessible educational game.

Table 4 Basic information of the accepted papers

ID	Title	Author(s)	Year
P1	*Towards a low-cost adaptation of educational games for people with disabilities*	Torrente Vigil, F. J., Blanco Aguado, Á., Serrano-Laguna, Á., Vallejo Pinto, J. Á., Moreno-Ger, P. & Fernández-Manjón, B.	2014
P2	*Community driven adaptation of game-based learning content for cognitive accessibility*	Westin, T.	2016
P3	*Combined method for evaluating accessibility in serious games*	Salvador-Ullauri, L., Acosta-Vargas, P., Gonzalez, M. & Luján-Mora, S.	2020
P4	*A device-interaction model for users with special needs*	Ojeda-Castelo, J. J., Piedra-Fernandez, J. A. & Iribarne, L.	2021
P5	*A method to develop accessible online serious games for people with disabilities: A case study*	Jaramillo-Alcázar, A., Cortez-Silva, P., Galarza-Castillo, M. & Luján-Mora, S.	2020
P6	*Serious games for people with mental disorders: State of the art of practices to maintain engagement and accessibility*	Francillette, Y., Boucher, E., Bouchard, B., Bouchard, K. & Gaboury, S.	2021
P7	*Method for the development of accessible mobile serious games for children with autism spectrum disorder*	Jaramillo-Alcázar, Á., Arias, J., Albornoz, I., Alvarado, A. & Luján-Mora, S.	2022
P8	*The need for universal design of extended reality (XR) technology in primary and secondary education*	Simon-Liedtke, J. T. & Baraas, R. C.	2022
P9	*Accessibility in video gaming: An overview and implications for English language arts education*	von Gillern, S. & Nash, B.	2023
P10	*Roadmap for the development of EnLang4All: A video game for learning English*	Alexandre, I. M., Lopes, P. F. & Borges, C.	2023

- P2 discusses the implementation of a system to evaluate the accessibility of texts in community-driven games.
- P3 considers the WCAG (W3C World Wide Web Consortium, n.d.) to evaluate the accessibility of 82 serious games.
- P4 designs an interactive adapted system and assesses its validity through a cognitive walkthrough and a think-aloud protocol with target users.
- P5 develops the video game *PC TRAVEL* in Roblox incorporating the guidelines from APX (AbleGamers, 2018) and GNOME (Gnome Developer, n.d.).
- P6 presents a state of the art of serious games for people with mental illnesses by analysing whether they apply available recommendations.
- P7 employs a user-centred design method to develop *SimpleTEA* for people with autism.
- P8 performs a literature review and gathers a series of suggestions for developing accessible extended reality (XR) experiences applied to education.

- P9 conducts a literature review to highlight how educators can re-evaluate and re-design aspects of their classrooms and instructional practices via the design of games with intentional learning.
- P10 works with volunteers to develop the video game *EnLang4All* using the GAG (Ellis et al., 2017).

With regard to the primary research question, the objective was to identify what recommendations are available in the literature to design educational games with cognitive accessibility features. The authors of the selected papers present them in a variety of ways. While some have explicit lists of recommendations, others describe their design choices more broadly. These are explained hereafter.

The analysis shows that the content and format of the information provided by the game are key aspects of cognitive accessibility. On the one hand, four papers (P4, P5, P6, and P8) mention different ways in which the player can receive feedback from the game, such as visual or audio cues, vibration, icons, and text in the form of subtitles or descriptions. This evidences the need for communicating information through multiple channels, which may take the form of transcriptions from audio or video to text, or speech-to-text/text-to-speech technology (P3, P4, and P8). On the other hand, the information should also be easy to understand, regarding either the simplicity of the language and its format (P2, P5, and P10), or the simplicity of the core concept of the game (P1, P7, and P9).

Other accessibility features that are recommended by the selected papers are related to pacing, difficulty, graphics, and control devices. Authors advocate for flexibility with regard to time constraints, not only allowing pauses or having a flexible pacing (P5 and P9), but also allowing the repetition of events or challenges (P5 and P7). This should be accompanied by a difficulty that gives a sense of progression (P5 and P7), and that includes transparent levels, from easier to harder (P10). For the game to be as compelling and attractive as possible, the graphic style should be carefully considered (P6, P7, and P10), so that it can portray facial expressions while still being eye-catching. To guarantee interaction, a variety of external devices should be supported: different controllers, headsets for virtual or augmented reality, and smartphones or tablets (P3, P8, and P10).

Certain features are mentioned less frequently in the selected papers but seem equally relevant. Button combinations should be simple and easy to memorize (P5 and P6), there should be options to adjust photosensitivity for those people that might experiment seizures (P3 and P5), and text size, colour contrast, controller layout, and height should be customizable (P7 and P8). In relation to navigation, a contextual help in the form of scaffolding or a similar method could serve as guidance (P3 and P9). Concerning the interface, what is seen on the screen should be as simple and uncluttered as possible (P6 and P8). Saving should be available in strategic points or throughout the whole game (P5 and P10). Regarding engagement, rewards should be offered as a way of keeping motivation, whose importance in education is fundamental, as previously mentioned (P5 and P7). Finally, people with disabilities should be included in the design of the video game's accessibility from the beginning of the development process (P1 and P8).

P6 adds two unique features not found in any of the other papers. These authors suggest, firstly, the avoidance of blood and gore, which may be triggering for some users, and secondly, the inclusion of a multiplayer option. This last feature has been used to foster engagement and social interaction for people with disabilities; concretely, it has proved to be effective in teaching social rules to people with autism (Gallup et al., 2016; Stone et al., 2019).

In Table 5, the recommendations for cognitive accessibility found in the selected papers are summarized. All of them may be applied to games that are not explicitly educational or even serious, potentially benefiting entertainment games as well.

Regarding the methods employed by the selected studies to develop recommendations for cognitive accessibility in educational games (SRQ1), there seems to be a two-direction trend. On the one hand, five papers (P1, P4, P5, P7, and P10) use the actual development of a game as a case study, putting the recommendations into practice and performing reception studies to evaluate the adequacy of the design. On the other hand, four papers (P2, P6, P8, and P9) carry out a literature review of a particular aspect of cognitive accessibility to gather and assess a series of recommendations proposed by other authors. An interesting case is P3, which does not fit in any of these two categories: the authors develop a method to assess the accessibility of serious games and implement it in a corpus to have a general view of the accessibility landscape.

The variability of the method in the selected papers elucidates the first limitation of this study. Some authors do not assess their recommendations; instead, they summarize results found in other research, as is the case of P8. Others use guidelines during the development process of a game (P1 and P10) or to check if they have been implemented (P6). P1 and P10 do include a validation process as part of their methodology: P1 evaluates usability with target users, but this concept does not equal accessibility, since being usable is just one of the several factors that make something accessible (Mangiron, 2011), and P10 evaluates the adequacy of the developed game, but with questionnaires that are addressed to volunteers with no mention to any disabilities. In conclusion, none of the aforementioned papers (P1, P6, P8, and P10) include target users in the creation or the evaluation of accessibility features.

Regarding the target users of the recommendations, the selected papers are aimed for as many users as possible with disregard to their abilities, but always including players with cognitive disabilities or learning difficulties (SRQ2). However, there are two papers, P4 and P7, which only address players with autism. Interestingly, their recommendations are not particularly similar among them, probably because P4 is aimed at students with autism, but also visual, motor, or hearing disabilities, while P7 uses a method specifically tailored for players with autism.

Likewise, analysed papers focus on different aspects of educational games: while P10 is centred on XR for educational purposes, P2 deals with the accessibility of community-driven games in education, and P6 includes in its review all kinds of serious games, whether they are educational, therapeutic, or other. As a result, some of these recommendations might be too specific or too broad to be applied to all educational games for people with any kind of cognitive disability or learning difficulty, which is the second limitation of this literature review.

Table 5 Extracted recommendations for cognitive accessibility from accepted papers

ID	Recommendations
P1	Consideration of accessibility from the design stage of the game Simple and easy to understand content and structure
P2	Text simplification
P3	Automatic transcriptions, from audio or video to text Sign language Photosensitivity settings External devices for virtual and augmented reality Contextual help
P4	Audio instructions Visual icons next to 3D objects Audio and visual feedback
P5	Adjustable sensitivity/error tolerance Simple language Voice or text repetition Subtitles Pause while the text is read Save points Explicit visual rewards Simple-to-difficult progression Simple controls Challenges repetitions Easy execution
P6	Multiplayer mode Avoidance of gore elements or blood Cartoon aesthetic Simple controls to be memorized Few interface elements simultaneously Symbols instead of text Option to modify feedback: vibration, sounds, or icons
P7	Customizability of play experience Evolving tasks Single objective Clear instructions Reward after good performance Repeatability of tasks and predictability of objectives Minimized and simple transitions Minimalist graphics and clear audio Sensory input Variability of stimuli: audio and visual

(continued)

Table 5 (continued)

ID	Recommendations
P8	Input controllers and more flexible headsets Emphasis on in-game flexibility (teleportation, observer-only mode, flexible time and reaction limits, focus indicators) Personalization and customization (text size, colour contrast, controller layout, height, sound management) Alternative communication means (keyboard support, speech-to-text, text-to-speech, captions) Improved multimodality (text, descriptions, captions, vibrations, complementing visual or auditory cues) Increased accessibility of the user interfaces Inclusion of people with disabilities in the design and development process
P9	Clean, simple text formatting Clear and precise instructions available on-demand in multiple modes Contextual, just-in-time guidance and scaffolding Additional time and flexible pacing
P10	Optional background music Effective tutorials Possibility of saving the game to resume it later Customizable in-game username for easy identification Eye-catching graphics Responsiveness in different devices (smartphones and tablets) Clear layout for changing between languages Improved readability Several difficulty and sorting levels

In summary, and bearing these two limitations in mind, Table 6 presents the main contribution of this literature: a set of recommendations to develop educational games with cognitive accessibility features.

Many of these recommendations are not specifically related to learning, but educational games have to be accessible in order for players to learn. That is, these suggestions potentially work for video games with purposes different to education or with the sole purpose of entertaining. Nevertheless, some of the recommendations gathered here, such as the cartoon aesthetic to portray emotions or the rewards to motivate learners, are not included in the guidelines for entertainment games, for example, XAG and GAG. To sum up, developers should apply the accessibility recommendations they consider feasible and appropriate depending on the purposes of their games, whether they are educational or not.

6 Conclusions and Future Work

The use of games for a purpose other than entertainment is on the rise. Among these so-called *serious games*, educational games are both enjoyable and instructive, as they are designed to teach players specific skills or new information. Interactivity

Table 6 Set of recommendations to develop an educational game with cognitive accessibility features

Recommendation	Definition
Alternative channels	Information should be provided through both visual and auditory channels when possible. Examples include automatic transcriptions and speech-to-text or text-to-speech technology
Simplicity	Content should be as simple as possible, including instructions, language, formatting, and objectives
Feedback	Players should be notified through visual icons, audio cues, or vibrations when they encounter an important event or are progressing adequately
Pace and repetition	Pausing should be allowed at any moment and additional time for tasks should be provided to ensure an adequate pacing. Events, dialogues, or challenges should be predictable and repeatable
Graphics	The graphic style should be simple but eye-catching. A cartoon aesthetic is a good option to show emotions
External devices	Different input controllers or headsets should be supported, and platforms such as smartphones and tablets should be compatible
Difficulty	A fair, simple-to-difficult progression should be offered, or the difficulty should be adjustable from the settings
Additional stimuli	Sensory stimuli should be added for dynamism, such as background music
Participation of disabled people	Games should be developed and tested involving people with cognitive disabilities or learning difficulties
Photosensitivity	Flashing or moving patterns that might trigger seizures should be avoided
Contextual help	Gameplay should be assisted through contextual reminders of controls or objectives, in-time guidance, or scaffolding
Controls	Button combinations should be simple and easy to memorize
Interface	Only necessary information should be displayed on the screen, and it should be simple and uncluttered
Personalization	Players should be able to customize as many aspects of the game as possible, such as text size, colour contrast, controller layout, or sound management
Rewards	Options to unlock levels, acquire abilities, or earn points or experience should be offered after overcoming challenges to keep engagement and motivation
Saving	Save points should be clear and numerous, or players should be allowed to save and resume the game at any moment

differentiates these games from other learning methods, and it contributes to keeping players engaged and interested. Moreover, educational games have shown to enhance cognitive skills, elicit emotions and motivation, and promote communication and teamwork among players (Barz et al., 2023; Mikropoulos & Iatraki, 2023; Plass et al., 2015).

However, educational games might present accessibility barriers for persons with disabilities, hindering their rights to education, information, and technology. Particularly, for players with cognitive disabilities and learning difficulties, determining the required response to progress in the game might be difficult, which could affect their self-esteem and trigger social alienation. Accessibility in this context may contribute to creating more inclusive educational experiences.

In this chapter, a literature review was conducted to identify which recommendations could be followed to create educational games with cognitive accessibility features. Ten papers were selected, and their analysis shows that the main suggestions to ensure cognitive accessibility are providing stimuli through alternative channels, allowing the pace to be customizable, and designing simple but engaging content. Other relevant features that should be considered are the graphic style, the control devices, and the difficulty. It should also be brought to attention the overall customizability of the game, the information available on the interface, and the rewards that are offered after an adequate progression.

On the one hand, selected papers followed mainly two methods: they either reviewed research on a concrete aspect of cognitive accessibility or they studied the development of an accessible educational game. On the other hand, they targeted players with all kinds of disabilities, that is, not only users facing cognitive barriers, but also visual, hearing, or motor ones. Only two papers focused on a single type of needs, namely those of players with autism.

This variability in the methodology and in the scope of the target audiences, which spans from being overly broad to extremely specific, implies that our concluding set of recommendations, as given in Table 6, may not be applied to every video game. Instead, developers should evaluate which ones are useful for the game's purpose (educational or not), mechanics, and users.

To validate these recommendations, future research should include developing a game following these recommendations. Then, a reception study with players with diverse accessibility needs and preferences should be conducted. This could be done by introducing the game in a real educational context to better understand how game-based learning fits in with more traditional practices, and how developers should treat certain educational content so as not to trivialize it, which is one of the main criticisms of educational games.

In conclusion, this research is a starting point for developers and researchers to create and analyse educational games with cognitive accessibility features. It aims to overcome the scarcity of resources regarding this topic and to bring together players, teachers, developers, and researchers to create more interactive and engaging educational experiences for all.

Acknowledgements This research is supported by grant PID2022-137058NB-I00, funded by MCIN/AEI/10.13039/501100011033 and by "ERDF: A way of making Europe". The authors are members of the TransMedia Catalonia research group, funded by Secretaria d'Universitats i Recerca del Departament d'Empresa i Coneixement de la Generalitat de Catalunya, under the SGR funding scheme (Ref. Code 2021SGR00077). Oliva-Zamora (2022FI_B 00308) and Larreina-Morales (2021FI_B1 00049) have also been awarded Ph.D. grants from the Catalan Government to carry out this research. This chapter is based upon work from COST Action CA19142—Leading

Platform for European Citizens, Industries, Academia and Policymakers in Media Accessibility (LEAD-ME) supported by COST (European Cooperation in Science and Technology).

References

AbleGamers. (2018). *Accessible player experiences (APX)*. https://accessible.games/accessible-pla yer-experiences/

Abraham, C., Jones, L. L., & Taylor, C. (2002). Self-esteem, stigma and community participation amongst people with learning difficulties living in the community. *Journal of Community and Applied Social Psychology, 12*(6), 430–443. https://doi.org/10.1002/casp.695

Alexandre, I. M., Lopes, P. F., & Borges, C. (2023). Roadmap for the development of EnLang4All: A video game for learning English. *Multimodal Technologies and Interaction, 7*(2), 17. https://doi.org/10.3390/mti7020017

Backlund, P., & Hendrix, M. (2013). Educational games—Are they worth the effort? A literature survey of the effectiveness of serious games. In *5th International Conference on Games and Virtual Worlds for Serious Applications (VS-GAMES)*, 1–8. https://doi.org/10.1109/VS-GAMES.2013.6624226

Barlet, M., & Spohn, S. D. (2012). *Includification. A practical guide to game accessibility*. https://accessible.games/wp-content/uploads/2018/11/AbleGamers_Includification.pdf

Barz, N., Benick, M., Dörrenbächer-Ulrich, L., & Perels, F. (2023). The effect of digital game-based learning interventions on cognitive, metacognitive, and affective-motivational learning outcomes in school: A meta-analysis. *Review of Educational Research.* https://doi.org/10.3102/00346543231167795

Bryman, A. (2012). *Social research methods* (4th ed.). Oxford University Press.

Calvo-Ferrer, J. R. (2015). Educational games as stand-alone learning tools and their motivational effect on L2 vocabulary acquisition and perceived learning gains. *British Journal of Educational Technology, 48*(2), 264–278. https://doi.org/10.1111/bjet.12387

Cassidy, R. (2019). *Cognitive accessibility guide. Can i play that?* https://caniplaythat.com/worksh ops/basic-accessibility-options-for-cognitive-accessibility

Cobb, B., Tzempelikos, N., Dowd, T., & Boyle, B. (2006). Cognitive—Behavioral interventions, dropout, and youth with disabilities: A systematic review. *Remedial and Special Education, 27*(5), 259–275. https://doi.org/10.1177/07419325060270050201

Derks, S., Willemen, A. M., & Sterkenburg, P. S. (2022). Improving adaptive and cognitive skills of children with an intellectual disability and/or autism spectrum disorder: Meta-analysis of randomized controlled trials on the effects of serious games. *International Journal of the Child-Computer Interactions, 33.* https://doi.org/10.1016/j.ijcci.2022.100488

Dutra, T. C., Felipe, D., Gasparini, I., & Maschio, E. (2021). A Systematic mapping of guidelines for the development of accessible digital games to people with disabilities. In M. Antona, & C. Stephanidis (Eds.), *Universal access in human-computer interaction. Design methods and user experience, 12768*, (pp. 45–63). Springer. https://doi.org/10.1007/978-3-030-78092-0_4

Ellis, B., Ford-Williams, G., Graham, L., Grammenos, D., Hamilton, I., Headstrong, G., Lee, E., Manion, J., & Westin, T. (2017). *Game accessibility guidelines.* https://gameaccessibilityguid elines.com

European Statistics Department. (n.d.). *Disability statistics.* https://ec.europa.eu/eurostat/statistics-explained/index.php?title=Disability_statistics

Fokides, E. (2018). Digital educational games and mathematics: Results of a case study in primary school settings. *Education and Information Technologies, 23*(2), 851–867. https://doi.org/10.1007/s10639-017-9639-5

Franceschini, S., Gori, S., Ruffino, M., Pedrolli, K., & Facoetti, A. (2012). A causal link between visual spatial attention and reading acquisition. *Current Biology, 22*(9), 814–819. https://doi.org/10.1016/j.cub.2012.03.013

Francillette, Y., Boucher, E., Bouchard, B., Bouchard, K., & Gaboury, S. (2021). Serious games for people with mental disorders: State of the art of practices to maintain engagement and accessibility. *Entertainment Computing, 37*, 100396. https://doi.org/10.1016/j.entcom.2020.100396

Gallup, J., Serianni, B., Duff, C., & Gallup, A. (2016). An exploration of friendships and socialization for adolescents with autism engaged in massively multiplayer online role-playing games (MMORPG). *Education and Training in Autism and Developmental Disabilities, 51*(3), 223–237.

Girard, C., Ecalle, J., & Magnan, A. (2013). Serious games as new educational tools: How effective are they? A meta-analysis of recent studies. *Journal of Computer Assisted Learning, 29*, 207–219. https://doi.org/10.1111/j.1365-2729.2012.00489.x

Gnome Developer. (n.d.). *Guía de Accesibilidad Para los Desarrolladores de GNOME.* https://developer-old.gnome.org/accessibility-devel-guide/

Hainey, T., Connolly, T. M., Boyle, E. A., Wilson, A., & Razak, A. (2016). A systematic literature review of games-based learning empirical evidence in primary education. *Computers and Education, 102*, 202–223. https://doi.org/10.1016/j.compedu.2016.09.001

IGDA-GASIG. (2021). *What and why.* https://igda-gasig.org/what-and-why

Jaramillo-Alcázar, A., Arias, J., Albornoz, I., Alvarado, A., & Luján-Mora, S. (2022). Method for the development of accessible mobile serious games for children with autism spectrum disorder. *International Journal of Environmental Research and Public Health, 19*(7), 3844. https://doi.org/10.3390/ijerph19073844

Jaramillo-Alcázar, A., Thompson, D., & Boada, I. (2020). A method to develop accessible online serious games for people with disabilities: A case study. *Sustainability, 12*(22), 1–22. https://doi.org/10.3390/su12229584

Keller, A. S., Leikauf, J. E., Holt-Gosselin, B., Staveland, B. R., & Williams, L. M. (2019). Paying attention to attention in depression. *Translational Psychiatry, 9*(1), 279. https://doi.org/10.1038/s41398-019-0616-1

Kenwright, B. (2017). Brief review of video games in learning & education: How far we have come. In *Proceedings of the SIGGRAPH Asia 2017 Symposium on Education (SA 2017)*, 1–10. Association for Computing Machinery (ACM). https://doi.org/10.1145/3134368.3139220

Laine, T. H., & Lindberg, R. S. N. (2020). Designing engaging games for education: A systematic literature review on game motivators and design principles. *IEEE Transactions on Learning Technologies, 13*(4), 804–821. https://doi.org/10.1109/TLT.2020.3018503

Lau, H. M., Smit, J. H., Fleming, T. M., & Riper, H. (2017). Serious games for mental health: Are they accessible, feasible, and effective? A systematic review and meta-analysis. *Frontiers Psychiatry, 7*, 209. https://doi.org/10.3389/fpsyt.2016.00209

Laws, G., Brown, H., & Main, E. (2016). Reading comprehension in children with down syndrome. *Reading and Writing, 29*(1), 21–45. https://doi.org/10.1007/s11145-015-9578-8

LoPresti, E. F., Bodine, C., & Lewis, C. (2008). Assistive technology for cognition. *IEEE Engineering in Medicine and Biology Magazine, 27*(2), 29–39. https://doi.org/10.1109/EMB.2007.907396

Mangiron, C. (2011). Accesibilidad a los videojuegos: estado actual y perspectivas futuras. *TRANS: Revista De Traductología, 15*, 53–67. https://doi.org/10.24310/TRANS.2011.v0i15.3195

Mangiron, C. (2012). Exploring new paths towards game accessibility. In A. Remael, P. Orero, & M. Carroll (Eds.), *Audiovisual translation and media accessibility at the crossroads: Media for all 3* (pp. 43–59). Rodopi. https://doi.org/10.1163/9789401207812_005

Marks, D. (1997). Models of disability. *Disability and Rehabilitation, 19*(3), 85–91. https://doi.org/10.3109/09638289709166831

Martinez, L., Gimenes, M., & Lambert, E. (2022). Entertainment video games for academic learning: A systematic review. *Journal of Educational Computing Research, 60*(5), 1083–1109. https://doi.org/10.1177/07356331211053848

Microsoft. (2023). *Xbox accessibility guidelines.* https://learn.microsoft.com/en-us/gaming/accessibility/guidelines

Mikropoulos, T. A., & Iatraki, G. (2023). Digital technology supports science education for students with disabilities: A systematic review. *Education and Information Technologies, 28*(4), 3911–3935. https://doi.org/10.1007/s10639-022-11317-9

Minecraft. (2023). *Minecraft education.* https://education.minecraft.net/en-us

Ojeda-Castelo, J. J., Piedra-Fernandez, J. A., & Iribarne, L. (2021). A device-interaction model for users with special needs. *Multimedia Tools and Applications, 80*(5), 6675–6710. https://doi.org/10.1007/s11042-020-10026-0

Oliveira, W., Hamari, J., Shi, L., Toda, A. M., Rodrigues, L., Palomino, P. T., & Isotani, S. (2023). Tailored gamification in education: A literature review and future agenda. *Education and Information Technologies, 28*(1), 373–406. https://doi.org/10.1007/s10639-022-11122-4

Plass, J. L., Homer, B. D., & Kinzer, C. K. (2015). Foundations of game-based learning. *Educational Psychologist, 50*(4), 258–283. https://doi.org/10.1080/00461520.2015.1122533

Rao, K., & Meo, G. (2016). Using universal design for learning to design standards-based lessons. *SAGE Open, 6*(4). https://doi.org/10.1177/2158244016680688

Retief, M., & Letšosa, R. (2018). Models of disability: A brief overview. *HTS Teologiese Studies/theological Studies, 74*(1), a4738. https://doi.org/10.4102/hts.v74i1.4738

Reynaldo, C., Christian, R., Hosea, H., & Gunawan, A. A. S. (2021). Using video games to improve capabilities in decision making and cognitive skill: A literature review. *Procedia Computer Science, 171*, 211–221. https://doi.org/10.1016/j.procs.2020.12.027

Riopel, M., Nenciovici, L., Potvin, P., Chastenay, P., Charland, P., Sarrasin, J. B., & Masson, S. (2019). Impact of serious games on science learning achievement compared with more conventional instruction: An overview and a meta-analysis. *Studies in Science Education, 55*(2), 169–214. https://doi.org/10.1080/03057267.2019.1722420

Salvador-Ullauri, L., Acosta-Vargas, P., & Luján-Mora, S. (2020a). Web-based serious games and accessibility: A systematic literature review. *Applied Sciences, 10*(21), 7859. https://doi.org/10.3390/app10217859

Salvador-Ullauri, L., Acosta-Vargas, P., Gonzalez, M., & Luján-Mora, S. (2020b). Combined method for evaluating accessibility in serious games. *Applied Sciences, 10*(18), 6324. https://doi.org/10.3390/app10186324

Sanford, K., Starr, L. J., Merkel, L., & Bonsor Kurki, S. (2015). Serious games: Video games for good? *E-Learning and Digital Media, 12*(1), 90–106. https://doi.org/10.1177/2042753014558380

Shapoval, S., Gimeno-Santos, M., Mendez Zorrilla, A., Garcia-Zapirain, B., Guerra-Balic, M., Signo-Miguel, S., & Bruna-Rabassa, O. (2022). Serious games for executive functions training for adults with intellectual disability: Overview. *International Journal of Environmental Research and Public Health, 19*(18), 11369. https://doi.org/10.3390/ijerph191811369

Simon-Liedtke, J. T., & Baraas, R. C. (2022). The need for universal design of eXtended reality (XR) technology in primary and secondary education. In J. Y. C. Chen & G. Fragomeni (Eds.), *Virtual, augmented and mixed reality: Applications in education, aviation and industry, 13318* (pp. 121–141). Springer. https://doi.org/10.1007/978-3-031-06015-1_9

Steel, E. J., & Janeslätt, G. (2017). Drafting standards on cognitive accessibility: A global collaboration. *Disability and Rehabilitation: Assistive Technology, 12*(4), 385–389. https://doi.org/10.1080/17483107.2016.1176260

Stone, B. G., Mills, K. A., & Saggers, B. (2019). Multiplayer games: Multimodal features that support friendships of students with autism spectrum disorder. *Australasian Journal of Special and Inclusive Education, 43*(2), 69–82. https://doi.org/10.1017/jsi.2019.6

Sun, P. L., Siklander, P., & Heli, R. (2018). How to trigger students' interest in digital learning environments: A systematic literature review. *Seminar-Net, 14*(1), 62–84. https://doi.org/10.7577/seminar.2597

Tops, W., Callens, M., Lammertyn, J., et al. (2012). Identifying students with dyslexia in higher education. *Annals of Dyslexia, 62*(3), 186–203. https://doi.org/10.1007/s11881-012-0072-6

Torrente, J., del Blanco, Á., Serrano-Laguna, Á., Vallejo-Pinto, J. A., Moreno-Ger, P., & Fernández-Manjón, B. (2014). Towards a low-cost adaptation of educational games for people with disabilities. *Computer Science and Information Systems (ComSIS), 11*(1), 369–391. https://doi.org/10.2298/CSIS121209013T

Tran, B. (2023). Gaming statistics: How many gamers are there in the world? *Games Publisher.* https://gamespublisher.com/gaming-statistics-how-many-gamers-are-there-in-the-world/

United Nations. (2008). *Convention on the rights of persons with disabilities.* United Nations Human Rights. https://www.ohchr.org/en/instruments-mechanisms/instruments/convention-rights-persons-disabilities#9

Vankúš, P. (2021). Influence of game-based learning in mathematics education on students' affective domain: A systematic review. *Mathematics, 9*(9), 986. https://doi.org/10.3390/math9090986

von Gillern, S., & Nash, B. (2023). Accessibility in video gaming: An overview and implications for English language arts education. *Journal of Adolescent and Adult Literacy, 66*(6), 382–390. https://doi.org/10.1002/jaal.1284

W3C World Wide Web Consortium. (n.d.). *Web Content Accessibility Guidelines 2.1.* https://www.w3.org/TR/WCAG21/

Westin, T. (2016). Community driven adaptation of game based learning content for cognitive accessibility. In T. Connolly, & L. Boyle (Eds.), *Proceedings of The 10th European Conference on Games Based Learning* (pp. 781–787). Academic Conferences International Limited.

Wilkinson, P. (2016). A brief history of serious games. In R. Dörner, S. Göbel, M. Kickmeier-Rust, M. Masuch, & K. Zweig (Eds.), *Entertainment computing and serious games, 9970* (pp. 17–41). Springer. https://doi.org/10.1007/978-3-319-46152-6_2

Wolff, J. (2009). Cognitive disability in a society of equals. *Metaphilosophy, 40*(3–4), 402–415. https://doi.org/10.1111/j.1467-9973.2009.01598.x

Yuan, B., Folmer, E., Harris, F. C. (2011). Game accessibility: A survey. *Universal Access in the Information Society, 10*(1), 1–19. https://doi.org/10.1007/s10209-010-0189-5

Gameography

Beyond Blue, E-Line Media, 2020.
Gears 5, The Coalition, 2019.
God of War: Ragnarök, SIE Santa Monica Studio, 2022.
Grounded, Obsidian Entertainment, 2020.
Oregon Trail, MECC, 1985.
Scratch, MIT Media Lab, 2017.
The Last of Us Part I, Naughty Dog, 2022.

Enabling Digital Literacy Pedagogical Sessions (#DLPS): The Case of Portugal

Sérgio Barbosa ⓘ

Abstract Since the increased digitization of everyday life, social media platforms have become key tools for how young people communicate and interact. However, there is little research on pedagogical initiatives that can bring digital literacy to stimulate critical thinking and public intervention on and with social media platforms. This chapter aims to foster an educational long-term campaign to bring digital literacy to the forefront of policymaking in Portugal and broader EU contexts. It showcases the Digital Literacy Pedagogical Sessions (#DLPS) designed to empower and nurture young people's post-digital futures. The data in this chapter is derived from a participatory pedagogy approach adopted at Portuguese schools during two periods: 2021–2022 and 2022–2023. The chapter suggests policy recommendations to consider how young people can actively participate in shaping digital society. Additionally, it advocates for a long-term educational agenda to promote public values as a key component in building a fair digital future.

Keywords Digital literacy · Young people · Participatory pedagogy · Postdigital Future · Portugal

1 Introduction: The Rise of Digital Literacy Pedagogical Sessions (#DLPS)

Digital literacy has become an essential framework for engaging with digital platforms in everyday life. (Livingstone, 2004; Masterman, 1985). However, we still struggle with understanding the impacts and ramifications of the rapid shift to a culture of connectivity (van Dijck, 2009, 2013) and how young people respond to this change. We are too often limited by the dominance of big tech for-profit companies, the so-called GAMAM (Google, Amazon, Meta, Apple, Microsoft), which lack insights from digital human rights perspective. Additionally, discussions about

S. Barbosa (✉)
Centre for Social Studies (CES), University of Coimbra, Coimbra, Portugal
e-mail: sergiosilva@ces.uc.pt

© The Author(s) 2024
A. Marcus-Quinn et al. (eds.), *Transforming Media Accessibility in Europe*,
https://doi.org/10.1007/978-3-031-60049-4_17

impact and responses often focus on individual users rather than on collective experiences. This is despite the fact that these platforms significantly shape and shift the makeup and meaning of marginalized and vulnerable communities and groups, influencing political, social, and cultural aspects. Therefore, how should we design pedagogical sessions on digital literacy? How are Portuguese young people affected by the increasing use of digital platforms in their daily lives, and what are their responses?

Portugal has a population of more than 10 million people and an Internet Penetration of 78% rate, with 49% of the Portuguese reportedly using Facebook and 24% reportedly using WhatsApp to share news (Reuters, 2022). With disinformation posing a challenge to the survival of democracies worldwide, a new Portuguese law was approved in May 2021, establishing the Portuguese Charter on Human Rights. This initiative puts Portugal at the forefront of efforts to combat disinformation. In addition to ensuring human digital rights, freedoms, and guarantees for citizens in their online environment, the legislation establishes that the state must protect citizens from people who produce, reproduce, and disseminate misinformation. This aligns with the European Action Plan against Disinformation, which is based on four core pillars, namely (i) improving the capabilities of European Union institutions to detect, analyze, and expose disinformation; (ii) strengthening coordinated and joint responses to disinformation; (iii) mobilizing private sector to tackle disinformation; and (iv) raising awareness and improving societal resilience (European Commission, 2018: 5).

With the rise of social media platforms, the spread of misinformation and disinformation has intensified globally. Propaganda and disinformation which once required detailed planning, can now be disseminated through platforms using algorithms (Gillespie, 2010; Howard, 2020). This culture of misinformation and disinformation endangers democracy and human rights, leading to a biased public sphere where objective facts are overshadowed by personal opinions and emotions in public debate. In the past decade, digital technologies and how young people use them have changed dramatically. Most teenagers use their smartphones daily, and almost twice as much as ten years ago (Baym, 2015). While platforms offer opportunities and benefits—enabling young people to interact with others, learn online, acquire job skills, and be entertained—these gains come with risks. These risks include exposure to disinformation and the potential to become passive users of these platforms (Barbosa & Back, 2020).

The chapter is composed of three parts. The first section provides a brief a literature review on the field of digital literacy and introduces the #Digital Literacy Pedagogical Sessions (DLPS) as a case study. The second section explains why the digital literacy sessions were selected for the case study, emphasizing the participatory educational initiatives. The third section is dedicated to discussing the methodology. The final section presents the lessons learned from the case study, highlighting its strong potential to increase youth participation and offering policy recommendations.

2 Digital Literacy as an "Umbrella" Concept

Digital literacy can be broadly defined as the development of knowledge, skills, and attitudes to provide users with essential framework for effective lifelong engagement with media messages on platforms (Christian, 2020: 7). It is a combination of literacy (learning how to read and write) and digital everyday life (learning how to use and engage with platforms). Here, the focus relies on #DLPS as a testbed applied in the Portuguese schools, as well as broader educational contexts. It aims to promote the dissemination of critical knowledge produced in the broader areas of social sciences, and humanities particularly through stimulating critical debates around the main challenges of contemporary democracies related to the platform society (van Dijck et al., 2018).

To contribute to the democratization of knowledge, the promotion of digital human rights is an essential clue. #DLPS advocates for participatory interaction, as well as bottom-up formats of pedagogy to foster basic competencies of digital literacy as an indispensable public value to nurture future generations. It also stimulates the construction of an ecology of knowledge toward an inclusive, fair, and democratic society oriented to understanding digital reality to transform it and promote inter-ventions (Tygel & Kirsch, 2016: 109). #DLPS has an approach based on collective learning that aims to make young people aware of how information travels faster on social media platforms while people live multiple online/offline lives. To do so, the pedagogical session enables young people to actively interrogate the digital infra-structure of platforms (van Dijck, 2020). As Hintz et al. (2018) remind us: "We cannot simply be seen as users of digital tools. The digital world is embedded in our lives and the larger structure that governs them" (2018: 16).

#DLPS was chosen as a case study for four main reasons: (i) to improve existing theoretical framework about policy interventions in digital literacy field, paying special attention to the Portuguese context; (ii) to foster public policies based on the different geographical and cultural school communities at an earlier educational stage; (iii) to adopt advanced methods, develop and validate instruments by using a range of participatory pedagogies to ensure digital literacy as powerful tool to nurture future generations; (iv) to develop a user-friendly pedagogical toolkit to be used in Portugal, EU and beyond. In sum, #DLPS reveals a sense of young people belonging that absorbs the diversity of the challenges of everyday digital life, while it provides a high degree of autonomy through the engagement of communal knowledge acquired by young participants and recommended to be used as practice of intervention in the coming future.

3   From Participatory Pedagogies to Platform Pedagogies

Helmond (2015) defines platform as a set of relationships, determinants, state, and market positioning all mediated through digital technologies. And what are their implications for pedagogies? Markham suggests that academics, teachers, and scholars should use long training in pedagogy and teaching and knowledge of interpretive and inductive/emergent methods of analysis to create better literacies in order "to help people to find modes and means of critically examining and understanding the contexts within which they are drawn into a neoliberal position through the seemingly innocuous practices of such things as making and sharing images, clicking on links, turning on the smartphone's GPS" (Markham, 2019: 759). While, Sefton-Green (2021) explores the relationship between platforms pedagogy and pedagogicisation of everyday life. The author dives into pedagogy to explain how people engage and interact with platforms: "paying particular attention to how users learn or are subjected to norms and behaviors as they read and write their section on digital platforms" (2021: 2) and how this relationship requires human agency within a larger process of control and re-conceptualization (2021: 10).

From participatory pedagogies to platform pedagogies, the #DLPS aimed to value the cultural and social aspects of platforms, support bottom-up educational pedagogies through mutual learning and strengthen participatory approaches (Barbosa, 2020). #DLPS provides practical experiences and knowledge exchange, such as presentations of the participants to the tutor through ice-breaking sessions; small talks followed by critical insights of the platform society, historical processes and their institutions of how platform power governs public and private life (Zuboff, 2019); and game dynamics on how to fight mis/disinformation. The goal is to activate meaningful engagement in collective teaching practices, while developing a critical consciousness into the digital world in a post-session moment.

Furthermore, young participants were presented to nominate their everyday routine on and with platforms, motivating themselves to be challengers, while creating forms of intervention in practical terms (Freire, 1968). #DLPS sessions provide Portuguese young people a direct contact with those who were carrying out initiatives related to interrogate and subvert the historical reflection on the development of platforms (van Dijck, 2014). Thus, the pedagogical format of the sessions promoted bottom-up discussions that were accompanied by "rodas de conversa" lasting 10–20 min at the end of each session. There, young people are invited to reflect together on their own practice experiences within platforms and provide feedback for their peers, while learning with each other.

4   Methods

#DLPS was developed under the guidance of CES—Centre for Social Studies, laboratory associated to the University of Coimbra. The so-called CES GOES TO SCHOOL (CVE) project constitutes one of the CES strategies for the dissemination of scientific culture, thus striving to foster contacts between its researchers and the wider community. To this extent, CES invites Portuguese schools to participate in the CVE project annually. This outreach project, which takes place between November and June of each academic year, is dedicated to students of various levels of education (2nd and 3rd cycles of basic and secondary education). It aims to contribute to the dissemination of knowledge produced in the different areas of social sciences humanities, through sharing the research work developed at CES and promoting debate around it. During 2022, CVE reached a noteworthy number of 4638 students in 91 sessions presented at Portuguese schools by CES researchers.

The #DLPS pedagogical sessions took place in 2021–2022 (3 selected schools)—Figueira da Foz, Peniche and Lisbon—and 2022–2023 (13 selected schools)—Sao Joao do Estoril, Arcozelo (Vila Nova de Gaia), Oliveira do Hospital, Aveiro, Ponte da Barca, Braga, Carregal do Sal, Porto, Vila Real, Leiria, Meda, Penacova—with the participation of the Portuguese schools involved with topics related to the agenda of digital literacy. The time period was up to two hours raging according to each school schedule. Most of the audience were young people between 12 and 18 years old. The selection of schools was done by the announcement on CES GOES TO SCHOOL web page, in collaboration with partner organizations, and with the full support of the project coordination team. The Portuguese schools were able to contact the researcher responsible for each seminar and book the pedagogical seminar through the online system. After the sessions, schoolteachers and students were invited to evaluate the school session.

To achieve its goal, #DLPS created a pedagogical toolkit applied to young people between 12 and 18 years old of elementary and high schools in Portugal. At the same time, it provided conditions for Ph.D. students to learn new techniques, gain access to information about digital literacy initiatives, instruments, and methods little explored at initial educational stages. The structure to create the session outline was conducted in three phases: (i) Desk Research of digital literacy: discussing the methodology and learning participatory (pedagogical) approaches. The desk research of digital literacy enabled the tutors to identify the driving forces of pedagogical practices and community values; (ii) Write-up the #DLPS teaching outline: showing how young people can absorb digital literacy skills knowledge from an earlier educational stage. Co-development of improvements of interventions considered promising for fostering digital human rights with the goal to provide policy makers with the knowledge on how to implement digital literacy sessions as effective long-term strategy, as well as to safeguard democracy in the coming future; iii) final discussion with the research team and application of #DLPS sessions all over Portugal. Integration of results with key EU policymakers' decisions, leading to the development of evidence-based policy recommendations to EU and Portuguese authorities. Table 1 shows how these

Table 1 Main features of # digital literacy pedagogical sessions (DLPS)

Participatory pedagogies self-reflection	Build, share, and produce self-flection among the young people Foster digital literacy activities through engaged conversations Joint face-to-face discussion on pedagogical process Argument discussions for a fair digital society with critical competences provided by an extensive cohort of stakeholders (policymakers, educators, digital rights activists, school community, and experts)
Digital literacy	Insights developed to critically reflect about the geopolitical power of GAMAM To foster daily practices to fight mis/disinformation on platforms Psychological inoculation to improve digital resilience against mis/disinformation Flying wheel to the physical library of the school Disseminate digital literacy lessons learned in an accessible manner to familiar members during the after-session moment Facilitate and disseminate online fact-checking platforms
#DLPS—digital literacy pedagogical sessions	Strong cohesion of all young participants Fostering creative interventions to claim a fair digital future Raising awareness against online manipulation shared on social media platforms Call to improve the dissemination of accurate information Collective manner to co-create solutions Digital community based on common values led by young people

topics embraced the #DLPS initiative, which issues related to digital literacy field were brought up by them, and reveals how youth organized in a participatory manner to interact with each other through a constructive pedagogical format.

5   #DLPS Outline

Ice-Breaking Session: The warm-up activity facilitates the beginning of interaction with the tutor. The challenge is to answer the four following questions in 20 s: What is your name? How old are you? What is your favorite hobby? And which platform do you most use?

Chat Apps and Affordances: This section points out the difference between the affordances of three chat platforms. It presents the main technological features of WhatsApp and Telegram, while disclosing the non-profit messaging service named Signal (Barbosa & Milan, 2019; Milan & Barbosa, 2020). Signal is presented to the young audience as an open-source project that is the favorite messaging platform among digital rights activists. It also supports one-to-one voice and video calling, like the siblings WhatsApp and Telegram. It performs end-to-end encryption (West, 2019), and it is developed/maintained by a non-profit Signal Foundation (Ermoshina & Musiani, 2019; Musiani & Ermoshina, 2017). From 2022, Meredith Whittaker became the president of Signal, while Brian Acton (former Yahoo! employee and WhatsApp co-creator) provided a loan of $50 million to transform Signal massive worldwide (Whittaker, 2023). The section also highlights that Signal is the safest chap app to send/receive nudes (Coding Rights, 2016).

Fact-Checking Platforms: To highlight the spread of dis/misinformation, this section presents the main fact-checking platforms available in Portugal. It discusses how to overcome dis/misinformation barriers by enhancing digital skills and competencies from the early educational age. Most of them narrate situations on how they check if the information is accurate or not. The section also points out the importance of accessing the library of the school.

Digital Colonialism: The idea of this section is to show and critically discuss the so-called Map of Internet Territories to illustrate the physical and geopolitical dimensions of the Internet structure (Varon et al., 2022). According to the authors of this project, the use of the term "cloud" refers to an imaginary technology that exists in the absence of a place or territory, something immaterial, abstract, timeless, and apolitical. But when the materialization of the cloud reaches different countries, the power relations become visible, from the physical infrastructure layer to the sphere of algorithmic decisions. In practice, oppressive relations, practices of digital colonialism, and establishment of monopolies are evident when students look at the map (Couldry & Mejias, 2018; Ghai et al., 2022). From the lens of the cartographic activity of the discipline geography, this section takes into account that situating where the students fit in all its dimensions of intersectionality such as gender, sexuality, race, class, ethnicity, culture, and nationality also matters in their relationship with the technology. Varon et al (2022) show that the Internet is a contested territory. To dispute it, it is necessary to know its dynamics through an engaged process of pedagogy. In addition, the map serves as a tool to kick-off conversations about digital colonialism and the role of technologies in the climate and socio-environmental justice debate.

Digital Literacy Gamified: In this section, we play the Go Viral! game (Go! Viral Game). The tutor shows how through ludic strategies the game helps to understand misinformation. In fact, Go Viral! nurture participants against COVID-19 misinformation, while highlighting the most common strategies used to spread false and misleading information about the virus. The idea is that young people will be able to fight dis/misinformation the next time they came across online (Hertwig & Grune-Yanoff, 2017). People who share misinformation often believe the information they are sharing is accurate (Wardle & Derakhshan, 2017). Lastly, it starts a small talk about Inoculation as psychological tool to prevent misinformation; in other words, it is a preemptive intervention that exposes people to a weakened form of common disinformation and/or manipulation strategies in order to build up their ability to resist misinformation and manipulation (Kumpulainen et al., 2020).

Roda de Conversa: The last section entitled "roda de conversa" shows a digital collage (Fig. 1) to conclude the pedagogical seminar, while generating food for thought. COVID-19 pandemic has revealed the depth of how important is to be online and how digital environments are becoming more and more complex. Globally, 71% of young people aged between 15 and 24 use the Internet (Global Connectivity Report, 2022), far more than any other age group, and in every country for which data are available, they are more likely to use the Internet than the rest of the population. By picking up one of the pictures shown in the digital collage, each student narrates an episode within the platforms and we promote a roda de conversation.

Fig. 1 Digital collage. *Source* Xanthe Dobbie Harriet (2018) still from the series "Wallpaper Queens"

6 Discussion

The data discussed here is derived from the own author's teaching experience. #DLPS provided both a reflection to activate youth generation through a bottom-up educational process, as well as foster digital literacy as key competence. The discussion sheds light on how young people responded to the #DLPS sessions, mediated by various stakeholders—educators, teachers, school community, and academic tutors. #DLPS concern is precisely to inform the challenges to discuss how "new media, particularly social networking sites, gives all of us, including young people, opportunities to share our civic identity and to connect with others about civic issues" (Christian, 2020: 244). After all, youth participants acquired critical skills by fostering a culture of engagement and critical discourse. Most of the young participants reported having smartphones and proved to be active users of social media platforms, which facilitated the curiosity about the topic discussion. Youth have been aware to share interesting doubts and pave the ways to engage during the seminars.

The pedagogical format of the seminar connected the knowledge acquired through the digital literacy initiative in which youth establish an intermittent dialogue to recognize and promote their agency. From this point of view, how can the lessons learned from the pedagogical initiative contribute to ignite even more intervention of Portuguese young people on this topic? What may change in participants' view of everyday digital life after this experience? The initiative not only fostered interactive and participatory approaches, but also revealed to be a pilot test to implement pedagogical activities at the school level. In other words: a bottom-up educational initiative to encourage young people to booster alternative solutions, thus paving a new orientation toward a fair digital ecosystem led by youth (Adjin-Tettey, 2022). In fact, digital literacy initiatives have become a key tool for education mainly after the COVID-19 pandemic. To understand how this influence processes occur, we should also look at how young people behave after the pedagogical session moments.

Young people did not choose intentionally to become passive users of platforms, however, the unpredictable, ongoing changes and transformations that participants created during these sessions served as a clue to keep them in the loop to be well informed about current opportunities and perils of platforms. The pedagogical initiative reveals that young participants are more and more curious about their personal interests and less about the issue of readjusting and qualifying their practice experience through platforms. On the other hand, the seminar promotes an engaged way to self-reflect about their everyday routine with digital platforms. It inaugurated a creative way to adapt the teaching curricula through participatory pedagogy. It advocates a new format of a teaching format, beyond the need to rely only on technological literacy as end-user. Here, digital literacy and participatory education combined foster a pedagogy to combat oppressive power structures—digital colonization, algorithmic violence, gender violence, class divides, and racism, among other forms of violence (Calzati, 2021), as well as to support cross-sector collaboration and new models for exchange on how to transgress the geopolitical power of the GAMAM. At the same time, the interrogation of platform dominance played in the Global North means also to be ready to overcome barriers of disinformation, while enhancing digital skills and competences from an early educational age.

#DLPS articulated educative, practice and accessible communication on the (digital) relationship since the advent of the Internet and related social media platforms (Marres, 2017; Baym, 2015). In this sense, #DLPS launched pedagogical instruments through an "engaged" approach (Milan, 2010), whereby the needs and values of promoting digital literacy educational initiatives become an integral part of the young people agenda which indicates an effort to social inquiry, making a difference for the community under study. It is noteworthy that digital literacy is not restricted to an open manner and training skills for the digital age (European Union, 2019). More than that: it is a *continuum* educative process of communication through which time to time, it is needed to be adapted and updated to target and nurture the digital skilled generation of young people, while to make them possible agents of intervention, presenting their points of view and their perspectives toward others, challenging themselves. It opens creative imaginaries after a discussion based on pedagogical approaches by and for young people.

In addition, #DLPS has been boosted by critical warnings about the use of platforms, considering that "rethinking democracy in the social media age must be multifaceted, thoughtful, collaborative and evidence-based" (Margetts, 2019: 120). In fact, the boundaries of public and private young people's engagement on platforms are most of the times very blurred (Boyd, 2014; Common Sense Media, 2012; Cortesi et al., 2020). Based on the #DLPS initiative, Table 2 suggests the following policy recommendations to the Portuguese government, European Commission, and European Parliament:

7   Moving Forward: Toward Pluriversal Pedagogies in a Postdigital Future

This chapter presented Digital Literacy Pedagogical Sessions (#DLPS) as a pedagogical tool to foster public values community practices, as well as to promote a critical understanding of the digital society in which young people are increasingly immersed. At the same time, it promotes the critical capacity to distinguish the quality and accuracy of information conveyed, particularly highly disseminated on and through platform ecosystem. Thus, if no concrete policy intervention is implemented to address the spread of false information, we will likely witness an increased denial of scientific expertise, reduced adherence to vaccinations among everyday citizens, and escalating political polarization on a global level (Roozenbeek et al., 2022). This process leads to the erosion of democratic values through the distortion of the public debate and numerous disinformation campaigns (Donovan & Wardle, 2020).

Many educational programs have already been established based on for-profit values under GAMAM group (van Dijck et al., 2018). However, in the context of

Table 2 Policy recommendations

Digital literacy public policies	Support and encourage the creation of national digital literacy initiatives as mandatory components of educational curricula, with long-term goals, evaluation metrics, and respective action plans, financed by European funds. In all member countries, the school curricula should integrate a digital literacy education course in which students are required to develop all dimensions of critical digital analysis and fact-checking platforms Integration of digital literacy in teacher training curricula, as well as more possibilities for in-service teacher training. Therefore, the focus needs to be not only on technological literacy as end-user, but also on digital literacy approach embodied in everyday routine of school community Improvement of an EU's digital literacy index for each member country in order to bring Europe closer to its neighbors, with evaluation criteria co-created by the school community and youth, adapted to each European country Participation of future generations in the processes of anticipatory governance of media accessibility. Ensuring youth participation in the processes of construction and public consultation of the EU legal framework for digital literacy
Dissemination of accurate news at the school community level	Massive campaigns to disseminate accurate information: tackle bad content uploaded on social media platforms with accurate information. Local authorities should promote the revitalization of young people's democratic agency at the core of society Spread accurate messages adapted to school-level contexts: flows of messages depend on socio-historical conditions, including local, social, cultural, political, geographical, and historical incorporated contexts. Local government, for instance, could work side-by-side with community schools supervised by engaged educators and experts on social media platforms Disseminate content on social media platforms in the form of videos, audio messages, and posts to enhance youth public trust in scientific expertise

the European Year of Youth (2022), the chapter suggests a two-pronged innovative approach. First, we should rethink and update traditional methods of developing and implementing digital literacy initiatives by undertaking three core practical actions: (i) returning to democratic principles by positioning young people as a central component of society, thereby fostering digital literacy initiatives at primary schools; (ii) empowering young people to act as promoters of human agency from an earlier educational level and (iii) avoiding the limitation of knowledge to a select group of experts, and instead promoting a recursive, iterative, transdisciplinary, and pedagogical process that engages young people, better informing them about their roles regarding the opportunities and risks of a platform society. Second, while exploring creative ways to disseminate new pedagogical formats, we should reinvent how governments and public authorities engage with young people. Academic experts could post training content on platforms using creative videos and short messages, ensuring that accurate information is accessible and adaptable to young people (Spurava & Kotilainen, 2022).

Far from providing a comprehensive pedagogical agenda, this chapter serves as a starting proposal for an innovative educational curriculum that integrates digital literacy into mandatory subjects such as geography, history, chemistry, physics, and math at the school level. This approach aims to better nurture young people and inform them about the spread of inaccurate content during turbulent political times (Margetts et al., 2016), while implementing best practices to combat polarization today. In conclusion, policy recommendations should be grounded in the everyday practices of young people as agents of social intervention and promoters of critical consciousness. Only through this approach can pluriversal pedagogical paths be co-designed by and for young people at the community level in a post-digital future (Escobar, 2018; Macgilchrist et al., 2024; Zakharova & Jarke, 2022). Future research should focus on improving #DLPS as a pedagogical platform through co-design (Costanza-Chock, 2020) and co-teaching (Pfeifer & Jovicic, 2023).

Acknowledgements This chapter is based upon work from COST Action CA19142—Leading Platform for European Citizens, Industries, Academia and Policymakers in Media Accessibility (LEAD-ME) supported by COST (European Cooperation in Science and Technology).

References

Adjin-Tettey, T. D. (2022). Combating fake news, disinformation, and misinformation: Experimental evidence for media literacy education. *Cogent Arts and Humanities, 9*, 1.

Barbosa, S., & Back, C. (2020). The dark side of Brazilian "WhatsAppers". In J. Sabariego, A. J. do Amaral, E. B. Carvalho Salles (org.), *Algoritarismos. Tirant lo Blanch: São Paulo-Valencia* (pp. 454–467). Brasil, Valencia.

Barbosa, S., & Milan, S. (2019). Do not harm in private chat apps: Ethical issues for research on and with WhatsApp. *Westminster Papers in Communication and Culture, 14*(1), 49–65. https://doi.org/10.16997/wpcc.313

Barbosa, S. (2020). COMUNIX WhatsAppers: The community school in Portugal and Spain. *Political Studies Review,* 1–8.

Baym, N. K. (2015). *Personal connections in the digital age. Digital media and society series.* Polity Press.

Boyd, D. (2014). *It's complicated: The social lives of networked teens.* Yale University Press.

Calzati, S. (2021). Decolonizing "data colonialism" propositions for investigating the Realpolitik of today's networked ecology. *Television and New Media Studies, 22*(8), 914–929.

Christian, S. E. (2020). *Everyday media literacy. An analogue guide for your digital life.* Routledge.

Coding Rights. (2016). *Safer nudes.* Available at https://codingrights.org/en/project-item/safer-nudes-2/. Access on 21 February.

Common Sense Media. (2012). *Social media, social life: How teens view their digital lives.* Retrieved from https://www.commonsensemedia.org/research/social-media-social-life-how-teens-view-their-digital-lives

Cortesi, S. C., Hasse, A., Lombana-Bermudez, A., Kim, S., Gasser U. (2020). Youth and digital citizenship+ (plus): Understanding skills for a digital world. The Berkman Klein Center for Internet and Society at Harvard University.

Costanza-Chock, S. (2020). *Design justice: Community-led practices to build the worlds we need.* MIT Press.

Couldry, N., & Mejias, U. (2018). Data colonialism: Rethinking big data's relation to the contemporary subject. *Television and New Media, 20*(4), 1–14.

Dobbie, X. (2018). *Harriet 'Wallpaper Queens' digital collage.* Available at https://xanthedob bie.wixsite.com/wallpaperqueens/gallery?pgid=kbt8isof-08340db5-b08a-4c21-a21f-784402 28f154 Access on: 21st March 2024

Donovan, J., & Wardle, C. (2020). Misinformation is everybody's problem now. Social Science Research Council.

Ermoshina, K., & Musiani, F. (2019). "Standardising by running code": The Signal protocol and defacto standardisation in end-to-end encrypted messaging. *Internet Histories, 3*(3–4), 343–363.

Escobar, A. (2018). *Designs for the Pluriverse. Radical interdependence, autonomy, and the making of worlds.* Duke University Press.

European Commission. (2018). Action plan against disinformation. https://www.eeas.europa.eu/node/54866_en

European Union. (2019). Policy and investment recommendation for trustworthy AI. https://ec.eur opa.eu/digital-single-market/en/news/policy-and-investmentrecommendations-trustworthy-art ificial-intelligence

Freire, P. (1968). *Pedagogy of the oppressed.* Heder & Herder.

Ghai, S., Magis-Weinberg, L., Stoilova, M., Livingstone, S., & Orben, A. (2022). Social media and adolescent well-being in the Global South. *Current Opinion in Psychology, 46*, 101318.

Gillespie, T. (2010). The politics of 'platforms.' *New Media and Society, 12*(3), 347–364.

Global Connectivity Report. (2022). Available at https://www.itu.int/itu-d/reports/statistics/global-connectivity-report-2022/. Accessed 21 February 2024.

Go! Viral Game. Available at https://www.goviralgame.com/en. Accessed on 21 February.

Helmond, A. (2015). The platformization of the web: Making web data platform ready. *Social Media + Society, 1*(2), 1–11.

Hertwig, R., & Grune-Yanoff, T. (2017). Nudging and boosting: steering or empowering good decisions. *Perspectives on Pyschological Science*, 1–14.

Hintz, A., Dencik, L., & Wahl-Jorgensen, K. (2018). *Digital citizenship in a datafied society.* Polity Press.

Howard, P. N. (2020). *Lie machines: How to save democracy from troll armies, deceitful robots, junk news operations, and political operatives.* Yale University Press.

Kumpulainen, K., Kajamaa, A., Leskinen, J., Byman, J., & Renlund, J. (2020). Mapping digital competence: students' maker literacies in a school's makerspace. *Frontiers in Education, 5*, 69.

Livingstone, S. (2004). Media literacy and the challenge of new information and communication technologies. *The Communication Review, 7*(1), 3–14.

Macgilchrist, F., Allert, H., & Cerratto Pargman, T., et al. (2024). Designing postdigital futures: Which designs? Whose futures? *Postdigital in Scientific Education, 6*, 13–24.

Margetts, H. (2019). Rethinking democracy with social media. *The Political Quarterly, 90*, 107–123.

Margetts, H., John, P., Hale, S., & Yasseri, T. (2016). *Political turbulence: How social media shape collective action.* Princeton University Press.

Markham, A. N. (2019). Critical pedagogy as a response to datafication. *Qualitative Inquiry, 25*(8), 754–760. https://doi.org/10.1177/1077800418809470

Marres, N. (2017). *Digital sociology.* Polity Press.

Masterman, L. (1985). *Teaching the media.* Routledge.

Milan, S. (2010). Towards an epistemology of engaged research. *International Journal of Communication, 4*(2010), 856–858.

Milan, S., & Barbosa, S. (2020). Enter the WhatsApper: Reinventing digital activism at the time of chat apps. *First Monday, 25*(12).

Musiani, F., & Ermoshina, K. (2017). What is a good secure messaging tool? The EFF secure messaging scorecard and the shaping of digital (usable) security. *Westminster Papers in Communication and Culture, 12*(3), 51–71.

Pfeifer, S., & Jovicic, S. (2023). Co-teaching postdigital ethnography. *CRC Media of Cooperation Working Paper Series* No. 34 November.

Reuters. (2022). Reuters Institute digital news report 2022. University of Oxford. Available at https://reutersinstitute.politics.ox.ac.uk/digital-news-report/2022. Accessed 10 December 2022.

Roozenbeek et al. (2022). Psycological inoculation improves resilience against misinformation on social media. *Scientific Advance 8*, eabo6254.

Sefton-Green, J. (2021). Towards platform pedagogies: Why thinking about digital platforms as pedagogic devices might be useful. *Discourse: Studies in the Cultural Politics of Education.* https://doi.org/10.1080/01596306.2021.1919999

Spurava, G., & Kotilainen, S. (2022). Young people as empirical experts of participatory research in the age of information disorder. *Media, Technology and Life-Long Learning, 18*, 1.

Tygel, A. F., & Kirsch, R. (2016). Contributions of Paulo Freire to a critical data literacy: A popular education approach. *The Journal of Community Informatics, 12*(3), 108–121.

van Dijck, J. (2009). Users like me. *new media & Society*, 1–19.

van Dijck, J. (2013). *The culture of connectivity: a critical history of social media.* Oxford, UK: Oxford University Press.

van Dijck, J. (2014). *The culture of Connectivity. A critical history of social media.* Oxford.

van Dijck, J. (2020). Seeing the forest for the trees: Visualizing platformization and its governance. *New Media & Society*, 1–19.

van Dijck, J., Poell, T., de Wall, M. (2018). *The platform society: Public values in a connective world.* Oxford.

Varon, J., et al. (2022). *Map of internet territories.* Available at https://www.cartografiasdainternet.org/en. Accessed 21 February 2024.

Wardle, C., & Derakhshan, H. (2017). Information disorder: Toward an interdisciplinary framework for research and policy making. *Report to the Council of Europe.*

West, S. M. (2019). Data capitalism: Redefining the logics of surveillance and privacy. *Business and Society, 58*(1), 20–41.

Whittaker, M. (2023). Building muscle in infrastructure. In: Cath, C. (Ed.), *Eaten by the Internet.* Meatspace Press.

Zakharova, I., & Jarke, J. (2022). Educational technologies as matters of care. *Learning, Media and Technology, 47*(1), 95–108.

Zuboff, S. (2019). *The age of surveillance capitalism: The fight for a human future at the new frontier of power.* Profile Books.

Exploring the Potential of Media Accessibility as a Pedagogical Tool: Students as Audio Describers

Marta Brescia-Zapata⊙ **and Sarah McDonagh**⊙

Abstract There is growing recognition of Media Accessibility as an educational asset in the classroom. More specifically, recent research has demonstrated its potential as a didactic tool for foreign language learning (Bausells-Espín in J Audiovis Transl 5(2):152–75, 2022; Talaván in Int J English Stud 19:21–40, 2019) and developing students' speaking, intercultural and digital literacy skills (Khanlou et al. in J Dev Phys Dis 33:1–25, 2021). In this chapter, we will focus on the creation of non-professional audio description (AD) by secondary students as part of a workshop carried out at Ítaca campus in Barcelona, Spain. During the workshops, students were asked to design and create an accessible, immersive story using the GreenVerse platform, developed as part of the GreenSCENT project (Smart Citizen Engagement for a Green Future, Nº 101036480). We begin this chapter locating this research within the growing body of work on the use of Media Accessibility as a pedagogical tool (Black in J Audiovis Transl 5:73–93, 2022; Herrero and Escobar in Transl Translanguaging Multilingual Contexts 4:30–54, 2018; Talaván in Int J Engl Stud 19:21–40, 2019), arguing the case for its integration in the classroom. We will then present the workshop methodology, followed by an analysis and comparison of the AD created by students. This analysis will assess where and how the AD aligns with or deviates from established guidelines and best practices, specifically following the ADLAB project recommendations (Remael et al. in *ADLAB audio description guidelines*, 2014) for English and the UNE 153020 Standard (AENOR, 2005) for Spanish. Our results show that students deviated from established guidelines in the areas of content selection, with students more prone to include evaluative statements in their ADs, owing to the purpose of the task at hand and students' unfamiliarity with AD norms and conventions.

Keywords Media accessibility · Language acquisition · Digital literacy · New technologies · Non-professional audio description

M. Brescia-Zapata (✉) · S. McDonagh
Universitat Autònoma de Barcelona, Barcelona, Spain
e-mail: Marta.Brescia@uab.cat

S. McDonagh
e-mail: SarahAnne.Mcdonagh@uab.cat

A. Marcus-Quinn et al. (eds.), *Transforming Media Accessibility in Europe*,
https://doi.org/10.1007/978-3-031-60049-4_18

1   Introduction

Media Accessibility (MA) refers to the practice of ensuring media content, such as films, television programmes, cultural events, videos, and online content are accessible to a wide range of people, including people with disabilities. As a research discipline, MA has grown to encompass a broad range of modalities that include, but are not limited to, audio description (AD), subtitling, sign language interpreting, easy-to-read, and different research contexts, such as archives (McDonagh & Aguiar, forthcoming) and the metaverse (Zallio & Clarkson, 2022). In recent years, MA has come to be recognised as a valuable educational tool in the classroom to develop students' linguistic, intercultural, and digital skills (Black, 2022) as well as offer the opportunity to create accessible content such as AD and captions (McDonagh & Brescia-Zapata, 2023). More recent initiatives have drawn professionals and non-professionals together to create access to cultural experiences, such as opera (Matamala & Orero, 2022) and theatre (Di Giovanni, 2018).

Taking this as our starting point, in this chapter, we will focus on the creation of non-professional AD by secondary students as part of workshops carried out during Ítaca campus in Barcelona, Spain. Students were asked to design and create an accessible, immersive story using the GreenVerse platform, developed as part of the GreenSCENT project (Smart Citizen Engagement for a Green Future, Nº 101036480). Drawing on AD guidelines and best practice in English and Spanish, we will assess the AD created by Ítaca students, examining where and how they differed or aligned to them. We begin this chapter with a broad overview of the field of AD, its prevailing norms and practices. We then follow this with a discussion of AD guidelines in both English and Spanish, before moving on to explore AD's application in immersive environments and its potential as a pedagogical tool in the classroom. In Sect. 3, we present the methodology followed in the workshops, after which we report on the main results in Sect. 4, highlighting where and how the students' ADs aligned or indeed deviated from established AD guidelines in both English and Spanish. Finally, we close this chapter with a discussion of ideas for future research, with a specific focus on the didactic potential of AD in the classroom and its future application in immersive media.

2   State of the Art

Traditionally, AD has been viewed as a service specifically designed to cater to the needs of blind and partially blind individuals, enabling them to engage with audiovisual content through a supplementary description of the essential visual components of a work of art or media product (Remael et al., 2014). Conceived as complementary to the primary audio track or physical object, the audio describer is tasked with creating an AD that fills in important gaps in visual information, ensuring that the content is accessible to those who cannot rely solely on sight. The overall success of an AD rests on how the translation of visual information into words is handled and conveyed by the audio describer (Taylor, 2014, p. 42). Through their choice of words and vocal delivery, the audio describer can transform a media product or work of art from dull and uninspired to engaging and immersive for users.

Over the years and as AD has matured as a field, a comprehensive body of guidelines and best practices has emerged to guide its effective implementation across diverse domains, including, but not limited to, traditional media such as film and television (ITC, 2000; Remael et al., 2014; Netflix, 2023), theatrical productions (Snyder, 2010), and museums (Neves, 2014). As the field of AD has grown, practitioners and researchers have refined their guidance accordingly to encompass a broad spectrum of diversity and identity-related concerns (Hutchinson et al., 2020). Taking as reference research by Rai et al. (2010) and Matamala and Orero (2013), we compiled a list of the main regulations, standards, and guidelines on AD that are relevant for our study (in English and Spanish), which are presented in Table 1.

In regard to *what* to describe, most guidelines and best practices advise audio describers to refrain from overly subjective descriptions, emphasising the need for impartiality. According to Snyder (2010), a prominent advocate for objectivity in AD, the audio describer should refrain from including their personal opinions into their work:

> The best audio describer is sometimes referred to as a 'verbal camera lens', objectively recounting visual aspects of an event. Qualitative judgements get in the way; they constitute a subjective interpretation on the part of the describer and are unnecessary and unwanted. (2010, p. 43)

In line with Snyder's recommendation, most industry guidelines and professional standards advise against overtly subjective descriptions (Rai et al., 2010). Notably, in the UK, the ITC Guidance on Standards for Audio Description (2000) cautions audio describers to carefully consider their choice of adjectives when describing a scene, ensuring that their description does not include their personal opinion or interpretation:

> A few well-chosen words can enhance a scene considerably, but they must not reflect the personal view of the describer'. (2000, p. 20)

According to the Spanish UNE 153020 Standard (AENOR, 2005, pp. 7–8), audio describers are advised to use appropriate vocabulary, carefully place descriptive units, and consider the sequential importance of the dramatic action and visual elements. The standard also mandates a stylistic finesse characterised by linguistic fluency, syntactic simplicity, and the avoidance of subjective nuances. These criteria aim to ensure the objectivity of AD, providing a comprehensive and neutral portrayal of visual content for diverse audiences. However, as highlighted by Orero (2005) and Orero and Wharton (2007), the Spanish UNE 153020 Standard is unclear and ambiguous in certain aspects on how to elaborate an AD. Font Bisier (2023) further emphasises the need for an update to meet current accessibility needs. For instance, the standard recommends using appropriate language, yet lacks a clear definition of what is meant by 'appropriate.' It also introduces some contradictions; while

Table 1 Summary of regulations, standards, and guidelines in English- and Spanish-speaking countries

Country	Regulation	Standards, guidelines, and recommendations
Australia	**Broadcasting services act** (2018)	**Audio description background paper** (Mikul, 2010)
Canada	**Broadcasting act** (2018)	**Descriptive video production and presentation of best practices guide for digital environments** (Miligan & Fels, 2013) **Described video best practices. Artistic and technical guideline** (Accessible Media Inc and The Canadian Association of Broadcasters, 2014)
EU	**Directive of coordination of audiovisual services among the member states** (Audiovisual Media Services Directive, 2010)	**ADLAB project** (Remael, 2014)
Ireland	**Broadcasting act** (2009)	**Broadcast authority of ireland guidelines audio description** (Broadcast Authority of Ireland, 2012)
Spain	**Law on general audiovisual communication** (2015) **Law 10/2005 on urgent measures for the stimulation of digital terrestrial television, of the liberation of cable television and the encouragement of pluralism** (2005)	**Audio description for people with visual impairment. Requirements for the audio description and creation of audio guides** (AENOR, 2005)
United Kingdom	**Equality act** (2010)	**ITC guidance on standards for audio description** (2000) **Code on television access services** (Office of Communications, 2017) **Audio description guidelines** (O'Hara, n.d)

(continued)

Table 1 (continued)

Country	Regulation	Standards, guidelines, and recommendations
United States of America	**Twenty-first century communications and video accessibility** (2010) **and video description: implementation of the twenty-first century communications and video accessibility act of 2010** (2017) **Rehabilitation act** (1973) **NY state accessibility policy** (2010)	**Audio description guidelines and best practices American Council of the Blind's audio description project** (Snyder, 2010) **Audio description style guide v2.5** (Netflix, 2023)
International		**Technical report: part 5: final report of activities: working group B 'audio/video description and spoken captions'** (International Telecommunication Union, 2013)

emphasising neutrality and objectivity, it concurrently suggests adapting information to the type of work. This tension between objectivity and subjectivity is echoed in the broader discourse around AD scriptwriting.

As other researchers and practitioners argue, while objectivity is a desirable goal, it is ultimately unattainable due to the intuitive nature of AD scriptwriting, which draws on the audio describer's own personal interpretation of a scene or artwork (Holland, 2009; Orero, 2008, p. 180). In the light of this inherent subjectivity, recent research has challenged the notion of absolute objectivity in AD, instead promoting alternative versions of AD that depart from established norms (Mazur & Chmiel, 2012a, 2012b). These alternative approaches embrace subjectivity in scene description and include information about the film language when pertinent (Netflix, 2023). In some instances, alternative accessible filmmaking techniques have emerged as viable alternatives to traditional AD, offering a more immersive and personalised experience for audiences (Lopez et al., 2020, 2021). Work undertaken by the *Enhancing Audio Description* project (2024), for example, demonstrated the potential of enhanced sound design and integrated audio features, such as binaural sound, to serve as a supplement or even substitute for traditional AD (Lopez et al., 2020, 2021). These shifts in approaches have emerged alongside increased collaborations between AD professionals and filmmakers and artistic directors (Romero-Fresco, 2022; Romero-Fresco & Chaume, 2022), which, in turn, have helped foster a more nuanced approach to AD, one that embraces the perspectives of both the audio describer and the creators of the content they describe. Disabled artists and researchers, who have long championed inclusive practices (Cavallo, 2015; Thompson & Warne, 2018), also have come to play an increasing important role in this evolving landscape, offering valuable insights and experiences that have helped shape new norms and conventions for AD, ensuring that it better reflects the diverse needs of its audiences (Romero-Fresco & Dangerfield, 2022).

Despite the growing body of AD guidelines, there are still some unexplored areas of study, particularly the application of AD in immersive media. In contrast to 2D media, where AD is normally delivered in between dialogues (Jankowska, 2015), AD for immersive media, such as 360 videos, requires a more dynamic and adaptable approach to adapt to the unique nature of the content. This presents a unique set of challenges for the audio describer, such as issues related to fixation and interactivity. In 360 videos, the viewer can freely rotate their virtual viewpoint, which presents a dynamic and ever-changing visual field. If the AD is too fixated on a single element, it may fail to capture the broader context and richness of the 360 medium. As an example, an emerging interactive medium that places a growing emphasis on accessibility is video games (Larreina-Morales & Mangirón, 2023). Addressing the challenge of interactivity involves integrating AD with screen readers and sound cues that align with the specific game mechanics.

While AD standards and guidelines in established media platforms like television and film have made significant progress, comparable guidelines for emerging media, such as immersive environments, are still lacking (Fidyka & Matamala, 2018). Recognising this gap, the ImAc (Immersive Accessibility) project (2017–2020) conducted a series of focus groups and experiments to explore the integration of AD into immersive environments. These experiments focussed on two key aspects: how to integrate AD into a 360 immersive environment and address the technical and production considerations for their successful implementation. In focus group discussions with audio describers, a key challenge identified was content selection in 360 environment. Researchers also assessed the preferences of end users, finding that they desired a balance of AD approaches. While describing the main action was essential, end users also appreciated description of visual details that enhanced their overall understanding and immersion within the 360 environment. To further enhance orientation and immersion, researchers suggested adding auditory cues, such as directional sound effect and spatial audio techniques, to provide end users with additional information about their position within the 360 environment, making it easier to navigate and appreciate the immersive experience (Fidyka & Matamala, 2018).

AD has not only evolved to suit new media environments but has also extended its reach into various fields such as education, emerging as a valuable pedagogical tool in the classroom (Kleege & Wallin, 2015). Similar to subtitles for the deaf and hard of hearing (Talaván, 2019), AD has been used to develop student's close visual reading skills, enhance their writing and critical thinking, and raise their awareness of the lived experiences of blindness[1] (Kleege & Wallin, 2015). In their research involving university students, Kleege and Wallin (2015) found AD to be an effective pedagogical tool for enhancing students' engagement and critical analysis skills. Through a series of practical exercises, they demonstrated AD's ability to foster student awareness of visual media and encourage critical examination of visual communication.

---

[1] In line with Kleege and Wallin (2015), we have chosen the term 'blindness' to refer to the broad range of visual disabilities and non-normative ways of not seeing.

Despite its recognised pedagogical value, AD's application in immersive environments has not yet been fully realised in the classroom. Seeking to remedy this critical oversight, the following sections present the methodology and results of AD workshops we conducted with secondary students using the immersive storytelling platform GreenVerse.

3 Research Methodology

This section details the methodology followed during the workshops and presents the GreenVerse platform used by the students to create their immersive stories. It also reports on the recruitment of participants for this study, which adhered to the ethical procedures as approved by the UAB ethical committee. In total, two workshops were carried out with four groups of students who took part in the Ítaca campus initiative, which seeks to promote the use of Catalan among secondary school students in the region of Catalonia (Ítaca, n.d.).

3.1 GreenVerse Platform

As previously described by McDonagh and Brescia-Zapata (2023), the GreenVerse platform is an interactive 360 storytelling platform created and developed as part of the GreenSCENT project. The platform allows users to create multimedia narratives, integrating static images, 2D non-immersive videos and 360 videos, and a blend of text and audio. Figure 1 illustrates the current landing page of the GreenVerse platform.

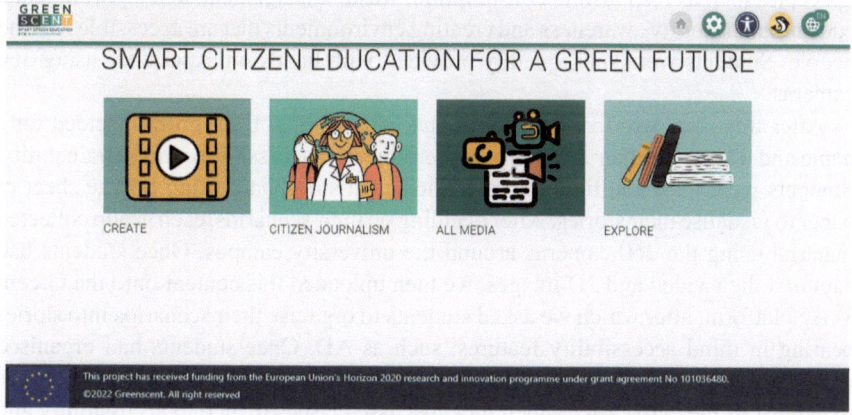

Fig. 1 Screenshot from the GreenVerse landing page

At the time of the workshop in July 2023, the platform was in its Beta version, with some bugs in the system. The workshop therefore served two purposes, to provide researchers with the opportunity to develop an educational workshop on audio description with secondary school students with a particular emphasis on sustainability, and for researchers to test the GreenVerse platform with potential end users, whose results fed back into the design process.

3.2 Workshop Participants

A total of two workshops were held, which involved students, aged between 15 and 16 years old, who were part of the Ítaca campus initiative. In total, 16 of students participated in the workshops, divided into four groups of 3–5 students each. Prior to the workshop, most students were unaware of MA, with little to no experience in creating accessibility features, such as AD, in either traditional or immersive media.

3.3 Design of Workshop

Each workshop followed a similar procedure, comprising ten steps, as illustrated in Fig. 2. Firstly, we introduced ourselves to students using self-descriptions. After this, we introduced the GreenSCENT project, as well as the GreenVerse platform. This introduction served as the foundation for the workshop's exploration of the interconnections between the concepts of AD and sustainability through immersive media. Using the example of the GreenVerse platform, students were introduced to the concepts of immersive media and asked to create their own 360 stories that addressed issues related to sustainability and accessibility. This involved exploring facets of both concepts, such as responsible consumption, waste management, and environmental education, disability awareness and creating environments that are accessible to blind people. Students were subsequently provided with hands-on experience using 360 cameras.

After this step, we divided the students into groups. Each group decided on a name and a topic for their 360 story on the subject of accessibility and sustainability. Students were allocated time to create their own storyboard using a large sheet of paper to visualise their stories. After deciding on their scenarios, each group collected material using the 360 cameras around the university campus. Once students had captured their video and 2D images, we then uploaded this content onto the Green-Verse platform, after which we asked students to organise their scenarios into stories bearing in mind accessibility features, such as AD. Once students had organised their stories and recorded and uploaded their AD, they then presented their stories to the rest of the class, after which they discussed issues related to accessibility and sustainability.

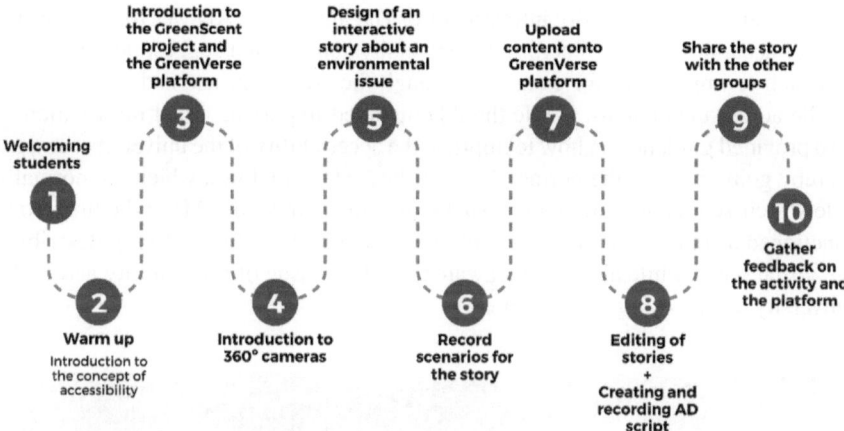

Fig. 2 Workshop workflow

To maximise the overall learning experiences for students, we deliberately withheld information about the prevailing AD norms and guidelines. Instead, we encouraged students to create their own ADs, bearing in mind the potential needs of the end user. The rationale behind this decision was driven by three key considerations. Firstly, Ítaca workshops were practical in nature, so a theoretical discussion about guidelines and standards was out of the scope. Secondly, time constraints prevented a comprehensive introduction to the intricacies of established AD guidelines. Finally, as educators, we were interested in observing how students, with no prior experience of AD, might approach this practice. Understanding where and how they might align or deviate from established AD norms constituted one of the main aims of our research.

4 Analysis

4.1 Student Stories

Due to the open and unrestricted nature of the task, each student group approached it differently. A common practice across all groups was that AD scripts were firstly written in Spanish and later translated into different languages, depending on the language ability of the group. This offered students the opportunity to practice their writing and speaking in languages other than Spanish, including Catalan, English, French, and German.

Group 1 focussed on accessibility barriers across the campus for blind students, highlighting the lack of accessible resources in the library, cafeteria, multimedia rooms, and overall university infrastructure. The aim of this AD was to raise awareness of accessibility issues across the university campus and suggest possible ways in which to improve it, for example, through the consistent use and placement of braille across the campus. While the AD included important visual information, it also provided guidance on how to improve the accessibility of the university campus, thereby going beyond the norms of established AD guidelines, which are normally solely focussed on describing the visual scene. In contrast, the AD of the first group functioned as both an informative and operative text type (Reiss, 1981), describing the visual scene while also raising awareness of the issue of accessibility across the university campus (Fig. 3 and Table 2).

Fig. 3 Screenshot from scene 1 in the story created by Group 1

Table 2 Audio descriptions by Group 1

Scene	EN	ES
1	In the library, there are not a lot of resources for the blinds. There are some possible solutions, for example: put texts in braille	En la biblioteca hay muy pocos recursos para los ciegos. Posibles soluciones: Poner textos en braille
2	They should put texts in braille, so the blinds could be able to throw the trash in the right side	Deberían poner textos en braille para que los ciegos puedan tirar la basura en el contenedor correcto
3	In the doors there are texts in braille and that's good but they are located in different places. A solution would be to put them in the same place	En las puertas hay letreros en braille. Esta es una buena idea, pero se encuentran en diferente sitio. Una solución es poner todos los letreros en el mismo sitio
4	A blind girl wants to go down the stairs and a boy helps her	Una chica ciega intenta bajar las escaleras y un chico la ayuda

Similar to Group 1, Group 2 focussed on providing practical solutions. However, both groups differed in their approach. While Group 1 focussed more on accessibility for university students, Group 2 placed a stronger emphasis on sustainability, specifically tailored to young children. Rather than adhering to established AD conventions, Group 2 went beyond these norms, creating a gamified approach that blended educational content with interactive elements. The group incorporated simple and creative instructions on waste disposal to educate children about sustainable practices in an engaging and interactive manner. While Group 1 provided an English and Catalan translation of their AD, Group 2 expanded their potential reach by translating their AD into French (Fig. 4 and Table 3).

Group 3 focussed their immersive story on the subject of sustainable practices, developing a series of scenarios in different locations across the university campus that showcased good and bad examples of these practices. Mirroring Group 1's approach, Group 3 translated their ADs into both English and Catalan, touching on diverse subjects such as littering, consumer habits, and transport. Group 3 focussed on education, guiding viewers through sustainable practices in a clear and informative manner in their AD, which functioned as both an informative and operative text type (Reiss, 1981). Deviating from traditional AD standards that prioritise objectivity,

Fig. 4 Screenshot from scene 1 in the story created by Group 2

Table 3 Audio descriptions by Group 2

Scene	ES
1	Para reciclar podríamos aplastar las botellas para crear juguetes
2	El cohete necesita pilas para poder despegar
3	No puedes tirar la basura al suelo porque si no el dinosaurio Eddie se enfadará contigo

Group 3 included evaluative statements, offering personal opinions and perspectives on sustainable practices. This departure from conventional AD norms reflected their willingness to engage in advocacy and encourage viewers to follow sustainable practices (Fig. 5 and Table 4).

Group 4 based their immersive story in three different locations across the university campus: the train station, library, and cafeteria. In each setting, they highlighted some sustainable practices that students could incorporate into their daily routines. At the train station, they highlighted the benefits of using a reusable travel card, instead of disposable paper tickets. This simple change, they argued, could reduce waste and contribute to a more sustainable campus. In the library, Group 4 underscored the advantages of digitising books, which could eliminate the need for physical books. Finally, at the cafeteria, they encouraged students to use reusable containers to

Fig. 5 Screenshot from scene 3 in the story created by Group 3

Table 4 Audio descriptions by Group 3

Scene	EN	ES
1	Margarita walks to the car, finishes the bottle of water, and throws it on the ground in the parking lot	Margarita camina para el coche, se acaba la botella de agua y la tira al suelo del parking
2	John is doing well because other children can use the same book and this way it doesn't take as many trees to make it	John no está haciendo bien porque otros niños pueden utilizar el mismo libro y de esta forma no se utilizan tantos árboles para poder fabricarlo
3	Two friends use the train to go to school to not contaminate so much	Dos amigos cogen el tren para ir al colegio y así no contaminan tanto el aire del planeta
4	Everyone is happy because they're taking care of the environment	Todos están felices porque están cuidando el medio ambiente

Fig. 6 Screenshot from the story created by Group 4

Table 5 Audio descriptions by Group 4

Scene	ES
1	Esta es la estación de ferrocarril de la UAB. Ahora puedes comprar una tarjeta o pagar con el teléfono para desplazarte con los ferrocarriles. Esta nueva tarjeta ayuda a reducir el consumo de papel
2	En la UAB existen muchas bibliotecas, pero cada vez se podría reducir el uso del papel y reducirlo para libros digitales
3	En cada facultad hay al menos una cafetería donde los estudiantes pueden comer a un precio muy bajo, para evitar el despilfarro de papel los estudiantes puedes traer su propio vaso de casa

help minimise the use of single-use plastics. Again, like the previous groups, Group 4 departed from traditional AD norms by incorporating evaluative statements and personal opinions, which ultimately shifted the nature of the AD into a call to action rather than simply scene description (Fig. 6 and Table 5).

4.2 Quantitative and Qualitative Data

After the workshops, a brief questionnaire designed to assess the effectiveness of the activity was sent to all participants, including students and instructors. This survey was designed by Ítaca and sought to gather insights into the participants' experiences. The completion of the questionnaire was voluntary, and the results are shown in Fig. 7.

In general, the workshops were well received by both instructors and students, who responded positively to the workshop activities and content. Both explanations

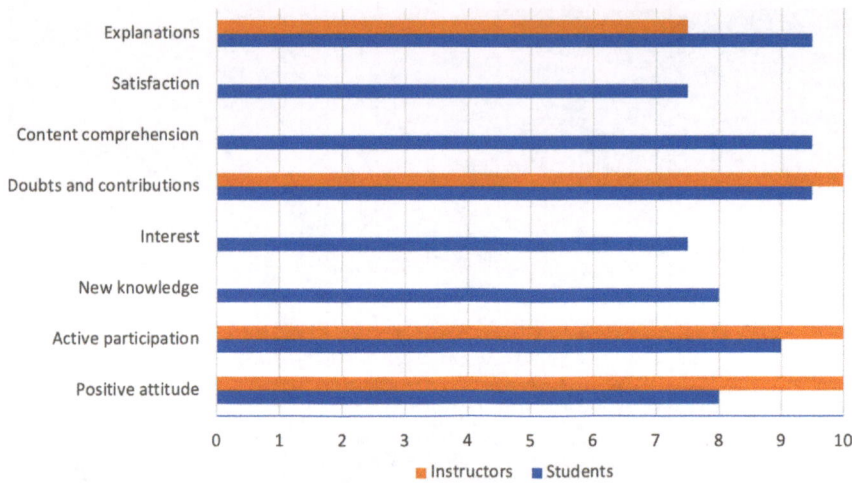

Fig. 7 Evaluation of the students and instructors who participated in the GreenSCENT activity

and content comprehension obtained similar results, indicating a satisfactory level of clarity and effectiveness of the workshops. Doubts and contributions and active participation reveal a highly participatory environment and almost perfect score. This suggests that the facilitators successfully created an atmosphere where participants felt comfortable asking questions and contributing to discussions. In this sense, positive attitude is also a critical metric for evaluating the overall learning atmosphere. Instructors maintained a perfect score of 10 out of 10, contributing to a favourable environment. Students scored the activity 8 out of 10, suggesting a generally positive attitude despite some room for improvement. While students' interest in the workshops scored 7.5 out of 10, indicating a moderate level of engagement, the lack of data from instructors limits our ability to fully assess their perceived interest level.

In summary, while Fig. 7 provides a snapshot of participants' feedback, a more comprehensive analysis involves delving deeper into the nuances of the data. The differences in scores between instructors and students, as well as the absence of certain data points, underscore the complexity of the teaching and learning dynamics. Addressing these variations and gaps is crucial for refining our approach, optimising participant experiences, and ensuring the continued success of our workshops.

5 Discussion and Conclusion

Given the inherent challenges of the 360 environment and the limited experience of workshop participants in AD practice, there were some deviations from established AD norms, specifically related to content selection. Traditional AD guidelines emphasise the importance of objectivity and neutrality (Snyder, 2010), aiming at providing a comprehensive overview of the visual content. However, in the context of immersive media, these conventions are not entirely applicable. The 360 format of immersive media presents several challenges for the audio describer, who must navigate the dynamic and interactive elements of the content. Unlike traditional 2D media, where the focus is fixed, the interactivity of 360 content makes it difficult to determine exactly what to describe. To address this challenge, workshop participants adopted a storytelling approach, focussing on their core message rather than attempting to describe every element in the visual field. The AD therefore served a specific narrative function, namely, to inform and educate the viewer on steps that they can take in their daily lives to be sustainable and accessible.

Despite the deviations from established norms, the workshops carried out as part of this study revealed the potential of AD practices to evolve in response to the changing media landscape. The storytelling approach adopted by participants not only addressed the intricacies of 360 content but also aligned with the goal of fostering engagement and awareness. This departure from strict objectivity towards a narrative-driven approach reflects an evolving landscape where the principles of AD can be adapted to meet the demands of evolving media forms.

A relevant aspect arising from the workshops was the use of translation as a means to produce ADs in multiple languages. While not a novel practice, its benefits in terms of time consumption, cost-effectiveness, and the overall quality of AD are highlighted, as noted by Jankowska (2015).

In addition to these considerations, the AD of 360 formats presents further challenges due to the abundance of visual information, surpassing that of standard AD (Fidyka & Matamala, 2018). The absence of established guidelines for AD in immersive environments underscores a critical academic gap. While some efforts have been made to understand how to integrate AD within immersive environments (Montagud et al., 2020), there is still a need for more extensive testing and research in this domain to develop guidelines and standards.

The results of the workshops reinforce the efficacy of AD as a pedagogical tool for educators. Beyond its primary role in providing accessibility, AD also enhances students' proficiency in translation, visual awareness, and storytelling techniques. Not confined to a singular purpose, AD is a valuable asset in the educational toolkit, facilitating multifaceted skill development among students.

In conclusion, our exploration of the challenges and adaptations of AD in 360 environments highlight the dynamic nature of this practice. As the landscape of immersive media continues to evolve, so too must AD principles and guidelines. This study contributes to the ongoing discourse, emphasising the need for flexible approaches and collaboration to further refine and standardise AD practices across diverse media formats.

Disclaimer This research has been partially funded by the H2020 project GreenSCENT (under Grant Agreement 101036480). The Commission's support for this publication does not contribute an endorsement of the contents, which reflects the views of the authors only, and the Commission cannot be held responsible for any use which may be made of the information contained herein. The authors are members of TransMedia Catalonia, an SGR research group funded by 'Secretaria d'Universitats I Recerca del Departament d'Empresa I Coneixement de la Generalitat de Catalunya'

(2021SGR00077). This chapter is also based upon work from COST Action CA19142—Leading Platform for European Citizens, Industries, Academia and Policymakers in Media Accessibility (LEAD-ME) supported by COST (European Cooperation in Science and Technology).

References

Accessible Media Inc. & The Canadian Association of Broadcasters. (2014). *Described video best practices. Artistic and technical guidelines.* Toronto, Canada: Accessible Media Inc.

AENOR. (2005). *Audiodescripción para personas con discapacidad visual. Requisitos para la audiodescripción y la elaboración de audioguías.* AENOR.

Audiovisual Media Services Directive. (2010). *Official journal of the european union L 95/1 (Directive 2010/13/EU).*

Bausells-Espín, A. (2022). Audio description as a pedagogical tool in the foreign language classroom: An analysis of student perceptions of difficulty, usefulness and learning progress. *Journal of Audiovisual Translation, 5*(2), 152–75. https://doi.org/10.47476/jat.v5i2.2022.208

Black, S. (2022). Subtitles as a tool to boost language learning? Children's views and experiences of watching films and television programmes in other languages with interlingual subtitles. *Journal of Audiovisual Translation, 5*(1), 73–93.

Broadcasting Act. (2018). *Official Gazette S.C. 1991,* c. 11, 12 December 2018, Ottawa, Canada.

Broadcasting Authority of Ireland. (2009). *Broadcasting Act 2009.* Retrieved from: https://www.irishstatutebook.ie/eli/2009/act/18/

Broadcasting Authority of Ireland. (2012). *Guidelines—Audio Description.* Retrieved from: https://www.bai.ie/en/codes-standards/

Broadcasting Services Act. (2018). *Official Gazette No. 110, 1992* (Compilation No. 94), 1 September 2018, Canberra, Australia.

Campus Ítaca. (n.d.). https://www.uab.cat/web/campus-itaca-1345780037226.html

Cavallo, A. (2015). Seeing the word, hearing the image: The artistic possibilities of audio description in theatrical performance. *Research in Drama Education: The Journal of Applied Theatre and Performance, 20*(1), Article 1.

Di Giovanni, E. (2018). Participatory accessibility: Creating audio description with blind and non-blind children. *Journal of Audiovisual Translation, 1*(1), 155–169.

Enhancing Audio Description. (n.d.). *About us.* https://enhancingaudiodescription.com/about/

Equality Act. (2010). *Parliament of the United Kingdom,* Chapter 15, 8 April 2010, London, United Kingdom.

Fidyka, A., & Matamala, A. (2018). Audio description in 360° videos: Results from focus groups in Barcelona and Kraków. *Translation Spaces, 7*(2), 285–303.

Font Bisier, M. A. (2023). Análisis de la norma UNE 153020 sobre audiodescripción: ¿Debería modificarse tras diecisiete años de vigencia? *Ética y Cine Journal, 13*(1), 41–52. https://doi.org/10.31056/2250.5415.v13.n1.40640

General Law on Audiovisual Communication. (2015). *Official Gazette 7/2010,* 1 May 2015, Madrid, Spain.

Green-SCENT Project. (n.d). *Homepage.* https://www.green-scent.eu/

Herrero, C., & Escobar, M. (2018). A pedagogical model for integrating film education and audio description in foreign language acquisition. *Translation and Translanguaging in Multilingual Contexts, 4*(1), 30–54.

Holland, A. (2009). Audio description in the theatre and the visual arts: Images in words. In J. Díaz-Cintas & G. M. Anderman (Eds.), *Audiovisual translation: Language transfer on screen* (pp. 170–185). Palgrave Macmillan.

House of Representatives of the United States of America. (1973). Rehabilitation Act (1973). *House of Representatives* 29 U.S.C. § 701, 26 September 1973, Washington, DC, United States of America.

Hutchinson, R., Loveday, C., & Eardley, A. F. (2020). Remembering cultural experiences: lifespan distributions, richness and content of autobiographical memories of museum visits. *Memory, 28*(8), 1024–1036. https://doi.org/10.1080/09658211.2020.1811874

ImAc (Immersive Accessibility) Project. (2017–2020). *Homepage.* https://www.imacproject.eu/

Independent Television Commission [ITC]. (2000). ITC guidance on standards for audio description. Retrieved from: http://audiodescription.co.uk/uploads/general/itcguide_sds_audio_desc_word3

International Telecommunication Union (Focus Group on Audiovisual Media Accessibility). (2013). *Part 5: Final report f Activities: Working Group B "Audio/Video Description and Spoken Captions."* Geneva, Switzerland: International Telecommunication Union.

Jankowska, A. (2015). *Translating audio description scripts: Translation as a new strategy of creating audio description.* Peter Lang.

Khanlou, N., Khan, A., Vazquez, L. M., & Zangeneh, M. (2021). Digital literacy, access to technology and inclusion for young adults with developmental disabilities. *Journal of Developmental and Physical Disabilities, 33,* 1–25.

Kleege, G., & Wallin, S. (2015). Audio description as a pedagogical tool. *Disability Studies Quarterly, 35*(2), Article 2. http://dsq-sds.org/article/view/4622

Larreina-Morales, M. E., & Mangirón, C. (2023). *Audio description in video games?* Universal Access in the Information Society. https://doi.org/10.1007/s10209-023-01036-4

Law on Urgent Measures for the Simulation of Digital Terrestrial Television on the Liberation of Cable Television and the Encouragement of Pluralism. (2005). *Official Gazette BOE-a-2005-10069,* 15 June 2005, Madrid, Spain.

Lopez, M., Kearney, G., & Hofstädter, K. (2020). Seeing film through sound: Sound design, spatial audio, and accessibility for visually impaired audiences. *British Journal of Visual Impairment,* 1–28.

Lopez, M., Kearney, G., & Hofstädter, K. (2021). Enhancing audio description: Inclusive cinematic experiences through sound design. *Journal of Audiovisual Translation, 4*(1), 157–182.

Matamala, A., & Orero, P. (2013). Standardising audio description. *Italian Journal for Special Education, 1,* 149–155.

Matamala, A., & Orero, P. (2022). Opera co-creation: From collaborative translation to artistic co-creation in audiovisual translation and accessibility. *Hikma, 21*(2), 41–63.

Mazur, I., & Chmiel, A. (2012a). Audio description made to measure: Reflections on interpretation in AD based on the pear tree project data. https://pdfs.semanticscholar.org/7d50/5dc4f1126335 17c9ca8a0d4d2d73e7d3539e.pdf

Mazur, I., & Chmiel, A. (2012b). AD reception research: Some methodological considerations. https://www.openstarts.units.it/bitstream/10077/6361/1/Chmiel_Mazur_EmergingTopics.pdf

McDonagh, S., & Aguiar, L. (forthcoming). Beyond preservation: Embracing participatory and accessible practices in the archive. *Collaborative Media Accessibility: Theory, Methodology and Practice.*

McDonagh, S., & Brescia-Zapata, M. (2023). Combining XR, accessibility, and sustainability in the classroom: Results of an exploratory study. In *Bridging the XR technology-to-practice gap* (pp. 67–79). AACE2023.

Miligan, B., & Fels, D. (2013). *Descriptive video production and presentation. Best practices guide for digital environments.* Toronto & Ottawa, Canada: Media Access Canada

Mikul, C. (2010). *Audio description background paper.* Sydney, Australia: Media Access Australia.

Montagud, M., Orero, P., & Fernández, S. (2020). Immersive media and accessibility: Hand in hand to the future. *ITU Journal.* https://www.itu.int/pub/S-JOURNAL-ICTS.V3I1-2020-2

Netflix. (2023). *Audio description style guide v2.5.* https://partnerhelp.netflixstudios.com/hc/en-us/articles/215510667-Audio-Description-Style-Guide-v2-5#h_01GZ20RE23YCC1QB27YT7F G7WR

Neves, J. (2014). Descriptive guides: Access to museums, cultural venues and heritage sites. In A. Remael, N. Reviers, & G. Vercauteren (Eds.), *ADLAB guidelines: Pictures painted in words*.

New York State Web Accessibility Policy. (2010). *Office of Information technology Services NYSP08-005*, New York, NT, United Stated of America.

Office of Communications [Ofcom]. (2017). Code on television access services. Retrieved from: https://www.ofcom.org.uk/tv-radio-and-on-demand/broadcastcodes/tv-access-services

O'Hara, J. (n.d.). *Audio description guidelines (for Film, Video and Television)*. London, UK: Independent Television Facilities Centre Ltd.

Orero, P. (2005). Audio description: Professional recognition, practice and Standards in Spain. *Translation Watch Quarterly, 1*, 7–18. http://www.translocutions.com/tsi/twq/tranlsation_watch_quarterly_December2005_issue1_sample.pdf#page=7

Orero, P., & Wharton, S. (2007). The audio description of a Spanish phenomenon: Torrente 3. *JoSTrans, 7*, 164–178. http://www.jostrans.org/issue07/art_orero_wharton.pdf

Orero, P. (2008). Three different receptions of the same film: 'The Pear Stories Project' applied to audio description 1. *European Journal of English Studies, 12*(2), 179–193. https://doi.org/10.1080/13825570802151454

Rai, S., Greening, J., & Leen, P. (2010). *A comparative study of audio description guidelines prevalent in different countries*. London, UK: Royal Institute of the Blind People.

Reiss, K. (1981). Type, Kind and Individuality of text: Decision making in translation. *Poetics Today, 2*(4), 121–131.

Remael, A. (2014). Combining audio description with audio subtitling. In A. Remael, N. Reviers, & G. Vercauteren (Eds.), *ADLAB audio description guidelines*. Retrieved from: http://www.adlabproject.eu/Docs/adlab%20book/#combining-ad

Remael, A., Reviers, N., & Vercauteren, G. (2014). *ADLAB audio description guidelines*. Retrieved from http://www.adlabproject.eu/Docs/adlab%20book/index

Romero-Fresco, P. (2022). Moving from accessible filmmaking toward creative media accessibility. *Leonardo, 55*(3), 304–309.

Romero-Fresco, P., & Chaume, F. (2022). Creativity in audiovisual translation and media accessibility. *The Journal of Specialised Translation, 38*, 75–101.

Romero-Fresco, P., & Dangerfield, K. (2022). Accessibility as a conversation. *Journal of Audiovisual Translation, 5*(2). https://doi.org/10.47476/jat.v5i2.2022.228

Snyder, J. (2010). *Audio description guidelines and best practices*. Snyder, (Ed.). Alexandria, VA: The American Council of the Blind

Talaván, N. (2019). Using subtitles for the deaf and hard of hearing as an innovative pedagogical tool in the language class. *International Journal of English Studies, 19*(1), 21–40. https://doi.org/10.6018/ijes.338671

Taylor, C. (2014). *"Cohesion" in audio description: New perspectives illustrated*. In A. Maszerowska, A. Matamala, & P. Orero (Eds.). Amsterdam, John Benjamins.

Thompson, H., & Warne, V. (2018). Blindness arts: An introduction. *Disability Studies Quarterly, 38*(3).

Twenty-First Century Communications and Video Accessibility Act. (2010). *House of representatives of the United States of America 111-260*, 8 October 2010, Washington, DC, United States of America.

Video Description: Implementation of the Twenty-First Century Communications and Video Accessibility Act of 2010. (2017). *Federal Communications Commission 2017-15526*, 8 October 2017, Washington, DC, United States of America.

Zallio, M., & Clarkson, P. J. (2022). Designing the metaverse: A study on inclusion, diversity, equity, accessibility and safety for digital immersive environments. *Telematics and Informatics, 75*, 1–12.

Assessing the Impact of Assistive Technologies on the Lives of the Hearing Impaired: A Bibliometric Analysis

Ekrem Bahçekapılı◉ **and Ahmet Ayaz**◉

Abstract This chapter provides an in-depth examination of assistive technologies designed to address the challenges faced by individuals with hearing impairments. Section 1 highlights the communication barriers and social interactions. Sect. 2 explores the effectiveness of these assistive technologies through bibliometric analysis, revealing how technological advancements are shaping trends in this field. The aim of this chapter is to elucidate how technological aids developed for individuals with hearing impairments support equal opportunities in every aspect, from education to professional life.

Keywords Accessibility · Assistive technology · Hearing impaired · Bibliometric analysis

1 Introduction

According to the 2023 report from the World Health Organization (WHO), approximately 5.3% of the world's population, or around 466 million people, are hearing impaired. This is an increase on 2018 when the percentage was 5.2% (World Health Organization, 2023). A person with hearing impairment is defined as an individual experiencing a loss in auditory capabilities, resulting in an inability to receive or rely on the auditory input necessary for understanding speech (Hauser et al., 2006). The primary challenge faced by individuals with hearing impairments revolves around communication. Sign language is the fundamental mode of communication for individuals with hearing impairments. Factors such as the limited number of individuals

E. Bahçekapılı (✉) · A. Ayaz
Karadeniz Technical University, Trabzon, Türkiye
e-mail: ekrem.bahcekapili@ktu.edu.tr

A. Ayaz
e-mail: ahmetayaz@ktu.edu.tr

A. Marcus-Quinn et al. (eds.), *Transforming Media Accessibility in Europe*,
https://doi.org/10.1007/978-3-031-60049-4_19

proficient in sign language and the lack of support for sign language in many information sources adversely affect the communication between individuals with hearing impairments and those with normal hearing.

Individuals with hearing impairments or hearing difficulties encounter significant challenges and multifaceted problems in various aspects of their lives, ranging from communication to education, health, and social interaction (Iezzoni et al., 2004). For instance, in the field of education, challenges arise due to the absence of suitable technological tools and inadequate accessibility and usability features in learning platforms, leading to difficulties in accessing educational materials (Batanero-Ochaita et al., 2021). Another example of inequality is observed in the workplace, where individuals with hearing impairments face technical challenges, including impacts on job performance and safety, a range of issues related to diminished ability to hear warning signals, as well as social problems such as communication difficulties, social isolation, and challenges in interacting with colleagues (Morata et al., 2005).

In contemporary times, rapid technological advancements and the widespread dissemination of the information age have significantly expanded individuals' access to information and communication opportunities. However, a group that may not fully benefit from these advancements is individuals with hearing impairments. Particularly, the increasing popularity of audio-based content and applications may pose barriers for individuals with hearing impairments in achieving equal access on these platforms. Tools such as voice assistants, podcasts, video conferences, and social media platforms enable us to exchange information, engage in entertainment, and foster social interactions within seconds. Nevertheless, these tools may create challenges for individuals with hearing impairments in accessing information. Accessibility is a concept of critical importance for individuals with hearing impairments in the digital age. The equitable, fair, and inclusive design of technological advancements plays a vital role in enhancing societal participation and equal opportunities for all individuals. To fully enable individuals with hearing impairments to benefit from this digital revolution, significant responsibilities lie with technology manufacturers and service providers. Therefore, accessibility is not merely a luxury but a necessity. While individuals with hearing impairments may not naturally acquire the ability to speak, solutions are being developed through technology and science to overcome these disadvantages (Schriempf, 2009). Assistive technologies play a crucial role in overcoming the communication challenges fundamentally faced by individuals with hearing impairments (Bishop et al., 2000; Gugenheimer et al., 2017). Many assistive technologies have been developed to address communication problems, especially for individuals with hearing impairments, through technology. Technologies that automatically generate subtitles for video content facilitate access for individuals with hearing impairments. Sign language translation applications expand the communication abilities of individuals with hearing impairments (San-Segundo et al., 2012), and specially designed hearing aids and applications assist them in being more active in their social and professional lives (Stark & Hickson, 2004).

The increasing importance and frequent research on assistive technologies for the hearing impaired makes it both necessary and important to present the current trends and outlook of this field. Therefore, it will be determined in which direction the studies in this rapidly changing field have evolved, which aspects should be emphasized, and new horizons will be opened for researchers working in this field. In this context, this study, which performs bibliometric mapping of research on assistive technologies for the hearing impaired, is important in terms of defining the field in detail and drawing a general picture. Bibliometric analysis aims to examine the evolution of published literature on a topic. The term bibliometrics is defined as the application of statistical and mathematical methods to texts. Bibliometrics has emerged as an important research area in various branches of science. Bibliometrics offers the possibility to study the productivity of any literature in detail (Mukherjee et al., 2022).

This chapter examines assistive technologies for communication difficulties that facilitate the communication of hearing-impaired individuals with normal hearing, provide access to various information sources, and improve their daily lives. Assistive technologies are classified under three main headings: sound enhancement and transmission technologies, communication and access technologies, and finally warning and notification technologies. In addition to this review, bibliometric analysis methods will be used to analyze the development, use, and impact of these technologies in detail. This analysis will play a critical role in identifying research trends, important studies, and future research directions in the field.

1.1   Sound Enhancement and Transmission Technologies

These assistive technologies can be divided into two categories: hearing aids and frequency modulation (FM) systems. Hearing aids are electronic devices primarily consisting of a microphone, amplifier, and speaker that capture and amplify external sounds, transmitting them to individuals with hearing loss. They come in analog and digital types, with digital variants converting sound into digital signals, offering improved sound quality and customization options (Zeng et al., 2008). FM systems, on the other hand, transmit the voice of a specific speaker directly to hearing aids, incorporating a microphone and receiver. By reducing background noise and echoes, these systems enhance the clarity of following the speaker (Lewis, 1994). While hearing aids capture and amplify sounds from the surrounding environment, transmitting them to the ears of individuals with hearing loss, FM systems transmit the sound from a specific source (usually a teacher) directly to the hearing aid, reducing background noise and ensuring clearer sound transmission (Pittman et al., 1999).

1.2   Communication and Access Technologies

Expanding on the section about communication and access technologies for individuals with hearing or speech impairments, recent literature provides a deeper insight into the advancements and critical analysis of assistive technologies (AT), brain–computer interfaces (BCIs), mobile applications, and among others. These technologies play a significant role in enhancing communication, accessibility, and overall quality of life for individuals with hearing or speech impairments.

Assistive Technologies (AT): Shanmugam and Marimuthu (2021) provide a critical analysis and review of AT, highlighting its significant impact on improving the quality of life for dysarthric patients by overcoming communication difficulties. The study emphasizes the importance of AT in the rehabilitation of individuals with speech disorders, including design considerations and the impact of technology.

Brain–Computer Interfaces (BCIs): BCIs offer potential improvements in communication for people unable to use traditional augmentative and alternative communication devices. Brumberg et al. (2018) discuss the current state of BCI, focusing on its application in AAC, its efficacy, and the future of BCI as an addition to AAC access strategies. This tutorial aims to provide AAC specialists with foundational knowledge for clinical application of BCI.

Hearing Aid Technologies: Advances in hearing aid technology have allowed for a more efficient, cost-effective hearing assistive system. Das (2021) reviews the advancements in hearing aid technology, emphasizing the potential of IoT for developing an effective hearing assistant device. This highlights the shift toward innovative solutions that improve the functionality and accessibility of hearing aids for individuals with hearing impairments.

Teletypewriter (TTY) or Telecommunication Device for the Deaf (TDD): TTY/TDD devices are equipment designed for individuals with hearing or speech impairments. They include a keyboard and display or printer, allowing written communication over the telephone line and connection to TTY/TDD compatible services. This technology has increased individuals' independence in telephone communication, but it has started to be replaced by internet-based communication platforms and more advanced technologies in contemporary times (Maiorana-Basas & Pagliaro, 2014).

Video Relay Service (VRS): Video Relay Service (VRS) enables individuals with hearing or speech impairments to conduct telephone conversations using sign language through a video device and an interpreter. This service facilitates more natural and fluent communication with other individuals (Saladin & Hansmann, 2008).

Captioning Systems: These technologies transform sounds and visuals into text and find application in various areas such as TV programs, movies, online videos, live matches, and conferences. Captioning systems, especially, make different types of videos more accessible for individuals with hearing impairments (Alsalamah, 2020).

Sign Language Translation Systems: Sign language is the primary mode of communication for individuals with hearing impairments. These technologies can work in two ways. The first method involves technological solutions that translate written or spoken text into sign language. These systems use computer-generated avatars or animations to represent information in sign language movements, thus facilitating access to information for individuals with hearing impairments (Sanaullah et al., 2022). The second method involves technological tools that detect sign language movements, converting them into text or spoken language, or translating written text into sign language. This helps individuals with hearing impairments communicate more effectively (Wadhawan & Kumar, 2021).

Mobile Applications: Mobile applications enhance the lives of individuals with hearing impairments by facilitating communication, access to information, and active participation in society (Alnfiai & Sampali, 2017). Mobile applications offer solutions tailored to the specific needs of individuals with hearing impairments, such as providing real-time transcripts for classes and meetings, finding accessible job listings, and granting access to entertainment content suitable for the hearing impaired.

1.3 Alert and Notification Technologies

Vibrating Alert Devices: Devices employing vibrations to notify individuals with hearing impairments of significant sounds or events contribute to enhancing their safety, independence, and overall well-being in daily life (Harkins et al., 2010).

Alerting Lights: Alerting lights are devices that use flashing lights to inform individuals with hearing impairments of important sounds or events. Alerting lights and vibration systems are often used together to draw attention to significant sounds and events for individuals with hearing impairments. While alerting lights provide visual feedback, vibration systems offer tactile feedback, each presenting different advantages and disadvantages based on the individual's needs and preferences.

The presence of individuals with hearing impairments worldwide and the opportunities provided by technology to improve their quality of life support not only individual success but also societal integration. As discussed in the first section, the challenges faced by individuals with hearing impairments hold a significant place in the general structure of society and technological advancements. In the second section, we will assess the impact, usage, and effectiveness of these technological developments on individuals with hearing impairments. Analyzing general trends and patterns in the scientific literature through recent innovations in access to information and communication, we will comprehensively examine the scope and impact of existing and potential assistive technologies for individuals with hearing impairments. This approach will unveil the practical applications and real-world impact of these technologies on the lives of individuals with hearing impairments.

2 Method

This chapter provides a comprehensive review of research trends in assistive technologies for the hearing impaired through of bibliometric analysis. It first describes the methodology used for the bibliometric analysis. It then provides a comprehensive assessment of the results, shedding light on key patterns and emerging themes in the literature on assistive technologies for the hearing impaired.

In this study, a bibliometric research design was employed to analyze articles related to the use of assistive technology in individuals with hearing impairments. As part of the bibliometric methodology used in this study, various aspects were examined, including the number of publications, authors, subject areas, and the inclusion of specific keywords in articles related to the research topic (Donthu et al., 2021).

Bibliometric analysis plays a crucial role as a statistical method in mapping the existing knowledge situation in a specific field, determining new research areas, and extracting critical data for various purposes, including supporting current scientific findings (Ayaz et al., 2021; José de Oliveira et al., 2019). The primary data source for this study was the Scopus database, recognized for its comprehensive coverage of multiple databases. The following query was executed to obtain data:

(deaf $*$ OR "hard of hearing" OR "hearing $-$ impaired OR "unhearing" OR "unable to hear") AND ("assistive technologies" OR (assistive AND techno$*$) OR (digital $*$ AND(tool OR tech$*$)))

Publications were selected to be included in this study based on predefined inclusion and exclusion criteria. Inclusion criteria encompassed articles discussing the use of assistive technologies for individuals with hearing impairments, published in scientific journals indexed in Scopus, and containing relevant keywords. Exclusion criteria covered publications with limited access (e.g., lacking full-text access), available only in abstract form, or not relevant to the research topic.

Various bibliometric software tools, such as Word Cloud Analysis, Trend Topics, TreeMap, and Clustering by Coupling, were utilized for visualization and analysis. Additionally, a descriptive analysis covering publication counts, authors, subjects, and keyword usage was performed on bibliometric data. The bibliometric study aimed to categorize and identify publications related to the use of assistive technologies in individuals with hearing impairments based on their topics, publication years, and authors. A co-citation network analysis was conducted to reveal relationships among publications related to the research topic.

2.1 Research Questions

1. How has the development of publications on the use of assistive technology in individuals with hearing impairments progressed in recent years?
2. What types of documents are frequently published regarding the use of assistive technology in individuals with hearing impairments?
3. Which countries demonstrate the highest level of activity in research on the use of assistive technology for individuals with hearing impairments in education?

4. In publications related to the use of assistive technology in individuals with hearing impairments, which language is predominantly used?
5. What specific research areas are commonly investigated in the context of the use of assistive technology for individuals with hearing impairments?
6. Which organizations are most actively involved in research on the use of assistive technology for individuals with hearing impairments?
7. Which authors are prolific in publishing research on the use of assistive technology for individuals with hearing impairments?
8. What are the most frequently cited documents in global research on the use of assistive technology for individuals with hearing impairments?
9. Which keywords are most commonly found in research on the use of assistive technology in individuals with hearing impairments?
10. How are publications on the use of assistive technology in individuals with hearing impairments visually distributed in a TreeMap format?

3 Findings

3.1 Number of Publications on the Use of Assistive Technology in Individuals with Hearing Impairments Over the Years

A total of 1294 studies were identified, and data were collected through comprehensive searches. The data presented in Fig. 1 demonstrate a substantial volume of publications on this topic over the years. From 1970 to 2012, the number of publications remained relatively stable with minor fluctuations. Particularly noteworthy is a significant increase in the number of publications between 2014 and 2019. A noticeable upward trend has been observed since 2014, reaching the highest number of publications in 2022 with a total of 120 publications. As of October 2023, the number of publications has been identified as 88. This analysis indicates a growing body of research in this field, highlighting the increasing significance of the topic in the scientific literature.

3.2 Number of Publications on the Use of Assistive Technology in Individuals with Hearing Impairments by Document Type

Figure 2 illustrates the distribution of publications categorized by document type in the utilized database. The analyzed documents encompass various types, including articles, conference papers, reviews, book chapters, conference reviews, books, notes, short surveys, data papers, and errata. The data reveals 588 articles, 485 conference

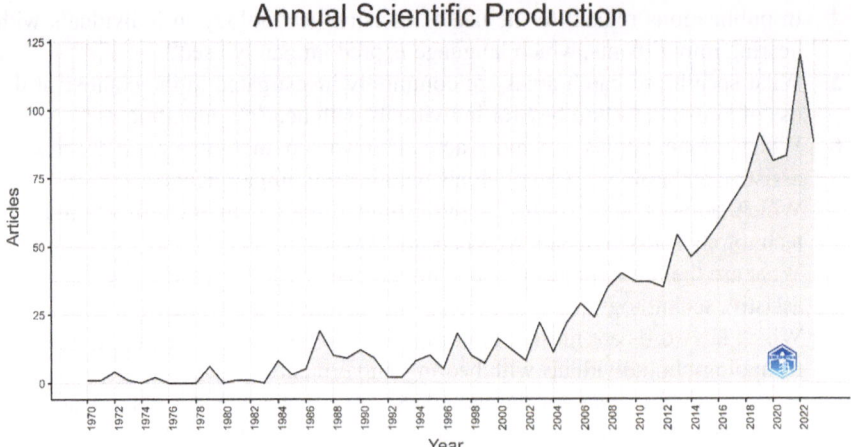

Fig. 1 Annual publication numbers

papers, 81 reviews, 61 book chapters, 61 conference reviews, 8 books, 6 notes, 2 short surveys, 2 data papers, and 1 erratum. While articles are the most prevalent document type, errata are the least common. The diversity of document types in this dataset underscores the variety of research approaches employed in examining the subject matter.

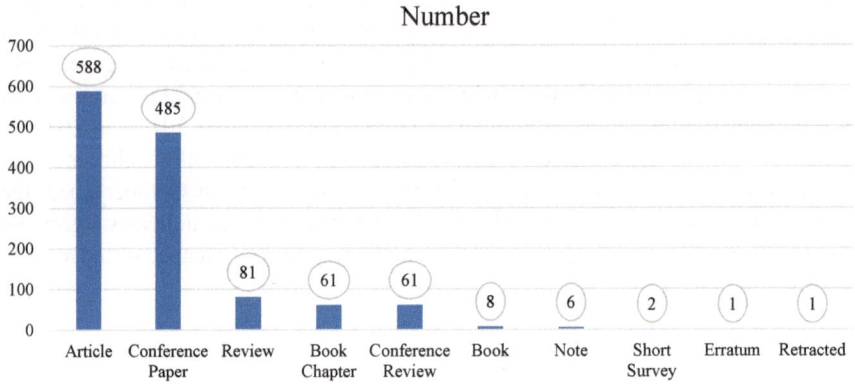

Fig. 2 Number of articles by document types

Number

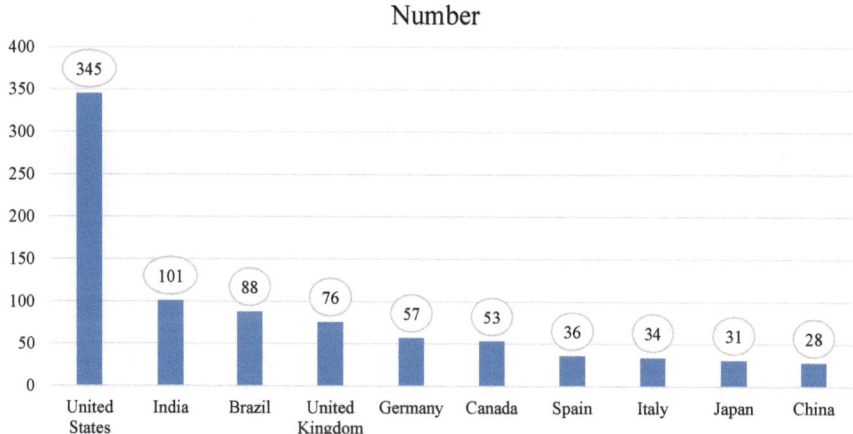

Fig. 3 Number of articles by country

3.3 Number of Publications on the Use of Assistive Technology in Individuals with Hearing Impairments by Country

Upon examining the Fig. 3, it is observed that contributions to publications on the use of assistive technology in individuals with hearing impairments have been made from a total of 86 countries. The United States leads in publication frequency with 345 publications, followed by India with 101 publications, Brazil with 88 publications, the United Kingdom with 76 publications, and Germany with 57 publications. The diversity of authors from various countries highlights global interest and participation in the field of assistive technology use for individuals with hearing impairments.

3.4 Investigation of Publications on the Use of Assistive Technology by Hearing-Impaired Individuals According to Languages

Figure 4 presents data on the distribution of publications related to the use of assistive technology by hearing-impaired individuals, categorized by the languages in which they were written. The dataset comprises 16 languages, with a total of 1220 publications, and English has the highest number of publications. Following English, there are 28 publications in Portuguese, 10 in Spanish, 8 in German, 6 in French, 4 in Russian, 3 in Korean, and 2 each in Turkish, Swedish, Chinese, and Japanese. Additionally, there is one publication each in Slovenian, Italian, Hungarian, Danish, and Czech.

Number

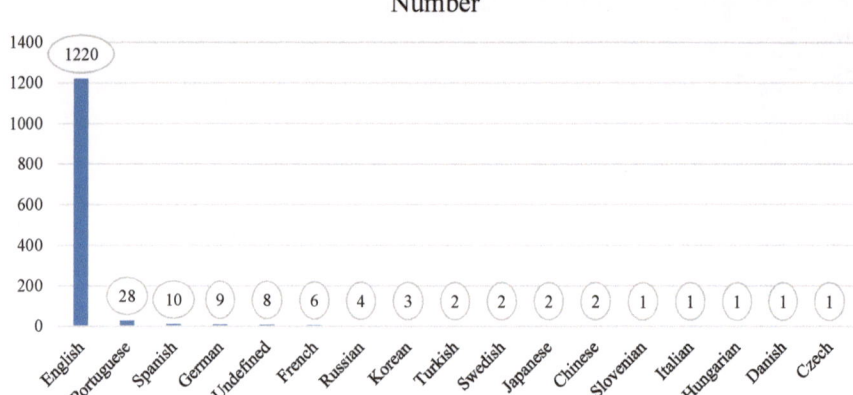

Fig. 4 Number of publications by language types

These data emphasize that English is the dominant language in research on the use of assistive technology by hearing-impaired individuals. However, it is important to note that research in other languages plays a significant role in achieving a more comprehensive understanding and addressing a more diverse audience.

3.5 Number of Publications on the Use of Assistive Technology by Hearing-Impaired Individuals According to Research Areas

The information in Fig. 5 categorizes the number of publications on the use of assistive technology by hearing-impaired individuals according to research areas. These areas encompass a wide range of fields, including Computer Science, Engineering, Medicine, Social Sciences, Health Professions, Mathematics, Arts and Humanities, Physics and Astronomy, Psychology, Biochemistry, Genetics and Molecular Biology, Decision Sciences, Material Science, Business, Management and Accounting, Neuroscience, Environmental Science, Nursing, Chemical Engineering, Energy, Chemistry, Multidisciplinary, Agriculture and Biological Sciences, Economics, Econometrics and Finance, Pharmacology, Toxicology and Pharmacy, Earth and Planetary Sciences, Immunology and Microbiology, and Dentistry.

Among these areas, Computer Science research stands out with 574 publications, followed by Engineering with 325 publications and Medicine with 303 publications. On the other hand, Dentistry Research is the least represented among all scientific fields, with only one article.

Number

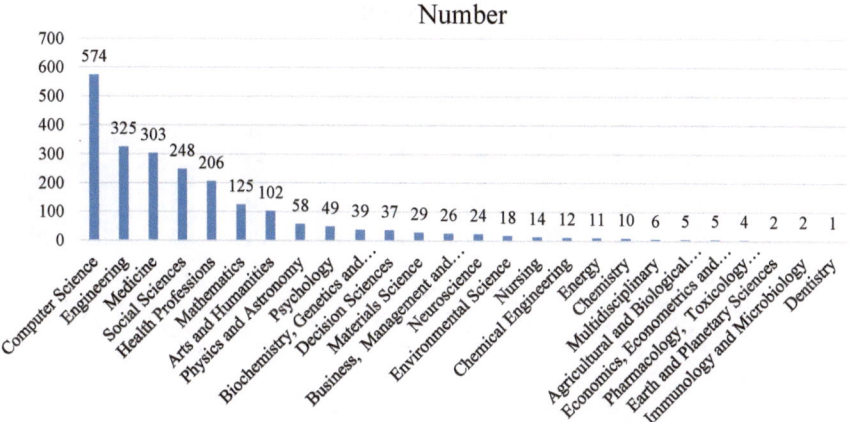

Fig. 5 Number of publications by research areas

3.6 Number of Publications on the Use of Assistive Technology by Hearing-Impaired Individuals According to Institutions

The dataset includes a total of 160 institutions, and their contributions to publications on the use of assistive technology by hearing-impaired individuals are illustrated in Fig. 6. The City University of New York (USA) leads in this field with 21 publications, followed by the Rochester Institute of Technology (USA) with 15 publications and Gallaudet University (USA) with 14 publications. Other significant institutions such as Instituto Superior de Engenharia do Porto (Portugal), Universidade de São Paulo (Brazil), and the University of Montreal (Canada) also have a noteworthy number of publications. These findings provide insights into the distribution of research conducted by various institutions on the use of assistive technology by hearing-impaired individuals.

3.7 Number of Publications on the Use of Assistive Technology by Hearing-Impaired Individuals According to Authors

A total of 159 authors have been identified in the dataset. Figure 7 categorizes the number of publications on the use of assistive technology by hearing-impaired individuals based on the contributing authors. There are 9 authors with the highest number of publications, each having contributed between 6 and 13 publications. Particularly noteworthy are authors with the most publications: H. Levitt with 11 publications, P. Escudeiro and W. Wittich with 10 publications each, and N. Cercone

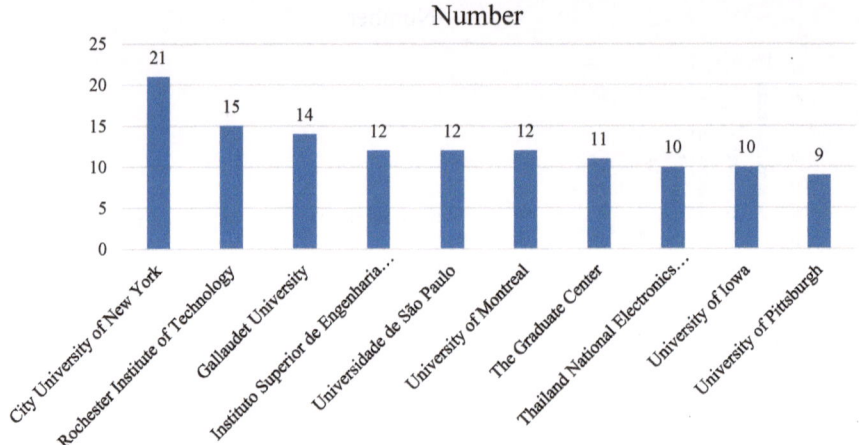

Fig. 6 Number of publications by institutions

and S. Nanayakkara with seven publications each. These data provide a general overview of authors who have made significant contributions to research in the field of assistive technology use by hearing-impaired individuals.

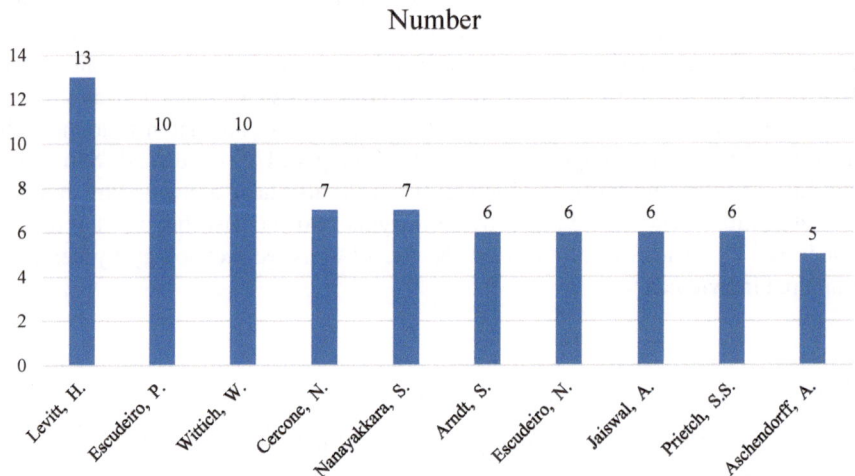

Fig. 7 Number of publications by author

3.8   Most Global Cited Documents

Figure 8 illustrates the top 10 most cited documents worldwide. The first article, written in 2012 and titled "Clinical Practice Guideline," was published in Otolaryngology–Head and Neck Surgery. This document has accumulated a total of 756 citations with an average of 63.00 citations per year. Additionally, its Normalized TC value is 19.09. The article discusses the interaction of technology with health-related assistive technologies and how it can shape guidance and applications in this field. Focusing on cases where patients present symptoms of sudden hearing loss (SHL), the study emphasizes how the accurate diagnosis and effective management of these symptoms can be enhanced through technology. In particular, this study encourages the use of advanced technologies in the diagnosis and management of sudden-onset hearing losses.

In 2006, the Trends in Amplification journal published an article titled "Effects of Age on Auditory and Cognitive Processing: Implications for Hearing Aid Fitting and Audiologic Rehabilitation." This article has received 300 citations, with an annual citation rate of 16.67 and a Normalized TC value of 13.18. The text explores questions triggered by age-related auditory and cognitive differences, highlighting developments led by research in these areas. The advancements discussed underscore the necessity of using technology to better understand auditory processing and the auditory needs of aging individuals. This is crucial in the design and functionality of hearing aids, headphones, and other auditory assistive devices. The text also mentions "intelligent" hearing aids and emphasizes advances in digital signal processing in auditory devices, reflecting the need to use technology to enhance the functionality and efficiency of hearing aids for aging individuals.

Additionally, in 2008, the Journal of Rehabilitation Research & Development published an article under the title "Cochlear implants: Current designs and future

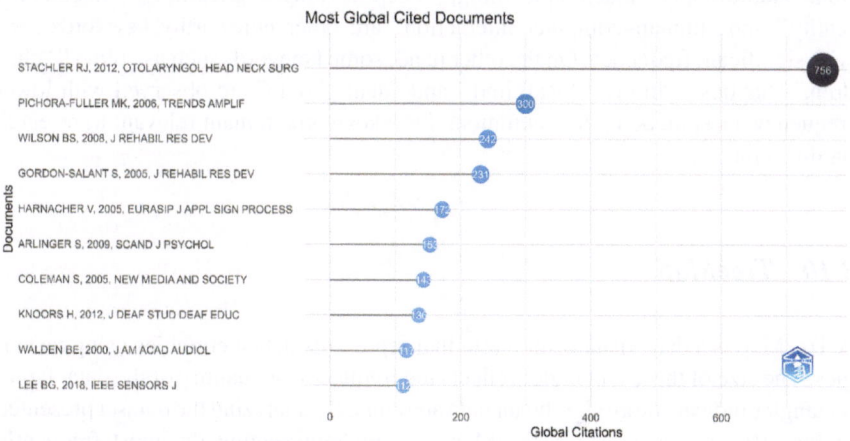

Fig. 8 Most global cited publications

possibilities." This document has received 242 citations, with an average annual citation rate of 15.13 and a Normalized TC value of 12.17. The article introduces cochlear implant technology as an advanced neural prosthesis for individuals with hearing loss, focusing on its development and effectiveness. The text indicates that cochlear implants are the most successful among neural prosthetics in restoring function. It provides information on how the design and performance of cochlear implants have been developed and improved, demonstrating the continuous evolution of technology to assist more people. The text emphasizes the current status and limitations of cochlear implant technology and highlights the potential for future improvements. This underscores the ongoing need for the continuous development of assistive technologies for individuals with hearing loss.

Finally, other prominent articles address the role and future development of assistive technologies in areas such as hearing loss, hearing devices, communication technologies, and language policies. Assistive technologies play a crucial role in improving the quality of life for individuals with hearing loss and facilitating their communication.

3.9 Keyword Analysis

Word clouds are a useful tool for visualizing the frequency of keywords in bibliometric data. They provide a quick and easy way to grasp the main themes of research topics. By analyzing the data presented in Fig. 9, we can create a Word Cloud that visually represents the most frequently encountered keywords in research related to "the use of assistive technology by individuals with hearing impairment."

In this research, the most prominent keywords include "sign language," "hearing aid," "cochlear implant," "accessibility," "speech perception," and "gesture cognition." Additionally, "machine learning," "deep learning," "e-learning," "augmented reality," and "human–computer interaction" are other noteworthy keywords seen with significant frequency. On the other hand, some keywords such as "blind," "children," "haptics," "libras," "deafblind," and "deaf people" are observed with lower frequency. Despite being less common, these keywords remain relevant to research on this topic.

3.10 TreeMap

A TreeMap is a data visualization tool that represents data hierarchies using rectangles. The size of these rectangles reflects the frequency or quantity of the data; larger rectangles indicate more significant data amounts. By analyzing the dataset presented in Fig. 10, we can create a TreeMap visually representing the most frequently occurring terms in research articles.

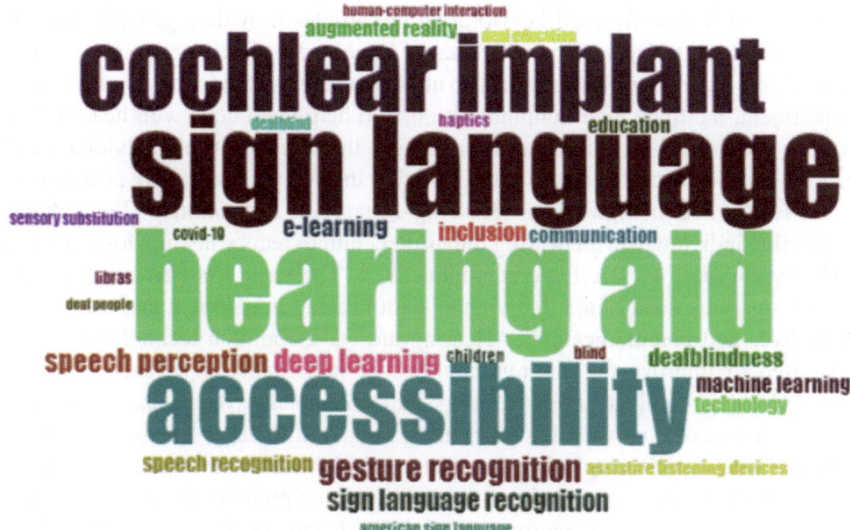

Fig. 9 Word Cloud

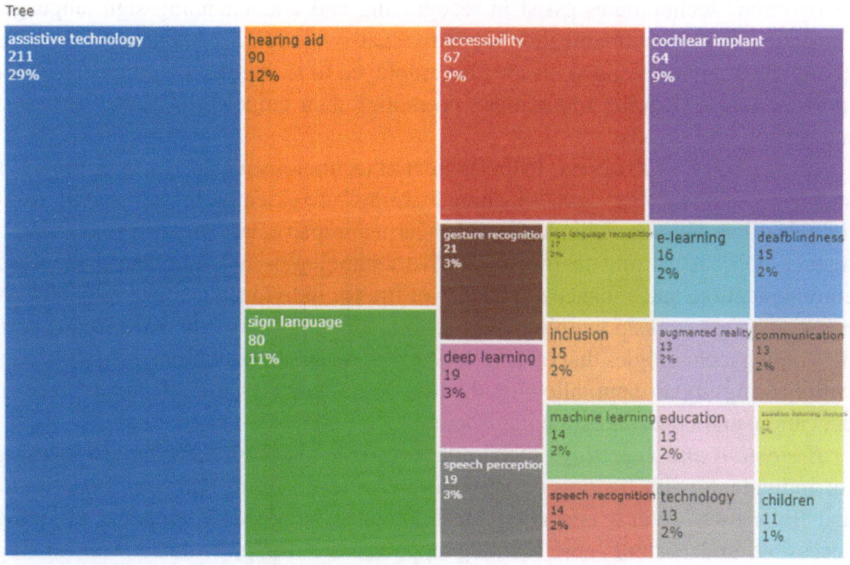

Fig. 10 TreeMap

The most frequently used keywords in the articles provide a general overview of topics related to individuals with hearing impairment. These encompass various technologies, terms, and subjects used to improve the lives of individuals with hearing impairment, facilitate their communication, and help them cope with hearing loss. Among the crucial topics aimed at enhancing the integration of individuals with hearing impairment into society and improving their quality of life are as follows:

Assistive Technologies for Hearing-Impaired Individuals: Technologies supporting individuals with hearing impairment aim to reduce hearing loss, enhance auditory abilities, and facilitate communication. The term "Assistive technology" includes various devices that individuals with hearing impairment can use in their daily lives and communications. "Hearing aid" is a common technological solution used to improve the auditory abilities of individuals experiencing hearing loss. "Cochlear implant" refers to a specialized implant system used to provide hearing abilities to individuals with hearing loss. Additionally, "Assistive listening devices" include technological devices that help individuals with hearing impairment communicate better, aiming to improve their lives and promote societal inclusion.

Sign Language and Communication: Sign language plays a critical role in effective communication for individuals with hearing impairment, enabling them to communicate with each other and individuals with auditory abilities. "Sign language recognition" technologies assist in recognizing and understanding sign language, facilitating better communication for individuals with hearing impairment. Various communication tools and skills are also employed to strengthen communication for individuals with hearing impairment, promoting their empowerment and increased integration into society.

Technology and Progress: In the context of technology and progress, approaches such as "Deep learning" and "Machine learning" are essential for developing technologies that support individuals with hearing impairment. These artificial intelligence approaches aim to make assistive technologies more effective, facilitate communication, and enhance the quality of life for individuals with hearing impairment. Progress in deep learning and machine learning represents advancements in developing technologies that offer increased access and opportunities for individuals with hearing impairment, allowing them to communicate more effectively, receive education, and better integrate into society.

Education and Learning: Technologies used to support education and learning for individuals with hearing impairment are crucial. Terms such as "E-learning" and "Education" refer to educational technologies and processes aimed at providing accessible and customizable learning opportunities for individuals with hearing impairment. Online education offers accessible and personalized learning opportunities, designed to meet individual needs and support communication. These technologies assist individuals with hearing impairment in continuing their education, enhancing their careers, and promoting their societal inclusion.

Accessibility and Inclusion: Concepts of "Accessibility" and "Inclusion" aim to make the lives of individuals with hearing impairment more inclusive and accessible. "Accessibility" refers to facilitating easier access for individuals with hearing impairment in physical, digital, and social environments, enabling them to access public buildings, online resources, and communication tools easily. "Inclusion" encourages equal rights for individuals with hearing impairment in all areas of society, including education, employment, culture, and social activities. Inclusion supports individuals with hearing impairment in living richer and more effective lives and celebrates the diversity of their communities. The concepts of accessibility and inclusion underscore the importance of studies and developments aiming to provide individuals with hearing impairment with increased access and opportunities.

These keywords reflect the technologies and related terms used to improve the lives, communication, and education of individuals with hearing impairment. Additionally, these keywords emphasize the significance of studies and advancements aiming to provide individuals with hearing impairment with increased access and opportunities.

4 Discussion and Conclusion

The outcomes of the bibliometric analysis on the adoption of assistive technology by individuals with hearing impairments provide a comprehensive depiction of the field's evolution over time. Notably, the pronounced surge in scholarly publications between 2014 and 2019 highlights an escalating interest in and acknowledgment of the pivotal role assistive technologies plays in ameliorating the life quality of the hearing impaired. This observation is in alignment with the findings reported by Valencia-Arias et al. (2022), corroborating the significance of these technologies. Such a trend not only mirrors advancements in technology but also indicates an increasing consciousness and commitment toward fostering inclusivity and accessibility within society.

The diversity in document types, with articles being the most common and errata the rarest, highlights robust scholarly engagement across a range of platforms, including peer-reviewed journals and conference proceedings. This variety indicates that the exploration of assistive technology for individuals with hearing impairments is advancing not only through theoretical frameworks but also through practical implementations and critical evaluations of existing technologies. Moreover, the international dispersion of publications, prominently featuring contributions from the United States, India, Brazil, the United Kingdom, and Germany, accentuates the global pertinence and applicability of assistive technologies, effectively transcending geographical and cultural boundaries. This scenario aligns with the observations made by Valencia-Arias et al. (2022), underscoring compatibility with their findings. Additionally, there is a noticeable trend of increased publication output from India, indicating a growing emphasis on contributing to this field of research within the region.

The linguistic analysis revealing English as the dominant language in this research area points toward the need for increased multilingual research dissemination. While English serves as a global academic lingua franca, the presence of publications in 16 different languages signifies the global interest and the necessity to cater to non-English speaking populations. This inclusivity could further enhance the understanding and application of assistive technologies worldwide.

The analysis of the most cited documents and keywords provides valuable insights into the research community's focus areas. The emphasis on clinical guidelines, auditory and cognitive processing, and cochlear implant technology underscores the critical intersections between technology, healthcare, and rehabilitation. Moreover, the frequent mention of keywords related to sign language, hearing aids, cochlear implants, and machine learning illustrates the dynamic nature of the field, incorporating both traditional and cutting-edge technologies.

In conclusion, the bibliometric analysis reveals a vibrant and rapidly evolving research landscape, marked by a significant increase in publications, a diverse array of document types, global participation, and a multidisciplinary approach. This growth indicates the field's critical importance and the ongoing need to explore, innovate, and improve assistive technologies for the hearing impaired. Future research should continue to build on this foundation, focusing on inclusivity, technological advancements, and the practical application of findings to ensure that assistive technologies become more accessible, effective, and tailored to the needs of individuals with hearing impairments. The trajectory of this research area promises further advancements and broader implications for enhancing the quality of life and communication for those with hearing impairments, offering a roadmap for researchers, practitioners, and policymakers alike. As this analysis does not assess the quality of the publications reviewed, the results provide only a quantitative perspective and therefore do not include a qualitative assessment.

Acknowledgements This chapter is based upon work from COST Action CA19142—Leading Platform for European Citizens, Industries, Academia and Policymakers in Media Accessibility (LEAD-ME) supported by COST (European Cooperation in Science and Technology).

References

Alnfiai, M., & Sampali, S. (2017). Social and communication apps for the deaf and hearing impaired. In *2017 International conference on computer and applications, ICCA 2017*. https://doi.org/10.1109/COMAPP.2017.8079756

Alsalamah, A. (2020). Using captioning services with deaf and hard of hearing students in higher education: A systematic review. In *American annals of the deaf*. https://doi.org/10.1353/aad.2020.0012

Ayaz, A., Celik, K., & Ozyurt, O. (2021). Pattern detection in cloud computing: Bibliometric mapping of publications in the field from past to present. *COLLNET Journal of Scientometrics and Information Management, 15*(2), 469–494. https://doi.org/10.1080/09737766.2021.2007038

Batanero-Ochaita, C., De-Marcos, L., Rivera, L. F., Holvikivi, J., Hilera, J. R., & Tortosa, S. O. (2021). Improving accessibility in online education: Comparative analysis of attitudes of blind and deaf students toward an adapted learning platform. *IEEE Access*. https://doi.org/10.1109/ACCESS.2021.3095041

Bishop, J. M., Taylor, L., & Froy, F. (2000). Computer-mediated communication use by the deaf and hard-of-hearing. *Kybernetes*. https://doi.org/10.1108/03684920010342143

Brumberg, J. S., Pitt, K. M., Mantie-Kozlowski, A., & Burnison, J. D. (2018). Brain–computer interfaces for augmentative and alternative communication: A tutorial. *American Journal of Speech-Language Pathology*. https://doi.org/10.1044/2017_AJSLP-16-0244

Das, A. (2021). Recent advances in hearing aid technology-A review. *International Journal for Research in Applied Science and Engineering Technology*. https://doi.org/10.22214/ijraset.2021.35762

Donthu, N., Kumar, S., Mukherjee, D., Pandey, N., & Lim, W. M. (2021). How to conduct a bibliometric analysis: An overview and guidelines. *Journal of Business Research, 133*, 285–296. https://doi.org/10.1016/j.jbusres.2021.04.070

Gugenheimer, J., Plaumann, K., Schaub, F., Di Campli San Vito, P., Duck, S., Rabus, M., & Rukzio, E. (2017). The impact of assistive technology on communication quality between deaf and hearing individuals. In *Proceedings of the ACM conference on computer supported cooperative work, CSCW*. https://doi.org/10.1145/2998181.2998203

Harkins, J., Tucker, P. E., Williams, N., & Sauro, J. (2010). Vibration signaling in mobile devices for emergency alerting: A study with deaf evaluators. *Journal of Deaf Studies and Deaf Education*. https://doi.org/10.1093/deafed/enq018

Hauser, P., Wills, K., & Isquit, P. (2006). Hard-of-hearing, deafness and being deaf. In *Treating neurodevelopmental disabilities: clinical research and practice*.

Iezzoni, L. I., O'Day, B. L., Killeen, M., & Harker, H. (2004). Communicating about health care: Observations from persons who are deaf or hard of hearing. *Annals of Internal Medicine*. https://doi.org/10.7326/0003-4819-140-5-200403020-00011

José de Oliveira, O., Francisco da Silva, F., Juliani, F., César Ferreira Motta Barbosa, L., & Vieira Nunhes, T. (2019). Bibliometric method for mapping the State-of-the-Art and identifying research gaps and trends in literature: An essential instrument to support the development of scientific projects. In *Scientometrics recent advances*. https://doi.org/10.5772/intechopen.85856

Lewis, D. E. (1994). Assistive devices for classroom listening. *American Journal of Audiology*. https://doi.org/10.1044/1059-0889.0301.58

Maiorana-Basas, M., & Pagliaro, C. M. (2014). Technology use among adults who are deaf and hard of hearing: A national survey. *Journal of Deaf Studies and Deaf Education*. https://doi.org/10.1093/deafed/enu005

Morata, T. C., Themann, C. L., Randolph, R. F., Verbsky, B. L., Byrne, D. C., & Reeves, E. R. (2005). Working in noise with a hearing loss: Perceptions from workers, supervisors, and hearing conservation program managers. *Ear and Hearing*.

Mukherjee, D., Lim, W. M., Kumar, S., & Donthu, N. (2022). Guidelines for advancing theory and practice through bibliometric research. *Journal of Business Research, 148*, 101–115. https://doi.org/10.1016/j.jbusres.2022.04.042

Pittman, A. L., Lewis, D. E., Hoover, B. M., & Stelmachowicz, P. G. (1999). Recognition performance for four combinations of FM system and hearing aid microphone signals in adverse listening conditions. *Ear and Hearing*. https://doi.org/10.1097/00003446-199908000-00001

Saladin, S. P., & Hansmann, S. E. (2008). Psychosocial variables related to the adoption of video relay services among deaf or hard-of-hearing employees at the Texas school for the deaf. *Assistive Technology*. https://doi.org/10.1080/10400435.2008.10131930

Sanaullah, M., Ahmad, B., Kashif, M., Safdar, T., Hassan, M., Hasan, M. H., & Aziz, N. (2022). A real-time automatic translation of text to sign language. *Computers, Materials and Continua*. https://doi.org/10.32604/cmc.2022.019420

San-Segundo, R., Montero, J. M., Córdoba, R., Sama, V., Fernández, F., D'Haro, L. F., López-Ludeña, V., Sánchez, D., & García, A. (2012). Design, development and field evaluation of a Spanish into sign language translation system. *Pattern Analysis and Applications*. https://doi.org/10.1007/s10044-011-0243-9

Schriempf, A. (2009). Hearing deafness: Subjectness, articulateness and communicability. *Subjectivity*. https://doi.org/10.1057/sub.2009.16

Shanmugam, A. K., & Marimuthu, R. (2021). A critical analysis and review of assistive technology. In *Handbook of decision support systems for neurological disorders*. https://doi.org/10.1016/B978-0-12-822271-3.00001-3

Stark, P., & Hickson, L. (2004). Outcomes of hearing aid fitting for older people with hearing impairment and their significant others. *International Journal of Audiology*. https://doi.org/10.1080/14992020400050050

Valencia-Arias, A., Patino-Toro, O. N., Rodriguez-Correa, P. A., Fernandez-Toro, A. C., Jimenez-Guzman, A., & Gonzalez, J. J. E. (2022). Bibliometric analysis of inclusive technologies for deaf people. In *Proceedings—2022 2nd international conference on advanced enterprise information system, AEIS 2022*. https://doi.org/10.1109/AEIS59450.2022.00022

Wadhawan, A., & Kumar, P. (2021). Sign language recognition Systems: A decade systematic literature review. *Archives of Computational Methods in Engineering*. https://doi.org/10.1007/s11831-019-09384-2

World Health Organization. (2023). *Deafness and hearing loss*. World Health Organization. https://www.who.int/news-room/fact-sheets/detail/deafness-and-hearing-loss

Zeng, F. G., Rebscher, S., Harrison, W., Sun, X., & Feng, H. (2008). Cochlear implants: System design, integration, and evaluation. *IEEE Reviews in Biomedical Engineering*. https://doi.org/10.1109/RBME.2008.2008250

Technological Innovations for Accessibility

Academic Training in Media Accessibility in Audiovisual Translation at a University Level: The Case of the Spanish University System

Juan Pedro Rica Peromingo ⓘ

Abstract In today's digital era, media accessibility has emerged as a critical element for ensuring inclusivity in content creation and distribution. With the growing demand for accessible media, academic and professional approaches to training have become instrumental in bridging the gap between content creators and the diverse audience they aim to reach. Academic institutions play a pivotal role in fostering a deeper understanding of media accessibility (MA). Educational programs provide foundational knowledge and critical insights into various aspects of accessibility standards and practices. With the emergence of media accessibility services within the mass media (subtitling for the deaf and hard-of-hearing, SDH, and audio description for the blind and partially sighted, AD, basically), the need for training professionals in these areas has arisen. MA has traditionally been regarded as a subfield in audiovisual translation (AVT) that is focused on audiences with sensory disabilities, mostly persons with a hearing or a visual impairment (Romero Fresco in Accessible filmmaking: Integrating translation and accessibility into the filmmaking process. Routledge, 2019). MA may be seen to include AVT and to be just as close to Translation Studies as it is to Film Studies or to the broader area of Accessibility Studies (Greco in *Journal of Audiovisual Translation, 1*(1): 205–232, 2018). This paper will provide answers to how academic training is carried out, what required skills and competencies, together with curriculum design, methodological approaches, training materials, and assessment are needed, how AVT training at a university level is, using the Spanish context and the Universidad Complutense de Madrid (UCM) as an example. Finally, information about those research projects nowadays which investigate media accessibility training used by instructors as reference for their teaching contexts will be included.

Keywords Training · Media accessibility · SDH · AD · Teaching · AVT · University

J. P. R. Peromingo (✉)
Departamento de Estudios Ingleses: Lingüística y Literatura, Universidad Complutense de Madrid, Madrid, Spain
e-mail: juanpe@filol.ucm.es

© The Author(s) 2024
A. Marcus-Quinn et al. (eds.), *Transforming Media Accessibility in Europe*,
https://doi.org/10.1007/978-3-031-60049-4_20

359

1   Introduction

In today's digital era, media accessibility has become a crucial aspect of content creation and distribution. Ensuring that media is accessible to all individuals, regardless of their abilities or disabilities, is not just a legal and ethical responsibility but also a significant step toward fostering inclusivity (Romero-Fresco, 2015, 2019; Rica Peromingo, *in press* 2024). Training in media accessibility plays a fundamental role in bridging the gap between content creators and the diverse audience they aim to reach. Media accessibility encompasses a range of tools and practices that enable individuals with disabilities to access and comprehend media content. It involves addressing various needs, including visual, auditory, cognitive, and physical impairments. Subtitles, closed captions, audio descriptions, sign language interpretation, accessible web design, and adaptive technologies are among the many tools used to make media accessible (Bogucki & Deckert, 2020, Tamayo, 2022).

Initially, professionals have been originally trained in the workplace (Arrés et al., 2021; Cerezo Merchán, 2019; Granell & Chaume, 2023; Mejías-Climent & Reyes Lozano, 2023). It was only later when universities began offering individual courses in media accessibility programs. Subsequently, degrees in Translation and Interpreting started to emerge in many European countries, with specific subjects on media accessibility (such as SDH and AD) incorporated into these degrees. Today, professionals continue to receive training through specialized courses, such as those offered by ATRAE (the Association for Translation and Audiovisual Adaptation) in Spain. Academics, on the other hand, are trained through subjects in degrees in Translation and Interpreting, Linguistics, and media accessibility in audiovisual translation. (Rica Peromingo, 2016; Silvester & Tuominen, 2021; Valdez et al., 2023).

Media accessibility has, therefore, emerged as a critical element for ensuring inclusivity in content creation and distribution. With the growing demand for accessible media, academic and professional approaches to training have become instrumental in bridging the gap between content creators and the diverse audience they aim to reach. Academic institutions play a pivotal role in fostering a deeper understanding of media accessibility. Educational programs provide foundational knowledge and critical insights into various aspects of accessibility standards and practices. With the emergence of media accessibility services within the mass media (SDH, AD, and sign language interpreting, SLI, basically), the need for training professionals in these areas has arisen. Media accessibility has traditionally been regarded as a subfield in AVT that is focused on audiences with sensory disabilities, mostly persons with a hearing or a visual impairment (Romero-Fresco, 2019). Media accessibility may be seen to include AVT and to be just as close to Translation Studies as it is to Film Studies or to the broader area of Accessibility Studies (Greco, 2018).

Although reference will also be made to professional training in accessibility, this chapter will provide answers on how academic training is conducted, detailing the required skills and competencies, curriculum design, methodological approaches, training materials, and assessment methods needed. It will examine how AVT training is implemented at the university level, using the Spanish context and the Universidad

Complutense de Madrid (UCM) as examples. Finally, it will include information on current research projects investigating media accessibility training, which university instructors use as references for their teaching contexts.

2 Media Accessibility: Definition and Components

Media accessibility refers to the strategies, techniques, and technologies used to make various forms of media content, including text, audio, video, and images, accessible to individuals with disabilities (Rica Peromingo, 2022). It aims to remove barriers that may hinder people with disabilities from accessing, understanding, and engaging with digital and traditional media. The importance of media accessibility cannot be overstated. Inclusivity and equal access to information are fundamental principles of a democratic society. Ensuring that media content is accessible to all, regardless of their abilities, is a matter of social justice and a legal requirement in many countries. In this section, the various aspects of media accessibility and its significance in today's world will be examined.

According to some authors, (Matamala & Orero, 2018; Mazur & Vercauteren 2019; Rica Peromingo *in press* 2024), the components associated with media accessibility include the following: closed captions, subtitling, audio description, sign language interpretation, alternative text or description text (Alt Text), accessible web design, and accessible document formats. Let us analyze each of these components:

1. Closed Captions: Closed captions provide a textual representation of spoken content, making audio and video content accessible to deaf or hard-of-hearing individuals. This component includes real-time captions for live events (Neves, 2021, Zárate, 2021).
2. Subtitling: Subtitles, created for both hearing individuals and those who are deaf or hard of hearing, offer textual translations of spoken content in a different language. This facilitates access and comprehension of multimedia content for individuals with limited language proficiency or certain degrees of hearing impairment (Díaz Cintas & Remael, 2021).
3. Audio Description: Audio description is essential for blind or visually impaired individuals. It provides a spoken narrative of visual elements in multimedia content, such as scenes, actions, and facial expressions (Matamala & Orero, 2018, Perego, 2021).
4. Sign Language Interpretation: The inclusion of sign language interpretation is crucial for the deaf community. Sign language interpreters convert spoken language into sign language during live events or recorded videos (Romero-Fresco, 2018; Rica Peromingo, *in press* 2024).
5. Alternative Text or Description Text: Alternative text is a textual description of images, graphics, and other non-textual elements in digital content. It benefits individuals who use screen readers to access the web (Georgakopoulou, 2019).

6. Accessible Web Design: Ensuring that websites and digital platforms are designed and developed with accessibility in mind is a fundamental component of media accessibility. This includes compliance with WCAG standards (Web Content Accessibility Guidelines) (Bywood, 2020; Georgakopoulou, 2019).

7. Accessible Document Formats: Creating documents in formats that are easily navigable and understandable by screen readers and other assistive technologies is crucial for providing accessible written content (Bywood, 2020; Georgakopoulou, 2019).

We believe that all these components related to media accessibility should be explicitly addressed in audiovisual translation and accessibility classes. Furthermore, these considerations should be incorporated into professional contexts where specialized audiovisual translators are trained with expertise in accessibility (Rica Peromingo, 2019).

3   Media Accessibility: Skills and Competences and Legislation

When thinking about the skills and competencies required for the training of academics and professionals in media accessibility, one is referring to those linguistic–cultural and technical aspects that every audiovisual translator should possess (Mazur & Vercauteren, 2019). These aspects are the ones that university educational programs should include regarding the technical knowledge required for the training of scholars and professionals in media accessibility (Rica Peromingo, 2016, 2022). The skills and abilities of every audiovisual and accessibility translator must be framed within a set of priorities (objectives) and constraints (obstacles) that influence the decisions that must be established with each audiovisual text that one may face, and "that must be re-established every time a new translation task is initiated" (Zabalbeascoa, 1997: 331–332). The following skills and abilities, among others, can be highlighted: software use (both professional and free programas), synchronization (subtitles and audio-described text), subtitles spotting, subtitles segmentation, speed, limit for characters per subtitle, ortho-typographical conventions, contextual information, identification of characters, emotions and sounds, music, songs, description, "empty spaces," tone of voice, intonation, excellent diction, etc. On the other hand, with regard to linguistic and cultural knowledge, university educational programs and professional training courses in media accessibility should cover aspects such as translation strategies, domestication, foreignizing, condensation or suppression of information, adaptation, mastering of the mother language and the target language, cultural elements, and registers.[1]

In addition to the linguistic–cultural and technical aspects just mentioned, it is crucial that the teaching or audiovisual translation and media accessibility also

---

[1] For more detailed information on the skills and abilities emphasized in the training of academics and professionals in accessibility in audiovisual translation, refer to Rica Peromingo (2016: 31–42).

includes training in the legislation or norms governing the provision of accessible materials (with SDH, with AD, with sign language interpretation, etc.) for an individual with visual and/or auditory disabilities (Martí Ferriol, 2020). This legislation should provide the rights of individuals with disabilities to access (and enjoy) audiovisual materials on equal terms with the non-disabled population. It should also regulate how accessible audiovisual products are presented for audiences with specific disabilities, such as those with hearing, visual, or cognitive impairments. Some of the international and national legislation (in the USA, the UK, or Australia, for example, in Europe, and particularly in Spain) that should be addressed in the training of expert audiovisual translators in media accessibility include the following (Bogucki & Deckert, 2020; Greco, 2019; Rica Peromingo, *in press* 2024):

- The Disabilities Act of 1990 in the USA, with some amendments in 2008 and specially Chapter 126 on "Equal Opportunity for Individuals with Disabilities," aimed at "to provide clear, strong, consistent, enforceable standards addressing discrimination against individuals with disabilities": https://www.cdc.gov/ncb ddd/disabilityandhealth/disability-inclusion.html.
- The Disability Discrimination Act 1992 in Australia, with some amendments in 2018, aimed at "to promote recognition and acceptance within the community of the principle that persons with disabilities have the same fundamental rights as the rest of the community: https://www.legislation.gov.au/Details/C2018C00125.
- The Equality Act 2010 in the UK, with an update in 2015, aimed at "to eliminate discrimination and other prohibited conduct [...] and to increase equality of opportunity": https://www.legislation.gov.uk/ukpga/2010/15/contents.
- The European Accessibility Act (EAA) approved in March 2019, aimed at "to contribute to the proper functioning of the internal market by approximating the laws, regulations and administrative provisions of the Member States as regards accessibility requirements for certain products and services by, in particular, eliminating and preventing barriers to the free movement of products and services covered by this Directive arising from divergent accessibility requirements in the Member States": https://eur-lex.europa.eu/legal-content/EN/TXT/? uri=CELEX%3A32019L0882.
- The International Organization for Standardization ISO/IEC TS 20071–21:2015, Part 21 in particular regarding information technology, user interface component accessibility and specifically regulating AD: https://www.iso.org/standard/63061. html. At present, there is an international committee with various professional and academic members, including Spanish universities such as the Universitat Autònoma de Barcelona and Universidad Complutense de Madrid, reviewing the standard for the publication of an update in 2024.
- The International Organization for Standardization ISO/IEC TS 20071–25:2017, Part 25 in particular regarding information technology, user interface component accessibility and specifically regulating the audio presentation of text in videos, including captions, subtitles, and other on-screen text: https://www.iso.org/sta ndard/69060.html. As with the previous case of the standard regulating AD, in

this instance, there is also an international committee involved in the revision of the standard for the publication of an update in 2024.

- Convention on the Rights of Persons with Disabilities (CRPD), especially Article 9 on accessibility in daily life and also in the media, aimed at "to promote, protect and ensure the full and equal enjoyment of all human rights and fundamental freedoms by all persons with disabilities, and to promote respect for their inherent dignity": https://www.un.org/development/desa/disabilities/convention-on-the-rights-of-persons-with-disabilities.html.

In the case of the Spanish context, and pending the update and implementation of the European ISO standards, there is specific legislation for the use of SDH, AD, and the use of the Spanish Sign Language interpretation in the media. This legislation will be affected in the near future when European standards on media accessibility become mandatory in the Member States of the European Union. Currently, the standards regulating real Access to the media for individuals with visual or hearing disabilities are as follows (Matamala & Orero, 2010; Rica Peromingo, *in press* 2024; Zhang, 2019):

- Norm UNE 153010 on subtitling for the deaf and hard-of-hearing (SDH) (2012): https://www.une.org/encuentra-tu-norma/busca-tu-norma/norma/?c=N0049426. This is the standard that regulates SDH in Spanish media. The initial standard was published in 2003. Subsequently, there was an update in 2012, and since then, it has been the operational standard. As mentioned before, it is currently in the process of being updated.
- Norm UNE 153,020 on audiodescription (AD) (2005): https://www.une.org/encuentra-tu-norma/busca-tunorma/norma/?c=N0032787. This is the standard that regulates AD and audio guides. The standard was published in 2005 and has not undergone any updates since then. Similar to the SDH standard, it is currently in the process of being updated.
- Ley 7/2010, de 31 de marzo, General de la Comunicación Audiovisual[2]: https://www.boe.es/buscar/pdf/2010/BOE-A-2010-5292-consolidado.pdf. This standard individually addresses the obligations of audiovisual communication service providers concerning minors and individuals with disabilities, who, in the view of the legislator and European institutions, deserve special protection. Especially important is Article 8 of the law, which is exclusively dedicated to the rights of individuals with disabilities (page 3).
- Estrategia Integral Española de Cultura para Todos. Accesibilidad a la Cultura para las Personas con Discapacidad,[3] published in 2011: https://www.mdsocialesa2030.gob.es/derechos-sociales/discapacidad/docs/Estrategia_Integral_Espanola_Cultura_para_Todos.pdf. The Strategy integrates, within a single framework, all the actions and accessibility measures that have been adopted within the scope of the General State Administration in favor of universal

---

[2] General Law 7/2010, March 31 on Audiovisual Communication.

[3] The Comprehensive Spanish Strategy for Culture for All: Accessibility to Culture for Individuals with Disabilities.

accessibility in the cultural domain. It also envisions new initiatives in cultural environments or activities where needs have been identified, all while following harmonized guidelines and the highest standards of quality, technology, and adaptability. The objective is to ensure, in accordance with the principle of universal design, inclusive cultural services and products that equally serve all individuals regardless of their abilities (page 6).

- Guía de buenas prácticas para la incorporación de la lengua de signos española en television,[4] published in 2017: https://www.siis.net/documentos/ficha/529550. pdf. This guide aims, with the invaluable support of end-users, to ensure the quality of sign language services through accessibility and linguistic criteria that meet the needs of deaf and deaf-blind individuals in accessing television content (pages 6–7).

All this international legislation, in conjunction with local and country-specific laws, should be integrated into the curriculum of audiovisual translation and media accessibility education. Technical, linguistic, and cultural knowledge cannot exclusively be the most emphasized aspects in university classes and professional training centers for audiovisual translators. An apparently complex field like legislation in the audiovisual domain becomes essential if one of the aims is to train academics and professionals in accessibility.

4   Media Accessibility Training: Methodologies Used

When thinking about the methodologies used for teaching media accessibility, one may be referring to the work that educators must undertake with their learners. Among the methodologies used, training in both technical and linguistic–cultural aspects is recommended. In the tradition of Spanish university contexts, this type of education has focused more on linguistic and cultural issues than on the "technical constraints" that influence the final outcome of the SDH or the AD texts in one way or another (Cerezo Merchán, 2019; Rica Peromingo, 2016). Therefore, trainers are strongly encouraged to explore technical aspects while teaching the linguistic and cultural elements necessary in the translation process. In almost all cases of audiovisual translation, it is the technical constraints that will "force" us to make linguistic modifications in the resulting translated text (Díaz Cintas & Remael, 2021). In the specific classes of audiovisual translation and accessibility at UCM, training begins initially with all the technical constraints that are typical and particular to each of the traditional audiovisual translation modalities (dubbing and subtitling for hearing audiences) and those related to accessibility (SDH and AD, along with sign language interpretation). It is emphasized that, as mentioned before, the technical constraints will influence the linguistic decisions made when translating the audiovisual text into the target language. Once this technical training is completed in class, training shifts

---

[4] Guide of Best Practices for the Incorporation of Spanish Sign Language in Television.

to linguistic and cultural constraints in the translation and accessibility of the audiovisual product. In the case of audiovisual translation and accessibility modalities, emphasis is placed on teaching the specific regulations in each of these modalities. This is the proposal that we are implementing in the university setting at UCM.

In our opinion and from our experience in our AVT classes, students in media accessibility should learn to use both professional software (provided it is available for acquisition in the specific educational context) and especially free software that yields fairly accurate results for practicing accessible modes of audiovisual translation: professional programs such as Spot, EZTitles, or OOONA (online subtitling), as well as free software programs like Aegisub (available both for Windows and Mac environments), Subtitle Workshop, iMovie, Audacity, Windows Movie Maker 2024, etc. (Rica Peromingo, 2016).

In technical matters, the main focus should not only be on the use of software programs for SDH or AD or the incorporation of sign language interpretation but also other characteristics more specific to the audiovisual product being dealt with, for instance, visual and auditory coherence, lip synchronization (in the case of dubbing), space synchronization (in the case of subtitles for hearing and subtitles for the deaf), "empty spaces" in audio descriptions, etc.

When dealing with the technical constraints that any audiovisual translation for any modality has to face, the teaching of aspects more related to linguistic and cultural conventions of both the source and the target languages can be interspersed. Students should be familiar with those aspects that are particularly conflictive and may cause translation problems when transferring information from the foreign language into their native language. In the case of the English–Spanish combination, for example, the following aspects can be mentioned: cultural and historical references, intertextuality, phraseological units, periphrasis, proverbs, accent (national, regional, idiolect), interjections, onomatopoeias, wordplay, rhymes, proper and place names, foreignization and domestication, loan terms and calques, orthotypographical norms, among others (Rica Peromingo, 2016). These are the methodologies that, from our point of view, have worked and continue to work in the university setting (specifically at UCM) for the training of academics and professionals in media accessibility.

The methodologies employed should incorporate the use of videos for SDH and AD practice with students, always for educational purposes: films, television series, documentaries, news programs, theater plays, operas, musicals, etc. Within these methodologies, some authors (Cerezo Merchán, 2019) propose the following methods for teaching media accessibility: comparative method (which means to compare accessible versions with non-accessible ones of the same content to highlight the differences and challenges of accessibility), progressive method (in which the instructors will gradually introduce levels of complexity in practicing accessibility, starting with simple subtitles and advancing to audio description and other forms of accessibility), participatory method (which actively involves students in the process of creating accessibility, fostering reflection and critical analysis), collaborative method (which encourages teamwork to address accessibility projects, allowing students to benefit from a diversity of skills and knowledge) and analysis and evaluation method (which develop critical analysis and evaluation skills for audiovisual content in terms of accessibility). These methods aim to provide students with a comprehensive understanding of the challenges and strategies related to accessibility in media.

Most specialists nowadays prefer competency-based training to AVT, that is, a combination of task- and project-based learning: contrastive, extralinguistic, methodological and strategic, instrumental, and translation problem-solving.

5 Media Accessibility Training: Educational Materials, Assessment, and Evaluation

One of the critical aspects in media accessibility training is the type of materials that can be employed in courses (both at the university and professional levels), designed for the education of learners in media accessibility. Within this methodology, a syllabus that encompasses the following progression of content and materials for implementation in the audiovisual translation classes is presented in the following pages.

At the moment, in the AVT and media accessibility classes at UCM, we are using this syllabus as an example of training for academics and professionals in this field. We have been using this methodology and class program for several years in our classes, and it has worked very satisfactorily (see comments on the AVLA and TRADAVAL projects later on). The results of the teaching evaluations by the students have been very positive, emphasizing the fact that in the classes, we promote technical, linguistic, and cultural training, as well as knowledge of the existing regulations in the different AVT modalities taught in the classes (Rica Peromingo, 2019). The contents of the syllabus in question are as follows:

1. A selection of audiovisual materials: video clips from different classic and recent movies, TV series, documentaries, theater plays, operas, news shows, etc.
2. An analysis of the technical and linguistic constraints of the audiovisual product.
3. An anticipation of the problems the trainees may face in the process of the AVT.
4. Training on the software used for both SDH and AD.
5. Research on the conflictive issues encountered in the process.
6. Discussion on the SDH and the AD produced by the trainees.
7. Assessment and evaluation of the trainees and also of the materials used.

At the Universidad Complutense de Madrid, within the framework of audiovisual translation classes, and specifically in the modules addressing media accessibility, we adhere to the outlined syllabus[5] which progressively heightens the difficulty of the activities from both technical and linguistic–cultural perspectives. At the beginning of the academic term, students are provided with this information, gaining awareness of the nature of activities and the effort required well in advance. Furthermore, the

---

[5] See Appendix 1 and Appendix 2 for examples of two real activities: one for SDH and another one for AD. Information about the results of the implementation of those activities is also included.

activity objectives, time commitment, and whether the task is to be carried out individually or in a group are explicitly stipulated. Up to the current academic year 2023–2024, the outcomes of this syllabus have yielded highly favorable academic results among students in AVT and MA programs. We are confident that this model can be effectively implemented in other national and international university contexts or in training enterprises for audiovisual translators specializing in media accessibility.

Regarding assessment and evaluation, the evaluation of materials should take place after completing the activities, allowing for the detection of their efficacy in achieving the stated objectives. Assessment of the students/trainees' activities should always be in line with the purposes of the course and the aims of the activities. The proposed syllabus advocates for both formative and summative assessment focusing on the results obtained from the activities and also on the evaluation of errors committed, both technical and linguistic and cultural ones. Finally, discussions and reports after the activities should also be part of the students'/trainees' assessment. All information regarding the outcomes of the activities can be incorporated into the forms used for each of the audiovisual materials employed in the classes. (Bogucki & Deckert, 2020; Rica Peromingo, 2019; Rica Peromingo & Sáenz Herrero, 2019).

In conclusion to this section, a component proposed in this methodology for teaching audiovisual translation and media accessibility is the final evaluation of the students' work by a group of individuals with hearing and visual impairments participating in the research project[6] and the research group[7] I lead at the Universidad Complutense de Madrid. These end-users analyze the production of students in AVT and MA classes to determine if the work has been executed as accurately as possible for a deaf or hearing-impaired audience. Furthermore, they assess whether the SDH and the AD have been created in accordance with legislation and regulations, specially those existing in Spain for SDH and AD. The end-users evaluate all student works by completing questionnaires that encompass technical, linguistic, and cultural data (for more information on the original questionnaires created by the UCM research group and project and some results of those evaluations, refer to Rica Peromingo 2019).

6   Media Accessibility Training: Research Projects to Develop Professional and Academic Profiles

In this final section of the chapter, a list of international research projects (primarily within the European context) and Spanish national projects whose primary objectives are related to accessibility research (SDH, sign language interpretation, and AD) are

---

[6] The AVLA (Audiovisual Learning Archive) Project. Information about the research project can be found here: https://www.avlaproject.com/.

[7] The UCM Research Group Translation, Audiovisual Translation and Linguistic Accessibility (TRADAVAL). Information about the research group can be found here: https://www.ucm.es/tradaval/.

presented. Ultimately, this aims to enable academic researchers and professionals to acquire more specific and up-to-date knowledge regarding the needs of the deaf and blind communities and how to enhance and improve their access to audiovisual products.

In the specific context being analyzed in this chapter (the university setting in Spanish public universities, specifically UCM), the syllabus, materials, evaluation, and methodologies used in audiovisual translation and media accessibility classes have been greatly influenced by the results obtained in the projects and research groups analyzed in the following pages. Specifically, European projects, national projects, and research groups in which the author of this chapter is involved have provided valuable information to design the accessibility courses being taught at the UCM.

The increased involvement and concern for teaching fundamental aspects of media accessibility have led to a significant number of European educational and institutional organizations (particularly in the Spanish context) financing research projects specifically focused on training academics and professionals in audiovisual translation and media accessibility. Some of these research projects are outlined below[8]:

1. Interlingual Live Subtitling for Access—ILSA: ILSA will identify the skills and profile of a new professional, the interlingual live subtitler (ILSer), develop, test, and validate the first training course on interlingual live subtitling (ILS) and provide a protocol for the implementation of this discipline in three real-life scenarios, namely TV, political/social settings, and the classroom. https://galmao bservatory.webs.uvigo.es/projects/interlingual-live-subtitling-for-access-ilsa/.

2. AVLA Project—Corpus of Linguistic Accessibility (CALING): The project (funded by the UCM) consists of the use of new methodologies and technologies applied to the teaching and learning of the different modes of audiovisual translation (AVT), specifically the ones related to accessibility: SDH and AD. The main goal is to design materials, resources, and evaluation processes in order to put into practice these new technologies and methodologies for teaching and learning. https://www.avlaproject.com/.

3. CALING Project—*Recursos educativos inclusivos, innovación y lingüística de corpus en accesibilidad en traducción audiovisual (subtitulado para sordos, audiodescripción para ciegos y lengua de signos): el corpus CALING y su aplicación en contextos universitarios* (Inclusive educational resources, innovation, and corpus linguistics in accessibility in audiovisual translation (subtitling for the deaf, audio description for the blind, and sign language): the CALING corpus and its application in university contexts): The project includes the compilation of the CALING corpus (Corpus de Accesibilidad Lingüística) which includes a database of different activities designed by the research group and used in different audiovisual translations university classes to teach the different modes of audiovisual translation: dubbing, subtitling for hearing population, SDH, and AD. The project also includes the evaluation by real recipients of the students'

---

[8] The information is taken from the different web pages.

activities compiled in the CALING corpus. https://docta.ucm.es/entities/public ation/029ce137-b676-4666-8063-478159a9e32d.

4. COST LEAD-ME Project: This Action aims to help all stakeholders in the field of Media Accessibility and cross-cutting topics (e.g., AI and Inter-active Technologies) in Europe to meet the legal milestones requested by the recently passed European legislation. Researchers, engineers, scholars as well as businesses and policy makers will be empowered by LEAD-ME with a common and unique platform which will collect, create, share, and disseminate innovative technologies and solutions, best practices, and guide-lines, and promote them. Furthermore, it will contribute toward existing and new standards on Media Accessibility among 28 European or associ-ated countries. https://www.cost.eu/actions/CA19142/?fbclid=IwAR363Utb7p oILGTU15WzFY9U8KM71U_FYPyq5Kngf5FrAL9gP2A_Upp-Uhc#tabs.

5. ATHENA—Bringing Accessibility and Design for All into Higher Education Curricula: Accessibility and Design for All are the base for more independent living and self-determined participation for people with disabilities, the aging population and many other groups in our society. Accessibility and Design for All are the anchors and entrance points to reach the ultimate goal of more inde-pendent living and self-determined participation in all domains, e.g., education, work, politics, administration, culture, leisure/sports, religion, and entertainment. Accessibility, Design for All, and the role of Assistive Technologies are accepted as a fundamental social, political, and legal requirement in an open, democratic, and inclusive society, best expressed with the globally accepted UN-Convention on the Rights of Persons with Disabilities. https://athenaproject.eu/.

Finally, and in addition to the aforementioned international and national research projects, it is essential to highlight two research groups that amalgamate the investiga-tive efforts of various scholars, primarily within the fields of translation, audiovisual translation, and media accessibility[9]:

6. Transmedia Catalonia: It aims to research audiovisual translation (dubbing, subti-tling, voice-over, etc.) and media accessibility (subtitling for the deaf and hard-of-hearing, respeaking, audio description, audio subtitling, and sign language) in various genres, platforms, and supports. After an initial period devoted to descrip-tive research, its focus is now on user testing and technological implementation. Further information can be found on its website: https://grupsderecerca.uab.cat/transmedia/.

7. TRADAVAL UCM Madrid: The Research Group focuses on translation in general, with a specific emphasis on audiovisual translation (AVT) and linguistic accessibility (including subtitling for the deaf, audio description for the blind, and Spanish Sign Language-LSE). The intention is to integrate professional and academic profiles from other language departments within the Faculty of Philology at the Complutense University of Madrid (UCM) and profes-sionals from Spanish Sign Language currently engaged at the UCM's Center

---

[9] The information is taken from the different web pages.

for Sign Language Interpretation (CSIM) in the near future. The team comprises researchers and professors in the fields of translation, audiovisual translation, and linguistic accessibility, the majority of whom have collaborated on various national and international research projects as well as UCM's educational innovation initiatives for several years. Further information can be found on its website: https://www.ucm.es/tradaval/.

The involvement of professionals and academics in national and international research projects, as well as their participation as members of research groups, is crucial for the training of specialists in audiovisual translation and media accessibility. The outcomes derived from research efforts significantly contribute to their application in both classroom settings and training courses. Simultaneously, this facilitates the cultivation of researchers capable of engaging with national and international standardization organizations (Matamala and Orero, 2018), such as the UNE standards in Spain[10] or the ISO standards within the European context.[11] The comprehensive training of professionals and academics underscores the necessity, as pointed out by Greco (2019: 40), "for a wider discussion on a new model for accessibility education and training, which could then support and be coupled with a new model for accessibility practices. A model of training and practicing that is diversity-based, user-led, proactive-oriented, politically-driven, and quality-centered."

7 Conclusion

In this study, the significance of designing educational programs that provide fundamental knowledge and critical perspectives on aspects related to standards and the practice of accessibility essential for the training of academics and professionals in subtitling for the deaf, audio description for the blind, and sign language interpretation has been examined. Following this study, it becomes evident that the field of media accessibility, traditionally considered a secondary aspect of AVT, constitutes an independent area of study that is closely connected not only to AVT but also to Film Studies and Accessibility Studies in general.

The methods employed for the training of audiovisual translators and accessibility professionals in an academic setting have been analyzed. Furthermore, the skills and competencies that, in our assessment at a university level, are requisite for the execution of high-quality academic work and teaching have been discussed. Our investigation has delved into curriculum design, methodological approaches, and materials applicable in AVT and accessibility classes, including those at the master's level. Lastly, with a focus on education in diverse settings, we have identified current international (and national, in the case of Spain) research projects and research groups that exert direct and positive influence on the teaching and learning of specific AVT modalities related to accessibility. Examples of activities (refer to Appendices 1

---

[10] Official webpage in English: https://www.en.une.org/encuentra-tu-norma/busca-tu-norma.

[11] Official webpage in English: https://www.iso.org/standards.html.

and 2), specific methodologies, and real university educational contexts where such teaching approaches are being implemented have been presented.

Another crucial aspect that has been analyzed is the importance of incorporating existing legislation regulating accessibility-related modalities into the training of professionals and academics in audiovisual translation and media accessibility at a university level. This encompasses both local and national perspectives (in our case, Spanish legislation) and an international scope (including the USA, the UK, and Europe). The regulations under consideration pertain to subtitling for the deaf, audio description for the blind, and the inclusion of sign language interpretation. We believe that familiarity with these regulations should be considered an essential skill for every audiovisual translator to acquire during their training.

In conclusion, we assert that academic or professional training in accessibility at a university level necessitates the considerations addressed in this study. In the near future, further exploration is warranted to identify additional requisite skills, assess the current methodological approaches, enhance knowledge concerning legislation pertaining to accessibility modalities, and actively promote the involvement of academics and professionals in ongoing research projects. Ultimately, our role as teachers, AVT academics, professionals and researchers in the field of accessibility, aligns with the United Nations mandate (International Convention on the Rights of Persons with Disabilities,[12] Article 21 "Freedom of expression and opinion and access to information"), which obliges all member states of the European Union "to ensure that persons with disabilities can exercise the right to freedom of expression and opinion, including the freedom to seek, receive, and impart information and ideas on an equal basis with others and through all forms of communication of their choice."

Acknowledgements This chapter is based upon work from COST Action CA19142—Leading Platform for European Citizens, Industries, Academia and Policymakers in Media Accessibility (LEAD-ME) supported by COST (European Cooperation in Science and Technology).

Appendix 1

Example of an SDH Activity Sheet: Movie **Agora**[13]

1. **Activity Explanation: What It Entails**—The activity involves creating subtitles for the deaf for a scene from the movie *Agora*, which is provided to the students in mp4 format through the virtual platform used for the class. Both linguistic and technical aspects of deaf subtitling and the specific legislation on SDH discussed

---

[12] The document can be consulted at https://www.ohchr.org/en/instruments-mechanisms/instruments/convention-rights-persons-disabilities [retrieved on November 25, 2023].

[13] Official information about the movie: https://www.imdb.com/title/tt1186830/?ref_=nv_sr_srsg_0_tt_8_nm_0_q_agora.

in previous classes will be taken into consideration. In contrast to previous activities where students received the movie script, translated it, and adapted the text for subtitles for the deaf and hard-of-hearing population, for this activity, they will receive the original subtitle file for hearing viewers in Spanish and will need to adapt it for SDH using the software program utilized in class.

2. **Necessary Audiovisual Support**—For this activity, we will require the video visualization program (VLC), the subtitling program (Aegisub), and Microsoft Office Word. Connection to the Internet for research will also be needed.

3. **Activity Objectives**—The objectives are to identify translation issues, priorities, and constraints in adapting subtitles for hearing viewers to subtitles for the deaf from both a linguistic–cultural and technical standpoint. Students must pay particular attention to the contextual information in the scene (sounds, noises, music, characters' way of speaking, feelings, emotions, etc.) essential for its comprehension.

4. **Implementation of the Activity**—Students can collaborate in class to address common doubts, but the actual activity needs to be completed individually at home.

5. **Time Invested in Carrying Out the Activity**—Students will need to view the movie scene clip that needs to be subtitled for the deaf. In class, each student will use the Aegisub software program to work with the subtitles for hearing viewers and adapt them for deaf and hard-of-hearing population (approximately 20 min). Subsequently, a few randomly selected examples from the students in the class will be screened, and their work will be discussed, with particular attention to the technical and linguistic–cultural aspects of the audiovisual product (around 30 min). In the final minutes of the class, students will ask questions of doubts they may have about the activity. After the class, the students will individually upload the file with the SDH to the virtual platform of the course.

Some Results Gathered from the Practice of the Activity During the Current Academic Year 2023–2024: Overall, the activity has performed quite well, as students have been able to analyze the process of SDH and the challenges that may arise in creating Spanish subtitles for the deaf, especially from a technical perspective, considering the most significant technical constraints. Evaluation has taken into account how contextual information (essential for a deaf viewer) of the scene has been included and the fact that students worked with a pre-prepared subtitle file for hearing viewers eliminating the need for translation from English to Spanish. The outcome has been quite satisfactory, as students have included this information with considerable precision, adjusting and formatting the SDH quite accurately, even when required to add contextual information. The students' assignments have also been evaluated by the end-users (a group of deaf people) who are part of the research project under my direction at the Universidad Complutense de Madrid.

Appendix 2

Example of an AD Activity Sheet: Movie **1984**[14]

1. **Activity Explanation: What It Entails**—The activity involves viewing the opening scenes of the movie *1984* and drafting the text in Spanish that will be needed for audio description of the scene. Students are encouraged to be mindful of the technical aspects of the audio description process, consider relevant legislation and regulations on audio description (especially those referenced in Spain), and contemplate the tone of voice and intonation they will employ.
2. **Necessary Audiovisual Support**—For this activity, the students will require a video visualization program (VLC), a voice recording program (Audacity for Windows environments or iMovie for Mac environments), the movie script for the original descriptive information of the scenes, and Microsoft Office Word.
3. **Activity Objectives**—The objectives are to identify the necessary and essential information that must be included for the audio description of the scene, taking into account prior instruction in class regarding this accessibility modality in terms of linguistic, vocal, and technical considerations.
4. **Implementation of the Activity**—Students can collaborate in class to address common doubts, but the actual activity needs to be completed individually at home.
5. **Time Invested in Carrying Out the Activity**—Students collectively watch the scene in class (approximately 5 min) and begin working on the activity individually (around 20 min). Once the preliminary draft of the text deemed suitable for inclusion in the audio description is prepared, it is presented to the rest of the classmates and discussed with them (approximately 30 min). The final minutes of the class will be allocated to address any questions or issues that may have arisen in the process. After the class, the students will individually upload the video file with the AD inserted to the virtual platform of the course.

   Some Results Gathered from the Practice of the Activity During the Current Academic Year 2023–2024: The activity proved challenging initially, although ultimately, the results of the students' work were highly satisfactory. Consideration was given to conciseness, the application of information condensation techniques, and the summarization of relevant information, emphasizing aspects crucial for audio description for the visually impaired in an audiovisual product. Additionally, from a more technical standpoint, evaluation included the tone (and intonation) of the voice used in the recording, the speed of the description, and the synchronization of the audio-described text with the original oral text of the movie. As in the case of the SDH, the students' assignments have also been evaluated by the end-users (a group of blind people) who are part of the research project under my direction at the Universidad Complutense de Madrid.

---

[14] Official information about the movie: https://www.imdb.com/title/tt0087803/?ref_=nv_sr_srsg_0_tt_8_nm_0_q_1984.

References

Arrés, E., Castillo, F., Rebollo, J., & Yborra, J. (2021). Luces, cámara y… traducción audiovisual. Guía para futuros traductores audiovisuales. Pie de Página.

Bogucki, L., & Deckert, M. (Eds.). (2020). *The Palgrave handbook of audiovisual translation and media accessibility.* Palgrave Macmillan.

Bywood, L. (2020). Technology and audiovisual translation. In L. Bogucki & M. Deckert (Eds.), *The Palgrave handbook of audiovisual translation and media accessibility* (pp. 503–517). Palgrave Macmillan.

Cerezo Merchán, B. (2019). Audiovisual translator training. In L. Pérez-González (Ed.), *The Routledge handbook of audiovisual translation* (pp. 468–482). Routledge.

Díaz Cintas, J., & Remael, A. (2021). *Subtitling. Concepts and practices.* Routledge.

Georgakopoulou, P. (2019). Technologization of audiovisual translation. In L. Pérez-González (Ed.), *The Routledge handbook of audiovisual translation* (pp. 516–539). Routledge.

Granell, X., & Chaume, F. (2023). Audiovisual translation, translators, and technology: From automation pipe dream to human-machine convergence. *Linguistica Antverpiensia, New Series: Themes in Translation Studies, 22*, 20–40. https://lans-tts.uantwerpen.be/index.php/LANS-TTS/article/view/776

Greco, G. M. (2018). The nature of accessibility studies. *Journal of Audiovisual Translation, 1*(1), 205–232. https://doi.org/10.47476/jat.v1i1.51

Greco, G. M. (2019). Towards a pedagogy of accessibility: The need for critical learning spaces in media accessibility education and training. *Linguistica Antverpiensia, New Series: Themes in Translation Studies, 18*, 23–46. https://lans-tts.uantwerpen.be/index.php/LANS-TTS/article/view/518

Martí Ferriol, J. L. (2020). Norms in AVT: A dual approach to a long-lasting and fundamental notion. *Journal of Audiovisual Translation, 3*(1), 72–86. https://www.jatjournal.org/index.php/jat/article/view/11

Matamala, A., & Orero, P. (2018) Standardising accessibility: Transferring knowledge to society. *Journal of Audiovisual Translation, 1*(1), 139–154. http://www.jatjournal.org/index.php/jat/article/view/49/8

Matamala, A., & Orero, P. (Eds.). (2010). *Listening to subtitles: Subtitles for the deaf and hard of hearing.* Peter Lang.

Mazur, I., & Vercauteren, G. (2019). Media accessibility training. *Lingüística Antverpiensia, New Series: Themes in Translation Studies, 18*, 1–22. https://lans-tts.uantwerpen.be/index.php/LANS-TTS/article/view/564

Mejías-Climent, L., & Reyes Lozano, J. (Eds.). (2023). *La traducción audiovisual a través de la traducción automática y la posedición. Prácticas actuales y futuras.* Granada.

Neves, J. (2021). Subtitling for deaf and hard of hearing audiences: Moving forward. In L. Pérez-González (Ed.), *The Roudledge handbook of audiovisual translation* (pp. 82–95). Routledge.

Perego, E. (2021). Audio description: Evolving recommendations for usable, effective and enjoyable practices. In L. Pérez-González (Ed.), *The Routledge handbook of audiovisual translation* (pp. 114–129). Routledge.

Rica Peromingo, J. P. (2019). El corpus CALING: Docencia e investigación en traducción audiovisual y accesibilidad lingüística. TRANS. *Revista de Traductología, 23*, 263–298. https://revistas.uma.es/index.php/trans/article/view/4990

Rica Peromingo, J. P. (2022). Accesibilidad y herramientas tecnológicas en traducción audiovisual (TAV): Productos audiovisuales accesibles. Tradumàtica. *Tecnologies de la traducció, 20*, 284–294. https://revistes.uab.cat/tradumatica/article/view/318

Rica Peromingo, J. P. (in press 2024). Accesibilidad lingüística: las normas europeas y nacionales de aplicación en aspectos traductológicos audiovisuales. In: M. J. Varela Salinas, & C. Plaza Lara (Eds.), *Aproximaciones teóricas y prácticas a la accesibilidad desde la traducción y la interpretación.* Comares.

Rica Peromingo, J. P., & Sáenz Herrero, A. (2019). Audiovisual translation modes as an L2 learning pedagogical tool: Traditional modes and linguistic accessibility. In C. Herrero & I. Vanderschelden (Eds.), *Using film and media in the language classroom: Reflections on research-led teaching* (pp. 127–140). Multilingual Matters.

Rica Peromingo, J. P. (2016). Aspectos lingüísticos y técnicos de la traducción audiovisual (TAV). In *Series: Linguistic insights—Studies in language and communication*. Peter Lang.

Romero-Fresco, P. (2015). *The reception of subtitles for the deaf and hard of hearing in Europe*. Peter Lang.

Romero-Fresco, P. (2018). In support of a wide notion of media accessibility: Access to content and Access to creation. *Journal of Audiovisual Translation, 1*, 187–204. https://www.jatjournal.org/index.php/jat/article/view/53

Romero-Fresco, P. (2019). *Accessible filmmaking: Integrating translation and accessibility into the filmmaking process*. Routledge.

Silvester, H., & Tuominen, T. (2021). Collaboration between subtitling academics and practitioners. *Journal of Audiovisual Translation, 4*(3), 108–125. https://www.jatjournal.org/index.php/jat/article/view/188

Tamayo, A. (2022). Sign languages in audiovisual translation. *Journal of Audiovisual Translation, 5*(1), 129–149. https://www.jatjournal.org/index.php/jat/article/view/167

Valdez, S., Secară, A., Perez, E., & Bywood, L. (2023) Audiovisual translation and media accessibility training in the EMT network. *Journal of Audiovisual Translation, 6*(1), 19–44. https://doi.org/10.47476/jat.v6i1.2023.238

Zabalbeascoa, P. (1997). Dubbing and the nonverbal dimension of translation. In F. Poyatos (Ed.), *Nonverbal communication and translation* (pp. 327–342). John Benjamins.

Zárate, S. (2021). *Captioning and subtitling for d/Deaf and hard of hearing audiences*. UCL Press.

Zhang, X. (2019). Accessibility manager: Creating a profile of a new profession. Linguistica Antverpiensia, *New Series: Themes in Translation Studies, 18*, 73–86. https://lans-tts.uantwerpen.be/index.php/LANS-TTS/article/view/510

Digital Media Tools for Accessibility and Inclusion: A Case Study of Ukraine

Valeriia Kostynets⊙ and Iuliia Kostynets⊙

Abstract Since Russia's full-scale military invasion of Ukraine, brutal military operations, and Russia's terrorist missile attacks on territory in Ukraine, tens of thousands of Ukrainians have partially or completely lost their mobility. Today, many military and civilian individuals have suffered wounds, concussions, and injuries, requiring support and learning to live with ongoing disabilities. At least 2 million Ukrainians face challenges of social inclusion. Ukraine's social sphere is directly focused on the development of an inclusive society aiding people with war-related physical limitations and safe refuges in isolation. Social adaptation and orientation for people with disabilities are crucial at both local and provincial levels. Considering the high level of digitalization in Ukraine, the use of digital media tools to ensure accessibility and inclusivity in all areas of everyday life is incredibly effective. One of these tools can be an interactive map of inclusion, which is divided into an online platform (mobile app), where in one place all the information about inclusive spaces in the country will be collected. A place where an inclusive infrastructure has already been created. Digital media tools play a vital role in securing accessible and inclusive coverage. Improvements in digital materials and special locations can be achieved through cooperation between public and private sectors.

Keywords Accessibility · Inclusion · Digitalization · Digital media tools

1 Introduction

A full-scale Russian invasion of Ukraine, cruel combat operations, and continuous rocket firing of civil infrastructure and peaceful cities of Ukraine by the Russian Federation significantly increased the number of citizens who have partially or

V. Kostynets (✉)
Vadym Hetman Kyiv National Economic University, Kyiv, Ukraine
e-mail: valeriya.kostynets@gmail.com

I. Kostynets
National Academy of Management, Kyiv, Ukraine

© The Author(s) 2024
A. Marcus-Quinn et al. (eds.), *Transforming Media Accessibility in Europe*,
https://doi.org/10.1007/978-3-031-60049-4_21

377

completely lost mobility (Felix, 2023). Today, Ukrainian society faces numerous challenges related to providing barrier-free access to education, employment, and administrative services for various low-mobility groups. Creating an unobstructed living environment in public spaces and infrastructure remains crucial.

Targeted audiences for state strategies, policies, measures, and projects to implement an inclusive living environment include those who have lost mobility due to the conflict and internally displaced persons from occupied territories. Additionally, around 80 million people in the EU are affected by some degree of disability, emphasizing the need to share experiences in accessibility to ensure full and equal participation in society.

The European Accessibility Act (EAA) aims to improve the functioning of the internal market for accessible products and services by removing barriers created by divergent legislation (Directive 2019/882).

Currently, efforts by state institutions, private entities, and civil society in Europe and worldwide focus on key areas: (1) transport; (2) information communications; (3) urban infrastructure; (4) education; (5) labor market and employment (Zubchenko et al., 2020).

These practices align with the UN's sustainable development goals, particularly Goal 11, which aims to ensure inclusivity, security, and resilience of cities and settlements (United Nations, 2023), as well as with statements for persons with disabilities on different levels. In total, there are eight priority areas of effort which could be identified based on the UN Sustainable Goals.

The accessibility of goods and services, promotion of auxiliary devices, and ensuring full use of EU citizenship benefits (such as eliminating barriers to public life and leisure and providing quality community services) should be studied and discussed. Employment accessibility increases participation of people with disabilities in the labor market, where they are currently underrepresented. This accessibility is linked to education and training, promoting lifelong inclusive learning. Social protection, including support for decent living conditions, combating poverty and social alienation, and ensuring equal access to healthcare, plays a crucial role in social and economic development.

And the eighth priority is external actions meaning promotion of the relevant agenda within the EU Extension Programs and International Development Programs (EGA, 2023; EUR-Lex, 2000, 2011; ICED, 2017; Lecerf, 2019).

Ukraine's social sphere is directly focused on on developing an inclusive society to support the social adaptation of people with war-related disabilities, civilians, and isolated refugees.

Considering the high level of digitalization in Ukraine, the use of digital media tools to ensure accessibility and inclusivity in all areas of everyday life is incredibly effective. Technological progress has made it possible to create special tools and devices that help people with special needs to orient in the world. Ukraine has already implemented several initiatives for providing specialized technologies to citizens with special needs, including several programs with a joint motto "Innovation for Inclusion", which provides an increase in funding for the development of specialized software and devices (Davydenko, 2023).

The main role of digital media tools is to help support accessibility and inclusion in Ukraine. Given the current situation in Ukraine, there is significant interest in foreign practices in the field of accessibility (Zubchenko et al., 2020) in the following areas: (1) social; (2) economic; (3) civic; (4) physical and digital, universal design of appropriate infrastructure (urban environment, electronic services).

The purpose of the study is to synthesize and categortize digital tools and media resources that ensure accessibility in Ukraine. Using digital tools to address accessibility issues for those affected by hostilities is appropriate given Ukraine's advanced digitalization. This chapter aims to share practical Ukrainian experiences using digital media tools for inclusion and accessibility. The unique experiences from the two-year war period could make a pivotal contribution to existing knowledge due to their unprecedented nature.

Structurally, this study consists of the following sections. Section 1 addresses the relevance of the research topic. Section 2 includes the literature review and observations on providing accessibility and inclusion within the modern environment. Section 3 outlines the purpose, tasks, and research methodology, and Sect. 4 covers the main research results. Conclusions and prospects for further research are presented in Sect. 5.

2 Literature Review

Proper application and use of digital technologies can deliver outcomes for people and societies (Kennedy, 2023). Digital transformation will eventually lead to a complete digital twin incorporating all digitalization solutions into one virtual eco-system which will benefit all consumers (Vrana & Singh, 2021). In this section we highlight the positive aspects of the impact of digital technologies on society due to the accessibility of information and space.

Social accessibility ensures that individuals and social groups have appropriate conditions to participate in community life, cultural development, leisure activities, and self-expression. It aims to create equal opportunities and free access to education throughout life, including retraining and skill acquisition (Yasenovska et al., 2023; Zubchenko et al., 2020). Social accessibility also promotes Social Cohesion in communities. EU documents define social accessibility as the ability to provide overall well-being, minimize irregularities, avoid marginalization, overcome differences and divisions, and satisfy the means of achieving well-being for all members of society.

Economic accessibility provides conditions and opportunities for employment, obtaining financial and other resources for entrepreneurship of such social groups as young people, women with children under 6 years, the elderly, and persons with disabilities (Albadawi, 2022; Zubchenko et al., 2020).

The concept of civil accessibility involes ensuring that all discriminated and excluded social groups have access to decision-making processes, especially on issues directly affecting them. Civil accessibility also promotes equal participation of male and female citizens in political processes and the operation of political institutions (Ienin & Kuhta, 2022; Zubchenko et al., 2020).

Leading democratic states pay considerable attention to the implementation of principles of good governance (Davydenko, 2023) in public administration, particularly through establishing digital communication systems that set new standards for civic relationships. This approach is recognized as crucial for human capital development and for practically implementing the concept of "equal opportunities" (Arts, 2017), where everyone has a fair opportunity to realize their potential and fulfill their aspirations.

Physical and digital accessibility means the creation and implementation of appropriate standards, plans, projects, reconstruction, etc. (Davydenko, 2023; Zubchenko et al., 2020). The environment (public buildings and public places), transport, and services (including public and online services) at the community and state levels should be physically accessible to all social groups, including people with disabilities, the elderly, parents with children up to 6 years, etc. In many economically developed countries, physical and digital accessibility is realized through the concept of universal physical and digital infrastructure design.

2.1 European-Specific Background

2.1.1 Germany

In Germany, the implementation of inclusive and barrier-free access to employment provides two instrumental goals: advanced training and general awareness (through structural changes and demographic tendencies, the need for highly skilled workers in the future) and further improvement (Zubchenko et al., 2020). Some measures help to improve the interaction of different entities in the labor market. The main goal is to provide more opportunities to categories of citizens (persons with disabilities, older people, mothers with children under 6 years, and young people) who are less represented in the labor market (Lecerf, 2019). These groups are a part of the general program that is implemented in stages.

The National Action Plan 2.0 on the Implementation of the UN Convention on the Rights of Persons with Disabilities (BMAS, 2016) involves efforts from not only the ministries and departments within the social sector but also from all other federal ministries across 13 areas. These areas include work and employment; education; rehabilitation, health, and care; family, children and young people; culture, sports, and leisure; housing; protection of the rights of women and the elderly; personal and transport mobility; ensuring socio-political participation; protection of personal rights; international cooperation; and public awareness.

In Germany, the "Education in the Digital World" Strategy, which includes a dedicated section on digital education (Kultusministerkonferenz, 2022) aims to continuously deepen and develop digital skills even after graduation, professional training, or higher education. Digital educational environments enable personalized learning tailored to individual needs and goals. Additionally, digital development impacts not only the learning process but also leads to progressive changes in teacher qualifications at all levels and improvements in infrastructure.

2.1.2 Denmark and Sweden

In Sweden, it is worth emphasizing the state support of employment of persons with disabilities and employers who employ them (through the Swedish Public Employment Service). For example: (1) individually adapted assistance when applying for a job provided by individuals/structures that have an agreement with the service; (2) personal support in the workplace or during training (providing a personal representative or assistant); (3) financial compensation for special conditions (adapted to special needs workplace and work schedule) to the employer who employs a person with disabilities; (4) providing literature and translator to persons with visual or hearing impairments (an employer may apply for a grant if a person with a disabled person is employed or learned which requires translation of sign language, translation of written materials, signing a translation, recording professional literature on audios, etc.) (Zubchenko et al., 2020). Similar mechanisms of subsidies and fiscal preferences for employers are also available in Denmark.

In Denmark, the principles underlying the national well-being model of national and social protection system include active social measures, feedback from recipients (involving citizens in policymaking and decision-making, especially at the local level), and cooperation between state and municipal bodies and other social players (private companies and public organizations) (Zubchenko et al., 2020). This approach addresses the social problems of each citizen in a broader context, enabling decisions that closely meet the needs of target social groups. For example, flexible access to the labor market can be tested to harmonize family life and work for women with children, people with disabilities, the elderly, and other low-mobility groups.

Examining Denmark's municipal strategy, particularly Copenhagen;s integration policy, reveals four thematic blocks: a good start of life for children and young people; an inclusive labor market; support for of vulnerable groups and areas; and economic and social involvement. Each thematic block has a designated municipal structure responsible for it, but inclusivity is understood as a shared responsibility between the authorities and citizens . Denmark had made significant achievements in infrastructure projects, exemplified by "Yes, Copenhagen" Copenhagen (Connecting Copenhagen) which is recognized as the world's best "smart city" project (2013).

2.1.3 The UK

In the UK, lifelong education is considered crucial for overcoming inequality and career growth barriers, ensuring employees possess the necessary skills. State and local programmes emphasise the importance of broadening labor market representation to include not only persons with disabilities but also mothers with young children, veterans of military service, older adults, guardians and teenagers transitioning out of care. The British experience highlights the importance of communication in fostering social cohesion and inclusivity. The Government Communication Service acts as an intermediary between state bodies, municipal structures, representatives of local communities, media, and civil society organizations. It offers a variety of tools to enhance communication and communication competence, webinars, thematic research, guides, and publications in blogs from advanced government communicators). Significantly, the Government Communication Service aims for "World Leadership in Integration of Practices in Diversity and Inclusion," and it has a dedicated strategy for equality, diversity, and inclusion. Additionally, the UK government portal, Gov.uk, provides a guide for employers on hiring persons with disabilities and health problems, with regular updates to reflect legislative changes (Zubchenko et al., 2020).

2.1.4   Finland and Norway

The governments of Finland and Norway focus on active qualification activities for both workers and employees. Additionally, employees retain their wages during training, retraining, or advanced training programs. These practices align with the ecommendations of the European Commission's "A New Skills for Europe" (EAEA, 2017) on vocational education and training. This agenda aims to promote specific working and transitional skills, facilitate the transition from school to work and address sectoral, regional and local needs. It also worth emphasizes efforts to increase the attractiveness of vocational careers, and the flexibility and quality of the vocational education system in collaboration with employers and considering their requirements.

Finland's civic and communication practices are noteworthy, where both at the national and local levels adhere to the principle of "Noting About Us Without Us" (Zubchenko et al., 2020). This principle ensures that a significant proportion of measures in the field of inclusion and accessibility are developed and controlled by the recipients of social services and their representative organizations. Additionally, the Finnish approach emphasizes engagement with primary local civil society institutions, fostering real communication. This process helps legitimize governmental decisions during policy formulation and increases public trust in the authorities.

Norway's policies, emphasize qualitative communications based on the principle of inclusivity and universal design, integral to the government's policy of equal opportunities and anti-discrimination policies (Kirkpatrick, 2023). The goal of of public communication policy is to update, simplify, and improve the public sector, by focussing on user needs, the development of digital skills, and increasing the involvement of all citizens in public life. Universal design is the core of these priorities enabling individuals to thrive in everyday life regardless of illness or social, psychological, or physical characteristics (Kryklii, 2022).

2.1.5   Poland and Estonia

In Poland, every employer must pay a special contribution to the rehabilitation fund for persons with disabilities. These funds are used to create and to equip work-places for people with disabilities (Zubchenko et al., 2020). Additionally, employers can receive full or partial reimbursement from the state for expenses related to hiring people with disabilities. The state also offers various benefits to these enterprises, including tax breaks and subsidies for the production of goods or the provision of services. Employers are exempt from mandatory contributions if they employ a certain number of persons with disabilities.

In Estonia, civil communication is regarded as a cross-sector platform that makes it possible to achieve social progress in all related fields (Kryklii, 2022). The role of information and communication technologies is emphasized not only for establishing quality e-governance and providing administrative services, but also in generating innovations, attracting foreign investments, creating new jobs and promoting inclusive businesses for the whole population (including vulnerable and low-mobility groups). At the same time, considerable attention is also paid to cybersecurity and personal data protection.

Considering this European experience, Ukraine, amidst the full-scale Russian invasion, should ensure the maximum inclusivity and accountability particularly in education and employment and access to basic social services for internally displaced persons from temporarily occupied territories, as well as for those with reduced mobility due to hostilities or rocket attacks.

3   Research Methodology

To achieve the research goal of generalizing and systematizing digital tools and media resources that ensure accessibility in Ukraine, the first step involves analyzing scientific literature (Carrington, 2022; Mullin et al., 2021 etc.) and European regulations. This analysis aims to generalize the approaches of several European countries regarding accessibility and inclusion in modern environments and examine the Ukrainian legal framework concerning digitalization.

Data analysis in the research was conducted using qualitative research methods, specifically through observations, descriptive methods, and thematic analysis. The research focuses on systematizing digital tools and media resources in Ukraine to meet the accessibility needs of internally displaced people and those with special needs affected by the hostilities in Ukraine. For this study, individuals with special needs include people with disabilities, those with limited mobility, and those with specific physical needs.

4 Research Results

In September 2019, a public presentation of the Ministry of Digital Transformation and the Digital State brand took place. Thus, the actual implementation of legislative changes in the "digital" industry should take place with the participation of the Ministry of Digital Transformation and the Digital State. The European Commission's comprehensive program document, "The Single Digital Market for Europe," outlines three main areas that serve as guidelines for Ukraine: improving internet access for consumers and enterprises, creating appropriate regulatory conditions for advanced digital networks, and developing the digital economy through investments, interoperability, and standardization. In our view, the primary challenges in establishing a digital society and state in Ukraine include bridging the digital divide, enhancing cybersecurity, advancing e-learning and media education, fostering an information culture, and building trust, among other issues.

We agree with the opinion of V. Pylypchuk, who states that "information security and protection of personal data are the main problems of our state, because information and computer technologies significantly increase the risks of violation of the privacy of personal data due to the fact that they involve the accumulation and storage of data not on computer hard drives, and on remote servers, with the subsequent possibility of using a large, territorially and technologically distributed amount of information (data) about a specific person" (Pylypchuk, 2016).

Digitization of Ukraine aims to achieve the following goals (Law of Ukraine, 2018):

- acceleration of economic growth and attraction of investments;
- transformation of economic sectors into competitive and efficient ones;
- technological and digital modernization of industry and the creation of high-tech industries;
- accessibility for citizens of the advantages and opportunities of the digital world;
- implementation of human resources, development of digital industries and digital entrepreneurship.

In accordance with the goals listed above and the "Concept for the Development of the Digital Economy and Society of Ukraine for 2018–2020", the following principles can be identified on which the digitalization of society is currently based (Law of Ukraine, 2018):

(1) digitalization should provide every citizen with equal access to services, information, and knowledge provided on the basis of information, communication, and digital technologies;

(2) digitalization should be aimed at creating advantages in various spheres of life. This principle involves improving the quality of health care services and education, creating new jobs, developing entrepreneurship, agriculture, transport, protecting the environment and managing natural resources, raising the level of culture, helping to overcome poverty, preventing disasters, guaranteeing public security, etc.;

(3) digitalization is carried out through the mechanism of economic growth by increasing efficiency, productivity, and competitiveness from the use of digital technologies. This principle provides for the achievement of digital transformation of economic sectors, spheres of activity, their acquisition of new competitive qualities and properties. All-encompassing digitalization aims at the comprehensive and deep transformation of existing analogy economic and social systems and spheres into new value and quality for their efficiency, development, ease of use, etc.;

(4) digitalization should contribute to the development of the information society and mass media. The creation of content, primarily Ukrainian, in accordance with national or regional needs contributes to social, cultural, and economic development, as well as strengthening the information society and democracy in general;

(5) digitalization should focus on international, European, and regional cooperation with the aim of integrating Ukraine into the EU, entering the European and world markets. Ukraine's integration into European and global systems and infrastructures is, in particular, the result of conscious and full implementation of information, communication, and digital technologies;

(6) standardization is the basis of digitalization, one of the main factors of its successful implementation. Building digital systems, platforms, and infrastructures that are to be used by citizens, businesses, and the state for participation, competition, and success in the global economy and open markets is unacceptable. An exception may be relevant programs in the field of defense and security, in which the application of other standards (national, interstate) is justified;

(7) digitalization should be accompanied by an increase in the level of trust and security. Information security, cyber security, protection of personal data, inviolability of personal life and rights of users of digital technologies, strengthening and protection of trust in cyberspace are, in particular, prerequisites for simultaneous digital development and corresponding prevention, elimination, and management of associated risks;

(8) digitalization as an object of focal and complex state management. The main tasks on the way to the digitalization of the country are to correct the weaknesses of market mechanisms, to overcome institutional and legislative barriers, to initiate national-level digital transformation projects, to attract relevant investments, to stimulate the development of digital infrastructures, to create need of digital technologies using by citizens, and to develop appropriate digital competencies, creating the right incentives and motivations to support digital entrepreneurship and the digital economy.

All of these principles prove that digitalization of Ukraine is based on the positive influence of digital technologies on society.

The digital services and media resources for internally displaced persons, as well as persons with disabilities affected by the full-scale Russian invasion of Ukraine should be categorized under educational services, management services, and public services (Kurylyak et al., 2022).

It should be noted that such Ukrainian services are mostly universal and designed for various digitally sensitive groups including adults with disabilities, elderly people, remote students and children with disabilities. These digital platforms often feature navigation options to differentiate usage for different groups. Conversely, mobile applications tend to be more segmented by digital sensitivity. (Davydenko, 2023).

The provision of access to Ukrainians with disabilities or other socially sensitive features through mobile applications has been guided by several regulatory and methodological measures. These include the adoption of the "Basic Standard of Digital Accessibility" and the state's proclamation of the general technological initiative "State in the Smartphone." (Davyko, Davyko. Castagna, 2023).

4.1 Systematization of Digital Tools and Media Resources in Ukraine

Among management services, the most significant event in recent years in terms of remote service for citizens has been the introduction of an application "Action". This is a mobile application launched by the Government of Ukraine in 2019 as an initiative of digital inclusion. The application has been created to give citizens a simple and convenient way to access various public services and information online. Its operation is determined by the Cabinet of Ministers of Ukraine Decree No. 1137 of December 4, 2019 (Verkhovna Rada of Ukraine, 2023).

One of the priority goals of the Action Appendix is to enable authorities to provide access to essential services such as passport or driver's license, business registration, tax payment, and access to social services. By providing these services online, the government hopes to reduce bureaucracy, increase transparency, and increase overall efficiency for all categories of the population (Davydenko, 2023).

In addition to providing access to public services, the Action Annex also contains a number of functions that help people with disabilities to interact with their community. For example, the program provides access to local news and events, as well as tools to report problems and offer improvements for the community.

The Action Appendix is part of the large-scale effort of the Ukrainian government to promote digital inclusion and extend technology access to all citizens (Davydenko, 2023). In making public services more accessible and convenient, the government hopes to encourage more Ukrainians to use digital technologies and to participate in the digital economy. It is noticeable that this "Action" Appendix is constantly evolving and providing online access to new and more flexible social services.

The next and most popular digital service is educational. The universal digital resource for digital services for education in Ukraine (2023) is an innovative tool designed to enhance education delivery in the country. This platform offers a wide range of services and resources for students, teachers, and educational institutions. Key features of the platform include online access to learning materials such as textbooks, interactive lessons , and videos. It also incorporates educational tools and services like Labster, Zoom, Google Workspace, Coursera, Udemy, edX, etc. (Davydenko, 2023). This platform allows students to study remotely at their own pace and at a convenient time, providing greater flexibility and accessibility for individuals with varying digital and social sensitivities, which is particularly crucial during the war.

In addition to resources for students, the platform also offers services for teachers and educational institutions. Teachers can use a platform to create and manage online courses, communicate with students, and track student progress. Educational institutions can use a platform to manage their resources, enroll students, and monitor success. Using the latest technologies and innovative approaches, the platform helps to create a more flexible, affordable, and effective learning environment for both students and teachers.

The third most common type of digital service is universal accessibility. An example of a universal service with the focus on management and self-management was the project EnableMe Ukraine (2022). This is a branch of the international digital platform EnableMe Foundation, which has been working in Ukraine since 2022 providing vital assistance and support for people with disabilities. The non-profit organization of the same name aims to empower individuals and to give them equal opportunities for social integration and professional development. The foundation's digital platform offers a wide range of services, including online training, vocational training, employment, and psychological support (Davydenko, 2023). These services are designed to help people with disabilities gain the necessary skills and knowledge to lead an independent life and become active members of society.

EnableMe Ukraine was established in response to the war to provide vital information and services and to facilitate communication among people with special needs, including temporarily displaced persons, individuals with chronic diseases, and those with disabilities.

The platform organizers are trying to create a communication community that brings together people and their families to exchange information and resources and support each other. This community-oriented approach ensures that people with high social and digital sensitivity, along with their loved ones, will be able to access the information and services that they need to maintain their independence and quality of life, despite the devastating effects of the war.

One of the most significant impacts of EnableMe Ukraine (2022) is the improvement of employment opportunities for sensitive groups, including internally displaced persons. The vocational training programs have already helped hundreds of people to gain the necessary skills to work in various fields, including IT, hospitality, healthcare, and more. Additionally, the project helped reduce the stigma around disability, contributing to a more inclusive and accepting society.

Electronic support (E-support) is a common and widely used service in Ukraine. This universal government project provides various digital support services to the general population. These services are designed to facilitate the use of digital technologies, promote innovation, and improve access to information and services (Davydenko, 2023).

One of the key areas where e-support is provided in Ukraine is the e-government. The government has made significant investments in digital infrastructure and launched a number of electronic services to facilitate access to public services and information. Citizens can now access public services and information online, including tax returns, apply for social payments, receive official documents, etc.

A special focus in the systematization of digital tools is on the technologies for fast mobile access, particularly mobile applications. These applications are tailored to specific needs based on medical conditions or age making them suitable for people with disabilities, the elderly or those with certain health issues. For example, PocketBraille is a program that allows people with visual impairments to read and write Braille on their smartphones Be My Eyes connects people with visual impairments with volunteer service that can help with information orientation (Right to Protection, 2022). The systematization of special mobile applications is shown in Table 1.

The above list is not exhaustive and may change as new programs appear.

Table 1 Systematization of special mobile applications for vulnerable groups

Functional	Users	Examples
Communication programs	People with difficulties of communication, such as speech disorders, sensory disorders	Ava—Live Transcription ProDeaf Translator RogerVoice Video Relay Service
Visual assistance programs	People with visual impairments	Be My Eyes Envision AI Seeing AI TapTapSee
Navigation programs	People with disabilities of movement and orientation	Access Earth Wheelmap Waze Moovit
Educational and developmental	For socially sensitive people who are unable to study offline	Dyslexia Toolbox My Autism App AutisMate iCommunicate
For health	People with a variety of somatic and mental health disorders	Pocket Yoga WaterMinder Medisafe Headspace
Household support applications	Mostly people with a violation of the musculoskeletal system and people of advanced age	Assistance App Assistive Touch Disability Answer Desk Todoist
Entertainment	All people who experience isolation/have hypersensitivity	Dance! Soundscape Audiobooks Voice Dream Reader

Source Davydenko (2023), Kryklii (2022)

The classification of available applications can be expanded by features or user types, and some applications may cover multiple categories. For example, programs such as Voice Dream Reader and Learning Ally give access to reading materials for vision, dyslexia, and other learning problems, and communication programs such as Ava or Google Live Transcribe provide transcription services in the text time that facilitates people with hearing impaired people who cannot quickly perceive information (Davydenko, 2023). There are multifunctional applications of Be My Eyes, which can help solve various household, reference or orientation in unfamiliar places.

Mobile programs are also increasingly used in health care for the treatment of chronic diseases and promotion of recreation, return to remission, rehabilitation, and more. For example, MyFitnessPal and FitBit applications help people control their physical activity and nutrition, and HeadSpace and Calm organize and manage meditation and relaxation techniques (Davydenko, 2023).

Table 2 shows a separate, demonstrative in nature, classification of mobile applications for people with different forms of disability, based on the adaptability of these applications to use in Ukraine.

As of 2023, the most relevant and most productive were the software applications, implemented, primarily by the domestic "BeWarned" startup. The result of his activity is the latest universal platform to help people with hearing impairments. There are four technical assistants on the platform: Sound Monitor, Connect, Dance i Emergency Call described on Fig. 1.

Table 2 Mobile applications for people with different forms of disability

Program type	Example	Specificity of functions
Universal for people with hearing impairments	BeWarned	Combines several technical helpers
Technological support for people with visual impairment	TalkBack Be My Eyes	Helps users with visual impairment interact with their devices
Volunteer support for people with visual impairments	Ava	Allows you to contact a volunteer that can use the camera on your smartphone to assist
Technological support for people with hearing impairments	SignSchool	Uses artificial intelligence to transcribe an up -to -date conversation. Provides sign language lessons
Educational support for people with hearing impairments. Technological support for people with speech disorders	PictoDroid Lite; Easy voice recorder TouchChat	Programs for visual communication, recording—voice reproduction
Developmental support for people with autism	ProstoRadost	Helps master social skills
Technological support for people with musculoskeletal disorders	TouchChat	Helps navigate people on wheelchairs

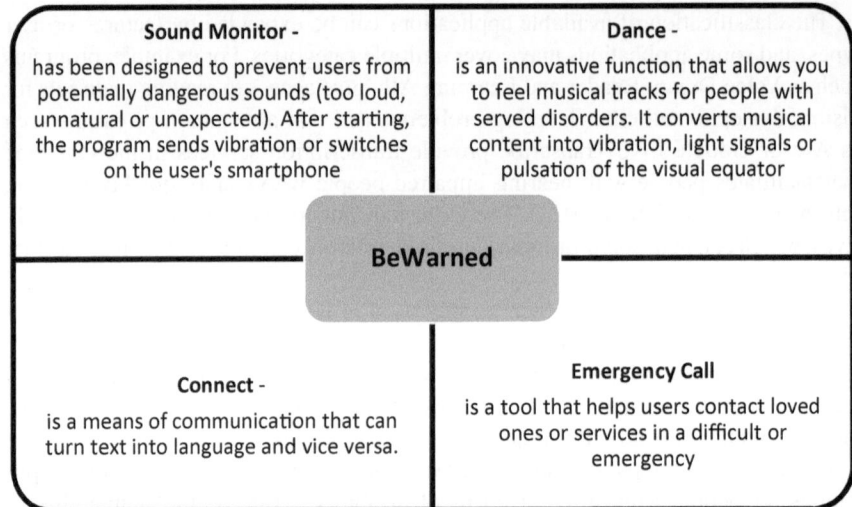

Fig. 1 "BeWarned" platform with its technical assistants. *Source* Built based on Davydenko (2023), Radanliev et al. (2023)

Be My Eyes is intended to assist people with visual impairments or orientation issues. It can be used to contact a volunteer network that can promptly help to solve several household and daily tasks (reading of labels, names of goods, checking their shelf life, etc.).

The advantage of the above applications is that they are available on both iOS platforms and Android and in a short time received high ratings from testers and users. These applications use the sensitivity of the smartphone (microphone, camera) to analyze the processor and the appropriate functional reaction (vibration, sound warnings, flickering, transmission of visual information to the volunteer, which can then help the user in real-time, etc.) (Radanliev et al., 2023). These auxiliary technologies have already improved the quality of life of thousands of people with sensory and motor disorders.

At the same time, "911Help" (Davydenko, 2023) has become one of the most universal mobile apps, filling a previously unmet need in Ukraine. It is an emergency response service that is aimed at improving the urgent and constructive digital response to emergencies in the country. It uses a special mobile app for communication of sensitive users with emergency services in their area, including police, fire service, and ambulance. The application can also track the location of the user and provide emergency services with important information about the history of the user's disease, his or her special needs, vulnerable areas, and more. The project was developed in response to hostilities.

Available platforms are advanced programs that provide profile or complex functions. The most popular in use are educational and entertaining, which require basic digital skills and often basic English (Table 3).

Table 3 Educational and entertaining digital platforms for people with different forms of disability

Platform type	Description	Example	Specificity of functions
Online training platforms with mobile accessibility features	Availability features for online training are now offered by many universal and special platforms to facilitate people with special sensitivity to access to educational content	Coursera	Offers closed subtitles and transcripts for video lectures
		Edx	Offers closed subtitles and transcripts for video lectures, as well as the ability to adjust the speed of video
		Udacity	Subjects' subtitles and ability to customize video quality according to individual needs
Game platforms with additional accessibility features	In recent years, the games' industry has succeeded in making games more accessible to all user categories. Often, such platforms are correlated with educational, reference, other services	Xbox	Offers several special features, including controlled controls, subtitles, and speech synthesis parameters
		PlayStation	Offers special features such as closed subtitles, text conversion options, and controlled controls
		Steam	Offers several special features, including controlled controls, Daltonics mode, and support for reading programs
Accessible software	These software and apps can help people with different disorders easier to use digital devices and software	JAWS	A screen-read program that helps people with visual impairment access to digital content on their computers
		Dragon Naturally Speaking	Speech recognition software that allows people with disabilities to manage their computers through voice
		TouchChat	A software that allows people with communication disorders to communicate with several characters, images, and words

Source Built based on Davydenko (2023)

Moreover, many video conferencing programs now offer accessibility features (Zoom; Microsoft Teams; Google Meet).

4.2 Interactive Map of Inclusion

Interactive Map of Inclusion "City without borders" (ACMC, 2023). This digital tool catalogs establishments, public spaces, and city infrastructure that have implemented measures for free access for low-mobility groups. The map highlights places where inclusive infrastructure has been created, such as sidewalk ramps, lowered curbs, accessible toilets, and traffic lights with sound signals. As of the end of 2023, approximately 800 locations have been added to the map, which continues to be regularly updated., (Fig. 2) (ACMC, 2023).

The primary goal is to compile spaces on a single platform that at least partially address inclusivity, thereby highlighting the need for nationwide changes. The project's inception stems from the fact that since the beginning of the full-scale war, tens of thousands of Ukrainians have partially or completely lost their mobility. For people with injuries and disabilities obstacles like stairs, high curbs, narrow doors hinder or prevent movement entirely. This project is intended to demonstrate that, society can no longer ignore the issues of free movement and access to services. It addresses not only the needs of disabled defenders who fought for the state but also those of civilians affected by Russian military shelling.

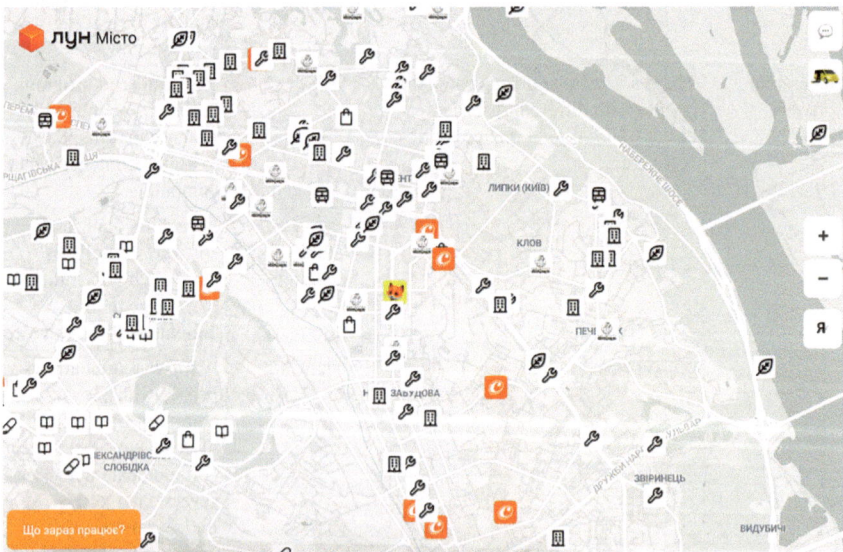

Fig. 2 Interactive map of inclusion. *Source* ACMC

5 Conclusion

Social inclusion and creating an accessible environment in Ukraine are certainly extremely relevant issues both during the war and in the post-war recovery period. Unfortunately, the number of Ukrainians, both military and civilian, who have partially or completely lost their mobility due to hostilities and become disabled, is increasing daily. There is an urgent need for social adaptation for both individuals with special needs and internally displaced persons. Utilizing digital tools to provide accessibility in all spheres of life is highly effective and promising in a digitized society. Further research in this area should focus on digital inclusivity to ensure accessibility in education for sensitive populations, including children studying remotely due to war-related reasons (Armstrong et al., 2021)

Acknowledgements This chapter is based upon work from COST Action CA19142—Leading Platform for European Citizens, Industries, Academia and Policymakers in Media Accessibility (LEAD-ME) supported by COST (European Cooperation in Science and Technology).

References

ACMC (September, 20, 2023). The interactive map of inclusivity "City without borders" was launched In Ukraine. https://acmc.ua/v-ukrayini-zapustyly-interaktyvnu-kartu-inklyuzyvnosti-misto-bez-mezh/

Albadawi, B. (2022). Leadership change for development inclusive education. *Journal of Positive School Psychology, 6*(2), 1085–1097.

Armstrong, A. C., Johansson-Fua, S. U., & Armstrong, D. (2021). Reconceptualising inclusive education in the Pacific. *International Journal of Inclusive Education,* 1–14.

Arts, K. (2017). Inclusive sustainable development: A human rights perspective. *Current Opinion in Environmental Sustainability, 24,* 58–62.

BMAS. (June, 28, 2016). Nationaler Aktionsplan 2.0. https://www.bmas.de/DE/Soziales/Teilhabe-und-Inklusion/Nationaler-Aktionsplan/nationaler-aktionsplan-2-0.html

Carrington, S. (2022). Leadership of inclusive culture. *Australian Educational Leader, 44*(2), 18–21.

Castagna, A. (November, 15, 2023). Digital inclusion and accessibility in Ukraine: Leaving none behind. https://www.promoteukraine.org/digital-inclusion-and-accessibility-in-ukraine-leaving-none-behind/

Copenhagen Connecting (2013). Copenhagen Connecting. Project. https://www.copenhagenconnecting.com/

Davydenko, H. (2023). *Digital inclusion and accessibility: social digitalization.* Vinnytsia. (in Ukrainian).

Digital Services For Education in Ukraine (2023). https://mooc4ua.online/en

EAA (2019) European Accessibility Act (Directive 2019/882). https://ec.europa.eu/social/main.jsp?catId=1202

EAEA. (2017). New skills agenda for Europe. https://eaea.org/our-work/influencing-policy/monitoring-policies/new-skills-agenda-for-europe/

EGA. (2023). DRIVE: A research project influence of digital transformation to vulnerable population groups. https://ega.ee/wp-content/uploads/2022/07/DRIVE_Ukraine_report_DVG_2022_UA.pdf

EnableMe. (2022). https://www.enableme.org/en

Equality, Diversity and Inclusion Strategy (2020). https://assets.publishing.service.gov.uk/media/6385e293d3bf7f7eb2ae56a7/EDI_strategy_Companies_House.pdf

EUR-Lex. (2000). Council Directive 2000/78/EC of 27 November 2000 establishing a general framework for equal treatment in employment and occupation. https://eur-lex.europa.eu/legal-content/EN/TXT/?uri=celex%3A32000L0078

EUR-Lex. (2011). Council Resolution on a renewed European agenda for adult learning. https://eur-lex.europa.eu/legal-content/EN/ALL/?uri=CELEX:32011G1220(01)

Felix, A. (March, 27, 2023). Immediate needs and an inclusive future: Persons with disabilities in Ukraine need more support. https://www.edf-feph.org/immediate-needs-and-an-inclusive-fut ure-persons-with-disabilities-in-ukraine-need-more-support/

ICED. (2017). Gender, disability & inclusion. http://icedfacility.org/category/resources/gender-and-inclusion/

Ienin, M., & Kuhta, M. (2022). The digital divide and the vulnerable in the digital aspect of social groups in Ukraine. In *Sociocultural transformations and geopolitical challenges in multipolar conditions the world*, pp. 216–221.

Kennedy, H. (2023) We're more and more aware of digital harms, but what is the digital good? https://blogs.lse.ac.uk/impactofsocialsciences/2023/03/06/were-more-and-more-aware-of-digital-harms-but-what-is-the-digital-good/

Kirkpatrick, K. (2023). Accessibility and inclusion through technology. *Communications of the ACM, 66*(11), 13–15.

Kryklii, O. (2022). The concept of digital inclusion. Essence, factors, elements. *Economic horizons, 3*(21), 62–71.

Kultusministerkonferenz. (2022). Strategie "Bildung in der digitalen Welt. https://www.kmk.org/themen/bildung-in-der-digitalen-welt/strategie-bildung-in-der-digitalen-welt.html

Kurylyak, V. V., Polumysna, O. O., & Shevchuk, A. V. (2022). People with disabilities in Ukraine. Trends of social integration media. *Cultural Almanac, 3*, 137–155.

Law of Ukraine No 67-p. (2018). On the approval of the concept of the development of the digital economy and society of Ukraine for 2018–2020 and the approval of the plan of measures for its implementation (dated January 17, 2018) https://zakon.rada.gov.ua/laws/show/67-2018-%D1%80#n13

Lecerf, M. (2019). *European accessibility act*. EPRS: European Parliamentary Research Service.

Mullin, A. E., Coe, I. R., Gooden, E. A., Tunde-Byass, M., & Wiley, R. E. (2021). Inclusion, diversity, equity, and accessibility: From organizational responsibility to leadership competency. *Healthcare Management Forum, 34*(6), 311–315.

Pylypchuk, V. (2016). Information security and privacy in the field of personal data protection. *Information and Law, 4*(19), 60–70.

Radanliev, P., De Roure, D., Novitzky, P., & Sluganovic, I. (2023). Accessibility and inclusiveness of new information and communication technologies for disabled users and content creators in the metaverse. https://arxiv.org/ftp/arxiv/papers/2308/2308.01925.pdf

Right to protection (2022). Experience in using digital public services. Monitoring report.

United Nations (December, 10, 2023). The 17 goals. https://sdgs.un.org/goals

Verkhovna Rada of Ukraine. (2023). Issues of the unified state web portal of electronic services and the register of administrative services. https://zakon.rada.gov.ua/laws/show/1137-2019-%D0%BF?lang=en#Text (in Ukrainian).

Vrana, J., Singh, R. (2021). Digitization, digitalization, and digital transformation. In N. Meyendorf, N. Ida, R. Singh, & J. Vrana (Eds.), *Handbook of nondestructive evaluation 4.0*. Springer. https://doi.org/10.1007/978-3-030-48200-8_39-1

Yasenovska, M., Zinenko, O., & Kormilets, K. (2023). Inclusion in Ukraine and beyond borders. https://library.fes.de/pdf-files/bueros/ukraine/20468.pdf

Zubchenko, S., Kaplan, Y., & Tyschenko, Y. (2020). *Creating a barrier-free environment and social inclusion: world experience for Ukraine*. Kyiv, NISD. (in Ukrainian).

A Multimodal Approach for Improving a Dialogue Agent for Therapeutic Sessions in Psychiatry

Karolina Gabor-Siatkowska, Izabela Stefaniak, and Artur Janicki

Abstract The number of people with mental health problems is increasing in today's societies. Unfortunately, there are still not enough experts (psychiatrists, psychotherapists) available. To address this issue, our research team developed a goal-directed therapeutic dialogue system named Terabot to assist psychiatric patients. This system features a voice interface, enabling verbal communication between the patient and the dialogue agent in Polish. Utilizing the RASA framework, the dialogue system is enhanced with text-based emotion and intention recognition. This enables the dialogue system to react "empathically," i.e., considering the patient's emotions. The purpose of Terabot is to provide extra support for mental health patients who require additional therapy sessions due to limited access to medical personnel. This will not replace drug treatment but rather serve as additional therapy sessions. Our study consisted of therapy sessions of patients talking to Terabot, conducted at the Institute of Psychiatry and Neurology in Warsaw, Poland. During these sessions, we observed several issues that have led either to interrupting the therapeutic session or worsening the patient's performance of the relaxation exercise. We suggest addressing these problems by implementing an eye-tracker in our dialogue system to make the dialogue flow more human-like. We propose a feedback loop in which the eye-tracker provides essential data back to the RASA framework. This gives additional information to the framework, and a more appropriate response can be given to the patient. Our main aim is to establish a feedback loop that will likely impact the way the conversation is conducted. Thanks to this, the dialogue system may perform better. As a result, the dialogue agent's responses can be improved, resulting in a more natural, human-like flow of conversation.

Keywords Dialogue system · Eye-tracking · Psychiatry · Cognitive-behavioral therapy · Feedback

K. Gabor-Siatkowska (✉) · A. Janicki
Faculty of Electronics and Information Technology, Warsaw University of Technology, Warsaw, Poland
e-mail: karolina.gabor-siatkowska.dokt@pw.edu.pl

I. Stefaniak
Faculty of Medicine, Lazarski University, Warsaw, Poland

397

1   Introduction

As the WHO reports, over the past few years, the number of patients waiting to be seen by psychiatrists has been growing constantly (the WHO highlights urgent need to transform mental health and mental health care, 2022). Unfortunately, waiting for a long time for an appointment or therapy is a disadvantage for psychiatric patients. As more people struggle with mental disorders, new solutions must be found to help patients. What could be helpful is the use of innovative technology to supplement the therapist's work. Some therapies, like cognitive behavioral therapy (CBT) (Fenn & Byrne, 2013) or exposure techniques in virtual reality (Sherrill & Rothbaum, 2023), have a straightforward, well-defined, and organized structure that enables them to be integrated into technological tools efficient (Dino et al., 2019). One example could be using chatbots for psychological therapies, e.g., the chatbot Woebot, designed for English-speaking individuals, which has helped treat depression (Fitzpatrick et al., 2017). Another example is an avatar-based dialogue system, although with human supervision, effectively treating auditory hallucinations (Craig et al., 2018; Stefaniak et al., 2019). When talking about these dialogue agents, one must bear in mind the different input signals these systems might receive. To achieve a similar level of intuitive interaction between humans and computers, the use of multimodal inter-faces is required (Duarte, 2007). From simple conversations to therapy sessions with specialists, human-to-human interaction is naturally multimodal, using speech, gesture, gaze, etc. In literature, multimodality is described as the combination of multiple senses and modes of communication, including sight, sound, print, images, video, and music, that make up a message (Dressman, 2019). To find better and more human-like results, multimodality is becoming one of the most important research directions to be followed. In the digital age, multimodality has become even more important for communication.

Multimodal fusion is a technique that uses a combination of different input modal-ities to enable systems to understand human behavior better. By combining multiple data sources, user intent can be interpreted more accurately and bring interaction closer to what users are used to from human-to-human interaction (Duarte & Carriço, 2006). As technology evolves, multimodal fusion will likely become an integral part of human–machine interaction. The popularity and frequency of multimodal capa-bilities are already increasing. One example could be the use of the eye-tracker in the field of human–computer interaction (Chandra et al., 2016; Majaranta & Bulling, 2014; Santini et al., 2017). Most eye-trackers use the near-infrared light spectrum to track eye movement interaction (Mulvey et al., 2008). The most important parameters obtained during an eye-tracking session include pupil diameter and eye movement parameters (saccades and fixations), among many others (e.g., number of blinks, blink duration, time to first fixation—TTFF) (Duchowski, 2017). Saccades are fast, simul-taneous movements of both eyes between two or more fixation points. The choice of a particular parameter for analysis always depends on the purpose of the experi-ment being performed. Therefore, the eye-tracking signal has become of interest to a broader public, e.g., in psychology (Hershaw & Ettenhofer, 2018; Krejtz et al., 2018;

Pfleging et al., 2016), education (Was et al., 2016), marketing (Białowąs & Szyszka, 2019; Wedel, 2014), medicine (Bartošová et al., 2018). For years, eye-trackers have also been used to study human–computer interaction. An example in this area is Embodied Conversational Agents (ECAs), which have received much attention. They use nonverbal behavior to establish contact with a human user (Bailly et al., 2006; Bee et al., 2009). For such a dialogue to become more reliable, these agents should be equipped with communicative and expressive abilities similar to those we know from human-to-human interaction (speech, gestures, facial expressions, gaze, etc.) (Bee et al., 2009). Increasingly, eye-trackers are used as an additional source of information during users' conversations with a dialogue agent (Bailly et al., 2006; Bee et al., 2009). Thus, the data obtained are then used to support or control conversational agents. An example of dialogue agents that take into account the behavior of the participant's eye movements in various aspects are: Gandalf (a humanoid agent), which can narrate planets and moons (Thórisson, 1997), an interactive storyteller Emma (Bee et al., 2010), or a dialogue agent who interacts with seniors (Amorese et al., 2022). Thanks to eye-tracking studies, it is possible to obtain several parameters characterizing, for example, a person's emotional state (Bradley et al., 2008) and concentration (Chang & Chueh, 2019). The human–computer interaction that is carried out is more natural, and as a result, dialogue agents can interact more realistically with people. It is a perfect example of how multimodal fusion can create immersive user experiences.

Concerning the growing problem in the domain of healthcare, our research team has developed a goal-oriented dialogue system called Terabot, which implemented elements of CBT. Initial results from dialogues with seven psychiatric patients are presented in Gabor-Siatkowska et al. (2023a, 2023b). We observed the accuracy of speech and intent recognition and compared the results with those of healthy subjects. During the therapy sessions at the Institute of Psychiatry and Neurology in Warsaw, Poland, we additionally used the Gazepoint GP3 eye-tracker to collect eye-tracking data from psychiatric patients while they interacted with the dialogue system. In this chapter, we will describe the problems encountered during these dialogues between the patient and the agent. Furthermore, we will show how integrating the eye-tracking signal into the dialogue system may prevent errors and miscommunication. Our chapter is structured as follows: Sect. 1 briefly reviews related work in our research field. Next, in Sect. 2, we describe Terabot, the therapeutic spoken-dialogue system. In Sect. 3, the conducted experiments are described. In Sect. 4, we present the ongoing problems that occurred during conversations between the patients and our dialogue agent. Section 5 describes our proposed solutions for these problems. The chapter concludes with a discussion and further work.

2   Terabot—The "Empathetic" Dialogue System

As mentioned earlier, the number of psychiatrists is insufficient due to the growing mental health problems in today's societies (the WHO highlights the urgent need to transform mental health and mental health care, June 17, 2022). As a response to this issue, to support psychiatric patients, we have developed "Terabot," a goal-oriented therapeutic dialogue system. This speech-to-speech system operates in the Polish language. It is designed to meet the needs of psychiatric patients dealing with complex and overwhelming emotions. It can be used to help them recognize their feelings and behaviors in difficult situations. In each session, the patient can choose from three emotional topics such as anger, shame, and fear. At the end of the session, Terabot offers a relaxation exercise to help the patient to calm down. Importantly, and to benefit patients, all of Terabot's responses have been reviewed and edited by psychiatrists. The dialogue flow has been designed according to psychiatrist recommendations using CBT therapy elements.

• The Architecture of Terabot

Our goal was to minimize the risk of the robot making a wrong response, so we designed a goal-oriented dialogue system. Figure 1 shows a schematic diagram of the architecture of our conversational agent.

When a patient starts speaking, an automatic speech recognition (ASR) system converts this speech to text (using GoogleWeb Speech API). This text is then further analyzed to identify the intents and slots for which the Dual Intent and Entity Transformer (DIET) classifier (Bunk et al., 2020), a multitask transformer, was used. It can handle both intent and entity recognitions. DIET uses a sequence model that considers the sequence of words. At the same time as the intent and slot recognition, the output

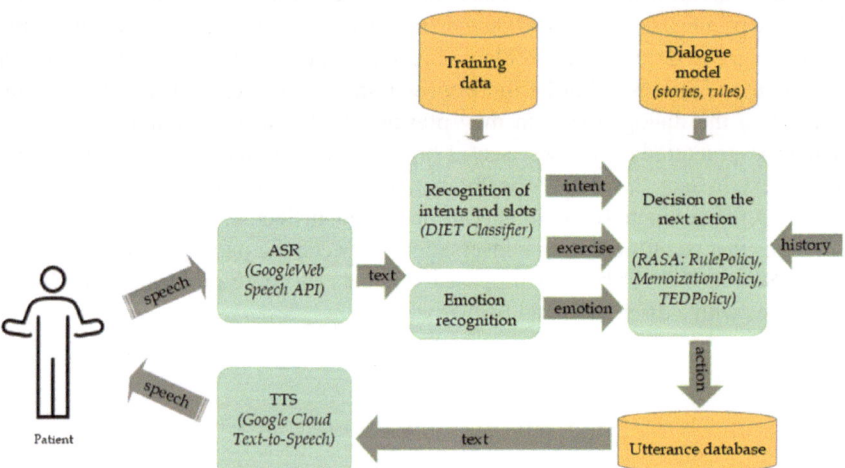

Fig. 1 Block diagram of Terabot dialogue system

of the ASR is passed to the text-based emotion recognition module (Zygadło et al., 2021). It is based on the Bidirectional Encoder Representations from Transformers (BERT) model with fine-tuning for emotion classification. The currently detected emotional state of the patient's spoken text determines the value of the "emotion" slot. Another slot is filled with the exercise type. The recent further development of emotion and sentiment recognition using big data and deep learning methods used in our dialogue system has been reported in our article (Kozłowski et al., 2023). Our system uses RASA to implement the action decision pipeline and the DIET classifier. RASA is an open-source dialogue management and natural language understanding (NLU) framework. This framework uses a weighted combination of the memoization policy (e.g., based on stories stored in memory), a rule policy, and a Transformer Embedding Dialogue (TED) (Vlasov et al., 2019) to decide the next system action. The TED policy takes into account the current state of the dialogue (patient's intent), slot values (including the recognized emotion), and previous states of the dialogue. If the next action is an utterance, it will be selected from the utterance database. The last step is to transform the selected text (utterance of Terabot) into a speech signal. The result is Terabot's response given to the patient. Since Terabot is a domain-specific dialogue system, we faced difficulty acquiring large samples of real data to increase the training database. In our research (Gabor-Siatkowska et al., 2023a, 2023b), we present how to enlarge the dataset using another commonly known AI tool, such as ChatGPT. Our proposed solution enabled the increase of the dialogue system's intent recognition accuracy of the spoken utterances by patients.

3   Sessions with Terabot

The therapy sessions with Terabot took place between March and August 2023 at the Institute of Psychiatry and Neurology in Warsaw, Poland. This study was conducted in accordance with the Declaration of Helsinki and approved by the Ethics Committee of the Institute of Psychiatry and Neurology in Warsaw. The first experiments with seven psychiatric patients talking to Terabot, which gave us 600 recordings, showed promising results (Gabor-Siatkowska et al., 2023a, 2023b). Most patients confirmed that Terabot understood their answers and emotions (around 3.5 on the Likert scale). All patients rated Terabot's speech as high quality, natural, and fast and liked how it was presented.

In total, there were 38 participants between the ages of 18 and 65 who took part in our study. All participants were admitted to a 24-h psychiatric hospital. There, they have been examined and classified by psychiatrists for additional therapy sessions with Terabot based on their diagnosed conditions. These patients have been diagnosed with F20.0 to F20.9 (schizophrenia) according to ICD-10 (WHO, International Classification of Diseases). They were treated with medication, including antipsychotics, mostly in combination with other antidepressants or mood stabilizers. They were randomly selected for the study after meeting the inclusion criteria and signing a consent form. It was a randomized clinical trial with random assignment

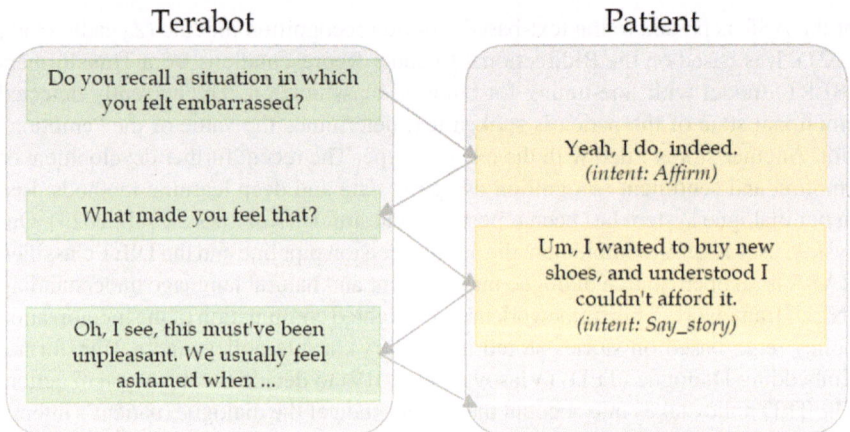

Fig. 2 The diagram is a fragment of a conversation in case the patient chooses the exercise on shame. As can be seen, the intention in the patient's utterance is analyzed, and the next Terabot response is matched to it

to different experimental conditions. Psychiatrists informed them about the purpose and conduct of the clinical trial and addressed any questions they might have had. Patients approved to record their voice and eye-tracking data. For conversational agents, which are designed for psychiatric patients, it is important that no image/video of the patient will be recorded during these conversations, as neither patients would consent nor would we get the bioethics committee approval. The anonymity of patients participating in the study was guaranteed.

In five sessions per week, this is one session per day, the patients talked to Terabot. Each conversation lasted for about 7–15 min. The patients could choose one of the three exercises: anger, fear, or shame, which could be then repeated or changed the next day. A fragment of such an exercise is shown in Fig. 2. The patients were sitting in front of Terabot, with an assistant invited to the same room. This was necessary because of the psychiatric institute's requirements for the patient's safety. Figure 3 shows a demonstration setup with a monitor and an eye-tracker at the bottom of the screen.

4 Frequent Problems During Dialogues

Despite the extensive testing, some unforeseen problems occurred during the therapeutic sessions. They caused some unintentional discomfort to the patients, sometimes leading to problems and misunderstandings during the conversation. As explained in Sect. 2, the RASA framework is responsible for sending follow-up utterances after receiving the appropriate information about the recognized intention

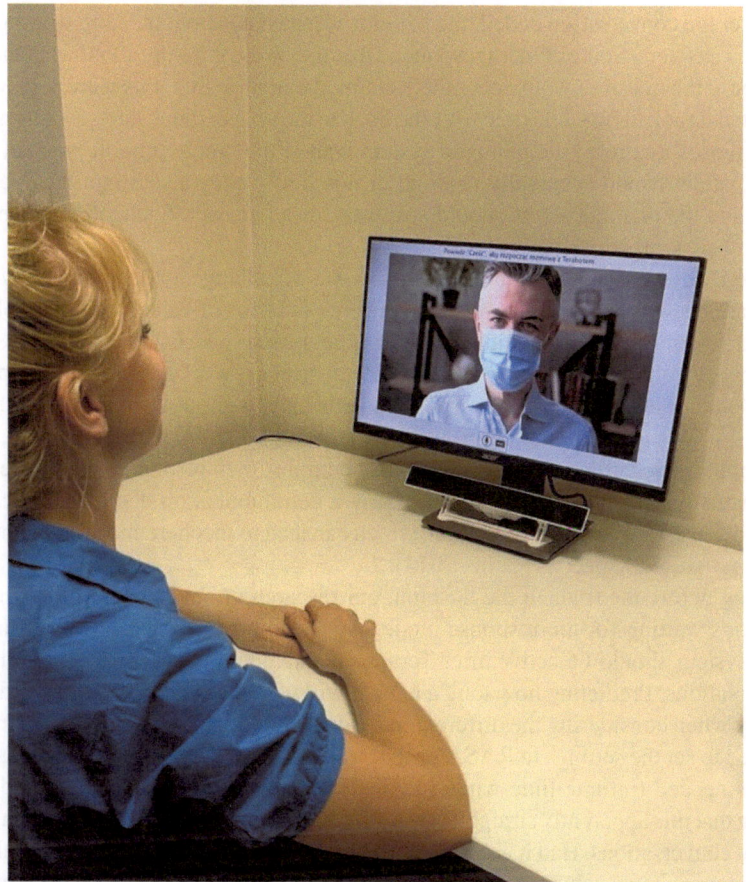

Fig. 3 Patient sitting in front of Terabot's interface. Their dialogue is conducted speech to speech. The eye-tracker is situated at the bottom of the screen

of the patient's speech. Even though we adapted RASA appropriately, as recommended by its guidelines, we found patterns of problematic issues. Some problems also occurred during the dialogues, which assistants have reported. All of these are described below.

- **Issue 1: Waiting Too Long for the Patient's Answer**

The first common problem is presented in Fig. 4. There have been frequently occurring situations in which the patient did not respond (to a question posed by Terabot) for an extended time. In these situations, there was no message from or to Terabot. It was also impossible for the assistants to ask the patient anything or to repeat the question of the dialogue agent—this would have interrupted the dialogue flow. The assistant did not know how the system would react to such a situation—if it would respond and remind the patient or hang up because it waited too long for the response.

After the conversation ended, the patients were asked about the long waiting time for their answers. Some of them responded that they were thinking about what the best answer to the question would be; others claimed that their thoughts were somewhere else, and it took them some time to come back to the conversation and give an answer. In all those situations, the dialogue system waited the whole time. It was not clear if the patient would eventually respond or not at all—they also might have left the room and the dialogue agent would still wait for an answer. Such situations had to be handled appropriately.

When it comes to the patient's speech, this was a challenge for our dialogue system. The patients who took part in our trials differed in terms of velocity and complexity of their responses. Some patients answered quickly and superficially, sometimes with low speech volume. Others provided complete, brief answers without much explanation. Another group of patients responded verbosely, without waiting for Terabot to finish the question. Yet another group of patients raised their voices at Terabot, literally shouting, regardless of how extensive or complex their response was. There were also patients suffering from logorrhea. It is a communication disorder that causes excessive use of words and repetition, which can lead to incoherence. It is sometimes called pressure of speech (Karbe, 2014).

Long before the trials in the hospital, our research group experimented with the Terabot's waiting-for-the-response mode. We tested how fast and for how long the ASR system should be active after Terabot's statement/question is finished during conversations. Predicting how long a patient will wait before responding is difficult, mainly when considering the different individual speech possibilities. Therefore, we decided to set the settings in RASA so that waiting for the patient's answer is as long as it is needed (infinite time when required). Unfortunately, it was unclear during testing that this apparently straightforward solution would cause problems during real patient conversations. Had it not been for reports of assistants, we probably would not have known about such a problem. This is, in fact, a situation that disturbs and affects not only a single question-and-answer conversation with the patient but also the entire therapy session as a whole. Such situations may lead to unwanted interruptions and could likely prevent the dialogue system from functioning correctly.

- **Issue 2: Lack of Knowledge About Patient Behavior**

Another common problem we have observed in the trials is shown in Fig. 5. As the dialogue progresses, at some point during the conversation, the patients are asked if they would like to participate in a relaxation exercise to help calm down their emotions. After a positive reply, Terabot proceeds with a relaxation exercise that lasts a few minutes. This exercise consists of therapeutic statements provided and recommended by psychiatrists. This is also the time for the patients to train their concentration. Unfortunately, in contrast to the domain of real human–human interaction, here, as the trials have shown, there is no way of knowing the patient's current behavior. During Terabot's utterances, no information is gathered, whether the patient was present and listened or maybe walked away. If the assistants were not present during this phase of the dialogue, we would not have any information about the patient's behavior. Only at the end of the relaxation exercise is the patient asked about the feelings and whether this exercise was helpful.

For patients staying at the psychiatric hospital, the speech-to-speech dialogue agent is also designed to train their concentration. The psychiatrists who co-designed this part wanted a sequence of significant sentences without having the patients to answer. During this part, patients could focus on their inner thoughts to calm overwhelming emotions. Unfortunately, here in the relaxation exercise mode, our dialogue system does not receive any feedback from the patient, so there is no certainty that the patient is even in front of Terabot's interface. The only way we can be sure of this is if the assistant sitting in the room confirms that the patient has been trying to follow the commands given during the exercise and trying to concentrate at all. Therefore, the performance of the dialogue system during the relaxation exercise needs to be improved.

Once again, during the experiments, we noticed different patient behaviors. These included, for instance, a group trying to concentrate and follow the instructions given

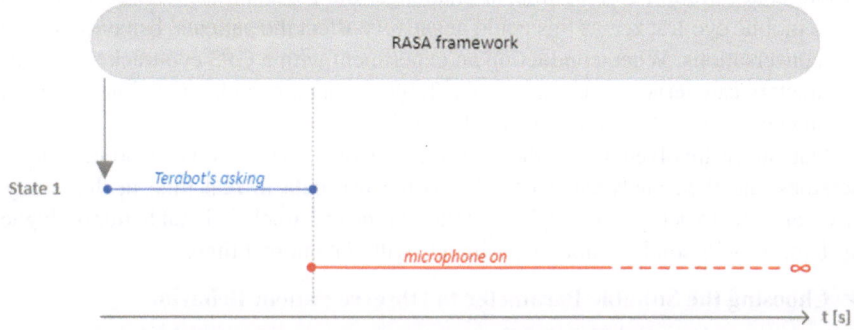

Fig. 4 Frequently occurring problem during conversations with the dialogue system: the microphone waiting infinitely for the patient's answer (the vertical gray arrow indicates the decision of the next chosen utterance of the system)

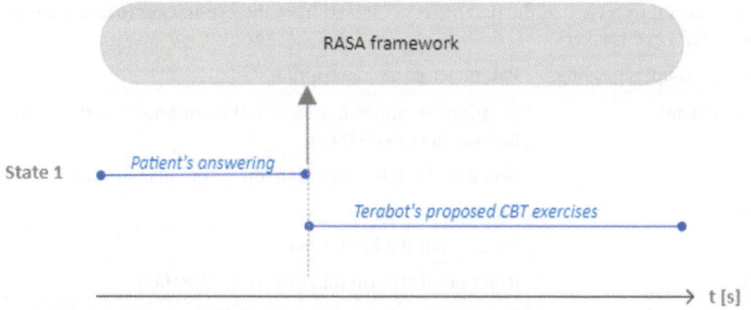

Fig. 5 Another frequently occurring problem during conversations with the dialogue system— no information on the patient's state or presence during Terabot's proposed relaxing exercise (the vertical gray arrow indicates the utterance going to the RASA framework)

to help them concentrate but also another group, e.g., looking away and thinking about anything else rather than coping with their feelings.

In our present dialogue system version, there are no means of contacting the agent other than voice commands. Our tests with patients have brought to light the need for more control or feedback on whether the patients were actually seated in front of the Terabot. It is crucial to gain information if the patients have been somehow participating in the relaxation exercise. This exposes the need for more than one modality for specialized dialogue agents, such as our Terabot.

5 Solutions by Using Eye-Tracker

In parallel to our dialogue agent, we used an eye-tracker to monitor the behavior of the patients' eyes during the conversations. It was a stationary Gazepoint GP3 model with a selected frequency of 60 Hz. As our study involved psychiatric patients, for whom concentration is a significant challenge, the psychiatrists advised us not to use a mobile eye-tracker, as this could negatively affect the patients' behavior during the conversations. When conducting an experiment with a GP3 eye-tracker, various parameters can serve as output signals. Table 1 contains a classification of output parameters divided by groups (general overview).

Our study involved using the eye-tracking data, which was recorded during sessions and then analyzed later. We did not use data in real time in this study. If we are able to achieve an implementation of the eye-tracker signal to our dialogue system, we will conduct more experiments with data in real time.

- **Choosing the Suitable Parameter to Observe Patient Behavior**

When considering implementing an eye-tracking signal for a feedback loop, it is important to determine which particular signal should be passed back (to the RASA framework). Researchers, especially in psychology or marketing, who are interested

Table 1 General overview of the parameters obtained from the eye-tracker (using the example of Gazepoint GP3 eye-tracker)

Parameter group, regarding:	Parameter group description
Eye movements	Fixations (number, duration, X/Y-coordinates of the fixation on the screen ($FPOGX/Y$))
	Saccades (number, duration, direction, magnitude)
Blinks	Identifier of a blink
	Duration of the blink [ms]
Pupils	Right pupil size (in mm or pixels) ($RPMM$)
	Quality flag of the right pupil—valid or not valid (RPV)
	Left pupil size (in mm or pixels) ($LPMM$)
	Quality flag of left pupil—valid or not valid (LPV)

in where the participant is looking typically analyze parameters related somehow to fixations (Krejtz et al., 2023; Porta et al., 2013); in our case, this would be the parameters, e.g., FPOGX/Y. These are the screen points (X and Y-coordinates) where the subject's gaze is focused. Unfortunately, using this parameter as feedback to the framework would not be desirable in our situation. Since this signal is responsible for the on-the-screen fixation information (in this case, either FPOGV or FPOGX/ Y), it would provide information only where the patient was looking directly at the screen. Selecting this parameter as feedback would result in undesirable actions by the dialogue system. While having dialogues with our dialogue agent, there will not be 100% eye contact throughout the whole conversation, as this also does not happen during human–human conversations. The patient's gaze may be focused (during conversation) on an object next to the monitor, providing no information about his fixation on the screen.

In our study, it is essential to determine whether the patient is present in front of Terabot's interface, not whether the patient is looking at the screen. Therefore, we suggest that our dialogue system considers the parameters regarding the patient's pupils, which are RPV/LPV or RPMM/LPMM. Even if the patient would not look at the Terabot's interface itself, just somewhere away from the screen, there is a broad acting window in which the patient's eyes (pupils) are still visible for the eye-tracker. Therefore, the pupil signal would be valid. Thanks to this approach, information could be sent back to the RASA framework indicating whether the patient is present.

- **Proposed Solution to Issue 1**

Figure 6 illustrates the solution proposed by our research team using an eye-tracker. The system activates the microphone, analyzes the patient's response, and verifies the presence of the patient's eye-tracking signal. According to this information, a better-adjusted intent for Terabot's utterance is chosen.

We evaluate four hypothetical situations:

(1) **Speech signal and eye-tracking signal provided**: The patient answers, and the microphone receives the patient's speech. In that case, providing feedback to the RASA by the eye-tracker signal would provide actual information that the patient is currently present in front of Terabot's interface. That would indicate that the patient actively participates in the discussion. It is noteworthy that maintaining 100% eye data signal (eye contact) is unnecessary, as such a large number is also uncommon in human-to-human conversations. A smaller amount of data retrieved from the eye-tracker is sufficient to classify whether the patient is present. If the patient gazes at Terabot occasionally while thinking or talking, the dialogue system might receive enough data for confirmation. On the other hand, when the waiting time for the patient's response takes too long, then initiation of another special utterance (acknowledging the patient) might be activated, e.g., utterance *Long_no_gaze:* "What are you thinking about? Should I repeat the question?"

(2) **Only speech signal provided**: The patient answers, so the microphone receives the patient's speech, but there is no signal from the eye-tracker. In this situation,

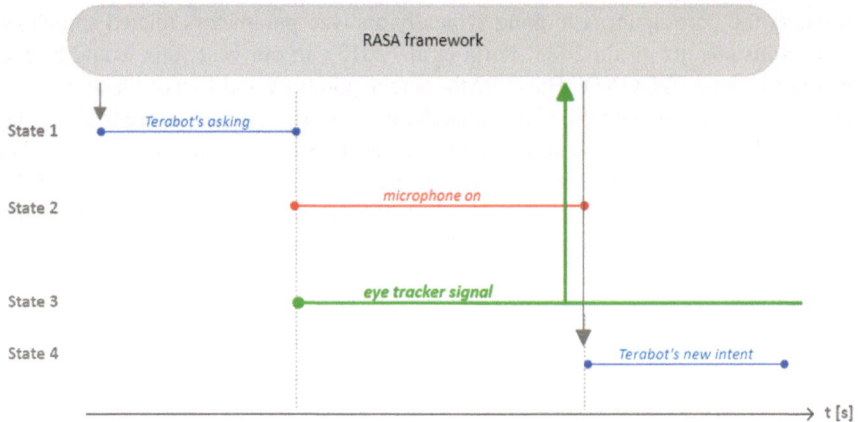

Fig. 6 Proposed solution to Issue 1: the vertical gray arrows indicate that an utterance has been selected for Terabot's speech. The vertical green arrow shows that the eye-tracking signal can give additional feedback to the RASA framework. Based on this, the utterances chosen for the following action of Terabot might be appropriately changed

another additional utterance could activated that can inquire about the patient's condition, e.g., utterance *Why_no_gaze:* "Is something wrong? Why don't you look at me at all?"

(3) **Only eye-tracking signal provided**: The patient does not answer, but the eye-tracking signal is present (and going back to the RASA framework). In this situation, one could consider for how long Terabot should stand still without any additional response, considering that the patient is present in front of Terabot's interface and may just need more time to focus on the answer. After some time, an utterance should be activated, e.g., utterance *No_looking:* "Is everything okay? Does something bother you? Should I maybe repeat the question?"

(4) **No speech or eye-tracking signal**: The patient does not speak, and there is no speech signal from the microphone or signal from the eye-tracker. In this particular situation, an important utterance would be needed, which would put the whole dialogue into a hold-on-modus. For example, an utterance *Are_you_there* with the statement "Hello, are You there? Do you want to continue our conversation?" should be activated to find out if the patient is still in front of Terabot's interface. Depending on the appearance of the eye-tracking signal or the patient's speech, further actions should be considered, taking into consideration whether to receive a response or not.

- **Proposed Solution to Issue 2**

Looking at the situation described in Fig. 5, additional information about the patient is missing that might somehow confirm the patient's presence during the relaxation exercise. Our solution to this problem is to let the RASA framework receive input from the eye-tracker while the patient participates in the exercise. If the feedback signal contains information about the detected pupil diameter of the patient, this would be confirmation enough that the patient is indeed present in front of Terabot's interface. We do not intend to consider 100% or even close to 100% of the eye-tracking data obtained as confirmation that the patient is present. A smaller amount of data sent to the RASA framework would be sufficient to confirm presence.

Then, RASA would be able to activate utterances depending on how the patient is behaving (understood here as the presence of the pupil signal received by the eye-tracker). For instance, if a patient consents to a relaxation exercise and the pupillary signal is recorded, various situations can be identified in which the dialogue system could enhance responsiveness (Fig. 7). The following scenarios could be considered:

(1) The patient **agrees to the exercise**, and the **system receives** feedback on the **pupil signal**—this is confirmation that the patient is present in front of the Terabot interface and wants to participate in the agent's relaxation exercise, during which one can focus on thoughts and emotions.

(2) The patient **agrees to the exercise**, but the RASA system receives an indication that there is **no signal** from the patient's pupil. In this situation, it can be assumed that the patient is not present in front of the screen or has closed eyes. As a result, another special utterance can be activated with an additional question or a request. This leaves room for the patient to respond to what is going on and for the system to adapt to the patient's behavior.

(3) The patient **does not agree** to the relaxation exercise—this situation is already handled in Terabot's dialogue scenarios.

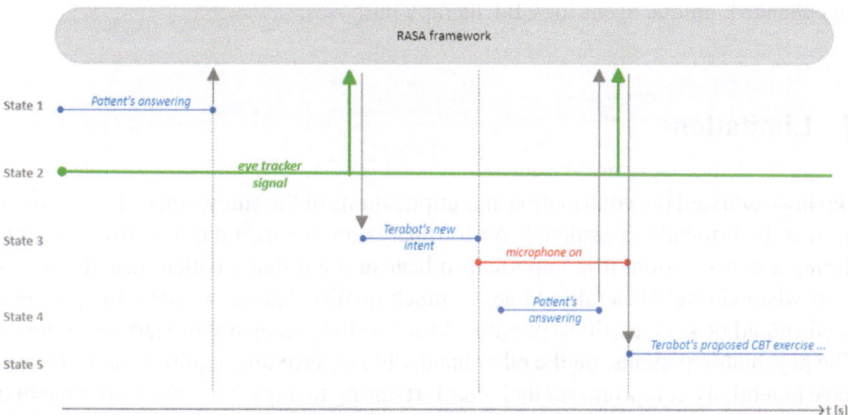

Fig. 7 Illustration of the proposed solution to Issue 2: Patient's utterance (vertical gray arrow) going back to the RASA framework and additionally the eye-tracking signal (green arrow) as an additional input signal. On the basis of these two signals (speech in utterance and eye-tracking signal), a suitable utterance will be formed as a response of Terabot

6   Discussion

We have highlighted the probable advantages and dialogue system enhancements that could be achieved by integrating the eye-tracker module into the conversational agent. In our example of our CBT therapy-oriented dialogue agent, we are also aware of the potential difficulties that could arise from such an extension. The following challenges may arise:

- Investing a considerable amount of effort in the developing part of the two systems: linking the eye-tracker module to the RASA system, taking into account pupillometric parameters.
- The need to remodel the dialogue flow diagram in the RASA framework.
- The need for expansion of the dialogue scenarios, which have to be accepted by psychiatrists.

Despite these challenges, we have shown that through the presence of the patient's pupillary signal, we found a way in which the conversations with Terabot can potentially be enhanced. We suppose that may change the dialogue flow with a benefit to the patient since the dialogue system would be more sensitive to human behavior. We believe that implementing a multimodal dialogue agent for therapy purposes would improve conversational adaptability. Through this multimodal approach, the interaction between the patient and the dialogue agent might closely resemble human-to-human interactions and conversations as we know them from casual therapeutic sessions with specialists. That multimodal approach would make it possible to obtain an enhanced, unique agent for CBT therapy purposes.

7   Limitations

Having discussed the contribution and implications of the study, some shortcomings need to be critically considered. As for analyzing eye-tracking data from patients during a conversation, it is important to bear in mind that a patient usually moves a bit when sitting. Generally, to get as much quality data as possible, the patient's head should be kept as still as possible during a study using a stationary eye-tracker. The psychiatric patients, on the other hand, did not have this requirement as it could have potentially compromised their comfort during therapy. Therefore, after the first analyses of collected eye-tracking data, we found many gaps due to the patient's head movements (e.g., in the relaxation phase of the exercises). Note that in our pilot study, Terabot was used to support drug therapy for psychiatric patients with schizophrenia.

Another aspect is that we have not yet implemented the integration of the eye-tracker signal into our dialogue system. Therefore, we cannot say whether the proposed solutions are fully satisfactory. We cannot predict whether the proposed solutions for improvement by combining Terabot with the eye-tracker will be able to cope with all the challenges during therapy sessions.

8 Conclusion

As technology continues to evolve, multimodal fusion will become a standard part of human–machine interaction. The use of multimodality features in dialogue systems is more and more common (Amorese et al., 2022; Bailly et al., 2006; Bee et al., 2009). New technologies in the fields of psychiatry and psychology are being designed to support or supplement therapy in various ways (Carroll & Rounsaville, 2010; Stefaniak et al., 2019).

In this chapter, we have shown how a pupillary signal can be used as an additional source of information for a goal-oriented conversation agent. The problems we encountered during our study using only a single-modal dialogue agent were pointed out. To overcome them, we have demonstrated the solutions of using an eye-tracker in such situations. When the pupillary signal is used as input to the RASA framework of the dialogue system, it can modify the utterances given back to the patient more appropriately.

9 Further Work

In our case, the next step will be experimental testing to determine whether the proposed solutions are effective for our dialogue agent. After that, we consider analyzing the eye-tracking data during the whole relaxation exercise. We want to find out if the Terabot-guided dialogues do have an effect, e.g., on either the patient's mental load or the achievement of the state of relaxation. If we can improve Terabot, we are planning to expand the research in two ways. First of all, in order to help people with different mental illnesses, we would also like to add other sets of exercises (emotions) that the patients could talk about. Second, expanding the research and testing the exercises on healthy people might also help persons in challenging circumstances. It could also help students struggling with strong negative emotions before an exam or a thesis defense.

We believe that although Terabot must not be a substitute for a visit with a psychiatrist, this dialogue agent can be helpful in managing to work through difficult situations in everyday life. As such assistive dialogue agents evolve, we believe that they can help patients and provide them much faster with therapeutic support.

Acknowledgements This research was funded by the Center for Priority Research Area Artificial Intelligence and Robotics of the Warsaw University of Technology within the Excellence Initiative: Research University (IDUB) program. The study was approved on April 27, 2022, by the Institute of Psychology and Neurology Ethics Committee in Warsaw, Poland; resolution No. IV/2022. This

412   K. Gabor-Siatkowska et al.

chapter is based upon work from COST Action CA19142—Leading Platform for European Citizens, Industries, Academia and Policymakers in Media Accessibility (LEAD-ME) supported by COST (European Cooperation in Science and Technology.

References

Amorese, T., et al. (2022). Using eye tracking to investigate interaction between humans and virtual agents. In *Proceedings—2022 IEEE international conference on cognitive and computational aspects of situation management, CogSIMA 2022* (pp. 125–132). Institute of Electrical and Electronics Engineers Inc. https://doi.org/10.1109/CogSIMA54611.2022.9830686

Bailly, G., et al. (2006). Embodied conversational agents: Computing and rendering realistic gaze patterns. In *Lecture notes in computer science (including subseries lecture notes in artificial intelligence and lecture notes in bioinformatics)* (pp. 9–18). Springer Verlag. https://doi.org/10.1007/11922162_2

Bartošová, O., et al. (2018). Pupillometry as an indicator of l-DOPA dosages in Parkinson's disease patients. *Journal of Neural Transmission, 125*(4), 699–703. https://doi.org/10.1007/s00702-017-1829-1

Bee, N., et al. (2010) Discovering eye gaze behavior during human-agent conversation in an interactive storytelling application. In *International conference on multimodal interfaces and the workshop on machine learning for multimodal interaction, ICMI-MLMI 2010* (pp. 1–8). ACM. https://doi.org/10.1145/1891903.1891915

Bee, N., André, E., & Tober, S. (2009) Breaking the ice in human-agent communication: Eye-gaze based initiation of contact with an embodied conversational agent. In *Lecture notes in computer science (including subseries lecture notes in artificial intelligence and lecture notes in bioinformatics)*. https://doi.org/10.1007/978-3-642-04380-2_26

Białowąs, S., & Szyszka, A. (2019). Eye-tracking in marketing research. In *Managing economic innovations—Methods and instruments* (pp. 91–104). Bogucki Wydawnictwo Naukowe. https://doi.org/10.12657/9788379862771-6

Bradley, M. M., et al. (2008). The pupil as a measure of emotional arousal and autonomic activation. *Psychophysiology, 45*(4). https://doi.org/10.1111/j.1469-8986.2008.00654.x

Bunk, T., et al. (2020). DIET: Lightweight language understanding for dialogue systems. http://arxiv.org/abs/2004.09936. Accessed November 25, 2023.

Carroll, K. M., & Rounsaville, B. J. (2010). Computer-assisted therapy in psychiatry: Be brave-its a new world. *Current Psychiatry Reports, 426*–432. https://doi.org/10.1007/s11920-010-0146-2

Chandra, S., et al. (2016). Eye tracking based human computer interaction: Applications and their uses. In *Proceedings—2015 international conference on man and machine interfacing, MAMI 2015*. Institute of Electrical and Electronics Engineers Inc. https://doi.org/10.1109/MAMI.2015.7456615

Chang, K. M., & Chueh, M. T. W. (2019). Using eye tracking to assess gaze concentration in meditation. *Sensors (Switzerland), 19*(7). https://doi.org/10.3390/s19071612

Craig, T. K., et al. (2018). AVATAR therapy for auditory verbal hallucinations in people with psychosis: A single-blind, randomised controlled trial. *The Lancet Psychiatry, 5*(1), 31–40. https://doi.org/10.1016/S2215-0366(17)30427-3

Dino, F., et al. (2019). Delivering cognitive behavioral therapy using a conversational SocialRobot. In *IEEE international conference on intelligent robots and systems* (pp. 2089–2095). http://arxiv.org/abs/1909.06670. Accessed February 18, 2024.

Dressman, M. (2019). Multimodality and language learning. In M. Dressman & R.W. Sadler (Eds.), *The handbook of informal language learning*. https://doi.org/10.1002/9781119472384.ch3

Duarte, C. (2007) *Design and evaluation of adaptive multimodal systems*. Universidade de Lisboa.

Duarte, C., & Carriço, L. (2006). A conceptual framework for developing adaptive multi-modal applications. In *International conference on intelligent user interfaces, proceedings IUI* (pp. 132–139). ACM. https://doi.org/10.1145/1111449.1111481

Duchowski, A. T. (2017) *Eye tracking: Methodology theory and practice.* Springer International Publishing AG.

Fenn, K., & Byrne, M. (2013). The key principles of cognitive behavioural therapy. *InnovAiT: Education and Inspiration for General Practice, 6*(9), 579–585. https://doi.org/10.1177/175 5738012471029

Fitzpatrick, K. K., Darcy, A., & Vierhile, M. (2017). Delivering cognitive behavior therapy to young adults with symptoms of depression and anxiety using a fully automated conversational agent (Woebot): A randomized controlled trial. *JMIR Mental Health, 4*(2). https://doi.org/10.2196/mental.7785

Gabor-Siatkowska, K., Sowański, M., et al. (2023a). AI to Train AI: Using ChatGPT to improve the accuracy of a therapeutic dialogue system. *Electronics, 12*(22), 4694. https://doi.org/10.3390/electronics12224694

Gabor-Siatkowska, K., Sowanski, M., et al. (2023b). Therapeutic spoken dialogue system in clinical settings: Initial experiments. In *International conference on systems, signals, and image processing.* IEEE Computer Society. https://doi.org/10.1109/IWSSIP58668.2023.10180265

Hershaw, J. N., & Ettenhofer, M. L. (2018). Insights into cognitive pupillometry: Evaluation of the utility of pupillary metrics for assessing cognitive load in normative and clinical samples. *International Journal of Psychophysiology, 134*, 62–78. https://doi.org/10.1016/j.ijpsycho.2018.10.008

Karbe, H. (2014). Wernicke's area. In *Encyclopedia of the neurological sciences* (pp. 751–752). Elsevier Inc. https://doi.org/10.1016/B978-0-12-385157-4.01189-1

Kozłowski, M., et al. (2023). Enhanced emotion and sentiment recognition for empathetic dialogue system using Big Data and deep learning methods (pp. 465–480). Springer. https://doi.org/10.1007/978-3-031-35995-8_33

Krejtz, K., et al. (2018). Eye tracking cognitive load using pupil diameter and microsaccades with fixed gaze. *PLOS ONE, 13*(9), e0203629. https://doi.org/10.1371/journal.pone.0203629

Krejtz, K., et al. (2023). A unified look at cultural heritage: Comparison of aggregated scanpaths over architectural artifacts. *Proceedings of the ACM on human-Computer Interaction, 7*(ETRA), 1–17. https://doi.org/10.1145/3591138

Majaranta, P., & Bulling, A. (2014). Eye Tracking and eye-based human–computer interaction (pp. 39–65). Springer. https://doi.org/10.1007/978-1-4471-6392-3_3

Mulvey, F., et al. (2008). Exploration of safety issues in Eyetracking. COGAIN EU Network of Excellence.

Pfleging, B., et al. (2016). A model relating pupil diameter to mental workload and lighting conditions. In *Conference on human factors in computing systems—proceedings* (pp. 5776–5788). Association for Computing Machinery. https://doi.org/10.1145/2858036.2858117

Porta, M., Ravarelli, A., & Spaghi, F. (2013). Online newspapers and ad banners: An eye tracking study on the effects of congruity. *Online Information Review, 37*(3), 405–423. https://doi.org/10.1108/OIR-01-2012-0001

Santini, T., Fuhl, W., & Kasneci, E. (2017). CalibMe: Fast and unsupervised eye tracker calibration for gaze-based pervasive human-computer interaction. In *Conference on human factors in computing systems—proceedings* (pp. 2594–2605). Association for Computing Machinery. https://doi.org/10.1145/3025453.3025950

Sherrill, A. M., & Rothbaum, B. O. (2023). Virtual reality exposure therapy. In *Encyclopedia of mental health* (3rd ed., Vol. 1–3, pp. V3-592–V3-600). Elsevier. https://doi.org/10.1016/B978-0-323-91497-0.00023-0

Stefaniak, I., et al. (2019). Therapy based on avatar-therapist synergy for patients with chronic auditory hallucinations: A pilot study. *Schizophrenia Research*, 115–117. https://doi.org/10.1016/j.schres.2019.05.036.

Thórisson, K. R. (1997). Gandalf. In *Proceedings of the first international conference on Autonomous agents—AGENTS '97* (pp. 536–537). ACM Press. https://doi.org/10.1145/267658. 267823

Vlasov, V., Mosig, J. E. M., & Nichol, A. (2019). Dialogue transformers. http://arxiv.org/abs/1910. 00486. Accessed November 25, 2023.

Was, C., Sansosti, F., & Morris, B. (2016). Eye-tracking technology applications in educational research. In *Eye-tracking technology applications in educational research*. IGI Global. https://doi.org/10.4018/978-1-5225-1005-5.

Wedel, M. (2014) Attention research in marketing: A review of eye tracking studies. *SSRN Electronic Journal* [Preprint]. https://doi.org/10.2139/ssrn.2460289

WHO highlights urgent need to transform mental health and mental health care. (n.d.). https://www.who.int/news/item/17-06-2022-who-highlights-urgent-need-to-transform-mental-health-and-mental-health-care. Accessed February 18, 2024.

Zygadło, A., Kozłowski, M., & Janicki, A. (2021). Text-based emotion recognition in English and Polish for therapeutic chatbot. *Applied Sciences (Switzerland), 11*(21). https://doi.org/10.3390/app112110146

'Control the Stream of Sounds': A Pilot Study on Intersemiotic Translation of Sound Effects and Music for Subtitling for the D/Deaf and Hard of Hearing in German, Spanish, and English in VOD Platforms

Vicente Bru García⬚ and Silvia Martínez-Martínez⬚

Abstract This study aims to address the need for standardization in intersemiotic subtitling of sound effects and music in audiovisual products through the revision of standards and guidelines in subtitling for the D/deaf and hard of hearing (SDH) and the analysis of a corpus consisting of SDH from German, Spanish, and English Netflix series. The results, examined using the classification identified by Martínez-Martínez in El subtitulado para sordos: Estudio de corpus sobre tipología de estrategias de traducción (2015), reveal differences in the three languages analyzed in terms of the most used intersemiotic translation strategy, as well as a lack of consistency in the translation of the same sounds in different subtitles. This article underlines the importance of establishing quality guidelines to ensure access to leisure for people with hearing impairments (Martínez-Martínez in Lo audiovisual bajo el foco del siglo, 2021, p. 353) and establishes a starting point in an interdisciplinary approach to subtitling sound effects and music.

Keywords Sound effects · Music · Intersemiotic SDH · Guidelines · Corpus

1 Introduction

Nowadays, there is a growing advocacy for the rights of people with disabilities (Toribio Camuñas & Jiménez Hurtado, 2022), especially following the United Nations Convention on the Rights of Persons with Disabilities (2007), and a defense

V. Bru García (✉) · S. Martínez-Martínez
University of Granada, Granada, Spain
e-mail: vicentebru@ugr.es

S. Martínez-Martínez
e-mail: smmartinez@ugr.es

© The Author(s) 2024
A. Marcus-Quinn et al. (eds.), *Transforming Media Accessibility in Europe*,
https://doi.org/10.1007/978-3-031-60049-4_23

of the right of people with disabilities to access leisure activities. Translation modalities such as audio description or subtitling for the d/Deaf and hard of hearing (SDH) are tools that enable people with disabilities to access audiovisual products found on video-on-demand (VOD) platforms.

Nevertheless, as noted by Martínez-Martínez et al., (2019: 411), despite the increasing availability of accessible products, the quality of these products tends to be deficient. This is especially true in terms of the translation of semiotic codes different from verbal code in SDH, i.e., sound effects and music. These fundamental components of the film soundtrack (Bordwell & Thompson, 2010: 298) are often inconsistently and arbitrarily translated, possibly due to professionals' lack of understanding of the characteristics and conventions of semiotic codes related to music and sound, or due to the absence of normative standards in SDH establishing patterns for translating these elements, thus requiring subtitlers to rely on their intuition.

This study represents an approach to the intersemiotic translation of sound effects and music in SDH of audiovisual products on VOD platforms in three different languages (English, German, and Spanish), analyzing the translation strategies used and the presence (or absence) of consistency in the translation of sound effects.

The proposed objectives are, firstly, to review the national guidelines of Germany, the USA, and Spain, as well as Netflix's SDH guides in English (EN), German (DE), and Spanish (ES), concerning the intersemiotic translation of sound, to ascertain their adequacy in achieving quality subtitling; secondly, to identify the most recurrent intersemiotic translation strategies in a corpus of Netflix series episodes in English, German, and Spanish and assess their relevance; and lastly, to determine if the intersemiotic translation of sound effects and music in the corpus episodes is consistent.

To accomplish this, we will start by describing the film soundtrack, the source text of the products analysed in this chapter, and the specific characteristics of the semiotic codes of sound and music. Subsequently, we will analyze the norms and style guides for SDH, particularly concerning intersemiotic translation, and their relevance in crafting quality subtitles. We will then describe the methodology used in the study to analyze Netflix's SDH and evaluate the results obtained through examples.

2   Film Soundtrack: Beyond the Dialogues

Understanding the nature of the source text, that is, the film soundtrack, is crucial for being aware of the relevance of intersemiotic translation strategies employed in SDH for music and sound effects. In this section, we will define the elements of the film soundtrack, their origins, and the characteristics of sound and music.

While cinema initially began with silent films, with sound limited to live music or commentary from a narrator (Martínez-Martínez, 2015: 33), it is now inconceivable to envision an audiovisual product without its corresponding film soundtrack. This auditory element, as highlighted by Bordwell and Thompson (2010: 298), encompasses not just the verbal code of dialogues but also incorporates sound effects and music, which operate in harmony and not in subservience to one another. Just as the selection of intralinguistic translation strategies in SDH can be analyzed through the study of verbal code and linguistics, an understanding of the sonic and musical codes governing sound effects and music, respectively, is necessary to appropriately use the most suitable strategy.

Sound possesses four primary characteristics that define any effect: pitch, intensity, timbre, and duration (Jiménez Hurtado & Martínez-Martínez, 2017: 246). Pitch refers to the speed of vibration of a sound, its quality being either high or low; intensity pertains to the amount of energy propagated by the soundwave and its proximity or distance from the sound source (loud, soft, distant); timbre denotes the distinction of sounds concerning their nature (telephone, guitar, voice), including the synesthetic attributes attributed to them (velvety, metallic..); and finally, duration indicates the length of the sound effect over time (long, short, intermittent).

Music also shares these four attributes, although its nature is intentional and organized compared to a sound effect, which tends to be natural and disorganized (Reybrouck et al., 2019).

Bearing in mind these characteristics, Martínez-Martínez (2015: 291) identifies three predominant strategies for describing sound and music in SDH: *categorization*, *attribution*, and *explanation*. *Categorization* involves identifying the sound source based on its nature (door, bell, music); *attribution* entails assigning a quality to the sound source (creaking door, high-pitched bell, pop music); and finally, *explanation* refers to the use of additional information or another attribution complementing a complex sound or describing music (distant creaking door, intermittent high-pitched bell, pop music by Britney Spears). The correlation between the sound's nature and the employed strategy was analyzed in a DVD movie SDH corpus within Martínez-Martínez's doctoral thesis (2015). However, the rise of VOD platforms has created a revolution for this translation modality, which makes this study a continuation thereof.

Concluding this section, it is crucial to acknowledge the significance of considering sound and its characteristics within cinematic language to select the most appropriate intersemiotic translation strategy.

3 Standards and Style Guides: Not Very Instructive Instructions

To better understand the decision for choosing a translation strategy over another, it is essential to study the regulations governing SDH in each country and language analyzed in our corpus, as well as the style guides of platforms like Netflix, where these subtitles are hosted.

While this analysis began in earlier studies (Martínez-Martínez, 2021), this study is innovative due to its focus on intersemiotic translation and the incorporation of an analysis of Netflix guidelines.

3.1 The USA

The USA was among the first countries to back the making of all television content accessible. In 1972, the program 'The French Chef' was first aired with closed captioning (Global Captioning Leader, 2011). This set up a precedent for the Americans with Disabilities Act of 1990, which mandated all public and private networks to provide their content with SDH.

The guide governing SDH in this country is the Captioning Key of the Described and Captioned Media Program (2024). Concerning sounds and music, this chapter comprises several technical instructions, such as position, format (bracketed and italicized if produced off-screen), yet the most significant aspects revolve around the prescribed translation strategies.

It emphasizes the importance of identifying the sound source and attributing it to a character, unless explicitly shown on-screen, while using specific terminology ('robin sings' instead of 'bird sings') and employing onomatopoeias to reinforce the sound. While onomatopoeias, as Pereira Rodríguez (2010: 93) suggests, may benefit post-lingually deaf individuals, the lack of established onomatopoeias for all potential sounds in a film soundtrack can impede SDH comprehension. Onomatopoeias like 'thrack' for a hit are somewhat arbitrary, as they might not be as recognizable as 'woof' for a dog, potentially causing added difficulty in sound comprehension.

As for sound duration, an instruction that can help the user to understand this effect is segmenting subtitles or using punctuation to indicate speed or rhythm of a sound, alongside employing the present participle ('barking') for continuous sounds and the third person singular ('barks') for abrupt or intermittent sounds.

Regarding music, the standard states that background music should be subtitled only if essential to the plot, explicitly stating the title, composer, or artist, accompanied by an adjective describing the conveyed emotions or mood. Interestingly, it advocates for using objective adjectives, avoiding value judgments like ('beautiful music') or ('melodic music'), which could influence the viewer's experience objectivity.

For songs, the Captioning Key recommends objectively reflecting their mood, indicating the song title and singer, and presenting the complete lyrics. However, the inclusion of title and artist might only be useful if they reflect the functional use in the film or if the artist is well-known, allowing the user to form a mental image of the piece's mood and the values associated with the artist's image. Otherwise, for obscure titles or unknown artists, these subtitles might be opaque or even puzzling for a deaf user.

Next, we analyze Netflix's English guidelines (2022a), which share similarities with those previously examined. For instance, in songs, it advises specifying the title of an instrumental piece only if widely recognized, which resolves some earlier ambiguity. However, to indicate ambient music, it recommends using a 'generic ID', which, by itself, is generic. Nevertheless, there is another instruction that mentions the need to present the genre or mood of instrumental pieces, which is a relevant strategy for better comprehension. Additionally, the guide underscores the importance of subtitling silence when pertinent to the plot, something that is as crucial as the sound itself, as indicated by Zdenek (2015).

Finally, regarding sounds, the Netflix guide emphasizes the importance of detailed and descriptive subtitles in intersemiotic translation. It focuses on the importance of describing voices, speech speed, or sound volume, referencing three of the sound qualities previously discussed: timbre, duration, and intensity, respectively.

3.2 Spain

Spain was also a pioneer in SDH, subtitling televised content for the first time in 1993 (Cuéllar Lázaro, 2016). Since then, the country has seen regulation of this translation modality twice through the UNE 153010 standards in (2003) and (2012), as well as laws emphasizing the need to safeguard the rights of people with hearing disabilities, such as Law 7/2010.

Focusing on the current guiding standard for SDH, UNE 153010: 2012, it also has two sections providing instructions for the intersemiotic translation of sounds and music. Regarding sound effects, the norm is limited, merely specifying, along with format, that the description of effects should be nominalized, avoiding action verbs in favor of nouns describing the sound source and prohibiting descriptions of the sensation produced by receiving the sound ('birds are heard') in favor of the emission source ('birds').

However, instructions for describing music are clearer and more pertinent to professionals' needs. The guide stipulates that each musical piece should be described by its genre, the conveyed emotion, or the identification of the piece. Yet, these instructions are not entirely clarifying or objective, because, apart from the identification issue analyzed before, the emotion conveyed can vary based on each subtitler's personal background, potentially contradicting the original author's intent.

Netflix's guide (2023) in Spanish provides some of the most detailed strategies for music description, the most specific among those analyzed in this study. It emphasizes subtitling diegetic music, something that is pertinent as diegetic sounds are part of the film's depicted universe. While identifying the piece is considered a useful strategy, the guide prefers describing the genre or mood over piece identification, given that potential unrecognized pieces can be difficult to understand only through the title and artist. It also recommends a structure for music description: music + genre + description, something that proves to be very useful for establishing a controlled language enabling more orderly and homogeneous knowledge access for users.

Regarding sound effects, the instructions are also pertinent, emphasizing concise and clear descriptions, using simple present tense if emitted by characters and nominalizing if diegetic effects. However, each subtitler's judgment prevails, as the instructions states ('please, use your best judgment in these cases').

3.3 Germany

SDH in Germany appeared earlier than in Spain, in 1980, on the ARD network (Cuéllar Lázaro, 2016: 149). However, its use was not regulated until 2014, when, under pressure from German associations for people with hearing disabilities, Germany included in its German cinema promotion law (*Filmförderungsgesetz*) the need for every produced film to have an audio-described version and one with SDH.

However, unlike Spain's UNE 153010: 2012 standard, Germany lacks a similar standard, although there are indications such as *Gemeinsame Untertitelrichtlinien für den deutschen Sprachraum* (Méan, 2013), formulated by associations of people with hearing disabilities from Germany, Switzerland, and Austria, establishing a set of minimum quality standards. For intersemiotic translation, the format (white on black in parentheses) for sounds and music is highlighted, preferring onomatopoeias (like 'wuff' for a dog bark), and paralinguistic elements if unclear, as well as indicating original song lyrics within hashtags, providing German translations when possible.

As for Netflix's own German guide (2022b), it mirrors the one analyzed for the USA, offering clearer descriptions of sounds based on timbre, duration, and intensity, yet as will be observed in the results section, it might not be sufficient.

Concluding this theoretical section, it is evident that the imprecision in providing instructions for intersemiotic translation may lead to inconsistency and heterogeneous strategies used in our corpus.

4 Methodology

In order to understand the most commonly used intersemiotic strategies in each of the studied languages, it is necessary to analyze a representative corpus of series from VOD platforms that can provide conclusive results.

For this reason, a corpus has been compiled comprising the SDH of several episodes from three similarly themed series (young adult crime) from one of the most representative VOD platforms, Netflix (Durrani, 2023), in German, English, and Spanish: *Kitz* (Reinbold et al., 2021), *How to Get Away with Murder* (Nowalk et al., 2014), and *Élite* (Salazar et al., 2018). To ensure that the sample is representative, four episodes were selected from each series. Subtitles resulting from intersemiotic translation and those describing the paralanguage of character interventions were the only chosen, given the nature of the study.

For the analysis, the labeling system developed by Martínez-Martínez (2015) was employed. It is a quantitative-approach labeling system for analyzing SDH based on two levels: sound origin and translation strategy used. On the second level, we will exclusively focus on the three major strategies described by the author for intersemiotic translation of sound effects and music: *categorization*, *attribution*, and *explanation*, strategies already defined in the previous section. Subtitles were labeled manually using the qualitative approach software, MAXQDA, and results are presented in the next section.

5 Analysis and Results

We now present the results of the predominant intersemiotic strategies in the SDH on the three languages. We first present the common findings in the corpus to establish the most frequently utilized strategies, followed by a discussion on the differences observed between languages (Fig. 1).

The figure indicates that the most used technique in all three languages is *categorization* (55%), followed by *explanation* (28%), and finally *attribution* (17%). This may be attributed to the frequent occurrence of *character identification* ('Wes', 'Roger', 'mutter' [mother]) in our corpus, which has appeared consistently. Therefore, in the subsequent figure, we have opted to exclude these subtitles to prevent this label from skewing the data.

We observe that in Fig. 2, the results vary across the three languages in the corpus. In DE, *explanation* stands out (47%), followed by *categorization* (37%)

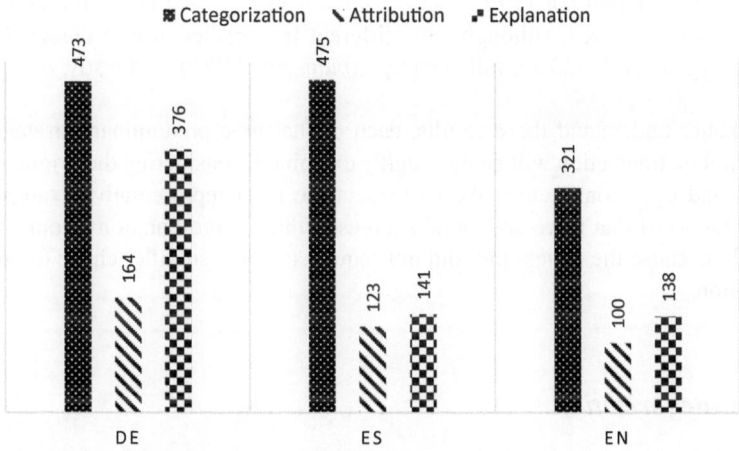

Fig. 1 Frequency of *categorization*, *attribution*, and *explanation* in DE, ES, and EN considering *character identification*. ALT: Table that describes the frequency of use in German SDH of *categorization* (473 subtitles), *attribution* (164 subtitles), and *explanation* (376 subtitles); frequency of use in Spanish SDH of *categorization* (475 subtitles), *attribution* (123 subtitles), and *explanation* (141 subtitles); frequency of use in English SDH of *categorization* (321 subtitles), *attribution* (100 subtitles), and *explanation* (138 subtitles); all of them if *character identification* is taken into consideration

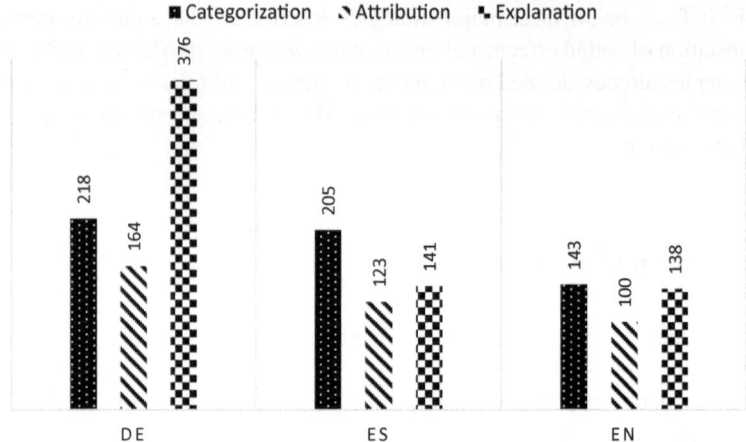

Fig. 2 Frequency of *categorization*, *attribution*, and *explanation* in DE, ES, and EN not considering *character identification*. ALT: Table that describes the frequency of use in German SDH of *categorization* (218 subtitles), *attribution* (164 subtitles), and *explanation* (376 subtitles); frequency of use in Spanish SDH of *categorization* (205 subtitles), *attribution* (123 subtitles), and *explanation* (141 subtitles); frequency of use in English SDH of *categorization* (143 subtitles), *attribution* (100 subtitles), and *explanation* (138 subtitles); all of them if *character identification* is not taken into consideration

and *attribution* (16%). In ES, on the other hand, *categorization* prevails (64%), followed by *explanation* (19%) and *attribution* (17%). In EN, a similar pattern to Spanish is observed, although with different frequencies of use: *categorization* prevails significantly (55%), followed by *explanation* (28%), and lastly, *attribution* (17%).

To better understand these results, each of the three predominant strategies in intersemiotic translation will be thoroughly examined, considering the origins of the sounds and their consistency. We will select the most representative examples. It should be noted that there are sound sources without representation in our corpus, possibly because the series' plot did not require it or the subtitler chose to omit its translation.

5.1 Categorization

Below is the cross-reference of labels between the translation technique *categorization* and the sources of the original sound text, following Martínez-Martínez's (2015) classification: 'nature', 'animal', 'human', 'object', and 'music' (Fig. 3).

As observed, the most common sound sources, excluding *character identification* (53.91% in DE, 56.84% in ES, and 55.45% in EN), are 'human' (41.44% in DE, 30.95% in ES, and 42.37% in EN) and 'object' (4.44% in DE, 8.84% in ES, and

CATEGORIZATION

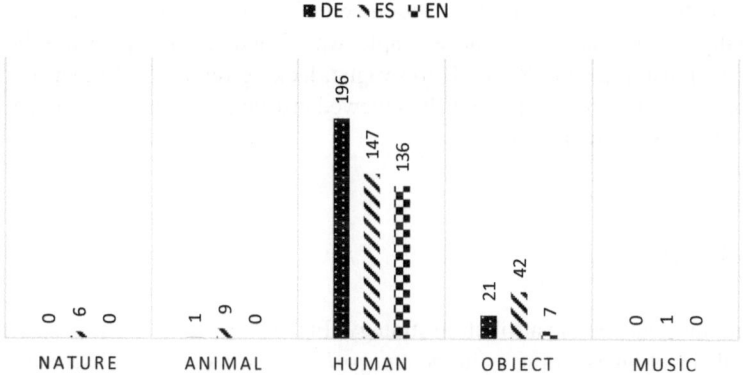

Fig. 3 Frequency of *categorization* in the corpus. ALT: Table that describes the frequency of use in SDH of *categorization* based on sound origin: nature (0 subtitles in German, 6 subtitles in Spanish, and 0 subtitles in English); animal (9 subtitles in German, 9 subtitles in Spanish, and 0 subtitles in English); human (196 subtitles in German, 147 subtitles in Spanish, and 136 subtitles in English); identification (255 subtitles in German, 270 subtitles in Spanish, and 178 subtitles in English); object (21 subtitles in German, 42 subtitles in Spanish, and 7 subtitles in English); and music (0 subtitles in German, 1 subtitle in Spanish, and 0 subtitles in English)

2.18% in EN). We will now analyze the sources 'animal', 'human', 'object', and 'music' to observe examples of inconsistency or typical structures in each language.

Despite the low number of subtitles found for sounds emitted by animals (1.9% in DE, 1.9% in ES, and 0% in EN), we would like to highlight an example found in the German series. It involves identifying the sound source + the sound produced ('Vögel zwitschen' [Birds chirp], 'Kühe mühen' [cows low], or 'Kuh brüllt' [cow bellows]). In the case of the cow examples, an inconsistency and terminological error can be observed with the verbs 'mühen' and 'brüllen'. The former is common for both cow and bull, while 'brüllen' is exclusively used for the male animal.

In sounds produced by humans, some very recurring structures are noted. In DE, sounds are inferred using separable ('schreit auf' [shout]) and non-separable verbs ('stöhnt' [moans]). In ES, explicit mention is made of transitive and intransitive verbs ('exhala' [exhale]) and reflexive verbs ('se mofa' [laughing at]), which are nevertheless clearly visible on the screen. In EN, there are interpretations of transitive and intransitive verbs ('chuckles') and verbs in continuous present ('grunting'). The case of the Spanish verb 'asiente' is noteworthy, as the visual component clearly shows the character performing the action, rendering subtitling it unnecessary, since it increases the cognitive load for the deaf person (Martínez-Martínez, 2022). It is important to note that the use of verbs is quite recurrent, with numerous examples, mostly related to alternating sounds.

In sounds from inanimate objects, linguistic codification often involves describing the type of sound produced by the object using a singular or plural noun (in

German 'Piepsen' [beep]; in Spanish 'pitidos', and in English 'beep'). It is also common to find nouns identifying the sound source ('Gong' [gong] or 'coche' [car]). Additionally, in the German series, action verbs like 'piept' (beeps) are presented.

Finally, in 'music', only one example was found in the Spanish subcorpus, 'música' [music], a subtitle that is too vague, lacking relevant information for the users and not following the previously reviewed instructions, making it an ineffective subtitle for describing the plot.

5.2   Attribution

We will now analyze the attribution strategy (Fig. 4).

In this label intersection, as in the *categorization* strategy, it is observed that the predominant sources of sound origin, reflected in a higher number of subtitles, are 'human' (72.56% in DE, 24.39% in ES, and 73% in EN) and 'object' (20.12% in DE, 39.84% in ES, and 22% in EN). Moreover, in ES, the use of attribution in 'music' is significant, in 35.77% of the *attribution* cases.

Let us start with the human source, which presents a variety in its attributions. The most frequent *attribution* consists of using adjectives that, on one hand, refer to mood or physical states altering voice modifiers. Examples include 'vorwurfsvoll' (full of complaints) in German and 'irónico' (ironic) in Spanish. On the other hand, attributions are related to sound intensity using adjectives in DE, EN, and ES ('laut' [loud],

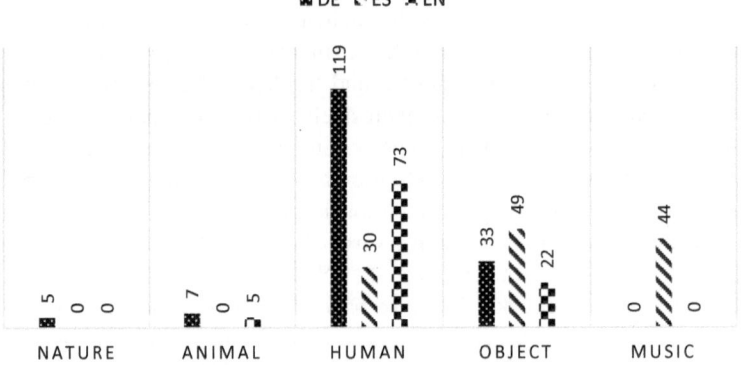

Fig. 4 Frequency of *attribution* in the corpus. ALT: Table that describes the frequency of use in SDH of attribution based on sound origin: nature (5 subtitles in German, 0 subtitles in Spanish, and 0 subtitles in English); animal (7 subtitles in German, 0 subtitles in Spanish, and 5 subtitles in English); human (119 subtitles in German, 30 subtitles in Spanish, and 73 subtitles in English); object (33 subtitles in German, 49 subtitles in Spanish, and 22 subtitles in English); and music (0 subtitles in German, 44 subtitles in Spanish, and 0 subtitles in English)

'lloroso' [tearful], 'seufzt leise' [sighs softly], 'respira fuerte' [breaths deeply], 'beathing deeply', or 'breathing heavily'). The last two examples in EN draw attention since 'breaths deeply' means the same as 'breathing heavily'. However, it seems that the emphasis in the former is on the depth of breathing, while in the latter, it focuses on the act of breathing itself. With less frequency, there are adjectives that add a quality to the original sound in EN with an adjective + noun structure ('indistinct conversations') and in ES with a noun + adjective structure ('conversaciones inaudibles').

Finally, in EN, there is a notable use of verbs ending in -ing following different pattern structures such as adjective + verb in -ing ('indistinct talking'), noun + verb in -ing ('voice breaking'), or verbs in -ing + adjective ('breathing heavily').

In object, a similar pattern emerges. In most cases, nouns representing the sound source are paired with adjectives indicating various sound qualities. In EN or ES, it is common to find nouns + verbs ending in -ing (in EN) or gerund (in ES): 'telephone ringing' or 'agua salpicando' (water splashing), respectively. In ES, there is a wide recurrence of structures such as noun + adjectives that refer to the characteristics of the sound source ('disparos electrónicos' [electronic shots]), nouns + participles not directly related to the sound, or at least not directly ('llamada desconectada' [disconnected call]), or noun + prepositional complements ('vibración de móvil' [mobile phone vibration]). In DE, there is a preference for using adjectives referring to sound intensity + nouns ('lauter Knall' [loud noise]) and the type of sound production ('skurrile Klänge' [funny sound]).

Lastly, in 'music', we have only found subtitles in the Spanish corpus. These subtitles identify the film genre associated with the music ('música de intriga' or 'música de suspense'), interpret the musical sound that sometimes embodies functions of cinematic music theory ('música triste' or 'música emotiva'), or interpret by referring to the proximity or distance of the sound source ('música distante').

5.3   Explanation

We will now present the explanation category (Fig. 5).

The prevalent sources for *explanation* are human sounds (37.77% in DE, 53.19% in ES, and 44.93% in EN), objects (14.89% in DE, 8.31% in ES, and 50.72% in EN), and 'music' (43.88% in DE, 35.46% in ES, and 2.17% in EN).

We will begin with human sounds, where we have found only two patterns to explain a sound produced in the audiovisual content. First, it locates the sound ('Kind schreit im Hintergrund' [Child is screaming in the background]) or 'indistinct shouting in distance'. The other pattern is focusing on the duration or temporal elements of the sound ('summt weiter' [continues vibrating]).

In objects, there is a clear parallelism with human sounds. The origin of the sound is located ('bandejas por el suelo' [trays on the floor]) or the duration or some temporal elements of the sound are explained ('Handy summt mehrmals' [mobile phone vibrates several times] or 'cellphone continues ringing'). Lastly, they

EXPLANATION

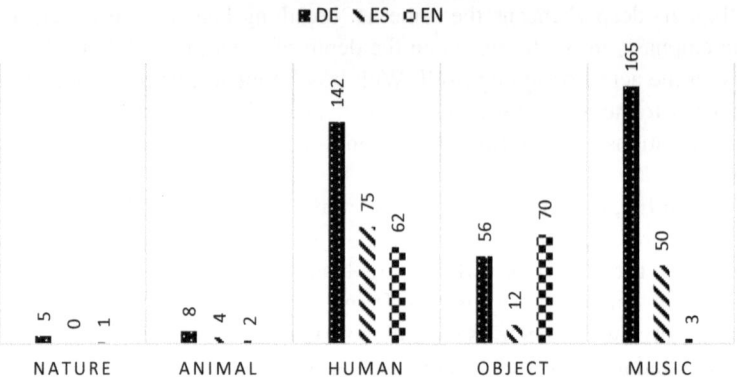

Fig. 5 Frequency of *explanation* in the corpus. ALT: Table that describes the frequency of use in SDH of *explanation* based on sound origin: nature (5 subtitles in German, 0 subtitles in Spanish, and 1 subtitles in English); animal (8 subtitles in German, 4 subtitles in Spanish, and 2 subtitles in English); human (142 subtitles in German, 75 subtitles in Spanish, and 62 subtitles in English); object (56 subtitles in German, 12 subtitles in Spanish, and 70 subtitles in English); and music (165 subtitles in German, 50 subtitles in Spanish, and 3 subtitles in English)

explain the concurrence of sounds, for example, 'Motor springt an und Wagen fährt weg' (Engine starts, and the car drives away). This sound, moreover, is redundant (Martínez-Martínez, 2022), as the user visually perceives the car moving.

In 'music', subtitlers often identify the sound intensity ('abrupter Übergang', 'Musik wird leiser' [abrupt transition, music fades]), or identify the song title and its performer, as indicated in the Netflix style guide ('"Home" von Somer', 'Naughty Boy's "No one's here to sleep" plays', or suena '"Fuel to Fire" by Agnes Obel').

6   Conclusion

The analysis presented in this study represents an initial description of current practices in the intersemiotic translation of music and sound effects in DE, ES, and EN. The prevalent use of *categorization* and *explanation* aligns with the instructions stated in Netflix style guides, although some instances have shown these techniques to be insufficient in describing film sound.

Additionally, some predominant syntactic structures have been identified in each language for describing music and sound effects, focusing on the sources of the sound. However, these structures are still inconsistent across languages and even among episodes within the same corpus. These identified structures represent a step towards establishing or creating a controlled language that could enable easier access to understanding film soundtracks for individuals with hearing impairments. Nevertheless, this inconsistency hampers knowledge accessibility and signifies a lack of understanding of the semiotics of the original text and its structural dimension.

The limitations present in this study are the lack of the analysis of other guidelines such as those by Disney, HBO, or Amazon and the fact that these guidelines are always evolving toward an improvement in intersemiotic strategies; and the analysis of just a genre, young adult crime, which limits the reality of SDH strategies for sounds and music.

Future research directions include expanding the corpus into different languages or with a broader sample, studying sound functions to identify associated strategies, or establishing a controlled language to help subtitlers ensure greater consistency in creating intersemiotic subtitles. Despite limitations associated with sample size and the source of subtitles being from a single platform, Netflix, we are confident that this study represents a step forward in research on intersemiotic translation in SDH.

Acknowledgements This research has been conducted within the TALENTO Research Project [Translation and simplified language of heritage for all. Analysis and consultation tool (PID2020-118775RB-C21)], funded by the Spanish Ministry of Science and Innovation (MICINN). This chapter is based upon work from COST Action CA19142—Leading Platform for European Citizens, Industries, Academia and Policymakers in Media Accessibility (LEAD-ME) supported by COST (European Cooperation in Science and Technology).

References

Bordwell, D., & Thompson, K. (2010). El arte cinematográfico: una introducción. Paidós.
Captioning Key. (2024). (7th December 2024). Described and captioned media program. https://dcmp.org/
Cuéllar Lázaro, C. (2016). El subtitulado para sordos en España y Alemania: Estudio comparado de los marcos normativos y la formación universitaria. *Revista Española de Discapacidad, 4*(2), 143–162.
Durrani, A. (February 2, 2023) Top streaming statistics in 2024. Forbes. https://www.forbes.com/home-improvement/internet/streaming-stats/
Global Captioning Leader. (2011). (22nd December 2023). A brief history of captioned television. https://web.archive.org/web/20110719060406/, http://www.ncicap.org/caphist.asp
Jiménez Hurtado, C., & Martínez-Martínez, S. (2017). ¿Qué se oye? El proceso traductor del subtitulado para personas sordas desde un estudio de corpus. In C. Gaona Pisoner (Ed.), *Temáticas emergentes en Innovación Universitaria* (p. 243–253). Tecnos.
Law 7/2010. 31st. March, General de la Comunicación Audiovisual (Spain).
Martínez Martínez, S. (2015). El subtitulado para sordos: Estudio de corpus sobre tipología de estrategias de traducción. [PhD]. University of Granada.
Martínez Martínez, S. (2021). Las plataformas de vídeo bajo demanda como recurso didáctico en la formación en subtitulación. In M. Viñarás Abad, A. Gregorio Cano, & R. Casañ Pitarch (coords.), *Lo audiovisual bajo el foco del siglo XXI* (p. 353–363). Tirant Lo Blanch.
Martínez-Martínez, S. (2022). Subtitling for the deaf and hard-of-hearing @ ENTI (Encyclopedia of translation and interpreting). AIETI. https://doi.org/10.5281/zenodo.6370763
Martínez-Martínez, S., Jiménez Hurtado, C., & Jung, L. (2019). Traducir el sonido para todos: Nuevos retos del subtitulador para sordos. *E-Aesla, 5*, 411–422.

Méan, Y.-M. (2013). Einheitliche Untertitel für Hörgeschädigte im deutschsprachigen Fernsehen— Chance oder Utopie? Ein Vergleich der Untertitelungsrichtlinien in Deutschland, Österreich und der Schweiz. [Master's Dissertation]. Zurich University of Applied Sciences.

Netflix. (2022a). English timed text style guide. https://partnerhelp.netflixstudios.com/hc/en-us/art icles/217350977-English-Timed-Text-Style-Guide

Netflix. (2022b). German timed text style guide. https://partnerhelp.netflixstudios.com/hc/en-us/art icles/217351587-German-Timed-Text-Style-Guide

Netflix. (2023). Spanish (Latin America & Spain) timed text style guide. https://partnerhelp.netfli xstudios.com/hc/en-us/articles/217349997-Spanish-Latin-America-Spain-Timed-Text-Style- Guide

Nowalk, P., D'Elia, B., Listo, M., Innes, L., Williams, S., Offer, M., Getzinger, J., Cragg, S., Wilkinson, J., Fuentes, Z., Allen, D., Stoltz, E., Zisk, R., Bary, K., Hardy, R., Katleman, M., Terlesky, J., Raju, S., Smith, M., Sullivan, K. R., Turner, J., Culpepper, H. M., Nowlan, C., & Rubio, N. (2014). [Directors]. How to get away with murder. [Serie]. Netflix.

Pereira Rodríguez, A. (2010). Criteria for elaborating subtitles for the deaf and hard of hearing adults in Spain: Description of a case study. In A. Matamala, & P. Orero (Eds.), *Listening to subtitles: Subtitles for the deaf and hard of hearing* (p. 87–102). Peter Lang.

Reinbold, V., Schulz-Dornburg, N., Becker, L., & Hübner, M. (Directors). (2021). Kitz [Serie]. Netflix.

Reybrouck, M., Podlipniak, P., & Welch, D. (2019). Music and noise: Same or different? What our body tells us. *Frontiers in Psychology, 10*, 1153. https://doi.org/10.3389/fpsyg.2019.01153

Salazar, R., de la Orden, D., Quer, S., & Torregrossa, J. (Directors). (2018). Élite [Serie]. Netflix.

Toribio Camuñas, S., & Jiménez Hurtado, C. (2022). Lectura fácil para el patrimonio: Fundamentos de un complejo proceso traductor. In R. Arroyo González, E. Fernández-Lacho, & D. Brao Sarrano (Eds.), *Investigación en comunicación inclusiva y multilingüe* (pp. 289–302). Comares.

UNE 153010: 2003. Subtitulado para personas sordas y personas con discapacidad auditiva. Subtitulado a través del teletexto. AENOR.

UNE 153010: 2012. Subtitulado para personas sordas y personas con discapacidad auditiva. AENOR.

United Nations. (24th January 2007). Asamblea General, Convención sobre los derechos de las personas con discapacidad: Resolución aprobada por la Asamblea General. A/RES/61/106. https://www.refworld.org.es/docid/497f08549.html

Zdenek, S. (2015). *Reading sounds*. University of Chicago Press.